THE

LEAP

THE

LEAP

R · T · W LIPKIN

cover art by Mat Yan | M. Y. Cover Design

Printed in the United States of America

First printing 2023

ISBN-13: 978-1-949059-30-4
ISBN-10: 1-949059-30-8
Library of Congress Control Number: 2023910906
Eclipse Ink, Ithaca, New York

The Leap is a work of fiction. References to historical events or
real people or places are used fictitiously. Other names, characters,
places, and events are products of the author's imagination, and any
resemblance to actual anything or anyone is entirely coincidental.

Visit my website: rtwlipkin.com

For Lorraine and Renée
with love

CHAPTER 1

THE FIRST TIME Sean Meade had the thought, she dismissed it. It wasn't possible, it couldn't happen, this wasn't how things worked, and besides, the thought arose at four a.m., it was propelled by the unexpected, unwanted, odd comm she'd had with Ethan, and by four thirty, when she finally got up, the thought had almost completely disappeared.

At five, when Sean was stepping through the waist-high maze of documents in her workroom, she was thinking of something else entirely: how to generate enough income to pay for the repairs she needed on the roof. Needed? She could just put more buckets and pails in the attic and wait another few days or weeks or months. Years, maybe. She had more interesting projects than roof repair to pursue.

Sean sat in the one corner of the workroom where there was space for her to sit down and leaned her head against the wall. Then she made the mistake of stretching out her legs, which resulted in one of the towering piles of documents becoming less towering and less of a pile and, worse, the papers now blocked one of the narrow paths in the maze.

Six months ago, Sean had had what seemed like everything, but five months and twenty-seven days ago, she'd taken that everything and morphed it into nothing.

She kicked at the fallen-down docs. She'd have to restore the pile. The order was vital. Necessary.

She tried not to think about what that everything she'd had had been and what the nothing had become even though she was aware that the not-thinking method always had the opposite effect.

What had the everything been? The job of her dreams as a detective on the elite squad of the Osada City Joukko, work on the most interesting case she'd ever encountered, an appointment with the impossible-to-pin-down expert who was going to repair her roof, and what had seemed at the time like the start of a promising relationship with Ethan Stiles, the sullen yet intriguing medical examiner and research geek.

Now? Nothing. The nothing was easy to not-think about, since it was, well, nothing.

Although she did have a case. She'd been doing private detective work since her escape from the joukko, and although her current job wasn't much, it was something. Wasn't something better than nothing? Wasn't that a reason to get up in the morning? Although she'd yet to find anything that was a reason to go to bed at night.

Sean pulled herself into a crouch and started re-creating the stack she'd knocked over. As she did, she glanced at each paper, reassuring herself that even though she'd lost a lot, she hadn't lost her mind, which was as sharp as ever. Each paper, as she replaced it in its proper position in the tower, was as familiar to her as her own name and address, as familiar as her former desk at the joukko, as familiar as the empty place in her heart, a place that seemed destined to stay empty.

Ethan. They'd ruined their friendship by attempting to make it into something it wasn't and couldn't ever be. Sean had suspected that from the beginning, but hoped she was wrong.

As she finished reassembling the tower, her meanderings congealed around her departure from the joukko and the job she'd always thought she wanted but as it turned out she didn't want it. Not just because they didn't want her—or didn't act like they wanted her—but because she didn't belong there. Having to do things in a prescribed way, a way that wasn't her way and that she couldn't force herself to fit into. Their useless, inefficient, bureaucratic, nonsensical methods.

Her comm interrupted her. Ziva Walls, her current client. Sean was still not used to having *clients*. A detective didn't have clients—a detective had cases and even that wasn't quite accurate. A detective had a job to find out the truth, and the people involved, no matter how much you might like them or think you liked or might like them, didn't matter. The truth was what mattered.

But now, as a private detective, it was the client who mattered, since Sean had to get paid. The client was the direct conduit to Sean's continuation as a person with a home and food and some new clothing when what she was wearing fell apart.

The stack reconfigured, she stood, walked through the maze and over to her desk, and turned the comm to voice.

"Meade," Sean said as she put her feet up on the desk and worked away at the burgeoning rip in her pants leg.

"It's Zee," said her client.

"It's early," Sean said, glancing at the time. It was 5:27 a.m., so maybe it wasn't so early. When your husband had been missing for nearly two weeks and the joukko hadn't helped you at all, 5:27 a.m. was probably already much later than you wanted it to be.

"I still haven't heard anything," Ziva said.

"I'm working on it." Sean didn't want to tell her client or herself that she'd made almost no progress. She *would* make progress. She had to.

"Work harder."

"Your case is my sole focus until it's solved." Sean's client had to be reassured and she didn't want to have to explain to Ziva Walls or to anyone that her focus was never on only one thing. It couldn't be. That wasn't who Sean Meade was. She needed a lot of things to focus on or she'd go mad. Hence the labyrinth of papers, documents, reports, bits of information—the towers, piles, stacks, and the maze itself.

"Morris has been missing for two weeks now. He's not like this. He's never been like this. He wouldn't do this to me. He's responsible. He's not the sort of person who would go missing, who wouldn't call his wife, who'd just disappear. I want answers. I didn't hire you to *work on it*. I hired you to find Morris."

"Zee, if anyone can find him, I will do it."

"Are you saying maybe no one could find him?"

"Yes." Sean hadn't wanted to say that, but it was true.

A not-insignificant number of missing persons stayed missing. Anything could've happened to them—abduction, accident in a remote place, and death were likely probabilities. Sean had a theory that at least 17 percent of the missing didn't want to be found, they'd wanted to escape their lives for any number of reasonable or unreasonable motives, and Zee Walls's husband, Morris, could be one of those. Sean had known Ziva Walls for only a few days but she could understand why Morris might not want to be found.

"He's not like that." That was one of Zee Walls's insistences: Morris just wasn't like that.

"I've seen odder cases." What Sean meant was that she'd found missing persons before who'd begged her not to let anyone, especially not their spouse or business partner or parent, know where they were. Know they were even alive.

"I'm coming in," Zee said, and Sean heard her unlocked front door opening.

One of the worst features of being a private detective, if not the absolute worst, was that her clients felt like they could drop by her house anytime they felt like it, although up until Zee Walls, no one else had. But none of her other clients had so far been this desperate.

Sean got up and wound her way through the maze in her workroom and out through the mountainous fortress of books and periodicals lining the corridor. Her living room, though, unlike most of the rest of her house, was spare, neat, and devoid of any trace of what someone else might refer to as Sean's hoard, but which wasn't a hoard but a collection of significant, useful, necessary, and often crucial information.

Ziva was sitting on the red-upholstered, sculpted, antique chair that was where Sean always sat, but she kept her mouth shut. That chair had set her back a month's pay, back when she got paid every month, and no one else had sat in it since she'd brought it home.

"You've gotten nowhere," Zee said. "Just admit it. If the joukko can't find him—not that they care to or are trying to—and if *I* can't find him, then I was a fool to think that anyone, much less you, could find him."

"Would you like some coffee?" Sean herself despised coffee but everyone else loved it, so she had it handy on the minimal chance someone would be at her house and want coffee.

"I don't want coffee," Zee said, "I want answers. I want to know where Morris is, why he left me, and what you're going to do about it."

"Whoa, whoa. Wait a minute. Morris left you? That's the first time you've said anything like that."

"I didn't mean it like you're implying."

"Maybe you did. Maybe the pressure's built up to the point where you're realizing things you didn't realize before. That can happen. Your subconscious can know things your conscious mind is unaware of." Or unwilling to face.

"That is not not not what's happening. He's gone. That's all I meant. He's gone. Disappeared." Ziva's harsh demeanor cracked and she fought back tears, but Zee Walls wasn't the kind of person who'd cry. Sean recognized the type, since she wouldn't cry either.

"Sometimes people keep secrets," Sean said. "And maybe you've discovered something you'd like to tell me about?"

"I ripped the apartment apart. It's not all neat and tidy and spare like your house is." Zee swept her hand in a big gesture around the picture-perfect living room while Sean held back her laughter. If Ziva

Walls saw the rest of Sean's house she wouldn't be speaking sentences with *neat* or *tidy* or *spare* in them.

"I thought you might be right. You said that the first day we talked—that he might have been keeping secrets from me."

"It's not uncommon."

"I ripped the apartment apart and found nothing. He's not like that. He wouldn't be like that. He's incapable of being like that. He's a nice person. Loyal. Reliable. Dependable."

Sean didn't want to tell her she'd heard all this before. That the loyal, reliable, dependable people were often the ones who were actually disloyal, unreliable, and unstable and the person they seemed to be was just a front.

"My place is a wreck now. Not like yours. You have to find him." Zee sniffled a bit and said, "Allergies. They're quite bad since Morris left me."

"Zee—"

"Since he disappeared. He did not not not leave me. He's not like that."

"Was Morris seeing anyone else?"

"Morris would never—"

"I don't mean necessarily a romantic interest. Maybe he had a new friend? Maybe a friend of a friend? Did he have any new business contacts? Someone at his job? A friend on the meshwork?"

Sean had asked her all these questions in their initial interview, but there seemed to be an opening now and Sean was going to take it. Ziva Walls was not telling Sean everything she knew. That was how people were—they told you what they wanted to and occasionally added in what they thought you'd like to hear. Everyone did it, not just clients or suspects or witnesses.

"He's not like that." Ziva's mouth settled back into a tight line, the line where it'd probably been since Morris's disappearance. Or since he'd left her. Or during their marriage.

"Well, everyone meets someone new every once in a while. Give yourself a minute to think about this."

"You mean someone new he met could've done something to him? Killed him?" Zee's voice quavered.

"Don't go there. We don't know what's happened to Morris—"

"See? I knew you didn't have any leads. You're just as useless as the joukko."

"Are you sure he didn't have any new contacts, either personal or professional? Or even peripheral? Maybe he and a colleague had lunch somewhere new?"

"Nothing like that. Morris had a routine and he stuck to it. I've told you all this before. That's how I knew immediately that he'd disappeared. He always commed me at five and he didn't. I knew right away."

"Yet you didn't report it until the next morning."

"I wanted to give him a chance," Zee said, rubbing her right hand against the arm of Sean's favorite chair.

"You might as well just tell me what it is you don't want me to know," Sean said. "How can I find him if I don't have all the facts?"

"You have as many facts as you need. Even if I suspected he was having an affair with his boss's wife, who's had an affair with almost everyone at the company . . . even if I suspected that, it'd just be my imagination. Nothing more. Nothing real. Morris isn't like that."

"What's her name?" Sean pulled out her notepad and waited for the name.

"What do you mean?"

"The name of your boss's wife, the one who has affairs with everyone."

"That's irrelevant."

"Let me decide."

"What if I refuse to tell you?"

"Look, I know where Morris worked."

"Works. He still works there."

"He hasn't been there since he went missing."

"But that's still his job. It has to be. He wouldn't lose his job. Not over something like this."

Sean sat up straighter. There was a *this*. Now she was getting somewhere with Zee, and maybe that somewhere was Morris's current location.

"The point, Zee, is that I know where Morris works. It'd be easy enough for me to find out who his boss's wife is. There's no point in your not telling me."

"Althea Pierce."

"Description?"

"Tall, red hair, very opinionated. Everyone wants her." Ziva Walls herself was tall and opinionated, but her hair was brown.

"Everyone but Morris?"

"Of course Morris wouldn't be like that."

"Right."

"I don't appreciate your sarcasm. My husband's missing—he's disappeared—and you don't have a clue about where he might be."

"I will find him," Sean said, reassuring not just her client but herself.

"Are you going to talk to Althea?" Zee was rubbing both hands on the armrests of Sean's favorite chair now and Sean was starting to worry she was going to have to have it reupholstered. That plus the roof repair were going to set her back even further than she was already set back. It was at moments like this that her spontaneous decision to leave the joukko started seeming foolhardy.

"Yes."

"You can't talk with her."

"Why not?"

"You just . . . can't."

"All right." Sean would talk to Althea Pierce as soon as she could. There was obviously something going on there but it might have nothing to do with Morris Walls's disappearance.

"Find him," Ziva Walls said as she stood up and pointed her right index finger at Sean. "I mean it."

After Zee left, storming out in the same abrupt way she'd stormed in, Sean wondered what was going on between Althea Pierce and Morris Walls. Or maybe between Althea Pierce and Zee Walls. She felt this would be the key to finding Morris.

It wasn't. And even if Morris Walls had been having an affair with Althea Pierce or with anyone else, by the time Sean Meade would find him it didn't matter anymore.

CHAPTER 2

EVERYTHING, IT SEEMED, in Oliver Hirata's life had slowed down. This had happened so gradually he hadn't noticed it until a couple of days ago and even then he thought maybe he was just tired. Anyone could be tired and Hirata had spent so many hours poring over a stream of never-ending numbers on the meshwork that he had a good excuse for this tiredness.

But his initial self-diagnosis, if he could call tiredness a diagnosis, wasn't quite right. Hirata wasn't tired at all, but he was slowed down or the objects, events, and perhaps even the people around him had slowed down. Or his perception of them had. Or the world was moving so fast that in comparison everything else seemed much slower than it should have been. He couldn't sort it out.

That was the other thing—the part of his brain in charge of focusing and sorting things out seemed clogged up, lagging.

Hirata had kept these symptoms, if that's what they were, from everyone he knew, including his current lover, a person he right at that moment couldn't name and was unable to call up an image of.

Was this early-stage dementia? Oliver's great-grandmother had died after years of dementia, but she'd been 218 years old and sickly—she'd never taken care of herself—not 37 years old and in superb health. Until now. If this was ill health and not just exhaustion.

Maybe Oliver Hirata was just sick of his work. He'd always enjoyed numbers, which was how he'd gotten into actuarial science to begin with, learning it from the ground up so that he'd eventually become one of the foremost programmers in the field.

He hadn't gone in to work yesterday, one of the rare at-the-workplace days in his schedule. Did he ever go in to work? But he'd woken up and it seemed like the moment he opened his eyes, the exhaustion—the slowness was more like it—had escalated. And this morning it'd been even worse. As though sleeping was causing this slowness, which made no sense, if there was anything that made sense anymore.

And, worse, working, which had always been his refuge, seemed to exacerbate the overall slowness of everything.

Right now he was lying on the floor of his garage. Why was he in his garage? How had he gotten here? How long had he been here? He didn't know.

He tried to summon up the name or the image of his current lover. Althea something. Yes, that sounded almost right. Was her hair red? He tried to imagine making love to her but his mind's eye showed him only a sequence of numbers with no pattern or purpose he could discern. Yet numbers always had a pattern and almost always had a purpose. Didn't they?

Three weeks earlier, Oliver Hirata had had no problem at all with anything. His life had been chugging along at the correct rate as had everything and everyone he encountered, his work was mildly amusing, and Althea—well, she was a stunning fringe benefit to his consultancy at Pierce Sangstrom.

The day when Oliver had had lunch with the ultra boring Morris Walls and Althea Pierce had stopped by had been a revelation. Not just because up until that moment he hadn't realized there was even one interesting meson in Morris Walls's corpus but because the moment Althea Pierce leaned down and kissed Morris, Oliver knew he and Althea were destined to have a fantastic interlude.

That interlude started two days later when Althea Pierce showed up, without warning, at Oliver Hirata's apartment. She was delivering sensitive Pierce Sangstrom documents, she said. Her husband, Charley

Pierce, couldn't make the trip and he'd entrusted the documents to her. She was the only person Charley could really trust. When Althea said that, she was laughing.

"Your apartment's beautiful," Althea said, staring over Oliver's shoulder into his living room. The wall of windows was one of Oliver's best assets, as it often made him seem even more enticing than he already was.

"Come in," Oliver said.

Althea came in and stayed for two hours and forty-seven minutes. That was the kind of thing—exact timing—that Oliver Hirata had formerly had a tight grip on. But now, lying on the floor of his garage— why was he there?—he once again lost the name of his current lover. Maybe he didn't have one. Didn't he? Wasn't there always an ongoing interlude? But . . .

His heart was racing but he was slow, or the world around him was slow, or both. He thought about turning over onto his side or maybe getting up but then he forgot he'd thought that. He stayed on his back.

Once upon a time, he thought. What did it mean? Why would he think that? And didn't he have work to do?

Once upon a time there was a forest and in that forest was a house made of glass shards. The glass had been manufactured at a seaside facility in a city whose name was now another missing element. The Lost City was famous for its glassmaking industry. One of the most convenient aspects of the glass-shard houses was that the shards could be broken off and used for many purposes, including piercing intricate shapes into your skin.

The garage floor was cold. Oliver Hirata remembered her name— Althea Pierce—but not what she looked like or why he knew her. Or if she was his current interlude.

Oliver sat up. Everything became clear. This was the moment he'd been waiting for, his return to normalcy when the slowness would end and the confusion and random oddness would stop. He stood and went back to his apartment.

A vivid memory of a conversation he'd had with Morris Wall jumped into his head.

"I'm having a hard time of it," Morris had said.

"I know what you mean." Oliver had stolen Morris's lover and from what Morris had said about his wife, the fantastic Ziva Walls, this was a big blow to him. But that wasn't what he meant.

"You and Althea—I don't mind," Morris said. "She's like that. Short attention span. Or maybe no one is as fascinating to her as she is to everyone else."

Oliver just nodded. He couldn't disagree. He himself wasn't half so compelling as Althea Pierce was, and Oliver Hirata thought he was damned compelling. But his ego had definite limits and he knew how to evaluate just about anything. That was his job.

"What is it, then?"

Oliver had to be responsive to whatever Morris was saying, since Morris Walls was his main contact at Pierce Sangstrom—not counting Althea, of course—and this consultancy was quite lucrative. He was going to make enough on this job to buy the apartment next door and expand his view after he knocked down the wall in the living room. The vista would widen and so would his prospects.

"It's this program," Morris Walls said. He put his hand on his forehead and grimaced. "Something's not right and—"

"You've been working too hard," Oliver said. Wasn't that what you were supposed to say?

"Maybe." Morris ran his hand back through his thick, curly hair. "Maybe."

"Take some time off," Oliver said.

"Althea," Morris said. "I think she has her sights set on someone new."

Oliver Hirata himself had his sights set on someone else. Once his interlude with Althea Pierce ended he'd see if Ziva Walls wanted another interlude. Planning was part of the game and sometimes it was the best part, although there was no way to tell until the interlude commenced.

Morris Walls seemed to be about to say something else, but he didn't.

The garage floor was cold, or maybe Oliver Hirata's back was cold. Hadn't he gotten up? Hadn't he just gone back to his apartment and into his living room and looked out over the grand vista of Osada City and the turbulent lake? Wasn't he going to buy the apartment next door and expand his view?

Once upon a time there was a dark forest where only one stream of light entered through a break in the trees. Everyone called the light Lux Fiat. Each person was allowed precisely two minutes a day to stand in Lux Fiat's beautiful glow. Lately the population of the Lost City had increased and your time in Lux Fiat had been reduced to one minute and thirty-three seconds. Too bad for you if you showed up late for your appointment.

Oliver had missed his scheduled Lux Fiat that day and was angry at himself. He went home and worked on his loom. He couldn't remember what he was making, but that was part of the process as he loosely understood it. The loom knew how to make things and you were more like a participant than a weaver.

"I feel desperate," Morris Walls said. He touched his balding head. Did lack of hair make you desperate? Oliver Hirata had a full head of hair, or at least he thought he did. If he could reach his head to touch it, he could verify this shaky fact but his hands didn't want to move at the same pace his memory thought they should. He'd have to wait.

Oliver Hirata wondered how many things he'd forgotten in the last few days or maybe weeks. When had things started to slow down?

He congratulated himself for being able to have these cogent thoughts. Logic. Logic would save him. No matter what rate the rest of the world was moving at, as long as he could maintain his logical focus, he'd be fine. He'd survive this. He'd survived worse, he was sure.

He'd stabbed himself with the glass shards of his forest home and lived, hadn't he?

But the day he'd missed his time in Lux Fiat. That had been very bad. Almost as bad as today, if it was today. Was it?

What was a day, anyway? A collection of thoughts and memories and activities? Chores and errands and achievements and accomplishments?

Right before Oliver Hirata's brain shut down he had a series of lucid, vivid thoughts.

Oliver Hirata. Thirty-seven years old. Actuary. Owner of apartment 9 in the Normandie, Osada City's most luxurious residential building. Owner of a garage on the outskirts of Osada City, a rare find in a city with limited space. His assets were accumulating. He had no debt. His life was on the right track, the one where it should be. He was, for the most part, satisfied with his life, his possessions, his interludes.

Current assignment with Pierce Sangstrom. Main contact at Pierce: Morris Walls, who was Althea Pierce's former lover. Next assignment in the works.

Last interlude with Althea Pierce. Next interlude with Zee Walls, if he could swing it, in the works. If not, there would be someone else. And then Zee.

The world had slowed down for Oliver Hirata exactly two weeks, three days, and twenty-two hours ago. Althea Pierce had just woken up and nudged Oliver, who was sleeping late. Very uncharacteristic. He always kept to a schedule. He never slept in, even during his interludes. Even during ultra interludes, which this one, with Althea Pierce, qualified as. She had a superior rating in his mental-only catalog of interlude appraisals and calculations. He excused himself from such vagaries since he was an actuary, and quantifying things was as natural and necessary to his life as breathing.

When he opened his eyes part of his being moved off-center. That's what he'd thought at the time, a fleeting notion. And now, during

Oliver Hirata's last lucid moments, he remembered this occurrence, this direct, unexpected sensation.

That day things had seemed just a tiny bit slower than they should've been. That morning, though, it worked out well for his time with Althea. He'd told himself it was just pure hedonic extravagance. Here in his luxurious apartment in the Normandie, where he was about to buy the apartment next door and expand all his horizons.

Oliver was certain this cascade of coherent, distinct, nonfantastic memories was a sure sign he was recovering from whatever it was that had been afflicting him for the last couple of weeks. It was over and he was himself again. He'd have to comm Althea right away. Then maybe he'd comm Zee Walls as well, get her set up for the next interlude.

Once upon a time . . . the phrase refused to go away. He tried to shake it out of his head, but his head was now moving at an even slower rate than the rest of the world. Than the rest of Oliver Hirata.

Once upon a time there were seventeen sheep in a dark forest. They had to pass under Lux Fiat every day so they could be properly accounted for and today Oliver Hirata had been chosen to give up his allotted time in the beloved light stream in order that the Lost City could make sure there were still seventeen sheep. Seventeen was the magic number of sheep that guaranteed that Lux Fiat would always be there for the residents of the dark, dank forest.

Oliver Hirata hadn't wanted to give up his time in Lux Fiat, since he relished it more than he relished anything else in his life, including numbers, including apartment 9 in the Normandie, including his interludes, past, present, and future.

He needed that light. Lux Fiat was life itself. While trying to reclaim his rightful place he tripped over the twelfth sheep, who had an unusual symbol sculpted, it seemed, into its coat. Oliver realized he was illiterate and that symbols that should've meant something and that did mean something to others had no meaning for him.

Shortly after Oliver Hirata's brain shut down, his body shut down.

Hirata's garage was located in a remote area of Osada City populated mostly by garages and storage lockers. By the time his body was discovered by Beryl Carson, who owned the garage next door to his, Oliver Hirata had been dead for nearly a week.

CHAPTER 3

THE ROUTINE WAS always the same: wake up, cleanse his computer, and, while this was taking place, scan the house for anything untoward, drink two glasses of purified water, go for a seven-mile run, take a shower, reconfigure his computer's operating system, and get to work.

Jonathan Lee Summers had been doing this for so many years that, had he chosen to, he wouldn't have had to think about any of it. It was as though the routine could power and execute itself. Yet he didn't let his own careful sequence run in the background of his consciousness. He was aware, present, and active in every step of the process. This was the only way to be absolutely certain.

A few months ago he'd had an argument with his former roommate, Ethan Stiles, about this. Ethan, as sloppy and haphazard as ever, had said that repeating the same routine day after day was bad policy, since it left no room for the odd, serendipitous revelation. Jonathan Lee was certain that having a daily routine was the sure path to revelation.

When they'd been at the Acres together, he and Ethan had done a lot of arguing and they still did, yet they remained good friends for the twenty-plus years they'd known each other.

Back at the beginning, Jonathan Lee thought a mistake had been made. The Acres was legendary for its uncanny ability to place the right two or three people together in the same dorm room—the people themselves were never consulted on this placement—but Ethan Stiles? Really? The guy was a slob, he never smiled, and, worse, he never slept and made a lot of noise while he was at his late-night, early-morning doings, whatever the hell they were.

"Look here," Jonathan Lee had said at two a.m. after Ethan's banging around had driven him from his scheduled sleep time, "you can't be like this."

"It's my method," Ethan had said. "I need it."

Despite his sullen demeanor, there was something so honest about what Ethan said that Jonathan Lee decided he liked the guy, that he'd get earplugs or listen to some kind of sleep hypnosis during his scheduled sleep periods, and he'd let his roommate do whatever he wanted to. It was his method, and Jonathan Lee respected method. After all, it wasn't like Ethan complained about Jonathan Lee's rigid habits, which must have conflicted with Ethan's scattered, disorganized style of living and thinking.

Jonathan Lee and Ethan didn't always argue, but when they did they used a style of disputation they'd developed that suited both of them. It had been honed to perfection during their sojourn at the Acres, where Jonathan Lee still was, since he was now a lecturer there.

The Acres had some kind of hold on not just Jonathan Lee Summers but on many of its students, graduates, dropouts, and most of its faculty. The place engulfed you, you became yourself there, and Jonathan Lee hadn't wanted to leave. So he stayed. He was now their premier lecturer on code formation, manipulation, and analysis, a field well suited to his regimented temperament, and one he excelled at.

Ethan, the fool, had become a medical examiner after shocking Jonathan Lee by going to the medical college at Keff instead of staying at the Acres like any less sloppy person would've done, but that hadn't put a dent in their friendship. Even now, with two very different careers and lives and being in different cities, their friendship was as strong as ever.

Jonathan Lee's stoic exterior—but not his regimen, which was ever-immovable—had disintegrated under the glance of Beryl Carson, who was getting her doctorate at Keff Institute in some obscure branch of botany, a subject Jonathan Lee had no interest in. But Beryl herself was of tremendous interest to him.

Ethan had introduced them to each other during one of Jonathan Lee's visits to Ethan at Keff, and Jonathan Lee never thought any of what transpired afterward was Ethan's fault. He couldn't've known. Jonathan Lee himself hadn't known that Beryl would marry him, give birth to Patterson Summers, and then abruptly leave him, taking Patterson with her. They lived in Osada City now and he seldom saw either Beryl or Patterson.

After Jonathan Lee's computer finished its cleansing routine that morning, he wasn't happy with something. He couldn't say what that something was, and it didn't matter. But once a computer got infected it was never the same.

Jonathan Lee's basement had a supply of new builds. He'd constructed all of them himself—it was a sort of hobby, although it was a necessary hobby—so he could be sure of each computer's integrity. And yet things happened. Computers were all vulnerable, even if you built them yourself. An attack could come from anywhere.

Gone were the days of a century or two ago when all you had to do was run one of many commercial antivirus programs, never open a message from someone you weren't sure of, and never ever execute any even mildly questionable program, and your computer was safe. Or relatively safe. That was ancient history.

Now your computer could get infected by almost anything. Stay on a site long enough—long enough could be a millisecond—and the site's origin could get a fix on your computer and even after you were off the site, the origin could launch a viral code that could eat away at all your most important data. Or steal it. Or modify it just enough that it still seemed fine, but it wasn't fine. It was corrupted.

That's similar to what had happened to Jonathan Lee's favorite game, Final Retreat, when he was eleven. He'd been so furious he'd thrown his computer out his second-floor window onto the concrete below. Jonathan Lee's emotions were under firmer control now, but to an eleven-year-old whose Final Retreat, his lifeline to escape from his ever-quarreling parents, had been destroyed, emotions were at a violent boil.

His parents had confined him to his room for a week after that, thinking it was punishment, but that was the week Jonathan Lee learned how to build his own computers from a physical book he'd received as a birthday present from a colleague of his mother's.

You had to be careful. Everyone knew it but no one practiced this care with the same diligence and regularity Jonathan Lee did.

After he had his new build set up, he commed Ethan.

"Did you see about Beryl?" were Ethan's first words.

"What about Beryl?" Jonathan Lee had commed Ethan to see how his friend was doing after the breakup with Sean Meade, a breakup Jonathan Lee still didn't understand. The two of them had seemed perfect for each other. "There's something going on with Beryl?"

"She's the one who found Oliver Hirata's body."

"Who?"

"Jay"—Ethan was the only person who could get away with calling Jonathan Lee anything other than his full name—"pay attention, man. I was just about to comm you. See what you thought. Sometimes I think you're psychic."

"There's no such thing," Jonathan Lee said, although he wasn't so sure he agreed with himself. One instance of his nonexistent psychic ability had been during his marriage ceremony when he had a clear picture of Beryl leaving him. Yet he'd gone ahead with it anyway.

"What about this Oliver Hirata?"

"I want to hash things over with you. I've never seen anything like it."

"Did you have to deal with Beryl?"

"Only for a moment. She acted like she didn't know who I am."

"That's just like her. She acts like she doesn't know who I am half the time."

"She found him by accident. His garage door was part open and she saw his legs and thought something had happened to him."

"I don't see what's so unusual about it. Other than how many dead bodies does anyone discover in their lives. None?"

"There was no odor."

"So?"

"He'd been dead for at least a week."

"Oh. Well, it's been cool this spring."

"Jay." Jonathan Lee could sense Ethan was shaking his head. He had his video feed turned off so he didn't see this but he could imagine it.

"All right. That is a bit unusual."

"It's unprecedented. But, forget that. That's nothing compared to the autopsy and the first of the labs. They're not just unusual or unprecedented, they're inexplicable. That's why I wanted to talk with you. Get your organized mind working on this."

"Finally. Some appreciation for my systematic thought processes. Has the slob method failed you?"

"I'm afraid it has." That Ethan wasn't arguing with him on this point was, Jonathan Lee thought, even more unusual than Oliver whatever-his-name-was's corpse having no odor.

"Start talking." Jonathan Lee looked out into his empty backyard and listened to Ethan.

"His liver is on the wrong side of his body, for starters," Ethan said.

"Couldn't that be congenital?"

"Perhaps, but I've never seen it and neither has anyone else I've consulted."

"I mean, Oliver whoever could just be a freak of nature. That would explain the lack of odor and the liver placement."

"Maybe if those were the only two things, I'd agree with your uncharacteristically unscientific explanation. But they're hardly the only things. His labs are all off, and while I was examining their odd results— I had them run three times and did one more myself—I discovered that Hirata's spleen was doing the work of a normal person's pancreas."

"What the hell?" Jonathan Lee was listening closely now.

"His pancreas looked like it'd been put in a dehydrator and then laid out in the desert sun for a few weeks."

"You're making this up. You're worried I'll screw up my next visit with Patterson over Beryl's having snubbed you."

"I wish I were making this up, Jay. There's so much more. Some of the cytology's unbelievable. Hirata has legions of cells without a nucleus and others that are like nothing I've ever seen in any living being."

"My first instincts say your corpse isn't a corpse."

"Well, he certainly seems like one. At least if you don't delve too deeply. So, Jay, if it's not a corpse, what is it?"

"It's some kind of manufactured being." Jonathan Lee Summers had no idea what he was talking about. The words just emerged from the cellar of his mind, unimpeded by any logical conscious process.

"I hadn't considered that. I'll have to mull it over."

"I don't know what I'm talking about."

"Maybe you do and you don't realize it."

"Have you talked this over with anyone else?"

"I commed Sean and we discussed it."

"I thought you and she were quits."

"That part—that didn't work out. But we're friends."

"She have any insights?"

"None. She said she'd think about it."

"I'm surprised she talked to you."

"This is business. It's different."

"How could this be her business? Didn't she leave the joukko?"

"I"—Ethan hesitated, then said, "She's still the best detective I know. I want her mind working on this. And yours."

"I've got to go." Jonathan Lee looked at the clock. In fifteen seconds he had to begin going over his students' papers, a task he despised.

"Let me know if you come up with anything. I'll send you the file."

"No," Jonathan Lee said as the seconds ticked down. "Don't send them. Meet me at Overtowns at two. You can give them to me there."

"All right."

The former roommates ended their comm. Jonathan Lee started reading his students' papers, saving the ones he knew would be the best for the end.

Beryl. He didn't want to think about her, about the discomfort, anxiety, and eventual despair. He still wasn't sure how or why anything had happened between them.

Jonathan Lee Summers couldn't have known it, but discomfort, anxiety, and eventual despair were three common symptoms of what had killed Oliver Hirata.

CHAPTER 4

S EAN'S SECOND IDEA, that something was wrong at the Normandie, Osada City's swankiest residential building, seemed plausible. She'd rejected her first idea, an insane idea, an impossible idea, an idea she'd had both while on the comm with Ethan and then later that night—this impossible, insane idea that was the correct solution and that would take her some time to return to.

Before she commed Ethan about her second idea, she went to the Normandie to investigate. She'd have to meet with Zee Walls, since she lived there, as had her missing husband, Morris, but she didn't make an appointment. She wanted to stop by unexpectedly and give herself time to explore before meeting with Zee.

That the Normandie was the residence of both the oddest corpse Ethan had ever encountered and also that of Morris Walls seemed like not just a clue, but a signpost. Whatever was going on with these two men, one dead and one missing and perhaps dead, had most likely started there. After she was done at the Normandie, she was going over to the garage where Oliver Hirata's body had been found. Maybe there was something there too, since the Wallses had a storage locker in the adjacent building.

Sean was no longer able to flash her joukko credentials, which could have gotten her in almost anywhere, but she'd made up an official-seeming ID for her private investigation business, and it usually worked wonders. Here at the Normandie, despite its reputation for having tight, military-style security, the entry clerk waved her in, barely looking at her or her quasi legit credentials as she sailed past her.

The building's "security" was abysmal. Anyone could get into the Normandie. That could be the source of the problem right there. Sean took out her notebook and circled the note she'd made about this on her previous visit. She felt like she was close to solving this case and getting the immense bonus for finding Morris that Zee Walls had contracted to pay her.

Sean wandered around the vast basement area. She'd gotten in through an unlocked door marked No Access. The door was trying to hide itself in a corner behind the second bank of elevators, but it was doing a poor job of it. After she was finished with this investigation, she'd contact the building owners and let them know they had to improve their security measures. Then she'd offer to draw up a plan for them, for a fee, of course. She made up a number five or six times what she thought this would be worth, then doubled it. She'd charge at least that.

The gray, utilitarian basement was in sharp contrast to the soigné entry and lobby areas, but the basement looked almost sterile. Overlarge cleaning apparatuses lined the corridors. The constant hum of what must have been some kind of machinery made her feel like she was in the belly of a large ship.

"Hey. No one's allowed down here." Sean heard the words but couldn't see their source. She kept walking.

"You. Stop. You're not supposed to be here." The voice was closer now. Sean turned around and saw a vehicle. The man inside was the owner of the voice she'd heard.

Sean took out her ersatz credentials and showed them to the man, who could've been young or old, tall or short. She couldn't tell from where she was standing.

"Okay, then," the guy said. "But be careful."

"I'm doing my best."

"Hey, get in. I can take you wherever you want to go. You could get lost down here or wear yourself out. There're kilometers of passages."

Sean got in the passenger side of the vehicle, which seemed like another of the cleaning devices.

"I'm just looking around for clues," Sean said.

"Floor polisher," the man said, gesturing around the vehicle's interior.

Sean still couldn't tell anything much about him. It was as though he was facilely anonymous, a trait Sean wished she herself possessed. Instead, she was a bit too memorable, with her big, dark, intense eyes and a head of thick, unmanageable hair that framed her face and accentuated the ridges of her cheekbones. She couldn't hide if she wanted to. Even shaving her head hadn't worked. She'd tried it once several years ago.

"If you want to know anything, just ask me," the floor polisher driver said. They were tooling around the expansive basement as he pointed out this and that. Nothing exceptional, although the tour was interesting somehow.

"Do you know Ziva Walls?" Sean would ask about Oliver Hirata later.

"Who doesn't know Ziva Walls?" the man said, rounding another corner and pointing to a series of red-painted doors. "I did that," he said. "Too gray down here. Thought it needed a little color. Red, for passion."

"Yeah."

"Well, Zee Walls. She's a very busy person. Never had any time for her husband. Too busy with other people. No wonder Morris left her."

Sean had to take notes in her head. She didn't want to stop the flow of information and was concerned that producing her notebook might intimidate the floor polisher driver, who Sean had taken an inexplicable liking to.

"Have you seen Morris recently?"

"No one has. He fled. If I were married to Ziva Walls, I might flee too. Can't blame the guy." The driver stopped the vehicle, and Sean realized the floor beneath them had been getting polished the entire time they'd been driving around. The machine made no noise. The source of the constant hum was something else.

"If you'd be able to tell me any particulars, it could help with my investigation," Sean said.

"They'd argue a lot. When they were both at home together and I'd happen to walk by their apartment . . . They're on the top floor, where there are a lot of problems because of the cheap material they made the roof covering from, so I'm up there a few times a week, sometimes every day. You could hear the shouting through the door and, say what you will about this supposed luxurious building, the apartments are well soundproofed."

"What did they argue about?"

"Mostly about the wife's liaisons. Morris—what a nice guy and very attractive—you see, Morris wasn't pleased with what Ziva was doing. The worst argument they had that I heard was when she was having it on with the Interlude Man, who lived in the apartment down the hall from theirs."

"The Interlude Man? Do you mind if I take notes?" This was getting to be too much to remember. Words she only heard seemed to vanish in Sean's memory, but anything she wrote down or saw written down and all images were forever embedded in her inner storage.

"Go right ahead."

Sean took out her notepad and jotted down several of the things she'd already heard.

"Can I ask your name?"

"Jordan Fields," the man said.

"Sean Meade," she said even though she'd already shown him her ID. "About the Interlude Man?" She wanted Fields to keep talking.

"Yeah. Oliver Hatori. No, wait. Hirata. The Hatoris live on five and that's a trio of sisters. Oliver Hirata is, I mean *was*, the Interlude Man."

"Could you tell me more about him?" Jordan Fields had given Sean an intro to talking about Oliver Hirata and she was going to run with it.

"Well, you see—and don't ask how I know this—Oliver Hirata was what you might call a serial lover. He had one lover after another, was passionate with all of them at the beginning, and then quickly tired of them. He called his encounters with them *interludes* and he was always on the hunt for a new interlude. He had interludes with all of the Hatori sisters on five, he had an interlude with Maizy, the woman on the front desk today, and in an unusual move for him, he had several nonconsecutive interludes with Ziva Walls."

Sean wrote as fast as she could.

"I guess Morris didn't mind the first one. After all, he might've had an interlude with Oliver Hirata himself, although I don't think he did. But it was the second or third one that got to him. He blew up at Ziva and told her she had to stop or he was going to stop her. Then he went missing. Probably decided it was easier to leave her than it was to argue with her all the time."

Sean wondered if it had been easier for Ziva Walls to kill Morris than it had been to continue to argue with him. Had she killed Oliver Hirata too? Maybe he didn't want another interlude and she did.

That Zee Walls was capable of murder had occurred to Sean more than a few times. But two murders? Sean had often encountered evil people in her work as a detective on the joukko. If Ziva Walls had killed two people, then . . . Sean would never get paid for finding Morris. She tried not to consider that part, but it was one of the biggest drawbacks of her current job. Her former job had had too many drawbacks, but at least she got paid no matter who was guilty.

Jordan Fields, who Sean thought would make a great friend, started up the machine again.

"Mind going around some more?"

"That's fine with me. Can you think of anything else? Anything unusual?"

"A missing person and a dead interlude lover aren't enough for you?" Fields was laughing and Sean joined in.

"An investigator can never have enough information."

"You know, now that I think about it"—Fields went around a close turn in a narrow corridor and Sean marveled at his skill with the machine—"I haven't seen Kaj Banerjee in a while."

"Kaj Banerjee lives here?" Banerjee was the current hottest artist in the hemisphere. His works were selling for phenomenal amounts, he seemed to be everywhere all the time, and his distinctive pieces had set off a host of copycats—one of them was being sued by Banerjee.

"He moved in right after he auctioned off that thing for two hundred million," Fields said. "Has two adjacent apartments. Paints, or whatever it is he does, in one, and lives in the other. You have to go out into the hall to get from one to the other, since the wall between the two places is part of the building's structure, so I sometimes see him in the hallways. A complete snob. Condescending. That type."

"No surprise there," Sean said. She put a couple of stars next to Banerjee's name in her notepad. This was one person who should be easy to locate, as he was familiar to everyone in Osada City and most of the rest of the world as well.

"It's been at least a week. No, more than two. He always makes a show of avoiding me, like I could contaminate him."

"Let's go knock on his door." Sean had an impulse and she always obeyed them. If it didn't work out, if Fields said no, then she'd move on to the next thing, which was confronting Ziva Walls about the lies she'd been feeding her.

"Okay. This way." Jordan Fields careened around three corners and sped down a long corridor that ended in a huge elevator. "I'll polish the floor when I'm up there. It's due tomorrow anyway." The elevator doors opened and after Fields drove the machine into the elevator he said, "Penthouse." The elevator obeyed.

"Kaj was one of Ziva Walls's 'friends,' I'm almost positive. I saw her leave his studio twice and saw him at her apartment door once. I guess she might've just posed for him, but I didn't get that impression."

Sean's brain flipped through her mental catalog of Kaj Banerjee's images of women and found one or two that might've been Zee. She'd verify when she got home.

Sean knocked on Banerjee's apartment door—no answer—and then on his studio door—also no answer. "Do you have a way to get in?" Sean looked at Fields.

"No."

Sean tried the door handle. Another unlocked door. This one wasn't the fault of the lax Normandie security system. She opened the door and looked back at Fields. "Want to join me?"

"I'll wait out here," he said, and drove the silent machine down the long, spooky corridor, polishing the already pristine stone floor.

Inside Kaj Banerjee's studio were paintings, one of which was definitely a painting of Ziva Walls, small objects made of crumpled pieces of paper, what seemed to be hundreds or thousands of art supplies, an open bottle of a liquor so pricey that only someone like the wealthy artist could afford it, and an orange tabby cat who was napping amid the chaos, but looked up and yawned at Sean, then stretched.

She made her way through the jumble, thinking Kaj Banerjee could use a maze like the one in her house where she'd made a clear path. Here, she had to avoid stepping on things.

Some of the paintings were astounding, more fantastic than they seemed when you viewed them on the mesh. Sean stopped staring and looked around.

In the far corner of the studio was an enormous computer, nearly fifteen centimeters across, sitting on a worktable, and on the floor underneath the table was Kaj Banerjee's lifeless body.

She knelt down. No pulse, no breath. She sniffed him. No odor. Not just lifeless—dead.

She looked at the computer and then at Kaj Banerjee's corpse, and her rejected first idea flitted in and out of her consciousness before she firmly replaced it with a far more plausible explanation, which was that something or someone here in the Normandie was responsible for Morris Walls's disappearance and Oliver Hirata's and Kaj Banerjee's murders, if they were indeed murdered.

Her number one suspect was her client.

After she sent a terse comm to Boyd McCormick, her former partner at the joukko and now the chief of detectives, she stared at the painting of Ziva Walls, waited for the joukko to show up, and wondered about too many things:

Where was Morris Walls? Was he alive?

If Ziva had killed Morris, why had she hidden him and not the other two victims, and why had she reported him as missing? Was she trying to take attention away from herself? Didn't she know her actions had had the opposite effect?

Would Sean find a paying client soon enough to avoid having to find another, far less desirable, job?

Could she convince whoever arrived at the scene to use Ethan as the ME even though the Normandie was just outside his jurisdiction? Sean couldn't stop thinking about her comm with Ethan, about the bizarre anatomical findings in Oliver Hirata's corpse, and she wanted Ethan to examine this body. See if the cells looked like ordinary cells. See if the pancreas and spleen were doing their correct jobs and if the liver was in the right location. And if they weren't . . . how had Ziva Walls managed that?

If Zee was the murderer of even one of these victims, how had she done it? She might be clever, she might be angry, she might be a murderer, but was she also a wizard? A magician? A conjurer? Witch? Alchemist?

CHAPTER 5

WE HAVE AN agreement."

Althea Pierce was slumped on the uncomfortable couch in her husband's office. The shades were pulled and the office was dark. Charley liked it that way and Althea didn't mind, although up here, in the clouds, it wasn't like they'd have an audience, as much as Althea might've enjoyed one.

"Did you kill him? That's not part of the agreement."

Charley had originally made the agreement with Althea since he thought he'd benefit from it. It hadn't occurred to him then that she'd take advantage of the terms and he'd have no desire to. Even after all her affairs and all her near-affairs, he still hadn't wanted to. Hadn't had to. His desires were concentrated on either expanding into an unreachable infinity the all-encompassing dominance of Pierce Sangstrom or on Althea herself.

Charley hoped Althea, who was trying to find a better position on the sofa, would never find one. He'd had the couch made for just this purpose. He wanted anyone who was looking for comfort to never find it. He ran a business from this office—not a vacation.

"Of course I didn't kill him. Why would I?"

"Jealousy is probably the first reason, followed by anger, frustration, or, in your case, fascination. I know how much you like trying out something new." He was hoping to make her even more uncomfortable.

"I do like new things, but I would never kill anyone," Althea said. She slumped down more, yet she was still thoroughly desirable. The moment he'd met her he'd known he'd marry her. But their agreement, whose terms he'd created, allowed either of them to pursue any other person they wanted to. Yet he'd pursued no one else, not really, and Althea had pursued, at current count, eighteen other people. That he knew of. There were probably more. There would always be more.

"And who would I be jealous of?" Althea straightened up, then moved to the corner of the sofa, the least uncomfortable spot on the torturous object.

"Anyone," Charley said. "Kaj Banerjee, for instance."

Althea huffed. "Don't be ridiculous. He's nothing but a con artist. And a terrible lover."

"Six months' worth of terrible?"

"It was only five months. Four. And you don't hear me complaining about your lovers."

Charley had convinced Althea that he also had lovers, although, other than Althea, there was no one he could properly term a lover. But he couldn't let her know that. He was currently in a supposed heated affair with Beryl Carson, a peripheral business contact he sensed Althea objected to, since Beryl was one of the most intelligent people in Osada, if not anywhere, and had a startling, stunning aura about her.

"But you did kill Oliver Hirata, didn't you?" He was enjoying blaming her.

Charley had purposely left Hirata's name out of this argument until now. Aside from Althea's affair with the disappeared Morris Walls, his most valuable worker, her affair with Oliver Hirata had bothered Charley to a greater degree than he thought it might. Althea seemed to be working her way through the Normandie, and Charley was concerned she'd get to the one person he never wanted her anywhere near. He might love Althea, but he had secrets from her and they had to be kept secret.

"Oliver's dead?" Althea looked so innocent. She was quite a good actor. Missed her calling, Charley thought, although the fabulas she wrote had made her an impressive fortune. He wasn't sure how much that was, as they kept their finances separate. That was part of another agreement they had, one that was official, unlike their other, unwritten, agreement.

"Don't act innocent."

"I didn't know." She crossed, then recrossed her legs. Charley congratulated himself for having had the idea for this sofa in the first place and for having had it constructed to his specifications. It never failed to work as he wanted it to.

"Murdered." Charley wanted to see Althea's reaction.

"That's ridiculous. No one would want to kill Oliver." Althea shook off her shoes and folded her legs under her body. She could try any position she wanted, but, guaranteed, nothing would work.

"Not even you?"

"You can accuse me of almost anything else and, with luck, hit on something I'm either capable of or have actually done, but murder? Never. Even I have limits."

"I hadn't noticed."

"If you weren't so busy with Beryl Carson, maybe you would notice."

Charley started thinking maybe he would get busy with Beryl Carson. Why not? What was holding him back? Nothing.

Charley got up from behind his desk, circled it, then sat on the edge, looking down at Althea, who seemed as though she'd actually found a comfortable position. Damn her. She was capable of the improbable, something he often warned himself to never forget.

"How did you meet Hirata?" This had been bothering Charley since he'd read that Hirata's body had been found, and by Beryl, of all people.

"That's not part of our agreement and you know it." Althea put her hand on her neck and looked over at the shaded window.

"Did Morris introduce you?"

"Don't be a fool. I'm not going to tell you anyway."

"Yet I could find out."

"Do that, then. I don't care."

"If you don't care, you could just tell me."

"How did you meet Beryl Carson?"

"You can't turn this around. I'm asking you. And you know how I met Beryl. She worked on that failed quantum project two years ago."

"Oh yeah. I'd forgotten." Charley suppressed a laugh. Althea would forget something, particularly something concerning his supposed lover? No.

"Morris did introduce you. He must have. The man has no social wherewithal." Morris was his most valuable worker and a good—no, a great—troubleshooter who had an immediate grasp of all computing relationships, but when it came to human relationships, he was a dud. Althea had no doubt done all the work during their liaisons.

"It's not part of our agreement. I don't have to and I'm not going to tell you."

One of the reasons he'd picked Beryl Carson to be his supposed lover was that he knew Althea envied her, although he wasn't sure why. Althea certainly didn't care how brilliant Beryl was, since she herself had an incomparable mind. Was it because of Beryl's ex, the onetime whiz kid who'd never left the womb of that overrated dump, the Acres? He doubted it. Or was it because of Patterson? Yet Althea had never wanted children. He hadn't been able to figure it out, but he'd sensed it would bother her, and it did.

"Did you enjoy your 'interlude'?"

Althea pulled her feet out from under her, slipped into her shoes, and stood up. He'd finally gotten to her. Finally something was working.

"You're *spying* on me?"

"Why would you say that?"

"How else could you know about the interlude?"

"There are many ways. You're not thinking."

"Are you trying to tell me you had an interlude with Hirata? That's interesting. When was this?"

"I am not telling you that. And if I had had an interlude with Oliver Hirata, I wouldn't let you know about it." Among the myriad of other things he wouldn't ever let her know about.

"Yet you keep telling me about Beryl."

"That's not an interlude. We're serious."

"That's news. You're serious? I suppose you'll want a divorce next. How tiresome." She sat back down, but this time she used the stiff-backed chair in front of his desk instead of the sofa.

Charley turned his back on Althea and opened the shades to reveal a deep gray sky. Why did nothing ever work on her? He was trying to get to her, but she'd gotten to him. Damn her. Damn his need for her.

"Is that why you're spying on me? Collecting evidence? It's not necessary. If you want a divorce, just tell me." Was Althea saying she wanted a divorce?

Charley turned back around and let out the breath he'd been holding in. "I do not want a divorce. Wipe that idea from your devious mind. I'm just concerned about you. Your goings-on have gotten out of hand lately. Scale back. You're playing around with volatile people."

"Morris Walls? Volatile?" Althea laughed, the very laugh that had hooked Charley Pierce on her the moment he'd first heard it.

"Banerjee. Hirata. You know who I'm talking about."

Althea looked away for the first time in the argument. Her eyes were fixed on something outside, although there was nothing to see except the clouds and the occasional bird.

"You don't really think I killed anyone, do you?" She sounded concerned, but she knew how to sound concerned. That didn't mean she was.

"I don't know what to think about you."

"We'll have an 'interlude' after you get home tonight. That should help you decide what to think."

"Don't mock me."

"I'm being playful."

"I'm seeing Beryl tonight." Now he couldn't go home. He'd have to use the apartment. Maybe he'd comm Beryl, although he didn't want to. He wanted to go home and have a damned interlude with his wife.

"Cancel."

"Why should I?"

"Because I'm asking you to."

"I'll cancel if you'll cancel your plans for the next two weeks."

"One week."

"Ten days."

"Nine days."

"Ten. I'm not moving from that." Charley should've stuck with two weeks but this argument had left him weak with need for Althea.

"Ten." She sighed and picked up her comm and said, "I have to cancel. See you late next week. Friday."

Althea got up. "Let's go home."

"I never should have married you."

"You mean you never should have made the agreement with me."

Althea was grinning now. She'd somehow won this argument. A trick she'd mastered. But Charley had tricks of his own.

Althea put her arms around Charley's neck and smiled at him. Not just her alluring grin, but a huge smile. Charley wound one hand around her waist and put the other into her dark red hair. As he was about to put his mouth on hers she said, "You haven't canceled."

"I don't have to. It's tomorrow, not tonight." He pulled her closer. He could feel her heart beating. Lust? Anger? Fear? Did he care?

"You're lying to me, Charley Pierce." Her lips grazed his. "You don't have to lie to me. Whatever else we've done, we've always been honest with each other. It's one of the things I like about you."

If Althea knew what he was doing or what the truth was behind his falling-out with Sangstrom she wouldn't think he'd always been honest with her.

"All right, I'm lying. I'm not going to cancel. I'm going to let her wait all night for me. Teach her a lesson."

"What lesson is that?" She moved even closer to him and pulled his lips against hers. He was igniting Althea's passion. Even if the passion wasn't for him but was for what he was lying to her about, it stopped mattering.

"That you're my wife and she comes second. That's the same lesson you should be teaching to all your 'interludes.' I insist on it." He lifted her onto the desk and pushed himself against her. She kissed him with a wild fury. "I insist on it." He said the words into her open mouth.

"It's not part of our agreement," she said.

"It is now." She was pulling on the neck of his T-shirt. He wore a pale blue T-shirt every day. He had hundreds of them, all the same. After they'd been washed three or four times, they didn't feel right. His discarded shirts were donated to some charity as a publicity move. Made him seem like he wanted to give back to the community.

Yet he'd sometimes see people on the street who were wearing what looked to be one of his discarded shirts, but it would have a disturbing slogan on it or, worse, a graphic depiction of the wearer's feelings about Charley.

"What if I won't agree to it?" Althea was touching his neck now, stroking him with her expert touch. The same touch she'd used on at least eighteen others since their marriage. On Morris Walls and on Oliver Hirata and Kaj Banerjee. Maybe Beryl Carson had a similar touch—or a better one. It wasn't that Althea was the most exciting lover he'd ever had—that position belonged to someone else, someone he despised—it was something else, something he couldn't quantify or even describe. But she had it, she *was* it. Or, if he were being honest with himself, she was the closest thing to it without being it.

He did something to her that always drew a response. "You'll agree."

"Maybe," she said.

"You will." As if he had any control over the impetuous woman he'd married.

Charley Pierce loved this woman, his wife, the volatile Althea Pierce. He couldn't explain why he'd fallen for her and he couldn't explain why he still loved her after all she'd done. All her lovers. She'd done it with Morris Walls in his office, which was just down the hall from Charley's. And she'd gone to their private island—the one he'd given to her as a wedding present—with Oliver Hirata.

She never should've started up with Oliver Hirata or Morris Walls. Kaj Banerjee. Lukas Adler.

"Charley," she said, whispering his name into his neck, driving him to an even more intense passion. "Do that again." He did that again.

He forgot about his plans to have his own interlude with Beryl Carson. He forgot about going home. He forgot about his demand for Althea to agree to his new term or what that term might have been. He forgot about almost everything but Althea, right there in his grasp, her breathing much harder now, her legs wrapped around his waist, her hands all over him.

He lifted her from the desk and laid her down right next to the uncovered window. Let the birds watch.

"Charley," she said, "I love it when you're like this."

"Is that why you infuriate me?" He helped her pull her clothes off.

She did something extraordinary with her left hand and Charley felt the world diminish down to that one point on his body that Althea's hand was on.

"Yes," she said. "It is."

She meant it, he was sure.

"Damn you," he said, closing his eyes.

"Is that why you married me?" She laughed and he opened his eyes to watch her seductive, laughing mouth. That wasn't why he'd married her.

CHAPTER 6

O VERTOWNS NEVER DISAPPOINTED. You could go there with your sworn enemy and still have a near-perfect meal. You could be having the worst day imaginable and just walking into Overtowns seemed to be a curative. If you were having lunch with your wife and she mentioned in passing that she was leaving you and taking Patterson with her, yet your lunch would be as delicious as it had been before the out-of-the-blue proclamation that would change everything in your life and destroy something inside you that you hadn't known was there.

Jonathan Lee hadn't been to Overtowns in a while, but the place was as welcoming as ever. There was nothing outstanding about it—it was just an ordinary-seeming restaurant, devoid of any deliberate design or theme. But it was alive in here somehow. If Jonathan Lee could get a fix on where that aliveness arose from, he could sell the formula and make a fortune.

Sitting in what Jonathan Lee thought of as the prime booth, which was located in the back-left corner of the joint, was Ethan Stiles, who looked the same as ever—like he'd been dropped here from five galaxies away and didn't know what the hell to do with himself. He stood up when he spotted Jonathan Lee coming toward the booth.

"I thought you'd never get here," Ethan said, handing him a thick envelope before he sat back down, scrunching himself into the booth's far corner.

"I haven't ordered yet and I'm starving," Ethan, ever the social inept, said.

Jonathan Lee sat across from Ethan and waved to the server, who he'd known for years.

"Be there in a flash," the server—and owner of Overtowns—Lane Overtowns, said.

Ethan looked at Jonathan Lee and tapped on the envelope. "Don't lose this."

"When have I ever lost anything?"

"Don't lose this. I'm serious."

Lane Overtowns came over to the booth and put his hand on Jonathan Lee's shoulder. "Haven't seen you in ages, Jonathan Lee. I thought you'd gone over to the opposition." He meant Keff Institute. Jonathan Lee would never consider going to Keff unless the Acres burned down or went bust—two improbable events.

"Ethan. What are you doing here? Aren't you at the joukko in Osada now?"

"Genesia," Ethan said. "Next door and two flights down."

Lane Overtowns started to laugh but when he saw that nobody else was, he stopped. Jonathan Lee thought it was insulting that Ethan, the joukko's best ME, was stationed in two-bit Genesia when he belonged in Osada City. Ethan's jokes about it weren't funny.

"You both want today's special?" Overtowns said. They did. Lane went over to the next table and Jonathan Lee resisted opening the envelope.

Jonathan Lee wanted to talk with Ethan about what was in the envelope and he suspected Ethan wanted to talk about it as well, but not in public.

Neither of them said anything. The sounds from Overtowns' other patrons did nothing to ameliorate the silence at the booth.

Finally Ethan said, "Don't lose it. I mean it." He tapped on the envelope again.

The food arrived. Admiring it, savoring it, devouring it, praising it, sighing about it when it was finished took up the rest of lunch.

Jonathan Lee and Ethan walked back to the Acres, using the longest of several familiar routes. Ethan would take the magrail back to Genesia after he was finished ruining everything Jonathan Lee had planned for the day. He'd set aside an hour before bed to read over Ethan's report. This walking discussion hadn't been in his agenda.

"What's on your mind?" Ethan said.

"I'm thinking of how you're wrecking my routine."

"Wait'll you see what's in the envelope. Then your routine will take a backseat."

Jonathan Lee and Ethan were on a well-worn dirt path through a fallow field that led into the forest. Ethan looked behind them to make sure no one was around.

"Open it. I want you to read some of this while I've got you right here to discuss this with."

Jonathan Lee obeyed. Ethan was rarely this insistent and although the two of them had talked over some of Ethan's findings in the past, he'd never given Jonathan Lee any material before. This case was obviously very different.

The two of them stood in the unplanted field while Jonathan Lee went through the contents of the envelope. It seemed Oliver Hirata had died of the failure of nearly all his systems, right down to the weird blood chemistry. Ethan was sitting on a tree stump by the time Jonathan Lee had finished.

"What do you think?" Ethan said.

"I don't think your Oliver Hirata is a human being," Jonathan Lee said. When you were finished considering all the likely explanations and they didn't add up, you were left with the impossible, or highly improbable.

"Up until his death, he certainly was impersonating one," Ethan said. "Didn't you read the medserv files on him?"

"Could be someone else went to his medserv appointments. Wouldn't be the first time that happened."

"Maybe." Ethan didn't seem convinced.

Jonathan Lee looked around for another tree stump, but there were none. Now that he was finished reading, he wanted to sit down. "Let's go back to my house."

Ethan got up and the two walked through the forest.

"Spring, when everything starts up anew. I always liked spring here."

"That why you stayed?"

"You know very well why I stayed. This is the only place I've ever felt like I belonged."

"Where do you think Oliver Hirata belonged? He was living at the Normandie and you should see the vehicle he had in his garage. The guy, or the semibiological machine, had impressive assets."

"Maybe he belonged right where he was. Maybe there are non-humans who look like humans who're all around us, only we don't know."

"How come none of them have ever turned up in an autopsy before?"

"Maybe they have, but the ME was so astonished they couldn't put it in their report."

"That's not the job of an ME. This is science. We report the findings, not some invented story to cover up for what we're too astounded to believe could be true."

"That's you, Ethan. That might not be every ME."

"I can't deny you have a point."

"You mean the workaday Prentiss. In Osada."

"I could mean Prentiss. Or anyone."

"Or the results could be quashed."

"It's happened before."

They emerged from the forest, picked up the pace, and went to Jonathan Lee's small house, which was on the western edge of the campus. The house was paid for, but the fee for the land use was deducted from his salary every quarter, a particular that bothered

Jonathan Lee, but he liked his house and had no intention of ever moving from it.

Ethan spread the papers out on the living room floor and the two men stared at them for a while before speaking again.

"At first I thought maybe a rare disease process could be the answer," Ethan said, "but I can't find anything close to this in any data, going back centuries. And what disease transfers the functions of one organ to another? Different parts of the brain can take up the work of a nonfunctioning sector, but that all takes place inside one discrete organ."

Jonathan Lee leaned back against the edge of the daybed in his living room. He often slept out here.

"What if someone were experimenting on Hirata, screwing around with his insides just to see what would happen?"

"Why would he have agreed to that?"

"They could've done it after he died."

"If they did, they left no outward signs. It's damned difficult not to leave scars on dead tissue. And this would've involved—I don't know what it would've involved. Seems incredible and unlikely."

"What's the cause of death, anyway?"

"Right now? Massive organ failure." Ethan snorted. "Which is about like saying the cause of life is organ function. In other words, it's nonsense. It's useless."

"I'm going back to my original hypothesis—Oliver Hirata isn't human."

"All right, Jay. What is he, then?"

"A mechanical-biological construct? An experiment of some sort? A species we've never encountered before?"

"Are you saying he's from another planet or even another galaxy?"

"Could be. Why not?"

"How did he get here?"

"The usual way—he traveled."

"Was anyone with him? And where's his vehicle? And why the hell did this advanced being from the great unknown become an actuary?"

"There's no accounting for taste, Ethan."

"Very funny."

"What if this is a disease?"

"Too early to tell. I'm waiting for the rest of the labs. But if it's a disease, it's unlike anything that's ever been seen before. And let's say it is—then where's it from? How did it get here? Is it infectious? Hang on. That's my comm."

Ethan reached into his pocket and pulled out his comm, put it on audio.

"Ethan," said the voice. "I know the Normandie's not in your jurisdiction, but—"

"I'm at Jay's."

"This is important," Sean said. "It can't wait."

"Hey, Sean. We could use your insights on this Hirata mess," Jonathan Lee said.

The more he looked over the data and the more he thought about it all, the more convinced he became that Oliver Hirata wasn't a human being. He might've looked like one on the outside, but inside he was something else entirely. Who knew where he'd come from? The mystery might never be solved. There might not be any way to solve it. Whatever Hirata was, though, Jonathan Lee wanted in. This was more interesting than anything he was currently working on.

"Jonathan Lee Summers," Sean said. "Did Ethan tell you about Oliver Hirata?"

"We're scrubbing our minds over it right now."

"There's another corpse at the Normandie. I want you to do the post, Ethan. If Prentiss touches this, it'll never be right."

"What part of the building's this corpse in?"

"Northwest corner."

"That's in Genesia. Officially. Unofficially it's in Osada City, since the Normandie wanted all its residents to have a classy address."

"What a relief. Can you work on this later this afternoon?"

"I'm out at Jonathan Lee's. Won't be back until late."

Before Ethan could say anything else, Jonathan Lee said, "Can you get out here? We need your investigative expertise."

"I don't—"

"It's okay, Sean. You should. The Oliver Hirata case is more important than—"

"And Kaj Banerjee."

"What about Kaj Banerjee?"

"He's the other corpse."

"I'd better get back to the morgue. I should be able to catch the next magrail. Come with me, Jay?"

Jonathan Lee Summers's day was already ruined. Why not ruin it further with an unplanned trip to Genesia to check out the corpse of Osada City's most famous artist? Maybe he could see Patterson tomorrow, if everything worked out.

"Sure."

Jonathan Lee threw some things into a bag, sent out a comm to his students, informing them that tomorrow's classes were canceled, and he and Ethan ran to the magrail, scaled the platform steps two and three at a time, and jumped onto the last car as it crawled out of the station before picking up speed.

By the time they got to Genesia, Jonathan Lee had devised an intricate, semiplausible theory about Oliver Hirata's origins.

He was from either another place or another time—a place where intergalactic travel was feasible or a time when time travel was the norm. He'd traveled to their time and place and in order to blend in had taken up a monumentally dull-seeming profession. But the atmosphere, the gravity, the food, the water, or something else had finally been too much for his system to bear up under, they'd failed, and he'd died.

As much as his theory seemed to account for Oliver Hirata's rare case, Jonathan Lee Summers was wrong.

CHAPTER 7

BOYD MCCORMICK HIMSELF had come to the Normandie. Sean figured he wanted to be in on the death of Osada City's most famous resident, even if this was technically Genesia. Before she'd been able to escape his questions, he started in on her.

"What the hell are you doing here, Meade?"

"I have a client in the building."

"You have a client? Someone trusts your abilities as a detective?"

Sean didn't answer. She'd quit, partly because of Boyd McCormick, and Boyd had been promoted. The man was untouchable. He'd cozied up to the powers at the joukko and in return they adored him. That was how the world worked, and no matter how much she resented it or how angry she was about it, she couldn't change it.

Instead of her abrupt departure from the joukko, she should've been the one promoted and Boyd should've been fired. He was the worst of the worst—but he was beloved. Even though Sean was independent now she still needed her connections at the joukko. Besides that, no one would ever believe her, not when it came to Boyd McCormick.

"That still doesn't answer the question. Was Kaj Banerjee your client? And you brought your cat with you?"

The orange tabby was standing next to Sean now, as though it were her cat.

"This is Banerjee's cat." Sean stuck her hands in her pockets to avoid using them to turn Boyd McCormick into a pulp.

"You still haven't answered the question."

"I didn't realize I had to."

"If Kaj Banerjee wasn't your client—and I can't imagine why he would be. If he needed a private detective he would've hired someone with experience and heft. You have neither. But if he wasn't your client, what the hell were you doing in his apartment?"

"The door was open and I'd heard that no one had seen him for a while. I thought I'd check on him. You know. In case."

"Some people never learn. You're one of them. Then, who is your client?"

"That's privileged information. You know that." Sean almost couldn't believe she was protecting Zee Walls, who might've been the murderer of three people. But Ziva was her client and she wasn't going to tell Boyd McCormick that—or anything.

"Everyone in the building's being canvassed. We'll find out anyway."

"You do that."

"You finished?" McCormick was addressing the head of the forensic team, someone Sean didn't recognize. Had that much changed since she'd left the joukko? While she was considering this, she heard McCormick say "Prentiss," and she cut in.

"No. Stiles."

"Are you still involved with that lummox?" Long ago, she'd trusted Boyd with facts about her personal life. She'd been a fool.

"That has nothing to do with this, and if you must know, we're still friends." She kicked herself for saying even this much. Boyd didn't deserve any avenue into her gone-from-the-joukko world.

"This is Prentiss's domain."

"This area of the building is located in Genesia."

"Hsu, get over here." At least this was someone Sean knew. Detective Toby Hsu had more info about the workings of the joukko than maybe anyone else on the force.

Hsu got up from the floor and came over.

"Sean. Good to see you. Are you back on the joukko? We need you."

"Sean Meade will never be back on the joukko, Hsu. Don't encourage her."

"I only thought—"

"Is it true that part of the Normandie is in Genesia and not Osada?"

"It is." Hsu was looking back and forth between Sean and Boyd. Sean made a mental note that perhaps Hsu would be able to help her in the future.

"And this apartment?"

"It's in Genesia," Hsu said. "I've already contacted Stiles. He's on his way over."

"I still want Prentiss here. I don't trust Stiles."

"He's the best ME I've ever worked with." Hsu said what Sean was thinking but couldn't dare say. She wasn't in any position to defend him.

"Healy"—Boyd addressed one of the forensic guys—"comm Prentiss. This is too important to leave to just anyone."

"Yes, sir," the sycophant Healy said. Sean was starting to remember everything she disliked about the joukko and congratulated herself for having had the impulse to quit. It was a relief to be disconnected from people like Vern Healy and Boyd McCormick.

"I'm going now," Sean said. She had to get out of there before Ethan arrived, and she had to see if she could talk with Ziva Walls before anyone on the joukko got to her.

"You still haven't answered my questions," McCormick said.

"Arrest me."

"You're lucky I'm not arresting you. You could be Banerjee's killer."

"No signs that this is necessarily a murder, Chief," Hsu said.

"Don't you have something else to do?" Boyd got that look on his angry face that made him look even angrier. Everyone on the joukko knew that look and no one wanted to be anywhere near him when he was sporting it.

"Getting to it, Chief." Hsu backed away.

The cat was now winding its way around Sean's legs.

"You know where to reach me." Sean bent down and petted the cat, who was acting damn nice for someone who probably hadn't eaten in a while. Sean had had Boyd over for dinner once back when he was her partner and she'd thought they could be friends.

She headed for the door, followed into the hall by the cat.

"I guess you want out of there too," she said as she went down the eerie hallway toward Ziva Walls's apartment. The cat raced ahead of her, as though knowing where she was headed.

No answer at Zee's door. Sean commed her, but got no reply. She'd have to talk to her later.

As she got in the elevator the one next to it opened and Ethan Stiles, looking disheveled and distracted, got out. He didn't see her and she pretended not to see him. After the elevator door closed, Sean saw that the cat was still with her.

"So you want to come home with me?" Like many witnesses she'd questioned, the cat avoided a direct reply. She picked it up and positioned it in her bag. The cat seemed fine with this arrangement.

"Mind if I join you?" While Sean had been fussing with the cat and getting off the elevator, she'd missed spotting Jonathan Lee Summers, who was leaning up against the Normandie's northwesternmost exterior wall.

"Jonathan Lee. What are you doing here?"

"Came in with Ethan. He's brooding over the Hirata case and promised to let me observe the Banerjee autopsy. Couldn't pass that up."

"Don't blame you." Sean herself wanted to observe the Banerjee autopsy but had to remind herself that she had no right to be there.

"What were you doing here?"

"I have a client in the building."

"Moving up in the world?"

"Right."

"The joukko's not all it's cracked up to be. This is a good thing for you. Getting away from them. Look how they treat Ethan. It's like they want to discourage all their best people. Is that a cat in your bag?"

"Yeah. I guess it was Banerjee's cat. Now it's my cat until I find someone who'd like to take it." Jonathan Lee scratched the cat's head and said, "Nice cat."

"So far."

"Don't be so suspicious."

"And you're not?" Jonathan Lee had been dumped and Sean knew all the details about Beryl's defection, as Jonathan Lee had called it.

"Only about a select few."

"Want to come over while you're waiting for Ethan?"

"Sure. I'm tired of waiting here."

"What's it been? Ten minutes?"

"Fifteen at least. I'm not good at waiting. Ethan'll comm me when he's ready to do the autopsy."

"I have to pick up something for the cat on the way home." Sean lived on the wrong side of Osada City, the side that no one who could afford to live on the right side would even consider living on but Sean liked it there, leaking roof and all.

"It'll give us something to do," Jonathan Lee said.

After gathering cat supplies and food—Jonathan Lee insisted on paying and Sean's finances were in no condition to refuse help—they went to Sean's house. She deposited Jonathan Lee in the pristine living room and took the cat back to the kitchen, which was also devoid of her hoard, and gave it food and water. While the cat was munching away, Sean went back to the living room, which was empty.

"What the hell?" Jonathan Lee's voice came from Sean's workspace. She squeezed her way down the hallway, holding her breath, relieved that Jonathan Lee hadn't disturbed any of the stacks there, but if he'd messed with the towers in her workspace she wouldn't hold back.

"No one invited you in here."

"That's exactly why I came in. You've never invited me past the living room. I thought you were hiding something. Is this why Ethan and you split up?"

"Ethan has never been back here." But what if Ethan had been back here? Would their nonrelationship have ended even sooner?

"I had no idea. You hide it well."

"This is my house. Not anyone else's."

"But you are hiding this."

"No one would understand."

"Ethan might. You've been in his apartment. The man's a diehard slob."

"He doesn't, um, collect things."

"What's this all about?" He was sorting through the current tower. "Is this why you were at the Normandie?"

"When did you become such a snoop?"

"I'm a natural snoop."

"Apparently."

"Who's this Morris Walls, anyway? Hang on." Jonathan Lee took his comm out and had an exchange with whoever it was on the other end.

"He's coming over."

"Who is?"

"Ethan. Isn't that who we were talking about?" She'd thought he meant Morris Walls was coming over. She shook her head. No case was that easy to solve.

"Isn't he doing the autopsy tonight?"

"Tomorrow morning. He's too tired. It's the Hirata thing. It's getting to him."

"Wait. You asked him to come here?"

"I didn't think you'd object."

"You might've asked me first."

"I'm always overstepping."

"True enough. Let's go back into the living room."

"You don't want Ethan to see this, do you?"

She didn't. She led the way back to the living room, where the cat had taken over the most comfortable chair, the same chair Zee had been sitting in earlier, and was cleaning its face.

"Morris Walls. Missing. I'm trying to find him. Failing so far. His wife, Ziva, is my client. You cannot tell anyone. I don't even think I want Ethan to know. But the thing is, Morris Walls lives—lived?—at the Normandie. So did Oliver Hirata. And now Kaj Banerjee."

"Did Ziva off them all?" Jonathan Lee had somehow intuited Sean's main theory and worst fear.

"I don't know, although, believe me, I've been thinking that exact thought."

Ethan's distinct knock sounded on her front door and he opened it, letting himself in.

"You got a cat?" were his first words. They hadn't seen each other in months but that was what he said.

"Yes, I did. Had to replace you." Ethan winced and Sean hoped she'd hurt him just a little, then hoped she hadn't. Just because two people didn't work out together didn't mean you had to retaliate. And what would she be retaliating for? She was just as much to blame.

"I think we have another one," Ethan said to Jonathan Lee, and sat down next to him on the worn-out couch.

"Going to let me in on the secret? Another what?"

"Another intergalactic or time-traveling visitor." Ethan leaned back and stretched out his legs. "I wanted to do the autopsy tonight, but my body objects. It'll have to be in the morning. You staying, Jay?"

"Wouldn't miss it. Already canceled tomorrow's classes."

"What are you talking about?"

"Oliver Hirata. Jay here thinks he's not human."

"I also think that's a possibility." Sean had thought this more than once.

"No wonder Ziva killed Morris," Jonathan Lee said.

"I thought I made it clear we weren't going to discuss this." It had been so long since she and Ethan had been a couple that Sean had forgotten there were no barriers between Jonathan Lee and Ethan and that anything she told one of them would automatically be transferred to the other.

"Who are Ziva and Morris?" Ethan kicked off his shoes. The cat stretched out his left front paw and did a combination yawn-meow.

"Ziva's her client," Jonathan Lee said. "Her husband—is he her husband? brother? uncle?—Morris is missing. Our Sean is on the case. They live in the Normandie."

"A hotbed of crime, her husband, and, Jonathan Lee, no thanks for filling Ethan in."

"You are very welcome. He'd find out anyway."

"It'd have to happen in my sleep," Ethan said. "I don't know how the two of you are so energetic."

"I'm pretending." Sean could lie down on the floor right where she was sitting and fall dead asleep. Maybe she wouldn't even have to lie down. The day had been long, stressful, eventful, angering, surprising, informative, and frustrating. And now Ethan was sitting on her sofa, just like he would have if they were still dating. Damn Jonathan Lee Summers for inviting himself over.

"We've been poring over the Hirata corpse. Well, the information. I haven't actually seen the corpse, not that I want to. Are you going to back me up on my theory?" Jonathan Lee looked at Ethan.

"The visitor-from-another-place-or-time theory? Go ahead, Sean, back him up. I'm out of options. If this is a disease, it's like no other known disease."

"Except it is like another known disease." Sean's original thought had been nagging at her subconscious and now it was full-blown in her conscious mind and had emerged, unbidden, through her mouth. She was too tired to care and much too tired and aggravated to censor herself.

"Tell me, Dr. Meade, what disease would that be?"

"You're the computer specialist, Jonathan Lee Summers. It should be obvious to you. This disease is a lot like a computer virus."

"But these are people we're talking about." Ethan's eyes were closed and he was shaking his head.

"Or biomechanical beings." Jonathan Lee was sitting forward now, his arms resting on his thighs. "If they're biomechanical beings, they could have a computer virus."

"If they're humans, they could have a computer virus." There. She'd said it. Her nutso theory was out in the open, ready to be flayed into subatomic particles by two ultra analytical minds.

"What you're saying is that you think there's a biological virus that's acting like a computer virus, right?" Jonathan Lee was fitting Sean's insane theory to something resembling logic.

"I'm saying that there's a computer virus that's infecting humans."

"Absurd." But Ethan's eyes were open now.

"I thought I'd throw it out there. It's the only explanation I've been able to come up with that fits the facts."

"But it's impossible." Ethan sat up. "It can't be."

"What if it can be?"

CHAPTER 8

BERYL LOOKED AT her comm—another message from Charley Pierce. He'd sent a few lately, but she had no idea why. Did she know him? Was she supposed to know him?

There was . . . well, she didn't have the wherewithal to think about that now. She had Patterson on her mind. Patterson wanted to spend the summer with Jonathan Lee, and Beryl was against it. She had to come up with an explanation that Patterson would accept. Maybe if she offered a choice: either Jonathan Lee or archaeology camp. That should do it. Patterson was wild for archaeology.

Her comm buzzed and she picked it up without looking at who was contacting her. She was sure it was Patterson, who always commed her in the afternoon.

"What do you think about archaeology camp?" Beryl put down her scroll and looked around the greenhouse. She'd strolled over here after her last class. She lectured only as a nod to the powers at Keff, who were grateful to have her on the faculty. By rights, she should've been head of the ag department at the Acres, but she'd no sooner be there than she'd—

"I'm afraid I haven't been to camp in years, but if you want to go, I'll be happy to accompany you," said an unfamiliar voice.

She looked down at the comm and saw Pierce's name, not Patterson's.

"Who are you?"

"It's Charley Pierce. From the quantum project you did such a great job on. Too bad it didn't work out."

"I meet a lot of people." She couldn't place him, couldn't picture him, didn't know which quantum project he could be referring to. She'd worked on several. She turned on the video on her comm and looked at him. She still didn't recognize him.

"I thought you were Patterson."

"Sorry to disappoint you."

"Patterson usually comms me right about now."

"I was wondering if you'd like to have dinner with me tonight."

"Why would I?" Beryl had no interest in anything other than Patterson and her work. Before Patterson, her work had been her only interest, and having to sustain a relationship with her husband, her ex-husband now, had taken up too much of her energies.

"I heard you were looking for investors."

Beryl had been about to end the comm, but if this Charley Pierce would invest in one or several of her ongoing or future projects, that was different. Her latest passion was an oceanic meadow that showed great promise as an almost-labor-free source of edible plant life. She had a few investors, most of them people she knew, but she needed more. The expense would be massive, but the results would be worth it.

"I am."

"I'm afraid you'll have to suffer through a dinner with me first."

"We'll have to go to Agretta's." That was the only restaurant that served the kind of food Beryl would eat, aside from what she or Patterson prepared.

"That's fine. See you there at seven?"

"Eight."

Beryl ended the comm, picked up her scroll, and researched Charley Pierce. He was *the* Charley Pierce, the head of Pierce Sangstrom, the megacorp whose ubiquitous programs were the mainstay of current technology.

After Beryl got home, Patterson emerged from the back of the house.

"I'm having dinner at Agretta's tonight. An investor. Want to come too?"

"Can't. Studying."

"Yes. That's more important."

"I want to spend the summer with Dad. I sent him a comm but haven't heard back yet."

"Wouldn't you rather go to archaeology camp?"

"Why would I want to do that?" Patterson was at that annoying age, although Beryl had thought almost every one of Patterson's ages had been annoying. It was as though Patterson had arrived in the world completed, needing no education, growing up, or guidance. Patterson already knew everything, including how to be annoying.

"Because you love archaeology."

"I was telling a friend just this afternoon how you are oblivious. More oblivious than ever. This proves it." Patterson's arms were folded across the chest of someone much older than Patterson could possibly be.

"Have a good dinner. I'll be studying. And, Mom, it's volcanology, not archaeology."

"Of course." Patterson's interest in archaeology was from two years ago. Or before that.

Beryl changed into her black dress, the one she wore when she was trying to get investors interested in her projects, and walked over to Agretta's, a few blocks away.

Why had Beryl ever been interested in Jonathan Lee Summers? Jonathan Lee wasn't a botanist, he wasn't all that interesting, and yet she must have fallen in love with him.

What was love, anyway? She sat down on a bench on the outskirts of the park across from Agretta's.

A huge, tall man was talking to her. It was as though the voice were being projected from the end of a long corridor in a sealed-off building.

"Are you all right?"

"Leave me alone." This was supposed to be a safe neighborhood, but here in Genesia, maybe nothing was all that safe.

"We're having dinner down the street together in a few minutes."

"I'm meeting Charley Pierce. I'm sorry." She wanted to have dinner with this man instead. He was helpful. Kind.

"That would be me."

"Oh. You look different in person."

"It's a trick I have. I like surprising people."

"You've succeeded."

Beryl had a weak grasp on what was transpiring. Was Charley Pierce, owner of the megacorp Pierce Sangstrom, flirting with her? Was she flirting with him?

"I haven't eaten all day," she said.

"Let's get you some food. Then we'll talk about business."

During the meal, Charley Pierce droned on about his business while Beryl mentally reviewed her day. Volcanology: that was Patterson's current interest. She thought about her lecture on wild sea-grasses and their effect on carbon pollution and how she could improve her arguments. Love? That was the way you felt when you wanted to be close to someone but it was, later, only a false memory.

"I told Althea that you and I were having an affair." Charley's words interrupted Beryl's musings. The man had the quintessential winning smile. That could explain his success.

And he was flirting with her. Beryl wondered who Althea was but was more interested in where this evening was leading. She hadn't been with anyone since she left Jonathan Lee, and Charley Pierce seemed like as good a place to start in again as anyone might be.

"Are you saying you want to have an affair with me?" She wanted him to make this clear.

"Are you saying you want to have an affair with me?" He was smiling. Charley Pierce had a good face, even if it wasn't the same face that had been on the comm this afternoon. That face had been stern. This face was kind.

"It depends."

He leaned over and placed a gentle kiss on her cheekbone. She shivered with need.

"Yes, that's what I'm saying." She was unprepared for this but need had replaced preparation.

"Good," Charley Pierce said. "I have an apartment at the Normandie. It's not that far from here."

"I've never been there. I hear it's beautiful."

"I've never done this," he said. "I hear it's beautiful." He laughed and took her hand.

They went to the Normandie, the most fantastic structure Beryl Carson had ever seen, like something out of a fairy tale. She commed Patterson that she'd be back in the morning.

When Charley Pierce opened the door to his apartment, Beryl was stunned with the views, with the furnishings, with the way Charley Pierce was touching her and the way she was touching him, the way each of them responded.

She was impressed. Charley Pierce was someone she could have an affair with, someone who could help fund her research.

After midnight, Charley woke up Beryl, who'd fallen asleep after their passion had played itself out.

"Beryl," he said. She sensed he was talking to her.

"I'm going to leave Althea."

"I left someone once."

"You could stay here with me."

"I can't leave Patterson."

"Patterson can come too."

"Have you noticed the way motion has been changing?"

Beryl sat up. Fear laced through her. Nothing was moving at the correct rate—not the world, not her body, not the flickering lights of

Osada City. Inside her, something was crawling and something else was racing. The sensations fought each other.

Charley Pierce made sounds that Beryl had no way to interpret.

Is this what having an affair does to you? Why?

Those were her last thoughts.

CHAPTER 9

ZIVA WALLS OPENED the door to her apartment, where she'd been hiding out. Morris was still missing, and now Oliver and Kaj were both dead. Ziva was afraid Morris had killed Oliver, although that would have been an extreme reaction to what had been merely some uninhibited fun on her part.

She'd been sure Morris hadn't even known she was friends with Kaj. But what if he had known? And what if he'd thought she was having an affair with Kaj too? Maybe he'd seen some of the paintings and made an assumption. Had he murdered both of them?

Zee and Morris had had a tremendous fight about Oliver. But Morris had no rights. Because of Althea Pierce.

Something was lying on Ziva Walls's feet. Had a package been delivered and it fell into her apartment when she opened the door? She'd told management several times that they should hold her packages downstairs for her. This might be the most luxurious building in the hemisphere, but that didn't mean there weren't thieves around. Or inept management.

Or murderers.

Lying atop Ziva Walls's feet was the head of a woman Zee didn't recognize. Her immediate thought was that a vagrant had made her way into the building, had gotten upstairs, and had fallen asleep outside her door. Or fallen into a coma, was more like it. This woman was inert.

But this was no vagrant. She was wearing a very pricey dress. Zee had a few from the same designer, so she recognized it.

She crouched down and pressed against the woman's shoulder.

"Wake up. It's morning."

No response. Drunk, probably, or on one of the fashionable drugs.

"I don't know why you're at my door, but you have to get up now. Go home."

Nothing. As though Zee needed something else to complicate her already overcomplicated life. She used to enjoy complexities but since Morris had gone missing she'd wanted to have a simpler existence.

Zee put her hand on the woman's wrist and felt for a pulse. There didn't seem to be one, but Zee wasn't a medical expert.

She looked out into the hall. No one else was around. Why hadn't another tenant seen this body before Ziva had? Today, just like nearly every day lately, was about to be upended. Why couldn't Kaj Banerjee still be alive? He hadn't seemed like the kind of person who would die. If he hadn't, she could go over to his place. He'd know what to do. He'd take photos and use them for a painting or a tableau. He'd have his manager take care of the woman.

But Kaj was dead. Oliver was dead, although he would've been useless in this situation. He knew what to do with women who were alive, not comatose or worse, which Zee didn't want to believe was the current state of this woman at her doorstep. Dead, that is. And how unlucky for Zee. The security in this building was abysmal.

Zee commed her private investigator, Sean Meade, who so far hadn't produced any results, yet Ziva could think of no one else to contact who wouldn't immediately think she'd hurt—killed?—this woman. At least Sean was on her side, or should be for the fees she was charging.

"Zee. I wanted to talk with you." Sean always sounded so positive, no matter how little she had to be positive about. Ziva both appreciated this and disdained it.

"Get over here. I have a gargantuan problem."

"Give me twenty minutes."

"Get over here. Now. Something has to be done before—" Before what?

"What's the matter? Did Morris come back?" Sean Meade now sounded less than positive. Sure. If Morris came back, she'd be out of a job and wouldn't get the promised bonus for finding him.

"He has not come back. It's something else altogether."

"I'm on my way."

Ziva put her comm in her pocket, put her fingers on the unmoving woman's neck, and felt nothing.

Three dead bodies—if this woman was another dead body—and all of them related in some way to Ziva Walls.

Although no one knew she was friends with Kaj Banerjee, and the only person who knew about her relationship with Oliver Hirata was Morris, who wasn't around to tell anyone. But what if someone else did know? And now this woman. At least there was no connection here, since Ziva didn't know who this woman was. Had been. She put her fingers on the woman's neck again, and again felt nothing. She put her fingers to her own neck and felt a wild, irregular pulse.

There was some sinister trap closing in on her and she felt powerless against it. She needed her private detective to do more than just find Morris. Now she needed her to find out how all these people had died and identify their murderers, if they had been murdered, before the joukko got to Zee. Or at the minimum she needed Sean to get her the world's best alibis. Isn't that what private investigators were good at?

Maizy at the front desk alerted Zee that Sean Meade was on her way up. Ziva leaned out into the hallway and waved at Sean as she got off the elevator. Sean waved back, then stopped walking. She was staring at the inert and probably dead body at Ziva's feet. The detective moved much too slowly toward Ziva.

"You have to do something about this woman." Zee was gesturing down at the strange body on her doorstep.

Sean crouched down and put her hand on the woman's neck, just like Ziva had done.

"Beryl, wake up."

"You know this person?"

"Not exactly, but I know who she is."

"What is she doing here?"

Sean Meade stood up. "What any other dead body would be doing. Nothing."

"Please take care of this for me." Ziva started backing into her apartment and while she was determining how she could close the door and not disturb the corpse, the detective put her hand on the door and said, "Don't move. I'm going to comm the joukko."

"Do we have to involve them?"

"Yes, we have to involve them. What did you think was going to happen?"

"You're the expert. I thought you'd take care of this mess."

"I am taking care of it." Sean took out her comm and left an unintelligible-to-Ziva message that sounded more like numbers than words. Then she commed someone else and now that she was no longer talking in the obscure language of the joukko, Ziva understood exactly what she was saying.

"Jonathan Lee, it's a good thing you're here. I've got upsetting news."

Sean's comm was on private, so Ziva heard only her end of the conversation.

"It's Beryl. Yes, I know, but. Jonathan Lee, I don't really want to tell you this way. Yes. All right. I understand. Beryl's—I called for the med team—but. Yes. I didn't—yes. No. No, it's not. It's all but hopeless. At the Normandie. Top floor. Not sure. This could be in Osada. All right."

"What could be in Osada?" Ziva was dying to ask a hundred questions, starting with who the hell Jonathan Lee was, but she had to start somewhere.

"This part of the building."

"What are you talking about? This building's in Osada City. It says so on the building's address."

"Part of the building's in Genesia."

"I would never live in such a place."

"Well, it's likely that you do live in such a place."

"I wouldn't consider it." Ziva Walls's fortune would be insulted to step foot in Genesia, much less live there.

"Today is even more horrendous than every other day since Morris left me."

"So he did leave you?"

"You're supposed to be on my side."

"I am on your side, but you need to give me the facts. How do you know Beryl Carson?"

"I don't. And that's her name? How do you know her?" Ziva wondered if Sean Meade had put this body outside her doorway in order to do whatever nefarious thing it was that a former detective on the joukko might want to do. Frame her for Oliver's death and then get an award? Did the joukko give out awards to private detectives?

"Yes. She used to be married to a friend of a friend of mine."

"Is that who you commed?"

"Yes. Why do you think she's here?"

"I have no idea. I don't know her and I was shocked when I opened my door just now. You have to take care of this."

"If you mean I have to help you disguise this somehow, that's not my job, but I will help you with the joukko. I won't let them question you without my being there and, Zee, you should call your attorney."

Ziva was still standing in her doorway although Beryl Carson's head was no longer resting on her feet. Sean was still crouched down next to the body that was looking more dead by the minute. Ziva felt like screaming but restrained herself. That would alert all her neighbors that yet something else was wrong.

"I meant you should take care of this. This has nothing to do with me. I don't know her. I didn't even know who she is. I mean, I still don't know who she is."

The elevator door opened and an angry-faced man strode toward her apartment. Ziva rather liked angry-faced men—after all, she'd married Morris, hadn't she?—but she took an immediate dislike to this particular one.

"Are you in charge of every incident at the Normandie now, Meade?"

Sean stood up.

"Boyd. I wouldn't've thought you'd be awake so early."

"Officer Boyd, I don't know who this woman is or what she's doing here." Ziva wanted to get that important fact out in the open right away.

"McCormick. Chief McCormick. And you are?"

"Ziva Walls."

"This your apartment?"

"Of course it is." How insulting. Of course it was her apartment.

"How well were you acquainted with the victim?"

"Victim?"

Just then the elevator doors opened again and a team of medical-seeming people dashed down the hall. Sean stepped aside and the medicals went to work on the dead-seeming Beryl Carson, ex-wife of a friend of a friend of Zee's private investigator who hadn't yet located Morris.

One of the meds looked up at Chief McCormick and shook her head.

"Estimated time of death?"

"Can't say. Have to wait for Prentiss. Or is it Stiles?"

McCormick looked at Meade. "Well?"

"I'm not sure. Let me take a look." She pulled out her scroll and studied a map. "It's a toss-up."

"Where's the head?"

"Probably Genesia."

"That's not correct." Ziva wouldn't be caught dead in Genesia, but she was smart enough not to say that to the joukko chief.

"This part of the hallway's mostly in Osada, though."

"Comm Prentiss."

"I think her husband—ex-husband—would want Stiles on the post." If Sean was saying this to somehow clear Ziva Walls of any suspicion, she couldn't tell how.

"I'm not talking to you, Meade. You're just another problem, as far as I'm concerned."

The medical waiting in the hallway said, "Prentiss is out of town at a conference."

"Damn this entire situation." Boyd McCormick's angry face expanded into rage.

By the time Stiles, who Ziva understood to be the medical examiner, arrived, Zee was tired of standing and holding her door open, so she sat in her entryway and propped the door open with her feet, which she wanted to scour, to get the death off them.

From her position down on the floor, she got a first-rate view of the victim's ex-husband, who seemed to be working with the medical examiner, but when the ME said, "Jay, let me do this and then you can take the time you need," Zee realized he was just the ME's friend and not working with him.

Stiles seemed very thorough and kept shaking his head. Sean had backed away and was leaning against the wall next to the elevator. The forensic team arrived just as Stiles finished. Then Jay—was this the Jonathan Lee Sean had commed?—knelt down next to his ex's body, picked up her hand, and whispered some things that Zee couldn't hear.

Ziva closed her eyes. She wanted all this to go away. There was no point to having a fortune if it couldn't get you out of situations like this one. She felt someone step over her legs.

"I didn't invite you in," she said to the tall man.

"You didn't have to." The now-furious chief looked like he'd kick Ziva aside if he had to. "This is our business and you'll have to let us do it."

"Sean?" Ziva stood up. "Do I have to do this?"

Sean, who'd been talking with Jonathan Lee, came over to the doorway and said, "Technically, you don't, but, Zee, let them in. It's the best way to clear your name."

"My name *is* clear."

"It shouldn't take too long. Once they determine there aren't any gen-tracings of Beryl in here, they'll be gone."

"I've told them already that I don't know this woman."

But she let the forensic team in. In less than an hour, they declared her apartment free of any of the victim's gen-tracings. The body was removed but the markers in the hall remained, her doorway was taped off, and Boyd McCormick, who fancied himself a chief, told Ziva to pack a few things because she couldn't stay at her apartment until the investigation was completed.

"But this is my home," she said.

"We'll get you a hotel room." Sean helped her pack. She was good for at least that, even if she'd failed to find Morris. But she'd made this morning somewhat easier than it might have otherwise been.

As they exited the Normandie and went out into the glaring sunlight, Ziva Walls thought that after all this was over, she'd sell her apartment and move as far away from Osada City as she could get. She'd go right now, but that would make her seem even more suspicious than she already did.

Three days later, when she was arrested, she regretted her faulty logic.

CHAPTER 10

I WANT TO go back to the Acres with you."

"All right," Jonathan Lee said. "After everything's finished. But you could just stay here. The house is yours now."

"I'm too young."

"Eighteen is too young?"

"I'm fifteen, Dad. Pay attention." Patterson's face was at least thirty years old, a maturity arrived at via Beryl's unexpected death.

Jonathan Lee wasn't happy staying at Beryl's house, a place he'd formerly only stood on the doorstep to while waiting to pick up Patterson. Now he was inside. Sleeping on the sofa since he couldn't bring himself to go into Beryl's bedroom. And anyway, Patterson had closed Beryl's bedroom door, declaring it off-limits.

With his classes canceled for the rest of the month, Jonathan Lee was free to spend as much time in Osada City as he needed to. Then he'd have to take Patterson home with him, although he was hoping to find an alternative. An acquaintance at the Acres was working on a multiyear study of a volcano whose dormant state was in question, and although Patterson was perhaps too young for this sort of thing, Jonathan Lee was hoping to get his kid a spot on the study team. They'd be gone for at least four years and during that time Patterson would become an adult.

After only three days in Osada City, Jonathan Lee had had his fill. He didn't know how to be a parent, Patterson was self-sufficient, and the house smelled like Beryl. He didn't want to be there.

But Ethan's autopsy findings were disturbing—Jonathan Lee couldn't dare tell Patterson about these as Patterson hadn't slept and had hardly eaten since Beryl's death—and somehow Jonathan Lee, Ethan, and Sean had started dedicating several hours a day to working on this problem together.

They'd been doing their work at Ethan's place, but they were meeting at Sean's late this afternoon, as Sean was concerned she was leaving the cat alone too much of the time, although the cat didn't seem to care.

When Jonathan Lee got to Sean's, Ethan was already there, sitting in the cat's chair with the cat on his lap. The results of the three autopsy reports were spread out on the floor. Sean wasn't in the living room.

"Where is she?"

"Said she had something to do and will be back in a while."

"So much for spending time with the cat."

"I'm doing the job for her. Nice cat. I want to name him Sebastian, but Sean objects. She said it's her cat and she'll name him when the time's right. In the meanwhile, the cat's name is Sebastian. Say, have you been back among the chaos?"

"I thought you'd never ask. Is that why you two broke up? Afraid she'd turn your sloppy place into a storage locker?"

"I had no idea. Saw it for the first time today. She kept it hidden from me. Clever of her."

"She's damned clever. I've been tossing her theory around when I haven't been figuring out what the hell to do about Beryl's house and how to get Patterson, who's too young to be a student at the Acres, assigned to the volcano study. Ethan, would you want to stay at the house until Patterson decides what to do about it? It's not that far from the lab."

"Maybe. I'll consider it. My lease is up in a couple months." The cat jumped off Ethan's lap and Ethan got down on the floor and started realigning the papers.

"I think Sean has hit on something."

"Look, Jay, a computer virus can infect only a computer. Don't be ridiculous."

"But don't biological viruses mutate?"

"That's beside the point."

The door opened and Sean came in. Why she and Ethan had called off their whatever-it-was was yet another great mystery to Jonathan Lee. If he hadn't sworn off relationships, he'd be interested in Sean himself. She was one of the oddest, if not the oddest, person he knew, and to him that was a huge attractor.

"I'm worried about Zee," she said. "Finding Beryl's . . . I mean . . . what I'm trying to say is that her encounter with Beryl pushed her over an edge she was already teetering on. And I still don't have one lead on the disappeared Morris."

"They can't hold her for much longer," Ethan said. He was barely looking at Sean. Instead he stared at the papers he was holding, comparing one against the other.

"They have no evidence. Of course they can't. And she's innocent."

"Do you think all your clients are innocent?" Jonathan Lee would've thought all his clients were guilty.

"Most of them are innocent. Well, some of them. Did you find anything else?"

The cat leaped off the chair, sailing across the room onto the sofa, which it seemed he was eyeing as his next territorial conquest. The three of them stared at the graceful, athletic feat.

"That's it, isn't it?" Sean said. She drew an arc in the air, starting at Sebastian's chair and ending at the sofa, where the cat was now ensconced and looking like the ruler of the universe. "It leaped from a computer to a person and now to several people. Maybe more people than we already know about."

"You mean this illogical virus idea you've gotten your brain hooked on?"

"Ethan, if you can't see this is a possibility, I don't know how to convince you."

"You could prove how it's possible. Then I'll consider it."

"Maybe I could prove it," said Jonathan Lee. The more he stared at all the autopsy reports, the more he was willing to consider Sean's theory. Something was indeed behaving in much the same way a computer virus would.

"I'm listening." Ethan dropped the papers he'd been holding.

"I didn't mean I could prove it at this instant, just that I could study it and come up with a logical explanation."

"For example . . . ?"

"Computer viruses have become quite sophisticated. Back centuries ago you needed a physical object to put inside your computer before the virus could get to the operating system."

"People put physical objects into their computers? What the hell are you talking about?" Sean sat in Sebastian's chair and looked over Ethan's shoulder at the papers he'd been holding.

"Something called a disk, although I don't think it was shaped like a disk, but who knows how these things get named. You had to put it into your computer in order to get it to start. There was a slot for it or a tray. Not sure—it could've been something else entirely. The first computer viruses were all on these disks. Later, after the internet came into use—"

"The what?" Even Sebastian seemed confused by this term. He was staring at Jonathan Lee along with Ethan and Sean.

"The internet. The web. You know, the crude predecessor to the meshwork. Ages ago."

"I never heard of it before."

"Prehistoric. My point was that after this internet was in use, you no longer needed a disk to use as a medium to infect a computer. You could just send a virus out through any program or something called an email—I gather that was a primitive comm program—and when the recipient received it, their computer got infected."

"Thanks for the history class on computer viruses, Jay, but what does this have to do with the current situation?"

"Is Jonathan Lee implying that computers aren't infected through the mesh but internally now and not by some outside agent?" Sean was catching on.

"There've been viruses that seem to have no point of origin." Jonathan Lee was in his element now. He had a team of his grad students working on a situation like this, a thorny problem no one had yet been able to find either a cause or a solution for.

"That hardly seems likely." Ethan was holding the two papers again and Sean was staring at them as well.

"Everything must originate somewhere but exactly where is the problem. There was a virus a few years ago that was found to be generated by the operating system itself and of course the infamous Milburn virus that arose from merely searching for Milburn's data, or even merely coming across a reference to him."

"That still doesn't explain how a computer virus could infect a human being. Last I checked, humans don't run on operating systems."

"I didn't say I could explain it right this second, but I'm thinking about it. What if someone's created a computer virus that's a biological virus? That's RNA- or DNA-based?"

"It'd still have to leave the computer and get into a person's body."

"Maybe that's easier than it seems like it could be." Sean pulled the papers out of Ethan's hands. "Look at this"—she pointed back and forth between the two pages—"this looks exactly like something a computer virus would do, rearranging data in order to destroy the system, only this has rearranged biological elements instead of computer ones."

"Very technical analysis, Sean." Ethan was shaking his head. Jonathan Lee would have to work harder to convince his friend.

"You have a better explanation, Ethan?" Sean reached over and petted Sebastian, who seemed disinterested now that the internet was no longer being discussed.

"I've come up with nothing." It was obvious that Ethan couldn't stand his inability to pinpoint or even explain the causes of three deaths.

"Massive system failure." Sean read from another of the papers on the floor. "That sounds exactly like the result of a computer virus."

"It still doesn't explain how the contagion would work."

"Don't biological viruses sort of leap from one area to another?"

"That's a simplistic explanation. It depends on the virus. Some of them require direct contact. Others are airborne. Others need blood or body fluids as a conveyance medium."

"But some of them jump, don't they?"

Jonathan Lee was enjoying this debate between the two ex-lovers, and while he was enjoying it, the undercurrents in his consciousness were working out the particulars.

"You could say that." Ethan was forced to admit that Sean had a point. "And one thing all viruses—computer and biological—have in common is that they need a host in order to live."

Sean's comm buzzed.

She looked up. "Ziva's been taken to the hospital. I'd better go over."

"I'm going with you." Ethan stood up.

"Wait." Jonathan Lee's mind had clamped on to the obvious. "What if she's infectious? She could have the same thing—whatever it might be—that's so far killed three other people. We have to be careful."

"Too late," Ethan said. "We've all been exposed."

On their way to the hospital, Jonathan Lee's mind turned over the facts, but one fact bothered him more than any of the others: Patterson might have been exposed too.

CHAPTER 11

"MORE COFFEE?" ALTHEA picked up the carafe and looked at Charley. They were on the terrace at their country estate, where they'd gone after Beryl Carson's death. As though fresh air—or fresher air than Osada City's—could have an effect on the thousands of dilemmas now churning their way through Charley Pierce's mind.

Althea had no idea what had really transpired, and Charley wasn't about to tell her. But he'd had to admit he'd had dinner with Beryl that night, since Althea often went to Agretta's and knew the chef-owner, so she'd find out soon anyway.

He'd been pleased Beryl had wanted to go there—pleased, that is, before her death—since he'd wanted Althea to have corroborating evidence that he was seeing Beryl, and Agretta was sure to tell Althea the next time she went there.

The apartment at the Normandie, though, was one of his many secrets. It had been included in his agreement with Sangstrom, who also lived there. What must Sangstrom think about everything that had been happening? Charley set that thought aside. Right now he had to calm down Althea, who'd become convinced she was going to be accused of three murders—her two ex-lovers' and her husband's lover's.

"Why did her body have to be found at the Normandie?" Althea had said this about a hundred times since they'd gotten up that morning, and maybe a thousand times since the news of Beryl Carson's death had hit the meshwork. "Oliver, Kaj, the Normandie, and now your Beryl," she kept saying.

"It's just an unfortunate coincidence. It's containable." In Charley's experience, everything was containable or suppressible or would soon be forgotten, displaced by whatever would come next. There was nothing so compelling that it captured an audience and held it for longer than a few days or a week or two.

"It'd better be." Althea sat down and pulled apart a croissant sitting on her plate, shoving the pieces into her mouth. Eating them at a rapid rate, as though she were starving.

She never ate breakfast but since Beryl Carson's death she was eating three or four meals a day. Very unlike her. Charley wondered if Althea could somehow be responsible for what had happened to Beryl. He'd already convinced her they were having an affair. But . . . Charley had other ideas—and other knowledge and suspicions.

"I've got a headache I can't shake."

"Since Beryl?"

Althea never complained about any physical ailment, and he'd never heard her say she had a headache. Most unusual. Guilt? Maybe. Maybe this could work out. He'd have something to hold over her and she'd finally quit her dalliances. That two or even three—depending on what had happened to Morris—of her lovers had died had certainly slowed her down.

"Since before Beryl Carson. Charley, why did you have to have an affair with her? Couldn't you have picked someone else?"

"You mean someone like Oliver Hirata?" He waited for her reaction while she ripped up another croissant and ate each segment with what seemed like an urgent need for nourishment.

"Oliver Hirata wouldn't've had anything to do with you." Not the response Charley had been hoping for. He'd have to try something else.

"Why did you have an affair with him?"

"Why not? You were with Beryl. It's not like you would care."

"I cared. I still care. Your actions forced me to do something."

"Charley Pierce, I know you better than that. Nothing forces you to do anything." She picked up another croissant and said, "These are delicious. We should get these more often."

"We have them every morning but you don't usually eat breakfast."

"How can you say that?"

"Because it's true."

"We never have these and I always eat breakfast."

"Let's not argue. That's not why we came out here."

"We're in hiding." Althea laughed and swigged down her orange juice with the same gusto she was showing toward the disappearing croissants.

"We're not hiding. We're reestablishing the foundations of our relationship."

"While we're hiding."

"The joukko would know where to find us. This isn't hiding."

"Well, I'm hiding. You can reestablish foundations all by yourself. Have you noticed how slow it is out here? We should come here more often. Or I should. Did you bring Beryl out here?"

"No, I never brought Beryl out here. But I intended to. She would enjoy the gardens. Would have."

"Oh yes. She was a plant person of some sort."

"Yes. Of some sort. A botanist."

"She has a kid. Your kid?"

"Don't be a fool. The kid's a teenager."

"But still. I have to get a sweater."

Althea went into the house while Charley ate the last remaining croissant. Today was more like summer than spring, with the temperature already in the eighties. Yet Althea needed a sweater. That and her unusual appetite added up to something, and Charley, who could solve quantum equations in his head, was no stranger to simple arithmetic.

When Althea came back out onto the terrace, Charley said, "Who's the father?"

"What father?" Althea stared at the empty place on the table where the last croissant had been and glared at Charley.

"The father of your child."

Althea started laughing then and in between gasps said, "I can't believe you think I'm pregnant."

"I'd have to say the evidence points in that direction—your food intake, the sweater, the way you've been acting."

"How have I been acting? Like a pregnant woman? And how do they act?"

Charley was stumped. He had no idea how pregnant women acted.

"It's freezing out here." Althea wound the sweater tighter around her and shivered.

"Althea, it's summer out here."

"You were always impervious to the temperature. Like I was saying to Kaj the other day—Charley Pierce is cold-blooded."

"Kaj Banerjee's been dead for weeks now."

"That can't be right."

"Althea, are you feeling well?"

"I told you, I have a headache, and it's damned cold out here. Kaj is a much better lover than you are, Charley. Are you a better lover than Beryl Carson's husband?"

Charley decided to travel along the route Althea's questions were taking.

"Yes, I am. Beryl Carson's husband is a talented lover but I'm an improvement over him."

"She probably just told you that to stroke your ego. As though it needs stroking. And isn't her husband dead?"

"Jonathan Lee Summers. He's very much alive. Lectures at the Acres. An expert in code manipulation and analysis. I tried recruiting him once but he turned me down."

"Too bad. I could have had an affair with him too. If only he were alive and working at Pierce Sangstrom."

"He is alive." Whatever game Althea was playing, it was stimulating Charley, although nearly everything Althea did stimulated Charley in some way, but some of the ways weren't enjoyable.

"Then maybe I'll find him when we get back to Osada. My supply has run dry."

"So you can kill him too?"

"You're the only person I'd ever consider killing." Charley wondered about the validity of this statement. Althea seemed like someone capable of killing almost anyone.

"I mean that much to you?" He prodded her some more.

"Oliver was having an interlude with Ziva Walls, you know."

"I didn't know. And how did you know?"

"He talked about her all the time. Comparing us. You'd think she was the world's best lover, from what Oliver said."

"She's in jail."

"I'd like breakfast now. I've waited long enough."

Charley kept playing along. Whatever Althea was up to, he wanted more of it, more of her. This was better fun than the two of them had had in years.

He went into the kitchen, grabbed a handful of croissants, congratulated himself for having had them sent out yesterday, and went back out to the terrace, where there was no sign of Althea. What the hell?

"Charley." He heard her muffled voice.

"Althea? Where are you?"

"Come and find me. And bring breakfast."

He took the plate of croissants and went in the direction he thought her voice was coming from. When he found her, the game took on a few new dimensions. She was lying on the grass and eating a blade of it.

"That can't be good for you."

"It's delicious," she said. "Have some."

He put the plate of croissants down next to her and sat down. She ignored the croissants and pulled more grass out of the earth and ate it, earth and all.

"Have this instead." He handed her a croissant and she bit off the end then crammed the rest in her mouth.

"Heaven." She grabbed another croissant, sprinkled grass on top of it, and ate the combination as though it were her first food after months of fasting.

"Althea, I've never seen you like this. You're a lot of fun today."

"It's the cold. It's gotten to me." Yet her sweater was open and she'd unbuttoned the top of her blouse.

"We should come out here more often." Maybe they should stay out here, although Charley couldn't abandon the Pierce Sangstrom offices, and Osada City was the hub of his business dealings. And of course Sangstrom.

"Kaj Banerjee wanted me to marry him but I told him I was marrying you."

"We are married."

"Oh, Oliver, you do love to tease me."

Charley sat back. He didn't want to play this game anymore.

"That's not funny."

"All right. I know this is just an interlude, but it's a good interlude, isn't it? Not like the one you had with Ziva."

"Whatever game this is, I'm out of it."

Althea rolled a croissant around on the ground, covering it with grass and sodden earth, then ate it.

"Oliver—"

Charley took hold of Althea's shoulders and stared at her. "I'm not Oliver Hirata. Stop calling me that."

"You want to play a game? What should I call you, then?"

Charley pulled Althea up to a sitting position and tried to wipe some of the soil off her cheeks and chin. "Althea. What's the matter?"

"Oh, Oliver, you know how it is. One day everything is fine and the next, everything is so screwed up. Charley wouldn't like it if he knew we were out here on the island together. But it's my island."

"Althea, stop it. You know perfectly well that we're out at Tuigen, that I'm your husband, and that Oliver Hirata is dead." Charley took in a deep breath and held it against the truth.

"A few years ago I came out to the island and Charley didn't know where I was. Don't worry, Oliver, he'll never find us here. He's not clever enough."

"Let's go inside. The chill must be getting to you."

"It's quite warm and the food is all out here. Let's stay." She took off her sweater and kissed Charley with the kind of passion she hadn't demonstrated since before they were married.

Maybe the game was worth playing, although if Althea had to call him by someone else's name, she could've picked someone else, someone she had no ties to, someone he didn't disdain. Someone he wasn't happy to have out of the way, even if he had ended up dead, although he wasn't sorry Oliver Hirata had died.

While they kissed, Charley started to make plans.

"Oliver, I'm disappointed in you." Althea drew back and stared at Charley.

"Why's that?"

"Don't you want to go swimming?"

"I thought you were cold."

"That was yesterday or the day before. It's warm out today. I bought this island so I could go swimming whenever I want to."

"Althea, we're at the country house."

"Oh, Oliver, I'd never take you there. What if Charley showed up with that Beryl Carson he's in love with?"

"I'm in love with her too." Charley was tired of jollying Althea along.

"I'd like to meet her. She must be magnificent if the two of you are both in love with her."

"She's dead."

"I've never done it with a dead person. Wouldn't there be some kind of legal problem with that?"

"Althea, Beryl Carson is dead, Oliver Hirata is dead, and we're at Tuigen. Not on your damned island."

Althea broke their embrace and stood up. "I have to go inside. My head is killing me."

She ran toward the house and tripped, falling onto her side.

Charley ran after her and helped her up. She wasn't as heavy as Beryl Carson had been, even though Beryl was smaller than Althea. But Beryl had been dead and couldn't help him. Althea was alive and driving him crazy with her antics.

But they were here together. She limped as they walked back toward the house.

"Kaj," she said.

"It's Charley." Did she not know who he was? Or did she want Kaj or Oliver so much that she was pretending Charley was one or maybe both of them? Or . . . ?

"Charley. Kaj was sick, you know. That's why he stopped seeing me."

"What was wrong?"

"He couldn't get in sync with his life. That's what he said. I'm not sure what it means. Something about the pace of everything and how his inner machinery had been poisoned. Is that what's happening to me?"

"Nothing is happening to you, Althea. You're just stressed. All this death. It's frightening."

"When I get to the other side, I'll send you a note." Althea was laughing and her breath was interrupted by what seemed like hiccups.

"Let's get you inside." Charley steered the reeling Althea into her suite, which was on the opposite side of the house from his office. The more they walked, the lighter her body felt, as though her bones had been hollowed out and her skin replaced with feathers.

"I'll send for a doctor."

But when the doctor finally arrived, Althea refused to see her. She was feeling much better. She'd be fine in the morning.

Charley should have been relieved but instead several other dilemmas rose into his conscious mind and refused to let go. He'd have to talk with Sangstrom soon. But that wasn't the worst of what was bothering him.

CHAPTER 12

THE RIDE TO the hospital seemed to take forever. Jonathan Lee kept glancing at his scroll but wouldn't say anything. Sean was sitting next to Ethan and feeling even stranger about their current situation. They'd stopped seeing each other and now he was over at her house, naming her cat, and acting like nothing had ever happened between them. Like they'd been friends only and still were.

And the way he kept disagreeing with her theory. She was grateful that at least Jonathan Lee found some merit in it. She could be wrong—the idea was far-fetched—but she didn't feel like she was wrong. None of it was very scientific of her, but science wasn't her specialty. She was a detective and all the clues pointed at one obvious suspect.

Sean flashed her official-looking ID at the hospital's front desk and the attendant let them all in. But upstairs, on the third floor, where Ziva's room was, they encountered a worker with a stricter personality.

"Only the joukko and family members are allowed in to see Ziva Walls."

"She's my mother."

Sean turned around to see a tall, lanky teenager with a mane of near-black hair.

"Patterson, what are you doing here?" Jonathan Lee seemed like he was about to lash out at the teenager but was restraining himself.

"I'm here to see my mother," Patterson said. "Ziva Walls." Clever kid.

"And I'm her husband." Jonathan Lee put his arm around Patterson's shoulders.

"You are not," Patterson said, shaking him off.

"This way." A nurse let Patterson through the barrier and they went down an endless corridor, disappearing at the turn. The guard at the front put up her hand and told Jonathan Lee, Ethan, and Sean they weren't allowed any further. They could wait here.

"If Patterson gets this thing . . ." Jonathan Lee was looking at the floor as he said this. The three went into the waiting area and tried to figure out what to do with themselves.

"What's Patterson up to?" Ethan was sitting on the plastic couch next to Sean. She made a point of looking past him.

"Probably saw Ziva was in the hospital and decided to do some investigating. Beryl's death has been hard to take."

"For you or for Patterson?" Sean liked the direct way the two friends talked to each other. Ethan was talking to her like that now as well, with the exception of an unaddressed topic.

"For Patterson. But, yes, for me. I don't know how to be a father. It's never come up before. We just pal around for a couple of weeks here and there and Beryl took care of the rest. I'm out of my element."

"But you're a teacher, a lecturer. Don't you deal with kids all the time?" Sean had no experience being a parent, but she couldn't see what was so hard. "You just love them, right? And the rest falls into place."

Ethan, sitting beside her, moved away just enough to show her he and she were not the sort of people who'd have kids together. Not that she wanted kids—or didn't want them. And not with Ethan. Maybe it was the word *love* that had caused him to edge away from her.

"I'm not sure it's that simple. What the hell is Patterson doing in there?"

"Talking with Zee, probably—or listening. She's a talker."

"What do you think happened with her husband. Morris?"

Ethan was reading his scroll and frowning and demonstrating how he didn't care what Sean and Jonathan Lee were talking about since the conversation had turned to Sean's client.

"Yeah, Morris. I think he left her and doesn't want to be found. I'm a pretty good tracer and I can't locate him anywhere."

"You don't have the resources of the joukko behind you now. Ethan, can't you get someone over there to help with this? Or give Sean the access she doesn't have anymore?"

Jonathan Lee didn't understand what he was asking. Ethan couldn't do anything to help her, not if he wanted to keep his job. He'd be found out immediately.

"No," Ethan said, not looking up from his scroll, while Sean said, "It can't be done. I quit the joukko without notice. Walked out one morning and never returned. It's not like I left on good terms."

"What happened, anyway? If you don't mind talking about it."

"I might mind, but—"

"Patterson. What the hell? Pretending you're Ziva Walls's kid."

Patterson had just come through the barrier, striding about like a member of the staff, like coming to the hospital was an everyday occurrence. If Sean ever had a kid, she wanted this theoretical kid to be like Patterson: self-assured, forthright, resourceful, unafraid.

Sean noticed the beads of sweat on Jonathan Lee's forehead. If this was a disease, a virus—whether computer or biological—and Ziva Walls had it and Patterson spent that much time with her, and . . . What if Patterson had it? Sean didn't want to think that but she was thinking that. Jonathan Lee must have been as well.

"Someone had to go see her, so it had to be me. The rest of you are inept." Patterson kept impressing Sean, who thought Patterson would make a much better partner than Boyd McCormick had been, although the comparison was an insult to Patterson, who didn't deserve insults.

"Hey, don't say that about Sean. She's doing the . . ." Ethan trailed off and pretended not to have said what he just said.

"We're all just too old to be Ziva Walls's kid." Jonathan Lee was trying to smile and doing a lousy job of it.

"What's wrong with her?" Sean was almost afraid to ask, but she had to know. They all did.

"Broke her ankle. Some belligerent inmate in the jail chased her down in the exercise area and she fell."

"How the hell did you explain yourself to her? She must know you're not her child."

"I told her I was consulting on her case as a project for school. I know more about her troubles than I do about yours, Dad. But I don't think she killed Mom. I nudged her a little in that direction but she told me how shocked she was to find Mom's body at her doorstep and how it was so sad and she was afraid to go back into her apartment or even into the building. As soon as she gets out of jail she's going to move."

Sean saw her one current client fading into the nonpaying distance, but there was nothing she could do about it.

"Did she say anything about Hirata or Banerjee?"

"The other two who died in the Normandie?"

"What are you, assistant investigator on this case?" Jonathan Lee was standing next to Patterson. More like looming over Patterson.

"Dad. Don't you want to know what happened? And, Ethan, why are you so quiet? There's something you're not telling me, isn't there?"

Ethan shook his head and kept his focus on his scroll.

"There is. I can tell. I may be fifteen, but this was my mother. She shouldn't be dead. Not for years. I want to know everything."

"It's just—"

"It's complex." Ethan cut Sean off.

"I can do complex. I'm better at quantum maths than Dad is. And he knows nothing about volcanoes."

"I don't know anything about volcanoes either." Ethan stood up, ready to defend his friend. He'd been ready to defend Sean too, before he realized what he'd been about to do.

"We think she might've died of the same thing the other people at the Normandie died of." Sean couldn't see any reason to keep the facts from Patterson, who'd find out eventually anyway.

Jonathan Lee glared at Sean but she could tell he was relieved she'd said it so he didn't have to.

"And what is that thing?"

"Let's talk outside," Jonathan Lee said. After waiting for too long for the elevator, the four walked down the dim staircase. No one said anything.

Outside, in the fierce glare, Sean suggested they pick up some food and go sit in the park, far away from anyone who might be listening.

Ethan accompanied her into the store while Patterson and Jonathan Lee waited outside. They got sandwiches and orange-flavored drinks for everyone, slipping into a routine they'd had when they'd been a couple. There was something so normal, so everyday, about it that Sean could almost forget they'd hardly spoken recently.

"Ethan." She wanted to say something but wasn't sure what that something was. He was paying, no doubt aware of her precarious finances.

"Don't say anything, Sean. Let's just leave it where it is."

"I don't know how to not say anything, Ethan. I'd thought . . . well, you know what I thought."

"No one can know what anyone else is thinking."

They emerged from the store and Jonathan Lee, who'd overheard, laid into Ethan. "Maybe not know, but you can have a damn good idea what someone else is thinking. Like right now. You're thinking you wish I'd shut up and leave your ex-relationship alone."

"I didn't know Ethan was dating anyone," Patterson said, grabbing one of the sandwiches out of the bag and starting in on it as the group walked toward the park.

"I'm not dating anyone."

"He was dating me," Sean said. "But it didn't work out."

"That's right."

"Now you're thinking you'd like to slug me, if you were the kind of person who'd slug anyone." Jonathan Lee was laughing—the first time Sean had seen him laugh. He looked like a different person, a happier, more relaxed-in-the-world person.

"I'm thinking you'd better shut up before you're sorry you started down this futile path."

"Let's sit here." Patterson had found a huge shade tree and no one else in the park was nearby.

Everyone sat and took a sandwich and an orange drink.

"Mom never let me have food like this," Patterson, enjoying the sandwich, said. "She was very picky. I miss her." Sean saw the tears forming in Patterson's eyes.

No one said anything for a while and Sean purposely looked at Jonathan Lee and Patterson and didn't make eye contact with Ethan.

"Do I have to ask again?" Patterson was looking through the bag and found another sandwich. "Okay if I take this?"

"There's enough for everyone," Ethan said. "You don't have to ask again. We're not sure what Beryl died of, but it seems very similar to what felled both Oliver Hirata and Kaj Banerjee."

"I don't think Mom knew either of them. Did she?" Patterson looked at Jonathan Lee.

"That's outside my realm of knowledge. But she never mentioned either of them to me."

"I don't know who Oliver Hirata was except for what I read on the mesh. But everyone knows Kaj Banerjee. She would've said something if she knew him. She was always looking for investors. And, anyway, he was Kaj Banerjee."

"Do you know what she was doing at the Normandie?" Sean asked Patterson. If Jonathan Lee knew, he hadn't said anything about it.

"All I know is she had a date that night with Charley Pierce." Sean stopped eating and put the remains of her sandwich back in the wrapper.

"Pierce Sangstrom? That Charley Pierce?" The Charley Pierce whose wife Zee Walls thought was having an affair with her husband, the missing Morris.

"Yeah. She put on her best dress, said she was hoping to raise the funds she needs . . . needed . . . for the seagrass project. And I was happy to see her going out." Patterson gave Jonathan Lee a look and Jonathan Lee shook his head.

"She could do anything she wanted, having nothing to do with me."

"It had everything to do with you, Dad."

"I don't usually wait this long to eat," Jonathan Lee said.

"Are you using that as an excuse for everything? For never being around? For not caring? That is weak as hell."

"It's just a statement, Patterson. Don't read anything else into it. I'm doing my best."

Patterson turned away from Jonathan Lee and addressed Ethan. "You still haven't said what killed Mom."

"It's an unusual disease process," Ethan said. "Unprecedented."

Sean couldn't bring herself to tell Patterson that Beryl might have been killed by a computer virus that had started infecting people. It sounded unbelievable. It was unbelievable.

"Do you use the same computer your mother did?" she said.

"Of course not."

"Jonathan Lee?" Sean turned to him.

Ethan looked at his friend and said, "We'd better dispose of it."

"Absolutely not," Jonathan Lee said. "We'd better examine it."

CHAPTER 13

DAMON GARZA WAS sitting on a fortune. Not that he wasn't already rich, but this was outright wealth coming his way. If only the coroner would finish with Banerjee's examination, Damon could get the ball rolling.

Kaj had never been easy to work with—in fact he'd been hell to work with—but now that he was dead his oversensitive personality would no longer be in play. Now there'd just be an intriguing store of works and a dead artist—an ideal combination. Every artist was always more appealing dead than alive, and Kaj Banerjee was the most successful artist of the century.

The value of Banerjee's works was about to skyrocket. Damon Garza, Banerjee's agent, would reap the rewards of their longtime relationship. He could taste the profits. He wouldn't even have to spend anything advertising, as the buyers would come to him. They were already flooding him with comms. Someone was offering to buy everything, and the sum they'd mentioned shocked even Garza. But he was still figuring out how he could maximize his profit on this unexpected windfall.

Here Damon Garza was, sitting in Banerjee's attorney's office, where he'd been summoned for the reading of the will. The legalities of Banerjee's death were still to be determined, as there was some talk he might've been murdered, but the fact of his death was unquestioned. He was dead and the will was about to be enacted, if that was the proper term for what happened after death.

Sitting next to Damon Garza was an exotic-looking woman with lush brown hair and a cast on her lower leg. Garza thought he recognized her, but didn't know why. Banerjee's lawyer, Werner Stinnett, had gone out into the hall without introducing anyone, so Damon introduced himself.

"Damon Garza. I'm Kaj Banerjee's agent."

"Ziva Walls," said the woman, not identifying herself any further. Haughty, he thought, or as haughty as anyone with a cast on their leg could be.

Then it hit Garza. Ziva Walls was one of Kaj Banerjee's models. He'd probably left her a painting of herself. Just the sort of thing Banerjee would do. He was always giving things away, against Garza's advice.

Great luck that this model was here today. Garza would offer to sell the painting for her, explain how she'd never get as much if she tried to do it herself. This could be the first of the proceeds in his upcoming jackpot. Sort of kick things off until he had time to inventory everything and create just the right atmosphere around the works.

Actually, the hesitation on the part of the medical examiner could be to Garza's advantage. The more mysterious or odd Banerjee's death seemed, the more his works would be worth. The longer the ME took to determine the cause of death, the greater the interest in everything about Banerjee. But the timing had to be right—too long and interest would die out. Garza had to be careful.

"My ankle broke," Ziva Walls said. "Freak accident."

"These things happen, but I'm sorry this happened to you." Garza could sound sympathetic when it suited him.

"So am I. Everything's been hellish lately."

"I know. Kaj's death has been difficult for all of us."

"Aside from that. I didn't want to come here today, but Stinnett insisted. I was expecting a crowd, but it looks like it's just the two of us."

"Looks like. Say, didn't you pose for Kaj? I think I recognize you from a painting."

Werner Stinnett came back into his office, ending Garza's probe into Ziva Walls's relationship with Banerjee. Garza stood up. Ziva stayed seated. When Garza sat down again he noticed the subtle, smoky aroma of Ziva's unusual perfume. He'd have to ask her about it. It was the sort of thing that would make a great gift.

Stinnett positioned the papers on his desk and looked up. "We're here for the unhappy occasion of the reading of Kaj Banerjee's will. He was a good friend and I was sure he'd outlive me and that my son, who'll take over the firm in a few years, would be the one reading this. Not me."

So Werner Stinnett was a good friend of Kaj's? Damon Garza had never heard of him until his office had contacted him a few days ago. Stinnett was no doubt exaggerating, trying to make himself seem important, being not just the attorney for but the "good friend" of the famous artist. Everyone had wanted to be Banerjee's friend, but he had very few of them. Now that he was dead, anyone could pretend to have been his friend.

"Let's get to it, then, shall we?"

"Please," Ziva Walls said. "My ankle's killing me."

Stinnett started reading, but the legalese was disinteresting to Garza. Get to the point already. The more legal bull that Stinnett read, the more impatient Garza became.

"Ziva, I would have shared everything with you if I were alive, but as that's now impossible, I am giving you all of myself that's left. For you to do with as you please. For your enjoyment. You can even share it with Oliver Hirata if you'd like and I won't be here to object."

Werner Stinnett looked up from the paper, stopped reading, and said, "Do you believe this is the deceased Oliver Hirata that Kaj was referring to?"

"Yes," Ziva Walls said. "I didn't realize he knew about Oliver. But we were all neighbors and it's hard to keep a secret at the Normandie. People talk."

"And to my agent, Damon Garza, I leave the task of auctioning off the works now in his possession, the auction to take place at the earliest opportunity, and the proceeds to be distributed in equal shares to my alma mater, the Acres, for an expansion of their art institute, to the city of Genesia, to fund their food bank, and finally to the Osada City Center for Pet Adoption, the wonderful organization where I found my cat, Egon.

"Ziva, I hope you will take care of Egon or find someone who will love him as much as I do."

Werner Stinnett put down the papers and stopped reading.

He was finished? Garza must have missed something, because it seemed like he'd left everything to this woman who'd modeled for him—what he hadn't left to those other organizations, none of which deserved this kind of generosity.

Damon Garza sat forward. "And?"

"There's no *and*. That's Kaj's will, although there are stipulations, most of them about the auction, which I'll give you a copy of and will be happy to explain in detail later this week."

Garza took a deep breath, the inhale tainted with the alluring, smoky scent Ziva Walls was wearing. Ziva Walls, who had just inherited the most impressive art estate in the history of art.

"I'll have so much to do now," she said. "I'm going to need your help."

Damon Garza's shock lessened. She'd need his help. There would still be profit here, although nothing like what he'd been anticipating.

But he was mistaken. She was addressing Werner Stinnett.

"I'll be happy to help you in any way I can," Stinnett said. "Kaj was very dear to me and I see he must have been very dear to you as well."

"He and I were close," Ziva said, "but this is a shock. I thought maybe he was going to leave me the last painting he did of me, since he'd promised it. But this—it's unexpected."

"You bet it's unexpected," Damon Garza said. "I'm getting my own lawyer. This is an outrage. I've been Banerjee's agent for years and years. He's left me nothing but a task I'll get all but nothing for."

"Correction," Werner Stinnett said. "You'll get nothing. One of the stipulations of the auction is that your usual fee will be waived."

"What do you mean, my usual fee will be waived."

"I think it's self-explanatory."

"I'm supposed to give away my valuable services because of some 'stipulation' in Kaj's will? I don't think so. You'll have to find someone else to hold this auction and, believe me, no one else will be able to get the kind of interest and proceeds that I would. I know Banerjee's work inside out. You want me to spend months on this enormous task and not get paid?"

"Well, Mr. Garza, as Kaj explained it to me, although it's not contained in the will, per se"—Werner Stinnett picked up the papers he'd been reading and shook them—"you've made quite a fortune for yourself from the sale of Kaj's works. He felt you'd already been properly remunerated and was sure you'd be happy to head the auction. If not, we'll have to discuss this further, although not today, as I have a meeting out of town this afternoon and have to leave shortly."

"You're damn right we'll have to discuss this further. You'll get a call from my lawyer. And you"—Damon Garza stared at the smug Ziva Walls—"you get ready to spend the rest of your life in court over this horrendous miscarriage of justice."

"There can be no litigation, Mr. Garza. You should speak to your attorney about that. After the Burrows fiasco, the international court passed a binding ruling prohibiting contests in clear-cut wills of this sort."

"What sort of will is this sort?"

"It was executed more than two years before the decedent's death, the decedent was able to make decisions for himself, the language is straightforward and unambiguous, and all the parties mentioned in the will are alive and of sound mind."

"It's obvious Banerjee wasn't able to make decisions for himself. Anyone could see that. Anyone *can* see that." Damon Garza could see it better than anyone.

"To be clear, Mr. Garza, I made sure Kaj was examined by two prominent psychiatrists as well as his having taken the standard medserv sanity exam. There's no question but that this will is untouchable."

"According to you," Damon Garza said as he stormed out of Werner Stinnett's office.

Yet his own attorney wouldn't touch the will, reiterating what Stinnett had said about some bogus international court ruling Garza had never heard of, nor could he convince any other attorney he commed to handle this travesty.

But he would find a way to make something for himself out of this mess. He'd start in on Ziva Walls tomorrow. He'd force her to make a settlement. She'd understand his position even if the coldhearted Stinnett refused to. If that didn't work, he'd become Ziva Walls's agent and help her sell off Banerjee's works. Who better to do it? She'd be thrilled to have him represent her. She'd need his expertise. Yes, this seemed like a great idea.

Too bad Ziva Walls disagreed.

CHAPTER 14

"ND, ON TOP of everything else, his cat's gone missing."

Sean had been listening on her comm to Ziva Walls go on and on and more on about her time in jail, about her painful broken ankle, about the nerve of the Osada City Joukko for arresting her for crimes she not only didn't commit but couldn't possibly think of committing, especially not the unfortunate Beryl Carson, someone she didn't know and hadn't heard of and didn't recognize, and, finally, about how she'd inherited all of Kaj Banerjee's "stuff" and now had the unwanted and enormous task of figuring out what to do with everything, which was going to be difficult if not worse and a burden to her, especially since Kaj's agent was a worm she'd have nothing to do with, and here she was, a woman whose husband was still missing and who Sean Meade had still not located.

Jonathan Lee and Patterson, who'd both stopped by that afternoon, listened along with Sean to everything Ziva was saying.

"I have his cat," Sean said when Ziva took a breath.

"Well, what a relief. Egon needs special food."

"Egon?"

"The cat. Named after some artist from eons ago, I think. Kaj told me."

"I've been calling him Sebastian. He doesn't seem to mind."

"Are you going to keep him?"

"Yes, unless you want him. I mean, Kaj did leave Egon to you."

Sean was hoping Ziva would say no. She was enjoying having the cat around and didn't want to give him up.

"No, that's all right. He's bonded with you and I've got enough to deal with. Sean, where's Morris?"

"I have some new ideas, but you have to be honest with me."

"I'm always honest with you." Sean looked over at the Summerses, sitting on her sofa. Jonathan Lee shook his head and Patterson smirked.

"Was there any reason why you think Morris would have left you?"

"Of course not. Why would he? We had the ideal marriage. Except for his affair with Althea Pierce, and anyway, I was willing to forgive him."

"Well, let me get back to you. I'm going on an expedition this afternoon, see what I can find out."

"And you'll help me with the estate?"

"That's not my area."

"At least help me sort through things? I can't face this alone."

"I'll think about it."

After Sean ended the comm, Jonathan Lee said, "Maybe you could make a few thousand stacks of objects over at Banerjee's place."

"Very funny. I'll have you know those stacks of objects are very valuable."

"Don't you have a computer?" Patterson looked around, but Sean's computer was back in her workroom.

"Of course I do. But some things aren't on the mesh. I gather what I can. You never know when something will come in handy, and last night I realized I had a document that could help me find Morris Walls. Interested in coming with me? Maybe Morris would know about—"

"Hang on. Ethan's meeting us here."

Sean couldn't seem to shake Ethan Stiles from her life. There was no emotion there but she wasn't happy about having to see him all the time. Yet he was the only other person who had deep knowledge about Sean's theory, and even though Jonathan Lee assured her he was making some progress in his work on this matter and had isolated something very unusual, neither she nor Jonathan Lee had any medical expertise.

That was Ethan's contribution. They needed him. Because Sean had come to think of these deaths as her case. Unofficial of course, but hers, Jonathan Lee's, and Ethan's.

"Ethan still hasn't said anything about Mom's death. Isn't it about time he knew something definitive?"

"Have you taken Patterson back to see the hoard?" Jonathan Lee gave Sean a look that translated to *Don't you dare say a word about your insane theory.*

"I prefer to think of it as the archives."

Nobody would dare disparage an archivist, but hoarders were universally despised. And Sean wasn't a hoarder. Everything she'd saved over the years had a purpose. Maybe that purpose hadn't yet been brought to light, but in a world where almost everything was stored on computers and scrolls, physical objects had taken on a new importance, one Sean hadn't fully appreciated until now: these objects were free of viruses and, barring a fire or a flood, their contents were immutable.

"I've seen the stacks already, Dad. Ethan showed me last week. Stop avoiding my question. Something's up and I need to know. You've spent hours taking apart Mom's computer but you still haven't said why."

"I'm looking into her contacts, her correspondence."

"You have pieces of the thing spread out all over the study. That has nothing to do with her contacts. And the joukko are working on it—they copied all her data the day her body was found."

"I think we should tell him, Jonathan Lee." Sean was tired of keeping information from Patterson, who seemed mature enough to handle almost anything.

"It's just a theory. Nothing's certain."

"If it's just a theory, then why are you keeping it from me? Maybe I could help."

"Beryl's death seems similar to two other recent deaths."

"Yeah. All of them were connected with the Normandie in some way. I heard. Shouldn't someone be testing the air there? Taking samples from surfaces? What if just breathing or maybe touching something—anything—is enough to kill you?"

"Ethan had the health department go to the Normandie, but I haven't heard about the results," Sean said.

"Nothing out of the ordinary was found or the building would've been evacuated." Jonathan Lee looked at Sean. "Didn't Ethan tell you?"

Sean shook her head.

"I still don't know why Mom would've been there," Patterson said.

"The joukko are investigating." Sean had no facts about what the joukko might be working on, but it seemed likely this would be the focus of their investigation. "There's something else, something Ethan's discovered."

As if on cue, Ethan walked into Sean's house. Like he belonged there. At one time Sean had thought maybe he did belong there but she'd been mistaken. He didn't belong there and they didn't belong together.

"Did you decide to finally tell Patterson?" Ethan picked up Sebastian, sat down on the cat's chair, and put Sebastian in his lap. Like he belonged there.

"I think we'd better." Jonathan Lee looked resigned to the inevitability that Patterson would find out at some point.

"It's an insane idea," Ethan said, "but I've come to the conclusion it's an insane idea we have to consider as a real possibility."

"What the hell are the three of you talking about?" Patterson stared, one at a time, at all three of them.

"Sean? I think you should explain. It's your idea."

Sean had been hoping either Jonathan Lee or Ethan would tell Patterson, who she'd known only since Beryl's death.

"You see"—Sean swallowed hard, ran her hands through her thick mop of unruly hair, looked away, and then looked back at Patterson—

"I think it's possible that not just Beryl, but also these other two people, Oliver Hirata and Kaj Banerjee, were infected by a computer virus. What I mean is, they might have been."

"That *is* insane. It's also ridiculous. Dad, you want to tell me what's really happening?" Patterson's face was red with frustration and rage.

"I thought it was ridiculous at first too, but it does explain some bizarre findings."

"Like what, for instance?" Patterson was defiant now.

"Oliver Hirata was the first. His spleen was more like a pancreas and his cytology was inexplicable by any reasonable explanation."

"That's not Mom. That's Oliver Hirata. I don't care about him."

"Don't say it, Ethan." Jonathan Lee's tone was harsh. He was trying to protect his kid. "Just do not."

"Jay, I'm not going to keep this from Patterson. Beryl also has several, let's say, unusual findings."

"Stop. Patterson doesn't need to know any more."

"Yeah, I do. Tell me. You might lie to me about Oliver Hirata, but you wouldn't dare lie to me about Mom."

"I'm not lying about anything. Beryl's—I'm just going to say it, Jay—her brain architecture was distorted."

"What do you mean?"

"There's a specific architecture to the lobes of the brain. But Beryl's brain—it was as though someone had taken the parietal lobe and manipulated it, had scrambled the neurons."

"That's ridiculous."

"And many of the cells in her prefrontal cortex had no nuclei."

"Patterson, did you notice anything odd about your mom before she died?" Sean said, hoping to distract Patterson from Ethan's medical evaluation.

"It wasn't like she was ripping open her skull and moving things around, if that's what you mean."

"I mean anything at all. Really. Think about it for a moment."

"She could be scatterbrained anyway but lately, well, she was distracted, I guess you'd call it."

"Examples?" Although Sebastian was still on his lap, Ethan had morphed into full-on Dr. Stiles, the analytic, often brusque medical examiner.

"She thought I'd want to go to archaeology camp this summer, even though I haven't been interested in it since I was six or seven."

"I didn't know you were interested in archaeology." Jonathan Lee turned half around to look at Patterson.

"You never visited that year."

"When did this start?" Ethan had his scroll out and was taking notes.

"Just recently."

"Can you be more specific? Last week? Two weeks ago? A year ago?"

"I'm not sure. Not that long ago."

"Before or after she discovered Oliver Hirata's body?"

"Probably after."

"Ethan, do you think Beryl was infected by Hirata? But he was dead when she found him. How could he still be contagious?" Sean had never heard of someone catching a disease from a corpse.

"Certain viruses can persist long after the host has died."

"Which is true of computer viruses as well," Jonathan Lee said. "It's one of the reasons I destroy my computers when they've been infected."

"So it won't infect other computers?"

"It's happened. There are certain computer viruses that still effectively transmit electrons even after they're inactivated. And if the electrons were infected, then—" Jonathan Lee didn't finish before Patterson cut him off.

"Are we talking about a human virus or a computer virus? It sounds to me the most likely explanation is that Mom was infected by Hirata, not by her computer."

"As soon as I'm able to pin down the pathogen, we'll be able to get a better grip on this. I'm waiting for the results of several different tests. But even then it still might not be feasible to discern the infection's origin, even if the pathogen that infected Beryl is the same as the one that infected Hirata. You and I could both have the exact same flu virus, but we could live in different hemispheres and have gotten it by different means. If there's one thing a virus knows how to do, it's infect a host. That's the only way it can exist. Outside of a host, a virus is dead—if it was ever alive, a debatable point—pretty quickly."

"But that still doesn't tell us how Hirata was infected. If he infected Beryl."

"Or Banerjee."

"What about us? Shouldn't you be examining all of us?" Patterson wasn't saying anything the rest of them hadn't already considered.

"Once I know what we're looking for, I will."

"I'm not sure I want to know," Sean said, "if there's nothing that can be done about it."

"Of course you want to know," Ethan said.

"Yes, maybe. I'm not sure. If there's no cure and I'm infected, and, then . . ."

"We'll find a cure. We have to. Even if it's a computer virus. Isn't that one of your specialties, Dad?" Patterson was sitting on the edge of the cushion, staring back and forth between Jonathan Lee and Ethan.

"Partly. But there've been computer viruses with only one cure."

"And biological viruses as well." Ethan's head was thrown back, his eyes were closed, and he was petting Sebastian.

"Then we'll find that cure." Patterson was determined. "With all of us working together, we'll be able to discover it."

"I don't think you understand what Ethan and Jonathan Lee are saying, but I'm pretty sure I do, Patterson." Sean had to say it out loud since Jonathan Lee wouldn't. "They mean the one cure is death."

Ethan lifted his head from the back of the chair and half opened his eyes. "I'm afraid so."

"I refuse to believe this is true about what's happening right now. Mom may be dead but we can't let this happen to anyone else."

Under other circumstances Patterson's determination and hope might've been contagious.

Ethan's comm alerted him and he pulled it out of his pocket. Sebastian jumped off his lap. Ethan stared at his comm.

"Gotta go. There's another body."

"Ethan?" Sean's heart pounded so hard she could hear it and thought everyone else might be able to as well. Please don't let it be Ziva Walls. Please.

"It's Vern Healy."

"Who?" Jonathan Lee looked back and forth between Sean and Ethan. Patterson's fingers drummed out a vengeful beat, in eerie sync with Sean's galloping heart.

"Ethan," she said, "he was at the Normandie with the forensic team. Unless you mean a different Vern Healy." As much as she disliked Healy, she hoped it was someone else, someone she didn't know.

"No, it's Vern. McCormick's going to be beastly about this."

"He's going to arrest Zee again."

"Sean, I'm more concerned that you were there that day. I can't wait any longer. You'll have to come back to the lab with me."

"I'm going with you," Patterson said.

"Yes, I mean all of you. Everyone in this room has had direct contact with someone who's been felled by whatever this is. Biological virus or computer virus or it could be something else altogether. A previously unknown pathogen—maybe not a virion but some other kind of organism. Something no one's encountered before.

"Its methods are still unknown, but the one thing I'm sure about is that it's deadly and it has to be stopped before this becomes an epidemic. Or worse."

CHAPTER 15

IN MANY WAYS Althea was back to her old self. Whatever had been wrong with her had disappeared, and Charley blamed grief—or simple jealousy. Even though Althea's supposed rival, Beryl Carson, was dead, Althea never countenanced competition.

Charley suspected there'd been competition from the other direction too, since Morris Walls was married. Had Charley known Zee Walls lived in that apartment, he would've left Beryl's body in front of someone else's door. Or put it in the stairwell or pitched it off the roof, which he'd thought of doing but had rejected both ideas when he realized he'd have to drag the body around even more than he already had.

The evening had started off so well. He was fascinated with Beryl, whose multiple interests were energizing and inspiring. Halfway through dinner he promised to invest in her project, which had to do with seagrasses, whatever they were. Charley wasn't clear about the details, but he'd've promised to invest in anything she'd told him about. Why hadn't he asked her out after the failed quantum project? He'd thought about her. He'd used her name to try to get to Althea. But he'd never done anything about it until that night.

He might've waited. Maybe if he had, Beryl Carson would still be alive. As it was, Charley would've preferred Beryl had waited to die until she'd returned to her own home instead of dying there in his apartment, one he rarely used, while he was asleep. She'd been a passionate lover, he was fascinated by her, and he'd started wondering if he was capable of loving someone else. Of course that was just one short evening, one meal, one moment of sexual ecstasy. He didn't really know Beryl Carson.

He hoped to hell Sangstrom wasn't aware he'd brought Beryl to the Normandie, but Sangstrom was the one person who knew about Charley's apartment there, since it had been Sangstrom's.

Charley, though, had more than the constant anxiety of Sangstrom to occupy his current slate of anxieties. Now that Charley and Althea were back in Osada City, Charley was looking over his shoulder all the time. He reassigned his two assistants to a facility in Wyngarden, since one of them had also worked for Morris Walls, who was still missing. Just something else eating at Charley's raw insides.

But at least the joukko hadn't contacted him. There was that one bright spot. They seemed disinterested in Morris's disappearance and unaware Beryl and he had been together. He'd been careful to remove all his gen-tracings from her. He had supplies at the Normandie apartment for this purpose, but he hadn't realized he'd need them for something like this—for a corpse. The cleansing kits were to protect him in case someone he brought there would accuse him of who knew what. But he'd never brought anyone else there and now he'd stay away for a while.

Charley sat in his office and stared out at the vista of Osada City.

Pierce Sangstrom had started out with a surprising success, a program Sangstrom dashed off one afternoon and which Charley refined over a marathon weekend. Three days later they put it on the market, a careless gesture, testing out their new enterprise. What had started off as a dare—could they create a program that'd bring strangers together without anything more than a simple list of predetermined preferences?—was an overnight hit.

Their creation, Meet Me, paired users up with other users who answered only a short series of simple yes/no criteria selected by each. The program then arranged for all the rest so the parties involved wouldn't have to do anything other than show up.

Neither Charley nor Juno had thought it would amount to anything, but Meet Me developed a vast user base almost instantaneously at its launch, was fast and easy to use, and created a surprising, often fulfilling, meeting between two—or more—strangers.

There were numerous Meet Me copycats but none was as popular as the original, and Sangstrom's spinoff creations had been equally successful, especially Find Me, which connected anonymous users in distant locations on the condition they'd never meet. All location data was suppressed and if users attempted to exchange contact or identity details, these were blocked before they could be transmitted. A supposed deep hack could supersede this sometimes agonizingly frustrating aspect of Find Me, and Pierce Sangstrom was happy to benefit from the proceeds.

Since the Pierces returned to their home in Osada, Althea had stopped her eating spree and was back to her usual self, but with a few changes, some of which Charley approved of and some of which he wanted gone.

One of the items on the approved list was her renewed interest in her sex life with Charley. She wasn't seeing anyone else—as the investigator he had following her assured him—and she was being especially loving and inviting. He reminded himself to comm the investigator later, since he hadn't heard from him in a couple of days.

Althea. Why couldn't Charley stop the attraction and be done with it? She'd been nothing but trouble from the beginning and now . . . Oliver Hirata and Kaj Banerjee both dead. Morris Walls missing and maybe dead. Beryl Carson dead. Althea wasn't directly responsible, but Charley felt she was to blame for his having taken Beryl to dinner, since he never would've done it had Althea not been the unfaithful, uncaring wife she'd turned into. Actually, that she'd always been.

And Althea's odd behavior and weird illness when they were out at Tuigen. He was convinced it had changed her somehow.

One of the unsettling changes was that Althea was now overinterested in gardening, spending hours in their two-acre yard, a luxury in Osada City, where space was at a premium and only the wealthy had any land at all. Althea had facilely memorized the scientific names of hundreds of plants, it seemed, and was busy eight or ten hours a day eliminating the work their landscaper had spent years cultivating, and replacing the former arrangements, designs, and plants with ones of her own choosing. She did all the work herself, which was not like the former Althea, the one who'd existed before she'd gotten ill.

Did this sudden interest in horticulture have something to do with Beryl Carson, the botanist? Was she trying to outdo her supposed rival, even though that rival was dead?

In his worst moments since they'd arrived back in Osada, Charley wondered if Althea had killed Beryl. These wonderings involved a lot of assumptions—that Althea knew Charley had a date with Beryl that night, that Althea knew about his apartment at the Normandie, that Althea was able to get to Beryl without his knowing it, that Althea was a murderer.

Some of these wonderings were easier to believe than others.

One of Althea's changes on the unapproved list was that she would still occasionally call him either Oliver or Kaj. He wasn't sure if she was needling him on purpose or if her illness had caused a sort of permanent glitch in her memory so that he, Oliver, and Kaj were somehow interchangeable to her. Knowing Althea—the former, pre-illness Althea—he thought it most likely she knew exactly who he was and was using her former lovers as weapons against him. Letting him know that by having an affair, as she thought he'd had with Beryl Carson, he'd committed an act that gave her limitless power over him.

Among the many other swirling thoughts eating their way through the whorls of Charley Pierce's mind was one that, no matter how hard he tried to contain it, compartmentalize it, or reject it, it kept resurfacing: What if Beryl Carson was killed by a contagious disease and now he had it? What if he was the next death? What if he'd unknowingly given this disease to Beryl Carson and it was lurking inside him, waiting for the right moment to emerge and do its worst?

Charley's inherent feeling of invincibility had been his birthright. His partnership with Sangstrom had eaten away at some of it, but his marriage to Althea had delivered much heavier blows to it.

Unlike his obsession with Althea, Charley had always been able to successfully shunt Sangstrom to an encapsulated place in his mind and his life, made easier, perhaps, by how encapsulated Sangstrom's life itself was, holed up there in the Normandie, never associating with anyone, hiding from the world.

Still, Sangstrom worried Charley, particularly the prospect that their past and their secret present could still harm him from several different directions. But he and Sangstrom had an agreement, and Charley always kept up his end of it, even when he hadn't wanted to. Yet, this week had been all right and maybe next week would be too.

And, if nothing else, Sangstrom was reliable—always inventive, creative, brilliant. Also . . . but he wouldn't go near any locked-off thoughts, current or historic.

Charley got up from his desk and the view and wandered down the hall to what had been Morris Walls's office. Morris was still registered as working at Pierce Sangstrom, but Charley had cut off his salary. No point paying someone who wasn't there and who might be dead. What had happened to Morris? Was he running away because he was afraid Charley would get angry about his relationship with Althea and figured he'd better leave before Charley fired him?

But Morris was a worker. He'd've gone to another company. Charley would've heard about it, but he'd heard nothing.

Althea didn't talk about him and Charley didn't ask.

Charley left work early. His mind wasn't there. He commed the private investigator and got no response. That's the way these people were. When they wanted to get paid or if they had interesting information and wanted to get paid more, they commed you. If not, they were unavailable since they were purportedly working on your case.

When Charley arrived home, Althea met him at the door, looped her arm through his, dug into his clean jacket sleeve with her garden-soil-heavy gloved hand, and dragged him out to the yard.

"I've planted over a hundred and fifty peonies today. Aren't they glorious?"

"Yes, they are."

Charley meant it. For all the work their landscaper had done, Althea's designs and choices of plants were far superior. The arrays were stunning, unique, and grabbed your attention, unlike any garden he'd seen in the past, including their former, overpriced one. Knowing Althea, this would be the start of a new business for her. She knew how to turn all of her ideas and schemes into riches, a skill he shared and appreciated.

"Althea, I can't believe you just started doing this. You're already an expert."

"Oh, Vern, really. It's not so hard. There's a lot of information on the mesh about it. I just did some reading."

"Who's Vern?"

"Don't be like that, Vern, darling. Charley will never find out. He thinks you're spying on me!" Althea laughed her hearty, I-don't-give-a-rip laugh and kissed Charley with her uninhibited, post-illness passion.

Charley pulled Althea toward him and argued with himself about whether he should start an argument or make love to her right there in their spectacular new garden. He wanted both.

"I'm not Vern. This is your husband, Charley. Or have you forgotten me?"

"Don't kid around. Charley will be home any minute now. Let's go down to the riverfront and . . ." She whispered her plans into his ear and Charley stopped caring what she called him and went to the riverfront, the perimeter of their property, with her.

An hour later, while Althea was asleep and the sounds of the water lapping onto their dock did their best to lull him into unconsciousness, Charley summoned his energies and commed his private investigator, the louse Vern Healy, telling him he was fired.

CHAPTER 16

JUNO SANGSTROM STASHED her scroll in a locked drawer well ahead of Charley's scheduled visit. Other than her odd friendship with Jordan Fields and Charley's on-demand appearances, Juno didn't usually socialize.

She knew people and would nod at them on the rare occasions when she was out of her apartment, but there was never any conversation. This kind of thing was usual at the Normandie, the exclusive residence Juno had moved into after Charley Pierce married Althea.

Juno held the keys to Pierce Sangstrom's success as well as the controlling interest, and she'd been able to negotiate a settlement of sorts with Charley. She'd given him one of the several apartments she owned in the building, thinking they'd have their liaisons there, but other than the first time, he would come to her apartment instead.

Juno had always counted on Charley to eventually tire of Althea. Juno had twice her brains and, more than that, she had something Charley couldn't get from Althea: she loved him. Althea didn't care about him at all and anyone who saw the two of them together knew that at once. Althea was always looking for someone else, bored by Charley Pierce, which boredom was a mystery to Juno, who thought Charley Pierce was the ultimate person, the only person worth her time.

Or, she had. But there were other things in the mix, and Juno Sangstrom always had several ongoing plans.

Juno had met Charley during their first week at Keff, and they took an instant dislike for each other. Charley thought the galaxy of himself, he'd insult just about anyone, including his instructors, and he had what Juno at the time had thought of as toxic ambition. But they'd been forced to work together on a study team and she'd been impressed with the way he was able to take her raw programs and refine them. He wasn't an innovator or an original thinker like she was but he was a skilled editor and she appreciated his input, since she hadn't either the energy or the inclination for mundane details.

Over time, Juno fell in love with him. He was not her sort of guy, if there was anyone who'd be the sort of guy an insular loner would be attracted to, but he stimulated a sensation in her that she wanted to keep on stimulating and Charley was the only person who could do it. For his part, Charley never professed love to her but she was sure he did love her. They spent so much time together and Charley was always following her around. Their third year, they moved in together and Juno assumed this was the start of how things would be for the rest of their lives.

They worked seamlessly together and they made a terrific couple— even some of their fellow students noticed and commented about this. Juno couldn't imagine ever being with anyone else.

Charley never indicated he wanted to escalate their relationship to the next level, the one with a legal commitment. Juno acted like she didn't care, but she did care. Yet she designed her own downfall.

Meet Me had been dashed off as the answer to a dare Charley'd devised, to create a simple program that would bring strangers together, the simpler the program, the better. Something requiring almost no effort on the part of the users yet it would create stupendous, electrifying outcomes. Could she do it? Could he edit it to perfection? She could and he did.

And then he used Meet Me to find Althea Livesy and ditched Juno without a good-bye.

Juno appreciated the timing, though, as Pierce Sangstrom had already been established by then and since she'd put up more of the capital, she had the controlling interest. She waited, convincing herself Charley was having a fling and would come back to her. All his possessions were still at their apartment, which he'd moved out of right after he met Althea, and Juno took this as a sign he intended to return. Instead he married Althea, and Juno donated all his possessions to a Genesia charity.

She bought a top-floor apartment in the Normandie and moved in before the building was finished, then bought four other apartments in case she wanted to move one day. Except for the apartment she'd given Charley, she still had the other three and they remained empty, waiting. She'd told Jordan he could stay in one of them—after all, he worked in the building—but he'd refused. The man had integrity, something lacking in Charley Pierce.

A year after his precipitous marriage, Charley came to Juno's and asked to work something out. It was too hard being business partners with someone who didn't want to talk with him and maybe they should dissolve Pierce Sangstrom before this went on any longer. He never said he was sorry. He never said he knew how unhappy she'd been.

"I won't sell and I won't buy you out and you're not allowed to sell your share." Their business contract stated neither could sell out without the other's approval.

"Juno, can't we come to some sort of agreement? We used to work so well together."

"We used to live together, Charley Pierce, in case you've forgotten."

"I fell in love. It'll happen for you one day."

Charley's words barreled through Juno's soul, leaving in their wake a million thousand scars. It would happen for her one day? It had happened and the man she loved was sitting right there, talking to her as if she didn't matter.

"You still love her? Althea?"

"Yes." He didn't try to soften the blow but made it worse by saying, "More than I ever thought possible. She's the woman I'd always dreamed about being with."

"I have another apartment here," Juno said. "It's yours, under a few conditions."

"I don't need a place to live." Charley got up and left but a few months later he was back, soon after Althea had started up with one of her innumerable dalliances.

"She can't resist him," Charley said, as though that were a reasonable explanation.

"I don't know why you have to tell me about this."

"Juno, I've been thinking about your offer. About the apartment."

"I see." She waited. He still didn't know what the offer entailed.

"It's very generous of you."

"Yes, it is." She smiled at Charley and he smiled back.

"There's more, isn't there?"

"Of course there's more."

"You want me to . . ." He couldn't bring himself to say it, so she did.

"I want you. Twice a month should be enough. How does the second and fourth Thursday sound to you?"

"Althea can never find out."

"Don't be a fool, Charley. Of course she'll never find out." And Juno would be there for Charley when Althea left him. He'd be devastated and would turn to the only person who loved him and understood him in the deep, thorough way that only Juno did or could. She'd known Charley before he was the Charley Pierce of Pierce Sangstrom.

Juno wanted Charley to come to her, to make his own decision, to understand, to know, that Juno Sangstrom had been the right partner for him all along and his marriage to Althea had been a mistake. She wanted him to tell her all this and she wanted to make him agonize while he waited to see if she'd be willing to take him back. And in the meanwhile, she'd have him to herself two days a month.

Yet her arrangement with Charley was a disappointment. He'd come by, they'd talk for a few hours, he'd fill her in on what was going on at Pierce Sangstrom, they'd go over business plans, and then he'd leave. Sometimes they'd have a meal. She'd intended more, but she wasn't going to throw herself at him. She would wait. She had waited and was still waiting.

While she was waiting, she befriended Jordan Fields, who'd worked in the Normandie since its construction. He'd always been helpful to Juno and had never asked for anything in return, refusing her attempts to remunerate him for the many tasks he'd done for her. "I'm happy to help," he'd say, and it seemed like he meant it. He'd even brought her flowers once, and she was sad when they'd finally lost their nerve and died.

Jordan had asked her if she wanted to have lunch with him that day but she'd had to postpone it since today was Charley's. Jordan didn't seem to mind. "Tomorrow, then," he said. "I'll bring dessert."

Charley arrived on time, as always.

"How're things at Tuigen?"

"I'm happy to be back in the city." Charley took his usual seat on the chair across from the sofa, where Juno sat in her usual seat, in the corner, protected on two sides from the forces of the world but leaving part of herself open, an invitation to Charley.

"Have you done any more work on the new program?"

"I've tinkered a little here and there."

"Whatever you think best," Juno said.

Everyone at Pierce Sangstrom had the application now, since it was on Charley's computer there and the spread was inevitable, built in to the coding. The program was hidden, as it was here at the Normandie, where it had also propagated and had unleashed certain consequences, which Charley was well aware of.

There was a tickling in the back of Juno Sangstrom's mind that told her of even more impressive things to come.

"Althea was quite ill," Charley said, as though he could latch on to the subtlest of Juno's inner sensations.

"I don't know why you're telling me this." She held back a smile.

"It was unusual. She's never ill. And now she's obsessed with the grounds at the house, redoing all the landscaping and plantings."

"Is she trying to be Beryl Carson?"

Charley flinched but tried to recover. "When we were out at Tuigen she got interested in—"

"I know you were here with Beryl Carson, Charley. You don't have to lie."

"It's not a lie."

"But you and Carson were here. The night before she died, wasn't it?"

"Certainly not."

Juno got up and sat on the coffee table in front of Charley's chair.

"Have you forgotten that that used to be my apartment?"

"What are you trying to say?"

"I have proof."

"Are you threatening me?"

"I'm merely informing you. I know you had Beryl Carson here and it's clear the joukko doesn't suspect you, hasn't made the connection."

"You wouldn't dare."

"Althea's having another affair, isn't she?"

"You couldn't possibly know about it."

"I know Althea, and I know her methods. Just because a few lovers have disappeared or died shouldn't be an impediment to her preferences."

"I should never have gotten together with you, Juno Sangstrom. I knew right away I didn't like you and I like you even less right at this very second."

"I often feel the same way, Charley, but Pierce Sangstrom is our creation and we're stuck with it."

"I'll buy you out. I'll up my offer. You can move on to something else in your life, something without me in it."

"You'll always be in my life, Charley. We can't change the past."

"But the future—we can stop this now. Stop torturing each other."

"What makes you think you're torturing me? I quite enjoy our meetings."

"I've got a wicked headache. I'm going to have to cut this meeting short." He stood up.

"Too bad." Charley headed for the door. Juno followed him.

"How is it you've got two neighbors who've died and yet you're still alive?" he said, his hand on the door handle.

"Ziva Walls just inherited Kaj Banerjee's entire estate and yet her husband's still missing. The world is full of injustices."

"Ziva Walls knew Banerjee?" Charley dropped his hand from the door handle.

"I'd say they more than knew each other."

"Althea will be furious."

"Oh? Doesn't she have enough assets?"

"I mean about Banerjee and Ziva."

"Yes, I'd thought the same thing."

Charley leaned against the door and folded his arms across his chest.

"You knew about Althea and Banerjee?"

"And Hirata. The Normandie is a small world and everyone knows each other. Especially here on the top floor."

"What else do you know about?"

"I know what you're doing, Charley, and I know that once you finish your work on the new program, we're going to be invincible."

"You seem invincible enough as it is." Charley gave her the ugly stare he used to use back at Keff when they were still rivals, before they got together.

"There's never enough."

Someone else would've laughed while saying those words, covering up their real intent. But Juno had no need to hide her meaning. Charley, like Juno, could never have enough. It drove them both. It was one of the foundations of Pierce Sangstrom's ongoing success.

"Wait till you really see it in action. You'll be astounded at how well it works."

"Have you come up with a name yet?"

"I have some ideas. Desire Me is my current favorite," Juno said.

"Not bad. I'll put in some more work on it. Out at Tuigen I didn't get much done. Althea was quite ill."

"So you've said twice now. As though I'd care."

"I care. One day you're going to have to stop this and accept that Althea and I are married and get on with your life."

"This is my life."

Charley left. One thing she could count on with Charley—he always left.

She locked the door, unlocked the drawer, took out her scroll, and went back to work on her new program. Desire Me, when she and Charley had initially discussed it, was to be more than the antiquated so-called interactive program—it would be reactive, responding to the users' activities and, eventually, after learning more about them, to their intentions. It would capture their desires and connect them with others without the user having to do anything at all except possess the program. It wouldn't even be necessary to open it or activate it.

At some future point it might not be necessary to have the program at all—anyone could have it and it would work on anyone in the vicinity, a vicinity encompassing hundreds of thousands of kilometers.

But Desire Me was so much more than that, as both Juno and Charley had discovered.

The most difficult part had been the transference. How to get it out of the program and into a person. Yet Juno had figured out how to do it and she was making it better with each modification of the configuration, as test versions had proven.

On her system, the program wasn't called Desire Me. It had a much simpler, more descriptive name: Virus.

CHAPTER 17

ARE YOU QUITE done?" Sean had had enough. Ethan had taken what seemed like a thousand liters of blood from her, had subjected her to more tests than she knew existed, and she thought he was about to do more. This had to stop. She had a tenuous lead on Morris Walls, which was her intended focus that afternoon. Sean had been neglecting her paying client long enough. Ethan, Jonathan Lee, and Patterson could work on the virus without her for a day or two.

"Yes, I'm finished." Ethan turned his back to her while he worked on labeling the samples.

"You don't really think—"

"I don't know what to think. I need results." He turned back around. "I need proof. Ideas are insufficient."

"But ideas are the start of finding out."

"I can't argue with that."

"Then don't."

"Sean, we can be friends, can't we?"

The blood left in Sean's body seemed to stop flowing. Here they were in the lab, two doors down from the morgue where the corpses of Oliver Hirata, Kaj Banerjee, and Patterson's mother were still in storage. Where Vern Healy's body was lying, since he'd died at his home in Genesia and not in Osada City, as Boyd McCormick would've preferred. Were Sean and Ethan about to have the very discussion they'd both avoided?

"I keep telling myself it couldn't be helped, but I should've known." Ethan wasn't looking at her but at her blood samples.

"The past is easier to solve than the present." What Sean meant was that she should've known as well.

"Then we're still friends?"

"Ethan . . . still?"

He turned around and leaned against the corner of the table where he'd put all the samples. His lab coat was open and his eyes were bleary. He hadn't been sleeping. None of them had been—even the energetic teenage Patterson was starting to look exhausted.

"It's my fault you quit. I didn't mean to—"

"What?" What was Ethan talking about? She quit the joukko because she had to, having nothing to do with Ethan or her nonrelationship with him.

"They had me redo the autopsy on Joe Crouse, and I found something Prentiss had missed. Then they lost the results."

"Who is *they*?"

"Prentiss sent the body over, but McCormick requested it."

"The bastard." McCormick was the reason she quit. One of them, anyway. "I knew there was something else going on with Crouse. But Boyd wanted the case closed."

"I was trying to help but ended up making things worse."

"It had nothing to do with you, Ethan. Boyd and his pals were busy sweeping evidence into the dustbin right from the beginning. That's their *procedural* method. I couldn't stand it there anymore."

"You seem to prefer what you're doing now. You seem much happier."

"This is happy?" Sean held out her bandaged arm.

"You're engaged and involved in a way I never saw when you were on the joukko."

"You haven't seen me for months. Not until Jonathan Lee got involved in this mess."

"But I know you, Sean. You have an energy about you that wasn't present when you were on the joukko. I get it. I've been thinking of leaving myself. Working here can kill a person's soul."

"I loved my job." The idealized version of it, the version that had compelled her to join the joukko. The version that existed only in Sean's imagination. She'd been forced to quit, pushed to her limits by Boyd, by his cronies, by the mass of foolish bureaucracy that served no one but the department itself. By disillusionment. And Ethan didn't know her anymore.

"If you insist." Ethan didn't seem convinced.

"Are you going to come with me this afternoon? I might find Morris Walls, and maybe your services will be required, although I hope not."

"I can't leave the lab. I need to take care of all these tests and do the post on Healy. And try to get in a few minutes of sleep."

"It had nothing to do with you, Ethan. Stop saying it did."

"But it doesn't seem like—"

Sean stopped him. "Nothing is like it seems. It seemed like we should have been a good match, but we weren't." Was she talking about Ethan or about the joukko? She wasn't sure.

Sean jumped down from the examining table just as Jonathan Lee and Patterson came into the lab.

"Aren't you done yet?" Patterson said. "I thought we were going to go on a manhunt."

Sean laughed. "Yes, we are, although I wouldn't call it a manhunt. It's more like a fact-finding mission."

"Whichever it is, we'd better eat something first. I've got to replenish the lost blood." Jonathan Lee pulled up his sleeve and showed off the bandages on his arm, then Patterson did the same.

"I'm faint with hunger," Sean said.

"You should sit here awhile longer." Ethan was back at work on the blood samples and didn't turn around.

"Let's go." Jonathan Lee motioned toward the door. Sean and Patterson followed him.

"Okay if we pick up something at the place around the corner and then head out?"

"Sure. Are you going to tell us where we're going?"

"Dad, it's more fun if we don't know."

But Sean told them anyway. "We're going to the Flats."

CHAPTER 18

MAIZY NEWELL HAD been back at her usual routine for a few months and she'd started to feel more like herself again, not like the self she'd become for a few thrilling weeks when she'd been interluding, as he called it, with Oliver Hirata.

She hadn't thought he even noticed her. She was a fixture at the Normandie's front desk, most of the tenants didn't know her name, and she was sure none of them would recognize her if they saw her out of uniform or out of context. Yet Oliver Hirata had stopped her on the street that day, and she'd been wearing a pair of ripped jeans and one of those modified pastel blue ex-Pierce T-shirts that signaled her contempt for the megacorp.

Hirata surprised her, approaching her on the street like he did, smiling at her in seeming approval of her anti-megacorp attire. Before then, she'd thought of Hirata as someone who probably loved Pierce Sangstrom and would be disinterested in someone like her, a lowly front-desk worker who didn't mind showing what she thought of Pierce. Yet later, after his interlude with Maizy, he'd started up with Althea Pierce. Maybe that was *his* way of showing his disdain for the man in the pale blue T-shirt, Charley Pierce himself.

Maizy's T-shirt had PS Delenda Est written on the front—Pierce Sangstrom Must Be Destroyed—a slogan the anti-megacorp movement had taken from an ancient Roman saying whose origins were unclear.

Not that anything was being done about destroying Pierce Sangstrom, the megacorp that controlled everything everyone touched. Someone had to do something about them. If wearing this shirt would help, Maizy was happy to do it and, anyway, it was good to protest. It made Maizy feel better about herself, someone who was in thrall to whatever megacorp it was who owned the Normandie, her uncaring employer.

"Maizy, isn't it?" Oliver Hirata had said to her, stopping as he passed by on the sidewalk.

"Mr. Hirata," she said. "Yes, it's Maizy. Maizy Newell." Out here, in the world, she had a last name, not like at the Normandie, where she had only one, a name no one noticed.

"I like your style. Much better than the awful uniform they have you wear."

"No kidding. And it itches." Maizy had a permanent rash on her neck where the uniform collar chafed against her skin. She'd asked if she could have a different uniform but the Normandie head office had turned her down. No one else who was at the front desk complained and she shouldn't either. Didn't she want to keep her job?

Outside, in the sunlight, Oliver Hirata's eyes sparkled in a way that reminded her of how Lukas Adler's eyes also sparkled. Maizy might be anti-megacorp but she was an avid follower of all of Adler's fabulas, and the most recent one, *Keeping the Promise*, kept her up at night with its complex storyline and thrilling intrigue. Althea Pierce might be married to the owner of the despicable Pierce Sangstrom, but her fabulas were Maizy's favorites. At least back then they had been.

"Today's my day off," Maizy said, as though she had to explain to a Normandie tenant what she was doing out of uniform, out on the street, not performing her sacred duties to the building and its self-important inhabitants.

"Want to have lunch with me? I've got the afternoon free." He looked at her like he saw her, like he was interested. No one was more interesting than someone who was interested in you.

Why would Oliver Hirata want to have lunch with Maizy Newell? But she said yes. He was drawing her past the perimeter of their former relationship as lowly clerk and wealthy tenant. The lure was impossible to refuse.

While they had lunch at a restaurant Maizy had never been to before and could never have afforded, Maizy took the time to look at Hirata. He wasn't exactly good-looking—he certainly wasn't half so beautiful as the devastating Lukas Adler, who Maizy thought of as an ideal man, was—and since they'd moved out of the sunlight his eyes had ceased to sparkle. But Oliver Hirata was capturing her hidden desires and pulling them from her depths and onto the surface, where they met with his, finding a mutual need.

"It was wonderful running into you so unexpectedly," Hirata said after they were finished eating. Maizy could hardly remember what they'd talked about. She'd been so mesmerized by Oliver's presence that that had taken up all her attention.

"Thank you for lunch. I've never been here before."

"Why don't we have lunch here at the same time next week? If that's your off day, I mean. We mustn't interfere with your work." He winked at her, showing her he knew the job was beneath her but he also knew she needed it.

"Yes, thank you. I'd enjoy it."

He left her in front of the restaurant and she was sure he'd never show up the following week. The Oliver Hiratas of the world weren't really interested in the Maizy Newells. She'd been just a whim, an impulse, for him. He'd be back with Ziva Walls soon—Maizy knew they'd broken up, because Ziva had been crankier than usual and had snapped at Maizy for no reason at all just a few days earlier—and maybe Oliver and Ziva would laugh together about how Poor Maizy at the Front Desk had been so grateful for such a deluxe meal.

Well, that was how life was. Maizy didn't need the high-and-mighty Ziva Walls, although she was a generous tipper, and she didn't need Oliver Hirata either. Although the lunch had been delicious and Hirata himself was . . . his presence had been . . . those eyes sparkling in the sunlight were . . . his seeming interest in her . . . Maizy told herself she wouldn't be devastated if he didn't show up the following week and that she wasn't disappointed that all he'd wanted to do was have lunch with her.

That week he'd pass the front desk in the lobby and nod, just like he always had before their lunch. As the days went by, Maizy became convinced he'd never show up for lunch. He was that kind of person. And Ziva Walls was back to her cheery, voluble self, so either she was back with Hirata or she'd found someone else or maybe her creepy husband, Morris, who Maizy couldn't stand, had decided to pay attention to Ziva for a change.

From her work at the front desk and endless hours of observation, Maizy knew a lot about the tenants at the Normandie, yet they knew nothing about her. Except for the little bit Oliver Hirata might know from their lunch.

A week after their lunch, Maizy got to the restaurant late. She'd debated with herself over whether to go, picturing herself standing out front waiting for someone who'd never show up and feeling humiliated, let down, and like the fool she probably was. She'd put on a flowery dress, taken it off, put it back on, then changed into one of her faded blue anti-Pierce tees instead. She wasn't going to get dressed up to impress anyone. And besides their anti-everything-she-despised message, the tees were quite comfortable.

At the restaurant, Oliver was sitting at a table at the window and when he saw her, he stood up, waved to her, and smiled the very smile that made his eyes sparkle. Was that the moment she succumbed to his well-honed charms? Afterward she felt like the fool she'd attempted to avoid becoming, but that day, there he was, as promised, and he was waiting for her. She hadn't had to wait for him.

During lunch he took out his scroll and showed her a chart full of impressive-seeming numbers. He was working as a consultant for Pierce Sangstrom and he said the megacorp was even more horrific than Maizy had any idea about. He was going to expose them as soon as he had enough ammunition but he was still doing research. Later his research would extend to an interlude with Charley Pierce's wife.

"I'd ask you back to the apartment, but I feel it would be awkward for you," he said at the lunch's conclusion. Maizy was still eating the dessert, a decadent chocolate torte that was making her heart race at a faster pace than Oliver Hirata's attentions already had.

"It'd be more awkward for you," Maizy said. "Dating the help."

"Maizy, you're not the help. Why would you say such a thing about yourself? You're one of the most amazing women I've ever met."

Hirata had met a lot of women—Maizy was sure of it. He brought them all back to his apartment. Now she was going to be another in a long line of his women. She didn't want to be that person. But she couldn't stop her attraction to him. He was like the Earth, catching her hurtling asteroid in his magnetic field, pulling her toward him. Inexorable.

"I want to have an interlude with you."

This was the first time she heard him use the word, a word she should've paid closer attention to. Interludes, by their definition, were short-lived.

"What is that?"

"It includes lovemaking and lunches and dinners. An interlude will be our time together, to get to know each other, to delve into each other's secrets and desires. An interlude is fulfilling and stimulating. What do you think?"

As though it were up to her. As though she had a choice. As though he hadn't already crashed through all her barriers and taken her to a place she'd never paid any attention to.

"We can go to my apartment," she said.

"I've reserved a room at the Thorne. Would it be all right with you?"

The Thorne. "Yes."

Maizy Newell, who in her lifetime had never thought she'd step foot inside the Thorne, much less have an interlude with anyone there, was walking down the street with Oliver Hirata's arm around her waist. The fabric of his suit coat's sleeve was smooth and silky, unlike the fabric of her itchy Normandie uniform. Hirata's eyes sparkled in the sunlight and Maizy thought her eyes must have been sparkling as well, lit by the sparks inside her.

The room at the Thorne was two rooms. One was a living room bigger than Maizy's entire apartment in Genesia, a fifth-floor walk-up with a view of a brick wall, and the other was a lavish bedroom. At home, Maizy slept on the couch. At the Thorne, she and Oliver Hirata used the plush sofa for other purposes, then moved on to the bedroom, where Oliver turned Maizy's world into a kaleidoscopic tumble of pleasure and desire.

Late at night, after they'd paused for a brief nap, Maizy said, "Is this what you meant by an interlude?"

"Maizy, my dear, you'll see. This is just the beginning."

The beginning lasted for about six weeks. Then things shifted, although at the time Maizy didn't realize it. By then her world was so filled with Oliver Hirata and their interludes together that she didn't catch on to the changes.

Now she could put the pieces together. See how he'd used his skills to keep her off balance, alternately igniting her passions and neglecting her needs. He had an appointment and he couldn't meet her. He was so sorry. He'd make it up to her. The top-floor suite at the Thorne, champagne, and a gourmet dinner were his apology. She could stay there all week and he'd visit when he could. She waited for him but he didn't arrive. She didn't hear from him. The last night just as she was gathering her things, furious at herself for ever having gotten involved with Oliver Hirata and determined to at least have the pride to not spend another night there in the suite he'd paid for, he showed up with gifts for her— a delicate bracelet made of a material she couldn't identify and front-row seats to the upcoming Convergence of the Senses, an extraordinary event and one so out of her budget that she had never allowed herself to fantasize about it. Now she would have a front-row seat. And the bracelet was beautiful. And Oliver Hirata was apologetic, attentive, interested, passionate, his sparkling-eyed self.

But the only time they were together after that extraordinary night at the Thorne was at the Convergence of the Senses, an experience Maizy would never forget, an experience inextricably welded together with her interlude with Oliver Hirata.

The Convergence, which was affordable by only the wealthy, was an intoxicating thrill building on each of your senses, starting with mysterious, hypnotic sounds playing with your mood—accelerating it, dropping it, raising it again, taking you to the very edge then lifting you beyond an exquisite limit. This was added to with a surround of images, shapes, colors, and patterns that seemed to penetrate your body, wrap themselves around your soul. They connected you to everyone in your vicinity. Once you were connected, the touches started, as though you were being caressed by a thousand lovers, all of them devoted to only you, and then you understood the connection itself. You tasted the essence of the universe, sweet and salty, a flavor you could never get enough of—and finally the last sense, smell, came into the Convergence, as you inhaled desire itself and exhaled your ever-escalating need.

Oliver Hirata was right beside her during the concert. She'd never felt closer to him, never been more enamored of him, and even afterward, when he'd dropped her off at her apartment—he'd never been upstairs as they always met at the Thorne—she was convinced their relationship had reached another level. That this was no longer an interlude.

But she didn't hear from him the next morning or the next day or the next week. He nodded to her at the front desk, his usual tenant-at-the-Normandie self, but that was all. As though he didn't know her.

She'd been right—it wasn't an interlude any longer. It was finished. He didn't need to tell her. She saw him talking to Ziva Walls in the lobby. Had he just used Maizy as a way to get back with Ziva?

Maizy convinced herself she understood. Ziva Walls was more his type, a fellow tenant, a sophisticate. She warned herself against all thoughts of jealousy or anger. But when he started seeing Althea Pierce . . . The day Oliver and Althea strolled into the lobby and Oliver stopped at the front desk to ask about a delivery, then introduced Althea to Maizy—that was the day Maizy got angry.

Yet she had nowhere to put her anger. And why was she angry anyway? Oliver hadn't made any promises to her. It had been an interlude only. She should have realized it couldn't last. After he dropped Althea Pierce or perhaps she dropped him, Maizy felt better. Hirata's death had been another blow, but Maizy alternated between being sad and being relieved he was gone. Then she forgot about him.

Now, lying on her couch, her thoughts muddled, her left arm not responding to her commands, the room and its contents having broken into indistinguishable fragments, she thought about Oliver Hirata again, lying there in his garage, dead, for a long time before anyone found him. Would she lie here for a long time before anyone found her too? Would her downstairs neighbor notice she hadn't heard Maizy's footsteps overhead lately?

Maizy pulled her shattered inner resources together and managed to comm the emergency number. "I think I'm dying," she said.

"Who am I speaking with?"

"Maizy. New-ell."

"Are you home?"

"Yes." Was that the correct word?

"Maizy. Someone's coming. Hold on. They'll be there soon."

"I don't remember how to think and the world is ending." Maizy was surprised she knew how to talk. Maybe she would lose the ability in another few minutes.

"Hold on, Maizy."

CHAPTER 19

S EAN HAD NEVER been to the Flats although she'd heard of it. Rumors, mostly, and she'd once worked on a case where the only eyewitness gave the Flats as their address. McCormick had thought this was hilarious and tried to block their testimony, saying no one would believe such a kook, but Sean had insisted. The witness proved to be articulate, observant, and believable, although the case had been lost on a technicality—caused by McCormick's careless handling of the evidence. Deliberate? Maybe. Probably.

The Flats weren't on any map, so there was no finding them through the meshwork, but Sean had a good idea where they were supposed to be and she gave directions while Jonathan Lee drove her falling-apart transcer. Patterson entertained them with running commentary on whatever they passed by, critiquing everything from front yards to variations in the color of squirrel fur.

As they got farther from Osada City and then Genesia and the outlying towns, the landscape changed from winding roads and stylish buildings to stiff grids and utilitarian dwellings, to rolling fields, horses, barns, and silos, with a decrepit house here and there.

"I've never been out here, Dad. You'd think Mom would've been interested. Look at all these plants."

"Beryl probably did come out here, but without you. Not many volcanoes in the vicinity."

"Not true. There are three inactive volcanoes within fifty kilometers of Osada. I've been to all of them. One of them's not far from here, although we came a different route."

"Maybe we can check it out on the way back." Sean hoped, if they did go there, that the volcano would still be inactive. She didn't need any more problems.

They drove for a while with nothing but Patterson's voice cataloging the landscape—tree, grass, grass, grass, three horses, barn, red squirrel—to break the silence.

"Dad, go back. You missed it."

Sean turned around to see Patterson pointing to a turnoff they'd just driven by.

"Why do you think the Flats are there?"

"Process of elimination. I know they're not straight ahead, since I was there to see the volcano. And we haven't passed anything else that looked likely. So it must be this way."

"Might as well try it," Jonathan Lee said, and Sean agreed. He backed up, at speed—Sean didn't realize her transcer was capable of such acrobatics—and took off down the unmarked road.

"No signage," she said. "A good omen."

"You believe in omens?" Jonathan Lee took a second from his duties as speeding driver to glance at her.

"Believe is too strong. More like wonder about."

"Dad, my comm's dead."

"I've got extra charges. Hang on a second." Sean searched through her bag for the loaded charge swipes she always brought with her, but Patterson interrupted her efforts. "I had plenty of charge. There's no signal."

"Another sign?" Jonathan Lee said, slowing down.

Sean took out her comm and saw it was also blank. "Damn it. We're out here without any way to contact anyone if something happens."

"Nothing's going to happen."

"We might find Morris, in which case I'll want to inform Ziva."

"You can let her know when we get back." Jonathan Lee had slowed down even more, and all of them were staring at the landscape, which had gone from rolling hills and farms to a seeming infinity of featureless emptiness.

"I hope to bring Morris back with me."

"Good luck with that, Sean. From what you've said, this guy does not want to be found and he certainly doesn't want his wife to know where he is."

"I'll tell her if we find him. That's what she hired me to do."

"Wait till you hear his side of the story."

"There aren't sides to this story, Jonathan Lee, only facts. He's her husband, he disappeared, and she wants to know where he is."

Jonathan Lee pulled to the side of the road, which had turned to dirt and gravel, and turned off the transcer. "There are never only facts. Even in computing, facts are malleable."

"Science is all facts, all the time," Patterson said.

"Science gets its ideas from insights and intuitions. I dare you to call them facts."

"They're facts. Why not?" Patterson was enjoying this intellectual exchange with Jonathan Lee, but Sean was trying to find Morris Walls, not engage in an academic debate.

"It doesn't look like anyone could live here," Sean said. "There's just, well, nothing, for what looks like forever. Flat, empty nothing."

"That could be a tent out there," Patterson said, pointing at a section of the monotonous landscape where no tent, or anything else, was visible.

"There could be a pterodactyl out there, but we won't know until Jonathan Lee stops arguing with you and we get going again."

"I think we should walk." Jonathan Lee got out of the transcer and stretched. "Coming with me?"

"We could be walking for hours," Sean said. "Why stop here?"

"Intuition. Something about using machinery out here just seems wrong to me. You know how our comms are all dead? People out here might not take kindly to any kind of device."

"I'm up for it." Patterson jumped out of the transcer and jogged in place for a bit. "Let's go."

Sean was reluctant to give up the transcer, leaving it here in the midst of a great emptiness, but she did anyway. Maybe Jonathan Lee had a point. One of the rumors about the Flats was that the residents used only the resources the land itself provided—computers, scrolls, comms, and transcers wouldn't be part of their life and might not be welcome. At any rate, neither Sean's comm nor her scroll worked out here. She'd have to take handwritten notes on her findings, assuming there were any.

The trio walked for nearly two hours before they saw the settlement, a haphazard array of tents, lean-tos, and crude wooden shacks, sprawled across the level ground and butted up against a field of what Sean thought was probably corn, if she remembered what a cornfield might look like. She'd seen a fabula once about a family who owned a farm, but other than a hazy memory of the story and the food she ate, Sean had no direct contact with agriculture.

"See? Tents. Told you." Patterson looked pleased, and Jonathan Lee put his arm around his kid and said, "Brilliant. A dominant Summers genetic trait."

"I see you've come back around to facts, Dad." Patterson laughed and Sean smiled.

"Sean, what are you thinking of doing?"

"I'm thinking of going over there and acting like we're lost, which we sort of are."

"Right with you." The Summerses followed Sean over to the encampment, if that was the proper name for this group of residences.

"I know you." Leif Mattox emerged from a tent and walked toward Sean, his hand out. "Sean Meade, good to see you again."

"Leif, this is unexpected." She shook his hand, then he hugged her in his bearlike embrace. Leif was a big man, and somehow he looked just right out here in the nothingness, like his body could finally have the space it needed. He was wearing worn overalls and had a straw hat on his head.

"How are you?"

"Did you come all the way out here to see me? I'm flattered."

"I'm afraid not, Leif. I didn't know you'd be here."

"We didn't know here would be here," Jonathan Lee said. "Jonathan Lee Summers. Pleased to meet you. And this is my kid, Patterson."

Everyone exchanged handshakes while Sean switched tactics. There was no reason to pretend with Leif. She might as well just tell him what they were doing.

"Leif, I'm here on a case."

"I heard you left the joukko," he said. "They lost their best person, but you're better off away from that slimy lot."

"I did. I'm a private investigator now." What Ethan had said—that she seemed happier now. Was she?

"I'm looking for someone who's been missing for a while and I thought there was a chance he might be out here."

She pulled the paper from her bag and handed it to Leif. The flyer had been in Stack #173, about a third of the way from the top. Sean had a pretty good idea of where everything was in her stacks, and this particular piece had kept nudging at her subconscious, so she had to look at it again, although she'd remembered most of what it said.

Tired of your days and nights in the cruel city? Had it with computers, scrolls, comms, and all those unnecessary devices that do nothing but tie you down to their demands?

We welcome everyone to the Flats, where we live life without attaching ourselves to any object. When you're ready we'll be here. Free yourself. You'll love your new life.

CHAPTER 20

AH, THAT," LEIF said, handling the paper, nodding as he read it, then giving it back to Sean. "Haven't seen one of these in years. How did you come by it?"

"It's in her hoard," Jonathan Lee said. "She's somewhat of a collector."

"Archivist," Sean said.

"We could use you out here," Leif said. "Our archives are in need of a reworking. Since Nasir died, no one has gotten a handle on it."

"That's too bad about Nasir."

"It's all right. It was his time. He always said that after his two hundred and thirtieth birthday he'd think about packing it in, but he persisted for another twenty years. I really miss him sometimes."

"Two hundred fifty? Are you sure?"

"Patterson, that's not polite."

"It's okay, Jonathan Lee. And, yes, Patterson, I am sure. Nasir had his birth records—you should get a physical copy of yours since who knows what could happen to the computer records—and he was just shy of his two hundred and fifty-first birthday when he died."

"That's amazing. Dad, why don't we come to live out here?"

"Patterson. How will you do your volcano studies without a computer? And you seem to have forgotten what my profession is."

"You can always have a new profession, Jonathan Lee, no matter what you used to do or what you're used to doing," Leif said. "Take me, for example. I was an attorney. Gave it all up after a tragic year. Much better out here, being a farmer. I prefer it. I'm doing something real now, a job that makes sense. People have to eat and someone's gotta grow the food."

"Leif, I didn't realize you'd been an attorney."

"Wouldn't've made any difference. Your partner was determined to get the case thrown out. Didn't matter what I saw or what I said about it."

"Ex-partner. I've been finding out a lot of things about him I wasn't aware of. Heard something else just this morning."

"You're better off," Leif said again.

"Leif, I came out here looking for someone. I think there's a possibility he might be here or he might've been here at one time."

"Well, I know everyone out here. Just ask me. But, Sean, I have to tell you, there are folks out here who are anonymous, and if he falls into that category, I won't be able to help."

Sean took out her comm, where she had an image of Morris Walls stored, then realized her comm was useless. She put it back in her bag.

"His name's Morris Walls. Used to work at Pierce Sangstrom. His wife is quite concerned about him as he's been missing for weeks now."

"Pierce Sangstrom? Those megacorp bastards. Anyone who had any sense would rush away from that evil place after five minutes there."

"Evil? Because they're involved in the computing business?" Jonathan Lee looked hurt. His very livelihood was being insulted.

"It's not the business they're in, it's how they conduct it." Leif shook his head. "But there's no one here who used to be at Pierce. I would've heard about it. And no one here named Morris Walls or even just Morris. But, Patterson, we do have a volcano."

Patterson looked across the flat expanse. "Where?"

"It's in the ground, but you can see the caldera. Want to have a look?"

"You bet."

Leif and Patterson went jogging off to the caldera, leaving Jonathan Lee and Sean standing there, alone. No one else seemed to be at the settlement, although there were many structures where it seemed people did live.

"No caldera for you?" Jonathan Lee looked at her and Sean shook her head. They walked toward the southernmost area of the settlement.

"I'm going to investigate," she said. "That's what we came out here to do. What I came out here to do. You just came to get away from the situation in Osada City and give Patterson a break from Beryl's death."

"I'm giving myself a break from Beryl's death. My brain likes to absent itself from problems for a while. Helps it to work things out while I'm not thinking about them, and going somewhere new is especially stimulating."

When Sean got to the nearest tent she said, "Anyone home?" No one answered. She got the same nonresponse from the next three tents she approached.

"I can tell you're dying to go into one of these places."

"I can't. No warrant. No matter what Ethan thinks, there are some things about being on the joukko that are better. You have more authority."

Jonathan Lee walked past Sean, opened a tent flap, and looked inside. "Maybe I should quit the Acres and come live out here. This is damn nice."

Sean looked under his arm—he was a foot taller than her—and said, "I knew I could get you to do the dirty work."

The interior of the tent was simple but beautiful—colorful blankets piled up in one corner, woven rugs in a fascinating pattern covering the ground, a small table with bowls and cups against one wall, and handmade shelves holding clothing and other necessary objects against another wall.

Did the roof leak? Sean looked up to the top of the tent, which was dry. The pails in her attic should be looked at soon. It had rained a few days ago.

Sean and Jonathan Lee looked into three more tents using the same method, but found no one.

"There's something calming about this place." Jonathan Lee looked at Sean and she wondered what it would be like to live out here with him and Patterson and Leif and the other residents, none of them currently visible. Would Sebastian like it? Would Ethan move here or come to visit?

"I'm having crazy thoughts," she said.

"If they're the same crazy thoughts I'm having, I understand. It's as though we were brought out here to investigate not your missing person but our own future."

Sean felt drawn to the Flats, like she was meant to be here, like all three of them were meant to be here. But before Sean and Jonathan Lee could delve further into these scudding thoughts, Leif and Patterson emerged from the eastern edge of the cornfield, palling about like they'd known each other all of Patterson's life.

"Dad! Leif said I could stay for a while. The caldera has never been properly documented and I've never read about anything like it. I could be the first. And I like it out here."

"You have to finish the school term, Patterson. Then we can talk about it."

"It's just another two weeks. They can live without my presence. It's boring anyway. And this—this is exciting. Intellectually stimulating." The last descriptor was no doubt aimed at Jonathan Lee's academic inclinations.

"We should be heading back," Sean said. "We're parked quite far from here."

"And I thought you'd walked from Osada." Leif grinned at Sean. He knew they hadn't walked the entire way. Then he answered her unasked question: "I have a bicycle. That's how I was in Osada. Needed to check in with a friend. But it won't help you get back to your ride."

"Leif, if you do hear about anyone who's left Pierce Sangstrom, or anyone named Morris, or someone who lives—lived—at the Normandie, could you try to get in contact with me? Here's my house." She scribbled her address on her pad, tore off the sheet, and handed it to him.

"I'll try, but I can't promise. Like I said, there're people out here who want to remain anonymous or have changed their names. Not uncommon."

"I've already decided on my new name. I'm going to be Pliny," Patterson said. "He was there, at Vesuvius."

"You're not staying, Patterson," Jonathan Lee said. "We'll discuss your coming back at some point after we're home. After you finish the term."

"I'm Pliny while I'm here," Patterson said. "And I'm not going back. I like it here. You like it here too but you won't admit it."

"Come on, Pliny," Sean said. "It's only another two weeks. Then you can come back."

"I never said Patterson could come back." Jonathan Lee was starting to fume.

"Pliny," Jonathan Lee's kid said. "And, Dad, no one out here has dropped dead of a mysterious disease. It's safe out here."

A surge of fear shot through Sean then and, judging from Jonathan Lee's expression, it had affected him as well.

"Leif. We shouldn't've come out here. I wasn't thinking. I can't begin to apologize. This wasn't right." Sean had been so intent on the possibility of finding Morris Walls that she hadn't considered they might be spreading the infection, one they knew all but nothing about.

"I don't mind. You're all welcome here. You read the flyer." Leif was unconcerned, but he didn't realize what was at stake.

"But, all three of us—we could all be contagious with an unknown disease that's killed several people already," Sean said.

"I'll quarantine myself for a couple of weeks. That should be enough. But I wouldn't worry about it, Sean. I'm in good health."

Sean didn't want to say that everyone who'd died had also been in good health. But she thought Leif had one thing that could be in his favor: he didn't have a computer.

Patterson was convinced to leave by the suggestion of a contagion factor and went back with Sean and Jonathan Lee. When their comms got reconnected, the three had the same message from Ethan. All clear.

The relief each of them felt was palpable. Patterson insisted they go back since there was no longer any risk of contagion, and anyway they should let Leif know he wasn't in danger. But Jonathan Lee, after a toxic back-and-forth, refused Patterson's demand. It was late and getting later. They'd get a message out to Leif tomorrow and they'd revisit Patterson's request after the term ended. Not before.

After leaving Jonathan Lee and Patterson at the Carson house, Sean took the transcer back to hers, fed Sebastian, and made a sandwich for herself. Sitting in Sebastian's chair with Sebastian on her lap and a half-eaten sandwich on a plate she'd put on the floor, she stared at the comm Ethan had sent and read it for the tenth time. All of them, including Ethan, had been subjected to the same tests. But nowhere in his comm did he report on his own results.

CHAPTER 21

THE ODD OCCURRENCES at the Normandie were ruining what had once been the sheer enjoyment of living in such a grand, exclusive residence. These days Ziva Walls wanted nothing more than to sell her apartment, get out of Osada City, and be done with the place, but with the unexpected added burden of Kaj Banerjee's estate, she couldn't leave just yet.

Ziva's days were so full of Banerjee's massive leavings that she sometimes forgot about Morris—not just that he was missing but that he had existed, that she'd ever been married to him, or that she had cared. If she had at one time, she no longer did. He was gone, that was the end of that, and she had more important things to focus on.

Sean Meade, her private investigator, had done a thorough job, and Ziva decided Morris was unfindable and she was satisfied. Although she didn't pay Sean the bonus she'd promised her when—if—she found Morris, she did give her a substantial final payment and also made an appointment to have Jordan Fields, who could fix anything, go to Sean's place and see what he could do about her roof, which Sean, in passing, had said was leaking. Ziva would pay. It was the least she could do to help out after driving her investigator crazy with her constant demands. Also, it was a lure, or perhaps a bribe, to get Sean to come over to the Normandie and help Zee with Banerjee's colossal collection of stuff. She intended to pay Sean for her time there as well.

Sean had thanked her, said her generosity was unnecessary, and said she'd spend as much time as she could helping out with the Banerjee collection. She was due to be there this afternoon and Ziva was in Banerjee's studio trying to get things organized before Sean arrived.

Zee had already sifted through all the paintings, since, unlike some of the other art pieces, they were easy to categorize, using the system Damon Garza had recommended. Garza, who, like Morris, had disappeared from the scene, had suggested these categories during one of the scores upon scores of sales pitches for his services, and Ziva thought they made sense, so she used them. She hadn't hired Garza to, as he'd kept suggesting, "dispose of the estate," because she wasn't sure disposing of it was the right thing to do.

She wasn't moving anything from its position in the studio, merely cataloging it. She'd had an idea about what to do with Kaj's apartment and she was waiting for approval from the building management, who'd told her they had to consider this with care, since this was, after all, a private residence and not a public museum space.

If they wouldn't agree, which she was beginning to think they wouldn't, she'd have everything moved to a building she'd noticed on the outskirts of the city, and would re-create Kaj's studio there. It wouldn't be the same as the actual studio. Kaj's essence would be missing, but she'd be able to configure the rooms for easy viewing and that might be better than using his actual apartment, which was still her preference, and she thought Kaj would've liked the idea, although he hardly would've liked the idea of his life ending so soon.

He'd left everything to Ziva for a reason, although she wasn't sure what the reason might've been. He liked her, certainly, and she had liked him as well. He hadn't had the same draw Oliver Hirata had—but Kaj was different, fun to be with, and he'd never interfered in her life outside their friendship. Also, the paintings he'd made of her were spectacular.

She'd taken her favorite immediately and hung it in a prominent place in her living room. After you walked down the entrance hall and the room was revealed, aside from the breathtaking view, your eyes were met with this painting. The few people who'd been over since she'd hung it had all been mesmerized by it, as Zee herself was. Even the down-to-earth Jordan Fields, who she imagined didn't care at all about art, had gasped when he saw it and said he'd never seen such a stunning portrait.

Jordan had of course seen everything in Kaj's studio, since he'd often been in there to work on the dysfunctional plumbing, a constant problem at the Normandie. The building's finishes had been done too quickly. Still, Zee had loved her apartment until recently, and everyone she knew at the Normandie was happy with their homes as well.

Although maybe not as much these days, since Kaj and Oliver were both dead and the young girl Maizy Newell at the front desk was in critical condition at the Genesia Clinic. Ziva had sent her flowers even though she'd heard Maizy was in a coma, but she thought it was the least she could do. Oliver would have done the same, as he'd always seemed concerned about his past interludes and, with one exception, would never say anything negative about them.

That one exception was Althea Pierce. Oliver had spent an entire night—a night when they could've been making love instead of talking—at Ziva's, telling her about his mistake of getting involved with Althea, a woman no one should be involved with. He couldn't believe a person as successful as Charley Pierce wanted anything to do with her. She was not just an inconsiderate lover, but she had a cruel way about her. She'd call him Charley sometimes and act like she didn't notice her own error or perhaps thought he was Charley.

He'd purposely called her Ziva once, to get back at her, but Althea couldn't be gotten back at. She told Oliver that Morris had married Ziva for her fortune and nothing else. Everyone knew it. Oliver told Althea she wasn't one-sixteenth the lover Ziva Walls was and he was ending their interlude. Althea had laughed it off. If Ziva Walls was so great, why did her own husband want Althea more?

That was so long ago now. Oliver dead. Kaj dead. Morris disappeared and in effect dead. Zee had talked with Werner Stinnett about having Morris declared legally dead or whatever it was they did with the status of someone who was no longer present and who couldn't be located. She wouldn't touch Morris's assets—what if he came back?—but she wanted out of the marriage, which had been a mistake anyway. She'd known that the moment she ran into Oliver Hirata after he'd moved in.

But the past was over. She'd forge ahead. She was going to relocate to somewhere warmer, somewhere near an ocean. Ziva had had her sights set on a beach house in the west, but someone had purchased it before she had a chance to go out there and see it. If Kaj hadn't left her his estate, she'd be there now, sitting at the beach, far away from Osada City and the Normandie, where things seemed to be plummeting down a steep slope.

The awful Boyd McCormick, who'd arrested Zee after Beryl Carson's body had fallen on her, had contacted her three times since her release. She sensed he wanted something more from her than information about Oliver, Kaj, or Beryl, but she never let him get to the point of saying so. It was obvious Sean had a low opinion of him as well, and Zee agreed. He'd had Ziva locked up to make it look like he was doing something, not because he had any evidence.

While Zee was waiting for Sean to arrive, she inspected the crumpled-paper sculptures. It was difficult for her to tell what were sculptures or assemblages, if either term was what they'd be called, and what were attempts that hadn't worked out or that weren't yet finished. She suspected no one would mind how they were described or whether they were finished, since Kaj Banerjee had made them and these wads of paper, regardless of Kaj's intentions for them, would be worth more than Ziva's ultraexpensive apartment would ever be.

Ziva couldn't believe the joukko had left Kaj's computer in his studio, but they had. Perhaps because it was used to exhibit exposirays, as he called his computer creations, they hadn't thought the object was anything more than a display mechanism, but in fact it was a working computer.

She and Kaj had played games on it and had been intrigued by a mysterious, nameless program that had seemed to come from nowhere. They never did anything with it—even deleting an unknown program could cause serious problems—but they didn't open it either. After that day their relationship had become deeper and they often joked about it, speculating that the program had had an effect on them both, a silly idea, but Kaj liked fantasies like this and Ziva was willing to play along.

The computer was off now. Zee had shut it down after she'd taken possession of Banerjee's studio. The last time she'd been there when Kaj was still alive, it had been off, so maybe someone at the joukko had switched it on. Now she decided to turn it on again, wanting to see Kaj's exposirays, since she should start cataloging them as well. But the device refused to start up. She tried every trick she knew, but nothing worked. For a moment she thought about the almost-forgotten Morris, whose expertise might've been helpful in this situation.

Ziva was engaged in one last effort, redoing the computer's connection to the antique Kaj referred to as his drawing board, when Sean arrived.

"I didn't know you were coming today, but I'm glad you're here. I've started to get overwhelmed."

"Zee, you didn't have to send Jordan over. I can't have the roof redone at the moment."

"Don't concern yourself with the particulars. Jordan will take care of everything—"

"But—"

"No *but*. It's something I want to do for you. The materials Jordan asked for will be delivered early next week and the whole thing should be completed pretty quickly."

"Ziva, I can't accept this. You overpaid me for my job looking for Morris and I didn't find him. I'm still looking though. I haven't given up, even if you have."

"I've got Kaj's attorney, Werner Stinnett, working on the situation. I wanted to have Morris declared dead, but it takes too long. Years, apparently. How could anyone wait so long to get on with their life? Well, I can't. So I'm going to get a divorce in absentia or whatever it's called. Werner's son is actually doing the documentation but Werner is my advisor."

"I'm happy to hear you're moving on, Zee. I think it's obvious that unless something untoward has happened to Morris—and we'd know by now if he'd been hospitalized or imprisoned or . . . well . . . you know—"

"Yes. I've thought of all those things myself. Thousands of times. But I'm tired of wasting my energies on it. On Morris. Our marriage had already fallen apart and it's time to end it, no matter what Morris is up to, if he's capable of being up to anything."

"You're happy with this?"

"Sean, it's not about being happy. I want to focus on something positive. Oliver's death was very tough for me, and I still can't quite understand it or Kaj's death. Sometimes I get up after midnight and wonder if I'm somehow responsible for what happened to them. It seems like too much of a coincidence that both of them, and Morris— and Beryl Carson. But I didn't know her."

"The joukko didn't have any evidence against you, Zee. You should be relieved."

"They could still find something, even though I don't know what it is they'd find. They know a lot about me. I think I told them too much."

"Yeah, that was probably a mistake."

"And usually I'd think of a broken ankle as a bad thing, but it turned out to be what saved me from another night in jail. Do you know anything about computers?" Time to stop talking about the past and get moving on what needed to be done right now.

"I—not really. Just the usual stuff you learn in school, and I don't remember a lot of it. Why?"

"Kaj's computer won't start up. I've tried everything, but it's just dead." Zee held up the connector, a demonstration of one of her attempts at getting the computer to work.

"Zee, put it down." Sean's tone was commanding and harsh.

"I don't know why you sound so adamant, Sean. It's not like it's going to electrocute me. All those connections are done through the, you know"—she gestured around the studio, indicating the airborne electrons that ran all the powered devices—"so there's no reason to be—"

"Just put it down. I'm going to comm my friend who knows a lot about computers."

Ziva put down the connector. "You must be under a great deal of stress. I've never seen you like this."

Sean wasn't even paying attention. She was on her comm, talking to someone. Ziva finally heard a name: Jonathan Lee. Beryl Carson's ex?

"You're not going to have Beryl's ex come over here, are you?" Ziva didn't think she could face him, not since Beryl's corpse had arrived on her threshold.

Sean put down her comm.

"Yes. Jonathan Lee's going to come over."

"But—"

"Zee, let me tell you what's been happening."

Sean then launched into an impassioned speech Ziva could grasp only parts of, but the parts she did grasp made little sense.

"You're saying the computer might've killed Kaj? But it's perfectly safe. No one's ever been killed by a computer, have they? I mean, it's not like it can throw itself off the desk and knock you out or anything." Ziva tried out a laugh but it felt wrong, so she stopped. "You're not joking, are you?"

"I'm not joking. We're still not sure about it. You might not re-member him, but Ethan Stiles, the medical examiner, is doing more research. We should have answers soon."

Ziva Walls remembered Ethan Stiles, a man she feared might possess the same capacity to ignite her desires that Oliver Hirata had had. Someone she wanted to stay far away from. She was tired of her life's persistent dramas.

"I don't understand. Isn't there a profound difference between the kind of virus a computer would get and the kind of virus that would infect a person?"

"Like I said, we're not sure. But—and I'm not going to go into the awful details from the autopsies—"

"I appreciate that." Oliver being autopsied. No. She couldn't think about it.

"But even though this might not've been possible before, it may be what's happening now."

"You're saying this is why Oliver and Kaj—and Beryl—died? They got a computer virus? That's—no. I mean, I don't know anything about this sort of thing, but it's absurd."

"Maybe it is."

"But you don't think so."

"I could be wrong. I'm not a scientist."

"But your scientist friends think it's true." Zee got that impression from the serious, concerned way Sean was talking.

"They think it's not impossible."

"That's a gigantic distance from *not impossible* to *truth*. Which is it?"

"Viruses have been known to leap from animals to humans. Now it's possible one's leaped from a computer to a human. Maybe from several computers to several humans."

Ziva backed away from Kaj's dead computer.

"Did the same virus that killed this computer also kill Kaj? I'd better go wash my hands. Maybe take a shower. Sterilize myself. Should I be in here at all?"

The hours she'd spent in Kaj's studio. Did she have the infection now too?

CHAPTER 22

J ONATHAN LEE WENT over to the lab to talk with Ethan. He was getting nowhere with Beryl's computer and he wanted to talk things over with his friend. He'd commed Sean, who was on her way to the Normandie to help out Ziva Walls. She'd come to the lab when she was done.

"Don't tell Sean." Ethan hadn't bothered with a greeting or any new information.

"Hello to you too," Jonathan Lee said. "What is it I'm not supposed to tell Sean?"

Ethan sat down on one of the lab table's high stools and Jonathan Lee took a good look at his former roommate, someone he knew better than anyone else, including himself.

"You've got it, don't you?" Jonathan Lee wanted Ethan to say of course he didn't. To say that that was nonsense. To reassure Jonathan Lee he was fine.

"Yes," Ethan said. "Although so far I don't seem to have any symptoms, if I even know what the symptoms might be. At this point I know only what the results are, not what might precede them."

"How did this happen? Ethan, you didn't infect yourself on purpose, did you? For research?" That was just the sort of thing he might've done back at the Acres, and maybe he was still capable of such a rash act.

"I wouldn't know how, but of course I wouldn't do it. I don't have a death wish."

"Said the medical examiner."

"I think of quitting twice a week. Now I might be forced to."

"Don't you even think of dying on me." Jonathan Lee didn't want to consider a future without his friend.

"I can't guarantee anything. I'm not even completely sure I have it, but it seems likely. My body's hosting some of the same odd microorganisms I've seen in all the victims."

"Odd microorganisms? You mean you tested us not knowing exactly what you were looking for?"

"I knew what I wanted to see the absence of—anything even remotely abnormal. But I hadn't examined all the victims' microimages yet."

"But now you have. And you found this microbe in your results—and theirs."

"That's about the size of it."

"We'd better find a cure for this thing immediately." Jonathan Lee's sense of urgency surpassed its previous towering height.

"Yes, that would be the best course of action, Jay. Although this might not be the terminal disease it's so far seemed like it must be. There's a patient at the Genesia Clinic who I suspect has the same thing, and she's still alive, although in critical condition. I've sent someone over to take samples, so I'll have a better fix on it after the tests are run."

Jonathan Lee sat down and pulled out his comm.

"It's Sean. It seems Kaj Banerjee's computer has died and she wants me to come take a look at it." He sent her a reply.

"Don't you dare tell her. It's bad enough she'll find out eventually."

"She's finding out right now. Did you really think I wouldn't say anything about this? We're all in it together. She has to know the facts."

"I spoke to the head of the Osada City health department, told her we might have an epidemic on our hands, and she just laughed at me. I couldn't tell her what I thought the source was—she'd never listen to me again. Not that she's listening to me now. They went out to the

Normandie and did the initial testing—air quality and surfaces—and nothing was out of the ordinary, so, to her, that seems sufficient.

"But from what I've so far seen this does appear to be a sort of a virus, although I'm hardly an expert in either biological or computer viruses. It's RNA, but the structure looks like no virion I can find anywhere on the mesh. I sent a microimage out to a friend of mine from Keff—I think you might've met Ed Sperry at one of those late-night parties—and she's intrigued, so I hope to hear back from her soon. I sent the microimage to you too. Thought you'd like to take a look at it."

Jonathan Lee fought back any thought that he could lose his friend. Wasn't it enough that Beryl had died? He hadn't been close with her in years but she had been his wife and they'd been close then, or at least he thought they had been, although she might've disagreed. Jonathan Lee had many acquaintances, yet he had very few close friends and none as close as Ethan. He hadn't even been very close with Patterson until now.

Sean sent another comm and Jonathan Lee read it, looked up, and said, "Is Maizy Newell this person at the Genesia Clinic?"

"Yes. How would Sean know?"

Jonathan Lee switched the comm to voice and turned up the volume. "Hey, Sean. How did you guess the patient at the clinic was Maizy . . . what was her last name?"

"Newell," Ethan said.

"Ethan," Sean said. "I'm so sorry—"

"Don't feel sorry for me. If I hadn't been infected it might've taken even longer to pin down this bug. But how in hell do you know the patient's name?"

"Maizy Newell's one of the front-desk people at the Normandie. Zee told me she was at the clinic. In a coma, I believe. And, guys, Maizy was one of Oliver Hirata's interludes."

"His what?"

"That's what he called his affairs. Zee told me. So Maizy had direct contact, so to speak, with one of the victims. And, you know, there's a computer at the Normandie's front desk. So she had direct contact with that as well."

"All the computers at the Normandie could be compromised." Jonathan Lee's brain was on fire. "I think we should disable every one of them right away. Wait. Let me get over there. Okay, Ethan?"

Ethan was staring at something over Jonathan Lee's shoulder and didn't answer.

"Ethan, are you feeling all right?" Sean said. Jonathan Lee thought she was doing a poor job of sounding unconcerned.

"I'll feel fine as soon as Jay gets out of here so I can get back to work."

"I think you should test Ziva too, Ethan. She had a lot of contact with both Hirata and Banerjee. And she lives in the Normandie and of course has a computer. And has used Kaj's computer as well."

"Can you work up a list of everyone at the building? Tenants, workers, frequent guests? I think we'd better get everyone tested."

"Ethan, I'm not on the joukko anymore and there's the additional problem of the building being in two different jurisdictions."

"Forget formalities, Sean." Jonathan Lee didn't care about them and cared even less now that Ethan's life was on the line. "Just get the list and the three of us will figure out what to do with it afterward."

"I'll have Ziva help me. She seems to know everyone here."

"I'll be there in a bit." Jonathan Lee signed off.

"Ethan, it does seem that Beryl's computer may have been infected with some odd virus but that's as far as I've gotten. Have you come around to thinking this could actually have been caused by a computer virus?" Jonathan Lee wanted his friend's opinion. If they were heading down the wrong path—and since Ethan had isolated the likely pathogen, he had a better take on this than anyone—he wanted to know now.

"I'm still not sure, Jay, but, yes, I think it's looking like more and more of a possibility. It bears no resemblance to anything else I've ever seen and, like Sean said, this thing's acting like a computer virus, destroying entire systems, reassigning tasks from one organ to another, and devastating its victims. I've ditched skepticism for pure facts. Let's get them and go forward from there."

Jonathan Lee nodded, then went over to the Normandie. Sean met him in the lobby and they got in the elevator together.

"Zee's a mess. She's been working in Banerjee's apartment—his studio—for days and she couldn't get his computer to turn on. She's the one who turned it off. Although who turned it on? It was off when I discovered his body. Now Zee thinks she's infected too and she's scared. She's worried the entire building is contaminated with this virus and she's furious she didn't leave here sooner. She'd been planning to sell her place and move, but since she inherited Banerjee's estate, she's been staying here to take care of it."

"Her fears may very well be warranted." Before he had a chance to explain, the elevator opened onto the top floor and they went to Ziva Walls's apartment.

"Oh, it's you," she said when Jonathan Lee went in with Sean. "I was hoping the medical examiner would come. Isn't he going to take samples? I could be dying."

"You're going to have to go to the lab. He can't leave right now and anyway he needs the equipment that's there."

"I'll go right now." Ziva got up, found her bag, and took out a key, handing it to Sean. "This opens Kaj's place, and you can just leave my door open. No one except another tenant would come up here anyway. But you have to lock the studio. Too many valuable objects in there. It's the lab at the Genesia morgue, isn't it? I'll be back in a while."

Ziva sailed out of the apartment.

"She seems awfully anxious."

"Jonathan Lee, she's terrified."

"Let's hope she's all right. She doesn't seem to have any symptoms."

"Ethan doesn't either, does he? You were just there."

"No, he seems fine, although exhausted. He's getting Ed Sperry in on it, sent her the microimage. And—"

Jonathan Lee stopped talking as mental images lined up next to each other. He pulled his scroll out of his back pocket and started searching through it. Rubbed his hand across his forehead. Looked up at Sean, then commed his friend.

"Ethan," Jonathan Lee said. "The microimage you sent me. It's real, isn't it? Not some kind of mocked-up rendering?"

"It's real," Ethan said.

"Ethan, it looks quite like a graphic embedded in the coding of the program on Beryl's computer."

"There're images in coding?" Sean said as she grabbed Jonathan Lee's scroll and looked at the microimage.

"Sometimes," he said. "There can be. I didn't know what it meant—sometimes coders are just doodling, like anyone would—so I wasn't concentrating on it. But, hell, I think it's the same thing as your microimage, Ethan. Or damn close to it."

"Jay, can you isolate it and send it to me?" Ethan said.

"I'm doing it right now."

"Does this mean the virus is definitely from the computer?" Sean was now staring at Jonathan Lee's scroll, as though her very gaze could produce an effect.

"It means your idea's relocated itself from the theoretical and gained significant traction in reality," Jonathan Lee said.

"They're very similar. Give me some time. I'll get back to you." Ethan ended the comm.

"This is the breakthrough we need," Sean said.

"It's a start, anyway."

Jonathan Lee and Sean stared back and forth between Ethan's microimage and the design in the code.

"It looks like an exact match to me," Sean said.

"It's close. Sean, after we're done at Banerjee's, I want to take a look at Ziva's computer too," Jonathan Lee said. "See what's different, if anything."

"You mean see why he's dead and she's alive and full of energy."

"If I can."

Sean took Jonathan Lee over to Kaj's studio. It took him a few moments to adjust to the myriad of paintings and other objects cluttering the vast space.

"This is making your hoard look organized."

"My hoard's organized, and it's not a hoard. It's an archive."

"To you." To Jonathan Lee it was a hoard, no matter what Sean called it, although she did seem to know where at least some things were located in the collection of stacks.

"To me. Be careful where you step. Zee's trying to keep everything just as it was when Banerjee died. She's hoping to turn the studio into a museum of sorts, although she told me the building management might rule against her."

"For all we know, this building might be declared a disaster zone. Evacuated. Did you have a chance to get the list of tenants and workers?"

"I sent it to Ethan already. You should have a copy on your scroll."

"Let's take a look at this broken computer, shall we?"

Sean directed him through the morass to Kaj's work desk, where, alongside Banerjee's computer, there was an object that was already a museum piece, a sort of drawing device that had been obsoleted centuries earlier. Jonathan Lee had never seen one in person, only images.

"This is something else again," he said, picking it up, admiring the outmoded workmanship, then putting it back down.

"Zee said Banerjee used this. Called it his drawing board."

"Damn. It still works. Which explains this"—he picked up the connector—"other antique device. Astounding. But let's get to the computer." Jonathan Lee was giving himself directions. What he really wanted to do was take the so-called drawing board apart and see the inner workings. He wasn't a computer archaeologist but he'd sat in on lectures about the subject and was intrigued by the device.

He sat at Banerjee's desk and Sean stood behind him, looking over his shoulder while he tried and failed to get the computer to activate, then he started taking it apart. He always had his tools with him. After a few minutes, he got the computer to turn on and was able to engage the displays.

"That was fast. What was the matter?"

"A switch—well, they're not really switches anymore but they're still called that—had jammed. More of a mechanical problem. Anyway, I unjammed it. Let's see what's in this baby."

While Jonathan Lee examined the computer's programs, he explained parts of what he was looking at to Sean. She'd rested her forearm on his shoulder and was leaning over, staring hard at the array and asking good questions.

This was not the time to say anything, but Jonathan Lee packed away the question he'd had on his mind for days. Later, after all this was resolved, he'd ask if it was really over between Sean and Ethan.

Patterson had accused Jonathan Lee of being interested in Sean, and Jonathan Lee had said he wasn't. That he was interested only in solving this problem and she had good insights. Patterson had said, "Sure, Dad," and had gone back to reading up on some fine point about volcanoes or their calderas.

"There," Jonathan Lee said. "Look." He pointed at the odd, convoluted code. "Damned inventive." He was even more impressed than he'd been the first time he'd seen it, on Beryl's computer.

"What is it?"

"Not sure yet, but Beryl has a similar thing on her computer—and it's unlike anything I've ever run across. I've been trying for days to crack the code, but I've made zero progress."

"What do you mean, crack the code?"

"I mean it's coded in an unknown language. Well, unknown to me. The coder knew it. I think it's likely the coder invented it. It's effectively hiding what exactly the program is and how it operates—and what it does, which makes me very suspicious, since viruses are often hidden in complex systems like this."

"You think this could be it?"

"Look," Jonathan Lee said, pointing at the array. "There's the image again, looking like the pathogen's twin."

He turned off the computer. Had he just exposed both of them to the virus? "We have to be careful. Let's go take a look at Ziva's computer."

Jonathan Lee wasn't surprised Ziva's computer had the same program on it, although the code had a slight difference that was obvious even though Jonathan Lee wasn't sure exactly what he was looking at. And the image was absent. He showed Sean, pointing out the location where the design had been on the other computers.

"Why is it different?"

"It could have mutated."

"How?"

"It's probably built into the code. When I finally figure it out, I'll know more. But maybe that's why Ziva's okay."

"Do you think Ethan got it from a computer, or was he infected by one of the victims?"

"Hell if I know. He has had contact with some of the victims' computers—at least he's been in the same room with them—and that might be enough. We'll have to wait for more results."

"I'm tired of waiting."

"You're not alone." Jonathan Lee was sorry he said that, a phrase with a more personal meaning, one he didn't want to express. "Let's look at the list of tenants. It can't be a coincidence that the victims all have a tie to this building."

"The person who wrote this code must live in the building or have a strong connection to it. Or to one or more of the tenants."

"Or has access to the building."

"Like Jordan Fields. I met him in the basement. He has access to all the apartments as he's the resident handyperson."

Jonathan Lee opened his scroll and started reading the list Sean, with Ziva's advice, had compiled.

"Who is 'strange lady in the corner'?"

"Ziva doesn't know her. She rarely leaves her apartment. Some kind of a recluse, the kind who can afford to live here. She's the first on my list to try to talk with. I've already knocked on her door a couple of times, but there's no answer. Maybe she's not there."

"Did you try the door?"

"It's locked. Our method out at the Flats won't work here."

"Too bad."

"I think it's time we got more organized. I should concentrate on finding the person who wrote the code, see if they do live in the building. I'm going to have to tell Zee I can't help her with the Banerjee mess until this is over. I'd like some help with this—there are over a hundred tenants in the building and at least thirty full- and part-time workers—but it can't be you. You have to do the computer end. And of course it can't be Ethan."

"Why not ask Ziva to help? She's already involved. Assuming she isn't infected. And she knows a lot of these people."

"Good idea. I'll do that. Would it be okay if I recruited Patterson?"

"The term's over soon—maybe afterward. If Patterson agrees."

"Of course."

Silence. Neither could bring the words out into the open. Then they'd be too real.

Beryl's computer had been infected and she didn't live at the Normandie, although she'd died there.

The unspoken words jammed up against one another. What if Ethan got too sick to help? Or if he died? Was Patterson infected? Was Ziva? What if Sean or Jonathan Lee had contracted the virus while they were in Kaj's studio?

What if the infection had already spread so far that it had become uncontrollable? If hundreds or thousands of people were already infected but hadn't yet developed symptoms?

Finally Sean said, "Can we stop this?"

"We damn well better," Jonathan Lee said. "We have to."

CHAPTER 23

A DAY OR two after Vern Healy's death, it had faded into forgetting, and Althea Pierce started looking around again. Charley was such a bore and if he'd hired another private investigator, Althea hadn't been able to figure out where they were or who they might be.

For a moment she thought about Morris Walls, but she didn't know how to locate him, if he was still alive, which he might not be. After all, he worked at Pierce Sangstrom so his computer had been infected early on. He was probably lying around dead somewhere but no one had stumbled upon him yet.

In the meanwhile she did have Charley, and her illness and recovery had seemed to infuse their faltering relationship with a new passion. Yet he wasn't enough and he knew it. His knowing it was probably why he wasn't enough. Life was full of circular problems like this.

Like the problem of the virus, which Morris had shown to Althea one afternoon when they were in his office together and were taking a pause during one of their marathon sex sessions.

"The entire office seems to be infected," he'd said. "Unusual program. It's written in a cryptic code. Fascinating, really. Not sure what it's doing or how it got here. It's kept me up a few nights."

"Who wrote it?"

"Has to be Juno. I don't know anyone else who'd be capable of something like this."

Up until that moment Althea hadn't cared about this supposedly unusual program. Computers were just tools to get you through life, not something to throw your energies into, like Charley and Morris both did. It was far more fun to write fabulas and see them come to life, to invent stories for other people to play out and be entertained by.

But as soon as Morris said Juno's name, Althea became obsessed with the program. Only Juno was capable of something like this? Juno Sangstrom was not the great genius everyone seemed to think she was. Well, Charley did and Morris did as well.

Charley had married Althea—she'd insisted on it and he'd agreed at once—but he had an attachment to Juno Sangstrom that seemed unbreakable and of course her name was always next to his—Pierce Sangstrom—making it seem like they were forever tied to each other. Now Juno had written some sort of phenomenal program that was on all the computers at Pierce Sangstrom? And that Morris was marveling over? Was Charley also impressed by it?

Althea, like everyone who'd ever spent ten minutes in school, knew how programs worked. She copied it to her scroll and spent hours examining it. The language was indeed cryptic but even though she couldn't decipher it, Althea would find a way in. The great Juno Sangstrom wasn't so genius after all, not if a rank amateur like Althea Pierce could break into her supposedly unique code and leave her mark on it, which she intended to do.

Althea commed Lukas Adler, who was between jobs. She kept track of him, in case she might need him, and right now she needed him. Charley had had the gall to call her Ziva last week, testing her, and although she'd passed the test, laughing at him, she was furious. It was one thing if she called him Oliver or Kaj, but he didn't even know Morris's wife, Ziva, who never came to the Pierce Sangstrom offices, although perhaps he sensed that Althea despised her, which had nothing to do with Morris and everything to do with Oliver.

While she was waiting for Lukas's reply, Althea's memory replayed the unexpected thrill she'd experienced when she'd found out Oliver Hirata had died. And that Beryl Carson—Charley's lover—had discovered Hirata's body was the icing on the delicious three-layer cake. What a terrific day that had been. Oliver dead. Charley's lover about to be accused of killing him. And Charley panicking, although he'd hidden it.

But nothing could equal the day Ziva Walls had stumbled on Beryl's body and was arrested. That glorious moment. Too bad she was out of jail now, but she wasn't out of jeopardy. Just because the joukko hadn't been able to pin the deaths on her didn't mean they wouldn't eventually be able to do it. Althea herself had become convinced that Ziva had killed Morris as revenge for his affair with her.

"Althea. Surprised to hear from you." Lukas's throaty bedroom voice came over her comm. Half his fame was based on that seductive voice and the other half on his exceedingly good looks. Of course he could act, but anyone could act. Acting was the easy part, no matter how much Lukas might talk about pride in his craft or how he was studying for a role, trying to make it seem like he hadn't just fallen into his fame, but like he'd worked at it.

"I have a new fabula I'm working on and wondered if you'd be interested." She was working on nothing but Lukas himself, yet he didn't have to know it, and anyway maybe she'd stop messing about in the garden and write another fabula instead. The garden, like Charley, was starting to bore her.

"I might be."

Lukas thought he was clever, acting like he might not be interested and hoping to get his fee raised, but Althea knew the truth. Lukas's success had reached a higher level since *Keeping the Promise* and he had to be ecstatic at the prospect of starring in another of her creations.

"I thought I might drop by this afternoon."

"Why not come over right now? We could go for a swim."

"All right. See you in a bit."

Althea signed off, found a swimsuit, in case she felt like wearing something—she'd decide after she judged Lukas's interest—and then fought off yet another headache. They'd become chronic since she'd recovered from the illness she got out at Tuigen. She blamed the place for having made her sick and had decided not to go there again. When she needed to get away, she'd go to her island instead. It was much nicer there anyway. More beautiful, more relaxing, and it was all hers. Charley owned Tuigen.

Lukas Adler lived in an isolated neighborhood out past Genesia. He'd bought several deserted houses, had them ripped down, and had his own very plain house, surrounded by acres of nothingness, built in their place. He could've lived anywhere, but instead he lived here, outside an area he referred to as the Flats. And his house was nothing special—an unimpressive single-story structure with no personality unless plainness could be considered a personality. But he had a lovely pool, also quite plain but just the right size and shape, in the backyard, and he and Althea had had many good times in that pool.

Lukas was sitting at the pool's edge, his feet and lower legs in the water, when she arrived. He saw her and slipped into the water and started doing laps. The man could swim. He'd been some kind of a champion swimmer in school and he still had the technique. He was a pleasure to watch, a fact his agent was also aware of, and Lukas was sometimes booked in fabulas where he could show off his near-naked body and swimming prowess.

Here at his home, he was completely naked. Althea stripped and dived in, meeting him at the far end of the pool just as he did his elegant turn.

He surprised her—not an easy thing to do and something he'd never done before—stopping his laps and embracing her, kissing her, pulling her under the water with him. She wrapped her legs around him as they descended, surrendering to each other's needs, and as they ascended their bodies merged. The air Althea breathed into her lungs seemed almost unnecessary, as though she needed only the water, only Lukas's mouth on hers, only her body enclosing his.

They continued, under the water then rising to the surface, for what was both an eternity and an instant. This was new and stimulating and Lukas was surpassing all his previous performances. Althea's headache dispersed itself into the water, her boredom cured itself, and the script of her next fabula burst full-blown into her consciousness.

After she and Lukas were done, he went back to swimming laps and Althea lay on the cool pavement near the pool's edge, watching Lukas and working out the casting of her new creation.

Lukas would portray a version of Morris—a better-looking version and one more willing to take risks, to push anything and everything beyond its supposed limits. He'd be trying to overthrow the head of the tech company where he worked. Charley would be the obvious choice to play that role but he was a terrible actor and even if he weren't Althea would never give him the opportunity.

No, the actor playing Charley would be Nolan East, a real-life rival of Lukas's. Their mutual animosity played out well when they were in the same production together. No need for acting there.

Charley, played by Nolan, would, by a serendipitous event, stumble onto the creation of a computer virus that would affect the user directly, stimulating an obsessive need for another user. The two infected parties would be inexorably drawn to each other, and in order to be together they'd destroy their former lives and professions and anything else getting in the way of their relationship.

Morris, played by Lukas, would find the program and change it in very subtle ways. Soon the edited programs would be causing their users to not just destroy but to murder anyone who got in their way, and when the two obsessed users finally got to be together, they'd kill each other as well.

The part of Althea would have to be played by Olyn Gil, an actor even more popular and beloved than Lukas was. Olyn had played

Lukas's devastated ex in *Keeping the Promise* and the audience adored her. Here, in the new fabula, Althea, played by Olyn, would be the only person who could save the world from this insidious program, which was upending lives and decimating the population. As the effects spread, Olyn would be under more and more pressure to solve the problem and save humanity.

Yes. Good. Althea would work out the details later, after she got home. This was a surefire hit and she couldn't wait to get started on it. The most delicious aspect was that she herself would be portrayed as the world's savior.

Who would play Beryl? She'd have to think about it. Someone the viewer would have little sympathy for. And of course Oliver deserved to die and he'd be depicted as a villain. Juno's character would be absent from the fabula. She was unnecessary.

Ah, this was all falling into place.

Althea turned onto her back, letting the cool pavement and hot sun sandwich her body in their embrace. Ever since her illness at Tuigen, her body had been not quite right but today she felt grand. Coming out here to see Lukas had been an even better idea than she'd planned, as now she had something new to work on, something that would write itself and would increase her substantial fortune.

One thing continuing to bother her was Charley's attitude. He hadn't been affected by his lover Beryl Carson's death. And he almost seemed to have enjoyed Althea's illness, her discomfort.

Oliver Hirata. Kaj Banerjee. Beryl Carson. Even Althea couldn't say she minded any of the deaths too much.

She shielded her eyes from the devastating sunlight out here in the middle of nowhere where Lukas had decided to live. He'd told her once that he had to get away from the scene, that it was all right while he was working but when he wasn't he wanted peace and simplicity, two states of total disinterest to Althea.

The sun seemed to split into three pieces while she was trying to avoid it. Her throat emitted a strange noise.

"Althea." She could hear Lukas's voice but couldn't place where it was coming from. She tried to turn over onto her side and couldn't.

"Come back into the pool. You'll get burned lying there."

Someone Althea recognized but couldn't place attempted to answer.

Water. Was that rain?

"Althea. Are you all right?"

Morris could be so nice sometimes. They'd had a picnic together but now it was raining.

"Althea!"

People who could drift away from you were so tiresome. It was better if they came toward you, even if they were forced to.

The sun broke apart, trailed by a black hole that devoured the object known as s-k-y.

A voice with no location. Frantic words. Unidentified sounds.

How the black hole welcomes its devotees.

CHAPTER 24

ETHAN HAD STARTED a handwritten journal, keeping track of his own hour-by-hour experience. So far there wasn't much to say. He was exhausted, but getting two hours of sleep out of every thirty or forty wasn't sufficient. Sleep, though, was the enemy, creeping up on you just as you were losing awareness, enveloping you, taking you away from what was important.

Maizy Newell had the infection. She was still alive although unconscious. The doctor at the Genesia Clinic kept referring to her as being in a coma, but Ethan thought that was a misnomer. Maizy seemed to have some awareness, although it was difficult to pinpoint. She'd responded with a grunt when Ethan came into her room, and although that might've been a coincidence, he didn't think it was.

After her test results had come back, Ethan asked the clinic to isolate her, explaining that she had a contagious disease whose impact was still being investigated. The clinic had complied, moving her to a private room before he arrived there.

He sat down in the chair next to her bed and spoke with her.

"Maizy, this is Ethan Stiles. I'm a doctor and I'm doing research into the microbe responsible for your illness. I've run several tests and your results are similar enough to others' who're infected that it seems clear all of you have the same thing."

Maizy's left hand moved slightly. This was definitely not a coma. She was unconscious but she was trying to communicate.

Ethan reached over to the bed and took hold of Maizy's hand. He wouldn't think of touching anyone else now that he knew he was infected—he'd had his assistant take all of Ziva Walls's samples—but it was doubtful he could further infect Maizy Newell, although there were viruses whose potency increased the more you were exposed to them.

Ethan was careful, wearing full protective equipment, including a hood. His gloved hand held hers.

"Maizy, if you can hear me, press on my palm."

Nothing happened, so he demonstrated what he meant, pressing on her palm. Still nothing.

"I'm just going to keep talking if you don't mind. It's pretty lonely in here and maybe you could use a friend."

No response.

"I have the same infection you do. What's fascinating about it—and even though you're not a scientist I think you might find this fascinating as well—is that it's not a regular kind of virus, like when you get a cold. This is a computer virus. Weird, don't you think?"

Her hand twitched inside his. Maizy Newell was definitely not in a coma.

"What's even weirder is that I'm not the one who figured this out and neither did my oldest friend, Jonathan Lee Summers, who's a code formation expert. Instead, an investigator who used to be with the Osada City Joukko had the idea, and I'm convinced she's correct."

He waited for another response but got nothing. Maybe this wasn't so interesting to Maizy Newell. Maybe he should be talking about the latest popular fabula, if only he'd known what it was, or giving her encouragement that she'd recover, which she might not, or telling her a few outrageous jokes.

"The investigator who came up with this idea used to be my girlfriend but it didn't work out. Now we're friends. Someone"—he didn't want to say Ziva's name, which might upset Maizy—"told me your former boyfriend lived at the Normandie. Oliver."

Ethan felt the slightest tap on his palm. A bead of sweat ran down Maizy's check and past her chin.

"Maizy, is it all right if I talk to you about him?"

No response. Ethan wanted Maizy to wake up but he didn't want to push too hard.

"There's a beautiful flower arrangement here in your room. There are many people who care about you." He didn't know if there was any truth to this, but a person needed to know that someone else cared, and, according to the official records, Maizy had no family.

"I know you work at the Normandie and I wondered if you had any idea what Beryl Carson might have been doing there. If you were on the desk when she arrived or if she was often there."

A sigh escaped from Maizy's half-open mouth.

"Maizy, if you think of anything, even if it doesn't feel significant, please let me know. I need all the help I can get to solve this thing."

As hopeless as the request sounded at the moment, maybe something would come of it. When Ethan had been a resident working at the hospital at Keff, he'd witnessed many seeming miracles. And patients often remembered what was said to them when they weren't fully conscious.

He started to pull his hand away and felt Maizy's hand move.

"I'll stay awhile longer."

Ethan stayed for another two hours, falling asleep, his head arched back over the chair where he was sitting. When the nurse came in to check on Maizy, Ethan woke up with a start. He hadn't meant to fall asleep. His hand was at his side now, no longer holding Maizy's.

Maizy's head was turned away from him.

"Did she wake up?" the nurse said.

"No, but she did move—she's changed position—and she responded to a couple of my questions."

"I told the doctor she's not comatose, but she doesn't do anything while he's here, so that's what it says on her chart."

Ethan told the nurse to comm him if anything changed in either direction.

Out in the hall, away from Maizy's room, the nurse said, "Aren't you the medical examiner? Are you related to Maizy? Her records don't indicate anyone."

"Yes—and no. I'm researching the disease she might have."

"I see."

"Be careful when you're in the room with her. We don't know how contagious this thing is or how the contagion spreads."

"I'm always careful. Have to be. Say, if you're researching a new disease, I've got another patient you might want to take a look at."

"Yes."

Ethan and the nurse went to the changing room and put on new protective equipment, then the nurse led him down the hallway to another isolation room. This patient was covered by a tent.

"They're calling this an anomalous allergy, but, well, you'll see. This is beyond any simple rash."

Ethan and the nurse stood outside the tent. The patient, a young, fit man who was asleep, had a reddish-purple rash, assuming it was a rash, on his neck and shoulders. It stopped before his biceps then reappeared on his forearms, where it was more blue than red.

Ethan read the nurse's scroll, taking in the man's history. Then Ethan saw his name: Jordan Fields.

"I have to go," he said. "Thank you for showing me this patient. I'll include him in my research. My assistant will be around to take samples later."

Ethan stripped off his protective gear and fled the clinic, running back to the morgue's lab. He commed Sean.

"The guy who's going to fix your roof."

"What about him?"

"How much contact have you had with him?"

"Ethan, what's the matter?"

"He's in the Genesia Clinic, down the corridor from Maizy Newell. I think he might have this thing."

"No. I just saw him a couple of days ago."

"He's in the hospital. Has a unique rash." He didn't add that they couldn't contain it or that, judging from the rest of his test results, it might kill him.

"But—Maizy doesn't have a rash. Does she? And the others—"

"We have no idea what this pathogen's capable of or how it might affect anyone or—"

"What about Ziva? Did you get her test results back yet?"

Ethan checked his scroll. "Not yet."

"I'd better go. I have another couple of floors I want to get to before I stop for the night. Then Jonathan Lee and Patterson are coming over. Why don't you come?"

"I see you more now than I did when we were dating."

"I've thought of that too."

"Maybe you've got something in your 'archive' that could help us." Ethan thought he sounded desperate. He was desperate.

"Maybe I do. I'll check."

But Ethan didn't make it over to Sean's. Instead he was back at the Genesia Clinic, where a new patient had been admitted, and Axel Booth, the doctor assigned to her case, wanted to consult with Ethan. Also, Booth thought Ethan might want to see a future autopsy while the corpse was still alive. Or as though alive, if this was life.

It wasn't until Ethan got to the clinic that he learned the patient was Althea Pierce.

CHAPTER 25

THE LAST DAY and a half had been torture. Ziva hadn't been able to eat, sleep, think, or even talk. Her thoughts were uncontrollable and her feelings were worse. When she saw Ethan's comm she hesitated before reading it. But surely he wouldn't leave a message if the news was bad, would he?

The message was simple: You're fine. Comm if you have questions. She commed him.

"What does it mean that I'm fine?"

"Ziva, you're fine. All your test results are normal."

"But Sean said you don't even know what this is, so are you sure?"

"Yes, I'm sure." Something in his tone of voice made her suspect there was more he wasn't saying.

"But I could still get it."

"Unknown. You might be immune. You've had a great deal of exposure to others who had this and you spent hours in Banerjee's apartment and you have no signs of it. You should be reassured."

"I'm not reassured. I'm scared. Is Sean really okay?"

That had kept her up last night—thinking she'd exposed Sean to this deadly disease when she didn't have to. Who cared if Morris was missing? He probably wanted to be missing. People were dying. Sean had said she was fine, but Sean had a way of not revealing too much about herself. Maybe she was lying.

"Sean's fine."

Zee didn't know what to do with everything swirling inside her. She'd been upset yesterday when Ethan hadn't taken her samples himself. He seemed to be avoiding her. Then she realized why.

"You've got it, don't you?"

"Ziva, you have other things to concern yourself with."

"I'm concerning myself with you." She'd promised herself she wouldn't get any more involved in this mess than she already was, but she liked Ethan Stiles, maybe more than liked him, and she couldn't stay silent.

"That's very kind of you."

"No, damn it, it's not. I'm not being kind. I'm concerned."

Ethan laughed. "I've never heard anyone slice those two concepts apart quite so easily."

"I've never heard anyone avoid answering a question quite so adeptly." She waited, something she'd been forced to do for the last day, so she had recent practice in this previously unknown art.

"Ziva."

"Ethan?"

"I'd better get back to it."

"All right, Dr. Stiles. Tell me what I can do to help." Now she was sure he was infected. Why else would he refuse to say anything?

"You could give Sean a hand in the Normandie. We have to get as many people tested as we can."

"I'd already intended to. I was just waiting to find out my status. Didn't want to infect anyone."

"We're not sure if this passes from person to person."

"You mean everyone who has it got it from their computer? Sean said something about this, but it seems, well, improbable."

Sean was a good investigator, but some of her ideas seemed a little out of line with reality. She'd told Ziva some wacky details about images or designs or microscopic whatevers but Ziva'd been too worried about everything going on to focus on the details.

"It is improbable but the more research we do, the more it seems it could be the source."

"I'm not turning my computer on again until this is over."

"We're thinking of shutting down all the computers at the Normandie anyway."

"There'll be a riot. Although at least the scrolls will still work."

"I've got to go, Ziva."

He signed off. No computer, and the message was clear: no scroll either. Should she also stop using her comm? Was it also infected? Didn't it run off some part of the mesh?

She dropped her comm and stepped back from it. She had to get in touch with Sean, but she was pretty sure she was on the fifth floor, knocking on doors, so she ran down the staircase—maybe the elevators were infected as well—and saw Sean emerging from the Parks' apartment.

"Sean, I've been cleared. I can help you out now. The medical examiner, Dr. Stiles—he's infected, isn't he?" She knew he was Sean's ex and thought she'd better not sound too familiar with him, not that she was at all familiar with him. And what must Sean think of her, a woman with a missing husband and two dead lovers?

"That's great news and, yes, Ethan's infected. But he doesn't have any symptoms."

"You're as scared as I am." Ziva could see the fear in Sean's eyes even though her face was doing its best to hide it.

"There's a clock ticking, Zee, and we don't know how long the countdown might be. I am scared but we have work to do. Why don't you start on the sixth floor and we'll alternate—I'll do the odds and you do the evens. I wrote out cards with the address of the lab so no one will have to use their computer to find it. Take some." She handed Ziva a stack of cards, which Zee stashed in her pocket.

"Sounds good. Meet me at my apartment for lunch. It won't be much but I do have supplies: cheese, crackers, fruit. Sound okay?"

"I've been forgetting to eat. And after hearing about Althea Pierce—"

"What about Althea Pierce?" Something had happened to the person who'd destroyed Ziva's marriage? Not that it hadn't already been collapsing. But Althea Pierce had done her best to incinerate it.

"It's all over the mesh. Didn't you see?"

"I haven't looked at the mesh. I'm not sure I want to. What if I can still get infected? What happened to her?"

"She's in the Genesia Clinic in isolation."

"Besides stealing my husband, she was one of Oliver's interludes, you know." No matter what Ziva thought of Althea Pierce—and none of it was good or kind—she didn't want her to die. She didn't want anyone to die. Each new death made the virus more terrifying.

"I didn't know about her and Oliver." Sean took out her comm and sent a message.

"The last time I ran into Charley I wondered if he was stalking his wife." Zee'd seen him on her floor but had acted like she hadn't noticed him. Well-known people didn't like to be approached by strangers, and even though her husband worked for Charley, Zee'd never met him. This was before Morris went missing. If it'd been after, she would've stopped Charley in the hallway and demanded information.

"Where did you run into Charley?"

"Right here in the building. I see him here every once in a while."

"Oh hell."

"What new hell is this?" Ziva wasn't sure she could take any more.

"Charley Pierce. He and Beryl Carson had dinner together the night before she died."

The beach house Zee'd missed out on was taunting her. She could've been there. She should be there. She wanted to be there. She'd be safe there.

No one in the west was dying of a computer virus that had figured out how to infect humans. Or thought that's what had happened.

"Sean. Charley Pierce has a direct connection to most of the victims."

"What do you mean?"

"I mean Althea was involved with both Oliver and Kaj, and since she wasn't very good at hiding her dalliances, Charley had to've known about it. Of course Morris worked at Pierce Sangstrom, and he could be another victim and we just don't know it yet. Everyone else works at the Normandie, and Charley must know someone here, so he's had direct contact with them as well."

"What about Vern Healy?"

"Okay, so not everyone. But almost everyone." Ziva realized this applied to her as well. Maybe even more to her than it did to Charley since she'd had direct contact with Vern Healy, who'd been at her apartment to investigate Beryl Carson's death. But this was different. Ziva knew she was innocent. The megacorp magnate Charley Pierce might very well be guilty.

Sean was comming someone again. Ignoring Ziva.

"What are you doing?"

"I'm asking Ethan if he knows Charley Pierce. I don't think he does."

But, as Ziva found out later while she and Sean took a break and gave their halfhearted attention to pear slices and a lackluster cheddar, Ethan did have a connection with Charley Pierce, through Beryl Carson. The two of them had worked together on a failed Pierce Sangstrom project a few months earlier.

CHAPTER 26

OTHER THAN IN a graveyard, the last place Charley Pierce wanted to be was in a hospital. He couldn't stand hospitals and right now he wasn't so sure he could stand the person he was here to see. Bad enough that Althea had carried on with Morris Walls, down the hall from Charley's office—although at least Morris's work had always benefited Pierce Sangstrom—but now Charley was forced to talk with the detestable Lukas Adler, who wore his fame and good looks like he was entitled to them or, worse, like he didn't care.

Charley had avoided Adler the night before, but today the man was unavoidable in the one small, cold sitting room in the isolation ward. As though the cruelties of life needed to be emphasized by putting patients' families in this restrictive, strangling space together. Adler wasn't part of Althea's family but because he'd brought her to the clinic the day before he'd been given special visitation rights. Or perhaps because he was Lukas Adler and the staff wanted to fawn over him.

"I don't know what the hell happened." Adler had already said this to Charley, but it wasn't enough. Charley needed information.

"You mean to say you were by yourself in your pool and suddenly there Althea was, as if by magic, lying on the ground, immobile."

"She wasn't immobile and she didn't appear as if by magic. She'd come out to my place to tell me about a new fabula she's working on and I was in the middle of my daily laps, so I asked her to wait. Althea said she'd get some sun."

"She's burnt." There was a huge red splotch on her chest and the nurse had told Charley Althea had one on her back as well. The staff assured him they were turning her over periodically.

"That's not a burn."

"Then what is it?" Charley agreed that it didn't look exactly like a burn but he didn't want to give Adler any satisfaction. The guy was self-satisfied enough for this lifetime and the next ten.

"They think it's part of the disease process."

"That's what the doctor told me as well, but that's not enough. What disease? Where's the diagnosis? What's the name of this disease? You get a faster diagnosis than this when you go to the medserv, which doesn't have any human staff."

"Charley, they'll tell us when they know."

"Why are you here anyway? You could be home. I have to be here."

"No one but Althea has to be here. You don't have to be here. You could go back to Pierce Sangstrom and swoon over your day's profits. I'm here because I care about her."

Charley wondered why, if someone had to be sick, it couldn't be Lukas Adler. Then Charley wouldn't have to be here, he wouldn't be troubled by the dark thoughts he was having, and he could be at Pierce Sangstrom swooning over the day's profits.

Adler opened his scroll and looked away from Charley.

Charley got up and went for a walk down the cold, impersonal corridor. As though this place were a computer repair center, not a hospital for human beings. He opened the door to the stairwell and started climbing. At least he could get some exercise while he was here. Six flights later he was at the top. The door to the roof opened and he went outside.

Gray sky and humidity. The world that had once welcomed him had turned on Charley Pierce. His wife, who'd had too many dalliances, including with Morris Walls, one of the few Pierce Sangstrom staff Charley had counted on at one time, was dying in a hospital bed, and

Charley had been forced to interact with the imperious Lukas Adler, who was treating Charley like he was a bit player in the fabula Lukas was starring in. And acting like Althea had come out to his house, out past the civilized world and into the remote wilds, just to talk to him about some new showcase for Adler's supposed talent.

Charley was starting to prefer the time when all Althea did was find a new lover every twenty minutes. At least he hadn't been involved, hadn't had to talk with them. Hadn't had to go to a hospital. Hadn't lost hope that she'd ever be the person he wanted her to be. She might not live to be the person even she wanted to be.

With nothing to do except harbor these and other, somewhat worse, black thoughts until the doctors were done with examining Althea, Charley took out his comm and, after glancing at it, turned it off and put it back in his pocket.

Juno Sangstrom. Wanted to have a meeting with him about the new program, Desire Me. Wanted to talk things over with him. Set a launch date.

If Althea died, if she wasn't already dead—maybe she'd died while he and Adler had been in the sitting area or while he was on the roof, avoiding Adler—Charley would use her fortune to buy out Juno. She'd be intolerable if Althea died, trying to work her way back into his life, trying to re-create the old days when they'd lived together.

Charley loved people with inventive, creative minds. He was attracted to them and needed to be near them. As far as flaws went, he'd always thought this one was more like an asset and, at its worst, a mere annoyance. But his two main attractions of this sort—to Juno Sangstrom and to Althea Livesy—were seeming less and less like assets and more like outright disasters.

Althea might be dying and all Juno cared about was her latest creation. Granted, it had immense possibilities and every time Charley looked at it or worked on it he was more impressed, but right now was not the time. He turned his comm back on, let Juno know Althea was in critical condition in the hospital, and said they'd have to delay their meeting.

Juno didn't respond. She was taunting him. She'd been taunting him for years, ever since he'd met Althea and moved out. Why hadn't he broken all ties with Juno back then? He could've insisted she give up her stake in Pierce Sangstrom, paid her off, and been done with her. Instead, not wanting to lose her far-reaching mind and innovative, lucrative creations, he'd put up with her, agreed to her arrangement, and met with her regularly, although those meetings hadn't been what Juno had intended. He never gave her any indication he might be interested in her the way he had been before Althea. Before he'd had the where-withal to examine the situation.

Meet Me—a brilliant invention made even more brilliant the moment he and Althea had found each other. Without Meet Me he never would've known her. She lived in a different world from Charley's. Her fortune was made and although Charley had been born with a fortune, he'd just started to accumulate his own. She'd already written and sold several fabulas back then and was getting more involved in the production process. Charley didn't care about any of that. Not only did it disinterest him—he had no need or desire for fictional entertainments—but he didn't care what Althea did.

It didn't matter. It had never mattered. She did whatever she pleased and Charley still wanted her. He wanted her almost as much as he needed her, since she filled a fundamental purpose, relieving him of a problem there was no escape from.

He leaned on the railing and looked out, across Genesia toward Osada. He could almost see the Pierce Sangstrom offices from the roof of the clinic.

Althea had been so ill at Tuigen but she'd recovered. She'd recover now. She wasn't the kind of person who succumbed to disease or to anything. She was the kind of person who'd stand at the shoreline during a tidal wave and after the wave had receded and everyone and everything within a hundred kilometers was dead or destroyed, she'd still be standing. She'd be thinking what a great setting a tidal wave would make for a fabula and she'd begin plotting it, right then, right there amid all the devastation, climbing over corpses and wreckage with all her attention on only her own burgeoning creation.

Althea would die only if she wanted to.

Charley went back downstairs. He had to check on Althea. What if something had happened while his comm was off and he wasn't in the waiting area?

But nothing had changed. Althea was still the same, still unresponsive and with the strange burn or rash, Adler was still in the waiting area, the corridors were still cold and eerie.

Charley sat down as far away from Adler as he could get in the small room and took out his scroll, skimmed through some tasks he had to do for work, and then his attention was drawn to the application Juno was calling Desire Me, a program that went far beyond any of her former creations, into a realm that could mean an even greater fortune for Pierce Sangstrom and, more to the point, for Charley.

Like they'd done at Keff, when Juno and Charley worked on a program together they used a special cryptic code Juno'd devised, one that no one other than Juno and Charley—and of course computers themselves—knew how to read. For their school assignments they'd translate the code back to something ordinary so their work would be transparent, and of course the Pierce Sangstrom programs that users could customize to their own needs were also written in a familiar machine language—at least the parts the user could access were.

But while their work was in the development stage, Juno's language was the one they used. Charley got involved in the new program, making a few tweaks. She might be a genius but without his methodical technical expertise, her programs would never be as complete, as refined, as devastating. She had raw talent but he had the finesse needed to make something raw into a smooth and effortless creation.

Yet now he came upon something even he didn't understand. Had Juno created yet another language? A sublanguage to the cryptic code they already used? He'd never seen anything like this and he had no idea what it could mean. Had this always been in the program and he'd ignored it since it was buried so far down that it seemed to be part of the essential underpinnings? He often ignored those things. They were boilerplate necessities. But this was no boilerplate.

Charley walked out into the hallway, stood in the stairwell, and took out his comm, sending a message to Juno, asking her about the code in location t523B.

Charley's mind brought forth an image of Morris Walls. This was no time to be thinking about the man who'd been his most trusted employee and who'd become his least trusted. But with Althea in an isolation room just down the hall, maybe it was inevitable that Charley would think about Morris.

He shook his head. Nothing was clear. Althea could be dying. Out here in the stairwell, Charley was spared having to look at Adler's chiseled body. Charley commed Juno on voice.

"Charley, how nice of you to contact me. Especially with Mrs. Pierce in the hospital."

"Althea's doing better. She should be back home in a day or two." No point in telling Juno what was really happening.

"Your home? Or someone else's?"

Juno could be harsh. He let it pass. This was more important.

"Juno, you have to tell me about what's going on in t523B."

"So you finally read through everything? I was wondering when you'd get around to it."

"Yes, I finally did. I've got nothing to distract me here."

"Other than Lukas Adler and a dying wife."

Juno never left her apartment yet she seemed to know everything that was happening in his life. Charley reminded himself that she could just be guessing. It'd been reported that Althea'd taken ill while she was at Adler's house. Adler might live in an isolated location but once he brought Althea into Genesia, his life was laid bare.

"I want to talk with you about this." Charley wanted to know everything Juno'd done and what she intended to do next, all while covering over his end of things.

"A couple of hours ago you were canceling our meeting."

"I'm uncanceling it. I'll see you in two hours."

"Three. I'm working."

Juno signed off. Charley leaned against the wall while his mind raced.

He checked in on Althea before he left. She was still unmoving. The rash seemed to've spread, but Charley could have been imagining it.

In his transcer, he raced through the rough streets of Genesia to get to the Normandie, where he could scavenge Juno's brain, find out what she was up to, and discuss what it could mean for their future.

But even though his mind was now focused on the code— forgetting about Althea, about her dead lovers, about Beryl Carson, about Adler—yet an image of Juno herself appeared in his mind's eye and refused to fade.

CHAPTER 27

SEAN WAS SITTING on the floor of her workspace, forging her way through Stack #3,426. Sebastian was sitting on her desk, looking down over the procedure, as though he were in charge. She'd wanted to keep him away from her archives, but in her small house, her intent had proven hopeless. Sebastian liked to run up and down the long hallway and he often slept on top of one of the stacks. He never disturbed anything, so Sean didn't mind.

"Finally," she said as she pulled out the paper she was looking for, an article she'd read almost a decade ago and had thought significant enough to make a printed copy of and add to her collection. Although she'd remembered the article she couldn't remember the details. Now as she read through it, she landed upon something she hadn't noticed at the time, since it was before she knew Ethan: Jonathan Lee Summers's name, right there, quoted as an expert in code formation and analysis. An authority who lectured at the Acres. Couldn't get more qualified than that.

"Find anything?"

She looked up and, as though she'd summoned him, there was Jonathan Lee himself, standing in the doorway, looking more worn out than she felt. His hair was sticking out in a hundred directions, his eyes were bloodshot, and she was pretty sure he was wearing the same shirt with the same stain near the collar, the shirt he'd had on when she'd seen him two days earlier.

"You look like hell."

"Thanks," he said. "So do you."

"At least I changed my shirt."

"Really?"

She looked down at herself and realized she was wearing the same shirt she'd had on since yesterday or maybe the day before. "Well, I meant to."

"Good intentions pave the road to the Flats."

"It's hardly hell out there." Did he somehow sense she was about to attack him for his former expertise on a subject he'd argued with her about and was redirecting the conversation?

"My humor mechanism's on hold. And, actually, Patterson's there. The term ended yesterday and Patterson went out to the Flats straight after school. Left me a note. Took a bicycle and a backpack. Never said a word about it beforehand."

"Other than begging you to stay when we were all there."

"Other than. Why are you seething?"

"I'm not seething, but, Jonathan Lee, what the hell? You knew about this a decade ago."

"What this could you be referring to?"

"The possibility that a computer virus could make the leap and infect a human. I was sure I'd read about it somewhere and I just found this." She handed up the pages of the article she'd been reading.

"No reason to seethe over it. This was just a symposium I went to. Speculation only. We talked about all sorts of wild ideas. Possibilities but not actualities. Distant, far, far, far in the future possibilities."

"You mean—and I quote—'My sense is that, with advances in computer RNA configurations, this sort of phenomenon is only a few years away' constitutes a possibility in the distant future?"

"I don't know who said that, but everyone at gatherings like that one says shocking things, tries to wake up the bored crowd, make waves."

"Is that what you were doing?"

"I wouldn't've said that or anything like it."

"Yet you did." Sean held out the paper and pointed to the quote, attributed to Jonathan Lee.

"Just because it says I said it doesn't mean I did."

"Don't deflect. You must've said it."

"I suppose I might've. It was just talk."

"Trying to wake up the crowd, hunh?"

"Trying to wake myself up. Enliven a particularly boring symposium."

"And you see who else was there?"

Sean pointed and Jonathan Lee looked down at the page. "Charley Pierce. Well, he would've been. Pierce Sangstrom's always been at the forefront of technical innovations."

Jonathan Lee sat down on the floor, making a place for himself between stacks.

"What else do you have?" he said.

"That's about it. Jonathan Lee, we've got to get to Pierce, find out how he's connected to all this. Do you know him?"

"*If* he's connected. If. A lot of people were at that symposium. And this topic has been discussed more than once."

"Jonathan Lee. And you acted like I was out of my mind."

"Look at this mess. You are out of your mind."

"Pierce is involved somehow. I can feel it."

"I'm not friendly with him, but I do know him."

"Then I elect you to talk to him."

"I can't stand staying out at Beryl's house since Patterson left."

"I have a spare room, but, uh, you know . . ."

"The sacred stacks."

"Yeah. There's a sleep mat in there and I could probably make enough room for you."

Sean couldn't believe she was inviting Jonathan Lee to come stay in her house. She felt disloyal to Ethan, even though there was nothing there. And, worse, she was confusing herself. She wasn't interested in

Jonathan Lee, so why would it matter if he stayed at her place? It wouldn't.

"You should just stay here. It'll be easier. If we don't solve this thing soon, Ethan could—I won't say it. Nothing's going to happen to Ethan. It just can't."

"He's my oldest friend. I couldn't bear it, and I can't hurt him."

Sean brushed aside the implication—that Jonathan Lee was as not-interested in Sean as she was in him.

Jonathan Lee started flipping through Stack #3,426 and Sean put her hand on his, stopping him.

"It's organized. You can't disturb the order."

He put his other hand over hers and leaned toward her.

"The order is already disturbed, but I'll be careful."

She pulled her hand away. "Please."

He took a part of the stack, put it on his lap, and started reading through it.

"Ethan told me you want to shut down all the computers at the Normandie, but he can't get permission from anyone in authority. I'm trying to figure out a way that we can do it anyway."

"So am I. Hey, what's this?" He held up a sheet, and Sean leaned across to look at it. She was much too close to Jonathan Lee, here on her floor, in her house, where she'd invited Jonathan Lee to stay while Patterson was at the Flats.

She took the paper. "I guess I was saving information about Charley Pierce. Not sure why. It seemed important at the time."

"This says Pierce and Sangstrom were lovers. Did you know that?"

"I didn't remember. I don't really know anything about Sangstrom."

"She's the genius behind the operation. That's what the brains at Keff think, anyway."

"Maybe we should be talking to her as well."

"Sean, I don't think I should stay here. I'll get used to it out at Beryl's place. It's just odd now, with Patterson gone."

"You're probably right. I'm just . . . and you'll be going back to the Acres . . . and I don't know what Ethan would . . . and also we have to concentrate on the task . . . and . . ." She leaned closer to him. She wasn't interested, she couldn't be interested, and they had work to do.

He moved closer to her, reached out, and touched her ear. Nothing had ever felt quite this . . .

"Jonathan Lee. We have to be careful."

"I've been careful ever since Beryl walked out on me. Now I'm too tired to care." His hand was still on her ear, and she put her hand over his.

"Maybe I am too." She moved closer still.

Stack #3,426 was between them, but it couldn't keep them apart. Sean pushed it over. Jonathan Lee pulled her toward him.

Hours later she woke up. Jonathan Lee's head was on her stomach, his arm wrapped around her. She brushed back the lock of hair that had fallen over his forehead. He moved his arm, hugging her closer to him.

When had she last eaten? What would Ethan say when he found out? She'd better tell him before Jonathan Lee had the chance. Wasn't there already enough going on? Why had she allowed this complication into her life?

"Would you like breakfast?" The shades were closed and she wasn't sure what time it was, how long they'd slept, but breakfast seemed like the right meal to have.

"Yes." Jonathan Lee lifted his head. "Are you going to tell Ethan or am I?"

"I am. After breakfast. I'll go over to the lab."

"I'll go with you. Sean, I hadn't intended for this to happen. Not right now. Later, maybe, depending, but not now."

"I hadn't intended anything. I didn't realize." She'd missed every signal, every indication. She was a competent detective but when it came to her own life she hadn't been paying attention.

Jonathan Lee's free hand was making a design on Sean's thigh.

"We should have breakfast," she said.

"We should make love again, while we're still in the haze of it, before our guilt takes over."

"Too late." Sean was already awash with guilt.

"Then we can't waste any time." He lifted his head, moved up so his face was next to hers, gazed straight into her center, as though he'd known her since the beginning.

Another person would have had the willpower to disentangle herself, get up, take a shower, get dressed, make breakfast. Feed Sebastian. That person wasn't Sean. Her hands were in Jonathan Lee's disarrayed hair, then her lips were on his, and their bodies closed the space between need and transcendence.

Afterward, in the shower, after they'd made love with the water streaming over them and were washing off, Jonathan Lee said, "I haven't been with anyone since Beryl left me. I don't know what I'm doing. It's unfamiliar. Shocking, almost."

"Since Ethan, I haven't either. Jonathan Lee, I have to tell him. We can't have secrets. We're all working with each other."

"I'll go with you."

"I'd better go by myself."

"Sean. We're in this together."

"Why? Why are we in this together? What's happening between us?"

"I'm a scientist. This is out of my area of knowledge."

Jonathan Lee smiled. Sean smiled. They stepped out of the shower and stood, laughing, under the gusts of warm air swirling around them.

"I don't know what's so funny," Sean said between bursts of laughter. She couldn't stop herself.

"It's absurd, isn't it?" Jonathan Lee looked like a different person when he was smiling. No longer the serious, established expert. More like a kid who'd just discovered his love of the wonders of science. "That we've found joy in the middle of this crisis."

Sean took Jonathan Lee's hand and placed it in the center of her chest.

CHAPTER 28

A FTER A COUPLE of days of knocking on doors and pleading with fellow tenants to get tested for a disease she couldn't name, was reluctant to describe in any detail, and was more and more concerned about, Ziva had to get out of the Normandie and do something, anything, else.

She and Sean had been somewhat successful in convincing many residents to get tested, but there were still several unanswered doors. The reclusive woman on her floor hadn't even touched the paper Ziva had put partway under her door, which was the method Zee and Sean were using to try to contact tenants who didn't respond. With an edge of the paper visible in the hallway, they could keep track of who had actually seen their request to go to the lab and get tested.

Ziva was planning to go over to Sean's later, but now she was headed to the Genesia Clinic, where Maizy Newell, Jordan Fields, and Althea Pierce were. Not that Ziva would visit Althea Pierce, but she wanted to check in on both Maizy and Jordan, let them know that at least someone at the Normandie cared about them and was working on their behalf.

Although Ethan's comm had said Maizy was still not conscious, Ziva was hopeful. Maizy was alive, and that was more than she could say for Oliver or Kaj. They were dead and Ziva hadn't even had the opportunity to say good-bye to either of them. Vern Healy was dead too, although Ziva almost didn't care. He was someone she didn't know.

And Morris. Where the hell was he? He hadn't commed, hadn't contacted her. As if he'd actually disappeared instead of merely disappeared from her life. Stinnett's son was working on the divorce. He'd insisted Morris's assets be put into a trust until he reemerged, even though Zee told Stinnett several times that she didn't want or need anything of Morris's. The apartment was hers, she had ample assets, and if Morris did return—or if he didn't return but wanted access to his own funds—he should have it. Stinnett set it up so that Morris, should he want any of his funds, which so far he hadn't, would be able to get to them without any difficulty. The trust was just to shield the assets and make them available to Ziva if at some point in the future Morris might turn up dead or be declared dead. Then Ziva wouldn't have to go through complex proceedings and could use the funds as she wanted to. She was Morris's heir anyway. Zee had found his will and the Stinnetts had ascertained it was unlikely he'd written another one, although there was no way to be certain.

Lawyers, wills, estates, diseases, deaths, a missing husband. Ziva had had it. And how was she about to spend her day? At a hospital, visiting two unconscious people and avoiding the Pierces.

Later, though, she'd go to Sean's, find out what was going on, and maybe she'd get lucky and Ethan would be there too. And she could check in on Egon, or Sebastian, which Zee thought was a much better name, making sure he was happy in his new home, although that was just an excuse. Ziva had to know what was going on, if they'd found the cause, the cure, anything. She was connected to these people now, people she hadn't known a few weeks ago, back before Morris went missing, before all the deaths, before she'd heard of the possibility of a computer virus that could transmit itself to humans, if that was what was really happening.

She'd stopped thinking of Sean as her private investigator. Sean was her friend. Because of that, Zee would have to forget about Ethan. Sean wasn't with him anymore, but he was her ex, some people get sensitive about these things, and despite Sean's professional detective demeanor, Zee sensed she'd be someone who'd be more than sensitive.

Ziva would be moving soon anyway. She couldn't get involved with anyone, and Ethan, who'd already contracted this horrendous disease, would be better off not knowing her, since every man she'd been involved with lately had died or disappeared.

In the meanwhile, she'd found another beach house and had put in a bid on it even though she'd never been out west. She had to get away from Osada City, from the Normandie.

At the hospital, Ziva breezed past the front desk. Acting like you belonged somewhere was always a good strategy and today it worked. She sneaked up the staircase to the isolation floor and slipped into the hallway unnoticed, leaning up against a doorjamb and acting as invisible as she could. She'd wait until she was sure no one else was in Maizy's room and then she'd go in.

"You killed her."

Ziva pressed her ear against the doorjamb, a perfect conductor of sound. Two men were arguing with each other in the room on the other side of her position in the hall. This was more interesting than knocking on people's doors and having them tell you to stop interfering in their lives even though you were trying to save their lives.

"Calm down. She's not dead."

"She might as well be dead. She died on your watch."

"There's no reason to believe she won't recover. I wouldn't be here every day if I didn't think she'd recover."

Who were they talking about? Maizy?

"Althea was absolutely fine until she made the mistake of going to 'visit' you."

Althea Pierce. One of the speakers had to be her husband, Charley, but who was the other?

"If she got sick at my place, how come I'm not sick?" The voice sounded a lot like the actor Lukas Adler. Was Althea involved with Adler? Zee didn't want to stop listening, but she'd need absolute quiet to contemplate how someone who'd been with Lukas Adler would also be interested in Morris Walls. Seemed impossible, although impossible was how things were going lately, so maybe it *wasn't* impossible.

"You could be sick and you just don't know it yet. You're a sick bastard anyway."

"Charley, you're just upset."

"Is that act supposed to convey some deep insight you're having about me? Well, here's my deep insight about you: Althea made your career and you're worried that if she dies and her new fabula doesn't get produced, your career will be over. You're just here protecting your own future. Go home. No one wants you here."

Ziva was holding her breath. She wanted to take out her comm and record this conversation so she'd have it to play for Sean, but she was afraid if she moved to do it, the sound would expose her.

"Althea wants me here."

"Prove it."

"Charley, you're being an ass. That's not going to help Althea."

"And you being here every damned day is?"

"We're through talking."

The door next to Zee opened and Lukas Adler himself stepped into the hall. The man was even better-looking in person than he was in fabulas. He walked past her, not noticing her, and turned a corner. Was he going to see Althea?

Ziva had lost track of whether anyone else was in with Maizy. That was the reason she'd come to the clinic, not to eavesdrop on Charley Pierce and Lukas Adler, so she tiptoed down the hall and went to Maizy's room.

At one time Ziva wouldn't've welcomed having a conversation with Maizy that consisted of more than a few benign pleasantries if they saw each other at the Normandie, but right now she'd be thrilled if Maizy were conscious and screaming at her for stealing Oliver Hirata from her.

Not that Ziva had stolen Oliver from Maizy or from anyone. Oliver was not stealable, for one thing, and Ziva hadn't said a word to him before he came back to her. He'd always come back to her. After she moved to the Normandie, they'd had many interludes together and Ziva had been sure there would always be more. But . . .

Zee was pleased the new flowers she'd sent to Maizy had been put on the windowsill where Maizy could see them, if she opened her eyes to see anything. But Maizy herself wasn't in the room. She was probably having tests done. The sort of tests they couldn't do with you lying in the bed in the room, the kind needing equipment that couldn't be moved. Maybe this meant Maizy was doing better. Or . . .

"You cannot be dead, Maizy. I won't have it."

"I think they took her downstairs for some tests."

Ziva turned around and came face-to-face with Lukas Adler. In another lifetime, one she'd been living only a few weeks ago but which seemed like it had been eons ago, Zee would've loved meeting the famous actor and talking with him. Now she didn't care. He was just someone else cluttering up her distorted world.

"You know Maizy?"

"I don't, but after you hang out in the isolation area for a while, you get to know who everyone is. There aren't that many patients here."

"Althea stole my husband from me." Ziva couldn't believe she'd blurted that out, yet she had.

"I don't doubt it. I've seen her in action. She's not even subtle."

"He worked for Charley."

"If you're trying to get me to feel sorry for your stolen husband, you're succeeding."

"Ziva Walls." She held out her hand and Adler shook it.

"Lukas Adler."

"Well, Lukas Adler, if Althea is such an adept husband stealer, why are you here?"

"I feel responsible. She was at my place when she got sick. And we're friends. I want to make sure they're taking good care of her. When there's someone here, the staff is more attentive."

"Doubly so for you. Trying to impress."

"Probably."

"Did they say what exactly is wrong with her?"

"I've been getting the runaround. A lot of *It's too soon to tell* and *We need to run more tests* and *We're doing everything we can*. I could write my own fabula and populate it with noncommittal medical professionals. I've got the real-life dialogues memorized. Are you a friend of Maizy's?"

"It's complicated. But in a way, we almost are. She runs the front desk at the Normandie."

"That's interesting. Althea was involved with that artist and he lives at the Normandie."

"Lived. Kaj is dead."

"I didn't realize."

"How could you not know Kaj Banerjee died? Don't you keep current?"

"I live out in the sticks, away from everything. I go on the mesh only for work. Otherwise, I ignore it."

"Probably a good policy."

"Yes."

"Even more so right now." Ziva told herself to shut up. She was talking to Lukas Adler like they were old friends.

"Why?"

"So much bad news. Sad news."

"But you meant something else, didn't you?"

"I'd better go. Maizy might not be back for ages and I have other plans."

"It's been good talking to you. Other than the staff, who all treat me like I'm a mythical being, the only person I've had any conversations with lately is the dreadful Charley Pierce."

"Then he and Althea deserve each other."

"I can't disagree."

Ziva left the room, left the hospital without having seen either Maizy or Jordan Fields, who she'd forgotten about while she was talking to Adler, and walked all the way to Sean Meade's house, nearly eight kilometers away. She hadn't intended to walk, but she needed time to turn everything over in her head.

She couldn't shake the feeling she'd learned something worthwhile, yet she didn't know what that might be.

By the time she got to Sean's house the feeling was gone and in its place was a sensation of impending doom.

CHAPTER 29

WOULD CHARLEY BE at the hospital every day for her if she were sick? Juno doubted it. He'd probably use her illness as another opportunity to avoid her.

He'd said he was coming over, said he had to talk with her immediately, had to ask her about location t523B, even called her a genius, something he hadn't said to her in years, but then he commed to say he had to get back to the hospital. Something was going on with Althea. He wasn't sure what. He'd see Juno later.

Juno paced around the apartment. With almost three hundred square meters of floor space, there was plenty of room to wander. That had been one of the main appeals of the Normandie—the oversize apartments. Juno thought better when she was on the move and she didn't want to have to go outside to do it. When she had an idea, it had to be taken care of without delay. She needed her computer nearby. A scroll wasn't good enough for the sorts of complex concepts and procedures that fascinated her, that were her life's work.

She hadn't heard from Jordan Fields in days. He was her spy at the hospital, but he was often unconscious, which was something Juno hadn't anticipated. He was infected, but it was with a very weak strain of the virus, one she'd let mutate over several months, keeping a close eye on its progress. The mutation caused a rash and some other minor symptoms. The loss of consciousness wasn't supposed to happen.

Jordan, without any hesitation, had agreed to her scheme. Maybe he was tired of polishing floors and waiting on the Normandie's needy tenants. He'd stopped by Juno's apartment after spending an afternoon looking at the damage to Sean Meade's roof. As soon as Juno heard he was in direct contact with the detective, someone who might be getting closer to the truth, she realized she had to do something to keep them apart. Jordan knew too much, although he might not know exactly what it was he did know, but he was a talker. And Sean Meade was an observant investigator. Too observant.

When Juno'd brought up the idea of Jordan spying for her, he'd said yes, of course he would. He would love to help out Juno. She thought he was going to say he loved her—she often thought he did love her but couldn't express it—yet he didn't say it.

When she'd told him what was involved, that he'd have to expose himself to a virus and get admitted to the hospital, he was still amenable. "Sure, Juno, if you say it's okay, then it's okay." She assured him it was okay even though she herself wasn't certain it was. The virus had already morphed in ways she hadn't expected it would, and what Charley'd done . . .

When she'd told Jordan to sit at her computer, he'd said, "Why?"

"Because this is the most convenient place for me to administer the virus. So I can keep track of it on the computer."

He nodded, but he couldn't have understood. She'd told him to enter information about himself into the computer while she was getting the virus ready and he'd complied. A gauze pad saturated with alcohol served as the supposed medium for the infection. She'd rubbed the alcohol into his upper arm and he winced, as though what she'd done had been painful and the virus had entered his body through this procedure.

But Jordan was already infected before then, since he'd been interacting with her computer and the virus was programmed to find any suitable host, computer or human. Like all viruses, this one needed a host to survive and flourish, and Juno had encoded it with instructions that biological organisms were preferable hosts to computers. As soon as a human was in the vicinity, the virus latched on.

Juno, of course, was immune. She'd been vaccinating herself all along with an mRNA concoction she'd manufactured while she was creating the RNA computer-to-human virus. If she hadn't been immune, she wouldn't've been able to work on certain sections of the code.

Juno was surprised at how quickly Jordan had become ill. She hadn't thought he would and also hadn't thought he'd be unconscious for so much of the time or at all. What good was a spy if he wasn't awake to do the work? Had he already been exposed to the virus through his various duties in the Normandie? Maybe.

You're a genius. Charley's words resonated in Juno's solar plexus. Wasn't that where the so-called soul was supposed to be located? The soul was a human invention. There was no such thing as a soul. No one had one. Souls were for people who didn't understand science, who were superstitious, who thought there was something beyond one's corpus, who had ideas that didn't conform to the immutable laws of the universe.

Juno herself, though, didn't conform to the laws of the universe. She was her own law, a law that was able to invent an RNA virus that could not only infect a computer but that could infect its user. It had taken her years but it had been worth the effort and the time. Especially now that Althea Pierce was infected.

Althea had thought she was so clever, inserting her own low-level code into the program. As though Juno wouldn't notice. At first Juno was going to delete it but the code, although crude, was amusing.

Whatever Charley might've suspected, Hirata's and Banerjee's deaths hadn't affected her. They were expendable, as all scientific subjects were. How could you know if and how anything worked unless it was taken out of the conceptual and theoretical stages and tested in vivo?

While she was pacing through the apartment she came upon the piece of paper stuck under her door. It had been there for days and Juno hadn't moved it although she was curious about what it might say, but the paper was upside down, and she didn't want to disturb it and signal she was home, so she couldn't see what was written on it. Probably someone in the building asking for a donation for their favorite charity or a notice saying the water would be turned off on Tuesday between eight and nine. She didn't care enough to pick up the paper and read it.

Her masterwork was no longer just a brilliant concept. It was alive and in play, infecting computers and people alike. Doing its worst, and to Juno, that meant it was doing its best. If she were a different person, she'd have to give some credit to Charley, whose elementary enhancements had improved the virus's potency and widened its range.

So far Charley'd done minimal work on the program. When he finally laid into it, Pierce Sangstrom would be unstoppable. They'd rule the world. They'd have control of the virus and its vaccine. They'd have control over people's lives, since there was a version of this virus that didn't cause a harmful infection but instead, without any action necessary, inserted itself into the user's world, both technical and biological, learning everything about the user and then turning that information into profit. For her and Charley.

His distinctive knock sounded on her door.

"How's Mrs. Pierce?" she said after he came in. He stooped to pick up the paper that had been lying in the doorway.

"Althea's doing much better."

"Keep lying to yourself, Charley. Why don't you come in and sit down?"

Charley nodded and followed Juno into her den, which was where they held most of their meetings.

"Have you eaten?" Charley had a gray cast along the perimeter of his thinning face.

"I don't think so."

Juno went to the kitchen, grabbed some boxes, came back to the den, and put the boxes on the table in front of Charley.

"Here. Eat something."

Charley opened one of the boxes, sneered, put it down, then opened another box, one with his favorite crackers in it. He started eating them, two at a time.

"Did you see this?" He held up the paper he'd taken from her doorway.

"I saw it was there, but I don't have time for trivialities."

"Sometimes I think you're not the person from Keff, the one I used to know. Then you say something like that and I understand that you haven't changed at all."

"You're just not here to experience the change. Not like you used to be."

"We're not getting into that."

"If Althea dies—"

"Althea is not going to die. She's doing much better. Improved. Her doctors are optimistic. She's on track for a full recovery. It's just taking some time."

Charley stopped talking and stuffed several more crackers into his mouth. Maybe Althea was already dead and Charley was lying to Juno. But she was getting ahead of herself.

"This paper says they're urging everyone in the building to go to the Genesia Clinic and get tested. There's a serious infectious disease—that can cause great harm—and they're trying to get ahead of it, before it spreads further. So, Juno, why do I think you're responsible?"

"How could I be responsible for a disease? I rarely leave my apartment." Juno did her best to seem nonchalant against Charley's accusations.

"Juno, I've never doubted your brilliance. You were a shining beacon at Keff and you're the bedrock of Pierce Sangstrom."

"So I'm a beacon and a bedrock? I'm always amazed at how you can come up with new ways to insult me, Charley. Without me, there'd be no Pierce Sangstrom. You'd be a second-rate code editor at Uhlmann's, struggling to survive."

"Without me, you wouldn't be living in this posh building, doing nothing but using your overactive brain to figure out clever ways to destroy the world."

"So I'm destroying the world now, am I?" She stared at Charley. "If I hadn't designed Meet Me, you wouldn't even know Althea."

Charley threw down the box of crackers and stood up. "And I'm supposed to thank you for that?"

"Among other things."

"Thank you for everything, Juno Sangstrom. I wish to hell I'd never met you. My family was pushing me to go to the Acres but I wanted to study with Ledyard. I should've known then what a mistake I was making."

Charley Pierce was an idiot. He had not-so-idiotic areas of his brain but none of them were of use in human relationships. Even Juno, who had no social skills, understood others better than Charley did or could.

"I meant you've never apologized. Not even indirectly."

Charley sat down and picked up the box of crackers, then threw it back down again.

"Don't you have any real food here?"

"Use your comm. There must be a hundred places that will deliver."

Charley took out his comm and Juno intensified her stare. He still hadn't apologized. Althea could be dead, a distraught Charley could restart his onetime relationship with Juno, and he still wouldn't apologize. He'd just act like he belonged there with her. And then he'd try to meet someone else.

"You're hopeless," she said when he finally looked up from his comm.

Charley picked up the paper that'd been under her door and waved it at her.

"You're responsible for this." As though he weren't also responsible.

"You have no proof."

"I have all the proof I need. Althea's in the hospital. People have died. All of them have one thing in common: you."

"I don't know any of these people." Although she knew some of them better than others, lying to Charley came as naturally to her as lying to Juno came to Charley.

"And they have something else in common. Their computers are all infected with your so-called program, which is really just a vehicle for the most sophisticated computer virus ever devised."

"You can't know that."

"Look, Juno, the program's astounding. You're the kind of genius who comes along once in a century. There's no doubt about it. You've just gone too far this time."

"I've gone too far?" Charley was pushing her. "This program will give us unlimited power."

"Then you admit it. Your program is the source of this infection. It's the reason Althea's on the verge of death—"

"I thought you said she was improving."

"I meant, well—she is improving, but she's critically ill. You have to stop this now, Juno, before it spreads beyond the Normandie."

Juno smiled. "It's already spread beyond the Normandie. For one thing, it's at the Pierce Sangstrom offices. How else do you think Althea was able to get her hands on it?"

"What are you talking about? Althea doesn't know anything about computers except that they exist. And the program's only on my computer at the company. No one else has access to it."

"But, Charley, the program knows how to populate itself. As soon as it's on one computer on a network, it's on them all. And at a certain critical point—although even I'm not sure what that point is or when it will be reached—it won't even need to be on the same network as other computers. It will just spread."

"You have to stop this now. Before more people die."

"But that's down to Althea." Juno watched Charley's reaction. She knew how his mind worked, which knowledge was one of her main weapons.

"You keep bringing her up. I know you're jealous. I know you've never forgiven me for leaving you for her. That's in the past. Something dire is happening right now. Because of you. And you're the only one who can stop it."

"The virus wasn't designed to kill anyone. In fact, I wasn't sure what effect it might have on anyone it infected. That was part of the experiment," she said. "I wanted to see if it could transfer itself from the computer to its user. Then I'd monitor the effects, if there were any.

"But after Althea got her hands on it, it became deadly. She might not know anything about computers but she has a sinister streak." Would Charley defend Althea? How far would he go? What would he admit? Juno waited.

Charley got up. "I'm going to expose you for the murderer you are, Juno Sangstrom. Count on it."

Juno sat back and listened as Charley worked his way to the foyer and let himself out, making sure to slam the door for effect.

Juno smiled. Charley would never expose her as a murderer. She'd immunized herself in every way possible.

CHAPTER 30

O F THE FORTY-SEVEN tenants of the Normandie who'd come to the lab for testing, thirteen were infected with the virus. Nine of the people infected had no symptoms, two had a rash, and two were having difficulties with both cognition and balance. Ethan had been able to admit those with symptoms to the Genesia Clinic, but the nine asymptomatic tenants all refused treatment.

Ethan had pleaded with them, but was unsuccessful. Their responses: If this virus is such a big thing, how come I've never heard of it? You medical types just like to experiment on people. Count me out. I don't have the time to waste. Aren't you the medical examiner? You can do whatever you want with me after I'm a corpse. Until then— no. This doesn't even have a name so it's not a real disease. I'm sorry I came in to get tested, and how do I know the test is accurate? This could all be a giant hoax.

"You're doing your best." Ethan heard his friend's voice over the din in his mind.

"Jay, it's not enough. I have to do more."

"You have to get some sleep, Ethan." Sean was sitting on the floor. Jonathan Lee was on the couch, behind her. Ethan, masked and gloved, was in Sebastian's chair with Sebastian on his lap. Trying to keep a reasonable distance from everyone couldn't be done in Sean's small house, already overcrowded with her "collection," and Ethan was somewhat concerned he might pass the virus over to Sebastian. Without having done any tests on animals, he wasn't sure if they could also get infected. But Sebastian had jumped into his lap and Ethan didn't want to disturb him.

"We have to give it a name," Sean said. "That will make it seem more real to the people who might need treatment."

"And I think it's time we stopped keeping this to ourselves. I've spoken to six different people at the joukko about this, but I'm not getting anywhere. Jay, can you do any better?"

"I'll try comming Dorian Song at the Acres. She heads computer research. Knows a lot of people. And we should get her in on this anyway. Use her expertise."

Something had shifted. Ethan didn't know what it was, but it had happened. Since Patterson had gone out to the Flats, Jonathan Lee was staying at Sean's house and maybe that had caused the shift. Whatever it was, it was good. Jay seemed more focused, more collected.

"I should really be at the lab, but I wanted to fill you in on everything and I'm tired of comming," Ethan said.

Sebastian stood up. He'd sensed someone approach the front door before any of them heard the knock.

Sean got up as the door opened.

"Zee. What are you doing here? And what's happened?"

Ziva Walls came into the living room, nodded at everyone, sat in the chair opposite Ethan's, and said, "I walked here from the hospital. Sean, could I get a glass of water? I don't think I can make it to the kitchen."

"Stay right there. I'll be back in a second."

"I can't get anyone else to come in for tests," Ziva said. "So I gave up. But just for today. I'll get back at it tomorrow."

"Here." Sean handed Ziva a tall glass of ice water, which Ziva downed in two gulps. Her usual sophisticated, put-together style had disintegrated, probably somewhere around the fifth kilometer of her long walk. Ethan thought she looked better like this, more like a human being and less like an idealized portrait.

"You cannot believe what's going on over at the isolation ward. Charley Pierce and Lukas Adler are at each other's throats while Althea's on the verge of death. And I can't find out anything about Maizy."

"She seems a bit better," Ethan said. He'd spoken to the medical team earlier in the day and although Maizy still wasn't fully conscious, she was showing some signs of revival, and the virus seemed not to have affected any of her other organs or functions, although it was still present in her cells.

"Althea's condition hasn't worsened. I wouldn't say she's on the verge of death. So far, the only people who've died are those who, as far as we know, didn't display any overt symptoms beforehand." Ethan was sorry he'd said it since he himself hadn't displayed any overt symptoms.

He watched as Ziva looked back and forth between Jonathan Lee and Sean, and he wondered if she was noticing the same shift he'd seen.

"Where's the kid?" Ziva said.

"Patterson went out to the Flats. Term's over and there's a caldera there. Much more interesting than a deadly virus."

"I need to do more to help, but I know nothing about computers. I don't even want to use my scroll now."

"I haven't found any infected scrolls. I think you're safe there for the time being."

"For the time being. I don't want to be the first victim who caught this thing from my scroll."

"There is another way you could help," Sean said. "We need a name for the virus. I think giving it one will help us get more people involved—get tests, join our efforts, whatever's needed."

"I can do that," Ziva said. "I named some of Kaj's works. Give me a few minutes." She leaned back and closed her eyes. Ethan reminded himself not to stare at her.

"I'm trying to get a complete list of the tenants at the Normandie," Sean said. "It's not as easy as it seems like it might be. The people there can pay for their privacy. I have Toby Hsu at the joukko doing some research for me but she can work only in short spurts as she has to be careful no one notices."

"Isn't it time the joukko got involved anyway?"

"Sure, Jay, you convince them," Ethan said. "I've failed. They think I've concocted the entire thing. McCormick threatened to have me transferred to some town I've never heard of if I bring 'the matter' up again. I showed Hirata's autopsy report to Prentiss, who laughed and accused me of having a forged medical degree."

"Don't look at me. I'm an enemy of the state as far as the joukko's concerned." Sean, on the floor, folded her legs under her.

Ethan looked over at Zee, whose eyes were closed, her arms hanging limp on either side of the chair. Maybe she'd fallen asleep. Sebastian was asleep as well.

"How about microfect?"

Everyone turned to look at Ziva, who still had her eyes closed and her head back.

"As a name for the virus. Or biomech. No. Wait. They sound like the names of companies. I can do better."

"Microfect could work."

"Give me another minute or two. And stop talking."

Everyone was so worn out it was easy to obey Ziva Walls's command. Ethan could freely stare at her now, as both Jonathan Lee and Sean were as well. Waiting for her to come up with the name, as though, having given titles to some of Banerjee's work, she'd become an expert in the art of naming.

"Machirna. Or comvirna." Ziva opened her eyes and sat up. "Thanks for the quiet. I think better in silence."

"Either could work." Jonathan Lee was the first to speak.

"I like comvirna. Has a menacing sound to it and we need it to be scary," Sean said.

Ziva looked at Ethan, waiting for his opinion, but before he could speak, she said, "No. Wait. This is all too complicated. We should stay simple and call it what it is: leap virus or just the leap."

"Perfect," Sean said as Ethan said, "That's it. Thanks, Zee. You did well. Having a name will make it easier to talk about, to convince people it's real. I think I'll use comvirna as the scientific name."

"Can we have something to eat now? I'm starving."

"Sure." Sean got up and Jonathan Lee followed her.

After they'd left the room, Ziva spoke to Ethan. "You don't mind?"

"No, they're great names. Thank you." Sebastian got up, turned around, and curled into a new position on Ethan's lap and Ethan petted him with one gloved hand.

"I didn't mean about that," Ziva said.

"I'm not sure what you mean, then." Did it have something to do with the shift?

"I mean about them." Ziva tilted her head in the direction of the kitchen.

"You noticed the shift too?"

"If that's what you want to call it."

"What would you call it?" Ethan tried to add up everything he'd noticed and what Ziva was getting at but hit a blank wall.

"I'd call it two people starting to fall in love."

"You're mistaken."

"I've gone too far. I shouldn't've said anything. I thought you realized it. I was just checking to see how you felt about the situation."

"Jay and Sean? You're mistaken."

"Well, you know them better than I do, but the atmosphere in here has definitely changed."

Sebastian, who'd never purred before, started purring. Ethan closed his eyes and tried to negate what Ziva had said. Yet maybe she was right. He opened his eyes. Ziva had her feet up on the chair and her arms were around her bent knees.

"You're not usually so casual," he said.

"I don't usually walk this far. I'm glad you're here. I was hoping to see you."

"It's good you came over. The name's perfect."

"Thanks."

Ethan and Zee both stopped talking. Sebastian's purrs provided the only sound in the room. The kitchen noises seemed far away, like they might be in someone else's house or on another planet or in another universe.

Lately Ethan had moments where he felt like he was standing aside from his own life, an occasional, disinterested observer. An effect caused by lack of sleep or perhaps the virus itself. He retested himself every few days, making sure nothing significant had changed. So far, nothing had.

"Are you feeling all right?" The voice came from across the room. Ethan opened his eyes. He hadn't realized they were closed.

"No. Yes. I'm fine."

"Ethan, do you have a fever?" Ziva unfolded her legs and got up from her chair. Ethan forgot what he'd been about to say. An insidious heat crawled over his upper chest and worked itself into his neck.

Voices merged into each other. One of them must have been Sean's, who seemed to be saying something about the clinic. Ethan summoned his control.

"I'm fine. Just tired."

"Ethan, you have a rash on your neck."

"I think he has a fever."

"I just need some rest. Let me sit here awhile." Had he said those words? Or was that Jay's voice?

"Maybe you should lie down."

"No." He couldn't disturb Sebastian, who'd stopped purring.

No one should see him like this, with a rash on his neck and the threads of his life unspooling themselves. Ziva was right about Sean and Jay. Ethan had seen it weeks ago and he'd seen other things as well. About Ziva, about the virus. What were those things?

"He should go to the clinic. This looks like more than just exhaustion."

Ethan wanted to say he was fine but instead he fell into a crevasse and sank down into its icy walls.

"We're going to take you to the clinic."

But if he was at the clinic who would work on the leap? A good name. Ziva had been right about it, about everything. He reached out to embrace her, to thank her, to show her what was going on, but the fog condensed between them, shutting off contact.

"We'll be there soon, Ethan. Hang on."

How could they be anywhere soon? He was sitting in Sebastian's chair in Sean's living room. Sean and Jay were in the kitchen. Ziva was across from him, and he could finally look at her without it seeming like he had any motive other than friendship. The heat burned his scapula.

The floor of the crevasse opened up. He grabbed onto the rocks and ice on the walls, ripped the skin on his palms.

The leap had to be stopped before it went any further. He had to tell Jay, but Jay was on the surface, kilometers above him. In another world, another universe.

"I'll take you to my new house. It's on the ocean. Out west. This will all be in the past."

Hallucinations. He'd reached a new stage of the disease process and should be taking notes but his notebook had been buried in an unstoppable avalanche, one that was gaining momentum.

"Ethan, Dorian's coming up from the Acres. She's bringing some friends. Reinforcements. Fresh minds. Not exhausted. We'll have this solved."

Ethan wanted to laugh, wanted to say things left unsaid for years.

There were cracks in the fog and he could see the people he knew best, Jay and Sean, and Zee, who he'd reach for if only he didn't have to hold on to the frozen crags.

"My notes." He managed to get out those two words. He'd been working out some paths to a vaccine and maybe even a treatment. But now . . . If Jay would understand. If anyone could hear him.

CHAPTER 31

DORIAN SHOULD GET here tomorrow morning," Jonathan Lee said. "I told her we couldn't wait. She's bringing her group with her. I'm going to set them up at Beryl's. There's plenty of room there."

Jonathan Lee, Sean, and Ziva were sitting in the small waiting area outside the isolation ward at the clinic, where they'd brought Ethan, who'd developed a high fever along with the ever-increasing rash covering his neck and parts of his chest and back.

"Have you heard from Patterson?"

"No, and I won't. The caldera is all-consuming."

"I have to feed Sebastian. I almost forgot." Sean got up to leave.

"We should all go. There's nothing we can do here," Jonathan Lee said.

"I'm staying." Ziva stretched and yawned. "I've got nothing else to do. And I want to be here when Ethan's feeling better."

"Zee."

"It's okay, Sean. I'll be fine. With you two gone I can get some sleep."

The corridor was dead silent. Sean had wanted to look in on Ethan before they left but the staff wouldn't let anyone near him. He had to be stabilized. Couldn't be disturbed.

As they rounded the corner toward the elevator, the silence was broken by the sounds of footsteps and loud whispers behind them. Jonathan Lee and Sean glanced at each other, then sprinted back. Something was going on, and if it was Ethan they had to know.

They met Ziva, who was standing in the doorway of the waiting area, her arms crossed over her chest, her face ashen.

"Zee, what's happened to Ethan?"

"No, no, no. It's not Ethan." Ziva put one hand over her eyes. "It's Althea Pierce. She's . . . it's that . . . Sean, I thought the deaths had stopped . . . but . . ."

"Are you sure?" Jonathan Lee never assumed anything.

Ziva nodded her head. "I heard someone saying it. They all went to her room."

"There's nothing we can do about it, Zee." Sean had her arm around Ziva's shoulders and was hugging her.

"I thought the deaths had stopped. And, Sean, I feel like I'm responsible somehow."

"No you're not," Sean said.

Jonathan Lee walked toward Althea Pierce's room and glanced inside. Four people in white medical jackets were standing around Althea's bed, talking in low tones. Jonathan Lee could make out only snippets.

"But it's down to me. I'm the lead."

". . . kill you. You've got no tact. I'll comm . . ."

". . . the autopsy? Stiles is . . ."

". . . already talked with Prentiss . . ."

". . . have to be in the basement. But . . ."

". . . for the last two days. Newell?"

Couldn't these people speak up or at least turn toward the doorway? Jonathan Lee needed information he could use.

One of the medical people left the group and went to the door. Jonathan Lee didn't react quickly enough and came face-to-face with her.

"And you are?" She looked like she'd be happy to slice Jonathan Lee in half to get him out of her way.

"Jonathan Lee Summers. I'm here with Ethan Stiles."

The woman's demeanor eased somewhat. "Dr. Stiles. He's been sacrificing everything to try to solve this. I'm Hollis Park. I used to think I was an infectious disease specialist. Now I'm not sure if I know anything at all about them."

"This one's different." Jonathan Lee didn't want to say anything further, since he was too tired to get into an argument. "I know Charley Pierce. Would you like me to tell him?"

"You were eavesdropping." Park's attitude reversed itself.

"I've got nothing else to do and I noticed the commotion."

"Hardly a commotion."

"But you couldn't save her."

"No comment."

"You mean she's alive? And you're all just standing there, doing nothing?"

"I mean it's not my place to say anything. Patients have the right of privacy."

"Even dead patients?"

"Yes."

"Look, this will be all over the mesh in a matter of hours. Maybe only minutes. You can't keep something like this a secret."

"It's Charley Pierce. And Lukas Adler. They're—I can't explain it to you and I don't know why I'm talking to you at all. I hope your friend Dr. Stiles recovers, Mr. Summers."

Jonathan Lee had to change the character of this conversation. Hollis Park was probably one of Ethan's physicians. He remembered something. A long shot, but he tried it out.

"Are you by any chance related to the Parks who live at the Normandie?"

"Do you know them?"

"In a way, I do."

"They're my parents." A slight softening.

"Dr. Park, you should convince them to get tested. They're on the refusal list."

"What are you talking about?" She hardened again. Jonathan Lee's attempts weren't working.

"We think it's likely everyone who lives at the Normandie has been exposed to the pathogen that just killed Althea Pierce and that's killed several other people. We've been contacting everyone in the building, urging them to come in for testing. But many tenants, including your parents, are refusing. They don't understand how serious this could be."

"I don't understand how serious this could be and I'm a specialist. How could they possibly understand? I have to go now." She turned away from him.

"The offer's still good. I'll talk with Charley Pierce."

Hollis Park glanced over her shoulder, showing Jonathan Lee that he wasn't worth her full, direct attention. "Dr. Booth, the lead physician on Mr. Pierce's wife's case, is the only person authorized for such a conversation. Stop eavesdropping, Mr. Summers, and stay out of things that don't concern you."

There was no longer anything or anyone not of concern to Jonathan Lee, but Park had walked away too fast for him to say that. He went back to eavesdropping but the meeting had broken up and the participants pushed past him on their way out.

After they were gone—and Jonathan Lee was thankful none of them had confronted him the way Hollis Park had done—he looked into Althea Pierce's room. The shades were closed and all but one light had been turned off. The assemblage of medical equipment no longer showed any displays, and Althea Pierce was lying there, motionless, on the bed, her arms folded across her chest in the traditional death pose.

Ziva hadn't misinterpreted what was going on. The ward's most famous patient had died and the clinic was going to have a helluva time explaining what had happened, especially to the corpse's big-deal husband.

Jonathan Lee had widened the margins of the truth when he said he knew Charley Pierce. Pierce had contacted him once, years ago, trying to get him to come to work for Pierce Sangstrom, but Jonathan Lee had turned him down. He preferred doing what he wanted, when he wanted, and, for the most part, not counting a few classes Jonathan Lee would rather not've taught, the Acres provided him with the ideal environment. He had no intention of leaving, especially not to work at a predatory megacorp whose unwritten motto must be something like Us Over Everyone.

"Jonathan Lee." He felt a tug on his shirtsleeve.

"Sean. I forgot I was standing here." He looked down the corridor, but they were the only ones there. Althea Pierce was in a section by herself, so other than collecting her body, there was no reason for anyone else to be there.

"Lost in thought?"

"Unproductive thought. Dorian and her group should be here soon and I have to get out to Beryl's, see if the place is presentable. Lock Patterson's room off since I don't want to touch anything in there and it's a wreck."

"I'm having lunch with Toby Hsu. Now that Ethan's ill, she'll be more helpful. She's close with Ethan's sister."

"Oh hell, Sean. I hadn't thought about Miya. She should know."

"Wouldn't make any difference. She couldn't get here anyway. She and her family are on Mars, part of the experimental settlement in the south, in the highlands."

"I'd forgotten. Ethan told me they'd gone, but back then I was trying to figure out what had happened with Beryl. I still don't really know and now I'll never find out. It bothers me almost more than her death does."

"I told Zee about, you know—us. She'd guessed anyway and I'm no good at keeping secrets. I'd been planning on telling Ethan today and then . . ."

Jonathan Lee put his arm around Sean. "Let's get out of here. We have work to do."

They said good-bye to Ziva, who was in the waiting room reading from her scroll, which was perched on the windowsill.

Jonathan Lee drove Sean's beat-up transcer to her house.

"Wait for me," she said, then ran in to feed Sebastian, who acted like he didn't care, but sauntered into the kitchen and munched on his food while she was leaving.

"I'll help you clean up," she said to Jonathan Lee, "and I want to meet Dorian and everyone else. I've got another two hours before I'm meeting Toby, and I'll go crazy at home."

"Thanks. I could use the help filling everyone in on this mess. And with the cleaning, although let's not go too far. No one will care."

"Jonathan Lee, what do you think happened to Morris Walls?"

"Damned if I know. Why bring him up now? Didn't you stop looking for him a while ago?"

"Maybe because we just left Ziva at the clinic. She's not just being nice about Ethan, if you hadn't noticed. She likes him."

"Did she say something to you?"

"In a way. While you were busy interrogating Dr. Park, Ziva was asking me oblique questions about Ethan. I assured her we've been over for a long time and, anyway, you weren't just my roommate. At least, not right now. I mean, later, of course, you'll be going back—"

"Stop right there, Sean." Jonathan Lee drove to the side of the road and turned off the transcer, which was more of an antique than a usable vehicle. Perhaps it was part of one of Sean's collections.

"There is no later. We can't think that way. We don't know what's going to happen, even five minutes from now. Everyone on the planet could get infected and die before we have a chance to do anything about it. Or maybe nothing will happen and this is the extent of it."

"I keep telling myself the same things, but I have to confront some hard facts about my current existence. I have no income at the moment.

I've turned down several potential clients because I can't do anything but work on the leap virus."

"It's a good name. Don't know why we didn't come up with it."

"Well, Zee did. She's a creative person. Maybe naming things is her niche."

"How about if I start paying you rent? After all, I'm living at your house. I've become another negative number on your budget."

"I have no budget. And I have savings from my time on the joukko."

"Ethan told me he thought you were happier, more yourself, since you weren't there anymore."

"It's not just that I'm happier. I feel so distant from that life, like I was someone else when I worked for the joukko, someone who was pretending to be me. Hell, maybe I've got the leap virus and just don't know it yet. I think it messes with your head, the same way a computer virus can mess with the computer's logic system. As I understand it."

"That's pretty much it, Sean."

"But, JL, why is it no computers are infected? They're hosting the leap but they seem immune to it. Are they?"

Jonathan Lee shook his head and turned to look at Sean.

"Damn it, Sean, why did this not occur to me?"

"Well, it hadn't occurred to any of us. We've been focused on the people, not the computers."

"All my attention has been on the computers. I can't do anything about the humans. Hell, this is great, Sean. You've opened up an entire new area, one that could very well be the solution to the problem."

"How?"

"If computers are immune, maybe there's something there we're missing, something that could help us find a way to immunize people. What if there's computer immunity built into the program? Because if the program kills too many computers too quickly, then the virus can't spread and it wouldn't be able to get to its intended targets—people.

Assuming people are the intended targets, which I think they are. Sean, think about it. Why else would someone invent a computer virus that can be transmitted to humans?"

"I've always thought humans were the intended target. That's probably why infections in the computers themselves didn't even occur to me."

"You have really hit on something big here, Sean. And just in time since the group from the Acres will be here in a couple of hours. I'm wondering if the computers are infected. Perhaps with something that causes them to be able to transmit the virus. But only that. I've got a lot to work on now."

Jonathan Lee turned the transcer back on and swerved into the road, racing toward Beryl's house. As he screeched into the drive, he said, "JL? I've been reduced to initials?"

Sean laughed. "You've been elevated to initials."

CHAPTER 32

WHAT A HELLISH time not to have his assistants in Osada City. Charley had banished both of them to Wyngarden and he was thinking of having them return. Or was he himself supposed to make all the arrangements for Althea's funeral? He didn't want to. He couldn't. Not just because activity of this mundane sort was beneath him but because he didn't want to admit to himself that Althea was really dead.

Like the fabulas she wrote, she herself had always been so dramatic. It'd be just like her to pretend to be dead and then at the last microsecond return to consciousness, in effect resurrecting herself. If anyone was capable of such a feat, Althea would be the one.

She had had the world at her disposal. There was no reason for her to have died. None Charley could face. Therefore she wasn't dead. The doctor, the insufferable, full-of-himself Axel Booth, had commed Charley to give him the news.

"I'm afraid the worst has happened," Booth said over the comm.

"I don't care if the treatment costs a fortune or is experimental, Booth. Do it."

Charley didn't need to say this as Booth knew exactly who Charley Pierce was and that he had unlimited resources, but Charley said it anyway. To remind Booth that even though the doctor thought he was a god, Charley Pierce was a far more powerful god, one who could atomize such a low-level would-be deity.

"You don't understand, Mr. Pierce. I'm trying to tell you—Althea has passed away."

After being told he didn't understand, Charley had stopped listening. He understood everything, far more than Booth did.

"Perhaps you don't realize who you're talking to. This is Charley Pierce, *the* Charley Pierce. I own Pierce Sangstrom. We have unlimited resources. If you can't find a cure for Althea, I'll have her transferred. I've always thought the Genesia Clinic was a fifth-rate operation anyway, and now I'm convinced of it."

"Mr. Pierce, please. You're not listening. Althea died this morning. I'm very sorry to have to tell you this, but this disease has been beyond our—"

Charley ended the comm, cutting Booth off.

The Genesia Clinic had killed Althea. Charley thought of comming Booth back and telling him off. Charley'd chosen Axel Booth to take care of Althea. Even though he was working at the lousy clinic, his credentials were impeccable. He was the acknowledged expert in serious infectious diseases and had been one of the key players in the discovery of the cure for anomyensa just a few years earlier. No one had a negative impression of him.

That was all about to change. Charley was going to sue Booth into oblivion, put the blame where it belonged. He'd never "doctor" anyone again, if you could call what he'd done to Althea doctoring. Charley called it murdering.

Charley thought of comming his assistants. They might be at Wyngarden but they could still be useful. They could plan the funeral. Charley wanted no part of it. He wouldn't even go. He'd be too busy killing Juno Sangstrom.

No.

Yes, he'd go. He'd have to go.

He tried to comm Morana first. She was the more efficient of his two assistants. Burman could be useless as an assistant but Charley didn't want him to work anywhere else. He knew too much.

"Yes?" Morana's ever-scratchy voice came over the comm. Charley had the video turned off. He didn't want to see anyone. Really, he didn't want anyone to see him.

"Althea's died," Charley said. The first person he was saying those words to was Morana. Words he didn't want to hear, much less speak. And to say them to a nobody like Morana. "You and Burman have to plan the funeral."

"Mr. Pierce, I don't think you've heard."

"I don't think you're hearing me." Charley should've just fired Morana and Burman. Neither of them was helpful. There'd be a hundred thousand applicants lined up the moment he posted the job. He'd fire her right now but he needed Morana for one last thing.

"Burman's gone," she said.

Charley didn't care about the personal lives of his assistants. They weren't people. They were the means to an end, fungible.

"Mr. Pierce. Burman quit a few days ago."

Charley got up from his chair. "What?"

"Burman, Mr. Pierce. He's quit. I thought you knew."

"You'll have to do it yourself, then," Charley said. He didn't care if Burman quit or moved to an outpost on Mars or was lying dead in a garage.

"I see, Mr. Pierce. When will the funeral be?"

"Tomorrow."

"Tomorrow?"

"I should have fired you instead of sending you out to Wyngarden. Either you're going to make the arrangements for this funeral or you can walk out the door right now and don't think for a second I'll have anything positive to say about you if you ever want to work again."

"Certainly, Mr. Pierce."

Morana was being her usual annoying, faux agreeable self.

Charley started pacing around his desk, then stopped. Juno paced. If Juno did it, it was the very thing he should never do. He sat back down.

"You get this right if it's the last thing you ever do. The ceremony will be out at Tuigen, on the riverfront. I want thousands of people in attendance—her friends, her lovers, the people in the productions she's worked on, famous actors, even her critics. Her ardent fans. Everyone. I want a funeral pyre. No, a bonfire. Make it happen."

"Certainly, Mr. Pierce."

"And, afterward, there'll be a small gathering indoors. Only the select few will be invited. Everyone else will have to stay outside. Decent food for the outdoor guests. A grand feast for those invited in."

"Who should be invited in?"

"I'll decide. No one will be invited until I personally ask them. In the meanwhile, let all the attendees know there'll be a celebration of Althea's life after the bonfire."

"Certainly, Mr. Pierce."

"Comm me back with the details in an hour."

"Yes, Mr.—"

He signed off. Morana might be obsequious but she was effective. If someone had to quit, better that it was Burman.

Charley got up and stood at the window, looking down on the slithering swine below. Out of everyone in Osada City and Genesia, Althea Pierce had had to die. Althea had at least another 215 years ahead of her, time for her to come around to finally loving Charley the way she should have from the beginning, the way she never did.

Charley felt sure the joukko wouldn't do anything about her death. Well, they couldn't. He wouldn't go to them with the killer's identity, since not only would the joukko never believe him, but Charley was in a bind. If he let it be known that the virus Juno'd created was the cause of Althea's death, Pierce Sangstrom would be ruined.

Their name would become synonymous with a lethal virus and no one would ever have any dealings with them again. Charley himself would be forever associated with the virus and the devastation it caused, including Althea's death, even though it was Juno Sangstrom's creation and not his. Even though Juno Sangstrom was a murderer and Althea was her victim and Charley had had nothing to do with any of it, which idea Charley repeated to himself, letting it sink into a fact of sorts.

He'd also become Juno's victim, or Pierce Sangstrom itself had. She had them both captive, held in the grasp of her extraordinary invention.

Mixed in with his near-uncontainable, infinite fury at Juno was an insurmountable conflict: if the lethal aspect of the virus would be removed from the program, Pierce Sangstrom could have control of the world. They'd have the ultimate application, one that would capture the users' desires and manipulate and control them in any way they wanted. The possibilities were almost as infinite as Charley's rage.

Charley had spent hours in the last few days poring over Juno's work. It seemed her deadly program would work even if it wasn't activated, much like the ubiquitous Milburn virus had done. Milburn had been a boon to Pierce Sangstrom's business, as its reach was universal and Juno had come up with a fix for it, positioning the company as the industry's leading innovator.

No one had ever discovered who'd created the Milburn virus. Juno had told Charley more than once that she was jealous of its programmer, as the code was both ingenious and groundbreaking. Since it had been written in plain machine language, Charley had never suspected Juno, but now he wondered. Had she been the mastermind behind that as well? Had she set up her new virus so she could be the world's savior? Or was she just an insane, murderous, jealous, angry, vengeful genius?

Charley left his office and walked down the empty corridor. No one was there, as he'd given everyone the afternoon off, not telling them why. But he didn't want anyone else in the building and he didn't want to go home. As he passed by Morris Walls's office he had a brief flash of a mental image he hadn't been able to get rid of.

He'd heard them going at it, right there in Walls's office, so close to Charley's. It was one thing that Althea didn't care—it wasn't like her job or her livelihood or her future depended on Charley's good opinion of her. She didn't need him at all. That thought had always cheered Charley up. She didn't need him yet she stayed with him. Eventually she would recognize his worth in her life and she'd love him. He'd been counting on it.

But now . . .

Morris Walls, though, was dependent on Charley for his job and livelihood and future. Yet he'd succumbed to his lust for Althea and had dispensed with all propriety. And now he was missing. How convenient for Morris Walls. He should be dead. He might be but Charley hadn't been able to find out.

Charley spent a few moments contemplating all the people he'd like to see dead. Juno. Morris. Lukas Adler.

If Charley could pick only one, the choice was easy: Juno Sangstrom.

Yet only Juno could finish the program, which would benefit Pierce Sangstrom and which Charley wanted for the myriad of possibilities beyond what it had already accomplished. He would refine it but Juno held the rest of the pieces to its intricate, convoluted composition.

Pierce Sangstrom needed Juno. And, worse, Charley needed her.

Charley pounded his fist into the door of Morris's office.

Juno had backed him into a corner he'd never be able to get out of.

CHAPTER 33

YEARS EARLIER, WHEN they'd just launched Meet Me, Juno and Charley had been basking in their newfound success. Juno, just twenty-five years old, was riding high, ecstatic about the success she'd already achieved and knowing there'd be more. This was only the beginning of the life she'd dreamed of.

She never let anyone, not even Charley, know that she was originally from the down-and-out Lansden, a town that made even the lousy Genesia seem like an unattainable Eden. There was a lot Charley didn't know about her, that he'd never know.

She'd been rejected by the Acres, which she'd been counting on as her ticket out of the desperate life she'd endured while growing up, subject to regular abuse and beatings by her father and abandoned by her mother. That her mother had left her father was understandable, but Juno had never been able to understand why she hadn't taken Juno with her. Didn't her mother know Juno would now be getting the same blows her mother had suffered under? Didn't she care?

After Meet Me's success, both her parents had contacted her. Juno, who thought she'd never hear from either of them again—the day she departed for Keff she'd threatened to kill her father if he ever came near her and of course she hadn't heard from her mother since she was five—was at first pleased. That her mother remembered her at all gave her sensations something like love. Soon after, these sensations were replaced by the truth: her parents were interested in her now only because they thought she was rich. She never responded to them.

After the Acres rejected her, Juno had written to them, pleading for their reconsideration. They were sorry, they said, but all the scholarship slots had been filled and perhaps she could try again the following year when things might open up. Wishing her all the best in her endeavors. She had no such wishes for them.

But Keff Institute had accepted her and given her the full scholarship she needed in order to be able to afford that, or any, school. Even though Juno had always thought of Keff as a distant second to the Acres, she was happy to be able to leave home and go just about anywhere. She'd been stunned by the beauty of Keff's campus and the caring nature of their faculty, something she didn't know existed. School in Lansden had been crude and disinteresting. She'd sailed through but her interests and her imagination had never been stimulated. School had been merely a break from the torture at home.

At Keff, though, the beauty, the atmosphere, the other students, the faculty, the materials, and the relief and joy of having finally gotten away from Lansden had unleashed her imagination. The first week she was there she invented her own machine language, a cryptic code that, other than Charley, who took forever to learn it, no one else would ever be able to translate.

The second week there, she'd spotted Charley Pierce and felt an instant connection to the cocky guy who was always wearing the same pale blue T-shirt. At least she'd thought it was the same shirt, but after she got to know him she found out he had dozens of them. Once the shirts got to the stage he considered unacceptable, he'd donate them to the store the students all called the Bin, since it was mainly a charity for the scholarship students who had limited finances.

Charley's discarded shirts still had his scent on them, and Juno had one of them, which she slept in but never otherwise wore. It wasn't like sleeping with Charley might've been, but it was comforting anyway.

Juno quickly rose to the top of her class. After the first few weeks of walking around the campus, gasping at all the wonders at her disposal, and learning not to cringe in fear every time her roommate came back to the dorm—this wasn't her father and she was safe here, not like at home—after that, she got serious. She was here to learn, to get everything she could out of Keff Institute, to solidify her future, to raise herself out of the depths. The professors and lecturers loved her and her fellow students were intimidated by her. All except Charley Pierce, who teased her and made fun of her unique ideas, as though anything he himself hadn't thought of wasn't worth his, or anyone's, attention.

Charley's put-downs had the reverse effect on Juno. The more he insulted her the more she wanted him. She knew it had something to do with her relationship with her father but she didn't care. The fact was that she wanted Charley Pierce and it didn't matter why. He was the person she was meant to be with and she would have him. He might be dismissive of Juno, he might act like a privileged snob to her and to everyone, he might not be as intelligent as she was, but Charley had that presence, that gloss, that something indefinable that magnetized Juno to him, that set her on fire.

She was in her room, working out the design of a program that Ledyard, the best brain at Keff, would later refer to as groundbreaking and astounding, when Charley knocked on her door. Her roommate was long gone by then—he'd had to return home after his parents were killed in an accident and he wouldn't be back for a year—and Juno had the large suite to herself. She used her roommate's former room as her study and just slept in her own room. The living area, in the center, became a staging area for her work, where she could spread out the papers she used as rough drafts before she'd transfer everything to the computer.

"What's all this?" Charley said, stepping into the room. The floor was covered with her new project.

"It's work," Juno said. "Perhaps you've heard of it."

"Oh sure," Charley said. "Something the peasants do."

"If you studied a little, you'd get better grades."

"Are you my mother?"

Juno kicked him, a light kick in the shin. Nothing hard, not like the blows her father had dealt.

"What the hell?"

"Stop insulting me." As much as she was attracted to Charley, she was still upset by his insults.

"Whoa. Back down. I'm just playing."

"Play with someone else." She didn't mean it. She wanted him to play with her. It was all she could do to keep herself from putting her arms around his waist and doing whatever it was people did with each other when they felt the way Juno felt about Charley. She didn't know what that doing could be as her only experience of it was in the fabulas she sometimes watched and it was obvious the actions in those stories were fabricated, but she'd figure it out.

"Juno, the thing is, I'm here for your help." Charley changed into a serious person, right there in front of Juno's eyes, in her room. Was he a chameleon? Could he change at will? Or did he just know how to behave the right way in order to get whatever it was he wanted? If he did have that skill, Juno would have to study it in depth, since she wanted it and didn't have it. And needed it.

Charley pulled out his scroll and opened it to the crude program he was working on. Juno did her best not to laugh. How had this guy gotten into Keff? And she'd heard a rumor he'd actually been accepted at the Acres and had turned them down. He was a jerk, an idiot, and the most captivating presence she'd ever encountered.

"I'm stuck," he said. "And this is for Ledyard. He's the only reason I'm here."

"He's the best," Juno said. She meant that. She'd signed up for every course he taught and was scheduled to work with him in one of the hard-to-get one-on-one slots the next term.

Charley handed over his scroll. His hand brushed against Juno's and she thought she'd forgotten how to breathe.

"Charley, look at this. You can't do it this way." She pointed at a section of his code that although somewhat interesting was wrong. In a few minutes, they were sitting next to each other on the wicker couch in the suite's living room and Juno was showing Charley how to fix his program, watching his every move and correcting him as he finally got up to speed.

Time went away. There was only the work, Charley, and Juno's need.

Early the next morning, when they'd finished, Charley said, "Thanks, Juno. You're a better teacher than Ledyard. I understand this now." He leaned over and kissed her, but not in a romantic way, more like the way you'd kiss your scroll after you'd finished writing a great program. A triumphant kiss, not an intimate one.

He left. Juno wanted more. But, apart from that, Juno had found a source of immediate income. She hadn't known she could teach, but now that she did she became a tutor. She already knew a half dozen machine languages fluently and she was picking up several more. Other students didn't catch on as fast as she did and she was highly respected. In a few weeks she'd signed up six students and had a waiting list for another ten.

The income from tutoring made it possible for her to purchase a better computer and a new scroll. She also, on a whim, purchased an almost-sheer floral-patterned dress, a departure from her usual wardrobe, which consisted of two pairs of khaki pants and a collection of secondhand shirts. The dress had been in her closet for months before she wore it one night when she knew Charley was coming over.

By then they had a smooth working relationship. Although Charley was still not great at creating code, he excelled at editing it. He could cut out needless routines and condense complex formulations into elegant flourishes. He was in her rooms or she was in his almost every day. Yet other than that first kiss, nothing had ever happened between them and Juno knew Charley had had at least three girlfriends since he'd started at Keff. She wasn't the only one who found him irresistible.

The other girls, though, probably wanted Charley for his status and wealth, which he had once referred to as an accident of birth, but Juno wanted Charley himself. It wouldn't've mattered to her if Charley had been from Genesia or even Lansden. That he'd grown up in a mansion in Osada City was only a fact to Juno, not an enticement. She was going to make her own fortune—she didn't need anyone else's. And Charley hadn't even worked for his.

That night, when she'd put on the floral-patterned dress and taken her hair out of its usual braid, letting it fall down her back, Charley noticed her—not the Juno who was helping him with his work, who was now partnering with him on several promising projects, but the Juno who'd always wanted him.

"Are you trying to seduce me?" he said when she met him at her suite's entryway. She was wearing nothing under the dress, and although it wasn't see-through the fabric had the effect of seeming to reveal what was underneath without actually revealing it.

"Yes," she said. "Yes, I am. Is it working?"

"It is," he said. He leaned back against the door, closing it behind him. He switched off the overhead light, but Juno turned it back on again. "I want to see," she said.

Charley Pierce's dark green eyes looked at Juno for what felt like the first time. His gaze moved and he put his hands on her. Juno wanted to tear off his light blue tee but instead she put her arms around his neck and moved closer. Soon they were in her bedroom. She'd changed the sheets in anticipation of this happening.

Although she had no one to compare him to, Juno thought Charley Pierce was an adept lover. He seemed to know what he was doing and he brought Juno along with him. He was gentle and did things with her that elicited new sensations, ones she was unfamiliar with, ones she wanted to experience again and again.

In the morning, with Charley lying next to her in her bed, their destiny together blossomed in her imagination. Meet Me, the program that would ignite her fortune and eventually destroy the future she'd planned on having with Charley Pierce, didn't exist then.

But back then, she hadn't known. Back then she had the raw talent, and coupled with her dreams and now with Charley Pierce, it seemed as though her future would be even brighter than those dreams had ever been. Their third year, Charley and Juno moved in together to a small apartment off campus. This was the start of the rest of her life, her life with Charley Pierce. They'd get married, maybe they'd even have kids someday although Juno couldn't really picture kids, but it was what other people did so maybe she'd do it too. As long as she did it with Charley.

They formed Pierce Sangstrom shortly before graduation. By then Juno had stopped caring about school and didn't realize she was the top student in her class until Ledyard commed her to say he was looking forward to her speech, he was sad to lose his best student ever, and would she consider taking a job lecturing at Keff?

She thought about it but as soon as Meet Me hit the market, she knew she'd found her career. Juno and Charley had investors begging to give them their backing, but they didn't need it. The simple-seeming, friendly, and accessible Meet Me was an immediate success.

Meet Me's slogan—"For an instant connection"—wasn't far from the truth. The interface was clear and direct, the user had little to do but answer a few simple yes/no questions, and the results were interesting, fun, enjoyable, and often amazing. Everyone loved it.

But when it turned out that that everyone included Charley, Juno closed herself off in what had once been her and Charley's apartment and was now just hers. He was gone. Meet Me had paired Charley up with Althea Livesy, the up-and-coming fabula writer, the tall redhead who made Juno seem even shorter and plainer than she already felt she was.

"It just happened," Charley said the afternoon he appeared at their apartment after she hadn't seen him or had contact with him for over a week.

"Is that supposed to be an explanation?" June said. Her program was a success but her plans had disintegrated. She'd have to do much better next time.

"It's the truth," he said.

"Now you're going to tell me you weren't looking for anyone."

"I wasn't," he said.

"The entire point of Meet Me is to find someone. What the hell were you doing?"

"I was merely checking it out, making sure everything was working properly."

"You could have done that without entering your own data."

"I was curious. I didn't know I'd meet Althea."

"Why did you have to do this?"

"I didn't have to. I just did. I wasn't expecting anything. Come on, Juno, you experiment all the time. Otherwise you'd never come upon anything new."

"You mean the way you came upon Althea."

"Don't be jealous. It's not like you."

With that statement Charley proved he didn't understand Juno at all. Jealous? Whatever the next most powerful emotion beyond jealousy was, Juno was already there. She sensed Charley would never give Althea up, so Juno wanted her to die. She had active fantasies about introducing her father to Althea and letting him do the rest. She pictured Althea in the kind of accident that had killed her former roommate's parents.

Would Charley murder Althea in a fit of rage over something she said or did? That particular fantasy included Juno being the only person who knew Charley was guilty. Then not only would Althea be dead but Juno would forever have something to hold over Charley's head. He'd never betray her again.

In the end, what happened would occur in an unexpected, yet perfect, way.

~249~

CHAPTER 34

T HERE'S SOMETHING WRONG with McCormick." Those were the first words Toby Hsu said to Sean, who got to the restaurant after Toby was already seated. Jonathan Lee was at Beryl's house, cleaning while awaiting the arrival of his colleagues from the Acres. The plan for Sean and Jonathan Lee to straighten up the house together had been supplanted by need and passion, and Sean had gone back to her house afterward to change.

"Sorry I'm late."

"Sean, you don't know how lucky you are that you're no longer on the joukko." Toby spoke between gulps of her drink, a tall green concoction that looked like it could be juice but Sean knew it was something more potent, something Toby couldn't seem to live without, yet it never affected her work and seemed never to affect her at all.

"I know," Sean said. Ethan had touched on a truth—she was happier since she'd left the joukko. "What do you mean about McCormick?"

"Ever since, I don't know, maybe since the day we were at the Normandie for Beryl Carson's death? Since then he's changed. At first I didn't notice it, or I didn't think it was anything, really. But now these changes have fallen into a pattern. He has moments where he just sort of shuts down. He'll be talking and then he stops, closes his eyes, becomes very still. In the beginning I thought he was starting to think harder—or at all—about things, but after he'd done this a few times, it became clear it has nothing to do with thinking.

"He'll stop in the middle of the most mundane statement. And it's not like he's forgotten anything. But when he comes to again, if he is coming to—I mean, I don't know that he wasn't conscious while he was in what I'm going to call the shutdown—when he comes back, he sometimes speaks in words I'm not familiar with. Like another language, only one I've never heard before. But I'm not a linguist. So . . . but no one else knows what he's saying either."

"It's spreading," Sean said.

"You mean the leap virus?" Toby took a long swig of her drink.

Sean had told her some of the details, but they hadn't yet had a chance to discuss it at length.

"Yes, although McCormick's symptoms are new, I think."

Toby waved to the server, lifted her glass, and nodded.

"I need about twelve of these," she said, finishing off her drink and putting the glass back on the table.

"Have you made any progress with the rest of the tenant list at the Normandie?"

Toby picked her bag up off the floor, rummaged through it, and brought out a folded sheet. Sean had warned her not to send any information over the mesh. Whoever had created this virus had an extraordinary set of computer skills, and Jonathan Lee had warned everyone that nothing was safe. They had to resort to the printed page or in-person meetings.

Sean opened the paper, glanced down the page, and was immediately struck by one name: Milburn.

"Milburn lives at the Normandie?"

"It's not *the* Milburn, not the one who, even though there was never any direct evidence, the virus was connected to. After the virus disaster he changed his name and moved."

"I didn't—"

"Sean, you can't tell anyone. I helped with his relocation. I'm not supposed to say anything, but this is different. If what you've been telling me is true, then . . ." She shook her head. "I don't know what goes after *then*. Maybe we'll all be dead by this time next week. Because now it's not just tenants at the Normandie. It's Althea Pierce—I mean, that was shocking—and Healy and now McCormick's got something wrong with him. I was there that day. I could be next."

"Ethan too."

"Oh, Sean. I didn't know. How is he?"

"He's at the clinic, in the isolation ward. I'm not really sure how he is but Booth, the doctor in charge, said he was stable." Sean was glad Ziva was there to keep watch.

Toby's new drink arrived and she downed it in three large gulps, then ordered two more.

"Sorry, Sean. Do you want one? I'll order a pitcher."

"Yes." Sean rarely indulged but when she was with Toby, she would sometimes join in. Toby called the server back and ordered a pitcher.

"I guess Milburn's not so unusual a name," Toby said.

"Maybe not, but this particular Milburn's gone to a lot of trouble to hide the fact that they live at the Normandie."

"I thought that too, although I didn't have to dig that hard for some of these names." She pointed to the list. "Maybe Milburn's an alias, you know, sort of a way to cover the person's real identity by calling themselves such an infamous name."

"Could be," Sean said. The server brought the pitcher and filled Sean's glass. The green-colored drink was a little too delicious and Sean reminded herself to be careful. It was easy to get drunk on something this tasty.

"I ordered already," Toby said. "I hope you don't mind. It's what we always get."

Sean nodded. She was thinking about the Milburn virus, how it had infected almost every computer in existence. Maybe all of them.

"The leap's reminding me of Milburn," Sean said. "Didn't that virus do something like rearrange the essential data in every computer's operating system?"

"Something like that. You know more about this technical stuff than I do. I just know it screwed everything up."

Sean sat back and pictured Stack 142. Her collection had increased exponentially during the Milburn crisis, since her computer had been infected early on and she couldn't use it and couldn't afford a new one. During that time every physical object had taken on a new importance for Sean and she'd had to restrain herself from collecting more than just documents. She was an archivist, not a collector, and certainly not a hoarder.

Sean took a long sip of the too-delicious drink and said, "Pierce Sangstrom."

"Yeah. I bet Charley Pierce is reeling. The leap virus could be hurting his business—he probably knows all about it because of Althea's illness—and now she's dead."

"No, Toby, listen. I'm thinking of something else. Pierce Sangstrom came out with the so-called cure for the Milburn virus. They were the first and their cure worked. The crisis ended rapidly as soon as everyone got ahold of their fix."

"Yeah, I remember. They gave it away. Free. Made the megacorp look good for a change. Almost not hateable."

Twenty centimeters from the bottom of Stack #142 was a flyer Sean'd taken from a little girl who was handing them out on the street in Genesia during the Milburn crisis. The headline read: PS Delenda Est. Underneath it said: Before It Destroys Us.

Sean was no fan of Pierce Sangstrom but she wasn't interested in destroying them and thought the fringe movement that wanted them eliminated had gone too far. Maybe Pierce Sangstrom was too big or too powerful but they did useful work, and without their programs and interfaces a computer was all but useless. There'd be no benefit in destroying them.

She'd saved the flyer as a piece of history, but now she remembered what else the flyer had said: Pierce Sangstrom had created the Milburn virus so they could fix it, shoring up their reputation. And that's exactly what had transpired.

What if someone inside Pierce Sangstrom was active in the anti-megacorp movement and was leaking information?

"Before it destroys us," Sean said while she refilled her glass. Their lunch arrived just then and both women took a bite of their pasta before either spoke again.

"I see that on those recycled blue tees," Toby said while she chewed on an olive, "of the anti-PS movement. I don't think anyone outside this area even knows they exist."

"Not a lot of people here know they exist. But, what if they are destroying us?"

"You mean with the leap? You think they're doing it?"

"They've got the technological know-how."

"But Althea Pierce. They'd hardly kill her. Charley's wife? No. Have you ever seen images of them together? Pierce Sangstrom wouldn't think of killing her."

"Maybe it was an accident, Toby. Maybe she used a computer they didn't think she'd have access to."

"I don't know. Maybe. You think this Milburn"—she used her fork to point at Sean's bag, where she'd stashed the paper Toby had given her—"is connected to Pierce Sangstrom?"

"I'm going to find out."

"This Milburn owns several apartments in the building. Maybe it's just a front, you know, a consortium using the name Milburn to disguise the actual ownership. An illegal operation laundering their income by buying up expensive apartments. It'd hardly be the first time something like this went on."

"I was thinking this was a person using the name, but you could be right."

"Milburn could be a corporation, a group, anything. I didn't dig that deep, Sean, just got the names." Toby put down her glass and pushed it away from her. "I'll spend the rest of the day on it, Sean. The office should be empty this afternoon and anyway, we have to get to the bottom of this. If it's a dead end, let's find out now so we can go down the right path."

"What if it's not a mistake? What if someone at Pierce Sangstrom wanted to kill Althea? What if the other deaths were just practice?"

"You think it's Charley?"

"He's at the top of a long list. Spurned lovers, spiteful producers, directors, and actors. Anyone jealous of Althea Pierce's flagrant lifestyle and fame. Oh hell."

"What is it?"

"Morris Walls."

"Who?"

"He used to work at Pierce Sangstrom. He's been missing for a few weeks now. His wife hired me to find him, but I still haven't and she's given up and is getting a divorce."

"Why would he want Althea Pierce dead?" Toby had abandoned her drink and was laying into the pasta with the same fervor she usually reserved for alcohol.

"Walls's wife thinks they were having an affair—Morris and Althea. Really, she's sure they were. Then he went missing and now Althea's dead. He's a computer person. Office down the hall from Charley Pierce's."

"And he was having an affair with Charley's wife? That's daring. I'd put him right under Charley Pierce on the suspect list."

"Yes."

"Did you see Charley's having Althea's funeral tomorrow?"

"What?"

"Yeah, I read about it on my scroll while I was waiting for you. Out at their estate, that Tuigen joint. I saw something about a procession on the river and a bonfire."

Sean scrambled to rearrange her schedule. She'd been planning to spend all of tomorrow at the Normandie but now she was going to spend it at Althea's funeral. What better place to find a killer and to observe Althea's friends and enemies?

"I'd better get going," Sean said. "Thanks for meeting me and for this." She lifted up her bag, which held the paper with the Normandie's hard-to-pin-down tenants listed on it.

"You going to the funeral?"

"You bet I am."

"Sean, I know things aren't like they were between you and Ethan, but . . ."

"He's going to recover. He has to recover."

"Has anyone recovered?"

Sean sighed.

Toby put down her fork and stood up. "Sean, I'm sorry I said that. I didn't mean to imply . . . anyway . . . and you know, but the leap is frightening. Even people at the joukko who weren't involved in Hirata or Banerjee or Carson are starting to talk about it. There was nonstop gossip at Healy's funeral and a lot of people are worried about themselves."

"Maizy Newell, the front-desk person at the Normandie, is in the isolation ward. She's been there for a while. Ethan told me she's improving."

"That's good. Over at the joukko, we just hear about the—oh hell, Sean. I'm so sorry. I'm going to ferret out who this Milburn is. I'll comm you as soon as I know."

"I'm going over to the Normandie. See what I can find out. I'm going to start by knocking on every one of the Milburn apartment doors. And these others too."

But no one answered at any of the Milburn-owned apartments, and Sean thought most of her door knocks sounded hollow, like the apartments were empty. Before she got to the top-floor apartment, Sean went back downstairs and outside and stared up at the windows corresponding to the Milburn apartments, hoping to discern if they were occupied, but the sun glinted off the crystalline windows, obscuring the interiors.

Once Sean was back inside and on the top floor, she saw the corner Milburn-owned apartment was the one where the notice to get tested had still been sticking out from under the door for days. It was gone now, so someone must have been in there at some point even if they weren't right now.

Sean knocked on the door and got no response. Yet the knock, unlike the ones at some of the other Milburn apartments, didn't sound as hollow. She decided to go down the hall and wait in Ziva's place. She'd given Sean an access code and Sean had intended to pick up some clothes and other necessities to take back to the clinic for Zee.

Sean left the door ajar so she could hear any sounds from the hallway, then looked for a while at Banerjee's painting hanging in the living room.

So many people had succumbed to the leap: Oliver Hirata, Kaj Banerjee, Beryl Carson, Vern Healy. Althea Pierce. And Ethan could be next. No. Not Ethan. He couldn't be. And what if Jonathan Lee was infected now? Or Ziva? A chill ran through Sean's body.

She slid down the wall in the foyer and sat on the floor, propping open the door with her feet. She stared out into the corridor. If someone came out of the Milburn apartment, she'd see them.

But by the time someone did open the door, she'd fallen asleep and awoke to catch only a glimpse of the apartment door as it shut.

CHAPTER 35

ONATHAN LEE HAD gotten Dorian and the rest of the group from the Acres up to speed on what they knew so far and what they suspected, and had instilled in everyone a similar sense of urgency to his, although no one at Beryl's had their oldest and dearest friend in the isolation ward at the clinic.

"This isn't an experiment," he said. "Too many people have already died and we have to find out exactly why so Ethan can start"—he paused and changed his words—"so medical experts can start working on a cure. And so we can halt the progress and expunge the leap before it spreads any further."

"Are you absolutely certain this is what's happening?" Jonathan Lee had thought Dorian would be accepting of the conclusions he'd reached, but she'd been the most skeptical of the group, prodding him and throwing questions his way from the moment she arrived.

"As certain as we can be. Before Ethan became ill, he'd isolated the microorganism that's infected several people, and although it's not identical with the image of the virus in the code on Beryl's computer, it's damned similar. Ed Sperry at Keff is working on the biological images and Ethan was able to send her some samples as well. Our job is at the computer end of things."

"So the virus mutated? Or is this computer-human similarity just a coincidence?" Glen Searl, who worked in Dorian's lab and who'd never done more than nod at Jonathan Lee in the hallway, was sitting in the place where Patterson usually sat, and Jonathan Lee was damned glad Patterson had gone out to the Flats. Away from this mess.

THE LEAP

"It's no coincidence."

"From what you've said about the first victim, Oliver Hirata, it sounds like he might not be—well, have been—a biological human." Dorian had made herself at home and was sitting cross-legged on the floor, her scroll open on her lap.

"We've gone over this and although it remains a possibility it's highly unlikely. All his medserv files are exactly what you'd expect from a human being even if what happened to him is, let's say, unusual."

"I think we should keep our computers off," Dorian said. "I'm surprised you haven't already destroyed every computer in Osada City and Genesia, Jonathan Lee. That's your usual modus."

"It's not that I don't want to, it's that none of us has been able to convince anyone in authority to take that sort of massive action. We can't even get to every resident of the Normandie to have them get tested, and several people who were tested and are infected refused to come back for any further observation or treatment."

"What would that treatment be?" Glen was making handwritten notes on an old-fashioned pad of paper.

"We don't know."

"And the one person working on this is now in the isolation ward?" Violet Rushman was leaning over Glen's shoulder, staring at his notepad while she was quizzing Jonathan Lee.

"Yes."

"We have to get some other people involved on the human side."

"Axel Booth at the clinic is working on it—he's attended all the patients—and I'm trying to get Ed Sperry out here. But she is working on it."

"It's not enough," Dorian said.

"It's all we've got right now."

"Have you talked to Ledyard about this?" Dorian held up her comm.

Jonathan Lee and Hal Ledyard were not exactly friends. Since Ledyard had come over to the Acres from Keff he and Jonathan Lee had had several disagreements and Jonathan Lee did his best to steer clear of the guy.

"No, I haven't. But you're right. This is too important."

"I'll comm him for you," Dorian said. "If you want."

"I'll do it. This had better come from me if we're going to get his cooperation."

Jonathan Lee went into Patterson's locked bedroom, closed the door behind him, and sat down on the bed. Ledyard already thought some of Jonathan Lee's concepts and methods were either foolish or useless so he had to be careful about what he said to him, how he phrased this.

Jonathan Lee looked at the east wall of Patterson's room—covered with images of volcanos, calderas, the remains of Pompeii and Auckland, and other volcano-related info—and thought of the looming disaster right in front of him while he commed Ledyard.

"Jonathan Lee Summers. You must be desperate or you would never have contacted me." Ledyard had answered the comm immediately. Jonathan Lee had the video active, so Ledyard could see his expression.

"Hal, I am desperate and we need your help."

"What is it?"

Jonathan Lee had thought of a hundred ways to present the problem in a gradual, yet believable, manner but now that he had Ledyard on the comm, he didn't want to waste any time.

"Several people have died and we're pretty sure they were infected by a computer virus."

"Who put you up to this?" Ledyard had the same look on his face he'd had the last time he and Jonathan Lee had gone at it, a mix of annoyance and incredulity.

"This is no joke, Hal. Ethan Stiles has been working on isolating the pathogen—"

"You know Stiles?" Ledyard's demeanor changed the moment Jonathan Lee mentioned his friend's name.

"Yes. We're good friends."

"You never told me. I might've liked you better."

"Ethan's in the isolation ward at the Genesia Clinic right now and he's one of the people who've been infected with this."

"You'd better give me more information." Ledyard turned around and closed the shades in his office. Jonathan Lee had heard a rumor that Ledyard liked complete dark when he was thinking, but he'd had so little contact with him that he'd never experienced this phenomenon.

"We're calling it the leap virus," Jonathan Lee said. "It seems likely—more than likely—it seems probable that this virus leaps from computers to humans. It's already killed several people."

"This sounds familiar," Ledyard said. "Didn't you give a talk on this exact thing at a symposium a few years back?"

"That was just one of many distant possibilities. Just a thought experiment. I never considered that it would actually happen."

"Well, someone else did."

"This in the literature?"

"In one of my classes. The best student I ever had. To call her that is almost an insult. She's probably the best student anyone ever had. I haven't thought about this in years, but since you brought it up, I remember it distinctly. She was at the symposium and took up where your talk left off, arguing that this could be done and said it would be done in our lifetime."

"We should talk with her, then. Get another mind working on this. Are you still in touch?"

"Not really. Juno Sangstrom isn't exactly . . . Well, let's say she's not interested in socializing."

"Juno Sangstrom—the Sangstrom of Pierce Sangstrom?"

"Is there another? There's only one mind like that every ten or twenty generations. I wanted her to become a lecturer—she's an extraordinary teacher. But she was too ambitious. Maybe we should get her in on this. She—"

"Hal," Jonathan Lee said, interrupting Ledyard, "one of the deaths is Althea Pierce."

"I saw that she'd died. But on the mesh it just said she'd succumbed to an infection."

"She did. She had the leap virus."

Ledyard stopped talking. Jonathan Lee couldn't see Ledyard's face, covered in shadows, but he could see him shaking his head.

"Hal?"

"Well, as brilliant as she is, there's always been something a bit strange about Juno. And after Charley up and left her for Althea, she became even stranger."

"I didn't realize—"

"She's a very private person."

"Do you know where she lives?"

"No idea. I'll comm her. Sometimes she answers me. Sometimes not. I'll let you know."

"Wait, Hal. Let's be careful here. We don't know how she's involved."

"You mean you don't know that maybe she's not the very person who created this virus, don't you?"

"Yes."

"You have a point. If anyone would be capable of it, Juno Sangstrom would be. She uses her own cryptic coding language. Have you come across that?"

"Hal, you have no idea how helpful you've been. If you can get out here, we could use your input."

"I'll be there this evening."

Jonathan Lee gave Ledyard the directions to Beryl's house, then commed Sean, who didn't answer.

Jonathan Lee went back out to the living room, where the group was deep into a philosophical discussion about computer and biological viruses. Were either of them living organisms? Had someone invented a computer virus that was just that? And how could it be transmitted?

"Are any of you familiar with the Sangstrom code?"

"I worked on it once, for the prize, but, you know, no one's ever cracked it," Violet Rushman said while she opened a shell and started eating a peanut. "I was hoping to win."

"Everyone's hoping to win," Dorian said. She was staring at the floor, gazing at something while she spoke. "Even I had a go at it once. But it's a complete waste of energy. It's like trying to figure out how to breathe in a vacuum—it'd be great to know how, but why spend the rest of your life on something that impossible?"

"Well, my friends, we're going to have to spend our time on something that impossible right now, because it seems more than likely Juno Sangstrom wrote this virus," Jonathan Lee said.

Violet put down the peanut she was holding and said, "Let me at it." She took out her computer and was about to turn it on, but Jonathan Lee said, "Use your scroll. Don't want you to get infected."

"No one's gotten infected from their scroll?"

"Not that we know of. I've been thinking the leap might be transmitted through the photonic filamentation and—"

"Dorian." Glen was standing up. "Dorian, shut it off."

Jonathan Lee looked over to where Dorian was sitting with Beryl's computer and saw she had the array cast onto the floor. The most common casting location was the air at eye level, but Dorian liked looking down. She'd been the one to suggest not turning on any computers, yet here she was, doing it herself.

"What?" Dorian said, looking up. "Sorry, I haven't been paying attention. This is so interesting."

"Don't—" But she'd put her hand on the filamental array before Jonathan Lee could stop her.

Glen jumped up and shut off the computer.

"What the hell?" Dorian reached out to turn it back on, but Glen picked up the cube and stuffed it in his pocket. "Pay attention. Use your scroll."

"But this is one of the infected computers. We have to examine it."

"You may've just gotten it yourself," Glen said. "We don't need another victim."

"Look," Jonathan Lee said, "we know Beryl's computer's infected and I've isolated the virus. I want you all working on the program itself. Now that, thanks to Ledyard, we have a lead on how it might be coded—that should help. And Ledyard himself will be here in a few hours. Hang on."

Jonathan Lee took out his comm and saw the message from Sean: *Ziva says Ethan asking for you. Meet you at the clinic.*

CHAPTER 36

WAS COMPETENCE THE most desirable virtue? With the world slowed down to a standstill, Charley Pierce had plenty of time to contemplate such pointless questions. Did it matter what the most desirable virtue was if you were dead? Althea had been one of the most competent people Charley had ever known, yet her competence was now irrelevant.

Charley's banished assistant Morana was competent and she was putting it to good use. She'd made most of the funeral arrangements in less than three hours—slower than Charley would've have liked but faster than anyone else might've done—and she'd sent Charley a list of the people he'd probably want to invite into the house for the private get-together after the ceremony and bonfire.

He was reading through the list when Morana commed him back, asking what fuel or fuel combinations he'd prefer for the bonfire. She was indeed competent. Maybe competence was the most desirable virtue. Goodness was supposed to be a virtue, but it was indefinable. Charley's idea of goodness and Althea's hadn't been congruent, yet even Charley could argue Althea's contrarian case, maybe even agree with it.

Then there was fidelity—an antiquated idea having something to do with the spread of disease, was Charley's guess. Back in the olden times when sexually transmitted diseases couldn't be cured and people died horrible deaths.

Now that people were dying of some unknown virus, what would the new virtue be? Unaccounted-for good health? He shook his head. He knew he was just distracting himself from the facts. That Althea was dead. That her funeral was tomorrow. That she'd died of an unknown ailment. That she should be alive. That by this time tomorrow his wife would be a scattering of ashes floating down the river at Tuigen. That he'd been—

Charley was about to comm his other assistant, Burman, but hadn't Morana said something about his quitting Pierce Sangstrom? Helluva time to do it, just when Charley needed him, no matter how incompetent he'd been.

It was too bad Beryl Carson had died. Charley could really use someone to talk to right now and she'd been intelligent and insightful. He should've been having an affair with her starting the day he'd first met her. Isn't that what he'd told Althea? Yet she'd been incapable of jealousy. If he had one lover, then she had a hundred. His one was nothing.

And his one was dead. Dragging her body down the hallway at the Normandie had been one of the worst moments of Charley Pierce's life. Looking over his shoulder the entire way, convinced the reclusive Juno was going to pick that very moment to come out of her apartment, just in time to witness Charley with Beryl Carson's corpse.

Beryl had been a wonderful dinner companion. Agretta's had been as good as ever. Better. Their lovemaking had been excellent, considering that neither of them had had any recent experience.

But when he woke up at four in the morning, there was Beryl, as still as death itself, he'd thought then. Because she was dead. If he'd thought she might not be, Charley would've called for medical assistance. He kept telling himself he would've done that because he wasn't the sort of person to leave someone else to die. Not if they could be helped. But Beryl was dead. Charley had checked everything on a dead person necessary to be checked—the instructions were all there on the mesh—and Beryl had no chance of being revived.

Honesty was a virtue Charley didn't much care about—another worn-out concept Charley figured had been developed by the upper classes to keep the peasants at their mercy. Honesty meant those below had to pay up. That expression—paying up—had likely originated from the practice of the poor paying the rich. And the rich had turned this into a poor person's virtue—pay your way, nothing in this life is free, and something about giving tribute where it was due.

Hard work was another overrated virtue, something else the ruling class had foisted off on their lessers. Charley himself never had to work another day in his life and he was one of the richest people on the continent. Had he gotten there through hard work? Charley always said he had, but that was an exaggeration. He'd just done what he was going to do anyway and the riches had come to him. Even more riches than the ones he'd been born with.

Vices, though, weren't the opposite of virtues, even if they were supposed to be. Useful vices, like greed, were beneficial to their practitioners. Useless vices, like gluttony, were neither here nor there. If someone wanted to be a glutton, let them. Charley knew a lot of successful gluttons. Their vice hadn't hindered them.

Maybe sins were the opposites of virtues. Charley thought about this while contemplating murdering Lukas Adler, one of the people who should've been dead. After all, she had two other dead lovers, and maybe a third, if Charley's guesses about Vern Healy were correct. He'd been spying on Althea and maybe she'd seduced him.

Althea had been unparalleled in the art of seduction—or maybe it wasn't an art but either a vice or a virtue, he wasn't sure which. Seduction was a natural part of her being. She didn't have to actively do anything. Her mere presence was seduction itself. It always worked on Charley. Even now that she was dead, the thought of her could seduce Charley. Maybe Althea had been Charley's vice. She lured him on even though she'd disappeared into death.

Charley thought of making some comms, saying the words *Althea died* a few times. That that would help the reality sink in, as though reality had to work its way into your bloodstream in order for you to grasp it, when in fact reality was existence itself, inescapable.

The first thing, now that the funeral was on schedule, was to get back at Juno. Charley had to figure out how to do this in a way that wouldn't jeopardize Pierce Sangstrom's future and that wouldn't stop them from using her new program to its powerful, ultimate ends. With Althea gone—she was dead, not just gone, Charley reminded himself—with Althea dead Charley could concentrate on increasing his reach, his power, his influence.

Why not? It'd be simple once Juno's new program was polished and refined in the way that only Charley Pierce could effect. The program that would enter the user's life and never let go, latching on to all their desires and motivations and turning them into even greater riches for Charley.

Yet Juno remained a boulder in his way. Juno was the only person who'd ever truly understand the program, who'd ever be able to expand it in ever more creative ways. Not killing its users but manipulating them, turning them toward whatever direction Charley wished, and all directions would directly benefit Charley.

But . . . Juno. Although now that she'd killed Althea—Charley'd convinced himself this was true—maybe she'd stop. After all, her intended victim was dead. Like other intended victims were.

Charley tried to arrange his thoughts in a logical pattern, moving them around like dice inside his skull. Some of these dice refused to budge and others seemed to be disintegrating before he had a chance to rearrange their placements.

Charley took off his pale blue tee and lay down on the floor of his office. Maybe he was in Morris's office. His body was both here and across the room, staring out the window. Great ideas were working their way into compact cubes inside his cranium. Stacking them on top of each other proved to be too difficult so he made sinuous patterns with them instead.

Tomorrow Althea would make her final journey, burned into oblivion.

CHAPTER 37

E THAN STILES'S BED was encased in a tent. Axel Booth had decided it was conceivable that this virus, a virus he was resistant to attributing to a computer, was so contagious that a tent was necessary. The other patients on the isolation ward, Maizy Newell and Jordan Fields, were also now inside tents. Booth wasn't too happy with himself for not having done this sooner, although no one on the staff at the clinic had gotten ill. Or seemed to be ill.

He'd had a long conversation with Ziva Walls, who was obviously out of her mind with a combination of fear and lack of sleep. She'd barged into his office and demanded he listen to her.

"Dr. Booth, something has to be done. None of us has been successful and I'm hoping you'll be able to wield your influence. After all, Althea Pierce just died of the leap and—"

"The leap? What are you talking about? Althea Pierce had a sort of viral infection"—Booth wasn't sure it was a virus, but it was so much like one that he wasn't uncomfortable with the nomenclature—"and she didn't leap from anything. I think you need some sleep, Mrs. Walls. You should go home. I'll contact you if anything changes with Dr. Stiles."

"The leap virus. I'm sure Ethan told you about it although we didn't have a name for it until recently. It's what Ethan has, what Althea Pierce had, what Maizy and Jordan have. They got it from a computer."

"You can't mean you think these people got infected because they read about a disease on the mesh? Of course there have been odd cases in the past. People are very susceptible to suggestion, particularly a certain kind of person who spends too much time thinking about themself and every possibility of what could go wrong. But these cases didn't involve multiple people. You see—"

"That isn't at all what I meant. And I know Ethan had to have spoken to you about this. The disease is transmitted from a computer. Not *a* computer but any computer that's already infected. It's a computer virus, you see, only it's capable of leaping across the divide between computer and human and then infecting people."

Axel Booth sighed. Stiles had told him some crackpot theory about this virus, but even though he respected Ethan, Booth had listened only in spurts. He had patients to take care of and couldn't be bothered with insane concepts, which this obviously was. Stiles had even gone so far as to show Booth what were supposedly autopsy reports on Oliver Hirata and Kaj Banerjee, but the information there was fantastical, unbelievable, hallucinatory. Someone had obviously faked the results and then convinced Stiles they were true.

"Mrs. Walls, please understand that what you're suggesting is impossible. Computer viruses and biological viruses aren't the same thing. A computer virus is just a program that infects—and that's really a metaphor, not an actual infection—other parts of the computer. It can't leap out of the computer and I don't even know what you think it would do. Jump into someone's body? Travel through a person's bloodstream looking for a computer program it could interfere with?"

"Ethan told us the computer virus is RNA-based, just like the kind of virus that can cause human illness."

"Still, it's limited to computers. An actual virus is something else altogether."

"I'm not an expert, but, as Ethan explained it, both computer viruses and biological viruses need a host. They can't survive without one. And this is a computer virus that needs a human host, that's seeking a human host. The computer wasn't good enough. Or something like that. I don't remember all the details. And anyway, I don't see the difference."

"Let me see if I can explain. The kind of virus you're used to thinking of, the kind that would infect a person, is an organism that . . . wait, that's not exactly right. It's an entity—that's better—because it's never been determined if a virus is actually alive. It has no cellular structure and without a host it can't exist."

"The same as a computer virus."

"I suppose you could think of it that way, but it's very far from the facts. A computer virus is an invention of a human being. Now, why someone would invent one is not my field. I'm a doctor. Do no harm and all that. But a biological virus is not manmade. It's not an invention. It's a phenomenon of nature."

Booth stopped himself. Maybe Ziva Walls wouldn't know this, but he did: there were plenty of synthetic biological viruses that had been created in labs. Viruses that could cause massive damage. Back a few centuries ago work on one particular virus had been banned and all known specimens destroyed. Afterward, science had moved in another direction and . . .

"I don't think this virus is a phenomenon of nature. I think someone wrote the code for this virus. I mean, I don't know what to think. It's what Ethan told us," Ziva Walls said.

"It's all very interesting, but it's a fantasy. A computer cannot infect a human. Not really. It could display lies or threats, for example, and you could become fearful. But nothing can jump out of a computer and somehow enter your body."

"Yet something did—and is. We're trying to get all the computers at the Normandie shut down and I'm hoping you'll be able to help."

"You're mistaking correlation for causation. Just because many of the patients have a connection to the Normandie doesn't make something at the building—"

"The computers there are infected."

"As I was saying, this doesn't mean something at the building is the cause. Maybe someone in the building infected all the others. Not a computer. Or there's a virus or something like a virus there that's transmitted through any number of ways—through the air, through touch, through exchange of fluids—"

"Through a computer."

"I have to go on rounds." Axel Booth got up and gestured for Ziva Walls to leave his office with him. Really, the ideas some people had.

Yet as Booth was putting on his protective equipment he flipped through some of what Walls had said about Ethan's theories, and one thought kept recurring: if a person could create a synthetic biological virus, then couldn't a person create a synthetic virus that could be conveyed through a computer? Why couldn't this happen? As far-fetched as it seemed, could it be that that was what was happening?

Maizy Newell. She kept fading in and out of consciousness, but when she was conscious it was a thin facade. She couldn't speak or convey her thoughts or desires. She could move in only very slight motions. She'd stir then fade back again. She'd never spoken since she'd been admitted. She definitely had the pathogen present in her body that the other patients also did, yet it had expressed itself in different ways in all of them. He had hope for her. She was young and was otherwise healthy.

This evening she wasn't stirring, her eyelids weren't fluttering, and her pulse was slow and regular. More like sleep than unconsciousness.

He left her room and changed his protective equipment. The leap virus. What an absurd idea. On his way to see Jordan Fields the idea of leaping preoccupied Booth. How viruses could make the leap from an animal to a human host. From a doorknob someone had touched onto the skin of the next person who touched it. Viruses were sneaky bastards, desperate, doing anything they could to find a new host. It was that or die. Or, more accurately, cease to exist, since it was never alive.

Could there really be a virus that was in a computer and then leaped onto people?

Jordan Fields was a different sort of case, although he also had this pathogen in his system. He was unmoving and semiconscious. He spoke—well, anyway, he made sounds—but these sounds were in no language Booth or anyone he'd contacted could recognize or decipher. Booth had sent samples of Fields's utterances to several linguists and some friends of his who knew more than a few languages and no one could figure out the words, if they were words, that Fields was speaking. Maybe Fields was just babbling, not really saying anything, but the pauses, the gestures, the cadence of it seemed to indicate an organized structure.

Unlike Maizy Newell, who had a few visitors, no one had visited Fields. So if there was someone who knew Fields and could interpret, they hadn't appeared.

The next patient was Ethan Stiles. Booth felt personally responsible for Ethan, not just as his doctor but as a colleague. Stiles was the premier medical examiner in the area yet he'd been stepped over by Prentiss for the position in Osada. And Ethan was a friend and a good person. He'd been at the clinic regularly since this entire mess began and was working away on trying to find a cure for this inexplicable disease. That a medical examiner was devoting himself to finding a cure for a disease was unheard of. The man should be a researcher, not a corpse butcher. If—when—he recovered, Booth would tell him so.

Booth entered the room, where Stiles was sitting up in bed and Booth saw his fever had abated.

"Ethan, you're awake."

"Barely. Say, did Jonathan Lee give you my notebook?"

"Your friend Summers?"

"Yes. I asked him to. I think. I . . . it's . . . my thoughts, my words—convoluted. Sorry, Axel. It's this virus. Can't seem to get clarity."

"No, Summers didn't give me your notebook."

"You need to see what I've been working on. I need to get out of here."

"No chance, my friend. You don't want to spread this beast, do you?" Booth needed to appeal to Stiles's altruistic tendencies. Telling him he couldn't leave because his own life was in danger might not be convincing enough to keep him here, where he belonged.

"I don't think I can spread it. I think only a computer can."

Booth laughed just as he heard a knock on the door.

"Jay. Did you bring my notebook?"

Jonathan Lee Summers, who was some kind of computer expert out at the Acres, came into the room. "Ethan. Sean commed me. She's waiting outside, but Ziva said you were asking for me."

"This is Axel Booth, Jay."

"I've seen you around, Doctor. Is Ethan going to be all right?"

"There are too many unknowns here, Summers, but he seems to be improving." Booth left out that no one he'd seen with this thing had so far recovered. Yet there could always be a first. And there were living, although not well, patients.

"Jay, I gather you haven't given my notebook to Axel."

"I didn't know I was supposed to."

"I told you. Out at Sean's."

"You weren't exactly coherent then, Ethan. Where is your note-book?"

"At the lab. Top drawer of the left-most table. I think I have to sleep."

Stiles put his head back and closed his eyes.

"Let's go outside, Summers. I think Ethan needs to rest. This is the most activity he's had in days."

Summers followed Booth to the changing room and they both discarded their gear, then showered and dressed and went to Booth's office.

"Your friend Walls has told me quite a tale about Stiles's ideas on this pathogen," Booth said.

"The leap," Summers said.

"Oh, she told you too?"

"It's not about her telling me. It is the leap, as far as we can tell."

"I thought you were a scientist, Summers. Ziva Walls is just, well, I don't know what she is, but she doesn't know what she's talking about."

"Neither do you. Ethan, Sean Meade, Ziva Walls, and I have been following this thing since Oliver Hirata's death. And when we put everything together, the leap virus is what we've come up with."

"Nonsense." Booth stopped himself from saying *insane*.

"I think the same thing, but that doesn't mean it isn't true. Let me go over to the lab and get Ethan's notebook and you can see what he's been working on. He trusts you, so I'm going to trust you as well. We need as many minds working on this as we can get. I have some colleagues from the Acres here, Hal Ledyard's on his way, and we're trying to get Ed Sperry to help as well. But you've been working with these patients—"

"Hang on, Summers. You mean to tell me you think this is a virus that leapt from a computer into a human? Or several humans?"

"Yes. That's exactly what we think."

"How, exactly, do you propose this could occur?"

"We have only theories at this point. At the computer end, the virus's methods have proven . . . well . . . difficult to pinpoint. They're almost certainly hidden in a program that's written in a cryptic code. But we're working on it. The pathogen Ethan's isolated is RNA-based and there are computer viruses with somewhat similar configurations."

"This is the stuff of coincidence or more like a story you'd tell your kids if you wanted them off their computers and outside playing." Booth had yet to find a tactic that would work with his own kids.

"It's neither. Let me go over to the lab and get Ethan's notebook. You can read what another medical expert is thinking about this."

"Say it is true—and I'm not conceding it is—how would a computer be able to send a virus from itself into a person? Or how would the virus itself be able to leave the computer? If someone had ever figured out a way to have anything leave a computer and get into a human, well, that would be grand. Think of all the knowledge we could carry around with ourselves, conveyed into our brains by our computers."

"It's still unknown, but we're working on a few possibilities. The photonic filamentation could be the transfer medium."

"You've lost me."

"You know how your computer's array can be displayed anywhere? In front of you, on your desk, on the wall, even on your skin if you want it to be."

"Some very odd things have gone on with people using it that way. But the array didn't infect them. It can't." Booth brushed aside mental images of all the craziness he'd witnessed working in emergency when he was in training. People who'd used the array in very creative ways. He'd removed computer cubes from . . . he didn't want to think about it.

"It's not the array that's doing the infecting. It's the virus itself." Jonathan Lee Summers meant this. He wasn't just spinning some fantasy. Booth was paying attention now.

"The method's still unclear," Summers said, "but the idea is that the virus is able to penetrate the filamentation and convey itself either directly into the user or perhaps into the air, which would make finding a prevention and a cure even more urgent. If the contagion's airborne and direct contact with a computer is unnecessary."

"Let's see Ethan's notes. I don't like this theory of yours at all, but if there's any possibility it could be true, then I'm forced to explore it. Althea Pierce's death . . . and of course I don't want anyone else to succumb."

When Jonathan Lee Summers returned to the clinic with Stiles's notebook, Booth sat in his office and read for hours. Ziva Walls had described Ethan's theories with remarkable accuracy. Stiles had included in his notes many of the ideas that Summers had told Booth.

In the early morning, his usual defenses shut down after not having eaten or slept for nearly a day, Booth realized he could no longer reject the impossible. Stiles had laid out his findings, his thoughts and theories, with an elegant logic.

The leap—a virus that originated on a computer and infected humans. This might not be the only explanation for what was happening, but as absurd as it seemed, it was a plausible explanation. The most convincing. And the most impossible to defeat.

CHAPTER 38

S EAN'D BROUGHT ZIVA a change of clothes and some decent food. Zee had been able to take a shower in one of the unused isolation ward rooms and she'd put on the clean skirt and blouse, but Sean hadn't seen her eat anything.

A few weeks ago when she'd first met Ziva, Sean would never have been able to predict she'd be the sort of person who'd keep a vigil for a friend or who'd be so helpful during a crisis. Yet she'd spent untold hours contacting the tenants at the Normandie, urging them to get tested. And now she was at the clinic, making sure Ethan was being properly seen to, waiting and watching, while Sean was going to a funeral.

She picked up Jonathan Lee at Beryl's house and they drove out to Tuigen together.

Jonathan Lee slept for much of the ride but woke up as Sean drove onto the rough road leading to the Pierces' country residence.

"Damn. That's the first rest I've had in a while. Felt good. Sean, have you been sleeping?" Jonathan Lee stretched, yawned, and ran his hands back through his hair. He was simultaneously familiar and stimulating.

The leap had brought them together, was keeping them together until it was solved. Afterward, though. Afterward was unknown. Sean wanted to pull over to the side of the road, darken the windows, and continue where they'd left off yesterday before she'd had to leave. But she couldn't. The funeral was about to start and she wanted to be there to investigate, to see who was there, who Charley Pierce was favoring.

Hear what people were saying. Be there in case anyone else had the leap and was showing symptoms. Eavesdrop.

"I don't remember what sleep is." Sean slept very little anyway. She'd never needed it. Three or four hours sufficed and now she was running on one or two.

"Want to tell me how you plan on getting us in to this spectacle?"

It was all over the mesh—the grand sendoff Charley Pierce was giving his dead wife. Thousands of invited guests, many of them celebrities and Osada City's most illustrious residents, some sort of performance by a famous singer so famous even Sean had heard of her, and what had been described as a pyrotechnic display for the ages. More like an overblown party than a funeral.

"Don't worry. I'll just flash my detective credentials—they look quite official—and they'll let us in."

"Am I your sidekick?"

"Absolutely. Just pretend you're part of the team."

"I am part of the team. You, me, Ethan, Ziva, and now we have more members. Dorian, Glen, Violet, and the rest of the group from the lab at the Acres. Hal Ledyard arrived this morning. I would've introduced you but he's already deep into it and I didn't want to disturb him."

"Ziva's been a surprise."

"Wait, I think you missed the turn."

Sean backed up. She had missed the turn. It wasn't marked well. Nothing out here was. Privacy and seclusion were part of the exclusive character of the place. Unmarked roads, keeping out the unwanted. Just the sort of thing the owner of a megacorp would indulge in—a primitive-seeming setting for a pricey, sophisticated estate and grounds. Out here the estate was hidden from view, disguised behind a surround of dense, untouched forest with a dirt road as the only hint that something was beyond.

"I like Zee," Jonathan Lee said. "So does Ethan."

"Is there something more there?"

"I'm oblivious. You'll have to ask Ethan after he's feeling better. Were you able to talk to him?"

"Just for a moment. Booth thinks he's improving."

"Let's hope so."

Sean was paying close attention and didn't miss the next turn, but it seemed like they were going away from everything instead of toward something.

"You think this is right?" Jonathan Lee sounded skeptical.

"Supposed to be. We'll find out. JL, while I have the chance—you know, in case I get the leap or anything else happens—I want to tell you—it's been great. You, me, us, I mean. And if this is all there is, that's fine. I'm no good at this sort of thing. Just ask Ethan when he's feeling better. After we've got the leap under control. Fixed, I mean. I'm trying to say something here but it's not coalescing."

"It's still great, Sean. Don't overthink it. Let's just keep going. Since I've been here, my entire life has been upended. My schedule's destroyed, my habits have been thrown out, my days have lost their rhythm. But it's fine. I get to be with you and—stop."

"What?"

"Stop right here. Pull over."

"We can't. Not right now. The funeral's going to start soon. Even though I want to."

"I want to as well, but it's not what I mean. Look over there." Jonathan Lee pointed to what looked like a clump of bushes. Sean stopped the transcer. Beyond the bushes was a sign she hadn't noticed. She'd been too busy trying to stay on the right road—to even see the road, which was often indistinguishable from the forest floor.

The sign said No Trespassing / Violators Will Be Disposed Of Accordingly.

"That's a bit ugly, isn't it?" Jonathan Lee said. "Disposed of?"

"These are the Pierces. They can do whatever they want. Well, except for Althea. She's pretty limited these days."

"I am going to decline a laugh here. After all, we're on our way to crash her funeral. I think we should show some respect."

"I can't help myself. My introduction to Althea Pierce as a person instead of just a sort of celebrity—you know, the person who wrote *Keeping the Promise* and Charley Pierce's wife—was when Zee came to me because Morris was missing and he'd been having an affair with Althea. She just seemed like a run-of-the-mill homewrecker. I didn't think I'd be sneaking into her funeral in a few weeks. Say, what if Morris is here? Maybe I'll finally find him."

"It wouldn't be the first odd thing that's happened lately."

Sean drove past the threatening sign and, gasping, stopped again. The forest was no more. Instead, in front of them was a rolling lawn, acres of the lushest grass Sean had ever seen, the brightest flowers, the most magnificent trees, and beyond that, an enormous, huge, gigantic, gargantuan house.

"That almost makes the Normandie seem small." Sean couldn't stop staring.

Jonathan Lee hadn't gasped, but maybe he'd seen something like this before. Sean never had.

"That can't be just the house of one couple. Well, one person now. Can it?"

Sean looked over and Jonathan Lee looked as shocked as she felt.

"It's hardly a house. More like a hotel. Or a castle."

"No turrets. I think you need them to call something a castle."

"Maybe. Maybe it's just an ordinary old palace. JL, they're going to notice us. We do not fit in here. And where is everyone?"

"Out back, I suppose. Didn't you say the ceremony was on the river? I don't see a river yet, so it's got to be behind the building. There could be thousands of people there. Millions, perhaps."

Sean drove farther in and to their left was an enormous parking area manned by a crew of people, all of them dressed in the same blue and silver outfit, just like the guards in *Keeping the Promise* had worn.

"This is too much," Jonathan Lee said. "Who would want a funeral like this?"

"JL, the corpse never gets a say in these things. The funeral is for the living."

"Odd expression, isn't it? The living? The only time we ever refer to ourselves that way is when someone else dies. But someone else is dying all the time."

"Let's not get too morbid, JL."

"Yet this is the only time it's justified."

"We have work to do."

"You're right of course."

One of the uniformed guards gestured and Sean drove up to where she'd indicated. The guard leaned over and Sean opened the window.

"Invitation, please," the guard said. "No entry without one."

Sean flashed her official-looking credentials. "I'm here on business," she said.

The guard took Sean's card and scrutinized it. Sean thought they were going to be turned away and concentrated on devising a plausible story, something about her being Althea's old classmate or maybe Jonathan Lee was her relative and they'd come a long way and—

"Over there," the guard said, pointing with one hand and giving Sean back her unimpressive credentials with the other.

Sean followed the directions and left the transcer amid a mass of other vehicles, some of them worth more than Sean's house, although Sean's house was more like a shack when you compared it to the magnificent structure they were now walking past.

"We're getting closer," Jonathan Lee said.

"Yeah, I can hear the crowd now." The voices were murmurs. It was a funeral and despite the unusual setting and upcoming dramatics, people seemed to be behaving like they were at a more traditional ceremony.

Sean and Jonathan Lee stopped while they were still separated from the sight of what had to be a huge gathering. They leaned against a stone wall at the side of the mansion. Jonathan Lee took Sean's hand in his. He spoke in an undertone, although there was no one nearby who could have heard him.

"Closer—I mean with the leap virus. The transmission, anyway. It seems likely it's being conveyed through the photonic filamentation on the array. The filaments can sort of buoy up the RNA particles, which is what they must be, as they're released from the program—although it's not yet clear how that happens but it seems the most likely mechanism—and as soon as someone comes in close contact with the display, the virus moves over to the human. One good thing here—I think scrolls are safe. Their display uses an entirely different technology."

"Zee will be relieved. She's been keeping her scroll on the windowsill and sitting as far away from it as she can while still being able to read it."

"Are you ready for this?" Jonathan Lee gave her hand a squeeze and they left their safe place against the wall and started walking again.

"I'm prepared but I'm not sure I could ever be ready."

The murmurs got louder as Sean and Jonathan Lee got closer to the river, and Sean gasped again when they were able to see the crowd.

"I've never seen this many people all in one place at the same time."

"I guess you've never been to a Convergence."

"Right. Like I could afford it. What's it like?"

"I've only heard of it. Beryl told me about it. She wanted to go but I don't know if she ever did. I hope she did. I hope she got to do everything she wanted to do before she died. But everything she was working on—it's all stopped. I don't know if she had any colleagues who'll take over."

"Do you?"

"There are students, and Dorian could pick up a lot of my work. But nothing's as important as this. I've lost interest in everything else I was working on anyway. Not sure how I can go back to it after we solve the leap. Stop it. Find a cure. A prevention. When I think of all the infected computers I've destroyed . . ."

"We should be destroying all the computers at the Normandie, shouldn't we? Have them destroyed, I mean. Convince the tenants it's in their best interests. It's not like anyone there wouldn't be able to afford to buy a new one." Sean shut down the part of her mental dialogue that was about to list all the things she couldn't afford to buy right now.

"Yes, it's something we were discussing—out at Beryl's, I mean. That's the consensus. Our best shot at shutting this down before it goes any further is to destroy the source. Although we have no idea how far the virus has spread now. It seems likely it's on all the computers at Pierce Sangstrom—"

"Well, they can certainly afford to replace all of them."

"But, Sean. They have offices in several cities. Who knows how far this has spread? And. Hell. Look at all these people. You think the river is out there somewhere? Past the seething masses?"

"Must be."

Sean and Jonathan Lee tried to work their way through the crowd, but couldn't do it. People were hundreds-deep on the lawn. Everyone, it seemed, was wearing a black ribbon tied around their arm, their wrist, or some of the women were wearing them around their necks, the ribbon ends trailing across their chests and shoulders and floating in the breeze.

Jonathan Lee leaned down and whispered to Sean. "Didn't we rate one of these ribbons?"

"Maybe they ran out."

"Mighty poor planning."

"This is no time for sarcasm."

The crowd's murmurings came to an abrupt halt. The people near the front must've seen what was going on. Sean and Jonathan Lee could see only the hundreds or thousands of people in front of and around them.

"To all of Althea's friends, colleagues, and—Althea, I will admit this, because you would appreciate it—lovers, thank you for coming today." The voice seemed to be emanating from a distant galaxy. It must've been Charley Pierce speaking. Some whispers wound through the gathering. Althea's lovers? Had there been that many? And if Morris Walls was here, it'd be a miracle if Sean would be able to spot him.

"Thank you for coming to see Althea off. We'd never discussed what either of us would want at such an occasion."

Charley Pierce paused and coughed. The murmurs picked up again as he remained silent.

Sean wished she could see him, because every telltale gesture, movement, tic, every word he spoke, every pause—it would all add up to form a picture of who this person was, of what he might be capable of. To help her discern if he was the mastermind behind the leap.

After years on the joukko, Sean had come to the conclusion that anyone was capable of anything, with perhaps the exception of someone under the age of one. Even a two-year-old could be capable of atrocities, although they wouldn't understand it, wouldn't know what they were doing, what they'd caused, what it meant and would mean. How it would affect anyone else. Sean had worked on such a heartbreaking case.

She shook her head, listened as Charley Pierce started speaking again.

"What I'm trying to convey is . . ." He coughed and paused again.

Sean wondered if Charley Pierce were holding back tears. Well, just because he might be upset now didn't mean he hadn't killed Althea. He could be upset at the thought of being caught. Or have some remorse. Or feel threatened by someone in attendance. Or be a good actor.

"You see, Althea—I never thought she'd die. Today though. And. She'd be so angry she missed this."

Small bursts of laughter pulsed through the gathering, and the murmurs started up again then stopped the moment Charley continued.

"She did love drama. You'd almost have to think she'd arranged to die this way, in such a dramatic fashion. I mean, if she had to die. Which . . . I can't . . . I'm not . . ."

Sean heard Charley sob and turned to look at Jonathan Lee. He put his arm around her and pulled her close. Pierce sobbed again, followed by the distinctive sound of his mic turning off.

As Charley Pierce's silence became more and more excruciating, the murmurs picked up volume, then became whispers. The whispers turned into speech, the words washing through the gathering in surging waves.

They were such a wonderful couple. Always so close. She had everything. Say, what did she die of anyway? I heard she was in Lukas Adler's bed when she got sick. I had her once. She thought she was the world's best lover, and maybe she was. Were you at the party in Osada? The one Althea had after she won the award? Her gown covered only a few, uh, select areas. Stunning. If Althea Pierce can die so young, and, say, was she sick a long time? Some kind of infection. I just came for the bonfire. Only worked with her once and vowed I'd never do it again. Hey, did you hear if they'll be serving anything? I'm starving.

Charley didn't speak again but the crowd was silenced by a powerful whoosh. Sean and Jonathan Lee couldn't see anything but they could feel the heat from the fire that must've been lit. The crowd started moving, the heat in front driving them back.

The wind picked up then and the fire roared. Sean's face burned with the rush of heat and she could finally see the flames arcing into the sky above the crowd. Someone pushed into her and she fought for balance as more people streamed past her, desperate to escape.

Jonathan Lee held tight to Sean's hand, leaned down, and shouted into her ear, "Run."

CHAPTER 39

EXCEPT FOR JORDAN Fields, who'd had an unexpected reaction to the virus and hadn't been able to report back to Juno, as she'd planned—although at least Fields wasn't blabbing about Juno to the detective Juno thought she might've spotted at the back of the crowd—but, except for Jordan, everything, including some un-intended developments, was proceeding well.

As difficult as it was for Charley Pierce, who'd broken down into tears over Althea's death, it wasn't any more difficult for him now than every day since Charley had walked out on her had been for Juno. Not days, years. And Juno had made it all worse for herself by staying with Pierce Sangstrom, by clinging on to Charley with their regular, dispassionate meetings, which were a sort of self-inflicted torture for Juno.

She was innocent. She congratulated herself. The deaths weren't her responsibility. She'd created the virus—and she was concerned her authorship would soon be discovered, since who else was capable of such an extraordinary feat?—but she hadn't created it to kill anyone. Not that she cared even somewhat about anyone who'd died or was ill, and as she watched the flames rise from Althea's pyre, Juno had to suppress a smile. Althea was gone. Juno's path was clear, free, open. Her only impediment had been eliminated.

Juno'd been absent from public life for so long that no one at the funeral recognized her or, if they did, they were too afraid to approach her. Either was fine with Juno. She had no desire to socialize with anyone other than Charley, and that was hardly socializing. That was living itself.

Charley was on his hands and knees, staring up into the pyre, his face lit red by the heat and flames. Juno, who'd been standing near the front and at the far side, away from Charley, was roasting in the heat. Someone pushed into her and she was turned around to see the massive crowd fleeing en masse from the riverfront.

She looked back at the pyre, only the pyre had disappeared. In its place was an indistinguishable stretch of the riverfront, engulfed in flames and billowing smoke. Where was Charley?

Juno inhaled a lungful of smoke and spat it out. She had to find Charley. She'd rescue him and he'd finally see she wasn't just the genius behind Pierce Sangstrom's success, she wasn't just Charley's business partner, she was Charley's life partner.

As she walked toward the river, toward the towering mass of fire and smoke that Althea's funeral pyre had become, Juno's hopes rose.

Charley would come to her, embrace her. In his broken-down grief over Althea's death, he'd reach for Juno. Yes. Charley would crawl to Juno as she stood strong against the increasing wind, against the building flames. Sparks and ashes flew into Juno's face. Her hair was singed. Pieces of Althea's corpus were scattered across her floral-patterned dress.

Charley, with his arms around Juno's knees, would beg Juno to come back into his life. To live with him. To be the lover he needed and wanted more than anyone. He'd still be sobbing but his tears would be for the years he'd wasted, for the life he and Juno could have always had if only he hadn't had the misfortune of meeting Althea Livesy.

But Juno couldn't see him. The smoke was impeding her view of everything. The heat was intense. She felt something burning and looked down at the hem of her dress, which had caught fire. A spark, probably. She bashed her hands onto it, put it out. Ran to the river.

Charley would be there at the safest place. She'd meet him there. She'd rescue him. No. He'd rescue her.

The river. Where was it? Juno couldn't see.

"Get down." Someone's voice shot through the flames.

Juno got down. Yes, it was better here on the ground, underneath the chaos above.

Althea deserved to die. She was a murderer. Juno'd practiced the explanation: Althea's additions to the program were the cause of all the deaths and illnesses. Althea was just the type of person who'd do something like this even if she didn't really possess the knowledge or expertise. She might've been clever, but she'd merely stumbled onto something and it had turned lethal. How dare she interfere with Juno's masterwork. Yes, it sounded right.

Juno crawled in what she thought was the direction of the river.

She'd glimpsed Hirata with Althea a few months earlier and knew they had a connection. Althea had probably had a so-called interlude with him.

Hirata had once asked Juno to have an interlude with him. As though she knew him. Just because they both lived at the Normandie. He'd come on to her but she didn't want him. He had a regular something-or-other, something more than a mere interlude, with that despicable woman who lived down the hall, Ziva Walls. Juno had refused Hirata and he'd brushed it off, like a refusal from Juno Sangstrom was unnoticeable. Yet Juno had had to admit to herself that he was unbearably attractive, stirring a pulsing need inside her.

Juno decided that Charley'd left his computer on and Althea had seen the program, realized it was something important, hacked away at it, and killed herself in the process. This explanation had depth and an air of truth to it even though the actual truth was more interesting. But this would do.

Juno's hands finally found something that wasn't the broiling ground. But even the water was heated. Yet it was safer here. Juno pushed off into the river and started swimming for the other shore.

She turned to look behind her. From the river, the sight on the shore was extraordinary. The colossal funeral pyre was collapsing into smoky ruins while all around it the ground was in flames and the trees at the perimeter were now engulfed in the increasing inferno as well.

To escape the pervasive heat, Juno went under the water. When she emerged, she came face-to-face with Charley Pierce, whose cheeks and forehead were smeared with soot. His tears had been washed away. He was the Charley Pierce she'd met at Keff, his original self, untainted by his marriage to Althea. The Charley Pierce she'd lived with, purified by the rituals of fire and water.

Her fantasy was coming true. She was going to rescue him.

"Juno." He said her name. He wasn't pleading with her yet, but he would be. Juno watched the moment unfold as she lived it.

"Charley"—she was panting in the thick, fiery air—"we have to get to the other shore."

"You think I'm going to let you get there? If I could've planned this, I would have."

"Charley, you don't know what you're—"

He grabbed her shoulders and Juno closed her eyes, searing every sensation into her memory—the smoke, the raging fire, the heat in the water, the moment when Charley Pierce understood just how important Juno Sangstrom really was to him, to his life and his happiness.

"I've been trying to work this out," Charley said.

He would declare his love for her, that he'd always loved her. She waited, his hands on her shoulders, the two of them treading water here in the river. Althea reduced to ashes. The crowd dispersed. Charley and Althea's Tuigen about to be consumed by the conflagration. She tried to lift her arms to put her hands on his shoulders, but Charley was pressing into her arms and she couldn't move them.

"How you can receive the punishment you deserve without Pierce Sangstrom being destroyed in the process."

"Charley, I don't know what—"

"Murderers deserve their punishments, Juno. It doesn't matter who delivers them."

"No, Charley."

"When I realized what you'd done I couldn't see my way around it. But you're right here in front of me. I'll explain it was an accident. I was trying to rescue you."

"You don't have to rescue me, Charley. I—"

"But I want a confession first."

Charley had never been romantic with Juno, not even when they were younger and living together. But now he was asking Juno to bare her heart, her soul, her very reason.

"Charley, I love you. It's so good you want to—"

The pressure on her shoulders increased and the water was over her head. She hadn't taken a breath and now she was struggling, kicking out, trying to get to the surface. Charley didn't realize what he was doing. She couldn't breathe and felt the water seeping into her mouth, into her lungs.

Charley pulled her back to the surface and she gagged, spit up water, shook her head.

"Charley, I couldn't breathe."

"I want your confession," he said again.

"How many times can I tell you? I love you, Charley Pierce. I always have. I confess. I loved you before you noticed me, before we worked together. When we sat on the couch and I helped you—"

"I want your confession."

Juno had never, even in her most complex fantasies, imagined Charley Pierce could be this romantic. That he'd beg her to tell him over and over how much she loved him. That they'd be this close to death— to a fiery corpse and to their own approaching ends, here in the heated river—and that he'd want nothing more than to hear Juno's loving words.

"Charley. I don't know how else to say it."

She tried to lean forward to kiss him, but his hold on her shoulders kept her in place.

"Say it the usual way, Juno. The way any murderer would. Say it."

"I—"

The water closed over her head again. Juno felt the pressure on her shoulders increase. Charley was disoriented. The funeral, all those people, the out-of-control bonfire. Now he was struggling and didn't realize what he was doing. Juno started breathing in the water. She'd never thought she'd have to die in order to save Charley, but if she did, then she would. Just as she was surrendering herself to a martyr's death, she was pulled back to the surface.

"I'm not letting you off this easily, Juno Sangstrom."

Bliss. Hearing him say her name. Juno puked out a liter of water.

"I'd do anything for you, Charley. I don't need to say it. It's true. You know it."

"I want your confession. I want to hear you say you killed Althea. Say it."

"Charley—I—" She must have misunderstood what he was saying. The spreading fire, pushed around by what was now a heavy wind, distorted his words.

"Althea. Charley, she's gone. We have our future together. Finally."

Something plunged into Juno's stomach. Was Charley kicking her?

"That's—"

"I'm asking one last time. Confess that you killed Althea. I want to hear you say it. Look at me."

Juno looked into Charley's eyes. The reflection from the fire on the shore had turned them orange. The current was pulling them downstream.

"Althea killed herself." Juno loved saying that. It sounded better than it had in her imagination. It sounded better than the truth.

"I'm not letting go. You might as well say it before you're finished."

"She killed herself, Charley. I never meant it to—"

She was underwater again. She kicked out, tried to push against Charley, but the water was becoming familiar, almost pleasant. It was cooler down here. She'd told Charley the truth—her unending love and devotion—but it hadn't been good enough. She wasn't supposed to die today. This was the day Charley would love her.

Something wrapped itself around her, under her armpits, an embrace. The world became brighter. She was breathing, gagging, struggling. Not the calm death she'd anticipated.

"You're safe now. Only a few more minutes."

Charley's voice had changed. Was this an effect of death? Juno could see the sky, clouds, a too-bright sun spreading across the horizon, igniting everything in its path.

Lying on the sand. Hands pressing into her.

"Breathe."

She breathed out the river that had become part of her. She breathed in life.

When she looked up, it wasn't Charley's face she saw but the face of someone she recognized—someone anyone would recognize.

"You're going to be fine," Lukas Adler said. "Take it easy for a bit."

CHAPTER 40

J UNO HAS OUTDONE even herself. If people weren't dying I'd be begging every awards committee in the field to honor her."

Hal Ledyard had spent the last twenty-four hours locked in what had been Beryl's bedroom, the shades drawn, the lights off, doing nothing but working on his scroll, poring over the code as he delved into the leap virus. The group's suspicions, that Juno Sangstrom had created the code, had to be correct. No one else was capable of this and, anyway, the code—most of it—was written in Juno's invented language.

Of course Charley Pierce also knew this code, but when Ledyard got to the meat of the program and saw an even more complex, more elegant language, one he'd never encountered, one he couldn't hope to crack—no one had so far cracked Juno's somewhat less complex signature coding language—he immediately knew that only Juno could have developed this, pulled this off. It would take decades or centuries for a team of coding experts to get to the point of approaching a theory regarding it, much less unwinding it. Only Juno Sangstrom could have thought of it. Hell, it was leaps and bounds ahead of anything he'd ever seen.

The leap. Even though the code itself was untranslatable, its effect on the visual array was unmistakable. Portions of the unique language had inserted themselves into the photons, no matter what was being displayed. Juno'd devised an ingenious pathway for this section of the code to be transmitted through the filamentation and then, presumably, into the user. An unprecedented breakthrough. Yet the virus it carried was lethal.

"But can we stop it?" Dorian Song looked up from her work. Ledyard had thought he'd never have another student who could equal Juno Sangstrom, but Dorian had come close, and when she'd gone to teach at the Acres and asked him to lecture there, he'd departed Keff. He'd been there long enough and he wanted to work with both Dorian and Jonathan Lee Summers, whose often bizarre theories had an uncanny way of turning into realities. The leap virus was the most striking of the lot of them. He might not like Jonathan Lee, but that never interfered with the work.

"Summers predicted this," Ledyard said. "I'd argued against it. Anyone could see this is impossible. It has to be impossible—but we're all witnesses. It not just possible, it's being done."

"I was at that symposium," Violet Rushman said. "I still read the notes I took there from time to time, for inspiration."

The group had worked through the night again. Glen had fallen asleep on the floor, but he was now lying on his side, his head propped up on his left hand, his right arm draped across the hip of Dorian Song, who'd fallen asleep next to him.

Everyone was awake now.

"Anyone know how to contact Juno? I lost touch with her after she graduated." Ledyard stretched out his legs and yawned.

"Pierce was one of your students, right?" Dorian said. "What was he like?"

"A rich, arrogant bastard," Ledyard, resisting another yawn, said, "but a rich, arrogant bastard with a sizable brain. Unfortunately for him, he was in the same class Juno Sangstrom was in, so he was eclipsed. Well, everyone was. Anyone would be. I myself was. To call Juno Sangstrom a genius is an understatement. We all accept Meet Me now as some kind of throwaway application, but its complexity, its nuances, its ease—we forget this paved the way for the hundreds of programming breakthroughs that followed in its wake."

Ledyard sat back. "I have to stop lecturing. Everyone in this room could give the same talk. And with hair on their head." Ledyard rubbed his bald scalp and laughed.

"I don't usually agree with Jonathan Lee's draconian measures, but I think at this point we must all be in agreement. Before we do anything else, we have to destroy every one of the computers at both the Normandie and at all the Pierce Sangstrom offices." Dorian sat up and leaned back against Glen, who repositioned his right arm so it was encircling her waist.

Violet looked down at her tattered pale blue T-shirt and everyone laughed the kind of uncontrollable laugh that only people who haven't had any sleep are capable of.

"PS delenda est indeed," said the stunning-looking woman who'd just come through Beryl Carson's front door.

Ledyard stood up. "Ed, I didn't think you were going to make it."

"I talked with Ethan last night and he convinced me I had to be here in person. He said something about 'proceeding in the path of the ancients' and I succumbed to the pressure."

Ledyard walked over to Ed and they embraced. Everyone in the room could see how pleased he was that she'd come since they all knew he and Ed Sperry had been seeing each other for years. That was one of the reasons Ledyard had departed Keff, where such relationships were taboo. But they'd never taken the next step even though they'd talked about it.

"The ancients never saw anything like this," Violet said.

"I've been studying the microimages Ethan sent me and one of the reasons I had to come is that I don't quite believe what I'm seeing. I have to inspect these in person."

"Believe it, Ed."

"I cannot accept it."

"You're going to have to eventually—might as well start now," Dorian said. "If you talked with Ethan, does that mean he's feeling better?"

"He's in and out of it. But there doesn't seem to be anything as serious as what's befallen the first victims. And Newell shows definite signs of improvement. Fields is another thing altogether. It's baffling—all of it."

"Welcome to Bafflement Central. But we're putting the pieces together. Jonathan Lee gave us a running start," Dorian said.

"Where is Summers?" Ed Sperry took a seat at the dining table and Ledyard sat down in the chair to her left. She rubbed his back, which she always did when she sensed how tired he was.

"At Althea Pierce's funeral, a big bash out at Tuigen. Pyrotechnics and a cast of thousands. Jonathan Lee went with Sean Meade, the investigator who's working on this. They're hoping to see Juno out there since no one has been able to locate her."

"I picture her as still living in the walk-up she and Pierce had together, but I guess not, hunh? That was a long time ago." Sperry patted Ledyard's shoulders, turned toward the tabletop, and pulled one of the open scrolls toward her.

"Hal, you want to tell me what this mess is? Oh, but look—I can read this part. Is this some sort of joke in the middle of this cryptic gibberish?"

"Seems like it." Ledyard had thought about it, but hadn't developed a theory yet. It definitely wasn't Juno's work.

"I guess there's no way to really test it," Dorian said.

"Maybe find someone who's going to die anyway?" Violet said, but immediately recanted after seeing the disapproving faces in the room, all staring at her. "No, that's a terrible idea. I don't know why I would have mentioned it."

"Because we're all thinking about it, that's why," Dorian said. "And we're all thinking the slogan on your shirt isn't a bad idea either. Pierce

Sangstrom must be destroyed. They're at the epicenter of this catastrophe-in-the-making. There's no getting around it."

"What the hell have I gotten myself into?" Ed Sperry looked up from the scroll and gave Ledyard her most direct gaze.

"Nothing much, Ed. Just a computer virus that's leapt over the divide and is killing its human victims, a code that can't be deciphered, a disease that expresses itself in a multitude of different symptoms, many of them leading to death, and . . . What have I forgotten?" Ledyard looked around at the group of weary scientists, mathematicians, and computer experts.

"That we don't know where Juno Sangstrom is." Violet rubbed the back of her neck.

"That we don't know how to or if we'll be able to get permission to destroy all the computers we want to destroy," Dorian said.

"That someone else must've written part of this code. Who the hell was it? And how did they do it? And why? And a thousand other things." With great effort, Glen pulled himself up to a sitting position.

"That's it?" Ed Sperry said, smiling. "That's nothing."

Through the laughter in the room, Dorian said, "Oh, yeah, and we have to save the world. There's that little thing too."

The laughter ceased. This was no joke. Pierce Sangstrom's presence and influence were worldwide. Everyone on the planet had at least a dozen Pierce Sangstrom programs running constantly on their computers, on their scrolls. The megacorp was everywhere, inextricable from everyday life. A necessity.

If they didn't stop the spread of the leap now, it might be unstoppable. It might be the end of everything.

CHAPTER 41

"AT LEAST IT'S cool down here," Jonathan Lee said.

"Always going for the bright side, aren't you, JL?"

"Wait'll I come up with a nickname for you. You'll be sorry you ever started this."

"When do you think it'll be safe to go back out?"

"Sometime in the next century, after the leap virus has been eliminated, but we don't have that long to wait and also, there's no food down here."

Sean and Jonathan Lee were in the cellar of the Pierces' house, which Sean had started referring to as a palace. She'd spotted the cellar's outside entrance while they were escaping the conflagration on the shoreline. The flames had spread to the trees at the property's edges and were working their way toward the palace, but the palace was constructed of stone and seemed safe, at least for a while.

With everyone rushing to the parking area, this seemed like the best idea. Hide out here and emerge afterward, when the crowd had thinned.

"There was rumored to be food at the funeral, but I guess that's out now."

"My comm's not working. What about yours?" Sean put her comm back in her jacket pocket.

"No. Nothing. It was working out on the lawn, though. Got a message that Ledyard's made some progress and Ed Sperry's at the house now. Ethan must be feeling better. He convinced her she needed to be here."

"I was hoping we'd spot Juno, but I didn't see her. I mean, I didn't see thousands of other people either. Are we absolutely sure she wrote this virus? Couldn't it still be Charley?"

"I talked with Hal about it before I left. It has to be Juno. He taught both of them and Charley isn't up to this sort of thing. He can fix something, he can make something better, but he can't create it—not something this complex."

"I cannot find out where Juno lives, and I thought I had above-average people-location skills. Toby can't come up with anything either. I talked to her this morning. A lot of dead ends."

The color drained from Sean's face. "Ethan is not going to die. He can't."

"He's doing much better. I think he doesn't have the lethal strain of the leap."

"There are different strains? Do you mean mutations?"

"Yes, but there might also be different versions, right from the start. We won't know for sure until we find Juno and get her to tell us what's what."

"You mean even you won't be able to read her coding? I thought you were making progress."

"I'm making as much progress as any normal human could, which is to say, not much. No one's ever been able to translate Juno's coding language into anything recognizable or understandable. Parts of it— well, the syntax is right there, staring at you, daring you to make sense of the arrangements it's creating. But after that, there's only speculation, none of which has ever led to a solution.

"There're contests with very enticing prizes. People have spent years doing nothing but trying to crack open the Sangstrom Complexity, but no one's come close. It's the modern equivalent of the Riemann hypothesis, which people have been trying to prove—unsuccessfully— for centuries. Something that seems accessible and almost familiar, yet no one can get underneath it. If she and Charley Pierce both die and don't reveal the workings of her code before they do, it'll be the mystery of the ages."

"Like finding Juno Sangstrom. Or Morris Walls. I thought maybe he'd be here as well. Althea had been important enough to him that he upended his entire life for her—his marriage, his job, maybe his very existence. If he hadn't had an affair with her, I wouldn't be involved in this. I wouldn't know anything about it."

"You're missing the point, Sean. No one might know anything about this. Every single clue we've gotten toward solving this thing has arisen in some way from your involvement."

"Well, I had nothing to do with the autopsies. I think we can pretty much say Ethan's at the heart of this—of discovering it and of working toward its cure."

"I think it's time we took a peek outside. If the coast is clear, we can make a dash for the parking area and get the hell out of here."

"It's too bad we've missed this opportunity to confront Charley Pierce. Or Juno Sangstrom herself."

Jonathan Lee and Sean climbed the stairs to the swing-out doors leading from the cellar to ground level.

"Ready?" Jonathan Lee said.

"Wait. Wait. I—oh hell. Yesterday I was at the Normandie and—Juno Sangstrom. She must be Milburn. The apartment on the top floor, the one where no one ever answers the door. That must be Sangstrom. She must be the reclusive woman Ziva's told me about."

"She might not be behind the Milburn virus and—" Jonathan Lee paused with his hands up against the doors, ready to open them.

"I didn't tell you, JL. Several of the apartments at the Normandie are owned by someone or some entity named Milburn. That's practically a confession. Juno must live there. She has to. She must be responsible for both the Milburn and the leap viruses. The Milburn was just practice. Now she's moved on to the big time."

"Why would she want to kill anyone? Or make them profoundly ill?"

"You could ask that of almost any murderer. Killing someone else is not so much a solution to a problem as it is the creation of a bigger, never-ending problem. Yet it's done all the time. Back millennia ago they used to talk about motive, like there was a reason people did what they did. Motive is still in play—it can be helpful—but we also know that many motives are unusual, unique, something no one else but the perpetrator would ever be able to define or describe. Or there is no motive other than something as simple as because it can be done or a sort of hobby."

"This is some heinous hobby."

"It is. But maybe to the person doing it, it doesn't seem that way. I wonder what Juno Sangstrom was thinking of when she did this. If she did this. It is Juno. Right, JL?"

"The large part of it is Juno's doing, but there're sections of the code that must have been done by someone else, probably Charley. I'm going to open this door a bit now and see what the lay of the land is. Hang on. Maybe go back down the stairs. We can't know how far the fire's already spread."

"We have to get out of here."

"I agree. This is no way to spend an afternoon. Crashing a funeral we couldn't even see and now trapped in the Pierces' basement. Not exactly the ideal day."

"It will be if we can make real progress toward solving this."

"Stand back."

Jonathan Lee pushed on one of the doors, opening it a few centimeters, then let it fall closed again. He looked down the stairs at Sean.

"I think we can risk it," he said. "There's a crew of firefighters out there now. The house seems relatively untouched by the blaze and they're drenching the roof. Amazingly, there're a number of people still on the grounds. I guess no one can resist a spectacle. I can't see the shoreline, so I don't know what state the fire's in."

"Let's go. Maybe Juno's out there. Or Morris. Or Charley. Or someone who knows something more than we do."

As they emerged, a collective gasp arose from the gathering at the rear of the house. Sean and Jonathan Lee turned around and, following the gaze of the crowd, looked up at the roof, which was now engulfed in flames.

"Good timing," Sean said.

Jonathan Lee grabbed Sean's hand and they sprinted toward the parking area. He was almost a foot taller than Sean, but propelled on by the pure need to survive, she was able to keep up with his long strides.

Although there were still many vehicles in the parking area, Sean's didn't seem to be blocked in. Jonathan Lee and Sean, both gasping for breath after the smoke-infused dash they'd just completed, nodded to each other as they got in the transcer.

Jonathan Lee turned to Sean and said, "Let's get out of here before it's our funeral."

CHAPTER 42

THE MAIN THING on Lukas Adler's mind was how to avoid the publicity. He'd come to Althea's funeral in a subtle disguise that often worked, since he looked quite different under the brim of a hat, but now that he'd rescued Pierce and Sangstrom from a certain death, he might not be able to stay out of this. And the hat was long gone, floating down the river.

"If you think I'm going to thank you for this, I'm not." Charley Pierce had been fuming at Lukas since he'd hauled him to the shore across from the estate, which Lukas saw was now also in flames. "This is your fault. And hers."

Pierce pointed at Juno Sangstrom, who was lying in the sand, half-conscious. Her breathing seemed normal. She hadn't said anything since Lukas had carried her onto the shore, helped her empty her lungs of what looked like several liters of water, and breathed life itself back into her. The summer he'd spent at the medserv, back when he was in school, had come in handy on several occasions, but never as dramatically as this.

"I sent for medical help. They should be here soon."

"Are they going to save my house? The two of you have destroyed everything I care about. Everything that has any meaning for me." Charley glared at Lukas, then at Juno, who grunted and rolled over onto her side. The two of them looked like they'd been in the water for a week, not twenty minutes.

There were so many ways Lukas could play this. He could confront Charley Pierce right now, letting him know he saw him trying to kill

Juno Sangstrom. Saw him push her under the water at least twice—
perhaps three times, he wasn't sure—and Charley'd tried to shove Adler
away while he was rescuing Juno.

Adler could keep silent. He had, so far, although Charley Pierce
had to know Lukas had seen more than just two struggling people in the
river. He'd seen an attempted murder.

Charley must have killed Althea somehow, too, although Lukas
couldn't fathom how it might've worked. Poison seemed a likely culprit.
And something had in fact worked. Althea was dead, and just a few
minutes ago Charley Pierce had been trying to murder his business
partner and would have succeeded if Adler hadn't seen them in the river
and gone out there.

Confronting a murderer was never a good idea. Adler always made
them rewrite scenes where his character was supposed to have a long
diatribe against the villain before the fight scene. He'd been playing
villains himself lately and felt even more strongly about this. Give the
bad guy a chance and he'd use it against you. Lukas wasn't about to give
Charley that kind of opening.

"Meds will be here soon," Lukas said.

"Charley." Juno Sangstrom's first word. She was half sitting up
now. She sounded like someone calling for her lover, not a half-
drowned person about to confront her would-be killer.

"I'm having you both arrested," Charley Pierce said. "Two killers.
How did I ever get involved with you?" He was staring at Juno, and
Lukas was aware Charley might try again to kill her. Then he'd have to
kill Lukas as well, since he'd be a witness.

"You know I had nothing to do with Althea's death. She was my
friend." Lukas stopped himself from telling Charley off. That wouldn't
help matters. Yet if there was ever anyone Lukas wanted to kill, Charley
right now was that person.

"She was at your place when she got sick. What more proof do I
need?"

"She could've been anywhere when she got sick—"

"But she wasn't. She was with you."

"One of her many lovers," Juno said. She was holding her knees to her chest. Her hair was plastered to her head, her floral dress—the only item of clothing she was wearing—was clinging to her body, and her expression was a mix of disdain and disappointment.

"Althea wasn't the kind of person who could be tied down," Lukas said. He'd asked her once if she'd leave Charley. He and Althea had been seeing each other for months and he'd started to think they could have more than just an affair. He could picture them together, as a couple. They each had enough assets to ditch everything and do whatever they pleased.

But Althea had turned him down. No hesitation. *I don't do that,* she'd said and he'd countered with, *You're married to Charley, aren't you?* She insisted that was different, that Charley needed her and that Lukas didn't. But they could still be lovers.

Althea'd been right—he didn't need her. And now he couldn't even talk to her, swim a few laps with her, have a surprise afternoon with her.

"Well, she's burnt to a crisp." Juno smirked.

"You should've let her drown," Charley, pointing at Juno, said to Adler. "What she so justly deserves."

"I should've let you drown," Lukas said to Charley. "I'm still wondering why the hell I rescued you."

"I didn't need you to rescue me. I can swim."

"Then I should've let you swim." Charley would've died if Lukas hadn't rescued him. The current was dragging both Charley and Juno under by the time Lukas, a well-conditioned, strong swimmer, got to them.

Where the hell were the meds? Lukas had commed for them ages ago. Of course there was a large crew across the river at Charley's ego mansion, but there must've been some meds left to do the rest of the work in the district.

Maybe he should just jump back in the river and swim to the other side. Leave Charley and Juno here by themselves to work out their problems. Or to kill each other.

"I'll never forget who saved me," Juno Sangstrom said. She was aiming her words at Charley but she was looking at Adler.

"I'll never forget you killed Althea and that you're trying to bring down Pierce Sangstrom," Charley said. "You're going to spend the rest of your life in a prison cell. It's too bad they don't execute killers anymore. Although I rather like the thought of you in prison, separated from your beloved computers, rotting away, going mad."

Charley had changed his accusations. He was now blaming Juno, not Lukas, for Althea's death. Lukas became more certain that Charley himself was behind it.

Even if he passed the two-century mark, which many people did, Lukas would never forget today. A day when he'd rescued both Pierce and Sangstrom even though he'd had a shining opportunity to let the two of their cruel lives end in the river.

Adler looked over at the opposite shore. The estate house was being consumed by the flames. The firefighters appeared to have given up on the house and were focusing on keeping the fire from spreading any further. Althea's funeral pyre continued to emit embers and sparks. Many people were still standing on the lawn past the house, watching.

Althea would've loved this. She'd be writing a fabula about it while it was happening.

Lukas should've done a better job convincing her she could leave Charley. She'd be alive now. Instead she was a heap of ashes being pushed around by the increasing wind. Gone, scattered, disappearing into the unknown.

No one spoke for a while. It was better like this.

Lukas closed his eyes. He could picture Althea, her fiery red hair blowing in the breeze, her naked body in his pool, her imaginative mind always at work.

"She killed herself," Juno said, as though she were reading Lukas's thoughts.

He couldn't let this pass by without saying something. "She didn't. I was right there. And Althea would never've killed herself."

"Her killer should know," Charley said. Lukas wasn't sure if Charley meant him or Juno. Maybe he meant both of them.

"But she did kill herself," Juno said. "I don't mean she intended to. I'm not sure who she wanted to kill, but it was her code that did it, turning my program into a murder machine. I hadn't meant—"

"Wait, wait. Wait." Lukas wanted to make sure he was hearing what he was hearing. "Are you saying a computer program—your computer program—killed Althea?"

"That wasn't how I'd programmed it. Look for yourself, Charley. You have it. You can see the part that's not mine. It was done by a rank amateur."

Was this what a board meeting at Pierce Sangstrom was like? The two principals heaving accusations at each other?

"Juno, you're forgetting how well I know you. How well I know your tricks. The code is entirely yours, including the crude parts. No one else has touched it," Charley said.

"You've touched it." Juno was shivering now, holding on to herself. There was no way to help her since Lukas had ditched his jacket before he went into the water—and it'd be soaked now anyway—and getting near her to hold her was out of the question.

"I did some light editing," Charley said. "I haven't even gotten into it yet. Not to any extent."

"Althea touched it too." Juno rubbed her hands over her arms and pulled her legs in closer. Lukas took off his shirt. It was sopping wet but it was better than nothing. He went over to Juno and draped his shirt around her shoulders. She pulled it close around her. Still staring at Charley. Still not addressing Lukas, who was wondering why he'd bothered. The world would be rid of two apex predators if only he hadn't saved them both.

"She didn't have access to it," Charley said. He was as drenched as Lukas and Juno were, but he was carrying it off as though he were in his element. Maybe he was an amphibian. Lukas had always thought there was something slimy about Charley Pierce. Why hadn't Althea seen it? Left him?

"Charley, sometimes I wonder why I ever fell in love with you."

So that was the connection. Sangstrom in love with Pierce, although she apparently hated him as well, and Pierce had been trying to kill her just a few minutes ago. That these were the people who'd given Meet Me to the world, bringing millions of people together, was extreme irony.

Lukas tried to shut his mind against the conversation. Pictured himself at his house, swimming laps, lying on the deck, then in the kitchen, preparing dinner. Watching the sunset. Away from everything except the calm he'd discovered inside himself many years earlier, the calm he wanted to honor, to nurture.

"Stop kidding yourself, Juno. You're not in love with me," Charley said. "You're in love with yourself. You're your entire world but it's not enough. You want everything for yourself. That's why you had to kill Althea. Don't think you can get away with this."

"Charley—don't."

Lukas came back outside himself to see Charley Pierce with his hands around Juno Sangstrom's neck, about to strangle her. Lukas got up and walked the short distance to where the two lovers, haters, business partners, killers—whatever they were, they had to be separated before one or both of them died.

Charley was a big man and somewhat taller than Lukas, but Charley's size was no match for Lukas's strength and athleticism. He did laps every day and worked out regularly. He pulled Charley away from Juno, then pushed him to the ground.

"Stay," Lukas said, like he was talking to a disobedient dog, although Lukas had never spoken to a dog in this way and wouldn't. Dogs were beautiful creatures and Charley Pierce was one of the ugliest humans on the planet. Lukas held out his right hand, palm down, as though that would keep Charley Pierce in place.

"Stop interfering. Who are you to come along and get between us?" Juno, whose life Lukas had now saved twice, was berating him?

"Say the word. Next time I'll let him kill you." But Lukas stood between the two, blocking Charley's access to Juno. No one was going to kill anyone. Not while he could stop it.

"Today was supposed to be a celebration for Althea." Charley had sat back down and was picking up some small rocks lying on the ground around him.

"It's just like you, Charley, to want to give a party for a murderer." Juno was sneering.

Charley threw one of the rocks at her, but Lukas deflected it and it fell to the ground at his feet.

"Stop it. Just stop it now," Lukas said. It was too bad Althea was dead and was missing all this. She would've relished it. But Lukas just wanted to leave, go back to his house, absent himself from the anger and accusations. Bask in the silence.

The meds finally arrived. Lukas had to bear up under the nonsensical obsequious awe people gave to celebrities. But he appreciated the blanket wrapped around him and how he was now well rid of the despicable Charley Pierce and Juno Sangstrom, who were being tended to by a team of meds. They'd stopped arguing and were putting on a convincing act of being cordial business partners. Lukas wanted to laugh but kept it to himself.

One of the meds was talking to Charley. "So sorry about your house, Mr. Pierce. And on the day of your wife's funeral."

"I can rebuild the house," Charley said.

Today. The same hours, the same cycles as any day had.

But the vibrant, talented Althea Pierce was dead.

Lukas had rescued two of the worst—and most powerful—people on the planet from an imminent death.

And there was apparently a computer program that could kill people.

Now Lukas did laugh.

CHAPTER 43

ETHAN WAS FAR from cured—if there could be a cure for the leap—but he'd come through the worst of it, at least he'd convinced himself he had, and was feeling much improved. He was still in his room in the isolation ward but Booth had removed the tent, as Ethan's viral load had all but disappeared. And, as Ethan had explained to Booth, there was no evidence the virus was transmissible from person to person. It seemed likely that only the virus that came directly from a computer was capable of causing infection, although this wasn't a certainty.

Booth had gone over Ethan's notes, and he'd started working on finding out as much as he could about comvirna, the leap virus. Ed Sperry was here now, and she'd work with Booth.

Ziva Walls, asleep in the high-backed visitor chair, stirred, then stretched.

"Ethan. You're awake." She looked over at him and stretched again.

"So are you."

"This was the most uncomfortable chair I've ever slept in, but it was wonderful. I suppose anywhere will do if you're tired enough."

"I've slept on a slab at the morgue. Not ideal but better than the floor."

"How very morbid."

"Do a medical examiner's job for a while and you'll eliminate the word from your vocabulary."

"Because everything's morbid?"

"Or nothing is. It's hard to tell after a while. Zee, you don't have to be here. You should go home and get some proper rest." Axel Booth had told Ethan that Ziva had been here since he'd been admitted.

"Oh no. I'm not leaving until you do."

"Stubborn, aren't you?"

"It's one of my best qualities." Ziva laughed and Ethan joined her. They had the sort of connection he'd thought he and Sean might develop one day, but they never had, yet he and Ziva hadn't needed to develop anything—it was just there.

"Zee, if I ever get out of this place—"

"When you get out."

"All right, when I get out. And after the leap's resolved . . . What do you think about us getting together for something other than, well, all this—solving the leap, lying around in an isolation ward? You know."

"It's not possible."

Ethan had been concerned she'd say something like this. After all, Ziva Walls had a far different life from Ethan's. She obviously had enormous financial resources since she lived at the swanky Normandie, and she seemed not to have a profession or a job of any kind. She'd had at least one famous lover, Kaj Banerjee, and although Oliver Hirata wasn't famous, he'd also been wealthy. And her missing husband, Morris, had been a key employee at the Pierce Sangstrom megacorp. Ethan Stiles couldn't possibly live up to Ziva's usual expectations.

She socialized with a different sort of person than Ethan could ever be or would want to be, although he wasn't sure he wanted to keep on with his current work. There had to be something else. After this was all over he'd find it.

Ziva came over and sat down on the side of Ethan's bed. She took his hand in hers. He steeled himself for the rejection he knew was coming his way. She was softening it by getting closer and holding his hand—for comfort or pity.

"Let me try to explain," she said. "It's not possible because it already is. It's not something that's going to happen in the future. It's something that happened almost as soon as I met you."

"I'm not sure what you're saying." He'd been expecting her to describe why they couldn't be together but she seemed to be saying something entirely different. Yet his mind was still foggy, although it was no longer as distorted as it had been when he first became ill.

"You're asking the wrong person to explain themselves, Ethan. I don't know how to. I just know that this feels good and true, that I knew you right from the beginning, and that I'm not going to wait until this crisis or any other event or circumstance is resolved.

"Look what happened to Oliver and Kaj. And to Althea Pierce. Everything could be over in a flash. I don't want to wait. I won't wait. But I'll understand if you don't—"

Ethan tried to sit forward, but he couldn't manage it yet, so he pulled Ziva toward him.

"Ziva." He put his hand through her cropped brown hair and she leaned over and kissed him then put her head on his chest. He put his arms around her and sighed.

"I don't want to do anything to hurt Sean," Ziva said. "She's been a good friend. She's been amazing. I understand why you and she were a couple. I like you both."

Ethan hugged her closer. "I don't think you have any worries there. Sean and Jay are—I don't know what to call it. They have something together that she and I never had. It's as though there's an inherent blockage of sorts between any two people and in order for it to be dissolved there has to be some compelling force that breaks through. Sean and I never found it. Never had it."

"It's wrong of me to be happy about that, but I am." Ziva sat up.

Ethan realized she was still holding his hand. She said, "Because if you and Sean were still together, then this couldn't happen. Or it would happen but I'd have to stay away or pretend. And I've already done enough pretending in my life. My entire relationship with Morris, for example. A complete pretense. I was supposed to love him because he was so perfect for me. Everyone said so. I said so. So I loved him. But the blockage, the barrier—it never budged. In fact, it grew larger the longer we were together. I'm getting a divorce, you know. Or maybe you didn't know."

"Sean told me. I think it's a good thing. For yourself, I mean. Don't want you thinking I'm so selfish."

"Be selfish, Ethan. I am. I want you. I want to be with you. I probably shouldn't tell you this but I'm in love with you. I know, it's too soon and I don't know you, but I do know myself. I know how I feel when you're around. When I think about you. Hell, I sound like a teenager."

Ethan laughed. "You're not saying anything I haven't thought myself. I'm just reluctant to say it. I don't want to create something that will end abruptly. In case I'm not really cured of this. There's been a lot of death, Zee. We can't ignore that or forget it."

"Maizy's still alive and so is Jordan Fields. Not everyone who's got the leap has died. And all those people at the Normandie who had positive test results—they're still alive and maybe they're not even sick. What if the leap kills only certain kinds of people? Well, I mean, I don't know what I'm talking about, but perhaps there's some certain kind of person, with a particular body chemistry or genetic whatever or diet, and the leap affects them in a different way."

Her words cleared the fog from Ethan's consciousness and he saw a new path forward. "Ziva Walls. I love you," he said. "That's the very insight I've been looking for. I've been so busy investigating each individual case and isolating the pathogen that I've failed to consider what the victims had in common and what the survivors have in common. I have to start in on this immediately. I should be in the lab but I'll have to get Booth and Ed to do it for me. And get Jay's crew over at Beryl's involved. Hell, it could be something as elementary as blood type or genetotemporal articulation. Damn it. I can't seem to get up." He tried again but his body wouldn't obey.

"Ethan, you were very ill. You have to recuperate. I might not know what genetotempy-something-or-other is, but someone who's been as sick as you've been needs to rest."

"Zee, before I alert Booth and we have to spend the next hour on our comms, I have a request."

"All right. Tell me."

"I'd like you to kiss me again. For its therapeutic effect, you understand. Not just because of—"

Ziva leaned down and kissed Ethan again, ending not just his words but his thoughts of anything but Ziva and how he never wanted to let go of this extraordinary sensation that being with her created, a sensation radiating throughout his very existence.

"Ziva," he said between kisses, "I had no idea what I was missing."

"Ethan," she said, her palm on his cheek, "thank you for coming back to life. I was damned scared. I thought we'd never get to this." She kissed him again. "And I wanted this so much."

"No excitement. Do I have to remind every patient about this? And Ethan? You should know better."

Ethan looked past Ziva and saw Axel Booth standing in the doorway, his arms folded across his chest, a smile on his haggard face. "And while I'm here, let me remind you both: five kids is a huge responsibility. I haven't gotten any rest at home for over a decade."

"We haven't gotten around to discussing the number of kids yet." Ethan thought his cheeks would hurt later. He hadn't smiled this much in a long time.

Ziva sat up, but stayed on Ethan's bed.

"We'll have two," she said. "I've already decided. No need to discuss it."

"How did you end up with five?" Ethan didn't know anyone else with so many children. But two sounded right to him. With Ziva. He could almost picture it. But first he had to get out of here alive and make sure the rest of the world wasn't felled by the leap before they could stop it.

"Two sets of twins and an accident." Booth was smiling along with Ethan and Ziva.

"Axel, I've got—and this was Ziva's brilliant idea—a new angle to investigate. This could be the break we've been looking for. It's time we started looking at what the commonalities are among the victims who died."

"I'm meeting Ed Sperry at your lab in a half hour. We'll get right to it."

"Ethan, I want to help," Ziva said. "What can I do?"

"Go home," Ethan said.

"But—"

"I'm not trying to get rid of you." Ethan didn't want Ziva to leave, especially not now that their connection was coalescing, but the leap had to be stopped before anyone else got ill or died from it.

"See if you can get to the residents of the Normandie who haven't responded yet," Ethan said, "and plead with the people who tested positive to make one more visit to the lab so Axel and Ed can take samples from them. Assuming those people are still alive, which I hope to hell they are. Maybe you could get Sean to help you."

"Didn't she and Jay go to Althea's funeral?"

"They did?" Ethan must have slept through this fact.

"Why would they go there?" Booth said as the smile left his face.

"I think Sean was hoping Juno Sangstrom would be there." Ziva looked back and forth between Ethan and Booth.

"Ziva. Ethan. I guess you haven't heard. It's all over the mesh. Althea's funeral—it turned into a disaster. The bonfire on Althea's funeral pyre—"

Ethan tried to pull himself further up but he still couldn't. "Who did the autopsy?" he said as he collapsed back into the pillows behind his torso.

"Ethan, you—"

"Prentiss? The incompetent hack?"

"I couldn't stop Pierce."

"What the hell are you trying to say, Axel?"

"There wasn't an autopsy. Charley Pierce intervened, got someone to authorize her release, and took her body. He said he wouldn't have her chopped apart. Her wishes and his were more important than 'mere science.'"

"And now it's too late. Damn it all. Althea Pierce was an unusual case. The first one who was improving and then succumbed. We need her data. Even Prentiss could have done something, no matter how lousy it was. And didn't someone tell Pierce her autopsy could give us the information we need about the leap?"

"I confronted him when he came here but he wouldn't listen to me, Ethan. In fact, no one in power will. They're all afraid of Charley Pierce, of what he could do to them."

"If I die, I want you to do the autopsy, Axel. Don't wait for anyone to give you permission."

"Ethan. You're not going to die." Ziva grabbed his hand again. "Don't say it."

"I mean it, Axel."

"I haven't done an autopsy since med school."

"Nothing's really changed since then. You'll remember. Promise me."

"All right, Ethan, if it'll make you happy."

"Talking about Ethan's autopsy isn't making me happy," Ziva said.

"Every time I feel like we're getting somewhere with the leap, something else happens and we lose ground. We can't afford to have any more setbacks. Ziva, you should get out of here, start getting to the residents at the Normandie."

"Dr. Booth, you were saying something about a bonfire?"

"Althea's funeral pyre was lit and the fire got out of control. I gather from what I read that the Pierces' house burned down along with much of the surrounding forest."

Ethan succeeded in pushing himself up a half inch. "Was anyone hurt?"

"There were thousands of people in attendance. Not everyone's been accounted for. Pierce himself was just found along with Sangstrom."

"Sangstrom was there?"

"Ethan." Ziva grasped his hand between both of hers. "I haven't heard from Sean in hours. Or Jonathan Lee."

She let go of Ethan's hand, pushed off the bed, and got her bag off the floor, rummaging through it until she found her comm.

Ethan saw her hands trembling as the abyss threatened to drag him back down into its depths.

CHAPTER 44

I WANT TO make love to you in my office and I don't want to lock the door."

Althea hadn't known Morris Walls could be so daring, but maybe the way Oliver Hirata had looked at her or the way she'd looked at him had urged Morris to try out new tactics.

"Doesn't Charley come by without warning sometimes?"

"Yes."

"Is that part of your fantasy?"

"He's just such a bastard. Head of the world's most powerful, most inescapable megacorp yet it's never enough for him. He wants power— he wants *ownership*—over everything and everyone in the universe. He deserves to see his wife making love with someone else, someone who can please her."

Althea wondered if Morris was just using her to get back at Charley and Pierce Sangstrom itself? Althea could use anyone she wanted to— and had—but nobody would use her.

"I'll think about it," she said, then cut off contact with Morris for three days.

Instead she had lunch with Charley, which she almost never did, and walked back to his office with him.

"This is a pleasant surprise, Althea. We should do this more often," Charley said.

"All right," Althea said. "Let's make a regular thing of it. Every Wednesday sound good to you?"

Charley agreed. She saw the look of hope in his eyes, the look that said he'd do anything for her, if only she'd ask. Anything, that is, that didn't involve Sangstrom.

On her way down the hall after leaving Charley, Althea stopped at Morris's office, opened the door.

"Busy?" she said.

"Not at all," he said, folding his scroll.

"Good to see you."

"Why don't you come in for a while?"

"Can't. In a hurry." She left and let her frustration and need build. If Morris didn't feel the same way, she'd forget about him.

The next Wednesday, after a dull lunch with Charley, she stopped by Morris's office again.

Morris got up from his desk, opened the door all the way, and said, "Come in, Mrs. Pierce. So good to see you. I have something that might interest you."

He shut the door behind her, not locking it.

They both stripped. His shades were open. His office, down the hall from Charley's, was on the seventeenth floor, so no one outside could see them, but it was still thrilling. Everything about it was thrilling— what Morris was doing, what Althea was doing, the open shades to the sky, the thought that Charley could hear them, the added thought that Charley might come in.

After Morris was finished for the second time, Althea said, "You were right. We should have done this immediately. We shouldn't've waited."

"I had a meeting with Charley yesterday and he told me how you were going to have lunch with him every Wednesday. Yes?"

"Yes."

"Made me wonder if he knows about us. Bragging you were meeting with him once a week, as though his wife were giving him special attention."

"Maybe he does know." Althea was overcome with an urgent need for Charley to realize she had a lover right down the hall from his office. Morris had been so right—doing it here with him made everything so much more exciting.

"I'll make sure not to have plans on Wednesday afternoons, then. Well, not plans anyone other than you will know about."

Two Wednesdays later, while they were taking a break and with Althea still astride his lap, Morris said, "I have something interesting you might like to see." He reached around her and grabbed his computer off the table by the sofa that was the scene of most of their Wednesday activities.

He cast the array behind them on the sofa and showed her what must have been some kind of application, but Althea couldn't make sense of it.

"What is this?" she said.

"It's Juno's latest."

"Are you working with her now?"

Was Juno going to come between her and yet another man she was more than a little interested in? Wasn't it bad enough that Juno Sangstrom was a permanent wedge between her and Charley? Even though Charley didn't care about her the way he cared about Althea—the way he loved Althea—but he did care about Juno Sangstrom's talents. Althea's many and glorious talents were useless to Charley. He tolerated them and would go to awards dinners with her, but it wasn't like she could do anything to further the inescapable, ever-present tentacles of the Pierce Sangstrom grip on the universe, not the way Juno could. And she suspected there could be more, although that was just a suspicion.

"Working with Juno Sangstrom?" Morris said. "Are you kidding me? Charley won't let anyone else near her. Or maybe it's Juno who won't let anyone other than Charley near her. No one's really sure. But it's like she's a god living on Mount Olympus and a mere mortal like myself isn't qualified to have an audience with her. Like I'd be struck down by the intense light emanating from her corpus. Or expire from the awe of merely getting a glimpse of her. She doesn't even come to important policy meetings here. I don't think she's ever been in the building. At least not since I started working here."

"Then how do you know this is Juno's?"

"No one else could do this. It's on another level, even another level from anything else Juno's ever done."

Althea started getting dressed although she and Morris weren't finished yet, if they could ever finish.

Morris put his hand on a place on Althea's body that usually caused her to forget everything else and turn her attention back to Morris, but even though it had the same effect as always, Althea closed the front of her dress and slipped into her shoes. She'd been in a silent competition with the supposed genius Juno Sangstrom for years. Juno was forever floating in the space between her and Charley and now she'd intruded herself into her passionate world with Morris.

"Is she as attractive as she was when she was young?" Althea had caught a glimpse of Juno on campus at Keff many years ago and had been shocked at her iridescent beauty, having previously been certain she was a plain, maybe even ugly, nobody. Physically. There was no arguing with her mental prowess.

"I've never met her," Morris said, trying to bring Althea back into their ecstatic connection.

Juno Sangstrom. Did Althea have to compete with her yet again? Was she inexorably attracted to the kind of man who'd love her but continue to worship Juno?

"I need some ice water," Althea said.

"Stay put. I'll get it for you." Morris got dressed and left his office just long enough for Althea to copy Juno's latest masterwork.

Althea might not be the coding genius Juno Sangstrom was, but she wasn't completely ignorant on the topic.

That night, while she was in bed with Charley, who always wanted her with great urgency when he sensed she was seeing someone else—and perhaps he'd heard her and Morris if not today but on another Wednesday afternoon—he said something that compelled her to delve even deeper into Juno's new program.

"I've got something new on the horizon. Something extraordinary. I'm going to own the world. The universe itself."

"You already own a lot of it." Althea owned a portion of it herself, but not half so much as Charley did.

"Not like this," Charley said. "Not the way I'm going to. Getting everyone in my thrall."

If Charley thought this vainglorious declaration would cause her to drop everyone else and come to him the way he wanted her to, he didn't know Althea, who now wanted nothing more than to destroy his plans.

Her first task would be to ruin Juno Sangstrom, the plan's obvious mastermind. Afterward she'd work on Charley himself. Although without Juno, Charley would already be ruined.

Just before three a.m., her most creative time, Althea crept out of bed and went into Charley's study. His computer was on and she easily found the program Morris had shown her. No point in using what she'd downloaded onto her scroll when she could work off Charley's own version. Ah yes. Right there.

Sometimes she was so clever, she amazed herself.

At five, when Althea went back to bed, she fell asleep smiling.

CHAPTER 45

"CAN YOU SEE?"

"Keep going. You must be on the road."

Black smoke and wafting flakes and chunks of charred material blocked the sightlines on all sides of the transcer. Sean had opened a window to try to get a better view but started choking immediately.

"The auto hasn't worked in years," Sean said.

"You mean it worked at one time?" Jonathan Lee was driving since he'd done a better job of pretending to be able to discern what was ahead of them.

"Before I bought it," Sean said. "Allegedly."

"Mine doesn't work either." And Jonathan Lee had a brand-new transcer but the auto functions were a bust. And anyway, it was back at the Acres. He'd taken the magrail to Osada City.

"Do you suppose some of what we're seeing is, you know, parts of . . ."

"I was trying to avoid that thought, but, yes, I think it's not unlikely."

"I missed my chance to talk with Juno Sangstrom. She must've been there, don't you think?"

"No one's seen Juno for years, not since her time at Keff."

"That's the last image I found of her. I might not've even recognized her if I had seen her."

The smoke started clearing. Jonathan Lee was driving on the grass on the side of the road and he swerved back into the lane.

"We should go straight to the Normandie. If Juno wasn't at the funeral, then she's at home, hiding behind her Milburn front. Two of those apartments are on the same floor as Zee's. She could've seen her and didn't realize it."

Jonathan Lee sped up, passing every transcer in their way. Sean talked with Ziva, who'd been worried about them. Jonathan Lee commed Ledyard, but heard Violet Rushman shouting in the backyard.

"The prize is mine. I knew I could do it." Violet's voice was overtaken by Glen's. "You're not going to give me any credit?"

"I'll thank you at the ceremony," Violet said over applause and whistles.

"What the hell is happening over there?" Sean said just as Ledyard's voice came over Jonathan Lee's comm.

"Violet Rushman's exceeded the impossible. She's broken Juno Sangstrom's unbreakable code."

"We'll get there as fast as we can," Jonathan Lee said, pushing Sean's beat-up transcer to a speed she couldn't believe it was capable of.

Now they could solve the leap without needing anything from Juno Sangstrom. It didn't matter where she lived or if they could talk with her. They had what they needed. For the first time since Oliver Hirata's death, there was real hope.

But just as they got to Beryl's house and were about to go in, the elation Sean and Jonathan Lee had been basking in was crushed into oblivion when Ziva commed.

Ethan had relapsed and was unresponsive.

CHAPTER 46

MAIZY NEWELL WAS having yet another hallucination. She'd been having a lot of them lately. Or maybe they were dreams. In one of these whatever-they-weres, she was in Oliver Hirata's apartment—a place she had never visited, since they had to be careful. He'd said so. He didn't want to do anything to jeopardize her job. Her lousy job at the front desk of the Normandie. Like she couldn't find a hundred other jobs just like it if that one had been jeopardized or terminated.

At the time she'd thought he was being protective of her, gracious, kind, considerate. Had he been? Their interlude had been the highlight of a terrible year for her. She'd thought they were falling in love although he'd never said so. She'd never said so either.

Now she was in his apartment. They must have gotten serious. Wait. They must have gotten back together. Hadn't he dropped her? Gone back with Ziva Walls or maybe he was with Althea Pierce. She couldn't remember.

That he'd invited her into his apartment was a stunning change. Yet he wasn't there. Instead, sitting on the sofa was a smiling skeleton.

"Why don't you sit down?" the skeleton said, patting the seat next to her.

Maizy sat. The skeleton seemed to have a lot of authority. Maizy didn't want to lose her job. It was replaceable but it was easier to just stay where she was. There was less to prove.

"I see you're wearing one of my husband's discarded shirts," said the skeleton. No longer smiling. Stern, disapproving.

Maizy looked down. She wasn't wearing her itchy uniform. PS Delenda Est, her worn pastel blue tee said. Maizy moved away from the skeleton, who must've been Althea Pierce. The skeleton didn't look quite like the same woman who'd sailed by her in the lobby of the Normandie, arm in arm with Oliver Hirata.

"Oliver is in love with me and doesn't care about you. Also, you should be aware that any protest against Pierce Sangstrom is always punished. Severely."

Maizy thought about saying she wasn't protesting, but she was. No one company—or person—should have the power Pierce Sangstrom had.

Charley Pierce came into the room. He was more recognizable than the skeleton of Althea Pierce, who Maizy would have recognized immediately if she'd had flesh on her bones. These were famous people. They were more than people, they were demigods.

"Ah, Maizy, how nice to see you." Charley Pierce knew who she was? How could he? She wasn't wearing her uniform so her name badge wasn't present.

"You are not permitted to visit with my wife," Charley said, but not to Maizy. She couldn't tell who he was addressing.

Maizy looked out over the vista of Osada City. The view was as spectacular as Oliver Hirata had told her it was. He'd told her a lot of things but he hadn't mentioned that he knew a skeleton and Charley Pierce.

"Have some snacks," Oliver Hirata said. He was naked and Maizy was impressed with how relaxed he was with no clothes on and Charley Pierce and Althea Pierce's skeleton in his apartment. And Maizy, who didn't belong there.

She turned over.

Maizy was driving a snazzy new transcer. Bright yellow. Oliver Hirata was sitting on the passenger side and laughing.

"Did you enjoy the Convergence?" he said, his voice seeming to emanate from outside the transcer even though he was sitting right there.

"I loved it," Maizy said. "Thank you for taking me. I love you."

"Don't bother," Oliver said. "I'm in love with Ziva Walls. You must love someone else. I'm dead anyway."

That's right. Oliver was dead. Yet here he was, in Maizy's shiny new transcer, an object she could never afford. How had she purchased this? Did Oliver give it to her? Why would he?

The humming sound she often heard got louder. She tried to speak. She tried to listen.

Now she was in a room that looked like a hospital room. Maizy didn't like hospitals so this was a nightmare. Was she sick? She felt fine although she couldn't feel anything.

Murmuring voices around her were speaking in a code she didn't understand.

She wanted to be left alone. She wanted never to be left alone again.

"I think she's doing better," someone said.

"Do you think Dr. Stiles . . . ?"

"Not in here."

The skeleton from Oliver Hirata's apartment came into the hospital-like room and laughed. "Life is wasted on someone like you," the specter of Althea Pierce said just as Maizy collapsed into a pitch-black trance.

CHAPTER 47

LUKAS ADLER COULDN'T decide what the best course of action was. Usually he made immediate, definite decisions and refused to look back. But this was different. What was the point of telling anyone, including anyone in authority, that Charley Pierce had been attempting to kill Juno Sangstrom when he'd rescued both of them? If Juno herself didn't want to press charges, then what business was it of his?

While the medservs were taking Charley, Juno, and Lukas to the clinic, Lukas had stayed silent while Charley and Juno put on an act so convincing that Lukas, a trained actor, had to admire it. He'd just seen the raw truth of what these two were really like, but with an audience they became the best of friends, congenial, even joking with each other about what they'd just endured, thanking Lukas for helping them out on such a sad, tragic day.

He left them at the clinic. The meds in attendance had wanted to observe Lukas, but he didn't want to be observed, so he signed a waiver and left, then wandered around Osada City, mulling over what had just occurred, trying to make sense of it. Althea dead. Charley Pierce a would-be murderer. The reclusive Juno Sangstrom out of her mind. And a computer virus that killed people.

After a while Lukas found himself back at the Genesia Clinic. Habit, he guessed, after having spent so much time there waiting in vain for Althea to recover. He walked inside and went up to the isolation floor, where he'd spent so much time. No one stopped him. He was

Lukas Adler. He could do whatever he pleased—one of the few advantages of being well known.

Lukas walked by Maizy Newell's room. He'd sometimes go in and sit with her, just to get away from Charley and their constant fighting. To get away from his dire thoughts about Althea's probable fate. Maizy Newell was someone he had no connection to and he was always left alone here in her room.

He went in and sat down in the chair by her bed. He'd been in here so often that he felt he knew Maizy. He recognized her, at any rate, which, to Lukas Adler's fans, was the equivalent of knowing someone.

Life was absurd. That was the conclusion he'd come to. Althea had been killed by a computer virus. Juno Sangstrom was in love with someone who tried to murder her and would have succeeded if Lukas hadn't shown up when he did. Lukas Adler was sitting in the visitor chair in the hospital room of someone he didn't know.

He started laughing.

"What's so funny?"

He looked up. Maizy Newell, who hadn't been conscious any of the times he'd been in her room, was sitting up in her bed, staring at him. Her hair was a wild mass, a tangle of brown seaweed, and her eyes were a deep black abyss.

"Life," he said. "And death."

"I just had a conversation with a skeleton," Maizy said.

"I don't doubt it."

"Althea Pierce."

"I used to know her," Lukas said. "She died. Her funeral was today."

"That explains it," Maizy said. She squinted at him. "Are you Lukas Adler?"

"Usually."

"I keep having these dreams or nightmares or hallucinations. You're probably another one. Are you alive? The people in my hallucinations are mostly dead."

"Last time I checked."

"Is Charley Pierce alive? He was there too. In Oliver's apartment."

Did she mean Oliver Hirata, the fellow who'd died in the garage? Althea had had an affair with him. An interlude. She was going to use details from it in a fabula she was working on.

"Charley's alive. I just saved his life."

"Too bad."

"No kidding. Say, did you know Oliver Hirata?"

"Sure. He took me to a Convergence. A long time ago."

"Should I get Dr. Booth?" Lukas thought maybe someone should come tend to Maizy, since as far as he knew, she'd been comatose or unconscious for days or perhaps weeks.

"Who?"

"He's your doctor."

"Then I am in a hospital. I thought so, but it's hard to tell. Everything's been kind of a muddle."

"You've been sick, but it seems like you're getting better."

"All except for my current hallucination. Having a chat with Lukas Adler. Ridiculous. But it's better than being berated by a skeleton."

"You have a point."

They both laughed, and Lukas stopped caring about Charley Pierce or Juno Sangstrom. Here was a genuine person. No pretense. No pose.

"I'll get Dr. Booth," he said.

"Thanks. Maybe he can explain what's happening."

"No reason he can't take a stab at it."

CHAPTER 48

WHY COULDN'T THIS have started earlier?" Charley Pierce was standing at the window of his private room at Osada City Hospital, watching the heavy sheets of rain while he waited for the results of the endless tests they'd put him through.

He was alone yet Althea seemed to be present somehow. He was speaking to her, not expecting an answer.

"Damn it. Tuigen could've been saved if only it had started raining a few hours ago."

"And some lives would've been saved as well," Charley's haughty doctor said, interrupting his thoughts.

"Althea died. Today was her funeral. Or didn't you know?" He saw the doctor reflected in the window. Hair piled up on top of her head and a golden chain around her neck.

Doctors were among the stupidest people Charley had ever had contact with, and he'd known some idiots. The medserv, another of Pierce Sangstrom's many triumphant creations, could outdoctor any doctor Charley had ever known or heard of. When you became unnecessary you lost your mental edge.

"Eight people died out at your house," said the doctor. Charley hadn't bothered to learn her name.

"Stop spreading rumors."

Charley didn't know if this was a rumor or the truth but he was hoping it was a rumor. Having eight people die at Althea's funeral wasn't a good look for Pierce Sangstrom, although it should be easy enough to cover over. One of Morana's few talents was damage control. He'd hand this over to her. Have her be useful for a change.

"Stop denying the truth," the doctor said.

"I agreed to stay here at your insistence."

Charley brushed past the doctor and got halfway down the hall before he realized he was wearing only a hospital gown. But, so what? He was Charley Pierce. Hospital gowns could become the latest fad, the way pale blue T-shirts had become and still were.

He continued down the hall and found the door to the stairwell.

When he got downstairs he saw Juno Sangstrom standing in the hospital entryway, fully dressed. She seemed to be looking for someone. Her ride, maybe. Charley held his breath. If he played this right, he could cause an accident when her ride arrived and he'd finally be rid of her. She was not just the most persistent annoyance in his life but also Althea's killer. One of them.

"Charley, my dear." Juno caught sight of him and half ran to his side. She put her arm around his neck and kissed him like they were a passionate couple and she hadn't seen him in decades. When she was finished, she stepped back. "Charley. You're not dressed. We'll have to go to your place and find you something."

Charley's imagination had its hands around Juno's neck and was strangling her, but he couldn't very well do that to her here at the hospital, not with other people standing just a few meters away from them.

"Yes, let's go to my place," Charley said, putting his arm around Juno's waist. His arm should have been around Althea's waist but she'd been murdered then immolated into oblivion. He leaned down and kissed Juno, nipping at her lower lip, the way he used to do when they'd lived together, back before he'd had the miraculous good fortune of meeting Althea Livesy.

Juno pressed herself into Charley. "I knew you still loved me."

"Of course I love you, Juno. I've always loved you." Charley wondered if he sounded convincing. In case anyone could overhear them.

"Wait till you see what I've done with Desire Me. It's even better than it was the last time you were over. I've extended its capabilities. Every impulse of the user will be recorded, processed, analyzed, and used to our advantage."

Juno was saying things Charley didn't want to hear. He had to get her out of the way, and if she kept improving Desire Me he'd never be rid of her. Hell, anyone could work on this program now. Charley would teach Juno's code to someone new and bind them to secrecy with an unassailable contract. Or he could just do what the powerful elite in the classical era purportedly did and use their services, then have them expunged when they were no longer needed.

"You should come to my place, Charley," Juno said, interrupting his plans. "I've got clothes there."

"What the hell?"

"I never threw them out. You left them at the apartment. I saved them for you."

Juno was even more deranged than Charley had suspected.

"I knew you'd return to me. I was sure of it."

"Yes, of course," Charley said, humoring her.

"Now that Althea's out of the way—"

Juno's comm flashed as her ride pulled up to the curb. She grabbed Charley's hand and pulled him through the front door and into the transcer, where she rested her head on his shoulder, the way she used to, the way he never wanted her to and felt even more repulsed by now than he had when they'd lived together and he'd tolerated her for the sake of his own advancement. Juno Sangstrom was Charley's ticket to an ultimate success, one so grand he hadn't even imagined anything like it back then at Keff but one which was drawing ever closer.

The transcer took them to the Normandie, not to Charley's house. Juno held on to him and took him through the lobby. The black onyx floor was cold against Charley's bare feet. When they got to the elevator bank, Juno said, "Look there, Charley. Your footprints are following you."

Charley turned around. His wet footprints, the trail left by a sodden ghost.

When they got in the elevator, Juno put her hand on Charley's flesh and he forgot who and what he was.

They got off the elevator on the Normandie's top floor.

Could he kill Juno in her apartment? Wouldn't there be too much evidence against him? Certainly the cipher at the lobby desk had seen them come into the building—the dressed-up Juno Sangstrom and the hospital gown–clad Charley Pierce. He couldn't do it here. The river had been the perfect place. No one would ever have known. And the river was still there. He'd take her back to Tuigen and finish what he'd started.

"Why did you infect Althea and not Lukas Adler?" Why had Lukas gone to the funeral? He could have stayed away as he should have, and Charley's most persistent problem would have been eliminated.

"Althea killed herself, Charley. I don't know how many times I have to tell you."

"Althea would never kill herself. I don't know how many times I have to tell you."

Juno walked behind Charley and undid the ties at the top of his hospital gown.

"Don't," he said.

"But you're soaked."

"I'll live."

"I infected you with the virus, you know, but—"

"You what?"

Charley would kill her, right here. He'd drag her body to Ziva Walls's door and let her take the rap for Juno's death. Although Ziva was no longer in custody, yet now two corpses would add to Walls's guilt. Create her guilt. Solidify it.

This was the least he could do to square things off with the traitor Morris Walls, his trusted employee, who Althea had desired more than she'd ever wanted Charley himself. Despite his power, his fortune, his intellect, his thorough love for her. His devotion. He'd heard them going at it, heard Althea's passionate encouragings.

Morris Walls was a nobody and he'd disappeared. A nobody and a coward. Let his wife, Ziva, bear his punishment.

He heard Juno's voice. "It was . . . I was feeling pretty low. Of course you never would have died. Not like Oliver Hirata, who tried to have a so-called interlude with me. Or that full-of-himself Kaj Banerjee, acting like he ruled the world. Like art is so all-fired meaningful and important. Like it influences anyone or has any power over them. You understand, Charley. I know you do. I know what you've done. We have the power, the influence, the importance. What we do is real art, since it affects so many people. It affects everyone. It molds them, directs them, changes them."

"It kills them, you monster," Charley said, no longer able to contain his fury, which needed a target. "You killed Althea. If you think you're going to get away with it because I need you, you are dead wrong. I do not need you."

"I killed Althea? How diabolical you are. You may not need me, Charley, but Pierce Sangstrom does. None of that matters, though, because I need you. That's what matters."

Something in Charley's brain skipped over a long-held belief. Like a fast-forgotten dream. He'd lost it and didn't know where to recapture it. Or how.

"I could have killed you," Juno said. She was smiling. Even though Charley hated her and wanted her dead and wanted to be the agency of her death, and knew how to be the agency of death, he told himself Juno had a beautiful smile. Incomparable. Thrilling.

Juno pushed gently on Charley's chest and he backed up and sat down on her small sofa, the one she always sat on when he came over for his forced visits. The one he sat across from on the chair with the tapestry upholstery. Only now he was sitting on the sofa too, and she was perched on his lap.

"But I didn't kill you, Charley. I couldn't. I tried, but I couldn't. I love you too much. Althea's out of the picture now—"

Charley tried to remember who Althea was. The name had a certain resonance, a known quality, but with this extraordinary woman right here, giving herself so freely to him, his mind couldn't focus on those melodies. Or were they words or aromas? A forgotten poem.

"Juno," Charley said.

"Yes, Charley. I knew as soon as I could get you over here, where the viral load is strongest, you'd understand. You'd realize we belong together."

Charley put his hands around Juno's neck and kissed her chin while his brain struggled with what Juno'd just said.

"Juno, what do you mean?"

"Desire Me is working perfectly. As I'd planned. As we planned. You can feel it too, can't you, Charley?"

He glanced behind her at the computer array hovering in front of the rear wall of her study. The patterns would hold then rearrange themselves. Mesmerizing. Just the sort of thing only Juno could or would create.

"I knew it would be a success from the beginning," Charley heard himself say. "You really are a genius, Juno." Charley remembered a passionate night he and Juno had spent together, long ago. How had he ever left her? "I'll never leave you again." His disappeared beliefs pinged in the back of his brain but they'd lost their hold. He hugged her close, closer.

"I couldn't do any of it without you," Juno said between kisses. "I need you, Charley. That was always the driving force. Always. That's why I've done everything I've done. Why I had to do it."

Charley's head throbbed as though it were being hacked into by a dull-bladed ice pick. The room became so dark he could no longer see her. "Don't leave me," Charley said, hanging on to Juno's exquisite body, but he forgot who it was he didn't want to leave him.

Charley almost remembered something someone once said to him. Almost. It drifted off. Unreachable.

"I'll never leave you," Juno said. "I love you, Charley."

With each word her voice rose, competing with the pounding on her door and the shouting in the hallway outside her apartment.

CHAPTER 49

"HOW MANY COMPUTERS have been infected?" Glen said.

As soon as Violet had solved the code and the celebratory atmosphere had dissipated, the exhausted group at Beryl Carson's house had found new energy. Ledyard took over, lapsing back into his professorial persona, assigning each person a section of the program to analyze.

Even Ed Sperry, whose specialty wasn't computers, was working on it. There was no time to lose. People were ill and dying, and as crazy as it had seemed at first, this viral program was almost certainly the cause. The more they got into it, the more certain everyone became. Not just because of the image Jonathan Lee had found but because of the code's routines and directions.

Ethan Stiles had relapsed and Jonathan Lee had gone to the hospital, but he was expected back soon. They needed him here. If they were going to save Ethan, if they were going to quash what could become the most deadly infection known to humankind, they needed Jonathan Lee's expertise.

"How many? So far we don't know," Dorian said. "Probably every device throughout the Pierce Sangstrom empire. And everything at the Normandie. At least."

"Beryl's computer was infected." Ed Sperry looked up from the array she was studying. "How might that have happened? Or did she have an apartment at the Normandie?"

"Not that I'm aware of." Ledyard picked up the sheaf of extensive notes Jonathan Lee had made and sifted through them. "Summers thinks the virus might've entered her computer through correspondence she had with Charley Pierce."

"This could be a worse disaster than I thought," Dorian said. "If merely having correspondence with someone whose computer's infected could infect yours."

"Not if it was done deliberately." Jonathan Lee stood in the open doorway. Dorian had never seen him look so bedraggled. He may not've been infected with the leap, but its discovery and the intensive search for answers had changed him from an organized, put-together, regimented presence into a rumpled mess.

"What would be the motivation? Did Beryl have a run-in with anyone at Pierce?" Violet talked into the floor, where her gaze was focused on her scroll.

"Patterson told me she had a date with Charley Pierce, trying to raise funds for her latest project, but beyond that I don't know anything. I'll have Sean look into it," Jonathan Lee said. He commed her a message.

"Well." Ledyard rubbed his eyes and asked the question on everyone's mind. "How's Ethan?"

"He's alive." Jonathan Lee sighed. "Booth wouldn't let us into the room, so we waited for a while but nothing's changed. Sean went back to her place to feed the cat but she'll be here soon."

"We should get someone from the joukko to go over to the Normandie," Dorian said.

"Sean's on it. She has contacts there. We thought of going ourselves, but we've been through enough today and confronting a killer didn't seem like such a great idea. Although Sean tried to convince me. She used to be a detective there."

"Nine people died out at Tuigen. So far. Some funeral. And—oh hell. Did you see this?" Glen gave his scroll to Ledyard.

"It's called Desire Me?" Ledyard stared at the scroll and passed it to Jonathan Lee, who was still standing in the open doorway, as though he didn't want to come inside. Maybe he didn't. His ex had lived here, and as far as Dorian knew, they hadn't had much of a relationship since they'd split over a decade ago. Dorian had met Beryl once but had only a vague memory of her.

"Yeah, that's the name," Violet said.

Jonathan Lee leaned up against the doorjamb and said, "How much of Desire Me is running?"

"Hard to say. Maybe none of it. It doesn't seem like the program's actually been activated." Ledyard, out of character, looked to the rest of the room for confirmation.

"I haven't even gotten there," Violet said. She'd run a hastily put-together program that did a rough translation of the entire code, then apportioned it out without looking at anything but her own section.

"I'm toward the end, but I may not know what I'm looking at." Ed Sperry, unlike the rest of the gathering, seemed to be as fresh and alert as she'd been when she'd arrived hours that seemed like eons ago. "The part I'm looking at seems poised to infiltrate the user, clamp on to their limbic system, and manipulate their memories and desires. But, like I said, this isn't my field and I could be misinterpreting something based on my own biases. But the chemistry looks right to me."

"That could be worse than dying," Dorian said. She didn't want anyone manipulating her desires and certainly not Pierce Sangstrom. Bad enough they had become such an integral part of daily life that there was no escaping their influence.

"Wouldn't the easiest thing be to disable every affected device until we can figure out something else?" Dorian said. "Or, better yet, destroy them all." The circumstances had compelled her to become an advocate of the Jonathan Lee Summers school of thought: if there's an infection, it's pointless to try to fix it—instead, destroy the source.

"It would be, but so far we've had no success. We couldn't even get most of the residents of the Normandie to go to the lab and get tested. And the ones who did test positive weren't interested in doing anything about it since they had no symptoms—that we know of. And we haven't been in touch with anyone at Pierce Sangstrom. I don't even know if we could get into the building."

Sean, the private detective, appeared in the open doorway behind Jonathan Lee and despite the dire nature of what they were working on, the dynamic between Sean and Jonathan Lee was unmistakable. Dorian understood that Summers had finally overcome his failed marriage.

"Toby Hsu and her team are probably at the Normandie right now," Sean said. "McCormick's been on sick leave since Beryl's death, so at least we've been spared having to deal with him and his BS."

"Are you sure Juno's there?" Ledyard sat up straighter. He probably wanted to talk to Juno himself. They'd been great pals back in the day. Or maybe, like Dorian, he was anxious to see her in prison, where she belonged.

"It's our best guess," Jonathan Lee said at the same time Sean said, "We're sure."

Lightning flashed through the sky behind them. Jonathan Lee finally came all the way inside and Sean shut the door against the renewed downpour.

"There's not a lot I can do to help here," Sean said. Her coding knowledge was elementary, at best.

"We need your brain working on this," Jonathan Lee said. "And it's better that you're here instead of at the Normandie with the joukko."

"I'm going to take a nap," Sean said, and went into the bedroom that Dorian figured was Patterson's and shut the door. "I think better when I'm awake."

CHAPTER 50

ACTUALLY SEAN THOUGHT better when she was dead tired, since her rational mind shut down, freeing her to imagine anything at all, without restriction, but she wanted to be left alone to let herself work through everything she knew and have her memory wander through the stacks at her house. She'd taken a look while she was there, but hadn't found anything that seemed relevant.

She sat down on the floor, leaned back against the bedframe, listened to the booming thunder outside, and stared at the pictures of volcanoes that were on every wall of Patterson's room. Thought about the conflagration out at Tuigen and imagined the flames emanating from a furious volcano.

Many years ago Sean had tried out Meet Me, when it was new. She hadn't met anyone at all. Maybe she hadn't entered the right information into the small, simple form. Maybe she'd been too preoccupied, since she was vying for a promotion and that had been her sole focus. Meeting someone could wait. Now she wondered if she'd ever really gone through with the entire process. If you didn't submit your information, you couldn't meet anyone.

People claimed astounding results. Charley Pierce was said to have met his wife, Althea, through Meet Me, which Sean had always thought was a promotional myth. But maybe it was true.

One of the posters on Patterson's wall was of a body in a fetal position, turned to ashes and petrified. Sean quit hugging her knees. She had too much to do yet in her life. Death was out of the question.

Althea, though. Her life was finished.

PS Delenda Est. The slogan on the secondhand pale blue tees that had once belonged to Charley Pierce.

Juno Sangstrom—the genius behind Pierce Sangstrom's success. Why hadn't she fought to have her name first? How had Charley won out? Sean didn't know either of them and even if she did . . . Jonathan Lee had told her about his talk with Ledyard. About Juno's exceptional mind. Although Sangstrom Pierce sounded like an action, not the name of an influential megacorp.

Juno had written Meet Me, she and Charley formed Pierce Sangstrom, then Charley married Althea. Well, maybe Juno and Charley were just business partners.

And what a business. Pierce Sangstrom was embedded in the life of everyone on the planet, and if Desire Me got out there and started manipulating people's desires . . .

No one would stand for it, would they? Being controlled, having their passions orchestrated by someone else? Or maybe no one would know. Like no one knew about the leap except the few people in the next room and Ziva, Ethan, and of course Juno herself.

Yet Desire Me wasn't just the most frightening program Sean had ever heard of, Desire Me had also been infused with a deadly computer virus that would leap over the divide and infect humans, making them ill or killing them. How was that to Pierce Sangstrom's advantage?

Sean let her thoughts wander through the stacks in her hallway. She'd saved a flyer for *Keeping the Promise*, the fabula that had put both Lukas Adler and Althea Pierce in even greater demand. Like everyone else, Sean had spent hours watching the series.

She'd seen Lukas Adler at the hospital earlier. What was he doing there?

Sean had enjoyed *Keeping the Promise*, had stayed up late watching the newest episodes and felt like she personally knew the fabula's characters. The lovely Olyn Gil played Lukas Adler's devastated ex. Well, anyone would be devastated if Lukas Adler left them, wouldn't they? *Keeping the Promise*'s allure was dependent on that.

Even though Olyn's character met someone new, someone played by the sexy Nolan East, supposedly Lukas Adler's real-life rival, but even so Olyn—Sean couldn't remember her character's name—spent most of *Keeping the Promise* trying to get revenge for what Lukas Adler's character, also named Lukas, had done to her.

Yet the Lukas Adler character was somehow sympathetic. At least he was to Sean and she gathered he was to most other viewers. Had Althea Pierce written his character this way on purpose or had it just evolved as the drama progressed?

Lukas was single, alone, brooding but hugely successful in some fancy business he owned for most of the series. He met his true love— a woman Olyn's character despised—only near the end, right before Olyn died of an unnamed malady. The penultimate scene had Nolan East sobbing over Olyn's corpse, hinting at his own revenge to come, but the final scene was Lukas and his new love, lying on the beach together, both of them happy and satisfied.

Sean was wasting her time. There was no reason to be thinking about an outdated fabula, although it was still popular. Yet this was what Sean was thinking about.

She put her head back on the bedframe and closed her eyes. The picture of the petrified corpse turned into Althea Pierce, and the poster of the erupting volcano became the conflagration out at Tuigen.

She was too tired to make sense of anything.

Jonathan Lee would go back to the Acres soon. No promises there, not from either of them. If Ethan died . . . If Desire Me took hold . . . If the leap was uncontainable . . .

A cacophonous roll of thunder woke Sean up. She'd dozed off without noticing.

Frozen in her mind's eye was the image of Olyn Gil on her deathbed in *Keeping the Promise*. Did this mean something? Or had Sean just fallen asleep thinking about this so she also woke up thinking about it?

Jonathan Lee knocked on the door and opened it a bit. "Okay if I come in?"

"I wish you would."

"I worry about Patterson," Jonathan Lee said as he sat down beside Sean.

"Patterson's the very model of self-assurance."

"True."

"Ethan?"

"Nothing new. Ziva's been comming me with updates although there aren't any."

"I had a reverie about *Keeping the Promise*."

"I never saw it."

"You're alone there. Everyone saw it."

"Almost everyone. But even Beryl liked it and she wasn't interested in fabulas. I don't know what it's about."

"It's too complicated to explain but, to simplify, Olyn Gil plays the kicked-over lover of Lukas Adler and she wants revenge."

"Does she get it?"

"No, she dies."

"Too bad. I like Olyn Gil."

"JL, I just realized something. Althea Pierce wrote *Keeping the Promise*. And maybe it's about her life, or the life she wished for."

"How so?"

"At the end of it, Lukas is with a new lover, a woman who's a successful fabulist, like Althea is. I mean was. And his ex—the Olyn Gil character—is killed by a mysterious, unexplained illness. Is there a parallel to Juno, Charley, Althea? If Charley deserted Juno. If she's wanted revenge for this all along."

"I think you've gone overboard."

"You thought that when I suggested Oliver Hirata had died of a computer virus."

"Good point. Very good point. But we have no idea what went on between Charley and Juno, if anything. Let's ask Ledyard. He'll know."

Sean dragged herself to her feet and followed Jonathan Lee out into the living room.

"Where's Ledyard?" Jonathan Lee said.

"He went into the other bedroom. Needs to be in the dark to think," Ed Sperry said without looking up from her scroll.

Sean turned around and knocked on the closed door to what had been Beryl's bedroom.

"Come," said Ledyard, his voice muffled.

"How's it going?" Jonathan Lee said. Except for the glow of Ledyard's scroll, the room, Beryl's former bedroom, was pitch-dark.

"Too damned slowly." Ledyard turned around in his seat and stretched out his legs in front of him. "And unfortunately it seems that Ed's right about Desire Me. But I'm confounded by the odd section in ordinary machine language, the one inserted into the virus portion. It makes no sense."

"Could anyone have written it?" Sean said.

"Possibly."

"Someone like Althea Pierce, maybe?" Jonathan Lee said. "Or Charley himself?"

"We'll never know, will we?"

"Were Juno and Charley involved with each other, you know, personally? Very personally?" Jonathan Lee sat on the chair next to Ledyard's.

"They lived together."

"In the same house or in the same bed?" Sean said.

"I don't really get involved in my students' personal lives, but Juno told me more than once that Charley was her ideal partner and she was so lucky he hadn't gone to the Acres or she never would've met him."

"So, the same bed."

"Most probably."

"Sean thinks she's come up with something," Jonathan Lee said, "and since the last off-the-wall thing she came up with proved to be true, I'm wondering if this is as well."

"Tell me."

"I think perhaps, maybe . . . Juno used the program to get back at Althea for stealing Charley away from her and Althea tried to turn the tables on her by changing the code in order to do away with Juno instead. Although, as far as we know, it didn't work out."

"That is convoluted, but it reminds me of something I saw once. *Keeping the Promise.*"

"You saw it?" Jonathan Lee sounded surprised.

"Everyone saw it, Summers. Didn't you?"

"No." Jonathan Lee smirked. A mere popular fabula was beneath him.

"That's what made me think of this," Sean said. "Because Althea Pierce wrote it and maybe it's what she wanted to see happen in life."

"But Althea's dead."

"Yes. I imagine she didn't know what she was doing. Her plans backfired."

"Or Juno is the sole force behind this and she's responsible for every victim," Jonathan Lee said. "That seems much more likely."

Hal Ledyard bent his knees, leaned forward, and rested his elbows on his thighs. "I hate to think so. Juno—she was the best of the best. But we have to consider everything."

"Before someone else dies," Sean said. She meant Ethan. She looked toward Jonathan Lee and could barely see his face in the dark.

Jonathan Lee's voice was determined and steady. "I'm not going to let him die," he said.

CHAPTER 51

"OPEN UP," SAID the voice outside Juno's door.

"Are you expecting someone?" Charley said. He'd been holding on to Juno, but he let go now. She touched his shoulder.

"Of course not. You're the only person I've ever let inside. Ever."

That wasn't true, since she'd let Jordan Fields into her apartment and other parts of her life more than once. She hadn't heard how he was doing, but she'd given him a small dose of the virus. He'd just had an extreme reaction to it. And if he didn't recover . . . Here was Charley, finally, and he loved her. As he always should have.

A loud voice, too loud, made its way into Juno's private domain. "Osada City Joukko. We have a warrant. You have exactly thirty seconds and then we're breaking down your door."

Juno tried to ignore the command, tried to return her focus to Charley, the only person—the only entity—in the universe who meant anything to her. She'd give up everything—her talents and skills, her beauty, her assets, all of it—for the absolute knowing that Charley loved her.

"I think we should answer the door," Charley said.

Juno kissed him, but his response lacked the passion she needed. His interest in her seemed to be weakening. She had to get him closer to the computer array across the room. She should have directed it right where he was sitting instead of so far away. Her mistake. But she could fix it.

"Fifteen seconds," said the voice at the door.

"Juno," Charley said. "Answer it." She could hardly hear him.

"Ten seconds," said the voice.

"All right," Juno said. "I'm coming. Wait a moment. Just wait."

"Five seconds," said the voice while Juno ran to the door. She didn't want it destroyed. With Jordan in the hospital it might take weeks to get someone to repair it. She flung open the door just as a ferocious-looking officer was about to bash it in.

"Juno Sangstrom?" another officer said. The one in front. The leader of this mob.

Juno nodded.

"Answer," the officer said.

"Yes, I'm Juno Sangstrom."

"Detective Toby Hsu. Osada City Joukko," said the officer in charge. There were another five officers behind her. "We have a warrant to search your premises."

"You'll have to come back another time," Juno said, holding the door against the onslaught. "I'm working on something—"

"Move aside," Detective Hsu said, and walked past Juno and into the foyer. The contingent of other officers followed her, like they had the right to be here, in Juno's inner sanctum.

"I'm comming my attorney," Juno said. "You can't do this."

"Comm away," Detective Hsu said, then, acting like she was the owner of this apartment and not Juno, started directing her minions.

Where was Charley? Was he still in the study?

For the first time since Charley left her for Althea, Juno felt exposed, vulnerable, helpless. She couldn't stop what was happening since there were too many other people. If she could get to her computer in time, she could direct the array at each individual, but the influential process, as well as the virus, developed over time. It was working on Charley only because he'd already been exposed to several doses of it—and because he really did love and desire Juno. She just had to coax the truth out of him.

But where was Charley? Had he left her again? No, he hadn't gone past her and he didn't know about the back door of her apartment, the one exiting into the service elevator. He couldn't. No one except Jordan knew about it.

She ran into the study, but Charley wasn't there.

The noise from the invading army set Juno on an edge that made her want to scream but she wouldn't give anyone the satisfaction of hearing her pent-up rage. She raced to her bedroom, where the joukko was doing its best to destroy her peace and comfort. And Charley wasn't there.

Juno hurried through her apartment, checking every room and not finding Charley, the only person worth finding, but instead running into more of the joukko. It seemed as though they'd multiplied since they'd barged into her home.

She wanted to call out for Charley, but didn't want the joukko to know he'd been there. He needed to be protected.

Frantic now, Juno went back into the study. Maybe she hadn't seen him. But he wasn't there. Then she saw the back door was indeed open. How had Charley seen it? It was hidden behind a bookcase. She'd never shown it to him.

She walked through the opening and went into the service elevator, where Charley Pierce, the very center of her life, was lying on the floor, motionless.

"Charley?"

Silence. Stillness.

"Charley?" She said his name louder this time and it seemed like he might've moved, but she could've been imagining it.

"Charley. Get up. We have to get out of here." They could ride the service elevator to the basement and escape. The joukko would never find what they were searching for because even if they could or did, they wouldn't know what they were looking at, and no one but Charley knew her coding. Why was she so scared? There was nothing to be scared about.

"Charley, we'll be safe. Let's go." But Charley didn't move.

Juno closed the door. The elevator, with Juno and the inert Charley in it, sped to the basement. They were free. Juno would get Jordan to help her move Charley to a safe place. Back to his house or out to Tuigen.

But Jordan was in the hospital. Tuigen had burned to the ground. No. Charley would get up and they'd go to Charley's house. But would the joukko follow them there?

Juno would figure it out. She'd always figured everything out. That was her specialty—taking the impossible and creating success.

"Charley, get up." Juno was kneeling beside him. He had a pulse, or what she assumed was his pulse, but he wasn't talking. "Get up." They were almost at the basement level.

But Charley didn't get up, and when the doors of the elevator opened, Detective Toby Hsu was standing right there, a disapproving look on her face, and with two of her lackeys standing beside her.

Juno wanted to run, but she couldn't leave Charley. "Call for help," she said, glancing up at Detective Hsu. "Charley—I don't know what's happened to him." She looked back down at Charley, then turned her gaze to the detective again. "You have to save him. You have to. Hurry."

She started crying, right there in front of the joukko, in front of the strangers who'd invaded her home, people who had no ability to relate to her, who had no idea what the inner life of someone like Juno Sangstrom could possibly be like.

"Help him," she said, crying harder now. "You have to help him."

CHAPTER 52

WHY? TELL ME again. I don't get it." Ziva Walls sat in Axel Booth's makeshift office in the isolation ward and tried to get some clarification as to why Ethan was unresponsive. Why he'd relapsed. And what could be done to help him.

"I can only guess," Booth said.

"Then guess." Guessing was better than not having any insight at all.

"Despite the leap's unprecedented origin, it's still an RNA virus and if you're infected with the type of biological virus I'm more familiar with, you have your ups and downs."

"So Ethan's in a down phase?"

"I hope that's all it is."

"Of course that's all it is." Ziva refused to let go of her optimism about Ethan's recovery. It was necessary to not just her own state of mind but somehow, she thought, to Ethan's progress.

"But we don't know."

"That's not what I want to hear."

"It's not what I want to say either, but we know so little about this."

"Even with all the work everyone at the lab and the computer group have been doing? They've gotten the code now. Shouldn't that be helpful?"

"Helpful, yes, but it's hardly a cure."

"But other people"—Ziva stopped herself from saying *victims*—"have survived."

"I think so, but I can't be positive."

"Maizy's doing better, isn't she?"

"Yes, she appears to have improved tremendously."

"See? And Jordan Fields. He's better too, right?"

Axel Booth turned away from Ziva. "Right?" she said.

"I can't discuss another patient with you."

"But you just discussed Maizy with me."

Booth sighed and shook his head. "I'm afraid Mr. Fields is on life support now. It's only a matter of time before . . ."

"But he wasn't even very sick, was he?" Ziva couldn't picture the energetic Jordan Fields being all but dead. It'd been hard enough to imagine him sick, but this?

"I've told you all I can. We're waiting to hear from his family. No one's gotten back to us yet."

"His brother's part of the experimental settlement on Mars." Jordan had told Ziva all about it one morning while he was fixing yet another broken pipe in her apartment. The ultra luxurious Normandie was constantly falling apart, piece by piece. Jordan had said how brave or maybe how crazy his brother was to go to such a remote place, knowing he'd never return to his real home. Now it seemed like Jordan might not return to his life. "I don't think there's any other family," Ziva said.

"We're checking into it." Booth looked almost worse than the sick Ethan did. He'd been working nonstop, dividing his time between the isolation ward and Ethan's lab.

"If there's a disease, there must be a cure." This sounded right to Ziva, who thought there was a cure for everything, not just diseases. The cure for Morris's disappearance, for example, had been to hire Sean, and the cure for his continued disappearance was to divorce him.

"If only." Booth shook his head. "Despite millennia of scientific advances and medical research, there are still several diseases without a cure."

"That doesn't mean there isn't a cure, just that no one's found it yet."

Booth huffed a derisive laugh. "I can't argue with that."

"Can I visit with Maizy? If she'll let me. We weren't exactly friends before all this happened. But we weren't enemies."

"I'll ask her and I'll let you know."

"I meant right now. I'd like to visit with her now, not tomorrow."

"I cut you a lot of slack because Ethan likes you so much."

"Thank you."

Fifteen minutes later, Zee was sitting in the visitor chair in Maizy Newell's room. Maizy was sitting up in bed, smiling, and maybe almost glowing.

"It's nice of you to drop by, Mrs. Walls," Maizy said.

"Ziva, please. And I'm here anyway. A friend of mine is a patient down the hall from here."

"I'm sorry."

"He's going to get better, just like you're doing."

"I'm still afraid I'm not better. Look what happened to Althea Pierce, and she could afford the best medical care."

"How do you know that?" Hadn't Maizy been unconscious during the time Althea was in the ward?

"Lukas Adler told me."

Ziva did a double take. "You know Lukas Adler?"

"Not really. He just comes to visit me sometimes. I think he misses Althea."

Ziva suspected a lot of people must miss Althea. Her fabulas had been the source of fame and riches for countless actors, directors, costume designers, art directors, production people, marketers, advertisers, and probably hundreds of others.

"I'm not sure how I'm going to pay for all this afterward," Maizy said.

"Don't worry about it. I'll pay for it."

"Oh no. I didn't mean—you don't have to, and, well, Oliver. I tried not to be jealous, but you don't have to feel sorry for me."

"Poor Oliver. He lived his life in interludes. Don't do that, Maizy. Find something—find someone—worthwhile and stick to it, to them." Ziva almost couldn't believe what she—someone who hadn't stuck to Morris or to Oliver or to anyone or anything, really—was saying, but she meant it. With Ethan, life was different, and Ziva herself was not the same person she'd been before Morris's disappearance, before she met Sean, before she got involved with Jonathan Lee, Ethan, and the leap.

"I *was* jealous, you know. I'd see the two of you in the lobby and Oliver barely acknowledged me. I'd thought we were in love."

"Oliver had that effect on his interludes. His gift."

"He took me to a Convergence."

"Really? I've never been. What was it like?" Ziva had tried several times to convince Morris to go, but he'd always refuse. He'd say it wasn't real and he didn't want to get caught up in a fantasy. She could have gone by herself but had never done so.

"It's—well, I can't describe it. The effect is like falling in love with the universe. But it wears off afterward, after you're back in the real world. Some of it, anyway."

"Maizy, I can't apologize enough. I never meant to hurt you. I didn't find out you and Oliver had had an interlude until long afterward."

"It's okay. That was before I got sick. Everything's changed."

"How so?"

"It just is. I feel like my body realigned itself. I'm going to quit the Normandie. I can do something better. And Lukas Adler told me I could come recuperate out at his place. If he meant it."

"I'm sure he did. He's a good person. I've had a few chats with him out in the waiting area. He was here every day for Althea and was devastated by her death. Maybe the two of you can help each other out."

"I don't know how I could help him, but I do like him, and I don't mean Lukas Adler the actor. I mean the person. They're very different."

"You can't tell how you could help someone else. It's one of life's mysteries." Ziva thought of Kaj and how she was trying to help him by making sure her plans for his legacy would be something he'd approve of and be happy with.

"Thank you for stopping by, Mrs.—I mean Ziva. Maybe when all this is over, we can be friends."

"Maizy. We can be friends right now. I'm through with waiting for anything."

CHAPTER 53

A S SOON AS Toby Hsu commed her, Sean left the group hard at work at Beryl's house and went to the joukko. Jonathan Lee's input would've been helpful, but he was needed where he was. There was an invisible clock ticking somewhere in Sean's head, ticking down the days or hours or maybe minutes or seconds until someone else got infected, got sick, or died. Until the leap would become uncontrollable as it spread through everyone's computer and attacked its victims without caring who it hurt.

That's how both biological and computer viruses were. They needed a host in order to survive and any host would do. What happened to the host wasn't the virus's problem.

The rain pummeled Sean's transcer as she made her way to the Osada City Joukko. The drive was familiar yet odd. Sean'd worked there for years before she quit in disgust but now they needed her. At least, Toby Hsu needed her. They had Juno Sangstrom in custody and Toby needed to know exactly what to ask her. Sean would sit in the observation room and feed Toby some questions, helping her to keep the investigation on the right track.

"But I don't know about going into the building," Sean had said to Toby when she commed. "I'm not exactly welcome there."

"McCormick's still out and I've hired you as an official consultant, so there's nothing to worry about. Get here. Sangstrom's a mess and we have to use this opportunity to try to get her to talk." Toby had ended the comm, not giving Sean a chance to argue.

That so many officers and detectives were happy to see her surprised Sean. They waved to her as she walked by, saying how they missed her. She hadn't realized anyone had even noticed she'd gone.

As soon as she sat down in the observation room, it was as though she was still on the force. She took a deep breath and watched Juno Sangstrom, sitting alone at the interview table, waiting for Toby to arrive. Sean waited too and tried to get a fix on Sangstrom, who looked almost exactly like the images of her from two decades ago: the same small, sleek frame, the same high cheekbones and bright, alert eyes, the same gentle beauty, as though the passage of time had had very little effect on her.

Sean looked closer and saw Sangstrom's eyes were bright because she was crying. Was it put on? Was she practicing until Toby arrived, hoping to get sympathy instead of an interrogation?

As soon as Toby entered the room, Sangstrom swiped at her eyes and sat up straighter. The half owner of the ubiquitous megacorp was hardly going to wilt under the questions of a mere joukko detective. Maybe she hadn't been crying. Maybe the interrogation room's glaring lights were bothering her.

Toby gave the usual pre-interview speech and was about to ask the first of what Sean suspected would be hundreds of questions when Sangstrom interrupted her and said, "How is Charley? No one will tell me where he is, how he is, or what's happening."

"Mr. Pierce is being attended to."

"But how is he? You have to tell me. He's not just my business partner."

"That's not why we're here."

"Avoid answering all you want, but I'm not going to tell you anything until you tell me how Charley's doing and where he is."

"Mr. Pierce's condition and whereabouts are none of your concern right now," Toby said.

R·T·W Lipkin

"But—" Juno Sangstrom started crying in earnest. She seemed genuinely upset. After what Hal Ledyard had told her and Jonathan Lee earlier, Sean suspected Juno was truly upset.

Sean talked to Toby via a direct comm, whispering in case there was any sound leakage, which had been a problem in the past: "Tell her. You've got nothing to lose here and everything to gain."

"He's at the Genesia Clinic in the isolation ward. I've been told he's in stable condition," Toby said.

"Genesia? Why would they take him there?"

"That's the usual venue in circumstances like these."

Sean knew Toby was lying—there was no usual venue—and if they'd taken Charley to Genesia it was because he was another likely victim of the leap, a fact Toby hadn't mentioned to Sean earlier. This was just getting worse and worse.

"I have to go see him," Juno said.

"You'll have to wait."

"But I'll be able to see him?"

"We'll see. It depends on your answers."

"I'll answer anything you want as long as I can see Charley. He needs me." Judging by the emotion in Juno Sangstrom's voice and her body posture and general demeanor, Sean suspected Juno needed Charley whether or not he needed her.

Toby nodded. "Then let's get on with it."

Before Toby had time to speak again, Juno Sangstrom said, "It's all down to Althea Livesy."

"You mean Althea Pierce?"

Sean started taking notes. Even though both she and Toby could see a simultaneous transcript of the entire interview on their scrolls, Sean liked to jot things down. It helped her focus.

"She conned Charley into marrying her, so I never considered her to be Althea Pierce. She's Althea Livesy."

"You realize Althea Pierce died, don't you?"

"I was at her funeral, you know." Juno crossed her arms over her chest and aimed her steely eyes at Toby.

"I didn't."

"Of course I was. I had to support Charley. And we both almost drowned."

So Juno and Charley had escaped the blaze by jumping into the river. And now she was complaining she'd almost drowned when nine people, as of the last time Sean checked, had died in the conflagration, unable to find a safe exit.

"What did you mean when you said it was all down to Althea Pierce?"

"Livesy. It was her fault. All of it. I'd just written the perfect program and she got hold of it somehow and used it to try to kill me. But it killed her instead."

"Could you explain what you're talking about?"

"I just did. Aren't you listening?"

"Details. I need details."

"Well, it's not like you're going to arrest her ashes, are you? What difference does it make now? It's all her fault."

"What is it that's all her fault?"

"The virus, of course. The infections. The deaths. It's all because of her. She did it. Trying to be so clever, like it was a joke, using coding language any little kid could understand. But it's no joke. She's a murderer—and she accidentally killed herself. I call that justice."

"You're going to have to be more specific. What virus?"

"The one she wrote into my program. She was trying to kill me."

"Back up. How did Althea Pierce get access to your program and write a virus into it?"

"How would I know? I just know she did. I figured she saw it on Charley's computer and worked away at it. Or maybe she had her own office at Pierce Sangstrom." Juno smirked.

Sean whispered to Toby that they suspected all the computers at Pierce Sangstrom were infected with the virus via the program Juno had written.

"All right. Let me get this straight. You wrote an ordinary program—"

"An *extra*ordinary program. My finest yet. It's going to change everyone's life for the better. Everyone's—including yours. We should be going live in a couple of months and this will be an even bigger success than Meet Me was and still is. No one will want to be without it. No one *will* be without it."

Sean couldn't believe Juno Sangstrom was sitting in the Osada City Joukko interrogation room, the prime suspect in multiple deaths, and was touting her latest creation, a creation that contained a deadly virus. Yet that's what was happening.

Sangstrom might be a genius, but she was out of her mind or so taken with her own talents that nothing else—except perhaps Charley—mattered to her. Althea Pierce's death was just a blip in Juno's forward trajectory.

And if Althea Pierce had been the one who wrote the part of the code that was in simple language, how had she gotten hold of the program and done this? They'd probably never know. Yet that section might have nothing to do with the virus's effects and Althea could hardly have known how to translate Juno's cryptic coding. Sean shook her head and trained her focus back on the interview.

"She was trying to kill me," Juno Sangstrom said. "You should be arresting her but she's out of the way. She killed herself."

Sean wrote down *out of the way* and commed Toby. Was Sangstrom unwittingly implying she'd killed Althea Pierce?

"When did you decide to kill Althea Pierce?" Hsu said.

"Althea Livesy. I keep telling you but you're not listening. She had no right to Charley's name. And the way she carried on with every man she encountered. And killed them too. Just to show that she could. Showing off. Not that anyone misses them."

Toby shifted in her seat and Sean got up and stood next to the viewing window.

"Who do you mean?"

"You have to have figured this out by now. Isn't it obvious?"

"No. Tell me." Toby Hsu's face was expressionless.

"Oliver Hirata. Kaj Banerjee. And who knows how many others."

"Are you saying Althea Pierce—Livesy—killed Oliver Hirata and Kaj Banerjee?"

"I'm saying you're not very observant if you haven't figured it out already. She fooled around with them then offed them when they weren't interested in her anymore. Oliver Hirata and his interludes."

Sean immediately commed Toby. Sangstrom would have no knowledge of Oliver Hirata's interludes unless she'd had one with him or he'd suggested it to her. Sean knew about the interludes only because of what Ziva had told her. Toby glanced Sean's way and gave her an almost imperceptible nod.

"How long did you know Oliver Hirata?" Toby said.

"This isn't about me. This is about the killer. You are not listening."

"I'm just curious," Toby, playing along, said. "Did he tell you he was having an interlude with Althea?"

"I just . . . knew."

"Did you have an interlude with Oliver Hirata?"

"How ridiculous. I'm in love with Charley. Why would I bother with such an insignificant person?"

"But Charley was married."

"He didn't mean it. He was seduced and made a mistake. Anyone could make a mistake."

"Like the mistake you made by killing so many people with the virus you wrote? Maybe you hadn't intended to kill them." Smart. Toby was giving Juno what seemed like an out—her crimes were unintentional.

"I never intended to kill anyone. Of course I didn't. Althea did it. It should be obvious."

"What's obvious to me is that only someone with unimaginable skill and talent could've written a computer virus that infects and kills humans."

Juno Sangstrom stopped talking. Toby had cornered her. Either Juno Sangstrom was the coding genius of the century or she'd been outdone by her rival for Charley Pierce's affections—and a rank amateur coder at that.

"She didn't write it . . . per se. She made the changes and . . . turned it into a weapon. I'd never intended that." Sean was sure Juno was making this up on the spot and whispered to Toby.

"How was she able to do it?" Toby said, pressing.

"She wasn't a complete idiot. She just saw an opportunity and took it. Trying to get rid of me. It must have infuriated her that after all these years Charley and I were still business partners, still in love."

"If Charley was in love with you why didn't he just divorce Althea?"

"You couldn't possibly understand," Juno said. "Charley and I live in a different world than someone like you. Things aren't so cut-and-dried."

"So what was Althea's motive to kill you if Charley wasn't going to divorce her?"

"Jealousy. Isn't that the usual motive? She knew Charley and I were forever tied to each other. She knew I was his original love and that he would never give me up. Plus, I have twice the brains and ten times the influence a two-bit fabula writer has."

"I see. But weren't you also jealous of Althea?"

"I don't believe in jealousy. It's a waste of time." Sean saw Juno had regained some control over her somewhat flimsy set of excuses.

"Nevertheless," Toby said, "you said you saw that Althea Pierce had written this change into the code in order to kill you. Why didn't you just rewrite it or delete it or fix it somehow?" Toby was asking the very question foremost in Sean's mind.

Juno looked past Toby, her eyes focused on the blank wall behind her. She was quiet for a long time. Toby let the silence just hang there and waited. Then Juno sighed and said, "I couldn't."

"You couldn't or you wouldn't?"

"I . . . couldn't. There was something different going on with what she had done, the way it was integrated into the rest of the virus, the program."

"Wait, wait. You mean there was always a virus, not just the one you say Althea Pierce created?"

"Althea Livesy, and yes, there was always a virus, but it was harmless. It couldn't hurt anyone."

Sean wondered if that were true, if anything Juno was saying were true. Sean had so many questions now that there was no way she could communicate them all to Toby. But Toby was doing a good job all by herself. Sean paced in front of the viewing window and wondered where all this was leading. If the great Juno Sangstrom was willing to admit someone else—someone untrained and outside of the field—was better at coding than she was, then what was the truth? Had Althea really been that good? Or was Juno just covering up for her crimes?

Toby stood up. What was going on?

"We'll have to continue this at a later time. You'll be escorted back to your cell."

Toby walked out, shut the door on Sangstrom, and went into the observation room. What was she doing? Sangstrom was talking freely. Toby had a golden opportunity here to get the facts.

"Come on," Toby said to Sean. "We're going to the Genesia Clinic."

Sean picked up her scroll and followed her down the hallway. Something huge had to be happening that had caused Toby to stop interviewing Juno Sangstrom at such a crucial moment.

Sean gasped. "Is it Ethan?" What if he'd died?

"It's Charley Pierce. Come on."

CHAPTER 54

JONATHAN LEE SUMMERS had always respected and sometimes admired Hal Ledyard's expertise and insightful mind, but he'd never liked the man. Something about his manner and attitude just rubbed Jonathan Lee the wrong way, and his encounters with Ledyard often ended in ever-escalating, increasingly maddening arguments.

But here at the Carson house Jonathan Lee Summers and Hal Ledyard were working together. It seemed almost comfortable, like they'd always been collegial, when in fact they'd never been.

Working with the code translation Violet Rushman had created, each member of the group was still focusing on a discrete section of the program, but Jonathan Lee and Ledyard were concentrating their efforts on the code as a whole. Besides the section written in ordinary language, which they were referring to as the insert, they'd come across several places where odd elements had been added, ones that didn't fit in with either the majority of the code or the insert. The configuration was different, as though yet someone else had written it.

"I don't like this," Jonathan Lee said, pointing to yet another peculiar area. "Did three different people work on this? Together? Separately?"

Hal Ledyard closed his eyes, probably to block out the light Jonathan Lee needed to have on.

"Juno told me something a long time ago, but I have only a partial memory of it. Charley would help her out. But that's not quite right. It'll come to me."

"Hey." Dorian Song poked her head into Beryl's former bedroom, where Jonathan Lee and Hal Ledyard were working. "I think I found something big. An accident. I was trying to do something else."

"No need for the preamble—spill it," Jonathan Lee said.

"The code can't be edited."

"What?" Ledyard's eyes were open now.

"There's a lock on it, here in this innocuous section." Dorian showed her scroll to Jonathan Lee and Ledyard. "I've never seen anything like it."

"I have," Jonathan Lee said. "In another Pierce Sangstrom code— Meet Me."

"How the hell did you get your hands on it?" Ledyard seemed shocked and aimed his accusatory stare straight at Jonathan Lee.

"It was just a lark," Jonathan Lee said. "I was trying to hack Meet Me—I had a bet I could do it—and ran straight into this roadblock. Very similar to this. Maybe the same as this. I don't remember the specifics."

"I mean how did you get your hands on the code to Meet Me? It's proprietary."

"Are you defending Pierce Sangstrom?"

If Jonathan Lee were ever to tell anyone how he'd gotten possession of Meet Me's code, Hal Ledyard would be the very last person to find out. And he'd never tell anyone. Not even his betting adversary, a former student and now fellow lecturer at the Acres, knew.

"I'm trying to find out if you're just talking nonsense."

"Are you implying I talk nonsense?" Jonathan Lee was remembering what his relationship with Hal Ledyard was really like.

"Stop it, guys." Dorian was friends with both of them. "We need to solve this, not bicker."

Jonathan Lee was about to dispute the bickering remark, but decided Dorian was right. Solving the leap, stopping it, keeping it from spreading any further, finding a cure, finding a prevention—those things were more important than Hal Ledyard's petty insults.

Hal Ledyard's eyes were closed again, and he said, "Charley was her editor. That's what Juno said. He fixed things that needed fixing. Finessed sections that were unnecessarily convoluted. He was a run-of-the-mill coder himself, but when he was given Juno's exceptional work, he was able to refine it in a way even she couldn't."

"Do you think he's responsible for any of this?" Dorian took her scroll back from Jonathan Lee. "For the lock?"

"I have no idea," Ledyard said. "It's not my area."

"It's not my area either," Jonathan Lee said, "but if I had to bet on it—"

Jonathan Lee got up. "I have to go. I'll let you know what's happening." He shoved his scroll into his back pocket.

Sean had commed him. She and Toby Hsu were on their way to the Genesia Clinic and could Jonathan Lee meet them there? Charley Pierce was asking for him.

CHAPTER 55

CHARLEY HAD BARRICADED his room in the isolation ward, shoving his bed up against the door, and was demanding to see Jonathan Lee Summers. "He'll be able to prove it," Charley Pierce kept saying. He wouldn't say what it was that had to be proven.

He'd finally regained consciousness about an hour after his admittance and had insisted on being discharged, but Dr. Booth said he had to have a few more tests before they'd let him leave. Did he want to end up like his wife?

"I'd say that's entirely up to me," Charley Pierce said.

"It would be except that you may be the carrier of a deadly virus and you can't just go back out there and infect others."

"And what deadly virus would that be?"

"The one that killed your wife and several other people as well."

"Well, you're the doctor. Isn't it up to you to find a cure? You let Althea down—you let her die—and now you're saying I'm infected? It seems to me you know absolutely nothing about what's wrong with anyone. Although there's nothing wrong with me."

Booth left Pierce's room and Charley heard him alert the staff to be on the lookout in case he escaped. But instead of leaving, Charley had locked himself in his room and demanded to speak with Jonathan Lee Summers, the only person Charley could think of who'd come close to understanding just what Juno Sangstrom had done.

While he was waiting, he paced between the bed and the window. The rainstorm had become brutal, and Charley indulged in a vivid fantasy where Juno was out at Tuigen, alone, unprotected, while the force of the rain was so great that she drowned, just as she should have drowned when she was out in the river with Charley. Before the oaf Lukas Adler had injected himself into what had turned out to be the perfect situation, the very situation Charley had long dreamed of. But no. Adler had to "save" them.

Could someone drown in the rain? The question snapped Charley out of his reverie. He'd never heard of this happening to anyone, but maybe it could happen to Juno. It would be a pleasant end for her. What he meant was Juno's death would be pleasant no matter how it happened. But he'd read once that drowning wasn't so bad, that you eventually were deluded into thinking you were breathing the water and became rapturous. Something like that. He hadn't concentrated on the details. And they didn't matter. Juno, on the other hand . . .

Charley imagined climbing up through the ceiling of his room, getting to the roof of the Genesia Clinic, and having a private conversation with Althea. She was always avoiding him. She was busy with Oliver Hirata, with Kaj Banerjee, with Lukas Adler, with Morris Walls.

Walls had been a useful worker up until his fatal mistake. Walls's wife had hired some private investigator to find him. But even Charley, with his limitless resources, hadn't been able to locate him. His computer had been infected, like the rest of them. He couldn't still be alive. He wasn't supposed to be, although the version of the virus on his computer was one of the initial tests, before Hirata.

A voice penetrated Charley's thoughts, which were now including the bloated corpse of Morris Walls, floating in the middle of an ocean somewhere. Sea vultures flew around his body, if there were sea vultures. If there weren't, Charley would breed them.

"Charley Pierce," said the voice on the other side of the door. "You asked to speak to me."

Who could that be? Charley hadn't asked to speak with anyone and the voice was unknown to him. He had to get out of here. The window was locked. The door was barricaded. They'd trapped him. He tried to put his fist through the window, which was impenetrable.

The impenetrable Juno Sangstrom. Always five hundred steps ahead of him. Smug, self-possessed. Charley had nightmares about her but he had plans about her as well.

The nonsensical addition to the code that Althea had written. She'd probably thought it would do something, or maybe she was leaving a note to him in her playful way, letting him know she'd seen the program.

Banging on the door. A man's voice. Was he still at Juno's? She'd lured him there and drugged him. He pictured her lying in a foot-deep pool of black water, drowned, as she should be.

The window wouldn't budge. The ceiling was too far away. Would Charley always be Juno's prisoner? Were his plans useless against her insidious powers?

"Charley Pierce. You sent for me."

More lies. Everyone lied to him—that much was clear. Juno, Morris Walls, Lukas Adler, Althea. Liars, all of them.

"Go away." He had to think. There was a way out of this, a way he must have written into the code.

CHAPTER 56

IT WAS ONE thing for Althea to have an affair with Morris Walls—or with anyone—but it was quite something else for her to flaunt it by having passionate sex with the traitorous employee right down the hall from Charley's office.

Althea knew that Charley knew. Even the ultra passionate Althea wouldn't've been so wrapped up in her latest conquest that she'd be oblivious to Charley's awareness of everything going on. No, she knew that he knew, even if she acted like he couldn't possibly know.

And she'd written the clever little addition to Juno's brilliant code. He'd seen her do it. Stood at the door of his study at their home in Osada City and watched her at three in the morning, her so-called creative hour. She'd thought she was one-upping Juno, but even Althea must've realized that was hopeless. No one could surpass Juno, who'd written the most advanced program in the history of computers—a program that would directly influence every user and eventually everyone, even if they never had any contact with the program.

The virus was ingenious, something only a devious mind like Juno's could come up with. Yet, like everything Juno created, it had possibilities even she wasn't aware of. Charley was, though. That was his job—taking the genius of Juno Sangstrom and turning it into real-life practicalities.

Like eliminating Althea's lovers.

His first focus had been on Oliver Hirata, who, besides romancing Althea, had also had an interlude with Juno. Killing him was like killing two people—the one who'd been intimate with Althea and the one who'd had the stupidity to get involved with Juno.

At one of their regular meetings, he'd mentioned Hirata to Juno and she'd acted like she didn't even know him. But of course she did know him. He lived next door to her. And Charley knew everything Juno did. He'd made sure of it from the beginning of their crazy arrangement, the one Juno had devised and he'd foolishly agreed to. But he'd had her under constant surveillance since the beginning. He'd never trusted her.

Juno Sangstrom and Oliver Hirata at back-to-back Convergences. Juno and Hirata in their suite at the Thorne, which Charley found out was where the creep took every one of his interludes. Charley had hired Hirata just to keep an eye on him, but even he hadn't suspected Althea would get involved with such a sleaze. Yet she did.

Hirata's end wasn't what Charley had hoped it would be. He'd imagined him succumbing to a gruesome death while Althea gazed on in horror. And Kaj Banerjee, who died alone and unnoticed, was an even less fulfilling event. Althea was untouched, going about her usual ways, unconcerned, as though nothing had happened to anyone she knew or cared about. If she cared about anyone other than herself.

Too bad, really, about Beryl Carson. She would've been the perfect shield of jealousy to hold up against Althea's onslaughts. Beryl's death was an accident, one whose origin Charley could only guess at. Although Beryl had been at his apartment at the Normandie, where a computer he used was located.

But he didn't care. Once Desire Me was up and running, no one and nothing else would matter. Except Althea, of course. She would always matter. In some way, a way that had started to recede with every passing hour.

Charley was on the brink. He would finally have the power he'd dreamed of ever since he first encountered Juno Sangstrom's brilliance. He knew right then she'd be the key to his glorious future. He'd lived with her, made love to her, brought her into his ambit, and taken what he needed from her.

If things were different, he'd thank her for Meet Me, since he never would've met Althea without it.

The brilliant Althea. Brilliant in a different way from Juno. Scheming—that was how Charley always thought of her. That's why she wrote such successful fabulas, their plots pulsating with intricate, surprising designs. But none of the fiction she wrote was as surprising to Charley as the code she'd put into Juno's program—her little joke.

Yet after Charley had seen Althea in his study, he'd been inspired to take a closer look at the program and saw new ways to refine it to his benefit. Then he'd locked the code. No one else, not even Juno, would be able to touch it.

CHAPTER 57

JONATHAN LEE SUMMERS sat out in the waiting area with Sean and Zee Walls. Toby Hsu had gone downstairs to get coffee.

"Why does he want to see you?" Sean had already asked Jonathan Lee this question several times, but she was hoping the repetition would cause him to come up with an answer.

"He can't know we cracked the code," Jonathan Lee said. He was leaning back against the wall, his eyes closed, his hands clasped behind his head.

"Maybe he suspects it," Ziva said.

"Implausible. He barely knows who I am."

"But he did want to hire you a few years ago so he must have a good idea of what you're capable of. And maybe he attended the conference where you originally suggested the idea of a computer virus that could infect people."

"Don't I already feel guilty enough?" Jonathan Lee took his hands out from behind his head, opened his eyes, and sat up. "It was just an idea, nothing more."

"But you must've thought someone would do it one day. Why else would you have thought of it?"

"Yeah. That's the guilt part. The more harm something can cause, the greater the chance someone will invent it, no matter how difficult it might be to create. Someone said that once, long ago. Aristotle or Pascal or Anscombe."

"I have to go home," Sean said. "The buckets in my attic are probably all full at this point and Sebastian needs his dinner."

"I'll take you," Jonathan Lee said. "Maybe by the time I get back here, Pierce will have figured out why he wanted to talk to me in the first place."

"If he's still here," Ziva said.

"What do you mean?"

"I mean I sat in this very waiting area with him when Althea was so—well, before. I got the impression Charley Pierce is capable of anything and won't stop until he gets whatever it is he wants."

"But Althea died," Jonathan Lee said.

"I'm not so sure he didn't want that." Zee shook her head. "He put on a good act, but half the time I was seeing through that act. Lukas and I talked about it when Charley wasn't here. Lukas knows all the tricks and can spot faulty acting. He should work for the joukko."

"Why didn't you say something before?"

"I didn't think much about it," Zee said. "I was too busy trying to take care of Ethan."

Sean stood up and starting pacing. "Is Pierce just manipulating us? Manipulating the entire situation?"

"Well, the guy does own half the known world."

CHAPTER 58

ALFWAY TO SEAN'S, the torrential rain had reduced the range of vision to less than a meter in front of the transcer. Sean slowed down and Jonathan Lee started talking.

"Juno's the murderer," he said. "But I think Charley helped her."

"How did you come to that conclusion?" Sean was hunched over, squinting into the unseen future.

"Charley's been Juno's editor of sorts since the beginning. He takes her genius and improves it, or you might say he fixes it, although it's hardly broken. Being able to see exactly what her coding is has been a revelation. Like discovering the origin of imagination itself."

"You're exaggerating."

"A bit, but it's unique and astounding—and I haven't seen very much of it yet."

"Why would Juno want to kill the people who've died? Althea . . . well, Juno was jealous. But Hirata? Banerjee? Beryl? Vern Healy? Jordan Fields? I got the impression she was pals with Fields. And why would she care about Maizy Newell? All she did was work at the Normandie's front desk. But maybe they're just covers for the people she really wanted to see dead."

"Hell, Sean. I can't answer that. How can you get into the mind of a killer? Don't you have to be a killer in order to figure it out?"

"I hope not, or we're doomed. Come in with me a minute?"

Inside, Jonathan Lee and Sean were met by a sopping wet, mewing Sebastian, a host of gushing torrents bleeding through the ceiling, and ten centimeters of standing water.

"Sebastian, let's get you out of here," Sean said as she bent over to pick up the drenched cat. He climbed up onto her shoulders and licked her hair.

"Want to inspect the damage first?" Jonathan Lee said.

Sean shook her head. "Look at this, JL," she said, pointing at the ceiling, where new cracks were forming as they stood there, releasing ever greater downpours into the living room. "I have to face it—my stacks are being destroyed. Or they're already destroyed. There's nothing I can do."

"You seem almost calm about it." Jonathan Lee put his arm around Sean, and Sebastian climbed off her shoulders and onto his.

"Seem," Sean said. Inside she was raging. Why hadn't she gotten the roof repaired years ago? How had she allowed this to happen? Why didn't she keep the stacks in a safe place? Who else was going to die of the leap?

"We'll stay at Beryl's and figure things out in the morning."

By the time Jonathan Lee and Sean woke up the next morning, the still somewhat damp Sebastian nestled between them, Hal Ledyard was standing over them, delivering the news.

"Ed and Dorian have come up with what might be a cure for the leap—or at least a preventative. It's right there in the code. Been there all along. Violet discovered it."

"Ethan?" Sean and Jonathan Lee sat up and Sebastian jumped down and raced past Ledyard.

"Doing better. He wants to be the guinea pig but he might not need to be. Too soon to tell." Sean thought Ledyard looked like he hadn't slept in five years but he always looked somewhat drowsy.

"What about Charley Pierce?" Jonathan Lee said.

"Pierce and Sangstrom are both under arrest."

"He didn't escape?"

"How did you know he escaped?"

"Zee thought he might."

"Climbed through a duct in the wall, but they found him. Toby Hsu said she wants both of you at the station as soon as you're up."

"I'm up," Jonathan Lee said, rubbing his eyes, then his neck. "Sean?"

"Wide awake."

CHAPTER 59

Three months later

THE COURTROOM WAS packed. Not only were the two legendary
owners of Pierce Sangstrom on trial, but Lukas Adler was
scheduled to give testimony today and no one wanted to miss
out.

Ethan Stiles, looking pale but collected and attentive, was finishing
up his testimony. Jonathan Lee Summers would be next.

"I think the charts speak for themselves," Ethan said. He pointed
to the array hovering over the front of the courtroom, where the dia-
gram he and Jonathan Lee had spent uncountable hours working over
was. A combination of careful precision and easy-to-understand
graphics displayed just how the virus had been able to transfer itself
from computer to human.

Half the room was dazzled by this while the other half shook their
heads in total disbelief. A computer virus that infected humans? Could
never happen. This had to be a fairy tale. The defense had been working
this angle the entire trial. There was no such thing as the so-called leap.
The very idea was absurd and even more absurd was the idea that either
Juno Sangstrom or Charley Pierce would ever want to kill anyone—by
this or any other method. These kind, philanthropic innovators. People
whose creations were in everyone's homes and businesses—helping
them, never hurting them. Making their lives smoother and easier, not
killing them.

That Pierce and Sangstrom had joined forces for the trial still
shocked Sean. She, Jonathan Lee, Ethan, and Zee had discussed into

the ground why and how this had happened. The conclusion they'd all come to was that no matter how Charley and Juno felt about each other—love, hate, jealousy, rage, vengefulness, disgust—nothing was more important than Pierce Sangstrom itself. Neither of them wanted to see their life's work destroyed.

Ethan got up, pointed to various parts of the array and explained yet again how the leap worked, how the photonic filamentation was the medium transmitting the virus from computer to human, how he was able to isolate the virus itself, and how the team Jonathan Lee had put together had been able to confirm each step of the process. How they'd found the cure.

When Ethan finished, the judge, who Sean thought might be coming around to believing the leap was real, called a recess. The participants and observers in the room seemed to breathe out a collective release of tension before everyone got up to leave. In the back of the visitors' gallery, Boyd McCormick, now fully recovered, whispered something to the person on his left and they both huffed out a suppressed laugh.

Zee had ordered a picnic lunch and the group sat out in the park two blocks from the courthouse, choosing a spot well isolated from prying ears.

"That went pretty well, I think." Ethan looked over to Ziva, who nodded.

"I can't imagine going back to the Acres." Jonathan Lee's non sequitur stopped Sean from taking another bite of her sandwich. She put it down and said, "Because you think your testimony could harm your academic reputation?"

Jonathan Lee laughed and Ethan said, "Like that could happen."

"I only wondered—"

"I just need to do something different. My priorities have changed." He looked at Sean.

They'd been living together at Beryl's house since the flood had destroyed Sean's place, but she'd always thought the situation was temporary. That he'd be going back to the Acres as soon as the trial was over and she'd be doing whatever it was she was going to do next. She had an idea, but hadn't talked to Jonathan Lee about it. Ziva was the only person Sean had confided in.

"Charley and Juno sitting there next to each other, like they're friends. Sometimes even I can believe it. Then I remember what Lukas told me about what happened in the river." Ziva took a drink of water and passed the bottle to Ethan.

"They're going to get away with it, Jay, aren't they? Despite all our work." Ethan turned to his former roommate and oldest friend.

"I hope to hell they aren't," Jonathan Lee said.

"Keep hoping," Sean said, "but if I had to stake my life on it, I'd say they *are* going to get away with it. The evidence seems clear to all of us, but have you been looking at the faces of the jurors? Most of them seem like they feel sorry for Charley and Juno. They're going to buy into the defense's position—these deaths were accidents, the science is shaky, and it's a mere coincidence the victims are said to have some connection to each other."

"But they *do* have a connection to each other." No matter how much Sean had tried to convince her otherwise, Ziva clung to her belief that justice would prevail, that justice always prevailed. Sean, though, knew firsthand that that wasn't always the case, even if she couldn't stand it.

"What are you going to do after the trial?" Jonathan Lee said to Ziva.

She looked at Ethan. "We haven't decided yet. I do have a property out west, but I've never been there. And I still have Kaj's museum to finish. It's not in the Normandie, but I've been able to re-create everything in the building I bought over by the river."

"Are you ready for your testimony, JL?" Ethan said.

"Juno Sangstrom's been making copious notes. I'm half afraid that whatever she feeds to her lawyer is going to crush me under the weight of her expertise."

"But you're an expert too," Sean said.

"Do you see me owning half the world's most influential mega-corp? I'm just a two-bit instructor who had the misfortune of discussing the possibility of a virus like the leap at a symposium a few years back. The defense has already called me a crackpot once, and I haven't given even a minute's testimony yet."

"You'll be fine. I survived," Ethan said. "And if they don't believe you, at least you tried."

"And at least no one else got infected," Ziva said. "We have your group to thank for that, Jonathan Lee. Isn't that the most important thing? All those lives that might have been affected but instead have been saved?"

Sean threw down her still-uneaten sandwich. "No, it isn't."

Everyone stared at her.

"I mean, yes, yes. Yes, of course it is, but it's not the *only* thing. Zee, I know you feel the same way. Justice has to be served. Juno Sangstrom and Charley Pierce can't just walk away from the deaths of half a dozen people like they had nothing to do with them. Like they hadn't planned them. Like they hadn't *enjoyed* them."

"But even you think that's not unlikely," Jonathan Lee said. He put his arm around Sean's shoulders and gave her a hug.

"Just because that's what I think doesn't mean I agree with the outcome. You'd better give the best testimony ever given at any trial in history," she said to Jonathan Lee. "I'm depending on you."

"You can always depend on me," he said.

"You should eat something, Sean. We have to be back at court in a half hour." Ethan lay down on the grass and put his head on Ziva's lap.

"Have some cashews. They'll sustain you." Zee tossed a packet to Sean.

Sean opened it and took out a cashew, examined it, then put it back. "They're going to get away with it. And then—Desire Me will be the next big thing. The trial's turning into an unpaid advertising campaign for it."

"I've been rehearsing for weeks. Stop worrying," Jonathan Lee said.

But Sean was worried, and even though Jonathan Lee's testimony was brilliant, concise, understandable, unwavering, accurate, and convincing, when the defense called Prentiss, the know-nothing Osada City medical examiner, to the stand, Sean sensed it was all over for them. For the truth. For justice.

CHAPTER 60

Six months after the trial

THEY'RE UNTOUCHABLE, AREN'T they?" Maizy was lying on her side by the pool, watching Lukas finish his morning laps. She'd done the first twenty with him—far better than the two or three she'd been able to manage at first—but she was no match for the champion swimmer.

Lukas finished his workout, pulled himself out of the pool and up beside Maizy, then shook his head, sending hundreds of water droplets onto her nearly dry body.

"Oh yeah. There's never been any doubt."

"Ziva doubted. She'd hoped. You know that. She's very disappointed. About that, I mean. Not about everything."

"I tried telling her, but she's a hard sell."

"Do you miss Althea?"

"You can stop asking me that in another week." Lukas figured he had to give Maizy a definite timeframe. He knew she still couldn't quite believe someone she thought of as a celebrity would be interested in her. But he didn't think of himself that way and he was interested in her.

"Only one more week? But you could answer in the meanwhile."

"I miss her fabulas. She was the best writer around and I haven't been offered a part since that I have any interest in doing."

"You're not going to quit, are you?" Maizy squinted into the sun.

"I'm all but quit right now."

"What will you do?"

"We'll figure it out."

"I like it out here, away from everyone, from everything."

"That's the idea."

"I keep thinking about the Convergence. Something happened to me there. Something still humming inside me, waiting to take form."

"You're still recovering, Maizy. Give it some time."

"Thanks for having me out here, Lukas. It's been wonderful."

Lukas turned around to face Maizy. He brushed sparkling water droplets off her shoulder then took her hands in his.

"It *is* wonderful. It's going to continue to be wonderful."

"How can you know?"

"I just know."

"I can't figure out if the leap was the worst thing that ever happened or the best."

"Both," he said. Lukas had wondered the same thing and had come to that conclusion. "Both."

"During the interlude I had with Oliver—"

"You don't have to talk about it."

"But I want to. I want to tell you how I felt then and how I feel now—it's completely different. Then I was whirling, carried along on a path someone else had built. But now, Lukas—now I feel like I'm home."

"You are home, Maizy."

CHAPTER 61

"I
N SOME WAYS, it's like it never happened. Except for ... but
sometimes I don't get the connection," Ziva said. "As though
something *else* happened to Oliver and Kaj. And it's not like I knew
Althea."

"Beryl," Ethan said. "What the hell was she doing with Charley
Pierce? Did she really think he was going to fund her research? Pierce
has never funded anything that wasn't to his direct benefit."

"Maybe she didn't realize that, Ethan. From what I gather, she
lived a life removed from that kind of common knowledge. Jonathan
Lee told me she was so involved in her specialty that even when they
were married, she barely knew what he was doing, much less what was
going on in the rest of the world."

"Or cared, I'm sorry to say. Jay had a lot of problems with their
relationship, but I'd always thought it would work out, especially after
Patterson was born."

"We'll find out how much of a difference it makes three months
from now." Zee looked down at herself. "Right, kid?"

"Kid will be born and we still won't have a name."

"Don't worry, we'll have a name. It's on my list."

"It's not so bad here at Keff, is it, Zee? I know it's not what you
might've had in mind. But after Prentiss pushed me out of Genesia, I
didn't want to turn this down."

"I like it here, and Ed's been introducing me to an interesting
group. I've got the Banerjee exhibition next month, the renovations for
the nursery, and so many ideas I don't know what to do with them all."

"You didn't have to buy this house. We could've lived in the housing they provide."

"Ethan, you still don't get it, do you? I could buy this entire campus and it wouldn't make a noticeable dent in my assets. This house is simply a comfortable place to live for now."

"For now?"

"Think of where you were a year ago. Not talking to Sean. Bored with your job. No leap to occupy your time. We can't know what could happen next."

"Think of where you were, Zee."

"I know. I was so upset that Morris had disappeared. Sean's still looking for him even though I told her to stop a long time ago."

"Jay left the Acres like he hadn't been rooted to the place for most of his life. Gave his classes to Ledyard and Violet and had them appoint Dorian to his post. I hope he's happy."

"Does Jonathan Lee know how to be happy?"

"He can apply his memories from the ancient times."

Zee laughed, and said, "The kid agrees with you. Check it out."

Ethan put his hand on Ziva's belly and felt for the kicks. Zee put her hand over Ethan's.

"Ethan, it still bothers me. No one except a few of us know what really happened—not just Juno and Charley's guilt, but the leap itself and all its insidious possibilities. Most people think it was some rare, mysterious ailment affecting only a few people. And that it's over."

"The defense did a good job of making the facts seem like a wild fantasy conjured up by a collection of fools. If I didn't know what I know, they might've convinced me."

Ziva shook her head. "Your presentation and Jonathan Lee's were perfect. No one could have done a better job, but—"

Ethan interrupted her. They'd been over this so many times. "The jury didn't want to believe it and the science was over their heads."

"Ethan, do you think it's really over?"

"I try not to think along those lines too often. Pierce Sangstrom's doing better than ever. Desire Me is a monumental success. And who knows what those two might be up to now that they've literally gotten away with murder."

"Sean told me she heard they bought the building next to PS and are turning the top two floors into their residence. But not even a year ago they were trying to kill each other and would have succeeded if Lukas hadn't shown up. It's craziness."

"Somehow, they need each other, despite everything."

"Maybe. I used to think I needed Morris. Anyone can make a mistake."

"Zee, thanks for taking a chance on me. After what you've been through—"

"This was never taking a chance. I knew right from the beginning."

CHAPTER 62

SEAN HAD BEEN out at the Flats for a while now but today was the first time she'd encountered this man—tall, lean, his skin glowing with sweat. He got up from the place where he was working and turned around, smiling, as she approached.

"Hah," he said. "You're the investigator Zee hired, aren't you?"

"None other," Sean said. "And—"

"I have a new name. Part of the culture here. Alexander. Pleased to meet you."

"I'm still Sean. Maybe I'll come up with another name eventually. Nice T-shirt you've got there." Sean pointed at the well-worn blue shirt with the familiar font and the PS Delenda Est slogan on it. Not exactly what she expected to see Morris Walls wearing when she finally tracked him down—although she hadn't exactly tracked him down even though at one time she'd suspected he'd be out at the Flats—but it made sense.

"When I designed it I was hoping more would come of it. A movement. A revolution. I still hope, but I'm no longer so involved."

Sean stepped back. "You designed this? But didn't you work—"

"I'm Alexander now. I have nothing to do with any of that. And, yes, I designed it. I started it. I used to enjoy history but, being out here, I've come to realize its meaninglessness."

"Why did you leave Zee?"

"It wasn't that I left Zee, although I gather she's doing quite well these days, it's that I had to get away from Charley Pierce before he killed me along with everyone else he had it in for."

"Everyone else?" Sean sat down on the tree stump next to her, and Morris-now-Alexander squatted like he'd never been a corporate bigshot but had always been out at the Flats.

"Sure. Of course I don't know what went on in the sick creep's mind, but after Althea showed me what she'd done with what must have become Desire Me, I wanted to see if Charley or Juno would get the joke. Althea was very funny, very entertaining.

"If you rearranged the elements of her addition, it could be interpreted as 'I'll have the last laugh.' Except she didn't. And anyway, Charley made vast changes afterward. I might not've been able to read the code but I could see it changing, expanding."

Alexander stopped talking and Sean stayed silent. When he started again, he looked away from her, out across the fields, and gazed up at the daytime moon.

"The way Charley would look at me in the hallways at PS. Not-so-subtle threats he launched my way when he thought no one else would hear. About how my time was limited and an implication he meant Althea's time as well.

"I tried to warn her, but she said I was being paranoid, it was all harmless. Finally I came to realize that as long as I stayed at Pierce, I was in danger. That was right around the time Althea lost interest in me, so I had my opening and I took it."

"Do you think he meant to kill her?"

"Thinking and knowing are very different."

"Which is it?"

"He meant to kill her. She was in his way and, worse, she'd escalated her infidelities and was carrying on right under his nose."

"He's back with Juno."

"I've heard."

"Leif asked me if I'd like to stay on and be the archivist, take over Nasir's job, but I haven't decided yet." Would Morris/Alexander tell her to get out? She now knew more about him than he might want anyone at the Flats—or anyone at all—to know.

"The place grows on you. Give it a while and see what you think. I'd never intended to stay here, but now I don't intend to leave. You know Pliny, don't you? Came out here to escape a dead mother and an uncaring father. Now Pliny's devoted to an in-depth examination of the caldera."

"Pliny's father cares. He just doesn't have any idea how to go about it. But he's trying."

"So that's who that fellow is. The one with the orange cat who's always following him around."

"Sebastian. Or Egon. He answers to both. The cat, I mean."

"Good to meet you, Sean." Alexander pointed to his chest, then patted the inscription. "There's still hope. The movement's not dead. And best of luck with Jonathan Lee Summers."

He turned away, effectively dismissing Sean.

So Morris Walls knew who Jonathan Lee Summers was and that he was Pliny's father. And knew Sean. And knew Charley was responsible for the murders. Not Juno. Although Sean wasn't convinced Juno wasn't also responsible. She'd started it. She was the one who designed a program that could insinuate itself into the user. Not a program, a *virus*. She'd admitted it the day Toby'd interviewed her.

Sean went back to the tent she shared with Jonathan Lee, the place where they made love every night, the place where they'd spent hours dissecting and analyzing what had happened, trying to get a sense of rightness about it but never succeeding. And talking about their pasts and their future. Making plans, turning over possibilities. Pliny was letting Jonathan Lee in little by little, a sometimes excruciating process, but Jonathan Lee was determined to see it through.

CHAPTER 63

THE TALENTED, BRILLIANT, beautiful Juno Sangstrom. That day, many years ago, when Charley'd understood that his future, his fortune—his very life—were forever entangled with hers . . .

He loved her but he'd never tell her, not in any way that would let her know he meant it. He rarely told even himself although he understood it throughout his being. No one else could ever take her place on the altar of his soul's imagination.

When they were developing Meet Me he saw his way out. Because as long as he stayed with Juno, lived with her, wrapped his life around her, he'd never have the singular power that was rightfully his. If the insightful Juno ever knew she was writing the code that would separate them, she never acted like she did.

Althea Livesy was perfection itself. He could love her freely, unencumbered by the weight of inescapable need. Her very existence protected him from Juno's insistent presence. He convinced himself he couldn't live without her, as though she were some sort of replacement for the irreplaceable Juno Sangstrom. As if anyone could fill that role.

Then Althea started flaunting her affairs. Charley was so enmeshed in his self-protective, self-invented role of needing her that he became incapable of containing his jealousy. Maybe it was more like fury. That Oliver Hirata had had interludes with both Juno and Althea had Charley hitting a breaking point, yet even that hadn't driven him over the edge.

No, Morris Walls had that distinction. Charley had hired him, trusted him, depended on him. Then he carried on with Althea a few meters away from Charley's own office, his private sanctuary. On Wednesdays, the days he was devoting to Althea.

If Juno hadn't written Desire Me, what might've happened? Charley wondered about this sometimes. Would he be here now? Would he have been subjected to the trial? To the scrutiny?

But Desire Me was itself irresistible, presenting the ideal avenue for Charley to get rid of everyone he wanted gone from his life, from life itself. Oliver Hirata. Kaj Banerjee, who Charley suspected Juno had also dallied with although he had no proof. Althea herself, who acted like she'd never needed Charley. And to think that the silly joke she'd written into the code had been the impetus for the work he'd done, ensuring her end.

Too bad about Beryl Carson—killed, no doubt, by Juno herself. Beryl could've replaced Althea for a while, distracting him from Juno, taking up that deep inner zone, the one Juno ruled over.

The day he'd asked for Jonathan Lee Summers, the only person Charley could think of who might offer credible support that Juno was to blame for everything. Should he have waited for his arrival? Would Summers have come? At the trial, he'd seemed a forceful adversary to the very foundations of Pierce Sangstrom, yet even his convincing testimony had withered under the glare of an embedded cultural certainty that what he was suggesting was not only absurd but an utter impossibility.

The new lodgings next door to Pierce Sangstrom were nearly finished. Charley and Juno were living on the upper floor now while the work on the lower level was being completed. Charley's life and work had merged. Desire Me was a thousand times more successful than Meet Me had ever been, helped along by the publicity from the trial.

Juno was working on something new, something even more compelling than Desire Me. She hadn't let him see it yet, but he knew it would be a success and that Pierce Sangstrom would soon be the all-powerful entity he'd always envisioned.

Charley rolled over toward Juno, put his arm around her slim waist, pulled her toward him, listened to her sigh in her sleep. Thought about the day of Althea's funeral, about the opportunity he'd had and how it'd been destroyed by Lukas Adler, one of Charley's intended victims. Yet it hadn't worked out, and after Althea died, he'd lost interest.

He could strangle Juno right now, in her sleep. She was much smaller than he was and she wouldn't be able to break his grip.

It was a burden to need someone else so much, to need someone else who was a hundred times more talented and more inventive and innovative than you could ever be.

But it was also a fathomless draw, insistent, necessary. Without Juno there would be no Pierce Sangstrom, he'd be someone else, some-one less than the powerful person he'd become, a person who could arrange for the deaths of everyone he wanted to eliminate.

Juno turned over and faced Charley, snuggled closer, put her mouth on his, and whispered his name.

CHAPTER 64

"CHARLEY."

He hadn't changed. Not really. He was, if anything, more himself than he'd ever been. The very person Juno Sangstrom had been inexorably attracted to, the one she couldn't let go of. Her need. Her desire.

Charley wasn't the experienced lover Oliver Hirata had been, and he never would be. There was something missing there or maybe it was more that Oliver had had a talent that could be improved upon and embellished but could never be learned by someone else. No matter how much instruction Juno gave Charley—and he was a willing pupil. But Oliver was a natural, like Juno was a natural, although at a different sport.

Charley was under the mistaken impression that Juno's talent was in writing code when in fact her talent was in manipulating the world to bend to her liking. The process was slower than she'd imagined it might be, but she enjoyed it anyway.

Years ago she'd made a miscalculation. All Juno had intended was that Charley would use the opportunity to understand without doubt or hesitation that Juno was the only one he truly loved, wanted, and needed. Yet he'd chosen Althea.

This time, though, Juno knew exactly what she was doing. This time her creation would be to her own benefit.

"Charley," she said, "make love to me."

He grunted and hugged her to him. He'd never be the lover Oliver Hirata was. No one could be—she was convinced of that. But Oliver was not Charley, and couldn't be.

The day she'd told Oliver it was over was still as clear to her as it had been back then.

"I have to get to work," she'd said to him, climbing out of their bed at the Thorne's best suite.

"You're not staying? You always stay."

"I don't *always* anything."

"Ah. Well, I'll see you for dinner."

"No. It's done, Oliver. I've had enough." Although the truth was that Juno had long ago promised herself that she'd never let anyone but her be the one to end things. Not ever again.

Oliver sat up in the bed and glared at her. "It's not over."

Juno laughed. Oliver had said he enjoyed her laugh, so it seemed an appropriate end to their interlude.

"You should try Althea Pierce next," Juno said while she was getting dressed.

"You're diabolical." Oliver shook his head. He stopped glaring.

Juno left the Thorne.

Oliver had at least three other interludes before he finally took Juno's advice and went after Althea. Now they were both dead. Just as Juno had planned. Beryl too—something she'd had to take care of herself. And Jordan Fields, who knew too much.

"Charley," she said.

She had the ideas and wrote the code, but Charley did the heavy lifting, just like he always did. So reliable, dependable. And the way he'd lock the code always amused her, as though she couldn't get past his puerile efforts, even though she never let him know she could.

Back in the beginning Juno'd wanted to find out if the virus she'd written in Desire Me was capable of everything she'd dreamed of, and

Charley had made sure it was. The virus could do more than influence its victims—it could kill them.

Juno had given the orders but in the end Charley was the executioner.

She was working on something new now, something that would make Desire Me seem like child's play. Juno hadn't yet allowed Charley to look at it, although he'd already been subjected to it that day in her apartment.

The program's working name was Mastery. It would surpass all of Juno's previous inventions, convincing the user they were in control.

But Juno would be in control, just as she'd always been.

CHAPTER 65

JONATHAN LEE SUMMERS sat at the rim of the caldera, Sebastian by his side. Patterson was working below with the same tireless energy the kid had previously devoted to avoiding doing anything Beryl or Jonathan Lee requested.

How had Beryl gotten caught up in this mess? Jonathan Lee still hadn't come up with a satisfying explanation. Sean'd suggested that perhaps Beryl was interested in Charley Pierce, but Jonathan Lee thought it more likely that she'd been interested in his money and how to extricate it and inject it into her projects.

Yet what had Jonathan Lee really known about Beryl? Almost nothing and now even less. Patterson too. Although Jonathan Lee was currently trying to make up for his past mistakes there. Every once in a while he thought he might be succeeding.

Sean Meade, though. There he'd made only minimal mistakes. She put up with him. Was living in a tent with him—although a damned nice tent. And without any pileup of stacks. Was talking with him. Listened to him. Shared with him.

Sebastian was a poor listener but he'd latched on to Jonathan Lee even though Sean had been his savior. Sean can't have been happy about this inexplicable loyalty but she never complained about it.

"There you two are," Sean said. She sat down on Jonathan Lee's non-Sebastian side.

"How's your day been?"

"Just had a heart-to-heart with Morris Walls. Nothing of consequence." She laughed.

"Morris Walls? He's here?"

"Currently known as Alexander. I think he left off 'the Great' out of a sense of false modesty." Jonathan Lee laughed along with Sean.

"What's his story?"

"It might be just that—a story. But I believed most of it. Especially the part where he's the founder and chief instigator of the PS Delenda Est movement."

"You're making it up."

"No chance. He's even wearing the iconic T-shirt."

"Why would a high-level Pierce Sangstrom employee want to get rid of the megacorp?"

"Resentment, maybe. He's got nothing nice to say about Charley Pierce. And Desire Me scared him. He was convinced Charley was going to kill him. That's why he disappeared."

"It's not over."

Sebastian rolled onto his side and started licking his chest.

"No one's got the leap anymore. That's over. Isn't it?" Sean said.

"In its previous form, it's finished. We made sure it would be. But in a future form? I can't answer to that. And both Pierce and Sangstrom terrify me. Particularly the Sangstrom half."

"Charley's no sweetheart either. I wonder if anything would've changed if you'd been able to talk to him at the Genesia Clinic."

"You mean would he be in prison for the rest of his life?" Jonathan Lee rubbed Sebastian's left ear.

"Along with Juno."

"Didn't you have the answer there in one of your stacks?"

"I think about it early in the morning. Maybe I'll remember something."

"If we stay out here are you going to take the archivist job?"

"We?"

"We could go somewhere else. Somewhere new. Let me know when you make up your mind." Jonathan Lee's former well-ordered life had been discarded but he didn't care. The disarray had its own rhythm and method, one he was in sync with. He had a new appreciation of his dear friend Ethan's haphazard methods.

"Pliny's here and you two still have a lot of territory to go over."

"There're a lot of other volcanoes to explore out there. This was just a convenience, since we'd been here. A thousand years ago."

"Ten thousand years ago. JL, I've been thinking of getting a PS Delenda Est T-shirt."

"Does it come with a target drawn on the back?"

"Doesn't need one. There's probably a tracking mechanism sewn into the collar."

"I wish I thought that were funny. You know, Sean, we can stay out here as long as you want. I need a break from everything. I think you might too." Jonathan Lee gestured behind them, in what he thought was the direction of Osada City and the rest of the non-Flats world.

"Zee and Ethan—an unlikely couple, don't you think?"

"Not really. Ethan's always had unpredictable tastes. Leaving the Acres for Keff's a good example."

"The exalted Acres. But you left too."

"I met Ethan there. In a way, it's the foundation for what happened with the leap. With us. Don't knock it."

"You still feel responsible, don't you?"

"Absolutely." Jonathan Lee felt more than responsible—he felt guilty.

"If you could go back to that symposium, if you had another chance at it, what would you do?"

"Hell, Sean. Are you suggesting I could?"

One of the reasons Jonathan Lee was so taken with Sean Meade was that she had a way of coming up with the extraordinary. Jonathan Lee had been the one to suggest a computer virus that could infect humans but Sean had been the one with the vision to realize it had actually happened.

"Hey, Dad, come look at this," Patterson shouted from the bottom of the caldera.

Sebastian stretched, yawned, and sauntered toward Patterson. Sean and Jonathan Lee followed.

Halfway down the slope, Jonathan Lee laced his fingers through Sean's and said, "You didn't mean it, did you? About going back?"

"There was something in stack number 5324, I seem to recall." Sean laughed, let go of Jonathan Lee's hand, and started running. Jonathan Lee followed her.

Just as Sebastian and Sean were nearing Patterson, Jonathan Lee stopped, remembering what he'd said at the symposium two years after the one where he'd riffed on the concept of a computer virus that could leap to humans. He'd brought up the idea that one day computers, with their vast powers to churn through all information, real and imagined, might be able to break through the barriers that had so far prevented time travel from being anything but a fiction.

Could this be on the verge of realization? Jonathan Lee shook his head. He wasn't really psychic, despite his occasional insights. And, unlike the leap, this was truly impossible. Yet Sean had a way of bringing his thought experiments out into the open and giving them the air they needed to manifest.

Sean knew what was in the stacks. He'd get her to tell him the details of #5324.

Pliny was holding up a rock, showing it off. Sebastian stretched himself out on the ground nearby.

Sean waved to Jonathan Lee, who walked toward her, his thoughts for their future taking on a new and unexpected shape.

AUTHOR'S NOTES

R. T.W. LIPKIN lives in New York with her husband and three cats.

The Leap was written during the covid pandemic, the writing slowed down to the sludgy pace of the world. The many processes involved in getting the book ready for publication were interspersed between periods of ennui, resistance, and determination.

Carthago delenda est (Carthage must be destroyed) is an abbreviation of the phrase *Ceterum (autem) censeo Carthaginem esse delendam* (Furthermore, I consider that Carthage must be destroyed). Cato the Elder spoke this phrase at the end of all his speeches in the Roman Senate prior to the Third Punic War. He said it even at the end of speeches having nothing to do with Carthage. Quite the war hawk. Eventually, in 146 BC, Rome did destroy Carthage.

As reassurance, understand that what's described in this book isn't possible . . . although, okay, pretty much everything's possible. And reassurances aren't necessarily reassuring.

If you enjoyed the book, leave a review, tell your friends, read my other titles. Forget reality and immerse yourself in fiction.

Made in United States
North Haven, CT
29 October 2024

The Life and Legacy

of

Lincoln-Grant School

Covington, Kentucky

1866–1976

THE LIFE AND LEGACY

OF

LINCOLN-GRANT SCHOOL
COVINGTON, KENTUCKY
1866–1976

by

JOSEPH M. WALTON

LITTLE MIAMI PUBLISHING CO.
Milford, Ohio
2010

Little Miami Publishing Co.
P.O. Box 588
Milford, Ohio 45150-0588
www.littlemiamibooks.com

Printed in the United States of America on acid-free paper.

ISBN-13: 978-1-932250-83-1
ISBN-10: 1-932250-83-2

Library of Congress Control Number: 2010932144

The Road Not Taken

Two roads diverged in a yellow wood,
And sorry I could not travel both
And be one traveler, long I stood
And looked down one as far as I could
To where it bent in the undergrowth;

Then took the other, as just as fair,
And having perhaps the better claim,
Because it was grassy and wanted wear;
Though as for that the passing there
Had worn them really about the same,

And both that morning equally lay
In leaves no step had trodden black.
Oh, I kept the first for another day!
Yet knowing how way leads on to way,
I doubted if I should ever come back.

I shall be telling this with a sigh
Somewhere ages and ages hence;
Two roads diverged in a wood, and I—
I took the one less traveled by,
And that has made all the difference.

—by Robert Frost

Contents

LIST OF FIGURES

LIST OF PHOTOGRAPHS

Acknowledgments

This author wishes to acknowledge several individuals and organizations whose written works, contributions of historical materials or information, general support, and other efforts aided in the writing of this book. The following listings may be incomplete.

Research and published articles by Theodore H. H. Harris, a 1962 graduate of William Grant High School, and an African American Historian, were extremely important to the development of information about the early Lincoln-Grant school locations, as well as the shared histories of black feeder schools, such as Southgate School in Newport and the Latonia Colored School. The author extends thanks to Mr. Harris for those contributions as well as other written materials and historical photographs. Several personal conversations with Mr. Harris and others resulted in very productive clarifications of various aspects of the early history of the school. The historical data on Lincoln-Grant and its black feeder elementary schools in Boone, Campbell, and Kenton counties were also aided significantly by the writings of Jim Reis, a *Kentucky Post* editorial writer, who often collaborated with Ted Harris in developing several helpful newspaper and Internet articles on Lincoln-Grant through a series entitled "Pieces of the Past." *Shadows of the Past, A History of the Kentucky High School Athletic League* by Louis Stout provided a statewide perspective on black, segregated public high schools in the Commonwealth of Kentucky through an historical accounting of their athletic teams.

The author would like to thank former Superintendent Jack Moreland of the Covington Independent Public Schools and his assistant, Jena Meehan, for facilitating access to the *Official Minutes of The Covington Board of Education*. The author also extends gratitude to William Weathers for providing a copy of Betty Lee Nordheim's book, *Echoes of the Past, A History of the Covington Public School System,* and Tim Herrmann of the History and Genealogy Department of the Kenton County Public Library in Covington and his staff for their assistance with various historical photographs and newspaper articles. Many thanks to Barbara Gargiulo of Little Miami Publishing for her many efforts in preparing this book for publication.

The author also thanks other individuals for providing class photographs and background information for this book: Sadye Bunyan, Eva Bunyan Clark, Aaron Ballard, Rev. Richard B. L. Fowler, Willa Hoffman Jackson, Barbara Jouett, Charles James, Wayne Mays, Charles Dickerson, Vanda Lovelace Langham, Jessie Mays Lattimore, David Johnson, and Martha Walton Mason. The specific names of persons and organizations contributing photographs are listed with each image. All images from the Lincoln-Grant yearbooks are used through the courtesy of the Covington Independent Public Schools, Covington, Kentucky. Photographs from the Kenton County Public Library, Covington Kentucky are provided through the courtesy of that library.

I am greatly indebted to my wife, Dr. Nancy C. Riley Walton, for her love, patience and her understanding of the necessary time away from home in search of relevant materials, as well as countless, seemingly endless hours well into any given evening spent on our home computer. Her support and encouragement enabled me to sustain a period of several years on this project as it went through many revisions, and met with occasional obstacles and points of diversion. Thanks also to our children—Lisa, Joseph C., Rodney, and Kendra—and their families, as well as our extended family members for their continued love and support.

The opinions and interpretations expressed herein are those of this author only. This book is dedicated to all who passed through the doors of Lincoln-Grant School.

Joseph M. Walton, Ph.D.

Prologue

This is the story of a school that was created for the education of African Americans in Covington, Kentucky, in 1866. The history of the school is revealed through the collective experiences of the people who were affiliated with it for more than one hundred years. That shared history is far more than a mere compilation of events that took place within the walls of several school buildings over time. When analyzed together, the human interactions associated with Lincoln-Grant School also disclose a certain way of life in Northern Kentucky, as well as the evolution of racial relationships through conscientious patterns of social behavior over many decades.

Such a school could not have been possible without a historical, geo-political context, and a prevailing will to maintain racial segregation at any cost. The long-term development of the black school in Covington would take place inside of a tangled web of mixed values and emerging racial traditions in Northern Kentucky. Within that environment, the moral fiber of those who endured inequities based on race and ethnicity would be constantly challenged by the persistent imposition of racially based policies and practices.

The general character and worldviews of human beings are closely related to, and shaped by the nature of their physical surroundings, as they develop ways of living and surviving in a given geographical area. With that principle in mind, the current work begins with a preliminary discussion of the geography of the area in which the all-black school was established, while revealing how that geography intersected with the culture, politics, racial practices, and belief systems of people in the region as time moved forward.

Part I, The Formative Period, examines the establishment of the school's precursor and feeder institutions in a unique physical and social environment, while Part II illustrates a period of growth and development for the self-contained, kindergarten through twelfth-grade, all-black school in a new building that was opened in 1932. Part III discloses the process involved in the gradual desegregation of Lincoln-Grant School, along with other black elementary schools in Northern Kentucky from 1954 to 1976. This book concludes with the end of an era of public school racial segregation in Covington, as it examines the enduring legacy of a black school that had existed in the city for more than a century.

Unveiling the complete story of Lincoln-Grant School required a variety of source materials, consistent probing, and a few logical conclusions, since not much of the beginning history of the school was preserved in writing. The author focused initially upon the *Official Minutes of the Covington Board of Education*, which were extremely helpful in weaving together much of the story. The board minutes pinpointed various events in a sequence that allowed the author to see fully several strategic points in the school's history. However, it was quickly revealed that about ten years of those minutes, from the mid-1880s through 1893, were permanently missing. Although most of the available board minutes were clear and orderly, those from the late eighteen hundreds and early nineteen hundreds were handwritten, abbreviated, and sometimes difficult to decipher. Examination of some historical documents such as the *Covington City Ordinances* presented a similar challenge.

Reliance on newspaper articles primarily from the *Covington Journal* and the *Daily Commonwealth*, two local newspapers published in the late eighteen hundreds and early nineteen hundreds, became necessary to fill in the gaps of the early history. Noncontemporaneous historical descriptions provided by various individuals were also useful, although some of them occasionally yielded conflicting information due to idiosyncratic human recollections, or varied personal interpretations of reasonably objective data. Despite some minor inconsistencies, each of those sources contained threads of common information that meshed with other verifiable data.

The author also located excerpts from a dusty, isolated University of Cincinnati masters' thesis written in 1929 by Leconia Franklin Crosby, a William Grant High School graduate and former William Grant High School science teacher, among the Kenton County Public Library archival materials in Covington. An examination of the total thesis revealed detailed descriptions of the physical facilities and the high school curriculum at the Seventh Street Colored School first hand from Crosby, who was a teacher in the building at that time.

Also, much to the delight of this author, the thesis included a personal letter from Mr. Samuel R. Singer, the third principal of the all-black school, and the founding principal of William Grant High School. The letter by Mr. Singer provided an important pathway to the origins of public education for black Covingtonians. It also listed the names of graduates of William Grant High School, beginning with the first graduating class in 1889 and ending with the year, 1900. The latter information was invaluable to this author, because the board minutes, which listed precise, typewritten information giving the full names of all Covington high school graduates (including William Grant High School) for many decades, did not yield much information on the specific names of graduates for that period. (This author provides a detailed listing of William Grant Alumni from 1889 to 1965 in Appendix 6).

Delving into the history of a unique and complicated educational enterprise required a passion for uncovering history carefully, as well as a fascination with learning about the hidden depths and thoughts of those who preceded us, without undue proclivity toward embellishing, or understating the facts. Tenacity for discovering objective truth while trying to detach one's persona from the role of a former student was important in authoring this work. Although a portion of this writing is necessarily subjective, it is hoped that the author presents a reasonably compelling and accurate historical account of Lincoln-Grant School, while viewing its history and the human context that surrounded it through a relatively objective lens.

This author will use the terms, *black* and *African American* interchangeably throughout this book when referring to persons of African American descent. Occasionally, I will also use the phrase *people of color* when that phrase seems to be appropriate within a given context. However, direct quotes from other writers, notably those who authored newspaper articles printed in the late eighteen hundreds and early nineteen hundreds, will reflect the actual ethnic label, or racial epithet employed by those writers when referring to African Americans. Even though some of that language may be racially offensive, this author believes that including those descriptors as they were actually used within a given historical period is necessary, since those labels reflect not only the racial stereotypes that were prevalent during those times, but also the evolution of racial views in Northern Kentucky, and in this country at large, from the eighteen hundreds through the present.

Part I

The Formative Period
1815–1926

Ohio River Valley, c. 1792.
Early settlers on the Kentucky side looking across
the Ohio River to a barely settled Cincinnati.

CHAPTER 1

Historical Settings

■ TWO RIVERS

The history of Lincoln-Grant School evolved in a geographical area near two intersecting rivers that had developed naturally during a previous age of glacier activity. That setting would foster the development of complex human relationships in a region located in the midwestern section of the United States of America. The cultural traditions that would eventually characterize the region would be greatly influenced by the presence of the two rivers.

Human beings have always been attracted to, and fascinated by, large bodies of water. In addition to providing sustenance for our existence, the rivers, lakes, and oceans reflect the flow of life itself on a magnified scale of grandiosity. Our presence near them seems to enhance our own sense of humanity and humility, as well as the comparative limitations of our individuality. Humankind is also challenged to "harness nature" and bend its will to our purposes when facing natural forces over which we appear to have no control. Those factors would be relevant to those who chose to settle close to the Ohio and Licking rivers.

The Ohio River, forming from the convergence of the Allegheny and Monongahela rivers in Pittsburgh, Pennsylvania, and flowing westward for some 981 miles to Cairo, Illinois, would reach its midpoint near the developing city of Cincinnati, Ohio.[1] When viewed at a distance from the local shores and hills, the river seemed to emerge suddenly as it rounded the bend in a wide,

---

1. "Ohio River Information," *U.S. Army Corps of Engineers, Pittsburgh District*, http://www.lrp.usace.army.mil/nav/ohioback.htm (accessed September 12, 2007).

seemingly motionless, snake-like configuration, while en route from southern Ohio and West Virginia. Intermittently clear skies would brandish the horizon as the large waterway, with its overtly steady and even flow, as well as its treacherous, underlying sandbars and swift, shifting currents, forged its way along the northwestern Kentucky coastline. Even though the river was smaller then than it is today, the breadth of the mighty Ohio would eventually widen to almost a mile as it passed through the Louisville, Kentucky, area, while pressing onward toward the ultimate task of emptying its contents into the great Mississippi River. The Ohio River would form the northernmost border of what would eventually become the Commonwealth of Kentucky.

As as a much smaller tributary to the Ohio River, the Licking River, with its uncertain depths and sudden turns, would foster hidden places as well as peaceful hills and valleys that shrouded the Northern Kentucky countryside. The Licking would begin in Magoffin County in Kentucky and flow northwest for about 320 miles to enter the Ohio River, almost clandestinely, next to the terrain that would become the riverfront settlement of Covington, Kentucky. The smaller river would nearly go unnoticed in the shadow of the much larger Ohio, until one suddenly confronted its potential for wrath and the destruction of life and property during floods, and at other times when it claimed human life through suicide, or the accidental drowning of innocent victims out for a casual swim.

The Native Americans who originally inhabited the territory must have found it to be a sanguine and enchanting land with a bountiful supply of resources for human survival. The topography provided natural abodes, and a shadowy mystic that shaped and supported ancient customs, as well as beliefs about the known, and the unknown. Although there were no significant Native American settlements found in Northern Kentucky when the white settlers arrived, tribes such as the Shawnees, who lived around the Little Miami River valley in southwestern Ohio, and the Cherokees, who came from other territories, used the land around the two rivers as hunting grounds.[2]

The hunting seasons would be supported by both rivers, which nourished abundant wildlife, and a plethora of lush, green forests. White-tail deer, coyotes, numerous smaller land-based animals, wild turkeys, and a wide variety of other birds would flock to the land around the rivers. The appearance of black bears in the area would also not be unusual before their natural habitats were eradicated during the eighteen hundreds.[3] The Ohio and Licking rivers would serve as sources of freshwater fish and drinking water, as well as a means of transportation from one part of the territory to another.

As one journeyed in a southwestern direction, the quiet, unfettered majesty of the Kentucky terrain would paint a picture of tranquility and calm with

---

2.   "Kentucky," *Wikipedia, The Free Encyclopedia*, http://en.wikipedia.org/wiki/Kentuky (accessed June 17, 2009).

3.   Ibid.

greenery that gave the appearance of shades of a hazy blue color from a distance. The broad, natural landscape would slowly unfold over long stretches of hills and slopes, as night drifted into morning, revealing breathtaking, homogeneous trees and grass that would be visible to the naked eye for miles ahead. The deceptive color of the foliage would eventually cause the Kentucky Commonwealth to become known colloquially as "The Bluegrass State."

The seasons in the northern part of the state would come and go as they reflected the friendliness of nature in the spring and summer, and its harshness during the cold, barren months of winter. Fall, the intervening period, would cause the forests to resound with hope and promise as an array of natural surroundings with a variety of vivid colors prepared the earth for the sullenness and uncertainty of a colder season.

The peacefulness and serenity of that era would change as new faces of humanity began to appear. Clashes of cultures would soon develop as people with different customs and world views began to converge upon shared geographical space. Some of the patterns of human behavior that would eventually emerge within the Commonwealth of Kentucky on the basis of cultural and ethnic differences, would belie the attractiveness of the surrounding countryside.

The conflict between England and France over the purchase of land from Native Americans would be resolved when England prevailed during the French and Indian Wars. During the westward expansion, which was temporarily halted by the American Revolutionary War, southwestern Ohio and northern Kentucky would become focal points of population growth and development in the Midwest. The new settlers would bring about major changes in the terrain along the riverside, while displacing native inhabitants and wildlife in those parts of Ohio and Kentucky. In a more unified effort, the U.S. government would relocate large numbers of Native Americans to reservations west of the Mississippi, thereby causing their identification and influence in Northern Kentucky and Southwestern Ohio to become even more extinct.

The development of the region had begun with a relatively "blank slate," which could have been filled in historically in a number of ways in terms of human interactions. Those who inhabited the area would choose a racially-based, segregated approach to the development of their relationships with other human beings. Somewhat metaphorically, the convergence of the Ohio and Licking rivers would mirror the growth of a dual society in Northern Kentucky: a smaller one with roots in Africa, emerging from slavery in the United States of America, and a larger one stemming mostly from people who rejected their European roots for various reasons and came to America. The two rivers flowed from different directions and eventually conjoined while maintaining separate identities, as did two racial groups in Covington during its early history.

■ COVINGTON ENTERS THE COMMONWEALTH

The Commonwealth of Kentucky joined the Union in 1792 as the fifteenth state.[4] The commonwealth name, which was shared only with Virginia, Pennsylvania, and Massachusetts, meant, "its government [would be] run according to the consent of its people."[5] The commonwealth designation gave the citizens of Kentucky and the other three states the independence to devise their own rules and regulations regarding such actions as when to hold state elections, how to construct their state governments, and how to form their state statutes.

Within the Commonwealth of Kentucky, that sense of independence would also be reflected not only in eventual legal mandates for racial segregation, but also in a variation of cultural identities in different population pockets. For instance, the southern areas of the state near the Appalachian Mountains and the Tennessee border, known geographically as the Cumberland and Mississippi plateaus, would produce groups of people with closely knit, culturally encapsulated orientations, while the inner Bluegrass Region in the center of the state around Lexington, which had a broader landscape and large pastoral areas, would reflect more of a casual, rural, plantation atmosphere. The latter area would eventually spawn an interest in breeding racehorses, and farming in a relatively flat, fertile area of the state. The Louisville, Kentucky, area, home to the Kentucky Derby and Triple Crown Thoroughbred horse racing events, would be founded at the widest portion of the Ohio River near southern Indiana. As the largest, and perhaps one of the more socially liberal and racially diverse municipalities in Kentucky, it would be affected by a variety of cultural orientations as different people passed through an expansive geographical area. However, Northern Kentucky, where Lincoln-Grant School emerged, would eventually be comprised of a series of independent, smaller riverfront towns with localized businesses, and commercially oriented communities in the northernmost, outer Bluegrass Region of the state.

A Kenton County Public Library publication reports, "After a quick succession of several owners between 1780 and 1801, the 200 acres which were to eventually become the city of Covington were sold to Thomas Kennedy for $750. Kennedy lived near what is now the approach to the Suspension Bridge, where he ran a tavern and a river ferry. In 1814, he sold 150 acres of his land to John S. Gano, Richard M. Gano, and Thomas Carneal."[6] The settlement of Covington began with that purchase. The initial riverfront enterprise was named the Covington Company in honor of their friend, Gen. Leonard Coving-

---

4. The Black Population Census of 1790 revealed that Kentucky had 12,430 African American slaves and 114 free people of color. See John Hope Franklin and Alfred A. Moss, Jr., *From Slavery to Freedom: A History of African Americans,* 7th ed. (New York: McGraw-Hill, Inc., 1994) 85.

5. "Kentucky," 2009.

6. Kenton County Public Library, *Covington/Kenton County Library,* Public Images of America. Charleston, S.C.: Arcadia Pub., 2003, 7.

ton. Covington, an officer who trained troops in this area, was killed in the War of 1812.[7]

The Kentucky General Assembly incorporated the municipality of Covington in 1815. The city of Cincinnati, Ohio, had already begun its development in 1788 directly across the Ohio River to the north, and the town of Newport, Kentucky, had emerged immediately east of Covington on the other side of the Licking River in 1795. The interaction of Covington citizens with both cities had a definite influence upon the physical, social, and economic development of the young city, as it looked to its more established sister cities for guidance in its growth and cultural maturation. Indeed, a certain sense of common synergy would meld the three cities together as they moved forward historically.

Carneal and the Ganos "prepared a plat for the new city that was approximately five blocks wide by five blocks deep. The platted streets lined up with the streets of Cincinnati across the Ohio River, symbolically tying the future of the fledgling city to the larger neighbor to the north. The first five streets . . . were named for Kentucky's first five governors: Shelby, Garrard, Greenup, Scott, and Madison."[8] In a similar relationship to Newport, Kentucky, two streets running east to west in Covington, Fourth Street and Eleventh Street, would eventually become linked to streets in Newport by two bridges across the Licking River.

The Ohio and Licking rivers, and the development of the steamboat, fueled economic development and population growth in the region, causing the number of inhabitants in Covington to increase from a mere 715 people in 1815 to 2,026 in 1840.[9] The latter number would include 89 black slaves and 11 free people of African American descent. The European revolutions of the middle eighteen hundreds resulted in the immigration of many Germans and Irishmen to Covington between 1840 and 1860. Their influence upon the social development of the city would be fundamental to its developing character. White migrant workers from the Appalachian areas of West Virginia, Tennessee and the southern parts of Kentucky moved back and forth between their original homes and Northern Kentucky seasonally and intermittently in search of better livelihoods. They also influenced the local social atmosphere.

Some people of African American heritage arrived in Covington in larger numbers immediately after the close of the Civil War. Significant population growth also occurred in the area during the 1930s and '40s, the period of the great southern migration when black people primarily from Alabama, Mississippi, Georgia, Arkansas, and the more rural areas of Kentucky sought to escape the failing agrarian economy in the south. But there was also a stable, fundamental core of African Americans whose roots in Northern Kentucky

---

7.   "Our History," *City of Covington, Kentucky,* http://www.covingtonky.com/index.asp?page=history (accessed August 3, 2007).

8.   Ibid.

9.   Ibid.

went back to the pre–Civil War era. Several black families were descendents of former domestic slaves in the city, or free people of color who lived in the area before the Civil War occurred. Some of them showed evidence of the direct blending of the white, black, and Native American ethnic groups in a city that was, from its origin, divided in its belief about the viability and morality of slavery.

Both black and white people were drawn to the city of Covington for similar reasons. The first would be geographical location. Initially, a vibrant area bordered by two rivers with the potential for economic growth attracted white settlers. Similarly, black slaves and freedmen who yearned for better lives were motivated by the proximity of the Ohio River, which provided immediate passage to northern states. Later, three emerging cities—Covington, Cincinnati, and Newport, contiguously situated, and separated only by the rivers—would offer a wide range of possibilities for developing a way of life. Living in one city and commuting to another for one's livelihood was reasonably easy, while simply involving a brief ride or walk across a bridge over the Ohio or Licking River.

The second rationale for locating in the region relates to the human support systems, through family members who were already established in the area, or through the involuntary servitude of many black people. Typically, relatives who find a comfortable place to live will communicate that message to other relatives and friends, while inviting them to relocate. In the case of whites from Europe during the middle eighteen hundreds, and black people from the South following the end of slavery, there were usually relatives or other acquaintances already settled in the region that could provide support to those who had just arrived. In the black community, for instance, it was not uncommon for local relatives to take newly arrived kinfolk into their homes temporarily until they could find jobs and begin to develop their own independence.

A third motive for people choosing Northern Kentucky was the evolution of educational opportunities that would eventually abound for both blacks and whites in a region that would become known as the *tristate area*. But unfortunately, the white educational institutions in Northern Kentucky in the early days were mired in the phenomena of racial segregation, and were therefore unavailable to people of color.

Much of the physical development of the city of Covington occurred during the late eighteen hundreds and early nineteen hundreds. An article in the June 17, 1914, edition of the *Kentucky Post* titled, "Covington is Outgrowing old Bounds" characterized the early residential development of the city for its white citizens as follows:

Early in the history of Covington the wealthy [white] people erected their homes in that part of the city between Front-st. and Fourth-st. and between Greenup-st. and the Licking River. That part of the city was built to the extent of its capacity and the people began to move farther south, keeping well eastward of Madison. Wallace Woods was then open and a grand rush was made for that section, until the last lot now owned by Col. Lew Applegate on Wallace-av. is now being built on. Eastern-av. in that section is nearly entirely built up. At the time Wallace Woods began its building people began building on the hills west of Covington, in the place now known as Ft. Mitchell, and the popularity of that district was so great that the residents of that place represent quite a thrifty community. South Covington, formerly Latonia and Rosedale during the last 10 years has been used so much for the purpose of building that for a residential section for the country loving, city class it is being rapidly used, and the movement continues out both the Lexington and Madison-pikes.

The article continues,

On To Devou Park

When Devou Park was given to the city many a sad eye was cast upon the ground and the dawning of "What a Place for a Home" came into the minds of the fresh air loving, cooped-up business class. The hope of many for a house on the very point of the hill with a view of the entire Ohio Valley in the vicinity of Cincinnati and Covington was lost.

Following the close of the Civil War, a growing population of lesser-included black people would occupy more modest housing located largely on the east side of the city. Their population growth and density over several decades would mostly be prescribed in an area confined by Ninth Street on the north and Pleasant Street on the south, and bound east to west by Greenup Street and the Licking River. Before floodwalls were constructed sometime after the 1937 flood, the ravaging floodwaters from the Licking River would reach that area first, due to its proximity to the rising section of the river. The white residential areas on the eastern side of town had been built closer to the higher riverbanks near Fourth Street, or further out toward the Wallace Woods area, away from the Licking River. The prime residential areas around Devou Park, which overlooked the Ohio River valley from a unique vantage point, were definitely "off limits" to black people during that period.

Although a few black people lived in sporadic locations outside of the east side parameters, and also in racially segregated pockets of outlying areas such as Latonia, Peaselburg, and Elsmere, black people in the region were generally restricted to social interaction within their own racial group. They would eventually develop their own cultural characteristics and way of life primarily on the east side of Covington, or in small areas outside of the city.

There would be significant riverfront development in Covington in later years, resulting in more modern city buildings. However, most of the core residential area, and much of the primary downtown area would continue to reflect the early physical character of the city. Some of the older buildings would eventually be upgraded for new usage, or replaced by new ones. But as decades passed the relatively narrow streets, and older, constricted, classic brick and frame structures with several vertical levels would be dominant within the city limits.

After a period of annexing several contiguous communities, such as Latonia, Rosedale, and West Covington, the city would eventually grow to a population of more than 60,000 people. In later years, with outward migration to the surrounding areas of Campbell, Boone, and Kenton counties the population in the city of Covington would settle to around 43,000 residents, while the general Northern Kentucky population would include approximately 450,000 people. In the long run, the city and the neighboring area would sustain a majority white population with a little over 10 percent comprising ethnic minorities, who were mostly of African American descent.[10]

■ EMERGING RACIAL SEGREGATION: THE COLOR LINE

The growth and development of Covington was inextricably linked to that of Cincinnati and Newport as all three cities developed with similar racial attitudes. However, although *de facto* racial segregation was evident in Cincinnati from its inception in 1788, unlike Kentucky, the state of Ohio was not a slave state, and would not adopt formal laws of racial segregation after the end of the American Civil War. The last two factors would be significant in the eventual development of alternate educational opportunities for black people in Northern Kentucky.

The Ohio River served as part of the "Mason-Dixon Line" that separated several northern and southern states. That natural phenomenon placed Covington, a border city in an ambiguous position relative to the implementation of slavery. In addition, some European immigrants, Germans in particular, were opposed to slavery because of the oppression that they had experienced in their country of origin. And although most German settlers did not go out of their way to embrace people of color, the German influence would not enhance the development of slavery in Kentucky.[11]

Within the context of a pro-Union position on slavery, there were early reports of lynching and runaway slaves in Northern Kentucky, particularly in Boone County in the eighteen hundreds, counterbalanced by the accounts of white abolitionists harboring slaves and escorting them to freedom across the Ohio River during that same era.[12] Some slavehunters were still roaming the territory capturing former slaves and returning them to their "rightful owners" in Boone and Campbell counties, even after the Civil War had been concluded.[13]

---

10. "Our History," *City of Covington, Kentucky.*
11. Joseph R. Reinhart, "Kentucky's German-Americans in the Civil War," http://www.geocities.com/kygermans/kgew.html?200712 (accessed September 12, 2007).
12. *Covington Journal*, "Stampede of Slaves—Arrest of the Fugitives (Runaway Slaves from Boone County are Caught)," June 17, 1854.

Northern Kentucky citizens were clearly conflicted in their approach to persons of color in the early days of the region's history. There were free people of African American descent living in Covington prior to the Civil War, as was evident in the 1840 census and the subsequent emergence of black community and educational leaders who had lived freely within the city limits well before the end of slavery. Franklin and Moss reported the existence of as many as fifty-nine thousand free black people in the United States in 1790. Cincinnati, Ohio, was one of six major population centers in which many free people of African American descent were concentrated before the end of slavery. Although their numbers were smaller in Covington, they traveled back and forth between Covington and Cincinnati with relative ease during that period, as long as each person claiming to be "free" could produce a valid Certificate of Freedom upon demand. Free people of African American descent, some of whom were the biracial descendents of white and black people, could own property, as well as pursue educational opportunities, as some did in the early and middle eighteen hundreds.[14]

Black people who were free often married others with the same status, and produced children who were automatically free, thereby increasing significantly the number of free blacks in a given geographical area. However, the marriage of a free person of color to an enslaved black person would produce a different set of circumstances, sometimes involving "bartering" or purchasing the freedom of the enslaved individual. Within a format fraught with social contradictions, some slaves, such as James Baker purchased or petitioned for their freedom, and lived in the area without restraint, while others were given their "free papers" by their former slaveholders for a variety of reasons, including sympathy, feelings of guilt, or kept promises to other relatives. The unsettled status of slavery in Northern Kentucky resulted in vague relationships between slaves and free people, black and white.

All of those factors would combine to produce a varied underclass of people of color in Northern Kentucky with clearly observable differences in physical appearance, such as skin pigmentation and texture of hair. In addition, there would be perceived variations in levels of educational accomplishments and privilege among some people of color who were more directly connected to non-black relatives.

An admixture of ethnicities, German and Irish immigrants, white southern migrants, black people from the South, and other people of color who had been born and bred in Kentucky, as well as the staunch laws of segregation created by the Commonwealth of Kentucky would produce a complex, yet simple

---

13. One example is the story of a fugitive slave from Boone County named Henrietta Woods, as cited in the *Covington Journal*, April 8, 1876. See Eric Jackson, *Northern Kentucky*, Black America Series (Charleston, S.C.: Arcadia Pub., 2005) 19.

14. See John Hope Franklin and Alfred A. Moss, Jr., "Quasi-Free Blacks," in *From Slavery to Freedom: A History of African Americans*, 7th ed. (New York: McGraw-Hill, Inc., 1994).

racial dynamic within the state. The laws of segregation would simplify the division of the races into two groups, irrespective of the degree of skin pigmentation, one's kinship to white relatives, an individual's otherwise diverse racial heritage, or their socioeconomic standing in the community. There would be a color line. All persons would be designated racially as either categorically "white" or "colored" immediately upon sight, and treated accordingly.

Racial division in Kentucky became formalized in law as the Commonwealth of Kentucky spoke swiftly, and unequivocally with a single legislative voice on the question of post-Civil War racial relationships. Rigid racial segregation would be the legal mandate for Kentucky, and laws stipulating the segregation of the races would be fundamental to every aspect of public life in the state, especially the area of public school education. Those laws were focused on the containment of black people, and approached by Kentucky legislators with a sense of urgency and inflexibility unmatched by any other social phenomenon since the inception and demise of slavery in the United States.

The racial factor, the fundamental underpinning of segregated schools in America, leads the current discussion more directly to an infamous part of U.S. history that many people would like to forget. But recalling that part of history is important to the present dialogue. Knowledge of that history illuminates a clear path to the establishment of racially segregated schools like Lincoln-Grant, and the total exclusion of black students from attending white public elementary and secondary schools in the Commonwealth of Kentucky until 1955.

With the specter of human slavery as a part of the early American experience, the United States of America seemed inimitably positioned on the question of racial relationships. The perspective, and indeed the sense of arrogance generated by the subjugation of one race of people by another would lead to an overriding belief in the racial superiority of whites over black people. A degree of success in the enslavement of people of color through brute force would be accompanied by a series of actions, rules, and intractable belief systems about race (some even believed to be biblically based) that were unique to this country, and perhaps rivaled only by Africa's *apartheid*. And although its founders stated a theoretical exhortation that "All men are created equal" that "self-evident truth," though extracted from the U.S. Declaration of Independence, would not be reflected in the early racial practices of a majority of white Americans.

After slavery was debated at the highest levels of discourse in the country, and then defeated through the American Civil War, the concept of racial equality in America would become compromised by the need for the North and South to coexist as one nation. Almost no one wanted to repeat the American Civil War, and see the country torn apart again with "brothers literally fighting against brothers." The era of Reconstruction would be very agonizing for white Southerners and others who resented the sudden access of blacks to political positions, voting rights, and property ownership. After a brief period during the late eighteen hundreds, firm laws of racial segregation would be put in place to mitigate any material gains or political power that may have accrued to black people during the era of Reconstruction.

Both divisions of the country embraced racial segregation, which was maintained on a *de facto* basis in the North, and defined in firm, unequivocal, legal terms in the South. Southerners had lost the war and their right to enslave people of color, but slavery would be replaced by the next best thing for Southern interests—firm, unmitigated laws of human segregation based on skin color, which were passed in unambiguous language in Southern state legislatures, and carried out forcibly, and often violently, in practice. The Congress of the United States, the U.S. Supreme Court, and the Executive Branch of the United States, all of which were at that time greatly influenced by Southern segregationists, would also accommodate many of the racial views of south.

The purpose of the laws that segregated the races in Kentucky seemed to be threefold: (1) to prevent, insofar as possible, the co-mingling of the races on a social and educational basis, thereby attempting to maintain racial "purity"; (2) to contain the possible economic growth and political influence of black citizens, with the predictable consequence of prolonging their underclass status; and (3) to place severe limitations on the education of black people by prescribing a school curriculum restricted to "reading, writing and common arithmetic" because only those fundamentals seemed necessary for people who were believed to be of limited educational potential. Those purposes would form the philosophical underpinnings of segregated schools in Covington.

Both blacks and whites in Northern Kentucky used the expression, *colored people* freely, and respectfully when referring to persons of African American descent until the 1960s, when black people sought to define our own identity and cultural heritage. *Black* replaced *colored*, *Negro* (for black males) and *Negress* (for black females), to indicate racial equality with whites. Later the descriptors, *Afro-American* and *African American* evolved as expressions of our connection to our African roots. (Some nineteenth-century black intellectuals preferred the term Afro-American during the days of the Reconstruction).

The colored or white designation was convenient for the practice of racial discrimination, but that approach was in reality a racial oversimplification. The ability to distinguish between colored and white people became somewhat difficult at the racial margins with a few black people whose skin color was fairer than that of some white people. In those cases, those who were prone to use racial discrimination as a tool had to employ more refined "cues" involving texture of hair, shape of nostrils, fullness of lips, or trying to detect the slightest hint of skin color on the person's body in order to make racial distinctions. And sometimes all of that failed with colored people who were so white that they could "pass." There were several people in the black Covington community who fit the latter description, and who very obviously had white relatives in their racial backgrounds.

In Northern Kentucky, the label of colored was applied exclusively to people of African American descent. It did not appear to extend to other racial minorities such as Asians, Hispanics, mideastern Europeans or Native Americans, although those groups were also subjected to racial discrimination. If there were people of such extraction in Covington, they were somehow classified separately from black people. Or perhaps they made their lives less difficult by avoiding Northern Kentucky altogether, and simply residing across the river in Ohio, where formal laws of segregation did not exist.

Some black Covingtonians also chose the latter option, rather than contend with the rules of segregation in Northern Kentucky. As the City of Cincinnati had provided an educational outlet for free black people prior to the end of the Civil War, it would continue to be an alternate source of education for some black people as time progressed. Even as late as the 1940s and '50s, some black Covington families with financial means found creative ways to enroll their children in the Cincinnati Public Schools, while sustaining their permanent residence in Covington.

But even the "escape" from the laws of segregation in Kentucky by simply crossing the Ohio River for a "better education" at a predominantly white school was probably largely cosmetic, since *de facto* racial segregation was also prominent in Cincinnati. While being colored or white mattered more in Kentucky, it also mattered to a large extent in southern Ohio, and in the entire nation at that time. The color line was indeed the driving force behind public life—all over this land. And that line would ultimately be supported by legal rulings and interpretations at the highest levels in the land.

■ THE SOCIAL, ECONOMIC AND CULTURAL EFFECTS OF RACIAL DIVISION IN COVINGTON

The cultural and industrial character of Covington was shaped by its arbitrary ethnic distinctions, as black and white people were socially and culturally isolated from each other. A few successful white merchants such as Robert Wallace, Daniel Henry Holmes, Eugene Levassor, and the Carneal family wielded great influence within the city through their ownership of substantial portions of land or businesses. While those individuals and their families, as well as others provided a hint of social gallantry and elitism in the community, Covington would not become distinct as a bastion of "cultural" phenomena such as art museums, symphony orchestras, and other trappings of "high society." White artists, such as Frank Duveneck provided early local artistic influence in Covington. But even those artistic elements would be captured in much larger measure across the river in Cincinnati.

The marginal status of people of color in the Covington community during the late eighteen hundreds and early nineteen hundreds was very evident in the news media of that era. The local newspapers during that period carried almost no social news on black people other than sporadic, negative reports, such as the occasional arrest, usually of a black male, for an offense such as petty theft, or the brief account of a black woman who went after her husband with a knife during a domestic dispute. Accounts of black people who obeyed the law; served in the armed forces (even during the Civil War); traveled abroad; graduated from college; had intact families; owned land; started their own businesses; and achieved much in spite of the odds, went mostly unreported.

In addition to more elaborate and detailed discussions of white high school commencement and class activities in the area, news for local white people described their vacations, marital difficulties and infidelities, politics, and lawsuits against each other in vividly embellished detail. The local papers also reported the deaths of white people either from natural causes, or through occasional shootings or drownings in the rivers (accompanied by elaborate descriptions of the emotional state of grieving relatives) along with all of the common events that one would normally associate with a growing, local society. But such phenomena were generally not reported in the local newspaper for a relatively "invisible" black community.

The positive news for local black people in Covington was usually reflected in brief accounts of educational issues, or annual, abbreviated articles of high school commencement activities at the two colored high schools, one in Covington, and the other in Newport. The early counter culture of social and cultural news about the achievements of black people in Northern Kentucky would eventually be reported through local African American newspapers such as the *Call and Post*, which was started in 1916, and the *Cincinnati Herald,* which came into existence in 1955.

Ethnic differences in Covington would be accompanied by a variety of approaches to religious worship. European immigrants would bring with them a sense of devotion to various faiths resulting in such edifices as the St. Mary Cathedral Basilica of the Assumption, Temple Israel, and several historically white Protestant church buildings. Black people established the First ("Colored") Baptist Church, the Ninth Street Baptist Church, and the Macedonia Baptist Church, as well as African and Christian Methodist Episcopal churches. Lane Chapel C.M.E. Church, Ninth Street Methodist Church, and St. James A.M.E. Church, along with the Church of Our Savior, and other places of worship in the black community were also available as religious outlets for African American people in Covington. While some churches developed their own schools, religious leaders would also exert great influence upon the development of the city's public schools.

One article reports the following relative to Covington's early economic and commercial development:

> In its infancy, most of the commerce in Covington was connected with the rivers that formed the northern and eastern boundaries of the city.
> . . . The city's first manufacturing concern, a cotton factory was built near the river in 1828, and three years later, another business, a rolling mill and nail factory, was established along Scott Street near the river-

front. . . . The first commercial center of the city was established around the "public square" platted between Third and Fourth Streets and Scott Boulevard and Greenup Street. . . . During the 1830s, along with [a] public market, retail stores, businesses, offices, and other commercial establishments flourished in this area.[15]

Covington's economic growth would be further enhanced by the development of the Madison and Pike Street commercial corridor in the 1850s, and the dedication of the John A. Roebling Suspension Bridge between Covington and Cincinnati on January 1, 1867.

In subsequent years, larger employers would hire skilled and unskilled white and black workers in a major slaughterhouse, the Duro Paper Company, and the railroad and riverboat industries, while local and federal governmental offices, the city fire department and the police force, as well as the city transit system of streetcars and buses were racially restricted to white people at the upper levels of employment. During that era of racial segregation the mail carriers and even the city garbage collectors were exclusively white. Many other whites found an economic advantage at the managerial and ownership levels, and through office work and public service employment, while people of color were generally limited to domestic and service work, food preparation, and common labor jobs.

The general socioeconomic fabric of the city of Covington would develop with a mixture of white "blue collar" workers who enjoyed local pubs and breweries reminiscent of European models, along with white "business class" employees in small shops, restaurants, clothing stores, banks, and other small businesses. However, black people would, of necessity, develop their own social outlets and economic strategies.

In spite of consistent racial discrimination, and even reported Ku Klux Klan marches and demonstrations in downtown Covington during the early nineteen hundreds, African American people would not be uniformly restricted to lower level jobs in Northern Kentucky. Extension to the outskirts of the city generated a more rural, agricultural atmosphere in the expanding areas of Boone County, where a few black people, such as the Wilkens and Lewis families, acquired land. Some developed their own farms in Boone County. In addition, Jacob Price, a black businessman and minister ran a successful lumber company on Madison Street in Covington from 1881 until 1914. By 1891 "sales had increased to $15,000 per year, and the firm was employing two delivery teams and two yardmen."[16]

Several other enterprising black individuals and families eventually devel-

15. "Covington, Kentucky," *Wikipedia, The Free Encyclopedia*, http://en.wikipedia.org/wiki/Covington,_Kentucky (accessed June 17, 2009).
16. "Price, Jacob (Rev.)" Covington Biographies. Genealogy and Kentucky History. *Kenton County Public Library.* http://www.kenton.lib.ky.us/gen/kenton/covington/covbio/pages/price.htm (accessed April 13, 2007).

oped small businesses in the black community during the early to middle nineteen hundreds. The first African American funeral home in Covington was reported to have been owned by Wallace A. Gaines. Most black businesses were located within a four-block, Greenup Street corridor between Ninth and Eleventh streets, where the majority of black people were concentrated at that time. Those business included: black barber shops and beauty salons; Lacey's "Gene-Bess" Grocery Store on Robbins Street; E. B. Delaney & Son Funeral Home at Ninth and Greenup streets (owned by Elizabeth B. Delaney, the first black businesswoman in Covington); Crittenden's Tailor Shop at the corner of Ninth and Greenup streets; a local tavern called the Silverfront located at the corner of Robbins and Greenup streets; and at least two small restaurants, one at Lynn and Greenup streets (managed at one time by the author's parents), and the other behind the Silverfront Café on Robbins Street. C. E. Jones Funeral Home, located on Scott Street near the downtown area, was in an exceptional location for black businesses in Covington. Several of the local black businesses formed the Black Businessman's Association of the 1930s and '40s. The black Utopian Club would also provide a social and business link among black professionals and business people in the area during the 1940s and '50s.

Dr. Simon Watkins, reported to be Covington's first black medical doctor, and Dr. Adam D. Kelly, also recorded as an "Early African/American Doctor"[17] in the local community provided medical services for local black people. Dr. James E. Randolph, a graduate of Meharry Medical College in Tennessee who served as a local, black family and school physician for decades, would follow them. His office was located at the corner of Tenth and Greenup. And intermittently, there was at least one black dentist in the community located in a glass-plated building at the corner of Robbins and Greenup streets. Local black churches that were pillars of strength and survival in the black community would also become sources of leadership and character development for black people, and Lincoln-Grant, the local black school would serve as a distinct professional outlet for black teachers.

---

17. Drs. Watkins and Simon are referenced in the Covington Book Project, Covington Biographies, Genealogy and Kentucky History (www.roneinhaus.com/covington book xls - 109k) 2009.

*Photograph 1: Portrait of General Leonard Covington,
the person for whom the city is named.*
COURTESY OF THE KENTON COUNTY PUBLIC LIBRARY, COVINGTON, KENTUCKY.

Photograph 2: Artist's Sketch of Downtown Covington, Early 1800s.
COURTESY OF THE KENTON COUNTY PUBLIC LIBRARY, COVINGTON, KENTUCKY.

Photograph 3: Oldest House in Covington, Kentucky, 1798.
COURTESY OF THE KENTON COUNTY PUBLIC LIBRARY, COVINGTON, KENTUCKY.

An undated picture of Covington's oldest house, a log structure that was located on West Ninth Street between Russell and Banklick streets. Foreground, a young black boy carrying a lard or beer bucket. The house was demolished in 1916 because of safety concerns.

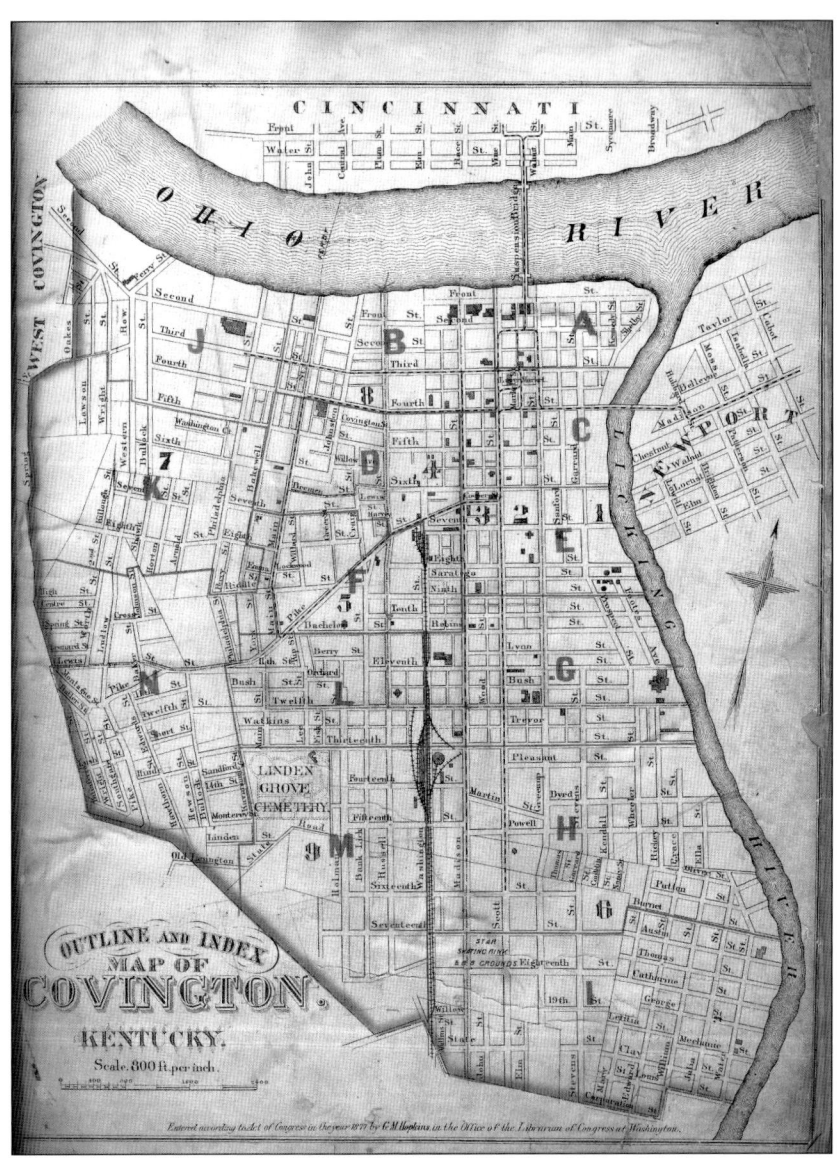

Photograph 4: Atlas Map of Covington, 1877.
Courtesy of the Kenton County Public Library, Covington, Kentucky.

Photograph 5: Unidentified Enslaved Couple.
COURTESY OF THE KENTON COUNTY PUBLIC LIBRARY, COVINGTON, KENTUCKY.

A portrait of an unidentified enslaved couple prior to the Emancipation Proclamation. Their attire would indicate their probable status as domestic slaves rather than field hands.

Photograph 6: Domestic Slave, Rachel Young at the
Wallace Family Mansion in Covington, Kentucky.
COURTESY OF THE KENTON COUNTY PUBLIC LIBRARY, COVINGTON, KENTUCKY.

Domestic slavery rather than slaves as field hands was the norm in Covington.

Photograph 7: Slave Quarters at the Carneal House in Covington.
COURTESTY OF KENTON COUNTY PUBLIC LIBRARY, COVINGTON, KENTUCKY.

Photograph 8: Superintendent Asa Drury.

Top left: *Asa Drury, First Covington Public School Superintendent (1856–59). Nordheim reports that Drury, an ordained minister, was from Massachusetts. He graduated from Yale in 1829*

Photograph 9: Holmesdale Castle.

Top right: *Holmes Castle located on the Holmesdale Estate, which would later be the site of the all-white Holmes High School in the early nineteen hundreds.*

Photograph 10: First District School, 1910.

Bottom: *First District School for white students, c. 1910.*

ORR'S FEMALE ACADEMY, COVINGTON, KY.

Photograph 11: Orr's Female Academy, Covington, Kentucky.
COURTESY OF THE KENTON COUNTY PUBLIC LIBRARY, COVINGTON, KENTUCKY.

The academy in the image above is identified as being located in Covington, Kentucky; however, there was a similar female academy listed in Covington, Georgia, in 1847. The principal of the latter school was a Georgia educator named Gustavas John Orr (1819–97). The school in Georgia was forced to close due to the Civil War.
(SOURCE: ORR FAMILY PAPERS, 1825–1970, EMORY UNIVERSITY LIBRARY ARCHIVES.)

Photograph 12: Old Covington High School, Class of 1890.
COURTESY OF THE KENTON COUNTY PUBLIC LIBRARY, COVINGTON, KENTUCKY.

Top row: *Frank Bailey, Lily White (teacher), Maurice L. Galvin, Charles W. Reynolds, James Terrill, and Superintendent John W. Hall.*
Middle row: *Professor T. J. Slattery, Jenny Snodgrass, Catherine Bowen, Mattie McDonald, Ruth Nelly, Florence Dailey, Lizzie Handy, and Seddie Grunkemeyer.*
Bottom row: *Kuper Hood, Georgia Lovell, Grace Culbertson, Oscar Roetken, Susan MacArthur, and Leila Bowen.*

Photograph 13: Kindergarten Class, Covington Public Schools, 1899.
COURTESY OF THE KENTON COUNTY PUBLIC LIBRARY, COVINGTON, KENTUCKY.

CHAPTER 2

The Beginning of a Racially Segregated School System in Covington

■ EARLY PUBLIC SCHOOLS FOR WHITE CHILDREN

The development of a racially segregated educational system in Covington reflected the evolution of a racially segregated society. While the emergence of both white and black schools had been less than orderly processes at several points, the schools for white children were started very early in the history of the city. Since public education in the United States was in its infancy, and many black people were still slaves in the early eighteen hundreds, the attention for the development of public schools had initially focused on white children exclusively. Private white schools were established in 1820, five years after the city was incorporated by the Kentucky General Assembly. Five years later, free public education would become available for white children, in addition to emerging, church-related private schools, which would also become an important part of Covington's white educational history.

Following the origin of a state system of education for whites in 1838, the Covington City Charter made provisions for white public schools in 1850. The city followed a typical model in the development of public schools for its white citizens. Rivaled by the emergence of private, religiously affiliated schools, the public school system was built historically by city "districts." Public elementary schools were eventually established in each district to serve the white children who resided within those districts, as that population expanded. The buildings were conveniently distributed geographically, and named for the city districts in which they were developed, such as First District School, Second District School, and Third District School. Covington Central High School (reported to be the oldest high school in the state of Kentucky) was established in 1853.[18] Central, the only white public high school in Covington was later named Covington Holmes High School due to its location on the Holmesdale estate, which had been originally occupied by the family of Daniel Henry Holmes, a white entrepreneur and businessman.

According to Nordheim, education for white students had progressed from 20 children and one teacher in a one-room schoolhouse in 1825 to an enrollment of 121 high school students in a four-year program and more than 1,000 in other grades by 1869. Soon the very first white graduates from Covington Central High School would emerge. Among them was "Miss Amelia Orr, who went on to become a second grade teacher in the Covington system."[19]

■ PRE–CIVIL WAR EDUCATION FOR BLACK STUDENTS

The first four city school superintendents, Asa Drury (1856–59), A. M. F. Randolph (1864–65), Ephraim Hardy (1866–67) and Z. F. Smith (1867–68)[20] would not be concerned about formal public education for black children, since slavery was still legal in the United States of America during much of their administrative tenure. "There was never a statute against educating slaves in Kentucky, but it was not widely encouraged; the schools were subject to being 'broken up, by Whites who opposed educating Negroes."[21] While Jones reports that whites burned several black slave schools in some parts of Kentucky prior to the Civil War, such activity in Northern Kentucky was apparently minimal or nonexistent.

Jim Reis and Theodore H. H. Harris indicate that African American education in Northern Kentucky began in "secret schools."[22] While that was perhaps true for some local domestic slaves, it is clear that free black people in Covington traveled back and forth across the Ohio River to be attend public schools in Cincinnati several years before the Civil War began, without interference from local white people. As will become evident later, a few local black people even attended colleges in Ohio and other locations prior to the Civil War. But since there were no systematic prewar educational facilities for black people in Covington, the early growth of education for white Covingtonians, with decades of progress, would compel predictable unevenness in the development of equal educational opportunities for white and black students in Covington.

---

18. Crystal Harden, "Holmes High to Celebrate History," Posted: September 29, 2003, http://www.covingtonky.com/index.asp?fn=news&id=1130 (accessed March 25, 2007).

19. Betty Lee Nordheim, *Echoes of the Past. A History of the Covington Public School System* [Covington, Ky.:The Covington Independent Public Schools, 2002.] 18.

20. Ibid., 123.

21. Wilson in Reinette F. Jones, "The Early Kinship: Kentucky Negro Public Education, Libraries, and Librarians," University of Kentucky. College of Communications Librarian. htpp://www.uky.edu/Subject/earlykin.html (accessed May 29, 2009). 21.

22. Jim Reis, "Education for blacks began in secret schools," *Kentucky Post*. Pieces of the Past, n.d. Accessed from the Kenton County Public Library, Covington, Kentucky, History and Genealogy Department Archival Files, 2007, 1.

■ THE AMERICAN CIVIL WAR AND FEDERAL POSTWAR INITIATIVES

The American Civil War, which began at 4:30 a.m. on April 12, 1861, with an attack by the Confederate army on Fort Sumter, South Carolina, would end four years later with Gen. Robert E. Lee's surrender to Gen. Ulysses S. Grant at the Appomattox Courthouse in Virginia on April 9, 1865. In spite of the fact that the Commonwealth of Kentucky was fundamentally a slaveholding state, Northern Kentucky seemed ambivalently pro-Union during the Civil War. Some of the towns in the region, such as Fort Mitchell and Fort Thomas retained the names of the Union fortresses that occupied those areas during the Civil War.[23] There were clearly mixed views on the war among Covington citizens.

The educational impact of the war on local white children was described by Nordheim as follows:

> Although Northern Kentucky never left the Union, the Civil War, of course, affected the area. The new [white] high school reflected the threat of the war and the economic uncertainty it generated. There were 105 [white] students enrolled at the beginning of 1856. At the end, there were 43. No mention is made of the particular cause for the sudden drop, but it is reasonable to assume that it was the unrest brought about by the uncertainty of impending war. In 1861 schools closed in May, which was early for that semester. The school board had run out of money and paid the teachers in scrip. Merchants would not honor the scrip, so the teachers were dismissed. This situation lasted only a few months, and the schools opened again on time in September. There were not very many Southern sympathizers in Covington, but four women teachers were not re-appointed to their jobs in 1863 because of their friendly feelings toward the South.[24]

The war and its outcome would influence the development of public education for both black and white children in Covington, and in the nation at large. The assassination of President Abraham Lincoln on April 15, 1865, would result in the ascension of Andrew Johnson, a Tennessee Democrat, to the presidency. A number of congressional acts designed to facilitate the transition of former slaves into full citizenship would follow, including the ratification of the Thirteenth Amendment outlawing slavery on December 18, 1865.[25]

Congress also passed the Civil Rights Act of 1866 on April 9, 1866, over the March 27 veto of President Andrew Johnson. That act, which gave citizenship status to black people, was followed by passage of the Fourteenth Amend-

23. "Covington, Kentucky," *Trailsrus: Civil War in Kentucky,* http://www.trailsrus.com/civilwar/region4/covington.html (accessed September 12, 2007).

24. Nordheim, *Echoes,* 12–13.

25. Phillip Gavin, "U.S. Civil War 1861–1865," *The History Place: The Past into the Future,* http://www.historyplace.com/civilwar/ (accessed September 17, 2007).

ment to the U.S. Constitution on June 13, 1866, and its final adoption after state ratification by three-fourths of the states on July 9, 1868.[26] In addition to confirming U.S. citizenship for black people, the Fourteenth Amendment guaranteed equal protection and due process to all U.S. citizens, regardless of race, color or creed.[27] Those actions would set the stage for educational efforts to move forward for black people in Kentucky and elsewhere. A series of educational initiatives for black people that consumed the next ten years would begin in Covington during the spring of 1866.

■ ESTABLISHING A BLACK SCHOOL IN COVINGTON—1866

The black population in Covington would increase following the end of the war. Public education for newly emancipated and previously free local black children in the City of Covington would emerge after the war as an "appendage" to decades of public education for white children. As a product of federally initiated post–Civil War efforts to assimilate black people as equal participants in a new social order, education for black people was, at best, a secondary concern in the minds of many local white citizens at that time. The fresh wounds of the recent domestic war over slavery, and a variation of feelings and viewpoints about its outcome would result in a mixed approach to educational opportunities for black people. Since there was no legal requirement at the local level for the education of black children immediately after the war, the priorities of Covington school superintendents would have been developing and strengthening the city's white schools that had been eroded by the war. As a consequence, black community leaders, who were supported in their efforts by the federal government, would take the initiative in advancing educational opportunities for black children.

A common view among those who have written different versions of the early history of the school is that "on April 17, 1866, a group of concerned citizens met in the Covington City Hall to establish a school for African American children. Among those present was Jacob Price."[28] Harris writes, "Following its usual procedure of opening a school in a church, the Freedmen's Bureau, with assistance from the Freedmen's Aid Commission, established a school in April 1866 at the Bremen Street Baptist Church. The Reverend Jacob Price served as pastor of the church with Jessie Wolfe of Cincinnati employed as the sole schoolteacher."[29]

26. The Commonwealth of Kentucky was one of several states that failed to ratify the Fourteenth Amendment. However, all states, including Kentucky were subjected to its provisions, once the amendment was ratified by a three-fourths majority of all states.

27. Gavin, "U.S. Civil War 1861–1865."

28. "Price, Jacob (Rev.)," Genealogy and Kentucky History, 1–2.

29. Theodore H. H. Harris, "Creating Windows of Opportunity: Isaac E. Black and the African American Experience in Kentucky, 1848–1914," *The Register of the Kentucky Historical Society* 98, no. 2 (Spring 2000) 159–160.

By September 1866 "The Freedmen's Aid Society had established a school [in Covington] consisting of 44 boys and 48 girls with Miss Wolfe as the teacher."[30] "Miss Wolfe was the first [black] teacher employed in Covington; later Miss Abbath and Mr. C. M. White were added. Both Miss Wolfe's and Miss Abbath's salaries were paid by the Freedmen's Aid Commission. Mr. White's salary was [paid] by subscription from the students."[31]

Jacob Price was not originally from Covington. A free man of color, Price was born in 1839 in Woodford County, Kentucky.[32] Woodford County is located more than ninety miles directly south of Covington, around the Lexington-Versailles area. Price moved to Covington in 1859, where he would marry Mary Singer, a member of a prominent, free black family, in 1868. At that point, Price would become a permanent resident of Covington. Mary Singer was born in 1841, and had been educated in Cincinnati, along with her siblings well before the end of slavery. Jacob Price and Mary Singer would rear four children in Covington—John, Charles, Anna Price (Hood), and a fourth child.[33]

Price was a minister at the Black Baptist Church on Bremen Street in Covington. The church, which was organized in 1864 by Rev. George Dupree with twenty-two charter members before the Civil War ended, eventually became known formally as the First ("Colored") Baptist Church. Price, who was listed as the church pastor from 1868 to 1870, and 1880 to 1881, would leave that church to form the Ninth Street Baptist Church at some point. Price's level of education is not defined, although he was described variously as a laborer and the owner of a local lumber business, in addition to being an ordained minister. His interest in the education of Covington's black children seemed to be born as much out of his role as a church pastor, as it was from the urgent need for post-war, black educational leadership in the local community.

The Bureau of Refugees, Freedmen and Abandoned Lands, commonly called "The Freedmen's Bureau," supported the initial work of Price and his colleagues. The bureau was established on March 3, 1865, with a primary purpose of assisting newly freed slaves in their transition into public life. "Organized under the War Department, with General Oliver O. Howard as its commissioner, and thus backed by military force, the bureau was one of the most powerful instruments of Reconstruction. Howard divided the ex-slave states, including the border slave states that had remained in the Union, into 10 districts, each headed by an assistant commissioner."[34] Northern Kentucky would be included in the Ninth district.

30. Ibid., "Organizing for the Education of Black Children, 1866–1872," *Kenton County Historical Society Bulletin* (July 2002): 3, http//www.kentonlib.ky.us~histsoc/ (accessed September 1, 2009).

31. Ibid.

32. "Price, Jacob (Rev.)," Genealogy and Kentucky History.

33. Ibid. The name of the fourth child was not identified in the article.

34. "Bureau of Refugees, Freedmen and Abandoned Lands," *Wikipedia, The Free Encyclopedia,* http://en.wikipedia.org/ wikiBureau_of_Refugees_Fredmen_and_Abandoned_Lands (accessed March 19, 2008).

The activities of the bureau in Northern Kentucky would embrace the development of schools for newly emancipated black citizens, including a school in Covington and one in Newport. Although the U.S. Congress did not fund the Bureau during its first year of operation, "by 1866, there were numerous missionary and aid societies working in conjunction with the Freedmen's Bureau to provide education for former slaves."[35] Price and his colleagues utilized the bureau as a catalyst for the black school in Covington.

Others in the community would quickly join Price in his efforts. Among them was Isaac Black, who was described in one local newspaper as "a light-colored Negro. . . . Born in Kentucky in June, 1848, Isaac Black lived his early years in Covington." He was an avid reader, who "apparently had acquired literacy during slavery."[36] As a previously enslaved, intellectually gifted individual, Black worked initially as a janitor in the Covington courthouse for several years, where he would become exposed to the local legal system. His insatiable appetite for reading would be served through his employment in the local public library. Black, who also reportedly studied to become a clergyman at one point, eventually found his true niche in life when he became a black practicing attorney, and cofounder of Harper and Black, one of the oldest black law firms in the Commonwealth. He seemed personally enigmatic in some respects, as well as conflicted in his political views and racial self-image. A man of obviously mixed racial heritage, Isaac Black was at the forefront of local efforts for a black school during his early adult years in Covington, although he was occasionally at odds with the local community in terms of some of his political views.

Two black church denominations would eventually emerge in Covington—one Baptist and the other Methodist. [37] Harris indicates that the Methodist congregation was actually an outgrowth of the original Baptist Church that was organized in 1864. Black Baptist churches have been historically independent of central control, while the black Methodist churches (i.e. African Methodist Episcopal (A.M.E.) churches or Christian Methodist Episcopal (C.M.E.) churches) were tied to hierarchically controlled, centralized organizations, and aligned closely with white Methodist organizations. To some degree, those religious variations reflected perceived differences in social standing *within* the black community. But in spite of such distinctions, members of both local church denominations had a vested interest in providing educational opportunities for Covington's black children. Hence, two black schools were eventually established—one in the Methodist Church and the other in the Baptist Church.

An elected board of local black men, influenced by Jacob Price and Isaac

35. Ibid.
36. Harris, "Creating Windows of Opportunity," 155.
37. John Boh, "The Old Colored Church on Madison Avenue," *Kenton County Historical Society Bulletin,* May 1992. Boh writes, "The *Covington Journal* (2-5-[18]70) reported that Afro-Americans have in Covington 'two church organizations,' numbering 250 Methodists and 75 Baptists."

Black, would provide early guidance to the two fledgling black schools. Harris reports a meeting on August 4, 1869 to elect a black school board. The board candidates from the black Methodist Church were King Gray, Jerry Moss, and Alexander White, while the black Baptist Church board candidates would include Jacob Price, Mr. Skillman, and Mr. Robinson. [38]

■ LOCAL, STATE AND REGIONAL COORDINATION

The oversight provided by the local black school board would be vital; however, the development of schools for African Americans in Covington would not merely be a local matter. Federal and state efforts, complemented by organized action from statewide and regional black citizens groups would become essential background forces that local leaders needed to create viable educational opportunities for black students in Covington.

As early as 1868, "African Americans from Kentucky and neighboring states would come together at a number of meetings to plan for the educational future of the race. A convention had been held in 1868 in Owensboro, KY, where Marshall W. Taylor was named president."[39] The following year, the Freedmen's Bureau held another convention in Louisville, Kentucky, at Benson's Theater.[40] "Seven hundred delegates were in attendance with Reverend H. J. Young of Louisville serving as convention president."[41]

A brief article in the *Covington Journal* dated July 10, 1869, indicated that "The colored people of this city, at a meeting held Wednesday night at the Methodist church on Third street between Scott and Madison appointed J. W. Grant and Isaac Black to represent them in the State Educational Convention, which meets in Louisville on Wednesday next."[42] Harris reports that, during the meeting in Louisville, Major Stone of the Freedmen's Bureau indicated that funding from the bureau would soon cease, and schools currently backed by the bureau would need to establish their own means of financial support.[43]

Harris also indicates that, at the time of the 1869 state convention, the two black schools in Covington had already been established. Those two schools had operated independently of financial support from the Freedmen's Bureau, but "there was a need to combine their resources" as they began to encounter

---

38. Theodore H. H. Harris, "Organizing for the Education of Black Children, 1866–1872." *Kenton County Historical Society Bulletin* (July 2002) http//www.kenton-lib.ky.us~histsoc/ (accessed September 1, 2009) 3.

39. Jones, "The Early Kinship," 2009.

40. Ibid.

41. Harris, "Organizing Schools for Black Children."

42. In separate column dated July 10, 1869, the *Covington Journal* also reported the annual election of the Covington superintendent and principal of the white high school as Dr. J. W. Hall. The appointments of school principals for the district's five white elementary schools, as well as teachers for those schools were also included in that article. The black school was not a part of the Covington school system at that point.

43. Harris, "Organizing Schools for Black Children."

financial difficulty. [44] The two schools united into a single school at the Methodist Church because of insufficient funding and a lack of cooperation from the Covington City Council or the Covington School Board, neither of which felt that it had jurisdictional responsibility for the black school under existing law at that time. As a consequence, the black school would struggle for funding, and even close temporarily in January 1871. But it would soon reopen in late February of that year.[45]

Educational funding for black students in Covington had been an ongoing issue since 1867, when

> The Kentucky Act of 1867 provided for the education of 'Negroes' and 'mulattos' in separate schools. There was a capitation tax of $2 for each 'Negro' or 'mulatto male.' This money and all other taxes collected from 'Negroes' was [sic] to be used for their schools, but the Covington School Board's charter did not provide for separate schools. The 'Negroes' of Covington felt that the Act of 1867 should override the Board's charter, especially since school taxes were being collected from 'Negroes' but were not being used for their schools.[46]

Harris writes that, in response to a subsequent request for the white city school board to provide funding from black property taxes that board declined to act. At a city school board meeting on February 17, 1871, the Board Committee on Law, chaired by Judge Pryor concluded,

> "The school board has not the authority to act in the matter, not having possession of the funds referred to in the petition. The account of taxes paid by the black people of Covington is quite small, not exceeding fifty or sixty dollars annually, and this money is in the hands of the Sheriff, and can only be reached by proper application to the County court." Based on that decision by the Covington School Board, the [black] school continued in the Methodist Church. They raised the necessary funds by other means. In September, 1871, the black school decided to hire a Principal for their school with John McLeod being selected.[47]

Eventually, the Covington City Council was persuaded to contribute $200 annually toward the support of the black school.[48] Boh writes, "On September 21, 1872 the *Covington Journal* expressed hope that the City Council would respond favorably to an appeal from Afro-American citizens for school money 'despite the state law excluding negro children from the benefits of the [white] school fund. . . . ' The Council's committee did recommend money for negro

44. Ibid.
45. Ibid.
46. Nordheim, *Echoes*, 98.
47. Harris, "Creating Windows of Opportunity."
48. Letter from Samuel R. Singer, third principal of the black school in Covington. See Leconia F. Crosby, "A Study of Pupil Marks, William Grant High School, Covington, Ky. 1918–1929," (master's thesis, University of Cincinnati, 1929).

education (Journal, 10-5-[18]72)." [49]

An article in the *Covington Journal* dated October 19, 1872, reported,

> The colored School Trustees of Covington, consisting of R. D. Cross, G. W. Durgins, Howard Haggard, Jacob Price, I. E. Black, J. H. Nixon [*sic*], William Blackburn, John Thomas, and W. J. Hamilton . . . organized by electing the following officers: President R. D. Cross; Secretary, W. J. Hamilton; Treasurer, Isaac E. Black. The board has employed Miss Mary L. Forte, of Cincinnati, as teacher, and the school was opened Monday in the basement of the Methodist Church on Madison street [*sic*] between Second and Third. About thirty-five scholars were present, but this number will be greatly increased.

At that point, the black school would be on more solid footing to begin making progress. The next step would include state legislation that created a common framework for black public schools in the Commonwealth of Kentucky.

However, some black leaders at the state level initially resisted the establishment of a separate state framework for black public schools in Kentucky. The split among black educational advocates was also reflected in some indecision about when a meeting slated for February 1873 would be held. The *Covington Journal* reported the following on February 15, 1873: "The colored people of this city have had a regular split on the subject of their educational Convention. A large number of them wanted the Convention held on the 18th instant, while some of them want to put if off until the weather clears up and streets are passable. In the meantime delegates have been elected all over the State to come here on the 18th instant. It is probable that the will of the majority will prevail."

The article continues,

> The following have been appointed on the
>
> COMMITTEE ON ARRANGEMENTS:
>
> Louisville – V. Helm, J. C. Smith, N. R. Harper, A. Roberts, William H. Lawson, G. B. Blakey, A. Fromen, Rev. P. Spillman, B. Butler, J. H. Taylor, Rev. R. G. Mortimer, Thornton Radd, William Spalding, Rev. J. Halliday, Dr. H. Fitzbutler, John Trabue.
>
> **Covington – Isaac Black;**[50] Frankfort – H. B. Lind; Berea – John Jackson; Shelbyville – W. H. Russell; Bowling Green – B. F. Thomas; Georgetown – James Bailey; Newcastle – E. P. Marrs; Brandenburg – John Bailey; Lexington – H. Scroggins; Danville – Gibson Doram: Paducah – G. W. Dupee [sic]; Cloverport – Rev. Scott Ward; Lebanon – Abram Menx; Owenton – Winslow Stanley: Bardstown – Rev. E. Sherman. [*Louisville Ledger*][51]

---

49. Boh, "Old Colored Church."

50. Bold lettering provided by this author to emphasize Covington's representation by Isaac Black.

When the "Colored People's Educational Convention" met later that month, The *Covington Journal* reported the following:

> We have watched with some interest the movement of the colored people of Kentucky to secure the advantages of education for their offspring. Delegates representing the colored people of Jefferson, Kenton, Campbell, Shelby, Nelson, Warren and Fayette counties met at Louisville on the 18th and organized an education convention. Dr. H. Fitzbutler of Louisville was made President; J. H. Dixon, of Covington, one of the Vice Presidents, I. E. Black of Covington, Secretary, and G. W. Guy, of Covington, Sergeant-at-arms.[52]

The newspaper article further indicates,

> The memorial [written by the black convention attendees] declares, "Regarding, as we do, education as indispensable to morality, and to the continuity of patriotism, we deem it a duty incumbent upon us who seek for our children equal educational privileges in common with other citizens of the United States; that we most earnestly request there be no special legislation in the State of Kentucky for colored people, since it is humiliating to us, detrimental to the finance of the State, and contrary to sound policy; that we sincerely believe that citizens, in general, of Kentucky are as ready to accord equal school privileges to the colored people of the State, as colored people are to receive those privileges."[53]

The declaration by black representatives championed principles with which few could disagree: (1) teaching morality and patriotism to newly emancipated black citizens of the United States; (2) providing them with educational privileges without humiliation as "second class citizens;" and (3) engaging sound fiscal policy for the Commonwealth of Kentucky by non-duplication of effort and resources. Such written expression and sophisticated language from black people, some of whom were enslaved a few years prior, seemed extraordinary. However, the fact that there were black men with such advanced communication skills in 1873 underscores the fact that some people of color in Kentucky and elsewhere were educated, even at the college level, well before the end of slavery, while others, like Isaac Black, had been remarkably self-educated even as enslaved persons.

■ SEGREGATION "FOREVER": THE KENTUCKY LEGISLATIVE ACT OF 1874

The following resolution was also adopted at the black convention: "That the present Legislature of Kentucky has our heartfelt thanks for the steps it has

---

51. *Covington Journal*, "The Colored Educational Convention," February 15, 1873.
52. Ibid., "Colored People's Education Convention," February 22, 1873.
53. Ibid.

taken in according our rights as citizens of Kentucky."[54] Kentucky legislators did not respond with enthusiasm to a published declaration and resolution that not only requested equal treatment for white and black citizens in Kentucky, but also seemed to infer the possibility of having black and white children learn in the same classrooms.

The immediate response in Covington via the *Covington Journal* (as a continuation of the same newspaper article cited above) was as follows:

> A permanent [black educational] organization was resolved upon, and to effect, its meeting is to be held in Covington on the Second Tuesday in July next. We wish the colored people complete success in every well-directed effort to secure proper educational advantages for their children. If they mean by 'equal education privileges' a pro rata distribution of the school fund for children of school age, regardless of color, but in separate schools, we second the motion. If, on the other hand, they intend to demand that provision be made for the education of their children in the same schools with white children, we enter a most emphatic protest. The colored people of Kentucky would be most unwise to demand anything of the kind. We cannot conceive of a proposition more likely to break down the system of common school education in Kentucky.

The point of view expressed by the editor or editorial staff of the *Covington Journal* in 1873 would foreshadow the Kentucky Legislative Act of 1874, as well as the "Separate but Equal" U.S. Supreme Court ruling that would become the law of the land in 1896. The message in the newspaper editorial was emphatic, and patently clear: Don't even *think* about the possibility of educating black and white children in the same schools in the Commonwealth of Kentucky!

Thus, the firm will to maintain racial segregation in Kentucky would neutralize any idea of fiscal responsibility through nonduplication of efforts, or other principled arguments presented in the aforementioned declaration and resolution from Isaac Black and his colleagues. Kentucky's white legislators would ignore that document, as plans for a separate framework for the education of black children of the Commonwealth moved forward in the state legislature.

A different group of black leaders had previously filed a petition with the state requesting the creation of separate, state-supported black public schools in Kentucky immediately after the Civil War ended,[55] followed by the Kentucky Act of 1867.[56] On those bases, the following framework, which insured *unequal* educational opportunities between black and white children in Ken-

---

54. Ibid.
55. Jones, "Early Kinship."
56. As previously indicated, the Act of 1867 provided for separate black schools in Kentucky based on taxation monies collected from black males. See Nordheim, *Echoes*, 28.

tucky, was put in place in 1874:

> In February of 1874 the Kentucky legislature approved an act to estab-
> lish a uniform system of common Schools for the education of the
> black children . . . but not on the same level as white children. . . .
> Taxes were to be collected from African American property owners
> for this purpose, and a separate Board of Trustees of African American
> men was to be set up to run the schools. The length of the school year
> could be shorter, even as brief as two or three months. The African
> American teachers had to pass an examination just as the white teach-
> ers did. However, the examination could not be extended beyond
> spelling reading, writing and common arithmetic. A school taught by a
> teacher competent to teach these subjects was considered to be a law-
> ful school.[57]

Nordheim further explains,

> There were two conditions Covington accepted as the rulings of the
> state act. First, it was not lawful for a white child to attend a Common
> school provided for the African American children, nor for an African
> American child to attend a white school. Second, no school house
> erected for a "colored school" could be located nearer than one mile of
> a school house erected for white children, except in cities and towns,
> where it could not be nearer than 600 feet. Covington did abide by
> these two rulings for almost the next hundred years.[58]

The act of 1874 also stated, "white and colored schools shall be forever
kept and maintained separately."[59] That act would leave not even the slightest
legal opening for the possibility of integrated schools in Kentucky.

Many racially segregated schools were created in Kentucky immediately
following the Kentucky Legislative Act of 1874 establishing common schools
for black children. Jones indicates that some 452 black schools, many with sub-
standard teachers, were reported in ninety-three Kentucky counties in 1875.
Those figures presumably included the black schools in Covington and Newport. As black citizens accepted a separate system of education for black children in Kentucky, another statewide convention "was held in Fayette County in
1875, led by African American ministers and Reverend E. H. Fairchild, President of Berea College. The purpose of these meetings was not only to address
educational needs, but also to coordinate the issues and present them to the
Kentucky Legislature to encourage better funding for Negro schools and teachers." [60]

57. Nordheim, *Echoes*, 21–22.
58. Ibid.
59. Ibid.
60. Jones, "Early Kinship."

■ A FLEDGLING BLACK SCHOOL IN COVINGTON—EARLY 1870S

The early black participants in the educational process in Covington would come largely from the ranks of people of color who were free before the Civil War. Black community leaders such as Jacob Price and the Singer family would first and foremost secure the education of their own children and relatives, while bringing other black children from the community into the educational process. Therefore, the students in the new school would be comprised of both black students who had been born into freedom as well as those who were recently emancipated.

"The Freedmen's Bureau published their own Freedmen's text book which was referred to as a reader. The Freedmen's Bureau pushed their particular philosophy of education for African Americans through the south by controlling the curriculum and resources that were provided to these schools."[61] However, the probable source of most teaching materials for the first black school in Covington would be books and other teaching supplies that were no longer used by white children in the community. That tradition would extend well into the future as Covington school superintendents passed on used books and materials from the white city schools to the black school after those books and supplies became outdated. That practice was even reflected in the Covington Public Schools as late as the 1940s and 1950s, when this author attended the school.

The more rudimentary educational curriculum of the first local African American school would soon be shaped around the state guidelines for "Common Schools" that were outlined in 1874. Though not specified in the state curriculum guidelines, singing would also be included for local black children. There was no black high school at that point, and black teachers with varying levels of preparation would be recruited to teach in the school. One teacher would normally handle several grades.

From 1866 to 1873 the black school in Covington continued to be located in either the black Baptist Church, the black Methodist Church, or both. When the church congregations relocated, the black school would relocate with them, while carrying the street name of each church location—e.g. the Madison Street School and the Robbins Street School.

It also seems evident that one early educational practice in some areas of Northern Kentucky (e.g. Latonia) was to house a few grades for black students in obsolete buildings that had been vacated by white students, even if such facilities were too large for the black student population, resulting in unoccupied classrooms. At some point in 1873 a vacated white school building like that became available on Greer Street in Covington.

Harris reports,

Earlier, the Covington board had constructed a new, larger school for

---

61. "Bureau of Refugees," *Wikipedia.*

white students and had decided to sell the Valley school building on Greer Street. Two attempts had been made to lease the building, but it still remained vacant. Members of the African American community suggested that the [white] school board either give them the structure or at least permit them to use it, but the board instead [proposed to sell] the property for an insignificant amount. That proposal apparently insulted Isaac Black [prompting him to tender his immediate resignation from the black school board]. . . . Soon, however, the Covington School Board recanted its decision and permitted the black community to use the Valley Schoolhouse. Black then rescinded his resignation.[62]

Nordheim also reports that a school for black children was established in one room of "the old Second District School building on Greer Street" in 1873 with one black teacher and several black students.[63]

By 1875, the black school was again reported in two locations: the church on Madison Street and the church on Robbins Street, with John McLeod as the principal, and Arzelia Ross and Constantia Taylor as assistants.[64] Black churches in the community would be logical places for a school, since they were (1) located in the black community, (2) equipped to handle large groups, and (3) not used regularly for church services during weekdays.

The efforts to establish a black school in Covington were predictably erratic and fledgling in status, while changing locations frequently. But the embryonic structure provided by the Commonwealth of Kentucky in the Legislative Act of 1874 would become the basis for the City of Covington to move forwarded with a more systematic approach to educational opportunities for black children.

■ JACOB PRICE AND ISAAC BLACK: A SHARED VISION

Soon the city would gain responsibility for the local black school, and its school principals and teachers would be "elected" by the all-white, all-male Covington Board of Education. At that point, Jacob Price would become less involved with the oversight of the black school in Covington. He would in fact concentrate more on his new congregation at The Ninth Street Baptist Church, and the growing lumber business on Madison Avenue that he operated from 1881 (the year that his brother-in-law Samuel Singer became principal of the black school) until 1914.[65] At the approximate age of seventy-four, Price reportedly jumped from a second floor window in his home at Tenth and Pros-

---

62. Harris, "Creating Windows of Opportunity," 163.
63. Nordheim, *Echoes*, 21.
64. Patricia Humphries Fann, "The History of William Grant," an unpublished manuscript.
65. "Price, Jacob (Rev.)," Genealogy and Kentucky History.

pect streets in order to escape from a severe fire in the home.[66] One article indicates that Jacob and Mary Price narrowly escaped death during that incident.[67]

As a church minister, a prominent businessman and a community activist, Reverend Jacob Price would continue to be a legendary and influential figure in the city of Covington until his death on March 1, 1923, at the age of eighty-four. An article in the *Kentucky Post* on March 2, 1923, reflected the following: "Rev. Jacob Price, negro minister, of 245 E. 10th-st, died Thursday morning and will be buried from the First Baptist Negro Church, Covington, Saturday afternoon at 1 o'clock. Rev. Price was one of Covington's oldest negro citizens. He organized the first negro church in Covington nearly 60 years ago, and was its first pastor. He also was the founder of the Lincoln Grant High School. He was held in high esteem by both races. His wife, to whom has been married 55 years; one son and one daughter survive him."[68] "Burial was in Evergreen Cemetery in Southgate, Kentucky."[69] Price's wife, Mary Singer Price died a year later, in 1924.

Although no school buildings would carry his name, Price's influence on conditions for the black population of the city would be formally memorialized when the federally subsidized housing projects for black people were dedicated in 1939, and named "The Jacob Price Homes" in his honor. One of the Price's surviving children, Annie Price (Hood) would be significantly linked to Covington's black educational history.

Isaac Black eventually left Covington and lived in Louisville for a number of years. He then resided outside of the Commonwealth of Kentucky "until 1886 when he married Rowena Saunders in Louisville. After living again in Covington a few years, Black and his family returned in 1891 to the Falls City"[70] where he practiced law.

In addition to striving for educational equity for black children, Isaac Black also seemed engaged concurrently in a pressing individual need to eradicate his enslaved past, as he sought an egalitarian personal presence with "white society folks" in Covington and other communities where he lived during the late eighteen hundreds. One incident reported in the March 27, 1875, edition of the *Covington Journal* was that "Isaac Black, a colored man, formerly janitor of the Court-house building in this city, now a practicing lawyer of Memphis, presented himself at the entrance of Trinity Episcopal Church, in this city, at the hour of morning service last Sunday. Isaac was accompanied by a colored brother. They demanded seats."[71] The *Journal* then presented two

---

66. *Kentucky Post*, "Negro Families Flee From Fire [Tenth and Prospect home of Jacob Price], February 21, 1913, 8.
67. "Covington Biographies," 2007.
68. *Kentucky Post*, "Negro Pastor Dies—Rev. Jacob Price Organized First Negro Church," March 2, 1923.
69. Ibid.
70. Harris, "Creating Windows of Opportunity," 174.
71. *Covington Journal*, "Civil Rights at Church," March 27, 1875.

versions of the event, one from Isaac Black, and the other from Mr. Botsford, a Vestryman at Trinity.

Isaac Black's account is as follows:

> As we entered we were met by Mr. Botsford, one of the Vestrymen. I asked him if he had any free seats at his disposal. He replied by opening a door leading to the gallery, and inviting us thither. I told him I did not wish to go upstairs; that if there were any *free* seats in the auditorium proper, I would be much obliged to him for one. He then informed me that the seats in the gallery were the only ones assigned for the use of colored people. He did not deny that there were free pews in the body of the church. I then told him I attended Christ Church in Louisville and Calvary Church in Memphis and in both I was always treated as any one would be who behaved as a gentleman. In those churches I always occupied seats in the auditorium. I did not go to Trinity Church for the purpose of testing any Civil Rights bill. I went there because I am a member of the Episcopal Church. [72]

The Vestryman's version, as reported by the *Journal*, is as follows:

> Mr. Black, on coming into the church asked if he could have a seat, simply, and did not at any time mention free seats; and further that when he (Mr. Botsford), in response to the request opened the gallery door, Mr. Black drew back and emphatically said 'No sir! no sir! none of your gallery seats for me, sir.' [sic] His companion then asked whether 'Mr.' Page was about. Mr. Botsford answering that since 'Mr.' Page's difficulties, he is no longer a Sexton. Mr. Botsford says that colored people do frequently come in and occupy seats in the body of the church, and no objection is made thereto, and that Mr. Black could have done likewise, but that he did not propose to usher Mr. Black and his companion up the aisle to seats. When asked for seats, that part of the church usually occupied by colored people was shown to him. Mr. Botsford says he did not tell Mr. Black that the gallery was the only place assigned to colored people. [73]

At the conclusion of the incident, Isaac Black reportedly "turned on his heel" and walked out of the church. The writer for the *Covington Journal* concludes the article with the following personal observation: "While a resident of Covington, Isaac Black conducted himself with propriety, and though filling a public position, knew his place and kept within its limits. His conduct at Trinity shows an instance of a good nigger spoiled by the mischievous Civil Rights Law."[74]

The Civil Rights Act of 1866 gave citizenship and equal rights to newly emancipated slaves. It was followed by the Civil Rights Act of 1870, which

72. Ibid.
73. Ibid.
74. Ibid.

made it illegal for two or more persons to conspire against the "enjoyment" of any right or privilege granted by the U.S. Constitution.[75] Several articles in the March 27, 1875, edition of the *Covington Journal,* including the church incident cited above, and two others in which black men entered white barbershops in Covington requesting service, but being denied the same, suggested that the Civil Rights laws were being "tested" by black citizens in Covington and other parts of Kentucky at that point. Isaac Black denied that as his intent in requesting that he and his guest be seated in "the body of the church" at Trinity. Mr. Botsford's elaborate attempt to rationalize the situation, while asserting his own lack of racial discrimination in the matter, reflected the sensitivity with which some white church people approached the subject at that point in Covington's history. On the other hand, the author of the newspaper article was quite explicit in his negative opinion of black people and their "place" in the Covington community.

That example of Black's quest for personal racial equality, and its reactionary magnification to a larger cause had been reflected earlier through his intense community activism in behalf of education for black children in Covington. Driven perhaps by the fact that he had been denied a formal education as an enslaved person, as well his inability to achieve equal social standing among white people, Black's participation at both the local and statewide levels was significant as he merged his intellectual gifts and legal training with the leadership provided by Jacob Price and other local black community people to form Covington's first black school.

> On April 18 1914, following an illness of several months, Isaac E. Black died at his home. . . . A Louisville newspaper gave this account: 'Isaac E. Black one of the oldest Negro attorneys of this city [Louisville]. Black was appointed by the late Police Judge W. R. Thompson, at one time a member of the Board of Children's Guardians, and was a member of the first Negro law firm of this city, Harper & Black which was admitted to the bar in 1871.' [76]

Jacob Price and Isaac Black, two men of color, were extremely significant in the historical development of Lincoln-Grant School. Price would be long remembered because of his longevity in the area, while Black would fall into relative obscurity in Covington upon leaving the area. Their beginnings had been different. One was a free man, and the other was born in slavery. Their practical worlds were also different. One was a laborer, businessman, and church pastor; the other a courthouse janitor, librarian, and attorney. But both shared a vision supported by deep commitment and action, which had resulted in the establishment of a black school in Covington. Another person in the local

75. "Civil Rights Act of 1866," *Answers.com,* http://www.answers.com/topic/civil-rights-act-of-1866 (accessed October 18, 2009).

76. Harris, "Creating Windows of Opportunity," cited by Harris from the *Louisville Herald,* April 20, 1914..

community, Col. William Letcher Grant, was also a significant participant in that vision.

CHAPTER 3

Covington Amends its Charter to Include a Black City School (1876)

■ THE INFLUENCE OF COLONEL WILLIAM GRANT

Placing the black school in Covington under the administration of the Covington Public Schools would become a primary goal of Col. William Letcher Grant. The son of former Covington mayor Moses V. Grant, and an older contemporary of Jacob Price and Isaac Black, William Letcher Grant, a white Covingtonian, was born on April 1, 1820. An article in the *Covington Journal* dated February 20, 1876, revealed that Grant "was born in Lancaster, Garrard county, Ky. His early education was received at the Lancaster Seminary, and he graduated at the Cincinnati College, Ohio. He studied law, and [was] a lawyer and speculator." Reis indicates, "William Grant worked in a grocery before taking up law. He studied in the law office of one-time Kentucky governor and senator John White Stevenson."[77] William Grant married Laura B. Southgate, a member of another prominent, white Northern Kentucky family, in 1845.

Although Grant was heavily involved in local and state politics, as well as the acquisition of real estate property in the area, he would apply much of his personal energy, community influence, and financial resources to those who did not have his opportunities in life. He was elected to the Covington City Council in 1854, but was defeated in his run for the Kentucky Legislature in 1859. William Grant was re-elected to the Covington Council as Third Ward representative in 1873, and was successful in being elected to the Kentucky General Assembly (or Kentucky Legislature) in 1875 as a representative from

---

77. Jim Reis, "School namesake an astute politician," *Kentucky Post*, January 19, 2004, http://www.kypost.com/2004/01/19/reissd011904.html (accessed March 25, 2007).

the Second District. His gaining the support of black males, who had been granted the right to vote in the United States by 1870, had facilitated his election as a state representative from Northern Kentucky.

An interesting personal characterization of black people appeared in the *Covington Journal* on October 10, 1872. The newspaper opinion article, apparently authored anonymously by the paper's editor or staff, was entitled "The Negro as a Politician." Reflected as a "voice of the people" commentary, it began as follows:

> We bear willing testimony to the general good conduct of negroes in Covington. In the main they are industrious and well behaved. Many of them are church members. Some of them take a lively interest in the education of their children. In their religious views they are tolerant— at least we know of nothing to the contrary. As a class they are perhaps over fond [*sic*] of parades and displays of that character. If they have a pic-nic [*sic*] they must go to it in procession. Then they have numerous emancipation days to celebrate by processions. All this however, is measurably harmless and nobody complains.[78]

The editorial continues,

> The negro in politics is a very different sort of negro. The moment he enters the political arena he becomes intolerant and overbearing. With those of his own color especially, he tolerates no difference of opinion. Less than six months ago the negroes of Covington were almost solid against [President] Grant. There was no exception. He was formally denounced by resolution as unworthy of confidence of association, and threats were made to mob him. They flopped over in a night, and are now solid for Grant.[79]

That opinion article was written within the context of the 1872 presidential election, wherein Ulysses Simpson Grant, the eighteenth president of the United States, was about to be elected to a second term. The commentary demonstrated how some white politicians could manipulate the black vote in the late eighteen hundreds. It also presented an interesting perspective of the "average" black person in Covington. Descriptors such as "industrious," "well-behaved," "church-going," as well as some black people having "a lively interest in the education of their children," reflected a point of view held by some whites in Covington in 1872.

The political support of African American males in Covington would become critical to William Letcher Grant, as he sought election to the Kentucky Legislature in 1875. At that point, Grant consulted with Isaac Black, J. H. Dixon, George Durgan, and Rev. Jacob Price, and gained the support of those influential black community leaders.[80] William Grant's consistent acts of

---

78. *Covington Journal*, "The Negro as a Politician," October 19, 1872.
79. Ibid.
80. Singer in Crosby, "A Study of Pupil Marks."

benevolence toward the black Covington community would definitely work in his favor, as he sought to garner the black vote.

The Grant name carried a lot of weight in Covington. Jesse Root Grant, who was the father of President Ulysses S. Grant, lived at 518–520 Greenup Street from 1859 until his death in 1873. Jesse Grant "was appointed postmaster of Covington by President Andrew Johnson in 1866, and he served in that capacity until 1872."[81] Local black men who had voted *en masse* for President Grant three years earlier would likely be more prone to vote for a local political candidate for the state legislature with the same last name.

As a shrewd politician, William Grant would solidify the vote of local black men by merging two realities in support of his candidacy for the state legislature: (1) the need for black people in Covington to secure appropriate educational opportunities for their children through an amendment to the Covington city ordinances, and (2) Grant's need for the black vote in the 1875 state election.

As a former Covington city clerk, and the son of a former mayor, as well as a former Covington city councilman, William Grant had political skill, an insider's knowledge of Covington politics, and the respect of Covington citizens, both black and white. Consequently, he was ideally positioned to follow through with his promise "that if Colored voters would support him as a candidate to the [state] Legislature, and if he were elected, he would have the Charter of Covington amended so as to provide for a public school for Colored children."[82] Grant won the election, and kept his promise. The charter amendment that Grant and his colleagues put in place on March 20, 1876, stated:

**Figure 1: City Charter Amendment Establishing a Black School
in Covington March 20, 1876**

that the Board of School Trustees of the City of Covington, out of any funds in their hand derived by taxation under and by virtue of the City Ordinances of said city, be and are hereby authorized and empowered to establish and maintain schools for the colored children of the city in such numbers and localities as in their judgment will furnish sufficient education facilities for the colored children of the city. Such schools shall be under the same control, rules and regulations as govern other schools of the city.[a]

a. Nordheim, *Echoes*, 28.

Thus, as of that date, the Covington Board of Education officially controlled the education of the city's black children. A separate black school board was no longer necessary. Funds previously collected from taxes on blacks in Covington would be sought from the state, and financial support for the black school would soon be provided in the same way that it had been supplied for the white schools.

81. Kenton County Public Library, *Covington/Kenton County Library,* 53.
82. Singer in Crosby, "A Study of Pupil Marks."

During the summer of 1876 The Covington Board of Education examined several individuals for positions in the "colored schools." An August edition of *The Ticket,* a local triweekly publication reported: "The following is the list of teachers lately examined for positions in the colored schools with their averages and amount of experience.[83] The article adds, "Mrs. M. Northrop, a white lady, an applicant for a position in the white schools underwent an examination which resulted: general average 82; experience, none."[84]

	General Average	Experience
J. S. McLeod	79 1/2	3 years
Arzelia Ross	76 1/2	3 years
Constantia H. Taylor	73 1/8	1 years [*sic*]
Mary Simmons	74 1/2	1 year
John Robinson	76	3 years
Samuel R. Singer	88 4-11	3 months
Eliza Weaver	73 1-10	none
Cora J. Warwick	75	6 months

The Covington School Board met in special session on Friday, August 18, 1876, to discuss provisions for the "colored schools" in Covington. The two primary items of business on the agenda were finding a place to house the black school, and the election of personnel for the school. "Mr. Hackathorn, from the committee appointed to find suitable buildings for the location of colored schools, reported that after considerable research, the committee was unable to find any structure suitable for the purpose, and recommended that lots be purchased and school houses erected."[85]

The article continues, "Dr. J. W. Hall, Superintendent of the Public Schools, called on, gave his advise [*sic*] in regard to the erection of the buildings, the management and grading of the schools, etc. The Doctor was of the opinion that for reasons of economy and utility, there should be but one school located in a central part of the city, the structure to consist of four rooms, all on the same floor. The school could then be the better graded and managed."[86]

John McLeod, who was also present at the meeting, expressed a different opinion on the matter:

Mr. McLeod was of the opinion that it would be impossible to get along with but one school, located in a central part of the city, as then

83. "Meeting of School Board," *The Ticket*, August 12, 1876.
84. Ibid.
85. Ibid.
86. Ibid.

[black] children from the suburbs would not then attend, etc. The Committee on School Organization were [*sic*] instructed to enquire into and report at next meeting upon the cost of a lot in the central part of the city; and also as to the cost of two lots differently located, with the erection of proper buildings, etc. The Committee were [*sic*] also instructed to procure suitable rooms for the temporary location of the colored schools.[87]

Next, "the election of teachers for the colored schools was entered into and resulted in the election of Mr. J. S. McLeod as principal over Mr. Singer by a vote of 8 to 2, and Miss Ross by 8 votes, and Miss Taylor by 9 votes, as assistants." In other business, "the Committee on Ways and Means were [*sic*] instructed to confer with the Superintendent of Public Instruction [at the state level] with a view to obtaining the money set aside for the education of the colored children. The Committee on Supplies were [*sic*] instructed to have 250 extra copies of the Rules and Regulations and course of study printed and bound separately. Adjourned at 10:55."[88]

The 1876 Covington city ordinance amendment creating a black school theoretically exceeded the more limited 1874 framework developed by the state. Board action regarding the printing of rules and regulations and course of study for the black school would seem to guarantee that white and black schools would offer the same curriculum to all students in Covington, regardless of race, color, or creed. But, while some may have expected an exact duplication of the curricular offerings at all schools in Covington after the city took control of the black school, that would not be the case.

The original state guidelines, the progress that had already been made in establishing a separate educational system for white students, and the core beliefs of some white system administrators would dictate that, at the outset, the quantity and quality of the curricular offerings for white students in Covington would be greater than those for black students. In fact, the curricular offerings at the segregated, black school would never reach parity with the more comprehensive, expanding educational opportunities provided for white children in the city.

Since a central purpose of education is to prepare children for the world in which they are expected to live as adults, the restrictions imposed on the early curriculum for black students at the state level seemed consonant with projected limitations of the functioning of black people in society as well as fundamental beliefs about differences in intellectual capacity between white and black children.

In addition to more advanced offerings in core academic subjects such as mathematics and science, the projected worldview for white students would include the need to teach Latin as well as German in the elementary grades. The

87. Ibid.
88. Ibid.

teaching of German, and the eventual establishment of a private German school would be relevant to the local German population. Latin would have functionality in their religious teachings, as well as provide language fundamentals for recent immigrants. The curriculum for white students in Covington would prepare them for a different "world of work" than black children. A domestic emphasis would soon become dominant at the black school, while white children would be prepared for a world that included business and industry.

The stark contrast between what white and black teachers were expected to teach in the Covington public schools was reflected in the differences in subject matter examinations required for black and white teachers. While teacher examinations for black teachers continued to be rudimentary, and linked to minimal state requirements outlined in the State Act of 1874, by 1895, white teachers were required to pass examinations in 12 to 25 subject matter areas, depending on their grade level, or their level of administrative appointment.[89]

John McLeod, who had been the principal of the all-black school since 1871, resigned in 1879 to become a "store keeper gauger," a government job that deals with the measurement and quantification of bulk merchandise. That position apparently provided McLeod with a better livelihood. Darius L. V. Moffett was elected to succeed McLeod as principal. Although Moffet's educational background is also not explicit, Harris reports that, when Moffet took over, the school opened in a new location with 200 pupils, "and two teachers, Hattie Todd and Clara Grandstaff."[90] Nordheim indicates, "By 1879 the [black student] enrollment had grown enough to require one principal who was male, two teachers (female), and a janitor for the instruction of 229 students.[91]

The successful amendment to the city charter was one of two major contributions that William Grant would make to the cause of educating black children in Covington. In a second act of benevolence and commitment, Grant deeded property on Seventh Street to the Covington Board of Education in 1880 for the specific purpose of erecting a new school building for black youth, thereby stabilizing the physical location of the school in the city. At that point, the school apparently was housed temporarily in some of the Seventh Street properties until a new building for black children could be constructed at 25 East Seventh Street. That action by Grant would spawn the eventual development of the Seventh Street Colored School, followed by the addition of a high school division for black students in the downtown area of Covington.

---

89. Nordheim, *Echoes*, 101–102.
90. Theodore H. H. Harris, "Covington amended charter for African-American schools." *Cincinnati Enquirer*, February 9, 2009.
91. Nordheim, *Echoes*, 26.

■ SAMUEL R. SINGER: THE FOUNDING PRINCIPAL OF WILLIAM GRANT HIGH SCHOOL (1886)

Samuel R. Singer took over the reigns of the city's black school enterprise in 1881. He would follow Darius L. V. Moffet, who held the position of principal for only two years. Singer had presented himself as a candidate for the job in 1876, but had lost to John McLeod that year. Although Singer had the highest teachers' examination score of all nine applicants who took the examination that summer, he was approximately twenty-four years of age, and only had three months of teaching experience at that point. McLeod, who was presumably older than Singer, also had the advantage of having been a principal and teacher at the black school for several years, before it became a city school. McLeod's continuation as principal provided natural continuity as the school transitioned to oversight by the Covington Board of Education in 1876. However, by 1881, Singer had shored up his credentials by not only gaining additional teaching experience, but also by earning a college degree. Given those accomplishments, as well as his high scores on the teacher's examination, Singer was well positioned to be elected as principal over Darius L. V. Moffett that summer.

Samuel R. Singer was born in Covington in 1852. His father, John Singer, was an emancipated, former slave from Virginia, and the Singer family had lived freely in Covington before the Civil War. A local barber by trade, John Singer and his family would become established and well respected in the Covington community. Samuel Singer and his siblings were educated in Cincinnati, since no public educational venue for black people existed in Covington before 1866. During the spring of 1868, Samuel Singer left Covington and took up residence in Ohio. He was approximately sixteen years of age at that point. Singer eventually enrolled in Oberlin College located in the northern part of the state of Ohio. Founded in 1833 by two Presbyterian ministers, Oberlin had been admitting black students on a regular basis since 1835. Samuel Singer graduated with high honors from Oberlin College in 1880 at the age of twenty-eight.

The *Daily Commonwealth* dated June 30, 1880, would carry two brief articles on Singer. The column titled "Marriage Licenses" would reflect two upcoming marriages: "John H. Duveneck, shoe finisher, aged 23 and Miss Mary Tungate, aged 19, both of Covington [and white]"[92] and "Samuel R. Singer, teacher, of Covington, aged 28 and Mrs. Frances R. Parrot, of Zanesville, O., 38, both colored." There were three items of significance about those two entries. The first was that social information about two people of color getting married was actually printed in the local newspaper—even on the front page—in 1880. The second was that white and "colored" engaged couples were

---

92. The *Kentucky Post* dated Sunday, May 3, 1931, would reflect the death of Mary Duveneck at the age of seventy-one, "survived by her husband, John Duveneck, brother of the late Frank Duveneck, famed artist, and one daughter."

entered in the same news column rather than in separate ones. (John Duveneck was the brother of the famous local artist, Frank Duveneck). The third item of significance was that Samuel Singer was getting married to a lady who had not only been previously married; she was ten years his senior.

Many of the "colored society folks" in Covington were caught up in that marital event, as the same page of the *Daily Commonwealth* carried a second article on Mr. Singer's impending betrothal: "S. R. Singer, a talented son of John Singer, Esq., the well known tonsorial artist, who is a teacher at Oberlin College, where he has just graduated with the highest honors, will be united in marriage this afternoon, in this city, to Mrs. Frances R. Parrot, of Zanesville, Ohio."[93] The fact that Singer's upcoming marriage merited two articles on the front page of the local newspaper reflected the relative social standing and respect that the Singer family had as "colored people" in Covington during that period. Singer and his new wife would become an integral part of Covington's social fabric, as Mr. Singer prepared to become the third principal of the city's all-black public school.

By the time that Singer took over in 1881, the black school had been under the direct authority of the Covington Board of Education for a little over four years. The Covington population had grown to some thirty thousand citizens, and the black school enrollment had expanded proportionately.[94] Rutherford B. Hayes, whose roots were in Ohio, and who had at one time resided in Cincinnati, was concluding his single term as the nineteenth president of the United States. Although Hayes had ended the Reconstruction, and signed a weakened bill against the enforcement of civil rights, black people continued to make progress as newly minted citizens of the United States. President Hayes expressed his view on the importance of public education with the following quote: "Universal suffrage should rest upon universal education. To this end, liberal and permanent education for the provision of free schools by the State governments, and, if need be, supplemented by legitimate aid from national authority." Though not specifically addressed to the education of black people in America, the strength of the president's latter statement would encourage the expansion of black schools, such as the one in Covington.

Singer, the brother-in-law of Jacob Price, would become a long-term principal at the school. His educational background, knowledge of the academic world, and leadership of the school would significantly advance the progress of the black school in Covington. Singer would stabilize the school within the Covington community, and also become the founding principal of its high school division.

The intersection of Singer's life with that of Col. William Grant would

---

93. *Daily Commonwealth*, "S. R. Singer, a talented son of John Singer, Esq.," June 30, 1880, 1.

94. The *Daily Commonwealth* on June 30, 1880, listed the Covington population as 30,735 by City Assessor Whitney, and 29, 697 according to the U.S. Census Department.

mark an important historical milestone in the life and legacy of the black school in Covington. Although Singer was approximately thirty-two years younger than Col. William Grant, he was personally acquainted with Grant, and spoke in laudatory terms of Grant's dedication to the cause of education for black youth in Covington. Therefore, when it was apparent that a high school would be established for black students for the first time in the history of the city, the Covington Board of Education agreed with Principal Singer's recommendation that the name of the new high school should be "The William Grant High School" in honor of Col. William Letcher Grant, a white man who had demonstrated sincere dedication and support for the development of educational opportunities for local black children through his words, as well as his deeds.

Unfortunately, Col. William Grant would pass away in May 1882 at the approximate age of sixty-two, a little less than a year after Samuel Singer became principal, and before a black high school came into existence in Covington. At the point of Grant's death, the new school building for black students on Seventh Street had not been constructed. An article in the *Daily Commonwealth* dated Wednesday, May 3, 1882, stated,

> It is our painful task to announce the serious illness of Col. Wm. L. Grant, who now lies at deaths' [*sic*] door. Although in feeble health for some time past he had been anticipating the meeting of the State commandery [*sic*] with a great deal of pleasure, and expected to witness the parade this morning. He was attacked by something like convulsions this morning about 8 o'clock, and his death is hourly expected. His immediate relations living out of the city have been notified by telegram of his critical situation.

Following Grant's passing, and burial in Covington's Linden Grove Cemetery on May 7, 1882, his widow, Laura Southgate Grant would succumb to pneumonia on January 25, 1883, at the age of fifty-seven.[95] In addition, their thirty-five-year-old son, Moses B. Grant would die from "paralysis of the brain" on December 10 of that year.[96] Four other adult sons of the Grants would remain to complete the work that William Letcher Grant had initiated.

The emotional events surrounding the proximate deaths of Grant, his wife, and one of his sons, as well as William Grant's obvious dedication and personal sacrifice in behalf of the black community would strengthen the resolve to name the new black high school division after him. Those events would also inspire Samuel Singer's later comment that "Any other name does violence to the origin and name of the school."[97]

Since the Seventh Street Colored School building had not yet been constructed, William Grant High School was established initially in 1886 within the "Colored School" building, wherever it was temporarily housed at the time,

95. *Daily Commonwealth*, "Death of Mrs. Laura S. Grant," January 26, 1883.
96. Ibid., "Death of Moses B. Grant," December 10, 1883.
97. Singer in Crosby, "A Study of Pupil Marks."

with an entering class of four black female students in a three-year program of study. William Grant High School was created as one of the oldest black high schools in the Commonwealth of Kentucky.

By 1888 a new building for black students would be erected on Seventh Street on a plot of land deeded to the Covington Board of Education in 1880 by William Grant. The new school building would be called "The Seventh Street Colored School," named simply for the street on which it was located and the skin color of its constituency. Those who wanted to de-emphasize the "colored" tag in the school's name would alternately call it "The Seventh Street Public School" or "The Seventh Street School." The two-year-old William Grant High School would also be contained on the upper levels of the Seventh Street Colored School building, with both the elementary and secondary units in the building under the leadership of Samuel Singer.

Nordheim reported that the "building, on Seventh Street between Madison and Scott streets was considered an equal to the other 'modern' schools recently built for use of the white children. Five teachers handled grades one through six, and the principal taught a few high school subjects. More teachers of the elementary and secondary courses were added as the school population grew."[98] However, the building was a ten-room, three-story classroom structure with no gym, auditorium, or cafeteria facilities, and without proper space for a growing domestic science program. The lack of the latter accommodations would cause major problems in the future, as the school's population continued to expand.

The William Grant High School class of 1889 would produce the first two black high school graduates in the history of the city of Covington from the initial class of four students. Annie Price would be one of the two graduates. She was the daughter of Jacob and Mary Price, and also Principal Samuel Singer's niece. The other graduate was Mary E. Allen, who would eventually become a career teacher at Lincoln-Grant School. It is reported that Annie Price (Hood) also was a teacher for a period of time, although this author could not document a listing of her name on the Lincoln-Grant faculty roster.[99]

Photograph 14: Tillie Young Gaines. William Grant High School, Class of 1892.

During the early years, the number of William Grant High School gradu-

98. Nordheim, *Echoes*, 29.
99. "Covington Biographies," 2007.

ates would continue to be limited to two or three students each year. The class of 1892, for instance, would produce two graduates—Frank Crawford and Tillie Young (Gaines). Tillie Young Gaines would become a teacher at the school.

Similarly, the class of 1894, would consist of two students—Carrie Frye and Nathan Fleming. Harris reports that the high school commencement for those two students "was held at the Odd Fellows' Hall in Covington." He adds, "This graduation attracted an enthusiastic audience. Board of Education president James A. Averdick's address to the audience was well received, and board superintendent W. C. Warfield spoke and presented diplomas."[100] One of the two graduates, Nathan Fleming would also become a career teacher at Lincoln-Grant School for several decades.

The disparities between the curricula at the newly established William Grant High School and the older, all-white Covington Central High School were patently evident at an early date. The board minutes in the late eighteen hundreds made no distinction in the high school programs completed by either William Grant or Covington Central graduates. However, while subsequent minutes continued to reflect no specific course of study for William Grant graduates (other than occasionally placing the descriptor, "general" by the black graduate's name during the nineteen hundreds), the Covington Central graduates were divided into three programmatic categories: Commercial Course, General (Academic) Course, and Manual Training Course. Students who were Scholarship Honors Graduates were also listed separately for Covington Central graduates. Honors graduates from William Grant High School were occasionally designated in the board minutes, but more often simply omitted. The development of Covington Central (Holmes) as a "comprehensive" high school, and William Grant as a "standard" high school began early in the history of the Covington Independent Public Schools.

In spite of narrow curricular offerings, the principal and teachers at The Seventh Street Colored School and William Grant High School were aware of the high school courses that students who were college bound would need in order to qualify for college admission. That knowledge was based in part on their own experiences as graduates of such institutions as Oberlin College, Otterbein College, Fisk University, and the University of Cincinnati. Principal Samuel Singer and his colleagues ensured that the basic courses required for college admission were offered at William Grant High School—even in the late eighteen hundreds. Accordingly, the first course of study at William Grant High School developed under the leadership of Mr. Singer was a three-year offering consisting of the following: [101]

Four units of English
Two units of Latin

100. Harris, "Covington Amended Charter," *Enquirer*, February 9, 2009.
101. Singer in Crosby, "A Study of Pupil Marks."

Two and one-half units of science
Three and one-half units of history and civics
Two units of mathematics
Two units of either domestic science and art for girls or mechanical
drawing and cabinet work for boys, respectively

That three-year program, from its inception, was more limited than the four-year high school program that was in place for white students as early as 1869. However the teachers at Grant would insist that their students master core academic subjects at the same level as their white counterparts. The black teachers seemed to have an optimistic view of the future for their students— one not circumscribed by curricular limitations, or a narrow vision of what black students could achieve in life. Regardless of the constraints imposed by racial segregation, there always seemed to be a belief among the black teachers at the Seventh Street Colored School and William Grant High School that their black students could achieve at the same level as white students. The Cincinnati educational enterprise continued to offer supplemental educational opportunities for black students in Covington whose families had the means to send their children across the river to take extra courses not offered in the black school.

Following are the names of the graduating classes that were listed by Principal Singer from 1889 through 1900.[102] Mr. Singer listed no graduates for the year, 1890:

Figure 2: List of William Grant High School Graduates, 1889–1900

[18]'89: Misses Mary E. Allen and Annie Price.
[18]'91: Messrs Isaac Lair, Charles W. Hillman and Charles Haggard.
[18]'92: Miss Tillie Young and Mr. Frank Crawford.
[18]'93: Miss Ozetta Wallace and Mr. Arthur Grant.
[18]'94: Miss Carrie Frye and Mr. Nathan Fleming.
[18]'95: Miss Hallie Boyd Dancer and Mr. Francis Marion Russel [sic].
[18]'96: Misses Julia Delaney and Lulu Smith.
[18]'97: Miss Ella B. Brown and Messrs Charles McGaines and Robt. Page Johnson.
[18]'98: Misses Elsie Amelia Gooch, Susie Emma Young and Pinkie Esther Delaney.
[18]'99: Misses Jessie B. Duke, Susie M. Duff, Grace Belle Johnson, and Josephine B. Woodson and Messrs Henry K. Gooch, William Oscar Miller and Elmer G. Douglas.
[19]'00: Misses Alice Chin and Elizabeth D. Wheeler.

In addition to the fact that the very first graduating class from William Grant High School included Principal Singer's niece, the small graduating classes at William Grant High School during the late 1890s and early 1900s tended to center on some family names, such as the Delaneys (1896 and 1898), and the Gooch family (1898, 1899, and 1902). Several of those classes of two

102. Ibid.

or three graduates also produced local black educators. In addition to Mary Allen (1889), Tillie Young (1892), and Nathan Fleming (1894), Lulu Smith (1896) and Robert Page Johnson (1897) also became teachers at Lincoln-Grant School. Mr. Francis Marion Russel [*sic*] (1895) served as a principal at Newport's Southgate School for several years. Were educational opportunities and the privilege of becoming an educator concentrated heavily among more economically and socially advantaged black families in Covington during those initial years? The reality was that children of families that had been free before the Civil War ended were probably better positioned to take advantage of educational opportunities in a postwar environment.

Segregated black schools had become the norm in Kentucky during the period of the Reconstruction, as mandated by Kentucky law. However, a ruling by the U.S. Supreme Court in 1896 would ensure the continued existence of racial segregation, not only in public schools but also in all other public facilities in the United States of America from 1896 through 1954.

■ THE IMPACT OF "SEPARATE BUT EQUAL" VIA *PLESSY V. FERGUSON*

There was indeed a sense of inflexibility about racial segregation in Northern Kentucky, and in the United States in general that would seem intractable from the late eighteen hundreds to the mid-1950s. Much of that stubbornness and personal comfort with segregation as a way of life was firmly rooted, not only in state statutes and the historical relationships of blacks and whites in America, but also in the "rule of law" as interpreted by the U.S. Supreme Court in 1896.

The high court's legal opinion stemmed from a "man of color" refusing to remove himself from a "white" railroad car in Louisiana. That seemingly trivial event would have ramifications for public policy throughout the country for many years. Cozzens[103] summarized the 1896 ruling as follows:

> On June 7, 1892, a 30-year-old colored shoemaker named Homer Plessy was jailed for sitting in the "White" car of the East Louisiana Railroad. Plessy was only one-eighths black and seven-eights white, but under Louisiana law, he was considered black and therefore required to sit in the "Colored" car. Plessy went to court and argued, in Homer Adolph Plessy v. The State of Louisiana, that the Separate Car Act violated the Thirteenth and Fourteenth Amendments to the Constitution. The judge at the trial was John Howard Ferguson, a lawyer from Massachusetts who previously declared the Separate Car Act "unconstitutional on trains that traveled through several states." (3)[104]
> In Plessy's case, however, he decided that the state could choose to regulate railroad companies that operated only within Louisiana. He

---

103. Cozzens, "After the Civil War."

found Plessy guilty of refusing to leave the white car. (4)[105] Plessy appealed to the Supreme Court of Louisiana, which upheld Ferguson's decision. In 1896 the Supreme Court of the United States heard Plessy's case and found him guilty once again. Speaking for a seven-person majority, Justice Henry Brown wrote:

> That [the Separate Car Act] does not conflict with the Thirteenth Amendment, which abolished slavery . . . is too clear for argument. . . . A statute which implies merely a legal distinction between the white and colored races—a distinction which is founded in the color of the two races, and which must always exist so long as white men are distinguished from the other race by color—has no tendency to destroy the legal equality of the two races. . . . The object of the [Fourteenth A]mendment was undoubtedly to enforce the absolute equality of the two races before the law, but in the nature of things it could not have been intended to abolish distinctions based upon color, or to enforce social, as distinguished from political equality, or a commingling of the two races upon terms unsatisfactory to either.(5) [106]

The lone dissenter, Justice John Harlan, showed incredible foresight when he wrote

> Our Constitution is color-blind, and neither knows nor tolerates classes among citizens. In respect of civil rights, all citizens are equal before the law. . . . In my opinion, the judgment this day rendered will, in time, prove to be quite as pernicious as the decision made by this tribunal in the Dred Scott case. . . . The present decision, it may well be apprehended, will not only stimulate aggressions, more or less brutal and irritating, upon the admitted rights of colored citizens, but will encourage the belief that it is possible, by means of state enactments, to defeat the beneficient purposes which the people of the United States had in view when they adopted the recent amendments of the Constitution.(6)[107]

And so it was done. The *Plessy* ruling would result in a "Separate but Equal" doctrine that would legalize the character of interactions between black

104. Cozzens, "After the Civil War." See internal notes (3) Keith Weldon Medley, "The Sad Story of How 'Separate but Equal' Was Born," *Smithsonian Magazine* (February 1994): 106 and (4) Edward W. Knappman, ed., *Great American Trials* (Detroit: Visible Ink, 1994) 218.

105. Ibid.

106. Cozzens, "After the Civil War." See internal note (5) Justice Henry Billings Brown, "Majority opinion in *Plessy v. Ferguson*," *Desegregation and the Supreme Court*, ed. Benjamin Munn Ziegler (Boston: D.C. Health and Company, 1958) 50–51

107. Ibid. See internal note (6) Justice John Marshall Harlan, "Minority opinion in *Plessy v. Ferguson*," in Ziegler, *Desegregation*.

and white people for decades to come. The Court had shrewdly crafted an interpretation that was designed with a twofold effect: (1) The "equal" part of the ruling would be consonant with the U.S. Declaration of Independence which begins with the "self-evident truth" that "All men are created equal," and thus give the *appearance* of racial equality. (2) At the same time, the "separate" interpretation of the ruling would give comfort to southern (and northern) segregationists who believed sincerely in the inherent inferiority of people of color, as well as the separation of the races based on skin color.

Cozzens concludes the following in her penetrating analysis of the *Plessy v. Ferguson* case:

> Over time, the words of Justice Harlan rang true. The *Plessy* decision set the precedent that "separate" facilities for blacks and whites were constitutional as long as they were "equal." The "separate but equal" doctrine was quickly extended to cover many areas of public life, such as restaurants, theaters, restrooms, and public schools. Not until 1954, in the equally important *Brown v. Board of Education* decision, would the "separate but equal" doctrine be struck down.[108]

The *Plessy* ruling facilitated state laws (some of which were already in existence) by the legislative bodies of the Commonwealth of Kentucky and other southern states, thereby providing federally mandated legal bases for schools like Lincoln-Grant all over the United States. The *Plessy* ruling did not *create* segregated public schools in America, since such schools existed well before 1896 during the era of Reconstruction. It simply gave *legal standing* at the federal level to racially segregated schools and other public facilities in the United States.

The *Plessy* ruling and other cases that used it as a legal precedent would sustain, both legally and in practical terms, an era of "Jim Crow" in America, a period of racial segregation and discrimination that lasted for many decades. The *Plessy* decision was indeed the *glue* that would hold racial segregation in place and give legal cover to segregationists in the United States of America from 1896 until 1954; and the history of Lincoln-Grant School would largely coincide with, and even overlap that period in American history. The *Plessy* ruling would support the educational and social shackles that would bind black people in America for what seemed like an interminable period of time.

■ CLIMATE CHANGE

The year was 1900. The *Kentucky Post* and the "Kentucky" section of the *Cincinnati Enquirer* had replaced the *Daily Commonwealth* and the *Covington Journal* as primary news outlets in Northern Kentucky. Those newspapers, which played a major role in shaping local public opinion, were trending away

---

108. Cozzens, "After the Civil War."

from the reporting of social trivia to national and local news of more general interest in the political, business, industrial, and educational arenas. Sustained by increased revenue from business advertisements, and still selling for one penny per paper, the local papers took on a bolder, flashier appearance, as they suddenly exploded with illustrations of the latest clothing styles and fashions from New York and Paris, as well as other expanded reporting.

The days of the "horseless carriage" as a routine mode of transportation were just around the corner; however the streets of Covington still reflected an abundance of trendy, privately owned buggies drawn by well-groomed horses, along with a few electrically powered streetcars running up and down the middle of Madison Street. As business and industry grew in Northern Kentucky, the streets of downtown Covington were alive with ladies in ankle-length dresses and fashionable headpieces, as well as men with uniform three-piece, early twentieth century suits, bow ties, humbug hats, long sideburns, and neatly-trimmed mustaches. Younger men and boys still wore knickers and high top boots, while school-aged girls demonstrated their sense of modesty in long, dark stockings, flat shoes, and plain, beltless dresses well below the knee.

The general population of the city of Covington had grown to almost forty-three thousand people, which included a proportionate increase in the number of black citizens. Two black public schools with high school divisions, one in Covington and the other in Newport, were becoming firmly established, along with several smaller black grade schools in outlying areas. However, the social climate in Northern Kentucky had become more rigid for black people. No longer were African Americans "testing" the civil rights laws of 1866 and 1870, or running for statewide political offices, as some had done in Kentucky during the days of the Reconstruction. Gone were the days when people of color, such as Isaac Black and "a colored brother" would walk into Trinity Episcopal Church on Madison Street with the expectation of being ushered down the aisle and seated in the "body of the church" along with John G. Carlisle, a nationally known politician, Gov. John W. Stevenson, and other prominent white Covingtonians.

Plessy v. Ferguson was becoming settled law, as black people seemingly accepted their "place" as second-class citizens in Covington and elsewhere. *Plessy* would soon be followed by the "Day Law," which provided additional reinforcement for segregated schools in Kentucky. Racial discrimination in public places became more predictable and acceptable, since the "separate but equal" interpretation of *Plessy* could now be used legally to restrict black people to certain public venues. Although the term, "colored" would continue to be used colloquially, the descriptor, "negro" (usually with a deliberate, lower-case *n*) was beginning to invade the newspaper print in reference to people of African American descent. Some whites felt that the term was more racially acceptable than the "colored" label—and some black people agreed. The pejorative racial epithet, "nigger" would continue to be used privately and offensively on a personal level, but that term would no longer be printed boldly in the local newspapers, as it had been in the late eighteen hundreds.

Changing attitudes toward prominent African Americans in the local community were reflected in a one-line local newspaper article printed under "Colored Notes" which stated rather callously one February day in 1893, "Prof. Singer's aged grandmother dropped dead yesterday morning from heart failure."[109] Nothing else was stated regarding her death, not even her name. That article would stand in stark contrast to the front-page article in 1880 announcing Singer's marriage, academic accomplishments, and the positive reputation of his family in the community.

■ AN ADMINISTRATIVE DILEMMA: "SENSATIONAL CHARGES"

Samuel R. Singer, the second longest serving principal in the history of Covington's black school, had led the Seventh Street Colored School since 1881. He had established William Grant High School in 1886, moved it from a three-year program to a four-year program thirteen years later, and produced a total of thirty black high school graduates from 1889 to 1900. Singer had also presided over the move into a new school building in 1888, and brought additional teachers on board to meet the needs of a growing black school in Covington. By the year 1900, Singer, a well-respected educator in the Covington community, was approximately forty-eight years of age. Everything seemed to be going well for him and the black school that he had nurtured in downtown Covington for almost two decades. But, in spite of those accomplishments, his social standing in the community, and his seeming indispensability to the school's operation, Singer's rather lengthy career in Covington would not end well.

Singer's administrative difficulty became public with a newspaper article dated July 30, 1900, which reflected the following:

> The most sensational charges that have been preferred against Samuel R. Singer, Principal of the Seventh Street Public School (colored), Covington [*sic*]. Essie Stowers, 18, colored girl, and a member of the Seventh Street School has sworn to an affidavit in which she swears that Singer assaulted her. She is at present in the hospital. The Affidavit was sworn to in the presence of Supt. John Morris, of the Covington Public Schools, and Trustee James Thompson.[110]

The article continues,

> Singer most emphatically denies the charges, and says that whole story is false and that it is merely spite work. The matter has been kept very quiet by the school board, as no proof could be obtained to corroborate

109. *Kentucky Post*, "Colored Notes," February 1, 1893, 1.
110. *Kentucky Post*, "Accuses the Principal—Charges Made Against Samuel Singer," July 30, 1900.

the girl's statement. The board is carefully investigating the facts in the case, and if sufficient proof can be obtained against Singer, he will be tried. He is regarded as a colored man of unusually good character, and the present charges against him have created furor among the colored citizens.[111]

Although there is no evidence that the matter reached the level of a criminal court trial, the local paper had published Singer's potential resignation, perhaps prematurely, by stating "The *Post* has it from a most reliable [undisclosed] source that the discussion of the Stowers charges brought out some sensational facts concerning the management of the colored school that was a revelation to the members of the School Board. A resolution was introduced in which the resignation of every teacher in the colored school was to be demanded." It is obvious that at that point someone who was privy to the confidential discussions of the Board of Education had begun feeding sensitive personnel information to the local press. The article continues, "After much discussion the [board] members came to the conclusion that the time was not opportune for such a radical move, and the resolution was withdrawn."[112] The article further states, "Then followed a motion to suspend Principal Singer. This was carried by the votes of every member present. The Clerk was notified to inform Singer that his resignation must be in the hands of the school board by next Wednesday."[113]

The newspaper article also reported, "Attorney Fisk [a board attorney] advised the board that no matter what action the Board took, the case would not end there, as it had been determined to push the damage suit filed against Singer in the courts."[114] The board attorney's legal advice seemed to suggest that, if Ms. Stowers pursued action in the civil courts, damages could be claimed against the Covington Public Schools, as well as Singer himself. Therefore, the Board should get rid of Principal Singer as soon as possible in order to reduce its potential liability in the matter.

The approach of the board was not to dismiss Samuel Singer outright, but rather to encourage his voluntary resignation. A *Kentucky Post* article dated August 22, 1900, reported, "Singer and Attorney Byrne [Singer's personal attorney] met Dr. J. A. Averdick and Col James Thompson of the board in the office of the Clerk Tuesday night. The members [Averdick and Thompson] announced to Singer that they thought his usefulness as a public educator had come to an end. As a consequence, it is thought that Singer will offer his resignation at tonight's meeting." [115]

But apparently Samuel Singer did not offer his resignation that night. On

---

111. Ibid.
112. *Kentucky Post*, "Singer Must Resign at Once," August 18, 1900, 1
113. Ibid.
114. Ibid.
115. Ibid., "Prof. Singer Will Resign—Result of the Board of Education's Stand—Trustees told Him He Must Get Out," August 22, 1900, 1.

August 23, 1900, the following day, Superintendent John Morris indicated, "I deem it my duty, by virtue of the power vested in the Superintendent by the rules of the board to suspend Prof. Singer from his duties as principal of the William Grant High School until his innocence can be fully established. This step is taken with the conviction that it is for the best interest of the school and that the damage suit now pending in court will establish the guilt or innocence of the accused." [116] By August 23, 1900, the coverage of the issue had moved from the front page to page three of the *Kentucky Post.*

Since public newspaper reporting on the subject appears to have ceased after August 23, 1900, the conclusion of the matter is unclear. A legal compromise may have been reached between the board attorney and Singer's personal attorney. It seems noteworthy that Singer's suspension was from the *William Grant High School.* The young woman who filed the charge was obviously a high school student, so any legal action on her part would not necessarily pertain to the elementary portion of the school. Singer's suspension from the high school division would demonstrate that the board and school superintendent had taken punitive action against Principal Singer, pending the outcome of any legal case pursued by Ms. Stowers, while presumably allowing Singer to continue to draw an administrative salary via the Seventh Street Colored School until he had the opportunity to retire from the Covington Public Schools.

There would not be a new principal at the black school in Covington until 1901. It is unclear how administrative matters were handled at the school during the 1900/01 school year. Given the board's apparent disaffection with all teachers at the school, no leader would likely have automatically emerged from the ranks of the teaching staff. But the real victims of those unfortunate circumstances may have been the students at William Grant High School. Although there had been consistent graduating classes of two or three students every year from 1889 until 1900 (except for 1890), there was no graduating class from the school in 1901, due in part to the conversion of the high school curriculum from a three-year to a four-year program, beginning with the fall of 1899. Superintendent J. K. Morris had recommended that conversion to the board during a meeting on July 7, 1899.[117] However, the implementation of that recommendation had apparently been confounded by the administrative dilemma over Samuel R. Singer.

The first class under the four-year program would not graduate until 1902. An article in the *Commercial Tribune* dated June 16, 1901, indicated, "For the first time in ten years there will be no commencement exercises of the William Grant Colored High School this year. This is due to the change in the course of study, which has been made four years instead of three. Last year there were seven graduates. Those who would have graduated this year will have to attend another year."[118]

---

116. *Kentucky Post,* "Singer out of Schools—Supt. Morris took definite action—The colored principal will have to retire," August 23, 1900.
117. *Cincinnati Enquirer,* "Covington—Board of Education," July 7, 1899, 8:3.

After leaving the Covington Public Schools, Singer reportedly returned to Ohio. Decades later, Samuel R. Singer authored the following correspondence to Leconia Franklin Crosby, a teacher at Lincoln-Grant, in support of Crosby's 1929 master's thesis at the University of Cincinnati. The letter, which appears to have been written in 1924, confirms many facts about the early history of Lincoln-Grant School, while not addressing the difficulties of Singer's final year at the school. It is apparent that, with a distant view of the unpleasant aspects of his career in Covington from decades ago, Singer was able to present a very valuable historical perspective of a seventy-six-year-old "elder statesman." See figure 3 on the following page.

Photograph 15: Triple funeral (husband, wife, and child), Philadelphia Street, Covington, late 1800s or early 1900s.
PHOTOGRAPH COURTESY OF THE KENTON COUNTY PUBL IC LIBRARY, COVINGTON, KENTUCKY.

Figure 3: Letter from Samuel R. Singer to Leconia Franklin Crosby, 1929

Up to the close of the Civil War, Kentucky made no provision for the education of the Colored Youth. Although I was born in Covington and lived there until the Spring of '68 [1868], I had to go, as did my brothers and sisters to Cincinnati. My entire education was obtained in Ohio. During the early years of Reconstruction the Freedman's Bureau of the General Government established a school in Covington. The Council of Covington then began to assist the Government school by giving annually two hundred dollars. This continued until the following interesting incident occurred:

At this time Gov. John Stevenson, a leading Democrat in Kentucky lived in Covington and during the time of slavery had a few domestic slaves. He became a candidate for the United States Senate. Mr. William Grant, an influential resident of Covington and a personal friend of Governor Stevenson, became interested. Mr. Grant was a fine man, genial and respectful to rich and poor. I knew him personally in my childhood, youth and early manhood.

Mr. Grant was a shrewd man. The Colored vote at that time was of much importance. Mr. Grant was a liberal democrat and was liked very much by Colored, who knew him. He knew the conditions of education for Colored and consulted with a few Colored men, namely; Isaac Black, George Durgan, Mr. Dixon and Rev. Jacob Price. He made this proposition to them; that if Colored voters would support him as a candidate to the Legislature, and if he were elected, he would have the Charter of Covington amended so as to provide for a public school for Colored children. He was overwhelmingly elected. His objective was the election of Governor Stevenson to the U.S. Senate, and he succeeded. He was also successful in having the Charter of Covington amended as he promised. So the Covington public school for Colored was instituted and in 1875 the first examination for the principalship was held.

John McLeod was elected. He held the place for a few years and resigned to be a store keeper gauger. Mr. Moffet was then elected. He held the principalship until the summer of '81 [1881] when I was elected, having graduated from Oberlin College in the class of '80 [1880].

From this time, to write in full the history of the Seventh Street Public School would be a long story. I shall close the account by a brief description of the William Grant High School. I wish very much to speak of the name. When the time for a high school came I asked the Board to establish a high school course and it acted favorably on my request and the name should be "The William Grant High School" in honor of Mr. William Grant. Any other name does violence to the origin and name of the school.

Now finally: The course was a three year course. My first assistant was Miss Minnie Moore. The first class i.e. entering consisted of Mary Allen, Annie Price, Amanda Cox and Emma Anderson, starting in '86 [1886]. I shall now give the names of the graduates up to 1900 inclusive: [The list of names was provided in figure 2.]

(Signed) Samuel R. Singer[a]

a. Singer in Crosby, "A Study of Pupil Marks." This is the full text of Singer's letter to Crosby.

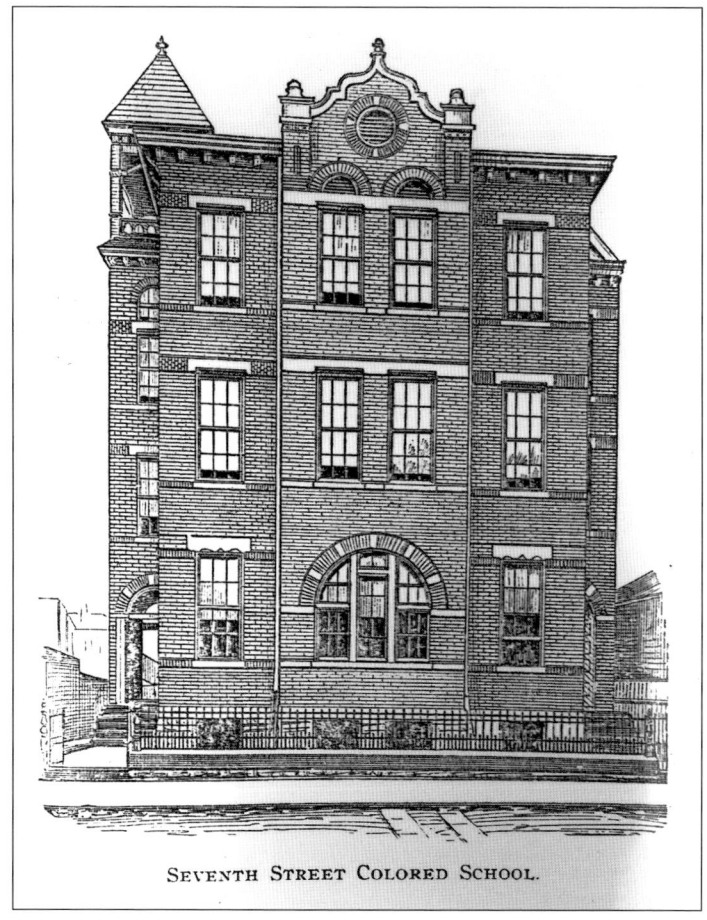

Photograph 16: Seventh Street Colored School, 1890.
COURTESY OF THE KENTON COUNTY PUBLIC LIBRARY, COVINGTON, KENTUCKY.

A drawing of the original Seventh Street Colored School building, Covington, Kentucky, 1890. The building was erected in 1888.

Photograph 17: Lincoln School, 1910.
CREATOR: ROMBACH AND GREEN
COURTESY OF THE KENTON COUNTY PUBLIC LIBRARY, COVINGTON, KENTUCKY

The Seventh Street Colored School was renamed Lincoln School in 1909 in honor of Abraham Lincoln, the sixteenth president of the United States of America. William Grant High School was also contained on the upper floors of the building.

Figure 4: Salary Schedule—Covington Public Schools, 1890s

Music Director, per month $125, per year $1250
Drawing teacher, per month $70, per year $700
Writing teacher, per month $70, per year, $700
Principal, High School, per month $160, per year $1600
Assistant Principal, High School, per month $125, per year $1250
Assistants, High School, per month, $85, per year $850
A & B Intermediate, per month, $65, per year $650
Principal, District Schools, per month $125, per year $1250
Primary & Grammar School teachers, per month $55, per year $550
Directors Kindergartens, per month, $40, per year, $400
Assistants Kindergartens, per month $35, per year $350
Janitors (white schools), per month $66.67, per year $800
Jan itors (colored school), per month $41.67, per year $500
Janitors (kindergartens), per month $8, per year $96
First substitute teacher, per month $25, per year $250
Superintendent, per month $166.67, per year $2000
Clerk, $75 per month

The total budget for running the entire Covington Public School System in 1894 was approximately $98,000, with about 5.7 percent of that amount being allocated to the operations budgeted for the "Colored School." The board minutes of 1894 reflect the following disbursements, and balance on hand as of July 1, 1894:

Figure 5: Covington Public School Budget, 1894

Disbursements:	
Bonds	$ 700.00
Incidentals	3198.10
Clerk	600.00
Supplies	1315.35
Prtg & Sta	367.28
High School [white]	9836.05
First District	7498.18
Second District	10435.43
Third District	9928.96
Fourth District	10872.00
Colored School	**5490.21**
Fuel	2612.67
Premium & Interest	6.33
School Furniture	858.00
Insurance	218.70
Repairs	10696.83
Salaries	7605.59
Tuition	20.00
[Total]	$82259.68

Balance on hand July 1, 1894

$14906.15

Figure 6: Covington Board of Education Agenda, 1899
BOARD OF EDUCATION MINUTES, 1899.

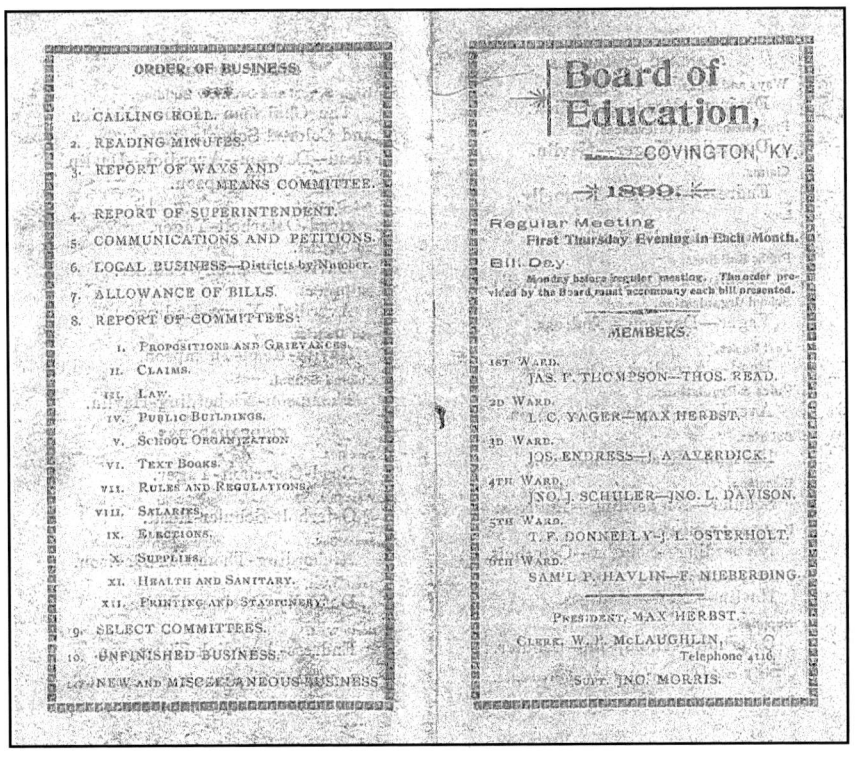

Figure 7: Covington Board of Education Committee Assignments, 1899
BOARD OF EDUCATION MINUTES, 1899.

STANDING COMMITTES.

Ways and Means,
Davison—Read—Averdick.

Propositions and Grievances,
Donnelly—Yager—Havlin.

Claims,
Endress—Havlin—Donnelly.

Law
Yager—Read—Havlin.

Public Buildings,
Thompson—Osterholt—Donnelly.

School Organization,
Yager—Davison—Endress.

Text Books,
Read—Averdick—Osterholt.

Rules & Regulations,
Averdick—Yager—Thompson.

Salaries,
Davison—Read—Thompson.

Elections,
Schuler—Nieberding—Endress.

Health and Sanitation,
Nieberding—Schuler—Osterholt.

Printing and Stationery,
Havlin—Read—Endress.

Supplies,
Osterholt—Thompson—Schuler.

The President is a member of each committee.

LOCAL COMMITTEES.

High School and Overflow Building.
The Chairman of the District
and Colored Schools.
Read—Davison—Averdick—Havlin
Thompson.

1st District.
Read-Osterholt-Yager.

2d District.
Davison-Donnelly-Schuler.

3d District.
Averdick-Yager-Endress.

4th District.
Havlin-Read-Thompson.

Colored School.
Thompson-Nieberding-Havlin.

KINDERGARTENS.

East End.
Read-Osterholt-Yager.

West End.
Osterholt-Schuler-Read.

South End.
Nieberding-Thompson-Davison.

South West.
Donnelly-Davison-Havlin.

North West.
Endress-Averdick-Thompson.

The President is a member of each committee.

Figure 8: Newspaper Advertisement for Jacob Price Lumber Company, 1882

Figure 9: Afro-American Mission Herald, Early 1900s

The Afro-American Mission Herald, *published in Louisville, Kentucky,*
was one source of positive newsprint for black people in 1900.
KENTON COUNTY PUBLIC LIBRARY, COVINGTON, KENTUCKY.

Photograph 18: Old First Baptist Church, Bremen Street, 1915.
KENTON COUNTY PUBLIC LIBRARY, COVINGTON, KENTUCKY.

The old First Baptist Church on Bremen Street in Covington was the center of many of Rev. Jacob Price's educational and community efforts in behalf of black Covingtonians in the 1800s. The church building (above) was destroyed by a tornado in 1915 and eventually rebuilt on East Ninth Street.

Photograph 19: Interior of New First Baptist Church, Ninth Street.
COURTESY OF THEODORE H. H. HARRIS.

Early 1900s interior of newly built First Baptist Church on Ninth Street in Covington, Kentucky. The church was originally founded by Rev. George Dupree in 1864.

Photograph 20: Ninth Street Baptist Church, c. 1921.
KENTON COUNTY PUBLIC LIBRARY, COVINGTON, KENTUCKY.

Photograph 21: A Corner Store in Covington, 1912.
COURTESY OF THE KENTON COUNTY PUBLIC LIBRARY, COVINGTON, KENTUCKY.

Photograph 22: A Wintry Scene in Covington, Twelfth Street, Early 1900s.
COURTESY OF THE KENTON COUNTY PUBLIC LIBRARY, COVINGTON, KENTUCKY.

Photograph 23: Covington Public Library, 1940s.
COURTESY OF THE KENTON COUNTY PUBLIC LIBRARY, COVINGTON, KENTUCKY.

A 1940s postcard setting of Scott Street showing the Covington Public Library. Unlike racially segregated public libraries in other parts of Kentucky, the Covington Public Library was racially integrated in 1901. The Carnegie Library Auditorium was frequently the setting for commencement exercises for both the black and white schools on separate evenings before new school buildings were built. Graduating classes for both schools were relatively small at that point.

CHAPTER 4

New Horizons at the
Turn of the Century

■ A NEW PRINCIPAL: FRANK L. WILLIAMS

The Seventh Street Colored School and William Grant High School needed a new principal in 1901. The ideal process was to have groomed prospective candidates for the position by giving them two or three years of teaching experience within the black school building, preferably at the high school level, then elevating them to the principalship. But there were apparently no internal candidates for the job at the black school after Samuel Singer was forced out. The superintendent and board had to look outside of the system to other black schools, particularly those within the Commonwealth. In doing so, they found Frank L. Williams, who came to Covington from Louisville, Kentucky, to replace Samuel Singer.

Photograph 24:
Principal Frank L. Williams

The Louisville Central High School records reflect that Williams had been the principal of that school from 1900 to 1901, for only one year prior to his arrival in Covington. He had also been a mathematics teacher at the school before becoming an administrator. Thelma Cayne Tilford-Weathers indicates, "Williams left [Central] to become principal of Sumner High School in St.

Louis."[119] Although that may have been his original intent, Frank Williams ultimately became the principal of the Seventh Street Colored School and William Grant High School in 1901 instead. (He would in fact go to St. Louis, Missouri, seven years later). It is unclear why Williams did not continue as the principal of a major black school in Louisville with which he had an obvious history. Principal Faustin S. Delaney would succeed Williams at Central.

The appointment of Williams as the fourth black school principal in Covington took place at the turn of the century during a period when education, both locally and nationally, was in transition from its rudimentary beginnings in the 1800s to a more progressive era. Normal Schools were emerging for the preparation of schoolteachers. The nation would also be recovering from the mortal wounding of President William McKinley on September 6, 1901. McKinley would die eight days later, and would be succeeded by Vice President Theodore Roosevelt. A change in the presidency would affect the area of public school education, as well as other public institutions in the United States. One of McKinley's goals had been to "banish illiteracy" in the United States, while his successor felt that "a thorough knowledge of the Bible is worth more than a college education." Those two presidential values, although seemingly at polar opposites, would each influence public school education in the nation during that period.

■ Teacher Credentialing and Teacher Supply

Teacher credentialing was an evolving matter in public schools across the United States during the late eighteen hundreds and early nineteen hundreds, and initially both black and white teachers were only minimally prepared. Nordheim reports that, pursuant to the passage of the 1874 State Act, "The African American teachers had to pass an examination just as the white teachers did. However, the examination [for black teachers] could not extend beyond spelling, reading, writing and common arithmetic."[120] Graduation from high school seemed to be a minimum qualification for taking the examination during the late eighteen hundreds. Black teachers in Covington needed to meet those rudimentary requirements in order to teach at the school.

By 1901, when Williams became the principal of the school, all Covington teachers were required to have a least one year of training in a normal school. Jones reports that as a result of lobbying by the Kentucky Negro Education Association, a State Normal School, which later became Kentucky State College, was established for training black teachers in 1887.[121] Located in Frankfort, Kentucky, approximately one hundred miles south of Covington, that

119. Tilford-Weathers, *A History of Louisville Central High School 1882–1982* (Louisville, Ky.: Printed by General Printing Co., 1982) 6.
120. Nordheim, *Echoes*, 21.
121. Jones, "The Early Kinship."

institution, along with normal schools at the University of Cincinnati and other local institutions in Ohio, would eventually provide outlets for upgrading the education of local black teachers.

Semiannual teacher examinations in subject matter areas continued to be necessary due to minimum teacher preparation at that time. A board report on July 7, 1904, by Superintendent John Morris reflected the following:

> The semi-annual teachers examinations was [*sic*] held on June 30th, and July 1st and 2nd, at the [white] High School building.

> There were seven applicants, but as some of the examiners are away from [the] city the results can not [*sic*] be reported tonight. Enough however is known to justify me in saying that but five certificates will be issued [*sic*].

The instructional staff at the Seventh Street Colored School could replenish and rejuvenate itself by producing several of its own potential faculty members under Williams's leadership. It was not uncommon for some William Grant High School graduates to become teachers at the school after completing the post-secondary educational requirements and passing the teachers' examinations in relevant subjects that were necessary during the early part of the century. (The white schools in Covington also employed that practice.)

The tradition of William Grant graduates becoming teachers at the school would be carried forward well into the future when other graduates returned to teach at Lincoln-Grant School after completing baccalaureate degrees at historically black colleges or local institutions. While one could argue the merits of recruiting faculty members from graduates of the school, and the degree to which that practice limited educational growth, that source of teachers seemed to be embraced by the Covington Board of Education as a matter of convenience, if not necessity. Teachers who were not William Grant graduates would be added to the faculty in larger numbers in later years.

■ ACADEMIC PROGRAMMING AND STUDENT ACHIEVEMENT

Kindergarten was introduced into the Covington Public School System in 1892 for white children. Nordheim reports that the Covington kindergarten classes were initially contained in separate buildings from the elementary schools. A different environment was thought to be necessary to prepare kindergarten students for entry into the larger body of students a year later. According to Nordheim, a separate kindergarten was opened for black children in 1894. However, the board minutes for the late eighteen hundreds and early nineteen hundreds do not reflect the assignment of a kindergarten teacher at the black school or a freestanding black kindergarten in the city. Also, the standing committee assignments for the board in 1899 show kindergartens for white children in five different city areas, but none at the "colored school."[122] The assignment of a kindergarten teacher on the Lincoln-Grant School faculty roster was not shown in the board minutes until 1940, with the appointment of Miss Betty Cleo DePriest.

The core high school curriculum initiated in 1886 would remain constant at William Grant High School throughout its existence, except for a foreign language variation from Latin to French, then Spanish, as well as other minor adjustments in the fundamental content areas. The high school course of study at William Grant had been changed to a four-year program in 1899 with little alteration in basic course content, but more academic depth in the courses offered. Although the numbers were relatively small, there would be a steady flow of high school graduates from William Grant High School.

A *Kentucky Post* article dated June 19, 1902, titled "Colored High School Exercises," would describe the commencement exercises for the first four-year graduating class at William Grant High School. That class also comprised the first class to graduate under the leadership of Principal Williams, as indicated in Figure 10. [123] One of the two graduates, Elizabeth Wotten Gooch would eventually become a long-term music teacher at the school. She was also an organist at the Ninth Street M. E. Church in Covington.

The Lincoln Grant and William Grant Reunion Program Booklet for 1979 indicates the following biographical information on Miss Elizabeth Gooch: She was born on September 16, 1883, in Covington. Miss Gooch attended Lincoln-Grant School from the age of six, until her graduation from William Grant High School in 1902. She was one of two graduates that year.[124] Before becoming a teacher of special subjects and music at Lincoln-Grant, she attended Oberlin College for two years, followed by St. Athanasius College in Georgia. She ultimately earned a bachelor's degree in education from the University of Cincinnati. Miss Gooch taught at Lincoln-Grant for thirty-nine years, from 1915 until her retirement in 1954.[125]

Photograph 25:
Miss Elizabeth Gooch

122. See figure 7 of the present work.

123. On June 16 and June 18, 1902, the *Kentucky Post* carried two separate articles describing in greater detail the commencement exercises of the white Covington High School, which yielded twenty-three graduates, including eighteen girls and five boys. One of the white male graduates was Harry Hinde Southgate, a young man with a familiar surname in the community; Henry K. Gooch, presumably the brother of Elizabeth Wotten Gooch, was a graduate of the William Grant High School Class of 1899, which had an unusually high number of seven black graduates.

124. *Kentucky Post*, "Colored High School Exercises," June 20, 1902. Two graduates were listed the Odd Fellows hall ceremony: Ruth Belle Johnson and Elizabeth Wotten Gooch.

Figure 10 Commencement Program, William Grant High School Class of 1902

"The twelfth annual commencement exercises of the William Grant Colored High School of Covington were held at Odd fellows Hall Thursday evening. The graduates were Ruth Belle Johnson and Elizabeth Wotten Gooch. The program was as follows: Chorus, 'Night Sinks on the Wave;' 'Daybreak;' salutatory and oration, 'Evolution of Industrial Arts,' Elizabeth Wotten Gooch; chorus 'Tramp O'er Moss and Pell;' oration and valedictory, 'Adversity, an Element of Growth,' Ruth Belle Johnson; chorus, 'Wood Nymphs;' presentation of class by principal [Frank L. Williams]; presentation of diplomas by Superintendent Morris; address on behalf of Alumni Association, Henry K. Gooch; commencement address, Dr. J. A. Averdick; chorus, 'O Hail Us, Ye Free;' Benediction by Rev. George W. Ward."

Additional graduates of the black four-year program emerged in 1903 under the leadership of Principal Frank Williams. Members of the William Grant High School class of 1903 included "Five graduates, one boy and four girls" according to the board minutes for July 2 of that year. No individual names of graduates were listed in the minutes.

Although children from age six to sixteen were required to attend school in Kentucky as of 1896, graduation from high school was still relatively novel in the United States during the early nineteen hundreds. Consequently, there were few high school graduates, black or white, in Covington during that period. The conclusion of the third year of Williams's tenure as principal was documented with the following article in the *Kentucky Post* on June 16, 1904: "The colored pupils of the William Grant School, Covington gave their third annual song service Wednesday night at the Ninth-st. M. E. Church. There were songs by the classes of the different grades and at the close of the song recital, exhibitions in sewing and millinery were given. The graduating exercises of the high school will take place Thursday evening at the [library] Auditorium."

The report of Superintendent John Morris (on July 7, 1904) revealed the following:

Gentlemen;

The following report showing the condition of the Public Schools of this City for the month of June, and also the official acts of the Superintendent for the same time is respectfully submitted.

The annual commencement of the Covington High School [Holmes] was held on the night of June 14th [1904].

There were sixteen graduates, eight boys and eight girls.

Arthur S. Pflueger was the valedictorian, having gotten the highest

125. The source of biographical information on Miss Elizabeth Gooch is *The 1979 Lincoln Grant and William Grant Reunion Program Booklet.*

averge [*sic*] scholarship for four years and Charles E. Hinke was the salutatorian. The attached report shows the standing of each member of the class.

The annual commencement of William Grant High School was held on the night of June 16th [1904].

There were five graduates, all girls. Miss Mary Margeret Page was the salutatorian and Miss Maymie Milla Williams was the valedictorian.

The schools in accordance with sec. 92 of the Boards [*sic*] manual were officially closed on Friday, June 17th [1904].

John Morris

By that time at least eleven additional black four-year graduates had received high school diplomas from William Grant High School under the administration of Frank Williams, including the five young women mentioned above in the report by Superintendent Morris. During Williams's tenure the number of William Grant graduates had increased from two to three annually under the previous administration to four or five graduates each year.

In the meantime, Covington Central (Holmes) High School had graduated more than 540 white students between 1853 and 1902. According to Charles S. Furber, historian for the school, "They [Central graduates] are scattered to all parts of the globe, they have entered all the walks of life, and they are represented in all professions, trades and business enterprises."[126] The white Covington high school had a much larger student base, and had been producing graduates since 1853. By 1902, William Grant High School had only graduated a total of 32 students since its origin in 1886.

Commencement exercises for both Covington Central High School and William Grant were often held in the Kenton County Public Library auditorium on alternate nights in the early days, with the white high school always having its commencement the first night, as reflected consistently in the minutes of the Covington Board of Education. The Odd Fellows' Hall was also used on some occasions for the William Grant High School exercises. High school commencement venues would change in the future with the construction of new buildings, but the relative dates of white and black high school commencement exercises in Covington would continue.

There were few extracurricular activities at the Seventh Street Colored School during the late eighteen hundreds and early nineteen hundreds. The school apparently had no band or orchestra at that point. However, singing, a black custom stemming from slavery, seemed to be a part of the school's tradition from its inception. An annual celebratory song recital by black students became a part of the end of the year activities at the Seventh Street Colored

126. Kenton County Library, *Covington/Kenton County Library*, 61. Excerpt from Charles S. Furber's letter to fellow graduates of Covington (Holmes) High School dated June 4, 1902.

School under the Williams administration. That emerging tradition would further enhance the cultural image of the school in the community. Since there was no auditorium in the school building on Seventh Street, the recitals were held in local black churches. A 1905 report by Charles M. Merry, who was superintendent from 1904 to 1906, reflected the following:

> The 4th Annual Song Recital of the 7th Street [Colored] School will be held at the 9th St. M. E. Church the 13th [of June, 1905] at 2 o'clock.[127]

The 1904/5 school year would end with twenty-one white high school graduates from Covington Central and four black graduates from William Grant. Braden S. T. Vaughn, Luvenia M. Kilby, Romeo S. Butler, and Josephine Ellen Smith would each meet or exceed the minimum graduation requirement of average grades above 70 in sixteen studies to form the William Grant High School Class of 1905, as indicated in the board minutes dated June 3, 1905.

Harris reports that Principal Frank Williams "was actively involved in the community. He was one of the founding members of the Progressive Building and Loan Association."[128] Williams seemed well positioned to enhance the standing and reputation of the black school in the community. His major contributions would include strengthening the music program, increasing the number of black high school graduates from William Grant High School under a four-year program, and improving the preparation of teachers at The Seventh Street Colored School.

There were apparently no unusual circumstances at the black school in Covington during the administrative tenure of Frank L. Williams. He seems to have strengthened the core mission of the school, and successfully guided its development through transitions in faculty and students. But after seven years, Principal Williams would resign and move on to a different position.

His final graduating class, the class of 1908 would be featured in two *Kentucky Post* articles: one on June 9, 1908, announcing the commencement at the Public Library Auditorium on June 10; and the other on June 11 which described the commencement exercises for the following "Colored Graduates:" Grace Frances Davis, Mattie Mae Horner, Ida Mae Morton, Horace S. Sudduth, and Susie Pearl Williams. Horace Sudduth would become the owner of the Manse Hotel in Cincinnati. That hotel, located on Gilbert Avenue in Walnut Hills, would become a prominent venue for black social events during the nineteen hundreds.

Frank Williams's positive tenure at the school would later be captured in an August 29, 1908 *Kentucky Post* article which was titled "Will Honor Negro Prof." The article stated,

---

127. Official Minutes of the Covington Board of Education (1905), Covington Independent Public Schools, Covington, Kentucky, 1894–1976 (hereafter cited as Minutes, Covington Board of Education).

128. Harris, "Covington amended charter."

An educational mass meeting in honor of Prof Frank L. Williams, formerly principal of the Grant Colored High School of Covington, will be held at the Ninth-st. M. E. Church tomorrow afternoon. The affair is in charge of the patrons, teachers and pupils of the Seventh-st. school. [*sic*] A splendid program will be rendered, the feature of which will be an address by Prof. Williams. Prof. Williams resigned his charge in Covington to take charge of a similar school in St. Louis.

■ THE "DAY LAW"

A statewide legal ruling regarding segregated schools in Kentucky was approved by the state legislature in 1904. Even though the U.S. Supreme Court had provided a legal definition for the relative status of black and white people in the *Plessy v. Ferguson* case, people did not always behave according to "the law" with regard to racial relationships in Kentucky. A stroke of independence from existing practices of racial segregation occurred at Berea College, which, as Jones reports, "had been integrated since 1863."[129] Tilford-Weathers writes, "In 1903, State Representative Carl Day of Breathitt County visited the campus of Berea College. According to an article in a Filson Club journal, he was 'shocked' to see black students sharing dormitories with white students. He was so inflamed by this 'mixture' of races that he presented to the Legislature a bill requiring separation of the races in all schools in Kentucky. The bill passed the Legislature in 1904, and was upheld by the Supreme Court in 1908."[130] The law which became known as the "Day Law," resulted in the segregation of Berea College, and the formation of Lincoln Institute as an alternative boarding school for black students in 1912.[131] While segregated schools had been present in Covington since the beginning of public school education in the area, the *Plessy v. Ferguson* ruling and the Day Law would provide additional legal assurance for segregated schools such as Lincoln Institute and Lincoln-Grant School within the Commonwealth of Kentucky on a "permanent" basis.

■ THE EVOLUTION OF THE NAME, "LINCOLN-GRANT SCHOOL"

The evolution of the name of the black school in Covington would be finalized shortly after Frank L. Williams left the school district. Early board minutes, prior to 1888 referred to Lincoln-Grant simply as the "Colored School" in order to distinguish it from "white" schools in the city. When the new Seventh Street building was completed in 1888 under the Singer administration, the name of the school became officially "The Seventh Street Colored School." That name was recorded in the Board of Education minutes from 1888 to 1908. By June

---

129. Jones, "The Early Kinship."
130. Tilford-Weathers, *A History of Louisville-Central High School*, 6.
131. Jones, "The Early Kinship."

1909, the year after Williams relinquished his position, the official name designation in the Board of Education minutes had been changed to "Lincoln School," in honor of the sixteenth president of the United States of America. According to James Reis, "A story in the *Kentucky Post* on May 7, 1909, said that the school's name was changed because the Covington Board of Education had decided to add its seventh school district. The board felt that a Seventh District School for white students might be confused with the Seventh Street [Colored] School, so they changed the name of the black school [to Lincoln School]."[132]

The official name of the high school section of the public school for black people in Covington was always reflected in the board minutes as "William Grant High School," particularly when listing the names of its high school graduates in the Board of Education minutes. The emergence of the names, "Lincoln (Elementary) School" and "William Grant High School" in a single-building enterprise would lead to the hyphenated name, "Lincoln-Grant School," a designation that had become the official school name by 1912, as shown in the Covington Board of Education Minutes. That name would be carried forward for many decades, while reflecting the presence of both the elementary and high school divisions in one building. But when one referenced the high school section only, for instance during high school commencement, the proper name continued to be "William Grant High School," while the elementary grades or the entire K-12 enterprise carried the full name of "Lincoln-Grant School." (The elementary section was not referenced separately as "Lincoln Elementary School").

The distinctions between Lincoln-Grant School, William Grant High School, and Lincoln School (compounded by the original Seventh Street Colored School designation), while perhaps confusing to an outsider, were well understood by those who knew the arrangements, and the evolution of the school names. All of the names referred to the same buildings, which eventually contained kindergarten through twelfth grade for black students in Covington. The name complexity of Lincoln-Grant School was simply another entanglement of segregated education stemming from one single purpose: to keep all black students segregated from white children—"forever," and by any means necessary.

Lincoln-Grant School had become a reliable community fixture by the early nineteen hundreds. The school had emerged as a convenient vehicle for segregated public education—one through which all educational concerns of "colored people" in Northern Kentucky, particularly those at the high school level, could eventually be addressed. However, another period of turbulence in the school's history lay ahead.

---

132. Reis, "Education for blacks began in secret schools."

▪ THE W. H. FOUSE YEARS: A ROUGH ROAD AHEAD

William H. Fouse succeeded Frank L. Williams in 1908, as the fifth principal of The Seventh Street Colored School (and William Grant High School). Born in 1868, and married to Elizabeth R. Fouse, he is reported to have been "the first African American graduate of Otterbein College in Ohio."[133] At the age of forty, Fouse would inherit from his predecessor a faculty that had grown in maturity, stature in the community, and job security, in addition to a building that would shortly undergo the name changes mentioned above.

The school's physical plant would also expand beyond the Seventh Street facility as additional courses were added, thus causing the entire black school operation to become somewhat unwieldy for a single administrator. For example, as Nordheim reports, "In 1909 a manual training department was

Photograph 26: Principal William H. Fouse.

opened for boys only in Lincoln-Grant. Due to space restrictions, it could not operate in the Lincoln-Grant building so it was placed in the Fourth District School, [perhaps temporarily] and a teacher was hired for $900 per year."[134] During that same period, the City of Covington annexed Latonia and Rosedale, and the school administration began the process of closing the Latonia Colored School, and folding that entire operation into the Lincoln-Grant facilities during the first or second year of Fouse's administration.

It would become necessary to secure annex facilities to accommodate the additional courses and the bulging student body at the Seventh Street Colored School. Annex property was rented at Sixth and Scott streets in 1911. To add to those complications, planning for an evening school at Lincoln-Grant would soon begin.

The Covington superintendency had also gone through several transitions during the period leading up to Fouse's appointment as principal. Charles M. Merry, who succeeded John Morris in 1904, would serve for only two years. Kirtley Morris, who was in the superintendent's office temporarily from 1906 to 1907, would follow him. A *Kentucky Post* article dated August 2, 1907, indicated, "After handing in his annual report last night to the Covington Board of

133. "Fouse, William H.," as cited in "Grade Schools & High Schools in Kentucky," Notable Kentucky African Americans Database, *University of Kentucky Libraries*, http://www.uky.edu/Libraries/NKAA/subject.php?sub_id=124 (accessed May 29, 2009).12.

134. Nordheim, *Echoes*, 23.

Education and making numerous suggestions for the continued success of the public schools, Prof. K. J. Morris, the Superintendent, vacated that office he temporarily held and Prof. Homer Sluss took charge."

Sluss had originally been brought in from Byfield, Massachusetts, in 1904 to replace John Hall, who resigned as principal of the Covington High School.[135] During the board meeting on June 3, 1904, at which Sluss's appointment as principal was confirmed, the board also passed a resolution that "hereafter the principals of the schools should be relieved from the duties of teaching," and function only as "Supervisors of the Schools."[136] Although that resolution, which was adopted in 1904 due to the apparent protests of white administrators in the school system, would benefit Sluss as principal of Covington High School, the black principal at William Grant continued to have teaching duties. Sluss ascended to the superintendent's job in Covington three years later, but apparently did not change that policy at the black school. Managing the complexities of the black school, and teaching a class simultaneously presented additional complications for Principal Fouse.

The number of high school students would steadily increase during that period. An article in the *Kentucky Post* dated June 15, 1911, reflected the following:

> The twenty-second annual commencement of the William Grant (colored) High School was held last night at the Covington Library Auditorium, and a class of nine were given diplomas for the successful completion of the school course. Prof. Kelly Miler of Washington, D.C. made the principal address of the evening on the subject, 'The Aim and End of Education,' and the class was presented diplomas by Vice President W. H. Mackoy of the Board of Education. The following were the graduates: Perry C. Thompson, Mildred G. Thornton, John N. Burnside, Mayme W. Byrd, Wm. H. Davis, Etta L. Hundley, Mary L. Marshall, Maude B. Ragan, and Chas. W. Russell.[137]

Etta L. Hundley would return to become a career elementary school teacher at Lincoln-Grant after receiving her bachelor's degree from Knoxville College in Tennessee.

Given the mix of expanding opportunities and changes described above, problems would seem inevitable. The location of the school building on Seventh Street, along with its annex facilities, placed it in a central, downtown section of Covington, where the school and its activities were, in fact, "on display" for all people from the community who came to the downtown area on a daily basis. That setting, and the daily movement of black students to and from different downtown buildings for their classes enhanced the probability that complaints about the behavior of the Lincoln-Grant constituency would come to the

---

135. *Kentucky Post,* "Homer Sluss Chosen to Succeed Hall," June 3, 1904.
136. Ibid.
137. Ibid., "Colored High Pupils Graduate," June 15, 1911, 3:7.

attention of the superintendent and the Covington Board of Education, which at that time maintained its offices close by in the City Building, downtown. That probability would soon become a reality.

Serious problems for Principal William Fouse became public when his letter of resignation was considered at the end of his third year as principal. A *Kentucky Post* article on August 4, 1911, titled "Board Retains Principal Fouse at Grant School" began as follows: "At a meeting of the Covington Board of Education last night the trouble in the colored school caused a great deal of discussion, and although the teachers and salaries committee reported favorably on the board accepting Principal Fouse's resignation, which had been submitted to the board, the board turned it down and he was retained as the Principal of the school by a vote of 8 to 4." The article continues, "The committee that has been investigating charges made against several of [t]he women [t]eachers repor[t]ed that they had not finished their investigation and were granted more time."

Although the specific incidents which formed the basis of negative charges against some of the teachers at Lincoln-Grant were not made explicit in the board minutes, Dr. J. A. Averdick, a board member, presented the following communication from nine women teachers at Lincoln-Grant School during the September 7, 1911, board meeting. The letter appears to be based on complaints from the 1910/11 school year (see figure 11).

The boldness of the Lincoln-Grant teachers in authoring such a letter to the board would reflect the emergence of teacher's unions, and the protection that they would offer faculty members, including those of color. The State Association of Colored Teachers had been established in Kentucky in the late eighteen hundreds. As Jones reports, "In 1877 the [white] State Superintendent of Public Instruction, H. A. Henderson, gathered 45 Negro educators and trustees and formed the State Association of Colored Teachers" That action would make Henderson the "head of the Negro and the White education associations." Jones further indicates, "In 1913 the State Association of Colored Teachers would become known as the Kentucky Negro Education Association (KNEA), the representative body of Kentucky's Negro teachers and a lobbying group for education issues."[138]

The teachers who signed the letter were apparently protected through long-term teaching contracts, as well as membership in the firmly established State Association of Colored Teachers and its local affiliate. The letter was referred to a Special Committee, consisting of three board members. Apparently the concerns of the board were resolved at some point, since there seemed to be no further official board action on the matter. But further difficulties were ahead.

Fouse would subsequently become the subject of personal controversy involving a corporal punishment incident near the end of his relatively brief tenure as principal. The January 6, 1912, issue of the *Kentucky Post* reflected

---

138. Jones, "The Early Kinship."

Figure 11: Faculty Grievance Letter, September 7, 1911

Gentlemen:

At the July meeting of your Honorable Board, bitter accusations were made against the character of teachers of the Lincoln Grant High School, by members of your honorable body, whereupon the Chairman of the Locals of the Lincoln Grant High School presented a resolution demanding an investigation of said charges and the Board placed it in the hands of the Grievance Committee to investigate and report back to the Board. At the August meeting the Committee reported progress and was granted more time. This being September 5, 1911, and no call of said Committee having been issued and your honorable body having your regular meeting Sept. 7, we, the undersigned teachers in the Lincoln Grant High School, cannot allow a stigma upon our good name [to] pass unnoticed and implore your honorable body to give this matter your immediate and earnest consideration, and to secure a Committee who will do their duty regardless of consequences, and if any of our number is found guilty, let them suffer the penalty, but do not allow our character to be blackened without proof, without investigation, and without giving us an opportunity of defending same, for which we pray,

With high regard,
Respectfully,

Tillie Young,
Mabel C. Leake,
Lulu Smith,
Eva E. Webster,
Georgia H. Reed,
Emma B. Kaye,
Ruth B. Johnson,
Maggie E. Bell,
M. E. Allen

an article, which was captioned: "Negro Educator Placed on Trial in Police Court." The article stated, "W. H. Fouse, principal of the colored high school in Covington, was tried in Covington Police Court this morning on a charge of breach of the peace, preferred by Mackie Harold, negress, who alleges that her 15-year old daughter Beatrice was beaten by the principal. Many witnesses, teachers and students at the school were summoned in the case over which the colored population of Covington is somewhat agitated." Fouse spent considerable time on the witness stand defending his actions, while indicating that he was simply trying to restrain the young woman when she attacked him in a classroom setting, after refusing to comply with a directive that he had given her.

Figure 12: 1911 Faculty Roster

Ruth B. Johnson	$700
Lula B. Smith ($700)	750
Donald McLeod	750
Nathan Fleming	750
M. E. Allen	750
Georgia H. Reed ($600)	650
E. E. Webster	800
M. E. Bell	750
Emma B. Kaye	550
Mabel C. Leake	750
Tillie Young	750
Robert P. Johnson	600
S. R. Showes	650
W. H. Fouse (Principal)	1350

Although it is unclear how the court matter was ultimately resolved, the corporal punishment incident and its legal involvement would be followed by Fouse's resignation in the middle of the school year, twenty-five days after the trial. The Board of Education Minutes reflected the following brief statement: "Principal W. H. Fouse resigned January 31, 1912 and left for Lexington to take up his new duties."

The educational career of William Fouse would actually take a turn for the better after he relocated to Lexington, Kentucky. Although his administrative experience at Lincoln-Grant School did not end well, Fouse had administrative skills and academic strengths that would demonstrate his great value as a prominent educator of African American students. He eventually became a very influential school administrator, while serving as the founding principal of Paul Laurence Dunbar High School in Lexington from 1923 until 1938, as well as holding other administrative posts. Fouse died in 1944 at the age of seventy-six.[139]

Following the midyear departure of William H. Fouse in 1912, Miss Frankie B. Watkins, the only female administrator in the school's history, was appointed temporary principal of Lincoln-Grant School. Miss Watkins, whose name was not reflected on the original roster of Lincoln-Grant teachers for the 1911/12 school year, apparently came from outside of the Covington school system. She appears to have brought the school year to a successful conclusion. In spite of a year of turmoil, and leadership change in the middle of the school year, William Grant High School produced three black male high school graduates. The Board of Education Minutes dated July 5, 1912, reflected that high school diplomas were awarded to John Stanley Blackwell, George Henry Givens, and John Garrard Hillman. George Henry Givens was recognized in the Board of Education Minutes as the recipient of a scholarship award.

---

139. "Fouse, William H.," Notable African Americans Database, 12.

■ NEW STRATEGIES

The great debate between W. E. B. Dubois and Booker T. Washington about whether or not newly emancipated black people should receive a classic, liberal education like white people, or one more suited to service in an emerging agricultural and industrial nation had already taken place. It is doubtful that most white Kentucky school administrators were attending closely to a discussion between two black intellectual leaders during the eighteen hundreds—a discussion that centered on higher education for black people, and took place on a more esoteric, philosophical level in geographical locations not even remotely close to Covington.

But some elements of the conversation between W. E. B. Dubois and Booker T. Washington, who advocated the alignment of "Negro education" more closely to the practical world, seem to have also been a part of the belief system of white school administrators who structured the educational courses for black students in Covington and other parts of Kentucky. However, such alignment was most likely coincidental. The white school administrators in Kentucky were probably guided more by prevailing views on race, and their own thinking about the educational potential of black people than they were by reflections from Dubois or Washington. Most white Kentucky school administrators, including those who were superintendents of the Covington Public Schools, thought of education for black children in terms of the practical world in which those administrators envisioned black people functioning in Kentucky.[140]

Superintendent Homer O. Sluss, who headed the Covington school district from 1907 to 1917, appeared to be an "activist" administrator whose primary mission was to upgrade the overall quality of the curriculum and teaching staff in Covington. Several curricular innovations were initiated in the Covington Public Schools under his administration. Nordheim reports that Superintendent Sluss also worked closely with the University of Cincinnati to improve teacher preparation among Covington teachers.[141] Some teachers at Lincoln-Grant took advantage of the opportunity to upgrade their teaching credentials at that institution.

Although some of the innovations introduced by Superintendent Sluss would be beneficial to black students and teachers, his views on curriculum development seemed generally consistent with those of most white school administrators in Kentucky. For instance, a new program proposed for the all-white Covington High School in 1912 while Miss Watkins still functioned as temporary principal at Lincoln-Grant, would not be made available to black

---

140. Some black schools in Kentucky, such as those in Trimble County and Owensboro functioned for only three months per year during the late eighteen hundreds, while others limited their curricula to such subjects as farming, poultry, along with reading, writing, and "common arithmetic."

141. Nordheim, *Echoes*.

students. Nordheim reported that in September 1912 "A two-year high school program was proposed by Superintendent Homer O. Sluss. This [program] would enable students who want to go to high school to get at least two years' studies in before they had to quit to go to work. It applied only to the Commercial Course and continued on into the early 1930s."[142] And, of course, Lincoln-Grant School did not have a Commercial Course.

Sluss also created summer school in 1910, and opened two white junior high schools for grades seven and eight in 1912. (The student body at Lincoln-Grant School would never be large enough to sustain a separately designated "junior high school"). Another innovation was the introduction of half-year classes that same year by Superintendent Sluss.[143] That program, which allowed students to complete their high school studies during the first semester of their senior year, was apparently available to both the white and black high schools; however it would not be actually implemented in the white high school until December 1917 and at William Grant High School in December 1930. Would there be a different approach to change and innovation at Lincoln-Grant School after a permanent principal was appointed?

■ PRINCIPAL ROBERT L. YANCEY: "YANCEY IN CHARGE"

Robert L. Yancey, a former school principal from Evansville, Indiana, assumed his administrative duties as the sixth permanent principal of Covington's all-black school on the morning of March 2, 1913. Since 1900, the school had gone through some peaks and valleys in its administrative leadership. Even though there had been seven years of reasonable calm and success under Frank L. Williams, the Fouse years had re-ignited the negative public press that had consumed the image of the school at the end of the Singer administration a little over a decade ago.

Miss Watkins had successfully supervised Lincoln-Grant School from February 1912 to March 1913. However, the school needed permanent leadership that would bring sustained civility and calm to the school and community. Consequently, there would be a sense of optimism reflected in the local

Photograph 27:
Principal Robert L. Yancey

142. Nordheim, *Echoes*, 106.
143. *Kentucky Times Star*, "Commencement in Mid-Season—First," December 21, 1917, 16.

paper, which reported on March 13, 1913: "Yancey in Charge."[144] Robert Yancey, who apparently had the confidence and support of Superintendent Sluss, would hold that position for the next thirteen years.

Miss Watkins remained as a member of the Lincoln-Grant teaching staff for a period of time after Yancey arrived.[145] Her previous appointment as acting principal had led to an annual teaching salary of one thousand dollars—a figure that exceeded the salaries of all other Lincoln-Grant teachers, and was second only to that of Principal Yancey. That phenomenon probably created a pay equity issue in the minds of a few more long-term teachers in the Lincoln-Grant building, while others would have felt that she had earned it for her previous administrative work. However, Yancey's firm hand would apparently quell the waters at Lincoln-Grant, as a new era of growth and development for the school was being implemented.

Although Superintendent Sluss initiated most of his curricular changes and innovations in the white city schools, he also made some changes at Lincoln-Grant School, with probable input from Principal Yancey. Evening classes were introduced for black students in 1914, but not offered on a regular basis until 1923. There were other gaps in the Lincoln-Grant curriculum that needed attention. One of the superintendent's curricular concerns was a "theoretical" approach to domestic science offerings for black females at Lincoln-Grant. The course relied heavily on students reading books only, without adequate laboratories for "hands on" experience. As a consequence, Superintendent Sluss asked in his March 9, 1914, report to the board that consideration be given to "a vital relation to a well-regulated home" in the domestic and manual training of Lincoln-Grant students.

The superintendent's report stated, "If ['colored'] girls are to be adequately trained for such [domestic] responsibilities, they must have the practice as well as the theory. To accomplish this, it is important that a flat or house be provided, that will be a model in its arrangement, and in its appointments and furnishings." Superintendent Sluss further stated that "A home should be secured that will be large enough to accommodate the cooking and the sewing departments of the school, both of which are now seriously handicapped by quarters that are too small, uncomfortable, and unsanitary."

Sluss simultaneously included an opportunity for a practical outlet for the

144. *Kentucky Post*, "Yancey In Charge," March 13, 1913, 2. Immediately under the Yancey article was another, titled "Sluss is Back." Superintendent Sluss had just returned from a weeklong trip to Philadelphia where he attended the annual meeting of the Department of Superintendents of the National Education Association. Sluss, an active, forward-thinking superintendent, who would only lead the Covington schools for a few more years before moving on, was reported to be back "at his desk in the City Building in Covington" that morning.

145. Miss Watkins was listed in a *Kentucky Post* article dated June 17, 1914, as the musical director at the commencement exercises for William Grant High School. By 1916 Miss Elizabeth Gooch was the musical director.

recently instituted Manual Training program at Lincoln-Grant, as he further recommended, "If the board approves of the plan, the ['colored'] boys of the Manual Training Department should begin to make certain articles of furniture for the house; while the girls may prepare the linens, curtains, etc. Thus the pupils are likely to feel a real interest in the project. It is further more recommended that a committee of colored ladies be selected, to act with the Board in an advisory capacity. Such a form of cooperation would probably prove very valuable."

Superintendent Sluss had offered what seemed like a positive, theoretically sound recommendation for upgrading the domestic science classes, while concurrently providing an outlet for student-crafted furniture from the manual training courses at Lincoln-Grant. Principal Yancey and the Lincoln-Grant teaching staff undoubtedly supported the recommendation. But, although the proposal seemed beneficial to black students on the surface, in reality, the superintendent's recommendation confirmed his belief that Lincoln-Grant students should be prepared exclusively for domestic work or other service jobs. Nothing in his proposed plan offered a view of service outlets for students completing the cooking, sewing and manual training courses at Lincoln-Grant School beyond work in the home. Even the proposed school laboratory, "a flat or house . . . that will be a model in its arrangement, and in its appointments and furnishings," supported the domestic emphasis. In stark contrast, the manual training, domestic science, and commercial programs for white students simulated settings in business and industry, as depicted in classroom photographs from the early nineteen hundreds.

The traditions of cooking and sewing for black female students and furniture construction for black males would eventually become institutionalized as a part of the Lincoln-Grant School curriculum. The domestic emphasis would be consistent with a segregated society that, in the real world, could only envision black high school students in service capacities such as cooking, sewing, ironing, repairing furniture—and cleaning an office instead of doing clerical work in it. Principal Yancey and the teachers at Lincoln-Grant adjusted to the physical expansion of the domestic science and manual training programs to other downtown buildings, as well as the superintendent's recommendation for a committee of "colored ladies" to provide advice.

The William Grant High School class of 1914 would reflect five graduates, as shown in figure 13. In spite of a limited view of how black students would function in the real world, many William Grant graduates would excel beyond those expectations. One glaring example of such excellence was Jewell Rebecca Smith, the only graduate in the William Grant High School class of 1916 (see figure 14). Miss Smith, whose family was originally from Flemingsburg, Kentucky, approximately seventy-three miles south of Covington, was born in 1899. She lived in Covington as a school-aged girl.

Jewell Rebecca Smith would go on to Fisk University, a distinguished, historically black institution founded in 1866 in Nashville, Tennessee, where she

Figure 13: Commencement Program, William Grant High School Class of 1914

Commencement[a]

William Grant High School
June 1914

Graduates:
Leonard Conley
Francis Davis
Della Givens
Preston W. Smith
Marguerite Stewart

Program

Overture by the William Grant Orchestra
Invocation by Rev. T. A. Thompson
Music, "Joys of Spring"
Oration of the "Growth of the Negro Race" by Francis Davis

Class Address "Fifty Years of Emancipation,"
By Prof William Pickens of the Talladega (Ala.) College

Presentation of the class by Principal R. L. Yancey
Presentation of diplomas by President A. A. Ranshaw of The School Commission

Benediction by Rev. S. H. Mitchell

****

Miss Frankie B. Watkins, Musical Director
Miss Ione Winchester, Accompanist

Class day was held by the graduating class June 12.
The sermon to the graduates was preached by
Rev. T. L. Ferguson of the Ninth-st M. E. Church

The annual picnic will be held Thursday at the Cincinnati Zoological Garden.
Friday the annual reception will be held at the William Grant High School.

---

a. *Kentucky Post*, June 17, 1914.

earned a bachelor's degree. After she graduated from Fisk in 1920, the Covington Board of Education hired her as an English teacher at William Grant High School. Principal Yancey, who would mentor Miss Smith as she initiated her teaching career in the Covington Public Schools, would undoubtedly be very pleased to have one of his talented high school graduates back to teach at Lincoln-Grant. Miss Smith would also acquire another teaching colleague at Lincoln-Grant—a fellow Fisk graduate, who was approximately fourteen years older than her, named Henry R. Merry.

Figure 14: Commencement Program, William Grant High School Class of 1916

Twenty-Seventh Annual Commencement

**William Grant High School
June 1916**

Graduate

Jewell Rebecca Smith

Program

*Photo 28:
Jewell Rebecca
Smith Jackson*

An article in the *Kentucky Post* dated June 14, 1916 indicated, "Twenty-seventh annual commencement of William Grant High School, Covington, will be held at Carnegie Library Auditorium, Wednesday evening at 8:15 o'clock. The program: Music, 'Come, Sweet Spring' (Thomas), chorus; invocation, Rev. S. R. Reid; music "Wind of Night" (Lohr), 'Smiling Morn' (Sprofforth), chorus, oration 'The American Girl,' Jewell Rebecca Smith; music, 'Merry June' (Vincent), chorus; class address, 'Education for Life,' Dr. J. W. E. Bowen, Atlanta, Ga.; music, 'Earth With Its Troubled Voices' (Costa), chorus; 'The Class of 1916,' Principal R. L. Yancey; awarding of diplomas, Edward W. Pflueger, President, Board of Education; music, 'Fairy Life' (Gung'l), 'America' (S. F. Smith), chorus; benediction, Rev. S. R. Reid. Miss E. W. Gooch, musical directress; Miss Anna Palm Fleming, accompanist. Annual picnic will be held Thursday at the Zoo, and the alumni reception will be held a K. of P. Hall Friday."

Miss Smith married Robert C. Jackson, a former railroad employee who went to night school and eventually became a teacher in the Cincinnati Public Schools. Mr. and Mrs. Jackson originally resided in Covington with one son, Robert Connelly Jackson, Jr.[146] Although she would not become a school administrator, Mrs. Jackson would exert strong influence upon the future direction of Lincoln-Grant School, the strength of its curriculum, and the educational advancement of its students for many decades. Her personal imprint would be evident during the entire span of the school's remaining existence.

Although there was only one graduate in the class of 1916, there would be nine graduates a year later (see figure 15). The class of 1917 would produce two additional educators, Leconia Franklin Crosby and Catharine Williams, who would also initiate their teaching careers at Lincoln-Grant School under the supervision of Principal Robert Yancey.

Leconia Franklin Crosby returned in the 1920s as a science teacher at Wil-

---

146. Robert Connelly Jackson, Jr., the son of Mr. and Mrs. Robert Jackson graduated from William Grant High School in 1951, and later became a high school science teacher in the Cincinnati Public Schools.

Figure 15: William Grant High School
Class of 1917

| Emma Mae Correll |
| James Henry Crosby |
| Leconia Franklin Crosby |
| Anna Palm Fleming |
| Wallace Edward Gordon |
| James Henry Johnson |
| Sigsbee Wilson Sheffey |
| Mattie Love Spiller |
| Catharine Williams |

liam Grant High School. He would hold that position until 1940. Some of Crosby's influence would be reflected in a master's thesis completed in 1929 at the University of Cincinnati. Although he was highly critical of several aspects of the school's development at that point, Crosby's thesis provided vital information on the early history of Lincoln-Grant School, as previously noted.

Catharine Williams, who was born November 26, 1896, in Lexington, Kentucky, attended Lincoln-Grant school from the age of seven through high school. After graduation from high school, Miss Williams attended Kentucky State College, and then returned to Covington as an elementary school teacher in 1921. Miss Williams, who taught at the school for forty-two years, completed her bachelor's degree at the University of Cincinnati. Later in her life, Miss Williams married a widower from her church, Deacon Webb.

Sigsbee Wilson Sheffey, another graduate of the class of 1917, served as a custodian at Lincoln-Grant School for several decades. He and

Photograph 29:
Mrs. Catharine Williams Webb

his wife, Jencie, raised several children who also graduated from William Grant High School.

In the meantime, a new school superintendent, Harry S. Cox, had been appointed to lead the Covington Public Schools in 1917. The Lincoln-Grant teaching staff would continue to expand under Robert Yancey's leadership, while a core of teachers who had served under previous administrators also continued to teach at the school. The May 29, 1918, Minutes of the Covington Board of Education reflected the assignment of seventeen classroom teachers to the Lincoln-Grant School Staff for the 1918/19 school year, as indicated in figure 16.

Student advancement would also continue under Yancey, as an upward trend in the number of graduates was sustained. The William Grant High School class of 1918, depicted below, included four graduates, as reflected in the board minutes of June 17, 1918: Zenobia Elizabeth Jones, Katherine Vivian Lambkins, Sarah Beatrice Stewart, and Robert Kirk Wilson.

Yancey's tenure as principal would include an unanticipated health epidemic that impacted the 1918/19 school year. The Spanish Flu outbreak reached the Northern Kentucky area in September 1918 and quickly infected thousands in the region, resulting in more than four thousand deaths in the area. Schools were closed for a portion of the school year. That worldwide flu epidemic, which followed an earlier measles outbreak in the Covington Public Schools, would heighten the concern for contagious diseases in the schools, resulting in due diligence in personal contact, as well as regular reports from the school system's medical examiner regarding the general health of the Covington school population. The flu virus proved to be an "equal opportunity" disease, as it wreaked havoc upon the black and white communities in Covington. In time the virus would be eradicated, but it would leave indelible marks upon the lives of many local families, including those whose children attended Lincoln-Grant School. Regrettably, many families, black and white alike, lost family members during that epidemic.

Figure 16: 1918 Faculty Roster

Mary E. Allen	$850
Maggie E. Bell	850
Gertrude J. Dansby	850
Nathan Fleming	850
Sallie P. Frazier	850
Elizabeth W. Gooch	700
Gertrude I. Holland	800
Emma B. Kaye	850
Donald McLeod	850
Chester A. Rice	800
Lulu B. Smith	850
Frankie B. Watkins	**1000**
Eva Webster	900
R. L. Yancey (Principal)	**1500**
Etta Hundley	850
Clara McGee	800
Lula Garnes	700
Willie Evans Taylor	800

Health concerns during that period would cause one member of the Covington Board of Education to complain of an inequity between the "Colored" school and one white school building in the city. While the Lincoln-Grant school building on Seventh Street had adequate water facilities, one older building constructed much earlier for white children in the district did not. The board member implored the immediate installation of proper water facilities in the aging white school building so that the children in the white school could "properly cleanse their bodies." He further opined that this was an especially pressing matter, since adequate water facilities were available "even in the Colored school." But of course that board member voiced no concern about the *curricular* inequities at Lincoln-Grant School, while feeling so strongly about "water inequity" in one white city school building.

Even though a pandemic health threat, as well as U.S. participation in World War I had drawn the local community together against common enemies, unrelenting racial segregation would continue to plague the Covington Public Schools. The rubric of a "standard" curriculum for black students and a "comprehensive" curriculum for white students continued to distinguish the depth of curricular offerings of William Grant and Covington Central (Holmes) High School.

But in spite of those differences, the number of graduates from William Grant High School would continue to increase. Influenced by the addition of high school students from Newport, there were ten graduates in the class of 1922: Elizabeth F. Crosby, Julia A Buckner, Minnie M. Corbin, Matthew F. Garrett, Emma B. Robinson, Sarah E. Murphy, Cora E. Carneal, Thomas Wilson Fleming, Freddie M. Mallory, and Albert J. Waugh. One member of the class of 1922, Minnie M. Corbin, would return to Lincoln-Grant to become a career teacher in the 1920s. She earned a bachelor's degree in Education from the University of Cincinnati. The number of William Grant graduates would grow significantly during the next three decades.

As time progressed under Robert Yancey's supervision, the curricular limitations at Lincoln-Grant were persistent, and aggravated by the aging physical facilities that housed the school. Yancey pressed for the upgrading of the physical facilities of the school. However, the domestic science and manual training classes at Lincoln-Grant were eventually housed in older, separate buildings, one on Sixth Street and the other on Scott Street under the administration of Superintendent Harry S. Cox. One school board member would later describe one of the buildings as a "veritable fire trap" and the other as only accessible by having students cross an "arterial highway." [147]

Photograph 30:
Miss Minnie Mae Corbin

An article in the *Kentucky Post* dated May 1, 1923, titled: "School Unsafe—Fire Hazard Seen in Negro Building—10 and 12 E. 6th. [Street]" would also highlight the perilous physical conditions in the annexed facilities at Covington's all-black school. Yancey took a leave of absence for the 1923/24 school year following the negative publicity on the black school facilities. Although the reasons for that leave may have been unrelated to the conditions revealed in the newspaper report, it

---

147. Minutes, Covington Board of Education, June 28, 1928.

is clear that Principal Yancey had been dissatisfied with the facilities at Lincoln-Grant School for some time.

The building constructed in 1888 as the Seventh Street Colored School and its annex facilities were obviously no longer adequate for the growing black population during the Roaring Twenties. Not only had the black population in Northern Kentucky grown significantly, but also Southgate High School in Newport, the only other black high school in the area, had closed in 1921 due to low enrollment. At that point, all black high school students in Northern Kentucky had to be accommodated at William Grant High School. That phenomenon would cause a steady increase in the overall school population, as well as the number of William Grant High School graduates.

A retroactive view of the school facilities is provided through the thesis of Leconia Franklin Crosby, who stated that in 1929 the Lincoln-Grant School building on Seventh Street had "ten class rooms, three . . . for the high school, [and] the remaining rooms for the grades." The building had a science laboratory in one room on the second floor, which was inadequate, and a small room on the third floor that was used for English and the library. Another room on the second floor was used for Latin and history class and study hall. "The Manual Training and Domestic Science classes [were] held nearby on Sixth Street in an old building which was formerly used as a store. The students had to travel to that building for their work in those departments" as reported by Crosby. The Covington Board of Education Minutes of April 1930 made reference to "annex property" at 707 Scott Street, which was also used by Lincoln-Grant students and faculty.

An external fire escape from the third floor to the lower level would adorn the outside of the Seventh Street Colored School building. It is reported by a former student that, during fire drills students on the upper floors of the school (usually the older students) were required to enclose the lower part of their bodies in "Kroger sacks," and slide quickly down the fire escape.[148] While this might have seemed to some a logical way to escape the building without using the inner stairwells, one can only imagine the pain and slight bruises to the body that would have occurred as a result of such an exercise, let alone the potential fire hazard that the "Kroger sacks" might have presented if a fire actually occurred.

There were no gym facilities for the school, which did not appear to have an athletic team until the 1920s when a football team was developed under the leadership of Mr. Paul Redden in connection with the local black YMCA.[149] Football would later be replaced by basketball after the black school relocated.

---

148. Conversation in September 2009 between the author and Sadye Bunyan, a former student and teacher at the school. "Kroger sacks," also called "gunny sacks" are large bags made of a burlap material used to transport bulk quantities (e.g. 100 lbs.) of vegetables, such as potatoes or onions. The term, *Kroger sack* is a local colloquialism resulting from the use of the bags by Kroger grocery stores, which were founded in the Cincinnati area in 1883. Today, the sacks are used in children's games.

The school board and the community would begin planning for the development and construction of a new facility for black students in Northern Kentucky. However, in 1925, the board decided to request a total bond issue of $525,000, a figure that included $425,000 for a new white school building, and only $100,000 for the black school. Principal Robert Yancey, who objected privately to what he considered to be inadequate funding for the black school and the lack of fairness in the funding proposal, was "called on the carpet" by school board members for not publicly supporting the bond issue.

A *Kentucky Post* article dated September 30, 1925, indicated, "After a sharp reprimand by members of the Board of Education . . . Yancey was given his choice of supporting the bonds or of resigning. He chose the former and promised to give public support."[150] The article continues, "A special meeting of the board was called to demand an explanation of the negro for his reported stand against the issue. Insubordination was the charge placed against Yancey by Elmer H. Heile, president of the board. The principal said he had made no public statements unfavorable to the bond issue, that whatever utterances he had made were made privately."[151]

The article continues, "Yancey's grievance was that the bond issue calls for an expenditure of $425,000 to build a school for white children, and $100,000 to build one for negroes. He told the board that negro voters felt their children were entitled to an adequate building and would support the bond issue if sure that they would get such a building. The board was unanimous in denunciation of the principal until Dr. Charles W. Reynolds moved to excuse him, after his promise to work for the bonds."[152] But clearly displeased with the situation, Robert Yancey resigned in 1926, and was succeeded by Henry R. Merry. Yancey's resignation, followed by a change in the superintendent's office, appeared to have some effect on the bond situation for the black school.

On May 21, 1927, a few months after Henry R. Merry became the new Lincoln-Grant principal, Superintendent Harry S. Cox would pass away. At that point, Glenn O. Swing, who had served as the principal of the all-white Holmes (formerly Covington Central) High School for the previous eight years would be named superintendent. After Swing's appointment, there would be expanded discussions among board members, Superintendent Swing and Principal Merry relative to the funding issue for a new Lincoln-Grant facility. A different funding approach would consider asking voters to approve a $250,000 bond issue, as well as the solicitation of additional funding from the Rosenwald Foundation in Chicago. The new school building would be planned as a state of the art

149. Jim Rice, "Many tried, few defeated William Grant in '50s, '60,'" Pieces of the Past, *Cincinnati Post*, February 23, 1998, http://www.kypost.com/opinion/pieces022398html (accessed March 25, 2007).

150. *Kentucky Post*, "School Head is 'On Carpet'—Negro Principal Scored for Bond Attitude," September 30, 1925.

151. Ibid.

152. Ibid.

facility that would accommodate local black elementary students, as well as all black high school students in the area as they emerged from black "feeder" schools in other parts of Northern Kentucky.

Photograph 31: Shorthand and Bookkeeping Classes, Covington High School, 1914.
Courtesy of the Kenton County Public Library, Covington, Kentucky.

Curriculum disparities were evident between Covington Central (Holmes) High School and William Grant High School as early as 1914, when shorthand, bookkeeping and typing classes were available to white students in Covington. In contrast, William Grant offered only domestic science and manual training classes. Classes in typing were not offered at William Grant High School until 1956, two years after Brown v. Board of Education.

Photograph 32: Typewriting Class, Covington High School, 1914.
COURTESY OF THE KENTON COUNTY PUBLIC LIBRARY, COVINGTON, KENTUCKY.

Photograph 33: Professional Cooking Class, Covington High School, 1914.
COURTESY OF THE KENTON COUNTY PUBLIC LIBRARY, COVINGTON, KENTUCKY.

Photograph 34: Cooking and Sewing Classes, Lincoln-Grant School, 1950.
GRANTONIAN YEARBOOK, 1950.

The Cooking and Sewing classes at Lincoln-Grant School continued to be highly theoretical, and oriented toward domestic work, even as late as 1950.

Photograph 35: William Grant High School Class of 1918.
PHOTOGRAPH PROVIDED BY THEODORE H. H. HARRIS, CLASS OF 1962.

The photograph above appears to include a mixture of the graduates, the principal, and William Grant High School faculty members. The gentleman in the center with the bow tie is assumed to be Principal Robert Yancey. To his right is Mr. Chester Rice, a relatively young Manual Training teacher, who was a career teacher at Lincoln-Grant (and one of the author's instructors). The persons on the lower rows would include the three female graduates, Zenobia Elizabeth Jones, Katherine Vivian Lambkins, Sarah Beatrice Stewart (not necessarily pictured in that order), and the only male graduate, Robert Kirk Wilson in the center of the front row. The other two adults in the picture are unidentified, but presumed to be a male and female teacher in the high school.

Photograph 36: The Whatley Family, Early 1900s.
COURTESY OF THE KENTON COUNTY PUBLIC LIBRARY, COVINGTON, KENTUCKY.

The Whatley family was well known in Covington. Two family members were graduates of William Grant High School. An undated family portrait.

Photograph 37: James and Leonard Castleman, Early 1900s.
COURTESY OF THE KENTON COUNTY PUBLIC LIBRARY, COVINGTON, KENTUCKY.

The Castleman family name was prominent at Lincoln-Grant School, with several graduates.

CHAPTER 5

Black Feeder Schools in Boone, Campbell, and Kenton Counties

■ AN UNOFFICIAL BLACK THREE-COUNTY SCHOOL SYSTEM

Racial segregation in Northern Kentucky had necessitated the development of additional black schools to service young black children in isolated pockets of Boone, Campbell, and Kenton counties. Therefore, it had become essential for white school administrators to conceive of the educational universe for black students in Northern Kentucky, not as a *city* educational system, but as an ad hoc, unofficial *three-county* educational system.

The fact that some black students lived in geographical areas run by different city and county superintendents with their own school boards would make a three-county effort somewhat cumbersome. But the determination to sustain racial segregation at any cost would cause white city and county school superintendents and school boards in Northern Kentucky to coordinate their efforts, and create what they thought were reasonable, albeit eccentric educational arrangements for black children.

While they were at the elementary school age, black children in the three counties would attend local, segregated schools in their general geographical areas, often with one or two teachers handling several grades, and sometimes located miles from where they lived. Elementary children within the Covington city limits would, of course, attend Lincoln-Grant School, which eventually contained all grades, from kindergarten through the Twelfth grade. If the black elementary schools in the outlying areas were not sufficiently staffed to handle the upper elementary grades, then those students would be sent to Lincoln-Grant School before they reached high school age. When black students were ready for high school, *all* black high school students in Boone, Campbell, and

Kenton counties (including those from Newport after 1921) would attend William Grant, the high school division of Lincoln-Grant School.

The black public schools in Northern Kentucky that eventually sent their students to Lincoln-Grant School had their own, unique historical beginnings. Reis points out that "The history of northern Kentucky's black school [Lincoln-Grant] is really the history of five schools, William Grant High School and Seventh Street Elementary School in Covington, Latonia Public School, Dunbar and Wilkens schools in Elsmere, and the Southgate Street School in Newport."[153] There was also reference to schooling provided at the elementary level in the black Burlington Baptist Church in Burlington, Kentucky. The Burlington School, according to Reis, "traces its history to 1881."[154] A black elementary school called Beaverlick School was also reported in the Walton-Verona area in Boone County during the nineteen hundreds. Mrs. Bessie Smith Conley, a 1910 William Grant graduate, taught grades one through eight at that school during one period. Covington's Our Savior Catholic School, not mentioned by Reis, also sent black students to Lincoln-Grant School.

■ THE LATONIA COLORED SCHOOL, C. 1890

Reis relied on Theodore H. H. Harris, a local historian, for some information on the Latonia Colored School. Harris stated that 'The Latonia School was started to educate the children of blacks, who worked at the Old Latonia Race Course.'[155] "Latonia Race Track on Winston Avenue in Latonia (Covington) Kentucky, six miles south of Cincinnati, Ohio, was a Thoroughbred horse racing facility opened in 1883. The track hosted a spring/summer racing series and a second in late fall. It was once regarded as among the United States' top sites for racing, and drew more than 100,000 visitors annually. . . . Financial difficulties during the Great Depression forced Latonia Race Track to close its doors with its last race card held on July 29, 1939. . . . Today the property is the site of the Latonia Shopping Center." [156] Black racetrack employees and other black Latonia residents sent their children to the Latonia Colored School.

The Milldale Colored School may have preceded the Latonia Colored School in that area. Jones reported that a school bearing that name "is listed in the Covington Directories for 1890 and 1892. The school was located on Williamson Street in Milldale (present Latonia) Kentucky." Jones further states, "In 1890, Martha Butler was the teacher, and in 1892, Susie Taylor was the teacher." [157]

Reis indicated, "The 1900–1901 City Directory listed Robert P. Johnson[158]

153. Reis, "Education for blacks began in secret schools."
154. Ibid., "Several schools taught black students," *Kentucky Post*, February 17, 2003.
155. Ibid., "Education for blacks began in secret schools."
156. "Latonia Race Track," *Wikipedia, The Free Encyclopedia*, http://en.wikipedia.org/wiki/Latonia_Race_Track (accessed June 17, 2009).

as the teacher of the Latonia Colored School and listed the school on Cherry Street, which is now 30th Street." Reis further stated, "The 1910 City Directory listed the Latonia Colored School on Kruse Avenues, off Main Street. By the 1914 City Directory, there is no listing for the school."[159]

Betty Lee Nordheim confirms some of the above information as follows: "In 1910 a school was established [for African American children in Latonia] on the Southwest corner of Kruse and Main streets. These two streets later became 30th Street and Decoursey Avenue. There was only one teacher in the school. He taught all the subjects in the elementary grades, and the students then went on to William Grant High School on Seventh Street."[160] Although Robert Johnson taught at the Latonia Colored School in 1910, his annual salary of $650 was reflected on the Lincoln-Grant School roster in the June 2, 1910, minutes of the Covington Board of Education. This would suggest that at some point after the annexation of Latonia and Rosedale by the City of Covington in 1909, the Latonia Colored School was officially placed under the aegis of the Covington Board of Education.

The minutes of the Covington Board of Education dated October 3, 1912, indicated that "Robert P. Johnson, teacher at the Latonia Colored School last year [the 1911/12 school year], was transferred to the Lincoln-Grant School to take charge of two High School Classes, of several classes of backward children, and of the Fifth Grade while Miss Frazier gives special instruction in music." This information seems to confirm that the formal closing of the Latonia Colored School occurred at the end of the 1911–12 school year.

After the Latonia Colored School closed, some black Latonia students were transported to the Lincoln-Grant building in downtown Covington by private car. The expense of that arrangement led to a 1914 Covington Board of Education resolution "That on and after Monday, March 16, 1914, the colored children of Latonia in the elementary grades be supplied with street car tickets to provide them transportation to and from school; and that the present plan of furnishing them a special car be discontinued. The Business Director and the Principal of the Lincoln-Grant School are authorized and directed to see that this order is carried into effect, provided this does not conflict with any existing contract." At that point, the Lincoln-Grant principal was Robert Yancey, and the Superintendent of Schools was Homer Sluss.

---

157. See Milldale Colored School (Covington, Kentucky) as cited in "Grade Schools & High Schools in Kentucky," Notable Kentucky African Americans Database, 23.

158. Robert Page Johnson was an 1897 graduate of William Grant High School.

159. Reis, "Education for blacks began in secret school."

160. Nordheim, *Echoes*, 36.

■ THE DUNBAR AND WILKENS SCHOOLS (LATE 1800S—EARLY 1900S)

Reis's oral interview with John T. Hopkins who, in 1979 was a seventy-two year-old "Elsmere City Councilman and former student in the Elsmere black school" provided insight into the origins of the Dunbar and Wilkens schools, which were attended by black students from Elsmere and Erlanger. According to Hopkins, the Dunbar School 'was originally started by the black people themselves and was called the Dunbar School in honor of Paul Dunbar, Negro poet. . . . At first, all the county provided was the coal, but later they started paying the teacher's salary.' Hopkins indicated that the Dunbar school provided a basic curriculum including 'writing, reading, arithmetic, civics and health.'[161]

In a separate article Reis reported, "The [Dunbar] school was located on Spring Street and had one teacher for 25 to 30 students. Later a new and larger school was needed to handle Elsmere's growing black population. The site selected was on Capital Avenue and the school built there was named Wilkens Heights [Elementary School]. After integration, the school became part of the Erlanger-Elsmere School District."[162] It is unclear when the Dunbar School ceased operation.

According to the former Reis article, Hopkins also reported that the Wilkens Heights Elementary School "was named after the Wilkens family, a prominent black family which owned the land on which the school was built." Wilkens students were sent to William Grant to complete their high school education. Reis stated that the Wilkens School remained open until after the public schools in Elsmere and Erlanger were integrated in the 1950s. It was then converted to a day care center.[163]

■ OUR SAVIOR CATHOLIC SCHOOL, C. 1943

There were black Catholics in Covington, and a black mission church and school to serve them. The Church of Our Savior is still located on Tenth Street, a few houses from where the author lived as a child, and one block from the Lincoln-Grant School building. For a period of several years in the 1940s and 1950s there was a school attached to the church, which provided an early education oriented to the Catholic faith for black Catholic children, as well as others whose parents preferred a parochial school education for their children. Like the public schools, Catholic schools in Northern Kentucky were racially segregated. Similar to Lincoln-Grant, Our Savior had been originally conceived as a church and school that would serve all black Catholics in Northern Kentucky.

161. Reis, "Education for blacks began in secret schools."
162. Ibid., "Several schools taught black students."
163. Ibid., "Education for blacks began in secret schools."

Rev. Paul E. Ryan, a church historian writes,

> In the summer of 1943, Bishop Howard began the erection of a church and school on East Tenth Street, in Covington, to serve Negro Catholics of the City, under the care of the pastor of St. Mary Cathedral. And until such time that other churches might be erected for the Negro people, it was to serve as a mission church for the Negro people of Northern Kentucky. At that time, two frame houses, a single family house and a two-family house on Tenth Street which had been recently purchased by the Diocese, were completely renovated to serve as a church and school respectively. The two-family house was converted into classrooms and a convent for the Sisters of Divine Providence in whose charge the school was placed. The school was finished before the church, and was opened in September, 1943, the first year maintaining an average enrollment of about sixty pupils, of whom fourteen were Catholic. Sister Francis de Sales, C.D.P. was the first Superior of the School of Our Savior, assisted by sister Rita Marie, C.D.P., and Sister Mary Clementia, C.D.P.[164]

During that period, Our Savior School became a viable competitor with Lincoln-Grant by enrolling fifty to sixty black elementary school children that would have normally gone to Lincoln-Grant. The elementary class size at Lincoln-Grant School would decrease somewhat with the opening of Our Savior School. A high school division was added to Our Savior School in 1946, thereby affecting, in a minor way, Grant's high school enrollment as well. "In 1947, Bishop Mulloy gave his approval for the erection of a new school building to serve the Church of Our Savior Colored Mission. The building designed on the one floor plan, was constructed of concrete blocks, containing four large size classrooms together with other facilities. The new school was blessed by Bishop Mulloy on September 19, 1948."[165]

When the children from Our Savior were ready for grades not offered at the school, they were sent to Lincoln-Grant School. A few black Catholic parents opted to send their children to Deporres, a black Catholic high school in downtown Cincinnati, instead of Lincoln-Grant in order to continue their children's education in the Catholic faith. Our Savior School closed after desegregation was mandated. However, The Church of Our Savior remained open for Catholic masses, while the school facility was used as a community center for black Cub Scouts, Boy Scouts, and other social activities. The local Catholic schools became integrated after the 1954 U.S. Supreme Court decision.

The Church of Our Savior "remained a mission of the Cathedral until it became an official parish in 1981. In 2002 Our Savior entered into a 'Cluster' partnership with Mother of God Parish."[166]

---

164. Rev. Paul E. Ryan, "Church of Our Savior, Covington, Kentucky," excerpted from *History of the Diocese of Covington, Kentucky, on the Occasion of the Centenary of the Diocese, 1853–1953*, http://www.nkyviews.com/kenton/text/kenton_text_ryan_cov_colored_church.htm (accessed December 13, 2009).

165. Ibid.

■ SOUTHGATE ELEMENTARY AND SECONDARY SCHOOL, C. 1867

There was only one public school available to black students in Campbell County from the late 1800s until 1955. The beginning of Southgate School in that county mirrored the beginning of Lincoln-Grant School in Kenton County. Reis and Harris report that the original school was opened by the Freedmen's Bureau "most likely" in September 1867 under the supervision of a black school board.[167] According to an unidentified author, "the property of Southgate School was conveyed to the City of Newport by Thomas and Susan Dodsworth by deed dated October 4, [1870] and of record in deed book 10 page 183 of Campbell County for a school for African Americans."[168] The school was under the control of The Newport Board of Education by 1873.

The article quotes from "The History of the Public School of Newport," authored in 1939 by James L. Cobb as follows: "In August 1873, the Board employed one Negro woman teacher [Elizabeth Hudson] at a salary of $35 per month. She began teaching the first Monday in September in a one room cottage between Saratoga Street and Washington Avenue. This marked the beginning of Negro education in Newport."[169] Reis reports, "Another teacher was added in 1878 with the faculty growing to three in 1892 and four in 1890. An account in the book *Newport Kentucky—A Bicentennial History* says enrollment at the school jumped from 55 in 1889 to 125 in 1900."[170]

The former article states further that the first high school commencement was held in 1893. There were two graduates, and a local newspaper reported the following: "Louisa Smith and Lavinia Ellis wore white gowns and addressed the audience with essays on 'Opportunity' and 'A view of Life,' which showed deep thought and careful preparation and reflected credit on the teacher, Professor Lee, as well as on the young ladies." An article in the *Kentucky Post* dated June 18, 1896, indicated, "On Friday evening the second annual commencement of the High School Department of the Southgate-Street School (colored), will take place at the Park Avenue Schoolhouse Hall. There is only one graduate, Miss Beatrice Genevieve Johnson."

Reis reports, "an early principal at Southgate Street School was Charles D. Horner."[171] Subsequent school principals included Francis M. Russell (1904–08);[172] W. S. Blanton (1909–21, Nora H. Ward (1921–40) and Charles L. Harris (1940–53).[173]

166. "Our Savior Church," *Mother of God Church*, http//www.mother-of-god.org/our_sister_church.htm (accessed December 13, 2009).
167. Jim Reis, "Southgate Street School stood alone for decades," *Kentucky Post*, February 17, 2003.
168. "Newport's First Black School, Southgate Street School Elementary and High School." African American Records. *Campbell County Kentucky GenWeb*. http://www.rootsweb.com/-kycampbe/southgateschool.htm (accessed March 25, 2007).
169. Ibid.
170. Reis, "Southgate Street School stood alone for decades."
171. Ibid.

The June 17, 1904, issue of the *Kentucky Post*, in an article titled "Colored School—Will Hold Commencement Exercises in Newport" reflected the following:

> The Newport colored school will hold its commencement exercises Friday night. The salutary and essay will be delivered by Miss Mayme Elizabeth Washington, her subject being 'Failure or Success.' The school essay and valedictory will be delivered by Miss Mary Lorinia Gee, the other graduate. Her topic will be 'Intellectual, Moral and Physical Education., Other numbers on the program are: Chorus by the school; declamation, "One of the Heroes,' Miss Ethel Horner; school essay, "Looking Forward,' Miss Lulu Howell; school declamation, 'Searching for the Slain,' Miss Ethel Baker; recitation, 'The Ride of Jennie O'Neal,' Miss Eva B. McConico.

Black students from Newport in grades nine through twelve were sent to William Grant High School after Southgate School closed the high school section in 1921 due to low enrollment. The elementary division of Southgate School remained open, and was staffed by a few black teachers who taught more than one grade. Located in Southgate Alley near a railroad track, close to the Ohio River, the building contained four classrooms with two grades in each room. Two restrooms were located in the basement—one for girls and the other for boys. The building was set up for grades one through eight (without a kindergarten), but with increasing enrollment, the eighth grade was discontinued, and those students were sent to Lincoln-Grant School early. There was no lunchroom. Students packed their lunch, and ate it at their desks during lunchtime.[174]

Southgate Elementary School closed in 1955 when the integration of the Newport Public Schools was implemented. According to a historical building marker currently placed in front of the building, "In 1955, a desegregation program was submitted to the [Newport] school board and the school was dissolved. All African American students through eleventh grade could then attend Newport schools. Twelfth-grade students continued at William Grant, and teachers went on to positions in other Newport schools." The building stills stands, and is "being restored as part of the Newport Historic District" according to the former article on Southgate School.[175]

---

172. Mr. Francis Marion Russel [*sic*] was an 1895 William Grant High School Graduate.

173. During Joseph M. Walton's conversation with Jessie Mays Lattimore, a former Southgate School student in June 2008, Mrs. Lattimore indicated that Charles L. Harris was a Canadian citizen who lived in the Newport area during the school year, and returned to Canada each summer.

174. Ibid.

175. Reis, Southgate Street School stood alone for decades."

■ ROUTINE BUSINESS

Maintaining racially segregated schools in Northern Kentucky, including the black public schools mentioned above, would quickly emerge as "routine business" involving: (1) racial identification and separation of "colored" children wherever they lived in the three counties; (2) transporting them to a "colored" school building, sometimes located a far distance from their homes, and (3) financial reimbursement to the Covington school system from other public school districts for accommodating black students from outside of the city limits.

Racial identification would be the least difficult of the three tasks. It involved either self-identification, or designation by an external observer, and then stipulating the school buildings in Boone, Campbell, or Kenton County that black students from a given geographical area would attend. The third task, financial reimbursement, would also be fairly simplistic. Financial arrangements were worked out among the various school districts by having the Covington Board of Education designate black students from outside of Covington as "tuition pupils." Reportedly at some point the Covington Public Schools received annually fifty dollars for each black student from the other school districts.

However, the second task, transporting black students to a "colored" school building was a bit more complicated. Black students from outside of Covington were shuttled past the white schools in their communities to the closest black elementary school in their geographical area by whatever means necessary. When they were ready to attend Lincoln-Grant School, several modes of transportation were employed, including a small school bus provided by the school system; private automobiles reimbursed by board funds, or purchased by the school board; having the black principal at Lincoln-Grant pass out "streetcar money" so that students could ride the city buses and streetcars; or by simply letting some black students walk from Newport to Covington.

The January 25, 1935, minutes of the Covington Board of Education reflected the following recommendation from Covington Superintendent Glenn Swing: "The Newport Board of Education through Superintendent Owens has requested that the Covington Board of Education supply street car tickets to tuition pupils living in Newport, and who attend the William Grant High School. I wish to recommend that the same be granted and that the same continue during the time of the construction of the new Fourth Street Bridge."

The author recalls a few of the Newport students who routinely walked across the Fourth Street Bridge en route to Lincoln-Grant during the 1950s occasionally running up Saratoga Street just before the first school bell rang, to avoid being listed as "tardy," and encountering school detention for that infraction. The author also remembers a small school bus that arrived at the Lincoln-Grant building on Greenup Street every school morning to deliver a few black children, mostly from one family. The Behanans lived in Morning View, Kentucky, located southwest of Walton, Kentucky. Although their "learning readiness" may have been questionable after an early rising, and such a lengthy ride into the city, two members of that family of five or six school-aged children became William Grant High School graduates.

All black families with children who attended Lincoln-Grant School were not of modest income. Some parents who were more financially secure either drove their children to Lincoln-Grant from outlying areas, or provided their children with private automobiles to drive to school.

In a 1979 article titled "Lincoln Grant"[176] Emma Sleet Wallace, a 1932 William Grant graduate, provided an additional perspective on busing black students from the Walton, Kentucky, area in the 1930s. She reported a daily trip of twenty-five miles each way to attend Lincoln-Grant. Emma Sleet "grew up in Beaverlick, a Boone County community near Walton." The article further states, "At first, she and four other students were bused to the new [Lincoln-Grant] school [building on Greenup Street] then the Boone county officials decided it was much cheaper to buy the students an "old junker car" than operate a school bus for their transportation.

The practice of racial segregation in Northern Kentucky seemed "matter of fact" in its orientation. The school boards in the early nineteen hundreds were made up of white male members who seemed to view themselves as charitable to the black community. There was obvious comfort on the part of the Covington Board of Education as it operated a dual system of education based on race in cooperation with other school administrators in Boone, Campbell, and Kenton counties. There seemed to be a sense of civility, even to "the colored" over many decades, in spite of occasional rifts and strong-spirited debates about other business matters among individual members of the Covington Board of Education. Minutes of all board activities, including personnel, instructional and business transactions for the white schools and Lincoln-Grant were maintained. The minutes documented most board business in an orderly fashion from minor, mundane matters to passionate discussions of more critical issues, while usually listing any information about Lincoln-Grant School after that of the white schools.

Similar black schools were established in other major cities in Kentucky, including Louisville and Lexington, as black school administrators such as Frank Williams and William Fouse moved back and forth between those cities and Covington. Louis Stout reports the establishment of at least sixty-nine black, segregated high schools throughout the Commonwealth of Kentucky during the late eighteen hundreds and early nineteen hundreds.[177] Those deliberately designed, politically inspired arrangements for racially segregated pub-

---

176. The source of the undated article, "Lincoln Grant" was the Kenton County Public Library History and Genealogy Department. The article was accessed in the library by this author in 2008.

177. Louis Stout, *Shadows of the Past: A History of the Kentucky High School Athletic League*, 2006.

lic education followed the dictates of the laws of the Commonwealth of Kentucky.

Such provisions for public education, spanning many decades in the Commonwealth of Kentucky and elsewhere in the United States were living manifestations of this nation's overwhelming preoccupation with keeping the races segregated in the early and middle parts of the twentieth century. The detail, cumbersomeness, and duplication of effort reflected in maintaining segregated public schools demonstrated the extreme, and perhaps incredulous lengths to which school authorities and politicians would go to sustain separate educational venues for black and white children in those days.

Photograph 38: Latonia Colored School.
COURTESY OF THE KENTON COUNTY PUBLIC LIBRARY.

A school building originally constructed for white students in Latonia that was eventually vacated due to its age. The building is believed to have housed the Latonia Colored School students for two or three years during the early 1900s. The facility was only partially used, due to its size in relation to the number of black students that were served.

Photograph 39: Latonia Racetrack, 1900s.
COURTESY OF THE KENTON COUNTY PUBLIC LIBRARY.

Photograph 40: Dunbar School, Elsmere.
COURTESY OF KENTON COUNTY PUBLIC LIBRARY, COVINGTON, KETNUCKY.

Photograph 41: Wilkens Heights Elementary Students.
COURTESY OF THE KENTON COUNTY PUBLIC LIBRARY, COVINGTON, KENTUCKY.

Students perform at Wilkens Heights Elementary School in Elsmere, Kentucky, 1940s or '50s.

Photograph 42: The Church of Our Savior.
COURTESY OF KENTON COUNTY PUBLIC LIBRARY,
COVINGTON, KENTUCKY.

Left: Church of Our Savior, Tenth Street, Covington. The grade school was located in a building attached to the left side of the church.

Photograph 43: Holy Communion at the Church of Our Savior, 1950s.
COURTESY OF THE KENTON COUNTY PUBLIC LIBRARY, COVINGTON, KENTUCKY.

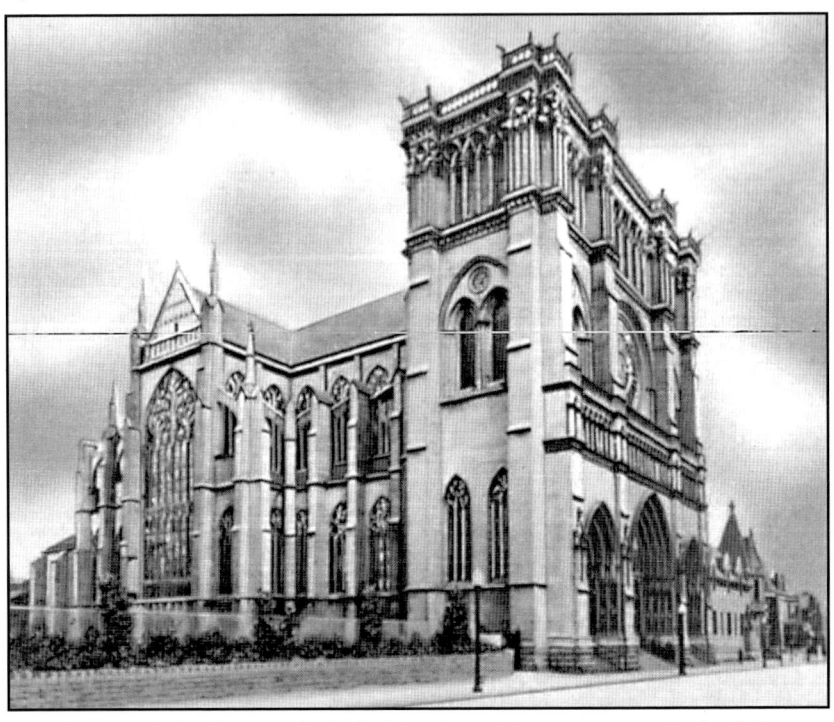

Photograph 44: St. Mary Cathedral Basilica of the Assumption, Early 1900s.
COURTESY OF THE KENTON COUNTY PUBLIC LIBRARY, COVINGTON, KENTUCKY.

Our Savior Catholic Church and School on Tenth Street operated as a mission of Saint Mary Cathedral Basilica of the Assumption on Madison Street in Covington. Our Savior Catholic Church entered into a "cluster" partnership with Mother of God Parish in 2002.

Photograph 45: Southgate School, Newport, Kentucky.
FROM THE AUTHOR'S COLLECTION.

Photograph 46: Historical Marker, Southgate School,
Newport, Kentucky.
FROM THE AUTHOR'S COLLECTION.

Photograph 47: Superintendent Glenn Swing and Associate, Early 1900s.
COURTESY OF THE KENTON COUNTY PUBLIC LIBRARY, COVINGTON, KENTUCKY.

A young Glenn Swing (right) and an associate at work in Swing's Board of Education office in the early 1900s. Swing served as the Covington Public School superintendent for a large portion of the segregated school era, from 1927 to 1960.

Photograph 48: Schoolmaster's Club, Northern Kentucky, 1900s.
COURTESY OF THE KENTON COUNTY PUBLIC LIBRARY, COVINGTON, KENTUCKY.

The Schoolmaster's Club was an all-male, all-white group of educators and community leaders in Northern Kentucky. That group played a key role in maintaining segregated schools in Northern Kentucky over many decades. Covington Superintendent Glenn Swing (front row, third from left) was a prominent member of that group.

Figure 17: Black Schools in Northern Kentucky

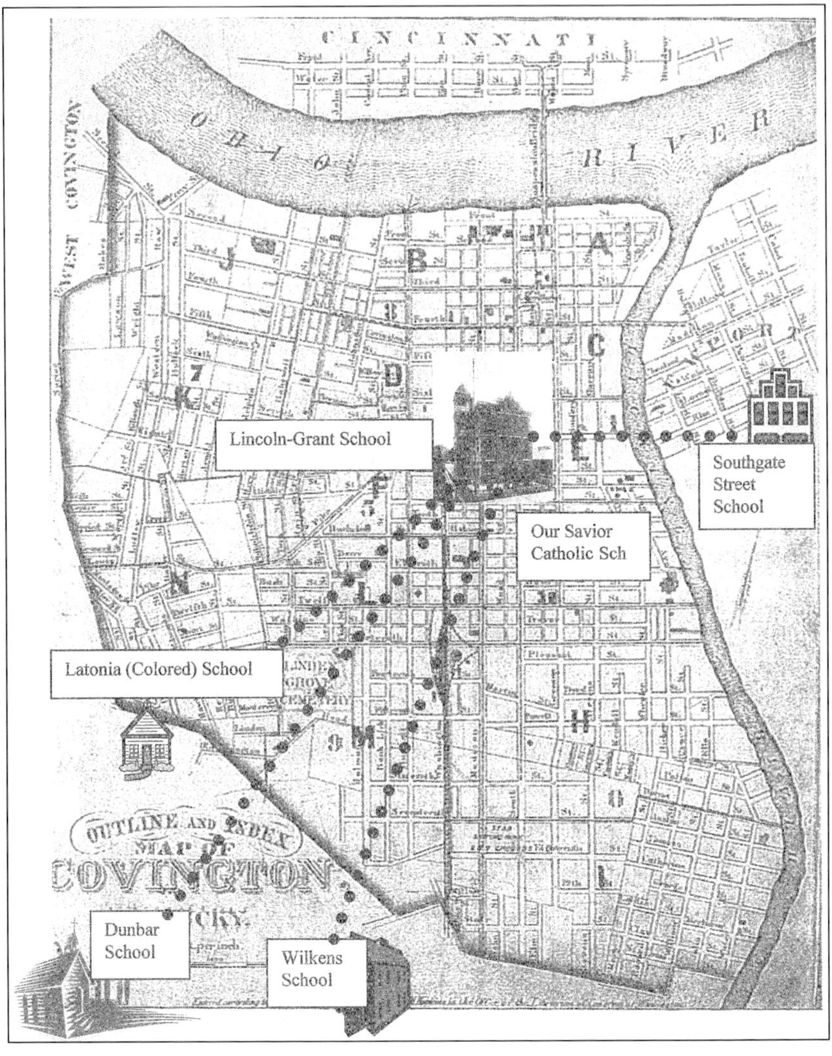

Black school linkages in Northern Kentucky during the early 1900s. Photo of Lincoln-Grant School courtesy of the Kenton County Public Library, Covington, Kentucky. All other building representations above are facsimiles.

MAP SOURCE: ATLAS OF THE CITY OF COVINGTON, COURTESY OF THE
KENTON COUNTY PUBLIC LIBRARY.

Figure 18: Educational Segregation in the U.S. Prior to *Brown vs. Board of Education*

Segregation Prohibited in 15 States:	**No Legislation in 12 States:**
Colorado Connecticut Idaho Illinois Indiana Iowa Massachusetts Michigan Minnesota New Jersey New York Ohio Pennsylvania Rhode Island Wisconsin	California Maine Montana Nebraska Nevada New Hampshire North Dakota Oregon South Dakota Utah Vermont Washington (State)
Segregation Optional or Limited in 4 States:	**Segregation Required in 17 States and D.C.:**
Arizona Kansas New Mexico Wyoming	Alabama Arkansas Delaware Florida Kentucky Georgia Louisiana Maryland Mississippi Missouri North Carolina Oklahoma South Carolina Tennessee Texas Virginia Washington, D.C. West Virginia

Source: *"Brown v. Board of Education,"Wikipedia, the Free Encyclopedia,*
http://en.wikipedia.org/wik/Brown_v._Board_of_Education (accessed January17, 2008).

Part II

An Era of Growth and Development
1926–1954

*Aerial View of the City of Covington with the Ohio River and
Suspension Bridge to the North, 1940s.*
COURTESY OF THE KENTON COUNTY PUBLIC LIBRARY, COVINGTON, KENTUCKY.

CHAPTER 6

From Seventh Street to Greenup Street

◼ THE LASTING INFLUENCE OF PRINCIPAL HENRY R. MERRY

As a graduate of Fisk University, the prestigious, historically black institution that produced Mrs. Jewell Smith Jackson, Henry R. Merry would soon become prominent in the Covington educational arena. His first administrative appointment in Covington was that of acting principal of Lincoln-Grant School for the 1923/24 school year, while Robert L. Yancey took a leave of absence. During that year, Merry apparently continued his teaching duties while supervising a teaching staff comprising thirteen elementary teachers from grades one through eight, two high school teachers, and four teachers of special subjects, including drawing, music (special), manual training and cooking.

Photograph 49: Principal Henry R. Merry

Mr. Merry apparently resumed teaching on a fulltime basis when Robert Yancey returned as principal for another two years, from 1924 to 1926. When Yancey resigned as principal in 1926 and left the Covington Public Schools for good, Henry R. Merry formally succeeded him, and became the seventh permanent principal of Lincoln-Grant at the approximate age of forty-one. Merry would take over in August 1926 and hold the position for several decades.

Henry R. Merry was a self-identified "colored man," whom many people assumed to be white upon first seeing him. While private speculation about Mr. Merry's racial origins might have occurred, his obviously mixed racial heritage was never explicit in the Covington community. Merry was born in 1885 during the post–Civil War era. His local family ties, apart from his African American wife and children were simply not discussed publicly. For a large portion of his adult life, Mr. Merry and his family resided at 1111 Russell Street in Covington, where his wife gave private piano lessons to black students.[178] In a different community, where his racial origins were unknown, he probably could have "passed," and lived successfully as a "white" man. However, Mr. Merry chose to live as a "colored" man in Covington.

Since race was at the heart of segregated schools, it is significant that a man with a mixed racial background would have a lengthy administrative career at the only all-black school in Covington. Mr. Merry was the most long-term principal at Lincoln-Grant, as he held the reigns of the school for a total of thirty years, and supervised the education of numerous black students until his retirement in 1955. When he first became principal, the school was still located in the Seventh Street building originally built in 1888. Merry had been chosen in anticipation of the relocation of Lincoln-Grant School from the Seventh Street facility to a new building on Greenup Street in 1932. Mr. Merry's presence during discussions on the selection of a site for the new school building, as well as the physical layout of the new facility, seemed necessary to the Covington school administration, which relied on him primarily to communicate with the black community regarding the construction of the new building.

Merry's overall influence on Lincoln-Grant School and its constituency was profound. He was a steady advocate for his black teachers and students as he represented the interests of Lincoln-Grant School to the Covington school administration, the Board of Education, and black educational organizations outside of the city. His relatively permanent status as principal would indicate that, in general, he had the consistent confidence of the Lincoln-Grant faculty, as well as that of the Covington Board of Education and central administration.

Merry's leadership style in relationship to students and teachers alike seemed relatively *laissez faire,* tolerant and benign, rather than authoritarian, stern, or intrusive. He had a "calming" demeanor, and seemed to be more of a consensus builder. Mr. Merry was not a person who was adversarial in his approach to most matters. While some people in the black Covington community would view him as perhaps not sufficiently aggressive in representing the interests of black people, or resisting some obvious curricular and policy disparities at Lincoln-Grant, others would see a "colored man" who could literally

178. Based on Joseph M. Walton's conversation with Vanda Lovelace Langham, August 2009. Mrs. Langham, a 1953 graduate of William Grant High School, took private piano lessons from Mr. Merry's wife in their home at 1111 Russell Street for several years as a young girl.

pass for "white" as a convenient foil to the external community.

A mixed racial heritage would allow Mr. Merry to "work both sides of the street" between white and black people effectively. Indeed, on important matters of administrative and educational significance some white people had more confidence in a "colored man" who looked physically like a "white man." On the other hand, Merry's mixed racial background benefited black people in some situations. For instance, Mr. Merry is reported to have wittily used his ability to "pass" to facilitate practical matters for his black teachers and students in other parts of Kentucky, during a period when racial discrimination such as refusal of food service to black people was blatant. While traveling into remote parts of Kentucky with some of his teachers or his basketball team, Merry would go into "white only" restaurants and secure food for those waiting outside in their automobiles for him. White restaurant owners who practiced racial discrimination would serve Mr. Merry, while refusing to accommodate his identifiably black colleagues and students.

Mr. Merry's son and daughter were both graduates of William Grant High School while it was still located on Seventh Street. His daughter, Elizabeth Page Merry graduated from William Grant in 1928, while his son, Charles Raymond Merry was a member of the class of 1931. A relative named Elizabeth Merry was shown on the roster of Lincoln-Grant School as a second grade teacher in 1928. She resigned her position as a teacher at Lincoln-Grant School on September 27, 1929.

Mr. Merry's daughter, Elizabeth Page Merry (Boone) would later become an elementary school teacher at Lincoln-Grant. After teaching at Lincoln-Grant for a number of years, she transferred to the Cincinnati Public Schools. His son, Charles Raymond, received a medical degree from MeHarry Medical College in Tennessee. However, Charles Raymond passed away at a relatively young age. The familial ties of Mr. Merry, and the interconnectedness of his family members to Lincoln-Grant School highlighted yet another idiosyncrasy of racially segregated education—the tendency for one family unit to center all of its educational associations in one all-black school building.

The Merry connections were but one such example at Lincoln-Grant. There were at least two instances where a husband, a wife, and their two children were concurrently engaged as teachers and students at Lincoln-Grant School. In several different cases, a parent and one or more children were simultaneously associated with Lincoln-Grant in the roles of teacher and student. In those situations, efforts were made to place the child (student) in a classroom setting apart from the parent (teacher). For example, if the parent taught one of two second grade classes, the child would automatically be placed with the other second grade teacher. But when the teacher/parent was the only person (e.g., in the high school division) who taught a given subject such as English, or special subjects such as physical education or music, even that separation became impossible. In at least two other perhaps less conflicting situations, two different sets of sisters were faculty members at the same time at

Lincoln-Grant. Those arrangements would, at the very least, obscure objectivity in teacher evaluations and student assessment for relatives in the same building.

Unfortunately, black teachers who lived within the city limits had no alternative for educating their children other than sending them to another city, such as Cincinnati, at considerable expense and inconvenience, or residing elsewhere and commuting to Covington. The unusual conditions described above were compelled by forced racial segregation since, consistent with Kentucky law, the Lincoln-Grant building was the only public school facility that black children and black teachers could access in the city of Covington. But the willingness of Lincoln-Grant teachers to educate their own children at the school also confirmed the high quality of instruction that Lincoln-Grant students received.

The August 21, 1928, minutes Board of Education minutes reflected that an expanded faculty of twenty elementary and secondary school teachers would be under Principal Merry's supervision at the Seventh Street building during the 1928/29 school year, as shown in figure 19.

Figure 19: 1928 Faculty Roster

Pearl Cowen	High School
Leconia Crosby	**High School**
Jewell Jackson	High School
Mary E. Allen	8th
Nathan Fleming	7th
Paul Redden	6th
Blanch I. Glenn	6-B, 5-A
Anna M. Snowden	5-B
Catharine Williams	4-A
Minnie Mae Corbin	4-B
Lulu B. Smith	3-A
Etta Hundley	3-B
Elizabeth Merry	**2-A**
Lulu G. McLean	2-B
Clara B. McGhee	1-A
Alberta E. Booker	1-B
Elizabeth Gooch	Special (Music)
Chester Rice	Manual Training
Eleanora W. Henderson	Domestic Science
Eunice Simpson	Special (Writing, Drawing)
H. R. Merry, Principal	

Leconia Franklin Crosby, a 1917 William Grant High School graduate who had returned later to teach in the high school, was also pursing a master's degree at the University of Cincinnati in the late 1920s. He further elaborated upon the high school teaching assignments listed above, when he stated in his 1929 master's thesis that, in addition to Principal Merry, the 1928/29 high school faculty consisted of a full-time English teacher (Jewell Jackson), a full-time history and Latin instructor (Pearl Cowen) and a full-time math and science teacher (Leconia Franklin Crosby) for an enrollment of twenty-seven boys and forty girls.

There were also three teachers who apparently were part-time in the high school, while devoting the other portion of their teaching load to the lower grades in the areas of music (Elizabeth Gooch), domestic art and science (Eleanora Henderson), and cabinet work and mechanical drawing (Chester Rice). Crosby indicated that the high school teachers all held bachelor's degrees and were also enrolled for graduate studies at the University of Cincinnati. Among the other three teachers who taught part-time in the high school section only one had a bachelor's degree, while the other two were "hastily in pursuit of it."[179] Ultimately, those two teachers would earn undergraduate degrees from the University of Cincinnati.

Educational preparation for teachers became more rigorous as the local curriculum for black students expanded. The bachelor's degree with specific academic and subject matter requirements would eventually become a minimum requirement. Lincoln-Grant teachers who were employed prior to increased teacher education standards would make diligent efforts to bring their credentials up to date with current educational requirements through study at local universities in Ohio, such as the University of Cincinnati and Miami University, as indicated above.

The faculty at Lincoln-Grant School would become stronger and better prepared under Mr. Merry's leadership. Properly certificated teachers with undergraduate degrees from historically black colleges, including premier black institutions such as Fisk University, Spelman College, Howard University, and Tuskegee Institute had joined the Lincoln-Grant faculty. Graduates of Miami University and Wilberforce College in Ohio, as well as Kentucky State College also taught at Lincoln-Grant. As time went on, the faculty steadily improved in quality, and continued to grow numerically in proportion to increases in the student body. Several teachers who were already employed at Grant completed master's degrees at the University of Cincinnati, while others arrived with graduate degrees in hand from other prestigious institutions such as Columbia University, the University of Wisconsin, and Miami University. Eventual retirements, and the occasional loss of good teachers to other school districts would produce minimal teacher turnover at a school that prided itself in having a significant core of long-term, professional teachers under one

179. Crosby, "A Study of Pupil Marks."

career administrator.

The improved strength of the faculty along with marked population growth would result in a significant increase in the number of graduates from William Grant High School. There were periodic adjustments to the graduation cycle and methods of securing a high school diploma as national events occurred. One such adjustment followed the 1929 Great Depression when the midyear graduation policy was implemented at William Grant High School. (That policy for the white high school had been in place since 1917). Students in the "half" classes for both Holmes and William Grant completed their high school courses usually around December or January of a given school year and had their high school diplomas conferred at that time. The Official Minutes of the Board of Education showed the midyear date as the student's date of completion. However, there was no official commencement in December, and those graduates were invited to participate in commencement exercises with the June graduates the following year.

The "half" classes appeared to be a response to economic times. That policy allowed students to exit high school a half year earlier and pursue post-secondary employment opportunities. Those bound for college had an extra six months to earn funds for their college education. The first half class at William Grant High School was the Class of 1930 ½. The final half class at William Grant High School was the Class of 1943 ½.

Photograph 50: Lincoln-Grant Faculty, 1920s.
GRANTONIAN YEARBOOK, 1950, COURTESY OF WILLA HOFFMAN JACKSON.

Row one: *Catharine Williams (Webb), Clara McGhee, Eleanora W. Henderson, H. R. Merry (Principal), unidentified, Martha Bishop, unidentified.*

Row two: *Paul L. Redden, Mary E. Allen, Blanche I. Glenn, Alberta E. Booker, Lulu G. McLean, Eunice Simpson, Elizabeth W. Gooch, Etta L. Hundley.*

Row three: *unidentified, unidentified, Wilma Carneal (Porterfield), Nathan Fleming, William H. Craig, Jewell R. Jackson, Chester A. Rice, Roscoe C. Vaught, Leconia Franklin Crosby.*

Photograph 51: Lincoln-Grant Faculty, 1930s.
COURTESY OF THE KENTON COUNTY PUBLIC LIBRARY, COVINGTON, KENTUCKY.

Row one: *Catharine Williams (Webb), Clara McGhee, Eleanora W. Henderson, H. R. Merry (Principal), Minnie Mae Corbin, Martha Bishop, Annie M. Snowden (Jones).*

Row two: *William Hargraves, Mary E. Allen, Blanche I. Glenn, Alberta E. Booker, Lulu G. McLean, Elizabeth W. Gooch, Lulu Belle Smith, Paul L. Redden.*

Row three: *Wilma Carneal (Porterfield), Nathan Fleming, William H. Craig, Jewell R. Jackson, Roscoe C. Vaught, Eunice Simpson, Chester A. Rice, Etta L. Hundley, Leconia Franklin Crosby.*

Photo 52: An Early Picture of Some of the William Grant High School Class of 1929.
COURTESY OF THEODORE H. H. HARRIS.

Second row, far right *is John "Jack" Delaney, who became a local attorney and mortician.*

The William Grant High School
Class of 1929

Velma Marie Arvin
Robert Lee Ayres
Richard Bailey
John William Thomas Delaney Jr.
Robert Edward Dews
Russell Lamont Frierson
Geraldine Elizabeth Fox
Josephine Russell Garrett
Bradshaw Holloway
James Henry Johnson
Maria Antoinette Reed
Jessie May Louise Temple
Melvin Waddell Walker

■ MOVING UP TO THE EAST SIDE

The era of growth and development for Lincoln-Grant School had begun at a point when the city of Covington was in a period of what would be described as an economic "heyday." The glory days for the city of Covington "as the commercial center for all of Northern Kentucky [were] the first two decades of the twentieth century. During those decades, particularly the 1920s, the city's downtown was a bustling place of activity, with numerous restaurants, department stores, shops, saloons, banks, theaters, and offices bringing swarms of people to the downtown commercial district."[180]

In addition to the construction of downtown buildings such as the Masonic Lodge at the corner of Fourth and Scott Boulevard, and the Kentucky Times-Star Building in the 500 block of Scott, Covington had also become "the financial center of Northern Kentucky, housing the following lending institutions, primarily on Madison Avenue: the First National Bank, German National Bank, Covington Savings Bank & Trust, Citizens National Bank, and Peoples Savings Bank and Trust Company."[181] Among the major stores on Madison Avenue, close to Seventh Street were Montgomery Ward, Herzog's Jewelry, Louis Marx & Sons Furniture, and the Madison and Liberty theaters.

In the middle of all of that commercial activity, virtually next door to F. W. Woolworth, and immediately across the street from the south side of Coppin's Department Store sat what was to some a disconcerting phenomenon—a segregated, black school building in downtown Covington, located at 25 East Seventh Street, close to Madison Avenue. Although the black school building had been situated there since 1888, the downtown area had grown exponentially around it. By the 1920s, the black school enterprise had also expanded to the point that storefronts nearby on Scott Street were being annexed to accommodate black children.

Something had to be done about what at that time had become a mushrooming cultural and social dilemma—"swarms of [white] people" coming to the downtown commercial district, along with several hundred black children and their teachers, who came from the black residential areas of the city as well as other parts of Northern Kentucky, and moved around daily among different school buildings in that same downtown area. One can only imagine the sense of personal irritation that some white businessmen and office workers had about "that downtown situation." Indeed, some older white residents and downtown business owners would still remember the negative public situations at the school from the days of Samuel Singer in 1900 and William H. Fouse in 1913. But the Covington Board of Education and its new superintendent, Glenn O. Swing, were already "on board" with a plan.

The circumstances described above, and the influx of black students from

---

180. "Covington, Kentucky," *Trailsrus*.
181. Ibid.

other counties along with the steady population growth of the city of Covington would collectively support a mandate for a new school building for Lincoln-Grant School. On June 29, 1928, "The Chairman of the Committee on Buildings of the Covington Board of Education presented the following" [resolution]:

> In view of the plight of the school situation for the colored children of the city of Covington, the old Seventh Street School House being in the crowded business section of the city, the old frame structure on Scott Boulevard—a veritable fire-trap, and the Manual Training and Domestic Science sections being two blocks away from the rest of the school unit—and can only be reached by crossing an Arterial Highway and another thoroughfare in addition to Seventh Street, it is moved that the Attorney of the Board draw up a suitable document so that the Board of City Commissioners may place upon the ballot in November, the Question as to whether or not Bonds to the extent of $250,000 shall be voted upon by the voters—for the construction of a building suitable for school purposes for Colored Children and also for the acquisition of a suitable site.

That resolution, the language of which was obviously designed to represent an urgent set of circumstances, would initiate the new building project for Lincoln-Grant School. It also concurrently addressed the school location issue (i.e. in the downtown business area), the inadequacy of the facilities, and a more adequate funding formula for the proposed new school building. The board resolution was immediately approved and "referred to the Committee on Buildings, the Superintendent and the Business Director for further report."[182]

Mr. Merry's voice and personal presence would help sell the plan to both the black and white communities. Jim Reis reported that Principal Merry "told a gathering in 1928 that he had traveled to public black schools in Louisville, Lexington and Hopkinsville and all had better facilities than his school, which lacked an auditorium and gymnasium."[183] Mr. Merry's point of view on the lack of adequate facilities at Lincoln-Grant was confirmed in a *Kentucky Post* article.[184]

Such a project would provide a strategic advantage to the white Covington community by effectively containing black teachers and children in one building. It would also help to sustain the racial segregation of *all* white schools in Kenton, Boone, and Campbell counties. That would be a selling point that would convince the white community in Covington to support the bond issue necessary for the new building. A majority of Covington voters, black and white alike, would view this as a "win-win" situation. Black people would have

182. Minutes, Covington Board of Education, June 28, 1928.
183. Jim Reis, "Long road to new school," *Kentucky Post*, February 7, 2000.
184. *Kentucky Post*, "Seeks support for bonds; Covington Lags in School Facilities, Speaker [H. R. Merry] says," November 3, 1928.

a new school building that would, in diminished fashion, mirror the classic Holmes High School building for white students built years earlier at a similar cost, and white people would be assured of continued school segregation without feelings of guilt over inferior building arrangements for black students. And as in important by-product, this undertaking would also move a rambling, somewhat embarrassing, multi-building arrangement for the education of black youth *away* from downtown Covington in the main business district to the east side of town close to the Licking River, where most black people lived.

But let's be clear. White people did not simply foist the building project upon black people without the agreement and cooperation of the black community. Black people during that era were willing participants and indeed strong advocates in a plan that would allow them to get a new school building. All of this must be viewed within the context of the Jim Crow era in America, wherein both blacks and whites accepted the status quo of "separate but equal." Black people knew that we were not "allowed" to attend school with white people in Northern Kentucky in those days. Within that historical framework, blacks were extremely receptive to the idea of having a brand new, well-built, organized single school building with adequate books and equipment, as well as properly trained and certificated black teachers, instead of an aging school structure with annexed facilities on different streets in downtown Covington.

■ SITE SELECTION, FUNDING, AND OTHER ISSUES

The task of actually constructing the new school building would be daunting, and fraught with many ills. The social and political climate would become poisonous as various factions of the community competed for influence in the planning and development of the new Lincoln-Grant building. There would indeed be a "Long road to (a) new school," according to a local newspaper article bearing that title that was authored by Jim Reis. "Politics (and) squabbles delayed (the) construction of Lincoln-Grant," according to Reis. There was an ongoing debate over the site for the new building resulting in emotional, "packed" board meetings, which included representatives from "the Covington Negro Minister's Alliance, the William Grant Alumni Association, the Utopian club, and the East End Property Owners Development Association." While other sites had been considered and debated, all of the groups mentioned above "supported a site on Greenup Street."[185]

By 1929 the board had settled on the site at the corner of Ninth and Greenup streets "and the construction thereon of a building suitable to the needs of the colored school children of the City of Covington"[186] Reis reported further that "whether or not it was a coincidence, the night after the board announced its decision on the site someone set fires in both the old Lincoln-Grant School

185. Reis, "Long road to new school."
186. Minutes, Board of Education, 1929.

building on Seventh Street and at the black Ninth Street Baptist Church. The school, in particular, suffered damage to the two-story addition on the rear of the building. It is not clear if anyone was ever charged in the fires."[187] Although there is a black Ninth Street Baptist Church close to where the new school was to be located, a *Kentucky Post* article dated June 3, 1929, identified the church as the "First Baptist Colored Church," which is also located on Ninth Street near the site for the new school. The article, titled "Believes Fires of Incendiary Origin," also identifies a person accused of the acts of arson. Ultimately, that individual was not charged formally with the crime.

There were additional complications. When the board attempted to purchase the land for the building following a lot of division among board members about the overall cost of the land purchase, some people were unwilling to give up their property by selling it to the school system. The board then had to go through the "eminent domain" process of condemning certain properties in order to clear the site, while paying too much for a few properties (and probably not enough for others), in the opinions of some people. The lawsuits would also cause resentment among a few property owners who were forced out of their locations through court orders in order to accommodate the new building.

Next came funding issues. The $250,000 figure for the bond issue represented the identical amount budgeted for the construction of a white city school building years earlier. However, that amount would not fund the same quality of school building in 1930. The initial projected budget for the new Lincoln-Grant building as reflected in the minutes of the Covington Board of Education on April 16, 1930, page 185, had grown to the amounts indicated in figure 20. Although almost 70 percent of the electorate approved the bond issue in the amount of $250,000 on November 6, 1928, the Board of Education had anticipated additional funding in the amount of a little over $61,000 from the Julius Rosenwald Fund in Chicago. Rosenwald was a wealthy philanthropist from Illinois who was influenced by Booker T. Washington to build rural schools for black people in the south during the late eighteen hundreds and early nineteen hundreds. His fund supported "more than 300 rural school buildings in southern states."[188]

In view of Rosenwald's generosity toward black schools, Superintendent Glenn Swing and the Covington Board of Education thought that there might be a good chance that the Rosenwald Fund would support one-fifth of the total cost of the new Lincoln-Grant School building. Communication with the Rosenwald people would extend over several months. The Rosenwald Foundation initially had interest in assisting in the construction of the new building, even to the point of expressing a preference for a specific site for the building. The board minutes reflect that Superintendent Glenn Swing and the business director were authorized by the Covington Board of Education to go directly to

187. Reis, "Long road to new school."
188. *New Georgia Encyclopedia,* "Rosenwald Schools."

Chicago to consult with the Rosenwald people and negotiate funding for the Lincoln-Grant building project.

Figure 20: Initial Projected Cost of Lincoln-Grant Building Project, 1930

Cost of Project

Cost of Site for Building	$ 75,037.50	
Cost of Purchasing Site	1,401.45	
Cost of Building	273,300.00	
Cost of Equipment	33,874.00	
Total		383,612.95
Cost of Building	273,300.00	
Cost of Equipment	33,874.00	
Total Ex. of Site		307,174.00

Assets (projected)

Bond Issue	250,000.00	
Premium on Bonds	5,017.84	
Interest on Bank Deposits to March 31, 1930	11,080.95	
Value of Old School - Appraised	37,875.00	
Appropriation from General Budget	18,204.36	
Rosenwald aid 1.5 of cost of Bldg. and Equip	61,434.80	
Total		$383,612.95

Reis reports that construction of the building was expected to begin in 1930, "but spring and summer of 1930 passed with no action. This was due, in part to negotiations with the Rosenwald Foundation over how much it might fund."[189] In spite of all of the efforts cited above, there is doubt about whether or not the Rosenwald funding ultimately materialized. An article in the *Kentucky Post* dated January 5, 1931, indicated that the Rosenwald Foundation sent a letter to the board indicating that it was "not interested in the school because it had learned that it was a combination grade and high school instead of just a high school."[190] Dr. J. A. Averdick, who did not believe that to be the "real reason" for withdrawal of interest in the project, stated "that the board will endeavor to find out who threw the monkey wrench into the plans of the Foundation to help the Covington School."[191]

The article further explicates the issue as follows: "The old [school] board

189. Reis, "Long road to new school."
190. *Kentucky Post*, "Ask Aid of Foundation For School," January 5, 1931.
191. Ibid.

in planning for the school contemplated a donation of $60,000 from the [Rosenwald] Foundation, which is giving aid to Negro schools throughout the country, but something went amiss, and when plans had been prepared, providing for the elaborate school, the Covington board was left high and dry."[192] The article continues, "The effort to go thru with the plans without the Foundation support led to the controversy, which finally resulted in the unseating of two of the old board members." Infighting and rancor among the board members were so persistent that those two members were denied re-election because of vicious campaigns against them.

Apparently, the Rosenwald funding did not materialize, resulting in a less elaborate new building than originally planned. "The Rosenwald Fund began to shift its focus away from school construction in 1928, as it moved toward funding other projects in education, medicine, and race relations."[193] Upon Rosenwald's death in 1932, the Rural School Building Program closed. The failure to secure Rosenwald funding might have been aided and abetted by the indecision and confusion generated by members of the Covington Board of Education. The hostility and disagreement among individual board members had stymied the Lincoln-Grant building project for several months.

Progress on building the school had also been delayed due to several court actions, and court injunctions issued as a result of board actions. The original architect, who was denied the opportunity to complete his work, filed a lawsuit. There was then a change in contractors and architects, followed by new building plans and a reduced budget. Determined to live within the limits of the $250,000 bond issue, the new board planned to hire a new architect to scale back the elaborate plans for the building.

But the bidding process for a new architect had revealed a significant problem with the physical site at Ninth and Greenup. It was found that the land at the site was too soft to support such a massive structure, and piles had to be driven into the ground before a foundation could be erected to bear the weight of the building. Another *Kentucky Post* article dated January 5, 1931, stated, "a resolution authorizing the business agent of the board to contract for the taking of tests on the soil will reveal that there is considerable doubt as to the erection of the building on the site which has been selected [i.e. Ninth and Greenup streets]. It is said that it will be necessary to sink pilings around the entire school property in order to erect a modern building upon it. This fact, it is stated, was known to the old board, and tests should have been made before the site was selected. The new board is confronted with the necessity of using the site, which has been purchased for a sum of $76,000, and every effort will be made to save the money which has been expended for the Ninth and Greenup street site. In view of the situation which had developed the new board may find it necessary to dig into the school funds in order to build the foundation, as

192. Ibid.
193. *New Georgia Encyclopedia,* "Rosenwald Schools."

the $250,000 voted for the erection of the building [did] not contemplate an expensive pile-driving job to safeguard the foundation."[194]

In the middle of all of those events, the U.S. stock market crash of 1929 would cause the U.S. economy to plummet into the Great Depression. That event would wreak economic havoc throughout the nation, and Covington would not be immune from its effects. "The Great Depression of the 1930s devastated many Covington businesses and residents."[195] A one-term U.S. president, Herbert Clark Hoover, would preside over what some would characterize as the most devastating financial period in U.S. history.

The Lincoln-Grant building project also became muddled in financial and political difficulty during this period. There was considerable angst between some Board of Education members and certain community people over the building issues, and even allegations of impropriety on the part of some board members leading to a grand jury investigation. Tension between some members of the Covington Board of Education and at least one community member erupted publicly when one board member, Dr. J. A. Averdick requested that the personal statement shown in figure 21 be recorded permanently in the Board of Education minutes on February 6, 1931, (p. 267).

Figure 21: Open Letter to the Board from Dr. J. A. Averdick, February 6, 1931

Gentlemen of the Board of Education:
Covington, Kentucky

In arising to a question of personal privilege, I do so to ascertain of possible who is responsible for the members of this Board and past Boards being called before the Grand Jury. Can anyone in this Board enlighten us as to what does it mean?

Seemingly some contemptible low down is anxious to place this Board and past Boards in bad repute. As for myself, I want to pass back the lie contemplated, yet I desire to be charitable by saying I am satisfied as to who he is, and that I believe he is suffering from Hallucination; in fact, that his many past acts give me the privilege as a physician to say I have believed it for several years. As to the charges brought before the Grand Jury in speaking for myself, I plead not guilty and am satisfied the public believe me and feel assured that none of this Board or any of the past Boards accused by him are guilty, and in justice to all concerned ask this to find a page on the Minutes of our Board.

J. A. AVERDICK
Member of the Board.

The name of the individual and the specific charges alleged are not a part of the board minutes. But it seems clear that Dr. Averdick, a man of German-

194. *Kentucky Post*, "Architects To Bid On Plans For School," January 5, 1931.
195. "Covington, Kentucky," *Trailsrus*.

Irish descent with medical and law degrees, and a fiery temper, had been at odds with at least one prominent member of the black community for some time. That individual was probably Charles E. Jones, a local, black community activist who was a primary advocate for the new school.

Charles E. Jones was president of the local chapter of the National Association for the Advancement of Colored People (NAACP) and the owner of C. E. Jones Funeral Home in Covington. According to an article by Jim Reis, he was born in Covington around 1882 and "died in 1947 at the age of 65." [196] He fought vigorously for the new building, and probably angered a few community people in the process. In honor of his leadership, the auditorium in the new facility would later be named "The Jones Auditorium."[197]

The relationship between Jones and Averdick was clearly adversarial when it came to issues about the new Lincoln-Grant building. J. A. Averdick was listed as a member of the Covington Board of Education as early as 1899, when city wards determined board membership. Averdick was a member of the board during the controversies surrounding Principals Samuel Singer and William H. Fouse several decades before, and was thus a familiar figure on the board during "tough" times. Although Averdick was perhaps one of the most influential board members due to his longevity with the board, Charles E. Jones was equally vociferous in his fight for the new school, while declaring publicly that he was "tired of [Lincoln-Grant School] being a political football" during the planning and preconstruction phases of the project.[198] Ultimately there were no grand jury indictments issued against board members.

The funding and location issues would eventually be settled, but there would be additional confusion and anger over construction bids and the letting of contracts for the project architect and the builder. New members would be elected to the Board of Education.

In spite of widespread economic losses and financial chaos at the national level, the Lincoln-Grant project would eventually move forward in the middle of the Great Depression, even though some of the more elaborate options for the building were scaled back. In fact, that building project would become a major source of renewed financial energy for some white subcontractors and businessmen in Northern Kentucky during a period when the total U.S. economy was failing. Several people wanted a financial "piece of the pie."

Finally, with most of the disputes over land and money behind them, board officials, and hundreds of people would gather on Monday, May 4, 1931, for the official groundbreaking ceremonies for the new school building. Many people would be dressed in their Sunday best for the occasion, including suits and ties for the men, and fancy outfits and coats, and an array of stylish headpieces for the women. Black cars and limousines from the 1920s and '30s would line

196. Reis, "Long road to new school."
197. Ibid.
198. Ibid.

the perimeter on Ninth, Greenup, and Saratoga streets, around the proposed building site, and the more prominent guests would occupy a raised platform constructed on the site for the event. Several hundred people would all gather in one large, nonsegregated group on a clear day for this momentous occasion. And there would be an overwhelming number of people of color among them.

An article in the *Kentucky Post* dated May 4, 1931, reported that "O. A. Kratz, city manager; Mayor Thomas F. Donnelly; Glenn O. Swing, superintendent of schools, and Rev. F. C. Locust, Negro minister, were the principal speakers. . . . Among others present were the Negro citizens' committee, Edward C. Landberg, architect, and numerous city and county officials." The article further indicates, "The program opened with the singing of patriotic songs by a group of the children [from Lincoln-Grant School]. Bernard J. Kathman, president of the board of education, acted as master of ceremonies. The ground was broken by Edward [C. E.] Jones, undertaker and chairman of the citizens' committee. Enthusiasm ran high as the Negroes saw the school, a dream of many years, actually underway. The Negro children are housed at present in the old Seventh-st. school structure and several annexes. The new brick and concrete construction will include all the details necessary to modern education."[199] Pictures of the groundbreaking would also reflect the presence of Principal Henry R. Merry, Dr. James E. Randolph, and the teachers from Lincoln-Grant School.

The program format for the groundbreaking would undoubtedly call for greetings or remarks from representatives of select groups. There would also be prayers in behalf of the teachers that they should continue to instill knowledge and truth into their students, as well as prayers for the school board and the administration, that they should make wise decisions in behalf of their constituents, and prayers that the new building for Lincoln-Grant School would be a major success story in the black community for decades to come. And among those gathered for the ceremony, and in the community at large, there would be disquieting memories, private musings about what went wrong in terms of site selection, funding, and building contracts, the burning of the old school and First Baptist Church and the alleged untoward behavior of some board members. But abundantly there would be a sense of excitement and positive anticipation about the future of the new school. There would also be a collective sigh of relief about having gotten to the point of this groundbreaking after so many months, even years, of delays and frustrations—and a nationwide financial collapse.

The events surrounding the construction of a new Lincoln-Grant building so far had included the following:

1. Extensive School board and community debates over site selection involving "packed" board meetings and heated discussions.

199. *Kentucky Post*, "Ground Broken At School Site—City Officials at Lincoln-Grant Ceremonies," May 4, 1931.

2. Several court actions resulting in delays and alterations in the plans for the new building.
3. Significant turnover in Board of Education membership.
4. Strenuous debates and division among school board members over the selection of a project architect and a builder, leading to long delays and months of inactivity on the project, even after the bond issue had passed overwhelmingly almost three years earlier.
5. The convening of a grand jury to investigate possible misconduct on the part of some of the Board of Education members, although ultimately no one was formally charged with wrongdoing.
6. Attempts by at least one individual to burn down the old Lincoln-Grant building on Seventh Street, along with the First Baptist Church the day after the site for the new school was finally selected.
7. The destabilization of the total U.S. economy via the Great Depression.

So what else could possibly go wrong? Well, since the first brick had not yet been laid for the new structure, there would surely be more complications.

After the high-spirited day of the groundbreaking, there would be additional difficulties in terms of the actual construction process. Construction was also delayed by the necessity of building a concrete retaining wall around the sides and back part of the property to support the ground and contain the playground area, so that the land surrounding the building would not eventually erode and drift away toward Prospect Street. Excavation was also necessary to raise and cement the area containing the floor of the auditorium. Those extra necessities would cause the cost of the building project to escalate.

In addition, Dr. J. A. Averdick passed away on August 1, 1931, at the approximate age of seventy-six, and would not live to see the new Lincoln-Grant building completed. His unanticipated death would cause a pause in board activity, followed by an additional change in board membership.

■   THE NEW LINCOLN-GRANT SCHOOL BUILDING

But pursuant to all of the political wrangling and confusion, and the initial problems with the site, a massive, some would even say "beautiful" structure would gradually emerge. Even though the board had put the facility on a "fast track" to be completed before school started again in September, it would not be ready for occupancy until the following spring. As it materialized from the ground up, people from the community and school officials would monitor its progress, and eventually stand in awe of its majestic qualities and regal appearance. The new Lincoln-Grant building, which encompassed Ninth Street on the south side, Greenup Street on the west side, and Saratoga Street on the north side would finally stand stark, unadorned, and unfettered against a brazen, open sky in anticipation of its use for many decades to come.

In the spring of 1932, Bernard J. Kathman, then president of the Board of

Education would put a "nice coat of polish" on the entire situation by recording the following in his Board of Education report:

> The past year has seen the completion of the new Lincoln-Grant School on Greenup Street. This piece of construction was accomplished in record time, and was finished and occupied on March 21. The William Grant High School has been advanced from a class "B" to a class "A" school by the inspectors from the State Department of Education at Frankfort. This high rating was given not only upon the basis of the new building and equipment, but more especially upon the high qualifications of the faculty of the school.[200]

Black people in Northern Kentucky were undoubtedly quite excited and proud when the new Lincoln-Grant School building was finally opened. "Colored folks" were quite anxious to demonstrate their ability to educate their own children in a new building. Black people wanted to make Lincoln-Grant a shining example of a school that could provide excellent education for black children by black teachers and administrators, who would insist upon the proper resources and equipment for the new school.

Excitement would permeate the air in the spring of 1932 as Lincoln-Grant students, and teachers settled into the new facility on March 21. Principal Merry would be quite busy answering questions and giving directions about the proper placement of teachers, classrooms, students and instructional materials in the new building, as well as coordinating a schedule of important public figures for the upcoming dedication ceremonies. Ten days after the school was opened, the local newspaper published an article on the new building which stated, "Many prominent educators and citizens will participate in the two-day dedication services of the new Lincoln-Grant Negro School, Covington, to be held in the auditorium of the structure Thursday and Friday night." The article continued, "The building will be opened for public inspection Sunday from 3 to 5 and 7 to 9 p.m. Bernard J. Kathman, president of the Board of Education will act as chairman of the services Thursday night, which has been designated as 'Citizens Night' while Glenn O. Swing, superintendent of schools will preside at 'School Night' Friday.[201]

An elaborate dedication program ensued. The ceremonies were punctuated by greetings and "well wishes" from many local and nationally recognized dignitaries, including several presidents of historically black colleges, and representatives from the State Department of Education. Robert L. Yancey, the former Lincoln-Grant principal who preceded Henry R. Merry, was also on the program. His presence was significant in view of the fact that he had fought hard for a state of the art facility for the new school before he resigned in 1926. The main speaker at the event was Dr. John W. Davis, president of West Virginia State College. The article concludes, "The new school faces Greenup st.

---

200. Minutes, Covington Board of Education, Spring, 1932.
201. *Post,* "To Dedicate New School," March 31, 1932.

Between Ninth and Saratoga streets, and is a three-story modern fireproof structure. It contains approximately 45 rooms with a spacious auditorium, gymnasium and cafeteria. It has been completed at an approximate cost of $300,000 and was made possible by a bond issue of $250,000 approved by voters in 1928."[202]

The physical layout of the building seemed well planned. The new school was a well-constructed facility with green hedges and grass all around the front, and a playground enclosed by a tall, chain link fence in the back. The playground had a full-length, outdoor basketball court as well as a painted baseball area in the other section of the schoolyard. Internally, the structure had well-equipped classrooms, a modern cafeteria in the basement, and good gym and auditorium facilities.

The school building was arranged so that the classrooms for grades kindergarten through eight were located on the first and second floors in ascending order, while the classes for William Grant High School (grades nine through twelve) were conducted on the third floor. There were special provisions for a science laboratory on the third floor, as well as a room for a small in school library on another level. The school building had four side entrances, two on Ninth Street and the other two on Saratoga Street. Limited parking was available for the principal and teachers on the Saratoga side of the building near the boiler room and the classroom for the metal shop.

One could also access the building through the gym doors in the rear, which led to the playground, but students mainly used those doors during gym classes. And of course there was the main entrance in the middle of the front of the building on Greenup Street. That entrance was a pavilion-like area with several glass entry doors, and a large entrance hall that led directly to the main internal doors for the school auditorium. The principal's office was on the right side, as one entered the building. Primarily parents and visitors to the building used the main entrance. Students usually avoided that entrance during the normal school day, since it was close to the principal's office and had sort of an open, intimidating feel to it. Students were instructed to use the side entrances closest to their homerooms.

The black custodians at Lincoln-Grant were especially proud of the new school building. For several decades, Mr. Conway, the chief custodian and Mr. Sheffey, the assistant custodian (both of whose children attended Grant) would work tirelessly to keep the building sparkling and clean inside and out, with neatly trimmed hedges and excellent lawn care on the outside.[203]

---

202. Ibid. It is noted here that the article does not reference any funding from the Rosenwald Foundation, nor does the figure of "approximately $300,000" appear to reflect the addition of $60,000 from Rosenwald. It is probable that the additional money over and above the $250,000 bond money was taken from the Board's school fund.

203. Mr. Conway's son, Woodson Coleman Conway graduated from William Grant High School in 1935. He became a long-term music teacher at Taft Senior High School in Cincinnati, Ohio.

The transition for students and teachers would be a rather easy one, after leaving the multiple facilities in downtown Covington. Although the William Grant High School class of 1932 had begun its senior year on Seventh Street, it would proudly take its place in history as the first class to graduate from the new building. No longer would graduation exercises for the black high school be held in the Public Library Auditorium or the Odd Fellows Hall.

Two students who had completed their high school studies at Seventh Street building in February 1932 would join fourteen others for the June commencement. The sixteen graduates, who comprised the class of 1932, and the members of every William Grant High School graduating class thereafter, would proudly take their commencement walk down the aisle of the school's Jones Auditorium. The new building, as well as population growth in Northern Kentucky would seem to inspire larger graduating classes in the future.

With public attention focused on the shiny, new yellow brick building on Greenup Street, the Seventh Street Colored School building located at 25 East Seventh Street would be demolished without fanfare after it was vacated in the spring of 1932. In its place would eventually stand a brand new facility for the Covington Board of Education, which was completed in 1935. As time passed, many local black students who had never experienced the Seventh Street Colored School would not know of its history, or its existence. And most people would not realize that those who enter the doors of the Covington Board of Education on Seventh Street are actually walking on a significant part of Covington's history.

■ OLD WINE IN NEW BOTTLES

But even with all the bustling, excitement, and "ruffles and flourishes" over the new building on Greenup Street, had there really been substantive changes in the *curricular* offerings at Lincoln-Grant School? One of the assurances that had been provided by the Covington Board of Education was the promise of adequate teacher staffing and proper equipment for the new school building. On April 15, 1930, the board authorized Superintendent Glenn O. Swing to send a letter to the Rosenwald Fund, which included the following language: "The Board of Education authorizes me to certify that it will provide an adequate teaching staff, including Manual Training and the Household Arts Courses. This letter would seem to satisfy the Trustees and Offices of the Fund on the two points which you raise in your letter of March 16." Providing "an adequate teaching staff" did not necessarily mean expanding the core curriculum at Lincoln-Grant School. The statement of declaration to the Rosenwald people from Superintendent Swing also carried with it an implied admission that the current Lincoln-Grant staff was "inadequate."

In spite of the fact that the Rosenwald funds apparently failed to become a reality, there were obvious efforts to strengthen the teaching staff at the new

Lincoln-Grant School. New black teachers with proper certification had been brought in to complement the existing staff, and some extracurricular activities had been added. The new facilities were all under one roof, and the accreditation of the school had advanced from "B" to "A."

In his dedication speech entitled, "The New Lincoln-Grant—an Opportunity," Mr. Merry had spoken of new possibilities for the school in its new facilities. High praise from various dignitaries had been heaped upon the new facility, and many in the community were extremely pleased with the outcome. But while all of that seemed to bode well for public discourse and excitement about the new building, it appears that there were not significant substantive changes in the *core curricular* offerings of the school after it moved to Greenup Street. For instance, although white students had been learning to type and take shorthand in Covington's public schools since the early nineteen hundreds, not a single student typewriter (there was one for the black school secretary), or business and commercial course was introduced for black students at the new school in 1932. And although the woodworking program for black males would flourish in the new building, auto mechanics for boys at the school would remain as an elusive, theoretical exercise in futility. There would also be no courses in science beyond biology, chemistry and physics, or mathematics beyond Algebra I and II.

The domestic emphasis of the school would also continue, as Miss Mary E. Allen, one of the two initial graduates of William Grant High School in 1889, and a long-term teacher at the school, presented "to the school furniture to be used in a model flat in the school"[204] during the dedication ceremonies. That action harkened back to a 1914 recommendation of former Superintendent Homer Sluss for "a vital relation to a well-regulated home" in the black school's domestic science offerings. Sluss had emphasized that "If ['colored'] girls are to be adequately trained for such [domestic] responsibilities, they must have the practice as well as the theory. To accomplish this, it is important that a flat or house be provided, that will be a model in its arrangement, and in its appointments and furnishings."[205]

The Sluss recommendation would finally be fulfilled in the new school building, as the domestic emphasis for the school continued, while being guided by a philosophical underpinning from Superintendent Glenn O. Swing. Swing's philosophy for black students in Covington resonated with an overriding belief that "The students of Lincoln-Grant School are being trained to serve the citizens of the Commonwealth of Kentucky."[206] That philosophy would stand in stark contrast to the one for white students in Covington, who were clearly being educated to participate in "all walks of life" as they scattered to "various parts of the world."

---

204. *Post,* "To Dedicate New School," March 31, 1932.
205. Minutes, Covington Board of Education, March 9, 1914.
206. This quote is based on a conversation with Miss Sayde Bunyan, a former Lincoln-Grant School teacher, in September 2009.

What a nice facility—a shining, bright yellow brick building for black people in Northern Kentucky located at the corner of Ninth and Greenup streets, just at the northern edge of the black community, and only a few hundred feet away from the Licking River. Was it all really just "smoke and mirrors," or "old wine in new bottles?" Some would undoubtedly argue, "They (black people) just got a brand new school building—and a nice, modern one, at that. What more should they want?" And many in the community, black and white alike, would agree with that perspective in the spring of 1932.

The Lincoln-Grant building, along with other structures in the Greenup Street corridor, would be significantly breached by the overflowing waters of the Licking River five years later, during the infamous 1937 flood. The solidly built structure would survive not only that event, but also another, milder flood in the late forties or early fifties. Shortly thereafter floodwalls would be constructed. The Lincoln-Grant building constructed in 1931 and opened in 1932 would stand tall well into the next century.

As the 1940s approached, racial segregation in Kentucky's public schools would be as virulent as it had been in the late eighteen hundreds. The long arm of the 1896 *Plessy v. Ferguson* ruling would reach well into the twentieth century in a legal case in the Commonwealth of Kentucky, which occurred in 1943, almost fifty years after the *Plessy* ruling. That case demonstrated the long-term effects of the *Plessy* decision:

> Seven-year old Bruce Asher was the son of Boyd and Hattie Asher. His parents wanted him to attend the school for whites in Letcher County, KY. He looked to be what was considered a white child, but Roy Huffman, the school principal, refused to let Bruce attend the school because, according to Huffman, Bruce was colored. The Asher's sued Huffman, hoping that a mandatory injunction would allow Bruce to attend the school. It was determined by the Kentucky Court of Appeals that Bruce Asher was indeed a colored child because his maternal great-grandmother had been a Negro slave. The Kentucky Constitution, KRS 158,020 sec. 187, was used to require that separate schools be maintained for white children and Negro children (children wholly or in part of Negro blood or having any appreciable admixture thereof, regardless of whether they show the racial characteristics of the Negro). Judge Roy Helm of the lower court had ruled in favor of Huffman, and the Ashers appealed. The Appeals Court affirmed and adopted the lower court's decision, the injunction was refused, and Bruce Asher was not allowed to attend the school for white children.[207]

Although that case did not involve the Covington constituency, it would resonate throughout the state as another firm example of continued, absolute racial segregation in all public schools in the Commonwealth of Kentucky.

---

207. "*Asher v Huffman*" as cited in Notable Kentucky African Americans Database, 4.

Photo 53: Greenup Street before Housing Demolition for New School Building, 1929.
PHOTOGRAPHS COURTESY OF THE KENTON COUNTY PUBLIC LIBRARY, COVINGTON, KENTUCKY.

Photographs on this page show the Greenup Street site (c. 1929) before the houses were razed to construct the new Lincoln-Grant School building.

Photo 54: Additional Picture of Greenup Street Site, 1929.

Photograph 55: Greenup Street, 1929.
COURTESY OF THE KENTON COUNTY PUBLIC LIBRARY, COVINGTON, KENTUCKY.

Picture of the Greenup Street site (c. 1929) before the houses were razed to construct the new Lincoln-Grant School building.

Photograph 56: Gathering for Groundbreaking for New Building, May 4, 1931.
COURTESY OF THE KENTON COUNTY PUBLIC LIBRARY, COVINGTON, KENTUCKY.

Photograph 57: Gathering for Groundbreaking, May 4, 1931.
PHOTOGRAPH COURTESY OF THE KENTON COUNTY PUBLIC LIBRARY, COVINGTON, KENTUCKY.

Groundbreaking for the new Lincoln-Grant School building on Greenup Street in Covington, Kentucky, May 4, 1931.

Photograph 58: Gathering for Groundbreaking for New Building, May 4, 1931.
PHOTOGRAPH COURTESY OF THE KENTON COUNTY PUBLIC LIBRARY, COVINGTON, KENTUCKY..

Groundbreaking for the new Lincoln-Grant School building on Greenup Street in Covington, Kentucky.

Photo 59: Groundbreaking Ceremonies, New Lincoln-Grant Building, May 4, 1931.
COURTESY OF THEODORE H. H. HARRIS.

Photograph 60: New Lincoln-Grant building, Ninth and Greenup streets, Covington, Kentucky, 1932.
COURTESY OF THE KENTON COUNTY PUBLIC LIBRARY, COVINGTON, KENTUCKY.

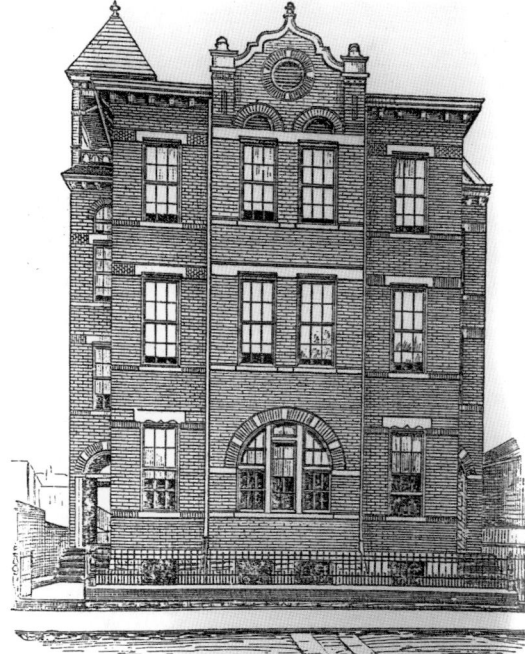

Photograph 61: (above): Board of Education Building (replacing the Seventh Street Colored School), 1940. PHOTOS COURTESY OF THE KENTON COUNTY PUBLIC LIBRARY, COVINGTON, KENTUCKY.

A new facility for the Covington Board of Education was completed in 1935 at 25 East Seventh Street, the previous location of Lincoln-Grant School. Above in the foreground is a 1940 representation of the Board of Education facility, shadowed by the demolished Seventh Street Colored School (old Lincoln-Grant School) building, which it replaced.

Photograph 62: Seventh Street Colored School, 1890 (comparative structure).
COURTESY OF THE KENTON COUNTY PUBLIC LIBRARY, COVINGTON, KENTUCKY.

Photograph 63: William Grant High School Class of 1932.
PHOTO PROVIDED BY THEODORE H. H. HARRIS, CLASS OF 1962.

The class of 1932 was the first class to graduate from the new Lincoln-Grant building on Greenup Street.

(Note: Graduates are not pictured above in the following order.)

February 1932

Madeleine Dilcia Frierson and Kathryn Louise Garrett.

June 1932

Lura Carnelia Baker, Anna Louise Butler, Nellie Lou Francis, Mae Margaret Frateman, Hazel Agnes Hamlin, Josephine Lavelle Harris, Marie Peggy Madison, Ella Marie Morton, Goldia Mae Elizabeth Moss, Melvenna Velma Paxton, Emma Elizabeth Sleet, William Wallace Edward Waugh, Samuel Reginald Webb, and Minnie Sheffield.

Bottom row: *Faculty, consisting of (l. to r.) William Hargraves (History) Eleanora Warren Henderson (Domestic Science), Roscoe C. Vaught (Latin), Henry R. Merry (Principal), Jewell R. Jackson (English), Elizabeth Gooch (Music).*

Second row from bottom: *(l. to r.) unidentified graduate, Leconia Franklin Crosby (Science), Chester Rice (Manual Training), and another unidentified graduate.*

SOURCE OF INFORMATION ON GRADUATES: MINUTES, BOARD OF EDUCATION, COVINGTON PUBLIC SCHOOLS, JUNE 24, 1932, 395.

Photograph 64: William Grant High School Class of 1933.
PHOTO PROVIDED BY THEODORE H. H. HARRIS, CLASS OF 1962.

Top row: *Alberta Henrietta Hawkins, Lillyan Hamilton, Commodore Russell Reid, William Lewis Jr. Jennie Belle Mitchell, Mary DuVal Burton.*

Second row: *Esther Lydia Harris, Ann Maie Helm, Elmer Downey Arvin, Bessie Maie Baker.*

Bottom row: *(Faculty) L. F. Crosby (Science), Mrs. J. R. Jackson (English), H. R. Merry (Principal), R. C. Vaught (Latin), William Hargraves (History).*

Photograph 65: William Grant High School Class of 1934.
PHOTO COURTESY OF THEODORE H. H. HARRIS, CLASS OF 1962.

Top row: *Alfred Alden Smith, William James Madison, Curtis Cortez Madison, Alfred Green Allen, Joseph Robert Howlett, Leconia Penn, Frederick Barbarossa Wiedmon, James Guthrie Butler.*

Second row from top: *Ramona Pinkins, Harriet Elizabeth Littleton, Ella Pollard Mitchell, Mattie Mae Baskin, Sarah Katheryn Johnsonne, Edythe Pearl Van Cleave, Vivian Jane Baker, Carrie Bernice Boyer.*

Third row from top: *Anna Frances Green, Kathryn Johnson.**

Not pictured, but listed in Board Minutes: *Robert Albert Frazier, Anna Pearl Ross (also listed with class of 1934 1/2), C, Mildred Yates.*

Bottom row: *(Faculty) William Hargraves, L. F. Crosby, R. C. Vaught, H. R. Merry (Principal), L. Spottswood, Mrs. J. R. Jackson.*

*Kathryn Johnson was not listed in Board Minutes with the class of 1934.

Photograph 66: William Grant High School Class of 1936.
PHOTO COURTESY OF AARON BALLARD, CLASS OF 1959.

Top row: *Rosetta Baker, Elizabeth Baker, Margaret Wilma Hendricks, Mary Beatrice Patterson, Melvena McCoy, Marie A. B. Jordan, Dorothy Thompson, Lucy Lee Hinton, Hattie Woodford Fortune.*

Second row from top: *Marguerite Louise Bunyan, Ruth Willis Hisle.*

Third row from top: *Lucille Robinson, William Assa Davis, Robert Conrad, Albert Brown Kilby, George Andrew Saunders, Andrew Leroy Hopkins, Earl Zinn Sleet, Neil Dunson, Nettie Ida Baskin.*

Bottom row: *(Graduates) Ernest Lee Miles, Woodrow Hinton, (Faculty) Mrs. J. R. Jackson (English), L. F. Crosby (Science), H. R. Merry (Principal), R. C. Vaught (Latin), William Hargraves (History), (Graduates) John Obie Tyler, Lawrence Reid Goggins.*

Photograph 67: William Grant High School Class of 1937.
Photo courtesy of Mrs. Eva Bunyan Clark, Class of 1937.

Top row: *Priscilla Fortune, Pearl Castleman, Glenna Sleet, Mattie Sleet, Sarah Harper, Eva Bunyan.*

Second row from top: *Mary M. Sweatt, Ottee Morton, Russell Conley, William Lewis, Ruth Harris.*

Third row from top: *William Williams, Benjamin Phelps.*

Bottom row: *(Faculty) L. F. Crosby, Mrs. J. R. Jackson, H. R. Merry (Principal), William Hargraves, R. C. Vaught.*

Photograph 68: William Grant High School Class of 1939.
PHOTOGRAPH PROVIDED BY RICHARD B. L. FOWLER, CLASS OF 1963.

Top row: *Frank William Payne, William Jackson Reed, William Frank Bannister, Henry Morris Higgins, William Bradley Merritt, John W. Brean, and Joshua Hinton.*

Second row from top: *Leara Hutchins, Alice Estella Sleet, Mary Whittaker, Armilda Booher, Alena Hughes, Gertrude Childs, and Clara Margaret Conway.*

Bottom row: *(Faculty) Mrs. J. R. Jackson (English), R. C. Vaught (Latin), H. R. Merry (Principal), William Hargraves (History), and L. F. Crosby (Science).*

Figure 22: Commencement Program, William Grant High School Class of 1939.

Fiftieth

Annual Commencement

of

William Grant High School

Jones Auditorium
Greenup Street at Ninth
Covington, Kentucky

PROGRAM

"Nymphs and Shepherds" . . . . Purcell
William Grant High School Glee Club

Invocation . . . . Reverend A. H. Tate

Music:
(a) "Ezekiel Saw De Wheel" . . . . . Arranged by Burleigh
(b) "Lo, a voice to heaven sounding" . . . . . Bortniansky
William Grant High School Glee Club

Address . . . . Reverend R. L. Bradby
Detroit, Michigan

Music:
(a) "Free As the Wind That Blows" . . . . . . Wilson
(b) "Kentucky Babe" . . . . Adam Geibel
Boys of the William Grant High School

Presentation of Classes . . . . Principal H. R. Merry

Presentation of Diplomas . . . . . Mr. Barnard J. Kathman
President, Board of Education

Music:
(a) "Neapolitan Nights" . . . . J. S. Zamecnik
(b) "Dark Eyes" . . . . Russian Folk-Song
Adapted and arranged by Riegger
William Grant High School Glee Club

Benediction . . . . Reverend A. H. Tate

Miss Elizabeth Gooch, Directress

GRADUATES
GENERAL COURSE

CLASS 1938½

William Frank Bannister
John W. Brean
Gertrude Childs
Leara Hutchins

CLASS OF 1939

Aratilda Boober
Clara Margaret Conway
Henry Morris Higgins
Joshua Hinton
Alena Hughes
William Bradley Merritt
Frank William Payne
William Jackson Reed
Alice Estella Sleet
Clarence Washington
Mary Whittaker

Wednesday Evening, June Fourteenth
Nineteen Hundred Thirty-Nine
Eight-thirty o'clock

Photograph 69: William Grant High School Class of 1940.
PHOTO PROVIDED BY RICHARD B. L. FOWLER, CLASS OF 1963.

Top row: *Edora Wallace Page, Ethel Lee Morris, Martha Spears (missing picture), Ida Kathryn Murphy, Sarah Elizabeth Ware.*

Second row: *Georgene Sweatt, John Earl Fisher, John W. Hisle Jr., Orval Lee Johnson, Mary Magdalena Sleet.*

Not shown: *Effinger Gaines, class of 1939 1/2.*

Bottom row: *(Faculty) R. C. Vaught, Mrs. J. R. Jackson, H. R. Merry (Principal), L. F. Crosby, William Hargraves.*

Photograph 70: William Grant High School Class of 1941.
PHOTO PROVIDED BY RICHARD B. L. FOWLER, CLASS OF 1963.

Top row: *Marvin Sanders McEntie, Robert Matthew Sleet, Samuel James Whatley, William Dawson Frye, Robert Painter Littleton, John Dockett Slaughter, George Walter Bunyan Jr.*

Second row: *Clarice Lee McEntie, Rosa Katherine Davis, Lucenia Ruth Hutsell, Gloria Jacqueline Johnson, Alberta Watkins Snowden, Alice Lynch Malone, Pauline Smith, Mary Louise Brown.*

Not pictured: *Lillie Mae Roundtree (1940 1/2), Russell Grant Banks.*

Bottom row: *(Faculty) l. to r. William Hargraves (History), Roscoe C. Vaught (Latin), Henry R. Merry (Principal), Jewell R. Jackson (English), William N. Jackson (Science).*

Photograph 71: William Grant High School Class of 1942.
PHOTO PROVIDED BY RICHARD B. L. FOWLER, CLASS OF 1963.

Top row: *Clarence William Baker, Amos Bothwell, John Thomas Hutsell, Anderson Louis Baughman, Hilliard Baskin, Arthur Arvin Sheffield.*

Second row: *John Marshall Payne, Annie Lue Hardin, Frances Aurelia Johnson, Vernon Tone Brown.*

Bottom row: *Thelma Mae Bufford, Geraldine Conway(?), Etta Mae Fishback, Alice Adeline Black, Everett Finnell, Geneva Sechrest, Lucille Hughes, Mary Gredderdine Davis.*

Not pictured: *Vernell Leroy Puckett (faculty not shown due to angle of photograph).*

Photograph 72: William Grant High School Class of 1943.
COURTESY OF THEODORE H. H. HARRIS, CLASS OF 1962.

The combined classes of 1942 1/2 and 1943 comprised the largest graduating class in the history of William Grant High School (32 graduates).

Bottom row: *Faculty, l. to r. William N. Jackson (Science), Unidentified faculty member, William Hargraves, (History), Henry R. Merry (Principal), Jewell R. Jackson (English), Roscoe C. Vaught (Math).*

Figure 23: List of Graduates, 1942 1/2 and 1943[a]

1942 1/2

David Zellars Brean
Rowena Mentlo Doyle
Walter Gilliard
Frank Hall
Ada Mae Trequela Harris
Dorothy Chase Hisle
Charles Andrew James
Winnefred Rebecca Lattimore
Christine Lindley
Charlotte Elizabeth Reed
Marjorie Katherine Simpson
James Edward Talley
Lida Belle Waters
Ruth Laverne Williams

a. Source of names of graduates: *Minutes, Board of Education, Covington, Kentucky, June 1943*, 199.

1943

Katie Lee Baughman
Eugene Clarke
Dorothy Rochelle Clinkenbeard
Richard Henry Collins
Thurston Thomas Grant
Rosa Lena Jamar
Florence Emma Johnson
Jasa France Parrish
Sarah Elizabeth Riley
Martha Louise Robinson
Inez Louise Roundtree
Sigsbee Louis Wilson Sheffey, Jr.
Anna Mae Sleet
Emma Addlene Sleet
Ella Pearl Stewart
Ruth Waveline Watkins
Forest Wells
Mae Louise White

Photography 73: William Grant High School Class of 1944.
PHOTO COURTESY OF THEODORE H. H. HARRIS, CLASS OF 1962.

Photograph 74: William Grant High School Class of 1945.
COURTESY OF THE KENTON COUNTY PUBLIC LIBRARY, COVINGTON, KENTUCKY.

Top row: *Julia Ann Shauntee, Mary Adeline Summers, Mary Alyce Martin, Marjorie Marie Flagler, Marion Elizabeth Harris.*

Second row from top: *Gladys Geneva Watkins, Viola Louise Gilliard, Marian Arletta Rhodes, Emily Elizabeth Brean, Alice Elizabeth Herndon, Lillian Mildred Jarman.*

Third row from top: *Ruth Ann Wilson, Virginia Lee Sheffey, Matthew Turner Garrett, William McClellan Jr., Sadye Irene Bunyan, Mary Elizabeth Williams.*

Fourth row from top: *Harold Fraker, Lorenzo Foster Jr., Charles William Stewart, William Glenn, William Robert Litmon, Charles D. Houston Jr.*

Bottom row: *(Faculty) l. to r. Henry R. Merry (Principal), Roscoe C. Vaught (Math, Birtill T. Barrow, William N. Jackson (Science), William Hargraves, (History), Jewell R. Jackson (English).*

Photograph 75: William Grant High School Class of 1946.
Courtesy of the Kenton County Public Library, Covington, Kentucky.

Top row: *Lorene Baskin, Lillian Louise Littleton, Dorothy Beatrice Johnson, James Henry Johnson Jr., Myrtle Olivia Harper, John Wilbur Doddy, Mary Frances Jones, Edna Earl Alexander, Harry Lee Lindley.*

Second row from top: *Ivery Lee Whatley, Naomi Elizabeth Green, Harry Franklin Riley, Imogene Allen.*

Third row from top: *Marian Lewis Clinkenbeard, Julius Conway Jr., Mr. H. R. Merry (Principal), Mrs. J. R. Jackson (English), Madeline Bernice Jarman, Walter Hadley Hutchins.*

Fourth row from top: *Charles Richard Conrad, Doris Mae Dale, Edward Alfred Riley, Marion Louise Talley.*

Bottom row: *Josephine Helen Perry, Chester Arthur Cowan Jr., Mr. R. C. Vaught (Math & Latin), Mr. William Hargraves (Social Studies), Mr. W. N. Jackson (Science), Mr. Birtill T. Barrow (Science), Mary Adelaide Spears, Rosetta Greene.*

Photograph 76: William Grant High School Class of 1948.
PHOTO COURTESY OF THEODORE H. H. HARRIS, CLASS OF 1962.

Top row: *Lucille Leachman, Arnold Spencer Gray, Thelma Russell, William Prentice McCullough, Norma Jean Dowell.*

Second row from top: *James Webb Jr., Sarah Helen Bradford, Charles Edward Harper, Betty Sue French, Alexander Green.*

Third row from top: *Mary Etta Shauntee, Theodore English, Margaret Lucinda Hutchins, Abraham Winston Johnson, Lucille Elizabeth Kenny.*

Fourth row from top: *R. C. Vaught (Math and Latin), Mary Jane Williams, Arcenia Bell Harris, W. N. Jackson (Science).*

Bottom row: *B. T. Barrow (Science), W. H. Hargraves (Social Science), H. R. Merry (Principal), Mrs. J. R. Jackson (English), Lee H. Pennington (Math and Science).*

GRADUATES

ROBERT BAKER	GLADYS BEHANAN	CHESTER DANDRIDGE
" Character is built on the debris of despair."	" Wise use of time will make for wise living."	" A penny saved is a penny earned."
Band Orchestra Baker's Bop Trio	Choir Glee Club	Varsity Basketball

FRANK DEAL	MILLARD GARRETT	JUANITA PEARL GRIFFIN
" The eyes of women are the eyes that ruin us."	" Where ignorance is bliss 'tis folly to be wise."	" Stand for the right if you stand alone."
Band Orchestra Grant Hi - Y Baker's Bop Trio Varsity Basketball	Choir Cheerleader Hi - Y Vice-President Glee Club	President Y - Teens Glee Club Choir

To have what we want is riches; but to
be able to do without is power. --George MacDonald.

Photograph 77a: William Grant High School Class of 1950.
GRANTONIAN YEARBOOK, 1950.

Top row: *Robert Lee Baker, Gladys Winifred Behanan, William Chester Dandridge.*
Second row: *Frank Louis Deal, William Millard Garrett, Juanita Pearl Griffin.*

Photograph 77b: William Grant High School Class of 1950.
GRANTONIAN YEARBOOK, 1950.

Top row: *Ernestine Hall, William Frederick Hargraves, II—93.7, Co-Valedictorian, Nettie Frances Humphries.*

Second row: *Granville Robert Ingguls, Collins Jackson Jr., Richard Douglas Jarman.*

HELEN JOHNSON

" He that loveth himself
knows no rival."

Y - Teen Treasurer
Choir
Glee Club

BETTY JEAN JONES

" The only way to multiply
happiness is to divide it."

Senior Class President
Student Council President
Choir
Glee Club
Y - Teens

CLIFFORD KENNY

" Though the way is
rugged thou must keep
trying."

Band
Orchestra
Grant Hi - Y

BETTYE JEAN MILLS

" I have made the begin-
ning not the end."

Senior Class Secretary
Y - Teen Assist. Sec.
Student Council
Choir
Glee Club

CLARENCE MORRIS
Salutatorian

" The beat of the heart
chooses its own time."

Senior Class Vice-Pres.
Grant Hi - Y
Junior Varsity Basketball

NORMAN REID

" Beauty is truth,
true beauty that
is all!"

Student Council
Varsity Basketball

Of all the lights you carry in your face,

joy shines farthest out to sea.

Photograph 77c: William Grant High School Class of 1950.
GRANTONIAN YEARBOOK, 1950.

Top row: *Helen Louise Johnson, Betty Jean Jones, Clifford Kenny.*

Second row: *Bettye Jean Mills, Clarence Morris Jr., Norman Patterson Reid.*

ROBERT RHODES
Valedictorian

"When in doubt whether
to kiss a girl goodnight
always give the girl the
benefit of the doubt."

Grant Hi - Y Treasurer
Choir - Glee Club
Student Council
Varsity Basketball

KATHERINE ROBINSON

" Giving is more than
getting."

Choir
Glee Club

MARY ELAINE WEBB

" The best today must be
improved for tomorrow."

Choir
Glee Club
Y - Teens

MARY MARGARET WEBB

" Experience keeps a dear
school, but fools will
learn in no other."

Choir
Glee Club
Y - Teens

PEGGY LEE WILLIAMS

" Have love above everything."

Glee Club
Choir
Y - Teens
Cheerleader

Reputation is what men and women think of us;

Character is what God and the angels know of us.

--Thomas Paine.

Photograph 77d: William Grant High School Class of 1950.
GRANTONIAN YEARBOOK, 1950.

Top row: *Robert Norman Rhodes—93.7, Co-Valedictorian, Kathryn Hood Robinson, Mary Margaret Webb.*

Second row: *Mary Elaine Webb, Peggy Lee Williams.*

Photograph 78: William Grant High School Class of 1951.
PHOTO PROVIDED BY RICHARD B. L. FOWLER, CLASS OF 1963.

Top row: *Ida May Washington, Edward Jerome Cunningham, Sarah Alice Weaver, Mary Elizabeth Hall, Robert Connelly Jackson, James Slaughter Jr.*
Second row from top: *Van Roy Clemons Jr., Robert Franklin Kelly, Gloria Ann Adams, Dorothy Benetta Humphrey, Carita Jean Sharpe, James Arthur Riley, Alfred Crawford.*
Third row from top: *William James Smith, David Lee Redden, Ezelle Lavonne Lee, Margie Lou Payne, Sylvia Marie Johnson, Devolzia Williams, George Andrew Patterson.* **Not pictured:** *Donald George, Bernice Lee.*
Bottom row: *(Faculty) William Hargraves, Roscoe C. Vaught, H. R. Merry (Principal), Mrs. Jewell R. Jackson, Birtill T. Barrow, William N. Jackson.*

Photograph 79: William Grant High School Class of 1953.
PHOTO COURTESY OF VANDA LOVELACE LANGHAM, CLASS OF 1953.

Top row: *Sue Belle Cavil, George Walter Harrison, Vanda Lovelace, Raymond Louis Clifford, Addie Mae Behanan.*

Second row from top: *Mattie Lee Royal, Eddie James Thompson, Juanita Dunson, John Weaver, Virginia Mae Rice.*

Third row from top: *Lueaver Jasper, William Herbert Riley, Marie Annette Slaughter, James Douglas Watkins, Ann Louise Turner.*

Bottom row: *(Faculty) William N. Jackson (Mathematics), Roscoe C. Vaught (Math & English), Jewell R. Jackson (English), Henry R. Merry (Principal), William Hargraves (Social Science), B. T. Barrow (Science).*

Photograph 80: Mr. William N. Jackson, Science Teacher,
1940s and '50s.
PHOTO FROM GRANT REUNION PROGRAM, 1979.

Photograph 81: Roebling Suspension Bridge to Covington, 1950s.
COURTESY OF THE KENTON COUNTY PUBLIC LIBRARY, COVINGTON, KENTUCKY.

Photograph 82: Downtown Covington, Madison Avenue, 1940s.
COURTESY OF THE KENTON COUNTY PUBLIC LIBRARY, COVINGTON, KENTUCKY.

Racial segregation was quite evident in downtown Covington during that period.

Photograph 83: Jacob Price Homes.
THE KENTON COUNTY PUBLIC LIBRARY, COVINGTON, KENTUCKY.

Many students who attended Lincoln-Grant School lived in the Jacob Price Homes in Covington. Situated three blocks from the school building, they were built in 1939 and dedicated to Rev. Jacob Price, an early black pioneer for Lincoln-Grant School.

Photograph 84: Walton Family Home, Tenth Street.
AUTHOR'S PERSONAL PHOTOGRAPH, 1950S.

Author's childhood home on Tenth Street in Covington, located one block from Lincoln-Grant School.

Photograph 85: Utopian Club, the Manse Hotel, Cincinnati, Ohio, 1950s.
Photo provided by Theodore H. H. Harris, Class of 1962.

Professional black educators and business owners developed a sense of identity and cohesion with each other through membership in the Utopian Club.

Above: *The Utopian Club gathers for a function at the Manse Hotel Ballroom in Cincinnati during the early 1950s.*

Attendees from far left rear: *Mr. Samuel Gaines, Ms. Lauraida Fitch, unidentified, unidentified, Mrs. William N. Jackson, Mr. William N. Jackson, unidentified (possibly Mrs. B. T. Barrow), Mr. Birtill T. Barrow, Mrs. W. H. Craig, Mr. W. H. Craig, unidentified, unidentified, Mrs. Annie Hargraves, Mr. William Hargraves.*

At head of table, l. to r.: *Mr. J. Conway, Mrs. Conway, Mr. Chester Rice, Mrs. Rice, Mr. Jay Hood (son of Annie Price Hood and grandson of Rev. Jacob Price), Mrs. Camille Hood, Mr. Horace Sudduth (hotel owner), Mrs. Sudduth.*

Right side of table, front to rear: *Mrs. H. R. Merry, Principal H. R. Merry, unidentified, unidentified, unidentified, Mr. Boone, Mrs. Elizabeth Merry Boone, Mr. Robert Crowder, Mrs. Mathe Crowder, Mr. Walter Gilliard, Mrs. Sara Fitch Gilliard, Mrs. Alice Martin, Dr. James Randolph.*

Photograph 86: Gene-Bess Grocery Store, Robbins Street, Covington, October 1933.
COURTESY OF THE KENTON COUNTY PUBLIC LIBRARY, COVINGTON, KENTUCKY.

Interior of black-owned Lacey's "Gene-Bess" Grocery Store on Robbins Street, October 1933.

Photograph 87: Dr. James E. Randolph, Family and School Physician.
COURTESY OF THE KENTON COUNTY PUBLIC LIBRARY, COVINGTON, KENTUCKY.

Dr. James Randolph was a family and school physician in Covington for decades.

CHAPTER 7

A Student's Perspective

■ THE GATEWAY TO THE SOUTH

By 1932, when Lincoln-Grant School relocated to Greenup Street, black and white people in Covington had developed many layers of racially segregated practices through decades of social experience. Routine social habits between the races had become so well ingrained that people from both races behaved automatically within their expected racial roles. While there were no signs in public places designating racial separation, such as Colored Drinking Fountain versus White Drinking Fountain, or Colored Waiting Room versus White Waiting Room, like those that existed in the deep south, there was unspoken racial discrimination in most public places. Although blatant, "in your face" personal racial animosity was not the norm, black and white people usually separated themselves from each other in most social situations.

During that period, there was a large, prominent sign on the Cincinnati side of the Suspension Bridge as one crossed the "Mason Dixon Line" going across the Ohio River into Covington, which proudly read, **Welcome to Kentucky, The Gateway to the South**. To add emphasis to its southern orientation, one primary thoroughfare that led from Covington to Fort Mitchell, Erlanger, and Florence was named Dixie Highway.

My family moved to Covington in the 1940s. I would barely remember the Deep South where I was born, and would only recall it through occasional summer vacations to visit relatives who still lived in South Carolina. My childhood memories would actually begin in Covington with a house on Johnson Street, followed by our long-term, small single-family home on Tenth Street, located one block from Lincoln-Grant School, where I would start kindergarten the year after we moved to Covington.

Our "way of life" as I grew up in Covington was centered on racial segregation. In the black areas of town, everybody knew everybody else and their families. There were many people in the black community who were cousins, aunts and uncles to each other. Some families had large numbers of children, and at Lincoln-Grant School, for instance it was not uncommon to have siblings and cousins who were scattered throughout several grade levels from elementary through high school. There were many traditional family constellations with fathers, mothers, and children, as well as others, where single parents raised their children. In some cases, aunts, and uncles raised the children of sisters and brothers, and occasionally, grandparents took care of their grandchildren in the absence of the parents. Though rare, there were also some foster care situations.

Some black families lived in "the projects," while other families owned small, modest homes within a few blocks of each other. There were also isolated pockets of black families in other parts of the city. Sometimes only a street or an intersection separated black and white neighborhoods. In certain areas, such as Russell Street, Johnson Street, or West Tenth Street, one or two blocks of "colored owned" homes might sit in the middle of an otherwise "white" neighborhood.

The city appeared to have a "schizophrenic" approach to people of color. While there was clear, definable segregation in this town of some forty to sixty thousand people, there was almost no overt racial animosity. There was an odd sense of "apartheid." The "approach-avoidance" attitudes of whites and blacks in Covington seemed to emerge with its ambiguous racial history. A conflicted approach to people of color resulted in various social inconsistencies between the races during the author's youthful experiences. The schools and residential neighborhoods were segregated by race, and while the several thousand black people who lived in Covington never went near the white schools, if black people ventured into a white neighborhood to do work for someone, or passed through a white area while going downtown, there was no ostensible racial conflict.

One white-owned, mom-and-pop grocery store operated exclusively in the black community at the corner of Tenth and Greenup for many years with cordiality and respect for its black customers from the husband and wife who owned it. And in some other venues, such as a local hardware store on Eleventh Street, there were genuinely casual and friendly relationships between some white and black adults. In the 1950s, two different white medical doctors would set up family practices that served black and white patients without regard to race on Scott Street.

In addition, the Covington Public Library, which had been racially integrated since 1901, was open to all people regardless of race, color, or creed. Thankfully, racial segregation had not deliberately invaded that facility in Covington, as it had in "separate but equal" public libraries in most other parts of

Kentucky, and in the South in general. I was an avid reader while growing up, and felt extremely privileged to be able to go into the public library on Scott Street and check out any book that I wanted. Reading about far away places and other ways of life would open a totally new world in my imagination from the one that existed in Covington. The white, female librarians were always friendly, smiling, encouraging, and genuinely helpful in our book selections in the children's area. We were even encouraged by them to sit at the library tables and peruse various books before checking them out, if we wished to do so. White children also came into the library sporadically, and while we did not mix with them, there was no racial animosity.

On the other hand, the personnel at the two movie theaters in downtown Covington, the Madison and the Liberty, actively and aggressively pursued racial discrimination against black people. The Liberty Theater was completely off limits to black people, as dictated by a racially intolerant owner with a Gov. George Wallace approach to the matter, while the segregated Madison Theater had about a dozen seats reserved off to the side with a poor view of the screen for people of color. Those "reserved" seats were almost never used, since most black people chose to go to Cincinnati, where we could sit wherever we wanted in a movie theater. But at some point in the 1950s the word spread in the black community that a new drive-in movie theater on the outskirts of town was accepting, even encouraging black people to patronize that facility. The younger, white owners had apparently voluntarily opened that drive-in movie to black people without having been coerced to do so.

Restaurants such as White Castle, Frisch's Big Boy, and the cafeteria in the basement of F. W. Woolworth's Five and Dime Store were carryout only for black people until those businesses were subjected to the sit-ins and demonstrations of the 1960s. Public accommodations such as buses and drinking fountains were never officially segregated, but there was a conscious avoidance of interracial interaction during the use of those services. Somehow, I can never remember using a public restroom in Northern Kentucky as a young person other than those at our black churches, at Lincoln-Grant School, and possibly the public library.

■ RIDING THE BUS

In many instances, the invisible wall between the races remained distinct and rigid, even sometimes to the point of absurdity. While seating on public transportation was random (probably because the Covington bus line ended in Cincinnati) most white people, white women in particular, would choose to stand right over a seated black person, while clutching the overhead support bars and struggling with their packages, as the bus moved in different directions, rather than occupy a vacant seat next to that individual. Some whites would either wait until another white person vacated a seat, or stand in the aisle defiantly from Cincinnati all the way to the end of the bus line in Covington if necessary, to steer clear of sitting next to a black person on the bus.

Black people would consciously seek unoccupied seats where no white person was sitting, but not necessarily at the back of the bus. Blacks would sit near the front of the bus if no white person were there, and whites would even sit near the back of the bus, if no black person were back there. But we all had to stand in close proximity to each other while waiting at the bus stop, and boarding the bus. Retrospectively, the bus situation between Covington and Cincinnati at that time was a foolish game of racial "musical chairs" driven by a convoluted personal interpretation of Kentucky's laws of segregation by those who rode the bus. Of course, when we rode the buses in Cincinnati, it didn't matter where people sat.

■   JIMMY AND CHARLIE

A six-foot, chain-link fence surrounded the Lincoln-Grant playground almost completely, except for two entry points close to the rear of the school building. That arrangement seemed designed to contain us during school hours, since we were not permitted to leave the grounds during the lunch hour. The baseball area on the south side of the playground, and a full basketball court on the north side were thoroughly used for after-school pick up games. Baseball and basketball games with a "full court press" often took place simultaneously, with all of the aggression, noise, and enthusiasm of "street ball." The play-ground normally was dominated for a couple of hours after school by the more skilled athletes from Lincoln-Grant School—those who had "made the team"—while a few of us with less athletic skill, simply looked on, and waited for the "tough guys" to wear themselves out. After the games were finished, and guys began to retreat to their homes to get ready for dinner, about five or six of us who had been sitting on the sidelines, would take to the court to test our considerably less viable, shoot-around basketball skills for a little while, before we also went home.

While all of this was taking place we would often notice two white guys around our ages, whom we would come to know as "Jimmy and Charlie," standing on the other side of the fence in their backyard, and peering through the chain links at the entire performance, while sometimes stopping their external observation to bounce a basketball vigorously on the ground. They lived in a two-family house directly adjacent to our schoolyard, separated from the school property by the six-foot chain link fence. Jimmy and Charlie also watched the more skilled guys perform, and noted when they left the playground. I suspect that, since Jimmy and Charlie actually lived closer to our schoolyard than most of us did, they would sometimes sneak around the fence and use our basketball court after we had all gone home.

But one day, after the skilled guys left the playground and two or three of us had taken over the basketball court, Jimmy and Charlie ventured slowly up Saratoga Street, while casually bouncing their basketball. The distance from their house to the end of the side of the chain link fence on Saratoga Street where one could enter our school playground was about a fifty feet. As they walked on the sidewalk, outside of the chain-link fence past the area where we were playing, still bouncing their basketball, we assumed that they were on their way to the corner grocery store, where Jimmy's mom worked, or somewhere else to play ball. But suddenly, they angled their way around the six-foot, chainlink fence at the open end, and entered our basketball area, while we were still shooting hoops at one end of the court. We wondered momentarily if they were trying to "start something" of a racial nature by walking onto our playground while we were there. Initially, they walked past us inside the Lincoln-Grant playground, while saying nothing, and started shooting their basketball into the basket at the other end of the court, which we were not using. We kept playing ball at our end of the court, as we glanced suspiciously at the two of them, and they glanced back at us for our reaction.

I am not sure how the ice was eventually broken. I think their basketball may have gone out of bounds at some point, and bounced into our area, while forcing us to interact temporarily. At that point, Jimmy and Charlie picked up their ball and started shooting it into our basket. Our reaction was to continue our game, and let them join us. After that incident, we started playing pick-up basketball with Jimmy and Charlie on a routine basis. They would never try to participate with the large group of more skilled athletes at Lincoln-Grant, but would always wait outside of the fence in their yard until the larger group of guys went home. Then they would come around the fence and "integrate" our small group.

We would learn that Jimmy and Charlie were cousins, although we only knew each other by first names. We did not go to each other's homes, or socialize outside of the basketball court, other than occasionally running up to the corner store on Eighth Street where Jimmy's mom worked, to get a bottle of pop and some chips together. Jimmy's mom would greet us as we came into the store together, and did not seem to object to her son and nephew hanging around with "colored kids." As we left the store to continue our game, she would usually say something personal and "mom-like" to Jimmy and Charlie, such as, "Be sure to be home in time for supper," thereby giving tacit approval to the situation on a limited basis.

What Jimmy, Charlie, and the rest of us did not know was that they were actually in violation of certain laws of the Commonwealth of Kentucky, which prohibited Jimmy and Charlie legally from entering our playground. We didn't know about those laws, which didn't seem to matter at that point. We just played basketball. But during the regular school day, Superintendent Swing and the laws of the Commonwealth of Kentucky ensured that Jimmy and Charlie went to their all-white school on the other side of town, while we attended Lincoln-Grant.

■ STRENGTHENING THE CURRICULUM

A comparison of the high school curriculum initiated by Principal Samuel Singer in 1886, and the 1957 high school curriculum is shown in figure 24:

Figure 24: Comparative William Grant High School Curriculum, 1886 and 1957.

1886	1957
Four units of English.	*English I, English II, English III (American Literature), English IV (English Literature)—one year of each.*
Two units of Latin.	*Foreign Language elective: Spanish I and Spanish II —each offered for 1 year, alternate years.*
Two and one-half units of Science.	*Two years of Science: Biology, Chemistry and/or Physics.*
Three and one-half units of History and Civics.	*Three years of Social Studies: American History; Economics; Vocation (1/2 year); Health (1/2 year).*
Two units of Mathematics.	*Math I (general); Math II (Algebra)—1 year each.*
Two units of either Domestic Science (Cooking) or [domestic] art (Sewing) for girls or Mechanical Drawing and Cabinet Work for boys, respectively.[a]	*Elective Subjects:* *Metal Work and Woodwork (boys)* *Cooking and Sewing (girls)* *Vocal Music* *Instrumental Music* *Typewriting I* *Typewriting II*
	Extra-curricular activities (after school; no academic credit): Student Council, Boy's Basketball, Cheerleading, Y-Teens, Hi-Y Club, Dance Club, and Jazz Combo, Drum Majorettes, and Drum Major.

a. Singer in Crosby, "A Study of Pupil Marks."

Although there were some changes, particularly in extra-curricular activities and elective subjects, certain gaps in the curriculum at Lincoln-Grant

School continued. In the fall of 1956, two years after the U.S. Supreme Court declared segregated public schools unconstitutional, and eight years before the high school would be closed permanently, sixteen typewriters arrived at William Grant High School to be made available to seniors only. And even then, all that was offered initially was the opportunity for seniors at William Grant to learn to type. There was no shorthand, or other business courses.

Study in the area of vocational education would involve a one-semester course that used another textbook entitled *I Find My Vocation* without any actual orientation or training for a post-secondary career. Initially taught by the school principal, the latter course was introduced at Grant sometime in the mid-1950s. Art courses were offered in the lower grades, and art appreciation was enhanced by occasional field trips to the Cincinnati Art Museum. There were no guidance counselors available at William Grant High School.

The photos from yearbooks shown on subsequent pages of the present work illustrate some of the curricular and extracurricular activities offered at Lincoln-Grant School after the school moved to Greenup Street.

■ THE INFLUENCE OF AN ENHANCED FACULTY

The Lincoln-Grant facility at Ninth and Greenup streets would become a major center of educational and social activity for black people in the Covington community. With an "A" accreditation, and a growing reputation for academic excellence among black schools, Lincoln-Grant School would eventually become a teaching laboratory for education students at historically black institutions, such as Kentucky State College. Not only did Lincoln-Grant School meet the needs of African American children in Northern Kentucky, it was a definite outlet for newly certificated teachers of color who sought employment after graduating from historically black colleges in the South. Many welcomed the opportunity to teach at Lincoln-Grant in the 1930s, '40s and '50s.

The teachers at the new Lincoln-Grant building were all black, and they were good at what they did, with rare exception. They were dedicated to their students, and they were well educated. Their typical backgrounds included undergraduate degrees, usually from historically black institutions in the South, and graduate degrees or advanced academic work at predominantly white institutions such as the University of Cincinnati, the University of Wisconsin, The Ohio State University, and Columbia University.

While it may have been disadvantageous to the careers of the school's black teachers to be so limited in where they could teach, their placement in our school gave their students the advantage of having a large number of exceptional teachers, who did not see them as inferior human beings. They were encouraging, nurturing, and supportive, and they continually pushed the Lincoln-Grant students toward academic excellence.

While all of my teachers were impressive in one way or another, I distinctly remember my first teacher, Miss DePriest. She was a small-frame, energetic, light-skinned African American woman with light colored eyes and naturally curly light brown hair. Her liveliness and enthusiasm were well suited for kindergarten children. She played the piano well, and would often gather us around the large, upright piano in her room to sing action songs, such as "Skip to My Lou," "The Whale Song," "School Days," and "My Bonnie." I believe that my kindergarten teacher actually influenced my early ambitions to play the piano by her example. Something must have "clicked" as I gravitated toward the old, upright piano in our home at the age of five after watching Miss DePriest play the piano in our kindergarten classroom day after day.

My kindergarten experience seemed typical. I was in the morning class, and after a half-day, we went home. I recall bringing my newly purchased rug to school for our designated group naptime on the classroom floor (we closed our eyes, but didn't really fall asleep), and the midmorning snack of white milk, chocolate milk, or orange juice supplied by the school, and cookies and Graham Crackers voluntarily brought in by our parents at previously assigned times each week.

Miss DePriest was responsible for teaching us all of our subjects during our half-day school experience including beginning to recognize the letters of the alphabet (a precursor to learning to read), learning how to spell our names (the antecedent to writing), rudimentary counting of various objects (the foundation for mathematics), singing, drawing, learning our colors, and doing physical exercises, as well as elementary instruction in the areas of health and nutrition.

At the end of the school year our class participated in kindergarten commencement, wherein we presented group actions songs for other classes and parents in the Lincoln-Grant auditorium. Examples of our class work and drawings were on display in the kindergarten classroom for our parents on the day of "commencement." Both the morning and afternoon kindergarten classes performed together as we were all dressed in white—even the boys, who wore white suits, usually with short pant legs. Miss DePriest praised our performance after it was over, and at the end of the program we each received a little "diploma" (actually a Certificate of Promotion to First Grade) as we prepared to enter first grade. (I believe the rationale behind kindergarten "commencement" was to start us on a road that would position us psychologically to look forward to graduation from high school. For many of us, it worked).

My first grade teacher was Mrs. Annie Hargraves, the wife of Mr. William Hargraves, who was a teacher of history in the high school upstairs. Mrs. Hargraves was a warm and nurturing teacher who smiled often and hugged us a lot. She appeared to be very fond of me, and provided me with excellent intellectual fundamentals. I remember Mrs. Hargraves hugging me and holding me close to her as she bragged to my mother about my academic progress at open house.

Mr. and Mrs. Hargraves had a son and a daughter, who were high-achieving students in the upper grades at Grant. In fact, they were both valedictorians of their respective graduating classes. The Hargraves' daughter would often spend her lunch hour practicing the clarinet alone in an empty classroom while other children played outside. I would sometimes pause outside the door and listen, as she would run through scales and arpeggios very flawlessly on her instrument before launching into a very spirited excerpt from a selection by John Phillip Sousa or other composers. I was fascinated by her ability to produce such melodious and accurate musical sounds on a clarinet without an accompaniment by any other instrument. The Hargraves' son was also an avid student musician who, in addition to playing the saxophone, was the designated student conductor for the band under Mr. Hutchinson.

My third grade teacher, Miss Etta Louise Hundley, was the consummate teaching professional. A 1911 graduate of William Grant High School, she had received her bachelor's degree from Knoxville College in Tennessee, and come back to Covington for what would become a lengthy teaching career at Lincoln-Grant. As a youngster I remember Miss Hundley as a rather stern teacher, but that was for our benefit as students. While I had no difficulty mastering third grade academic material there were others who did. Miss Hundley sincerely believed that every child in her classes could learn, and she insisted that they do so before they left her classroom. With a reputation for retaining students in the third grade, Miss Hundley was known to say to individual students, "You are going to learn how to tell time before you leave my classroom," or "I'm going to hold you back until you master proper English in my room," or "You'll certainly know how to count before you leave here!" While this approach might have seemed harsh to some, it guaranteed that students in Miss Hundley's class would be assured of having basic academic fundamentals, rather than just being passed on from grade to grade without academic mastery.

While our teachers provided a lot of positive reinforcement for our academic achievements, they also were not reticent to advise us continuously in practical or personal matters, including personal hygiene, good manners, and respect for our "elders." We were also taught humility and respect for our fellow human beings as we learned to accept and deal with the epileptic seizures of one of our classmates, and the rheumatic heart condition of another, that caused her to have fainting spells in the classroom. We also discovered the reality of death as well as racial tolerance when one of our fifth grade schoolmates was struck and killed while walking home from school by an elderly white woman who lost control of her automobile on Russell Street.

My intellectual curiosity grew as we completed scientific experiments in high school biology, chemistry, and physics classes under the tutelage of Mr. Birtill Barrow, who originally came from "the islands." Armed with a master's degree from Columbia University, Mr. Barrow *demanded* our academic excellence, as he approached the classroom setting with a sense of rigor and formality (an apparent carryover from what I believed to be his early formal education in the Virgin Islands). His time and energy seemed totally devoted to his students. Mr. Barrow was short in stature, and generally employed a lecture-type format, while standing in front of the class. He always addressed the young ladies by the title "Miss" and their last names, while simply using last names only for the males in his classes.

Mr. Barrow had little patience for academic sophistry or "foolishness." When a student gave a serious, but only marginally correct answer, he would respond thoughtfully with "Well . . . almost, but not quite," as he tucked his grade book and notes under his chin with folded arms, and moved on to another student. But if a student were clearly guessing at an answer he would respond immediately and sharply with: "Quit guessing! If you don't know, just say you don't know, and let's go somewhere and find out!" (the answer). His narrowed eyes reflected extreme displeasure with the person who had just guessed at the answer. When I raised my hand after no one else seemed to have the answer to the question, Mr. Barrow would turn to me and say in a calm, compassionate manner with a small hand gesture in my direction: "Tell 'em, Waldon." (For some reason, he never pronounced the hard "t" in my surname). I usually responded with the correct answer. He would then corroborate my answer for the class, smile briefly, and go on to the next topic.

A few of us were privileged also to take two years of Spanish from Mr. Barrow. We saw ourselves as intellectually advanced because only the potentially college-bound students took Spanish, the only foreign language offered at Grant at that time. After the first few weeks, all communication in the classroom had to be in Spanish. My classmates and I thoroughly enjoyed Spanish classes as we eventually spoke Spanish with reasonable fluency and gained knowledge about the culture of our U.S. neighbors south of the border.

I received particular encouragement from Mr. Samuel Gaines, who was the instructor of record for Metal Work, and who later also taught Typing when it was introduced into our curriculum. Mr. Gaines always specifically encouraged me to pursue greater educational heights. I remember even now his continual admonitions to me: "*You* have great ability. *You* will achieve much. *You* will go *far!*" (His firm articulation would trail the word, "fahhhh," as he embellished it with a stretch of his arm and open palm). I believe those comments went a long way toward pushing me to achieve at successively higher educational and professional levels after I became an adult.

And the fundamentals learned in my Wood Work class with Mr. Chester Rice have followed me throughout my life. The process of making lamps and tables "from scratch" in his class (which we displayed, and some of us even sold at the end of the school year) gave me knowledge of wood crafts and tools that I have used continuously in maintaining the homes in which we have lived. I am generally fairly "handy' around the house in terms of "fixing things."

I also received support, guidance and encouragement from Mrs. Jewell Jackson, who was always the senior class advisor. As the only high school graduate from William Grant in the class of 1916, Mrs. Jackson occasionally reminded us of the hard work and perseverance that it took for her to get to where she was in life. She talked about how proudly she marched down the aisle alone to receive her high school diploma. Mrs. Jackson emphasized her undergraduate degree from Fisk University, and her master's degree from the University of Cincinnati, while imploring us to do something similar with our lives. As she taught us correct English, she also instructed us on how to become well-educated, productive citizens. She emphasized ethical and moral values through the media of American and English literature. On the practical side, Mrs. Jackson taught us to "brush our little tongues, as well as our teeth," and she always urged me to "keep climbing."

Mrs. Jackson also encouraged a strong work ethic in her students. On more than one occasion while I was in the ninth grade, she engaged my services to help with her spring cleaning after having sought my parents' permission. She and her husband picked me up from our house on Tenth Street on Saturday mornings and drove me to their Victorian style home in the Walnut Hills area of Cincinnati, where I would spend about a half day scrubbing woodwork and dining room walls, washing windows, and polishing furniture. After I finished my morning's work Mrs. Jackson would serve me a light lunch at her large dining room table, pay me a modest fee for my services, and have her husband bring me back home. Eventually, I learned the bus route to and from her home. In the process, I was learning the "work ethic" and earning pay as well as being exposed to how well some professional black people lived. The Jacksons had a nice, well-maintained older home, and somewhere in the back of my mind, I wanted to achieve something similar in my lifetime.

I progressed through elementary school as a strong student academically, as I moved from the first floor of Lincoln-Grant to the second floor, and finally to "high school" on the third floor of the building.

■ GRADUATION DISPARITIES

In addition to providing significant insight into the staffing and building arrangements of Lincoln-Grant School on Seventh Street, Leconia Franklin Crosby's master's thesis seemed highly critical of the school, particularly with regard to graduation rates among blacks in Covington as reflected in 1929. Crosby believed that the primary factors affecting the relatively low graduation rate for black high school students at William Grant prior to the relocation of the school to Greenup Street included (1) significant population growth in the black community, from two thousand in 1915 to five thousand in 1929; (2) "the economic status of the Colored Population of Covington"; and (3) an apparent lack of "social and religious leadership." [208]

Crosby also seemed frustrated by the fact that some blacks that had migrated from the south seemed more economically advantaged, particularly in

208. Crosby, "A Study of Pupil Marks."

the area of home ownership than did some black people who had been born and bred in Covington. All of these factors contributed to a low number of graduates between the years of 1918 and 1929, according to Crosby.[209]

After the school relocated to a new building on Greenup Street in 1932 the quality of the faculty and the accreditation status of the high school improved, and the graduation classes suddenly ballooned significantly in numbers. One wall on the third floor contained the pictures of students in each graduating class, beginning with sixteen students in the class of 1932, and showing increasing numbers of graduates in subsequent years. The images, which included some of the teachers who had gone away to college and returned to teach at Lincoln-Grant, provided a legacy and an instant sense of school history. Through those pictures and other efforts, teachers encouraged students to know the history of the school, and take pride in it.

There was also an educational accommodation for veterans of the armed forces who returned home after World War II. In order to facilitate their readjustment to civilian life, President Franklin Delano Roosevelt signed the Servicemen's Readjustment Act, commonly known as the "GI Bill" in June 1943. That act provided for assistance with low interest mortgage loans, unemployment insurance and educational benefits for veterans. Several veterans took advantage of their GI benefits to complete their high school education, with a view toward entering college. "GI" graduates from Covington had to meet residency requirements for the City of Covington and pass the General Education Development (GED) test in order to qualify for their high school diplomas. Beginning in 1947 several black veterans completed their high school diplomas at William Grant High School through evening classes. GI graduates were often listed as members of various graduating classes at William Grant High School through official board action. Similarly, nonmilitary persons who completed their high school diplomas through GED courses were occasionally included in William Grant's graduating classes.

Prior to school integration, GI and GED graduates were kept racially segregated in the Official Board of Education Minutes by listing the names of the black GI and GED graduates under William Grant High School, while listing white GI or GED graduates in a general GI or GED category during some school years. An alternate strategy for segregating black and white GI or GED graduates in the board minutes was to list the black graduates under William Grant High School and white graduates under Holmes High School during other years. In either instance, a person reading the board minutes would be able to distinguish between white and black GI and GED graduates, although they all had to pass the same GED test in order to qualify for a high school diploma.

In the final analysis, William Grant High School would produce at least 792 graduates from 1889 to 1965. In contrast, Holmes High School would

---

209. Ibid.

graduate thousands of students during that period.

A close examination of the list of graduates from the early part of twentieth century revealed the names of the parents of several schoolmates, all of whom were William Grant High School alumni, going back as far as the early nineteen hundreds. The marriages of schoolmates, and the children they produced later were evident. Several prominent, long-term members of the local black community were William Grant graduates. Those findings confirmed the significant role that Lincoln-Grant School played as it served the black citizens of Northern Kentucky for many decades over several generations.

■ RACE, AND HIGH SCHOOL ACCREDITATION

Consistent with racial separation in all aspects of public education in Kentucky and other southern states, a separate evaluation process was employed for "Negro schools" while only comparing them with each other. White officials from the Kentucky State Department of Education administered a dual, racially based evaluation program for black and white high schools in Kentucky with assistance from the Southern Association Committee on Approval of Negro Schools.

"In 1924 the Division of Negro Education was formed within the Kentucky Department of Education, and Professor L. N. Taylor was hired as supervisor of Negro rural education."[210] After Taylor's retirement in 1943, "Sam B. Taylor was named Supervisor of Negro Education." Both men were white. The article further indicates, "From 1945–1947 Whitney M. Young, Sr. served as the Assistant Supervisor and Coordinator of Negro Education, the first African American to be hired in the Division of Negro Education."[211] The Division of Negro Education coordinated the accreditation reviews for black high schools in Kentucky.

The academic success of William Grant High School was reflected in consistent accreditation ratings of "A" from the Kentucky State Department of Education after the new building opened in 1932. L. N. Taylor wrote the following to Covington superintendent Glenn Swing, on June 15, 1942, ten years after the new building had been in operation: "Dr. [George] Howard's report on your William Grant School is more favorable than that on any of the other [black] secondary schools visited. It is exceedingly brief, as follows: 'This school is to be commended on splendid building and equipment and evidence of fine spirit and work. An excellent school.'"

The accreditation status of William Grant High School would continue at the "A" level for the remainder of its existence. But in spite of the fact that William Grant High School was considered to be "an excellent school," there was a

---

210. "Grade Schools & High Schools in Kentucky." Notable Kentucky African Americans Database. See Division of Negro Education (Kentucky), 9.
211. Ibid., 10.

racial qualification attached to the "A" rating. An analysis of the Board of Education records regarding Accredited High Schools revealed a problem with interpreting the accreditation status of William Grant High School. William Grant High School, and other black high schools in Kentucky were systematically designated with a parenthetical "C" or "Colored" tag beside the name of the school in the accreditation literature for the state as follows:[212]

School	Rating
Holmes High School	*A*
William Grant High School (Colored)	*A*

That label made anyone reviewing its accreditation status aware of the fact that Grant was a segregated, all-black high school. The label implied that the graduate of the "Colored" school had received an education that was, at best, "different" and at worst, inferior to that received by white students.

Separate review processes and the identification of black schools as "Colored" in the accreditation literature were not positive indicators for William Grant graduates and graduates of other black high schools in Kentucky. Black high school graduates would not receive objective treatment and evaluation based solely on their academic accomplishments and abilities as they emerged from high school into the real world. But racial separation in all aspects of public education, including the high school accreditation process was obviously more important to white school officials than objectivity or equity in the evaluation of high school programs.

The accreditation issue became a personal one for the author and his family in 1954. After joining the air force the author's brother, a 1954 William Grant High School graduate, was attempting to take a course of study that required a high school diploma. However, after air force personnel received his high school transcript, he was informed that he could not enroll in the program because he had not graduated from a "properly accredited" high school, even though William Grant High School was rated at the "A" level. It is probable that air force personnel reviewed the accreditation status of William Grant High School and found that William Grant High School was designated as "Colored." On that basis, they chose to deny that William Grant High School was "properly accredited."

In reaction to that incident, the author's mother and other active parents from Lincoln-Grant went personally to the Covington Board of Education seeking answers about the accreditation issue. They could not get a resolution to their concerns at the local level, so they drove to Frankfort, Kentucky, as a group to meet directly with officials at the Kentucky State Department of Education about the accreditation status of William Grant High School. The outcome of that meeting at the State Department is unknown, but at some point after the *Brown v. Board of Education* 1954 ruling was reaffirmed, the special

---

212. Minutes, Covington Board of Education, April 24, 1953.

designation of "Colored" beside the name of black schools in Kentucky was eliminated from the accreditation literature and the Official Minutes of the Covington Board of Education.

In response to the "separate but equal" accreditation issue, the author's mother pursued sending his younger sister to a different school by initially trying to get her into the then all-white Holmes High School. Her visit to the Kentucky Department of Education had apparently made her more aware of the impending integration of all schools due to the 1954 Supreme Court decision. However, she was told by the local board of education that Holmes High was "not quite ready yet" (for integration). She then went physically to LaSallette Academy, an all-white Catholic girls high school two or three blocks down the street from Lincoln-Grant and asked to speak with the administration. Although she had no money for private school tuition, she and another parent (our distant cousin by marriage) convinced the officials at LaSallette to allow Martha and Jean W. to attend LaSallette on a "scholarship basis." Although Jean W. did not like the rigor of the Catholic academy and quickly returned to Lincoln-Grant, my sister mastered Latin and the culture of the school, and became one of the first black graduates of an "integrated" high school in Covington a few years later.

The wall of racial discrimination and separation in Kentucky (and the nation at large) had become a fortress with many support systems and layers of racially based policy that seemed insurmountable during that period in American history. Separate but equal would become stretched to the point of absurdity through such policies and practices as those described above. And those extremes would become the tipping point that would lead to the ultimate demise of public school segregation.

■ PARENT-TEACHER ASSOCIATION, BAND BOOSTER'S CLUB AND PARENTAL INVOLVEMENT

The Parent Teacher Association and Band Booster's Club were both active groups designed to make the school better for the children. Routine activities took the form of raising money for band uniforms and helping to select outfits for cheerleaders and majorettes. The PTA and Band Boosters helped the school by sponsoring bake sales, school bazaars, and other community events to raise money. They also worked with teachers as they took on various projects as "helpers" in the school.

> The Band Booster's Club was organized in 1948 under the leadership of the School Bandmaster, Mr. Conrad Hutchinson, Jr., who felt that there was a need for raising funds for purchasing uniforms for the band, [and] also help[ing] in other activities concerning the school band. Officers elected were: Mrs. Mattie Reed, President, Mrs. Alice Finnell, Vice; Mrs. Maisie M. Price, Secretary; Mrs. Hermoin Deal,

Assistant; Mr. Sigsbee Sheffey, Sr., Treasurer. During the short time the club has been in existence, it has sponsored two dances during the Christmas seasons of 1948 and 1949, and has brought humor to the public in the form of two programs which featured an all male cast in skits and Fashion Shows. With Mrs. Jencie Sheffy as Chairman, sandwiches were sold at the ball games to raise additional funds. As a result of the Club's works, with the aid of other organizations, uniforms were purchased for fifty members of the band [*sic*] also one drum major suit and uniforms for the three drum majors. The Club's greatest thrill came when the band made its first appearance in full uniform at a Sunrise service on Easter Sunday 1949.[213]

On the academic side, some parents, such as the author's mother took an active role in shaping school policy and procedures. Although she was not a PTA officer, or even an official dues-paying member (due to lack of funds), the author's mother was diligent in her role as a "concerned parent." If there were weakness in our education at Lincoln-Grant they were thoroughly addressed by my mother and other concerned parents, who had strong records of "parental involvement." Throughout our school years, my mother monitored our teachers to ensure that we were "learning something." If a teacher appeared to be "weak" as evidenced by a lack of homework, or our reports that we weren't learning much in a particular classroom, my mother went immediately to the school to seek a change of teachers or other adjustments.

■ THE AUDACITY TO LEARN TO TYPE

Then there was the matter of the typing class during my junior year. Typing was introduced at Lincoln-Grant School for the first time in its history when I became a junior. But Mr. Lett, our principal, stated very firmly that the typing class was to be offered to *seniors only*. Since fifteen seniors were expected to enroll in the fall of 1956, exactly fifteen student typewriters (plus one for the instructor) had been purchased and placed in the typing classroom on the third floor of the building. But when fall classes started, there were only fourteen seniors. One of the seniors did not return, or was retained in the junior class. This left at least one seat in the typing class vacant. My brother, who was a senior made me aware of the vacant seat in the typing class. I wanted that seat. I wanted urgently to learn to type, and could not see why a vacant seat should be wasted, when I could be learning to type—especially since I had a study hall during the time that the typing class was offered.

The principal was steadfast in the policy that typing was "for seniors only" —until my mother paid a visit to his office. The end result was that another junior and I were allowed to take Typing I with the senior class. (The instructor relinquished his typewriter to the second student from the junior class). At the

---

213. Quotes excerpted from the *Grantonian* Yearbook, 1950.

conclusion of the Typing I class, the two of us then moved to Typing II while the rest of our class peers enrolled in Typing I. In my mind, typing was much like playing the piano. Looking at words on a piece of paper and responding with one's fingers on the typing keyboard was virtually the same as looking at notes on a sheet of music and responding with one's fingers on a piano keyboard. I excelled ultimately to about ninety words per minute—the first or second best in the class. I was so enthusiastic about the typing class that I went downtown and purchased my first typewriter, a used, portable Royal *pica elite* (with my own money), which would serve me well during the rest of my high school years, and throughout college.

My academic progress in college would be facilitated by my ability to type my papers and "themes" for English classes, as well as other written assignments. Students who turned in handwritten papers in college seemed to get lower grades on such papers. In my view, denying black students at Lincoln-Grant School the opportunity to learn to type until 1956 on the grounds that such a skill was not necessary for us because of our ethnicity, was a particularly vituperative act of racial discrimination on the part of the Covington Pubic School administration. It is worthy of restating at this point that typing, shorthand, and business courses, i.e., a commercial course of study, had been available to white students in the Covington Public Schools, males and females, since the early nineteen hundreds!

The principal felt that, since he had capitulated and allowed me to take the typing class, I was obligated at his request to type his papers for master's classes that he was taking at the University of Cincinnati. While I thought that in one sense he was taking advantage of the situation by having me use my study halls to type his papers, from another perspective I was learning something. I only had to type two or three of his papers during the semester, and as I read what the principal had prepared for me to type for his classes in school in administration, I remember thinking to myself, "I believe I could do this level of work with no problem at all." I could even see occasional concepts in some of the material that he had prepared that I would have written differently, although I would not dare suggest corrections. I typed what I was given exactly as it was given to me. I was also a bit surprised at the brevity of some of the papers for a master's level class in college, as I used that situation to begin to shape my own educational future.

Photograph 88: Flatwork Ironer, Lincoln-Grant School, 1941.
COURTESY OF THE KENTON COUNTY PUBLIC LIBRARY, COVINGTON, KENTUCKY.

Mae White and Florence Johnson with their teacher Eleanora Henderson work at the flat work ironer at the Lincoln-Grant School, Covington, Kentucky, 1941.

Photograph 89: Typing and Chemistry Classes, Lincoln-Grant School, 1957.
GRANT WARRIOR YEARBOOK, 1957. PHOTOGRAPHER: CURTIS BENION, CLASS OF 1958.

Top photo, Front row: *Joseph Walton, Robbie Patterson, Willa Hoffman.*
Second row: *Jessie Mays, Charles Jouett, Norma Brown.*
Third row: *Raymond Webb, Joan Jasper*
Bottom photo, foreground left to right: *Rosetta Collins (seated), Geraldine Tyler and Patricia Gray (both standing), Janice Warmack (with head turned).*
Background, left to right: *Charles Dickerson, Mr. Birtill Barrow (teacher), William Riley and Auguster Roberts (both seated), LaVera Givens (holding test tube), Eleanor Slaughter (face concealed). Three students standing in far background are unidentified.*

Photograph 90: Metal Work and Woodwork Classes, Lincoln-Grant School, 1957.
Source: *Grant Warrior* Yearbook, 1957. Courtesy of the Covington Independent Public Schools. Photographer: Curtis Benion, Class of 1958.

Top photo, left to right: *Wayne Mays, Charles Jouett, George Offutt, Leonard Phipps, Robert Scott.*

Bottom photo, left to right: *William Reed, Milton Jasper, James Moore, Jackie Young, Aaron Ballard (seated, Alfonza Davis, Mr. Chester Rice (teacher), Robert Phipps.*

Photograph 91: Fourth Grade Class, 1956.
SOURCE: *GRANT WARRIOR* YEARBOOK, 1956.
COURTESY OF THE COVINGTON INDEPENDENT PUBLIC SCHOOLS.

Photograph 92: Miss Lincoln-Grant and Miss William Grant, 1956.
SOURCE: *GRANT WARRIOR* YEARBOOKS, 56 AND 57.
PHOTOGRAPHS COURTESY OF THE COVINGTON INDEPENDENT PUBLIC SCHOOLS.

The Miss William Grant and Miss Lincoln-Grant contests were held each year. The 1956 court: J. Wideman, C. Jones, E. Hopkins, V. Sheffey, J. Barnes, B. Henderson.

Photograph 93: Eighth Grade Classes, Lincoln-Grant School, 1957.
Source: *Grant Warrior* Yearbook, 1957.
Courtesy of the Covington Independent Public Schools.

Photograph 94 (left):
Miss William Grant, 1957.
SOURCE: *GRANT WARRIOR* YEARBOOK, 1957.
COURTESY OF THE COVINGTON INDEPENDENT
PUBLIC SCHOOLS.

Top: Charlene Bedford.

Bottom: G . Tyler, R. Collins, S. Rhodes.

Photograph 95 (right):
Miss Lincoln-Grant, 1957.
SOURCE: GRANT WARRIOR YEARBOOK, 1957.
COURTESY OF THE COVINGTON INDEPENDENT
PUBLIC SCHOOLS.

Top photo: *Joan Herron.*

Photograph 96: Speech Class and Hi-Y Conference, 1950.
SOURCE: *GRANTONIAN*, 1950, COURTESY OF WILLA HOFFMAN JACKSON, CLASS OF 1957.

EIGHTH GRADE

Teacher, WILLIAM H. CRAIG

SEVENTH GRADE

Teacher, CLARENCE H. WILLIAMS

Photograph 97: Seventh and Eighth Grade Classes, 1950.
SOURCE: *GRANTONIAN*, 1950, COURTESY OF WILLA HOFFMAN JACKSON, CLASS OF 1957.

Photograph 98: William Grant High School Prom, 1954,
Manse Hotel Ballroom, Cincinnati, Ohio.
PHOTOGRAPH COURTESY OF WILLA HOFFMAN JACKSON, CLASS OF 1957.

William Grant Junior/Senior Prom, 1954, Manse Hotel, Cincinnati, Ohio.

Seated: *D. Sheffey (Prom King) and J. Clemens (Prom Queen)*

Left to Right, Standing: *L. Butler, B. Hargraves, C. LaBordeaux, G. Slaughter, D. Lightfoot, B. Roberts, D. Crawford, J. George, unidentified, N. Smith, J. A. Walton, R. Crawford, G. Walton, W. Hall, E. Graves, C. Mabrey, C. Herron, H. Davies Jr.*

Photograph 99: Drama Club, Lincoln-Grant School, 1957.
SOURCE: *GRANT WARRIOR,* 1957. COURTESY OF THE COVINGTON INDEPENDENT PUBLIC SCHOOLS.

The Drama Club was an important extracurricular organization for female students.
Dancers, clockwise from extreme left: *R. Patterson, P. Offut, Y. Humphries, C. Bedford, B. Stutson, M. Ferrell, D. Burton.*

Photograph 100: Class Play, Cyclone Sally, *Class of 1957.*
SOURCE: *GRANT WARRIOR* YEARBOOK, 1957.
COURTESY OF THE COVINGTON INDEPENDENT PUBLIC SCHOOLS.

The class play was a method of fundraising for the junior classes, as well as an outlet for their theatrical talents. **Above from left:** *Allen Thomas, Willa Hoffman, Rosetta Hampton, and Toney Walton, Jr., play their roles in* Cyclone Sally *to raise money for the Junior-Senior prom in 1957.*

Photograph 101: Hi-Y Club, Lincoln-Grant School, 1950.
SOURCE: *GRANTONIAN,* 1950, COURTESY OF WILLA HOFFMAN JACKSON.

Photograph 102: Student Council and Hi-Y Club, Lincoln-Grant, 1957.
SOURCE: *GRANT WARRIOR* YEARBOOK, 1957.
COURTESY OF THE COVINGTON INDEPENDENT PUBLIC SCHOOLS.

The Student Council (above), R. Patterson, president, and Hi-Y (below), L. Stewart, president) organizations represented additional opportunities for student leadership development at Lincon-Grant School.

Photograph 103: Y-Teens, Lincoln-Grant School, 1957.
SOURCE: *GRANT WARRIOR* YEARBOOK, 1957.
COURTESY OF THE COVINGTON INDEPENDENT PUBLIC SCHOOLS.

First row, left to right: *Activity Committee, G. Boston; Club Reporter, B. Dickerson; Program Committee, M. Miller; Program Committee, M. Jasper; Chaplain, B. Housley; Worship Committee, A. Walker, R. Johnson; President, A. Patterson.*

Second row: *L. Barnes, D. Stewart, Secretary, M. Walton; Chairman of Activity Committee, L. Grant; Activity Committee, D. Webster, L. Phipps, J. Montgomery, R. Banks, M. Lacey; Chairman of Program Committee, J. Wideman.*

Third row: *M. Castleman, J. Ramssy, M. Brown, Chairman of Worship Committee, C. Sharpe; Vice President, E. Hopkins; L. Salters, M. Mann, Treasurer, E. James; L. Doyle, M. Collier, L. Finnell, Worship Committee, J. Herron; K. Frye, J. Golbsy, S. Banks, M. McGee, B. Reed, As. Secretary, C. Stewart.*

Not photographed: *Minnie Mae Corbin, Y-Teen Advisor; Helen D. Braybay, Y-Teen Director.*

Photograph 104: Kindergarten Classes, Lincoln-Grant School, 1957.
Center, top row, both photos: *Mrs. Annie Hargraves, Teacher.*

Seventh Grades

Photograph 105: Seventh Grade Classes, Lincoln-Grant School, 1957.

Photograph 106: Lincoln-Grant Faculty, 1930s or '40s.
SOURCE: RICHARD B. L. FOWLER, CLASS OF 1963.

First row: *M. Beaver, B. Depriest, C. Williams, M. Corbin, W. Hargraves, E. Henderson, P. Redden.*

Second row: *unidentified, unidentified, unidentified, A. Vaughn, S. Gaines, B. Glenn, H. R. Merry.*

Third row: *unidentified, unidentified, unidentified, A. Booker, L. McLean, E. Hundley, J. Jackson.*

Fourth row: *C. Rice, C. Williams (Webb), E. Simpson, L. Crosby, N. Fleming, R. Vaught.*

Fifth row: *W. Craig.*

FACULTY

locis parentium!

H. R. MERRY, Principal

Fisk University A. B.
Graduate Study:
University of Cincinnati
University of Wisconsin
Atlanta University
Hampton Institute

JEWELL R. JACKSON

Fisk University A.B.
University of
Cincinnati M.E.

English
Adviser Senior Class
Grant Y - Teens

WILLIAM N. JACKSON

Morehouse College B.S.
Atlanta University M.S.
Graduate Study:
Ohio State University

Science and Mathematics

WILLIAM F. HARGRAVES

Miami University A.B.
Miami University M.A.
Graduate Study:
University of
Cincinnati

Social Studies & History
Member of Band & Orch.
Advisor Student Council

ROSCOE C. VAUGHT

Knoxville College Prep
Knoxville College A.B.
University of
Wisconsin M.A.
Graduate Study:
University of Cincinnati

Mathematics and English

BIRTILL T. BARROW

Bates College A.B.
Columbia University M.S.

Science and Modern
Languages
Member of Band &
Orchestra

MAUDLYN S. GARRETT

Spelman College B. S.
Graduate Study:
Atlanta University

Librarian

(No Picture)

Photograph 107: Lincoln-Grant Faculty, 1950.
SOURCE: *GRANTONIAN,* 1950. COURTESY OF WILLA HOFFMAN JACKSON.

Top photo: *H. R. Merry, Principal.*

Second line from top: *Jewell R. Jackson, William N. Jackson.*

Third line from top: *William F. Hargraves, Roscoe C. Vaught.*

Bottom photo: *Birtill T. Barrow, Maudlyn S. Garrett (no photo).*

ELEANORA W. HENDERSON

Howard College Diploma
University of
  Cincinnati B.S.
University of
  Cincinnati M.A.
Graduate Study:
  University of
  Cincinnati

Clothing

SAMUEL GAINES

Hampton Trade School
Hampton Institute B.S.

Auto Mechanics

CHESTER C. RICE

Normal School - Miami U.
University of
  Cincinnati A.B.

Industrial Arts

SARA WRIGHT

Kentucky State
  College B.S.

Home Economics

EUNICE SIMPSON

Wilberforce University
University of
  Cincinnati B.S.
Cleveland School of Art

Art and Weaving

PAUL L. REDDEN

Wilberforce University,
  B. S.
Graduate Study:
Miami University
University of
  Cincinnati
Kentucky State College

Physical Education
Hi - Y, Advisor

CONRAD HUTCHINSON JR.

Tuskegee Institute
  B.S. Music
Graduate Study:
Western Reserve
University of
  Cincinnati
New England Cons.
  of Music

Bandmaster

MARY G. DAVIS

West Virginia
  State College B. A.
Graduate Study:
Atlanta School of
  Library Science

Acting Librarian

ELIZABETH GOOCH

Oberlin College
University of
  Cincinnati B. S.

Vocal Music

(No Picture)

Photograph 108: Lincoln-Grant Faculty, 1950.
SOURCE: *GRANTONIAN*, 1950. COURTESY OF WILLA HOFFMAN JACKSON.

Top row: *Eleanora W. Henderson, Samuel Gaines.*

Second row from top: *Chester C. Rice, Sara Wright.*

Third row from top: *Eunice Simpson, Paul L. Redden.*

Bottom row: *Conrad Hutchinson Jr., Mary G.. Davis.*

Not pictured: *Elizabeth Gooch.*

ELEMENTARY TEACHERS

L. to R. Front Row-- E. Wilson, C. Bowers, E. Hundley, A. Vaughn,
C. Williams, M. Corbin,
Second Row-- A. Hargraves, C. Taylor, G. Gamble, D. Jackson,
M. Beaver.

STUDENT TEACHERS

L. to R. S. Sheffey, L. Cavil, C. Lett, N. Green, S. Gilliard,
C. Hines, W. McClellan, W. Gilliard.

Photograph 109: Lincoln-Grant Faculty, 1950.
SOURCE: *GRANTONIAN,* 1950. COURTESY OF WILLA HOFFMAN JACKSON.

Top photo, front row L. to R.: *E. Wilson, C. Bowers, E. Hundley, A. Vaughn, C. Williams, M. Corbin.*

Second row: *A. Hargraves, C. Taylor, G. Gamble, D. Jackson, M. Beaver.*

Bottom photo L. to R.: *R. S. Sheffey, L. Cavil, C. Lett, N. Green, S. Gilliard, C. Hines, W. McClellan, W. Gilliard.*

Photograph 110: Lincoln-Grant PTA, 1940s.
SOURCE: THEODORE H. H. HARRIS, CLASS OF 1962.

Lincoln-Grant School had a very active Parent-Teacher Association.

Photograph 111: Lincoln-Grant PTA, 1957.
SOURCE: *GRANT WARRIOR*, YEARBOOK, 1957.
COURTESY OF THE COVINGTON INDEPENDENT PUBLIC SCHOOLS.
PHOTOGRAPHER: CURTIS BENION, CLASS OF 1958.

CHAPTER 8

A Musical Tradition

■ VOCAL MUSIC

A long-standing musical tradition was an integral part of the educational experiences at Lincoln-Grant. Singing had been a part of the curriculum since the inception of the school, as noted by Fann and others in their descriptions of the Robbins Street and Madison Street schools in the eighteen hundreds. A tradition of "Song Recitals" by students at the Seventh Street Colored School had begun in the late eighteen hundreds, as reflected in the 1898 board minutes and the 1905 superintendent's report cited earlier. Also, as previously noted, the board minutes made reference to a teacher named "Miss Frazier" who, while apparently teaching other subjects, also gave "special instruction in music" at Lincoln-Grant School in 1912. Miss Sallie Frazier and Miss Elizabeth Gooch are both listed as members of the Lincoln-Grant teaching faculty in the May 29, 1918, board minutes, with Miss Frazier as the more senior faculty member of the two. Subsequently, Miss Frazier would no longer be affiliated with the school, and Miss Gooch would become the vocal music teacher. Miss Gooch would remain in that position for several decades. She was listed as the school's musical director as early as 1916, during the graduation exercises for Jewell Rebecca Smith (Jackson).

The sense of school pride that developed over the years for students of Lincoln-Grant was reflected in our singing the "Lincoln-Grant School Song" during school assemblies and at commencement each year. The words were set to the traditional Alma Mater melody, "Annie Lisle," sometime in the early nineteen hundreds during the tenure of Miss Frazier and/or Miss Gooch.

Figure 25: The Lincoln-Grant School Song.

Traditional Alma Mater melody based on the ballad, "Annie Lisle" by H. S. Thompson. The words are attributed to the music staff of Lincoln-Grant School during the early 1900s.

The "Annie Lisle" tune was a very popular Alma Mater melody. During the late eighteen hundreds and early nineteen hundreds numerous colleges, public schools, and private academies used that melody as their Alma Mater, while endowing it with wording appropriate to their individual school histories. The "Lincoln-Grant School Song" was in the same "league" as such institutions as Cornell University, the University of Akron, Emory University, Indiana University, Vanderbilt University, Swarthmore College, the University of Alabama, and Xavier University of Louisiana. Those institutions all used the "Annie Lisle" tune for their Alma Mater song.

The author was a music student under Miss Gooch and several of her successors. After Miss Gooch retired in 1954, she would be followed by several younger vocal music teachers including Miss Witherspoon (1954/55), and Mrs. M. Ruth Brown-Phillips (1955–1957). Mrs. Brown-Phillips received a B.S. degree from the University of Cincinnati, and completed graduate work at the Cincinnati Conservatory of Music. After leaving Grant, she became an educator in the Cincinnati Public Schools. Ms. Ann C. Blackwell, who succeeded Mrs. Brown-Phillips in the fall of 1957 would leave at the end of the 1957/58 school year. Mr. William Martin, Jr., a 1949 graduate of William Grant High School, succeeded Ms. Blackwell in 1958. A graduate of Kentucky State University, Martin would be the last vocal music teacher assigned to the school. He would eventually become the founding director of the Northern Kentucky Community Center, the name of the building on Greenup Street after the school closed in 1976.

The music teachers at Lincoln-Grant wanted their black students to perform some of the same musical repertoire as students in the white schools. While the author was a student at Lincoln-Grant School, the choirs performed standard choral music and Negro spirituals, such as "The Battle Hymn of the Republic," "God of Our Fathers," "He, Watching Over Israel," and "I Hear A Voice A'Prayin.'" The choirs performed in maroon choir robes for the entire period that the author attended the school.

■ THE INSTRUMENTAL MUSIC PROGRAM

The beginning point for the instrumental music program at Lincoln-Grant is uncertain. However, according to an article in

Photograph 112: R. Hayes Strider.
COURTESY OF THE KENTON COUNTY PUBLIC LIBRARY, COVINGTON, KENTUCKY.

the June 17, 1914, *Kentucky Post*, the William Grant Orchestra performed an overture at the Twenty-fifth Annual Commencement of William Grant High School. Miss Frankie B. Watkins, the former acting principal, was listed as the musical director in that article. The existence of an instrumental music program would be reflected in a 1933 *Kentucky Post* article announcing a Christmas celebration program on the lawn of the First Baptist Church on Ninth Street. The program featured as its speaker, Charles E. Jones, and music was "furnished by the Lincoln-Grant High School band," along with Christmas carols by the children of the church.[214] The development of the instrumental music program seemed to be sporadic until 1940, when Mr. R. Hayes Strider, was shown as a faculty member at Lincoln-Grant School in the board minutes. He was specifically assigned to the instrumental music program, while Miss Elizabeth Gooch continued to be in charge of the vocal music program.

By 1942, Mr. Conrad Hutchinson, who earned a B.S. degree in Music from Tuskegee Institute, and also completed graduate work at Case Western Reserve University, the University of Cincinnati, and the New England Conservatory of Music, had become the instrumental music teacher.

"Hutch" (the name that students called him affectionately when they were not in his presence) was a tall, lanky, very popular teacher who brought a certain level of musical "activism" and showmanship to the band as it performed the marches of John Phillip Sousa and others. His charismatic personality and musical style drew numerous students to the Lincoln-Grant Band, including one or two students who were severe disciplinary problems in other classrooms. Mr. Hutchinson's young son, Conrad III, was also a member of the band. One can only imagine the pressure of having to attend school in the shadow of a father who was a very popular and effective teacher. Mr. Hutchinson developed such a dynamic musical organization that two teachers, Mr. Birtill Barrow and Mr. William Hargraves, also joined the band and participated with students in parades and school concerts.

The marching and concert bands performed selections such as Elgar's *Pomp and Circumstance,* (for commencement exercises), *El Capitan, The Great Gate of Kiev,* and Fred Waring's arrangement of "The Battle Hymn of the Republic." The marching band also performed additional instrumental selections from the compositions of John Phillip Sousa and other well-known composers of famous marches for that period.

Early band attire consisted of white shirts with dark neckties, and dark trousers and skirts with uniform band caps that may have been "hand me downs" from the white schools. Used instruments also came from the white schools. But during Mr. Hutchinson's tenure, with help from a newly formed Band Booster's Club, the band received new uniforms that included washable white pants with a blue strip, and matching, bright blue waistcoats trimmed in gold. The new uniforms, which were secured in 1949, would endure for the rest

---

214. *Kentucky Post*, "Celebration at Church," December 23, 1933.

of the school's existence.

Mr. Hutchinson would remain at the school for a number of years. The author's instrumental musical training was initiated under his tutelage. The band was so large that when I entered the sixth grade, I could only observe, and turn pages for other French horn players, while sitting in that section of the concert band, because there was no instrument for me to play on a regular basis. I was at that point a beginner, and the more advanced students had preference. (Purchasing or renting my own instrument was not an option, given my parents' financial circumstances). I was looking forward to the following school year, when Mr. Hutchinson had promised to move me into the concert band as a seventh grader. I would then have a school-owned instrument to play regularly. However, all students who were looking forward to band membership would be disappointed when the Lincoln-Grant instrumental music program was put on hold in the fall of 1951.

The December 20, 1951, Board of Education Minutes would reflect the following recommendation from Superintendent Glenn Swing: "This is to report to the Board that Conrad Hutchinson, Jr., a teacher of Instrumental Music at the Lincoln-Grant School, is no longer identified with the Covington Public School System. Salary accumulations since September 1951 have been fully paid. Mr. Hutchinson has taken no steps toward re-establishing himself with the school system. I recommend that this resignation be accepted."

Despite an abrupt ending to his employment in Covington and a great disappointment to Lincoln-Grant band students that year, Mr. Hutchinson had been highly regarded by the Lincoln-Grant constituency. His very successful tenure at Lincoln-Grant for almost a decade had positioned him to continue a stellar musical career in higher education at Grambling State University, which had recruited him to bring his vibrant energy to that campus.

Mr. Robert Crowder, a graduate of the University of Illinois, succeeded Mr. Hutchinson the following year. Crowder, who earned B.A. and B.F.A. degrees from the University of Illinois, and also completed graduate work at Western Reserve University, had the task of reviving the instrumental music program. Some former band students had shifted to vocal music when they found out that "Hutch" was not returning. After Mr. Crowder arrived, a significant number of former band members did not resume their band membership, while some would implement dual enrollment in band and choir.

Mr. Crowder's personality was more conservative than that of Mr. Hutchinson. He was musically very solid, but not a "showman" like Mr. Hutchinson. Over time, Crowder rebuilt the band, although it was never again the size that it was under Hutch. The instrumental music program would sustain student interest for many subsequent years under his leadership. Mr. Crowder would be the last instrumental music teacher at Lincoln-Grant School.

As a continuing band member through high school, the author played several instruments under Mr. Crowder's direction. When Mr. Crowder arrived, I wanted to continue with either the French horn or the trumpet. However, he convinced me that my "embouchure" (i.e. the size and contour of my lips) was better suited for a larger instrument. At his request I played the trombone and the baritone horn in the marching and concert bands. (Actually, I believe Mr. Crowder had enough trumpet and horn players, and needed someone to play the latter instruments).

Later, when Mr. Crowder developed a small jazz combo, he requested that I learn to play the bass fiddle. I easily mastered that instrument. I played a "mean" bass part when our jazz combo performed at a school assembly. I recall several young ladies jumping up from their seats and screaming in "groupie" fashion while I plucked out my jazz solo improvisation on the bass fiddle. Then one of my buddies took over with a jazz saxophone improvisation followed by another musical buddy playing his part on the trumpet. (Mr. Crowder played the piano). We "brought the house down" as we concluded our musical jazz *debut* at Lincoln-Grant with such tunes as "Take the A-Train," and "Stompin' at the Savoy. " We also played for a couple of school dances in the gymnasium. However, it appeared that our brand of jazz music was better suited for listening than for dancing. For the purpose of dancing, the kids really wanted rhythm and blues and rock and roll and the hits of the fifties rather than the jazz tunes of the 1930s and '40s.

■ SPRING FESTIVALS AND SPECIAL MUSICAL EVENTS

During the period when the author attended Lincoln-Grant School, the musical tradition was enriched by annual spring events featuring elementary class performances and skits by individuals or groups of students, as well as music provided by the band and choir from the high school. During the variety shows, select students who were sometimes the children of our teachers, completed individual musical selections including solos excerpted from Broadway musicals, as well as small comedic acts.

The author remembers the son of his second grade teacher, a fair-skinned youngster, dawning a fancy white tuxedo with tails, and a matching top hat and cane as he tap-danced and sang across the stage in a spotlight to the song, "The Easter Parade." He sang and danced in the same style as the famous entertainer, Fred Astaire. The teacher's son was skilled musically, and his parents, who both taught at Lincoln-Grant, had obviously sent him for private singing and tap dancing lessons. A young, attractive "lady" performed as his partner as she strolled across the stage in her long dress and "Easter bonnet" while he pursued her with his song and dance. The act concluded with his singing to her: "With your Easter bonnet, and all the frills upon it, I'll be the proudest fellow in the Easter parade!" The song was very effectively executed. He also sang and danced to "Red Roses for a Blue Lady" with a bouquet of red roses in his hand for his lady friend.

Another youthful couple acted out the equivalent of a "Tom Thumb" wedding as they also performed and sang on stage. They were dressed up as a bride and groom while being accompanied by a youthful "minister." Their scene was effectively designed to evoke laughter from the audience as they performed various "antics" in the guise of a mock wedding ceremony. A lot of creativity, costuming and background scenery was involved in those productions.

There was usually an in-school performance for all of the student body at no charge to the students, as well as evening performances for the community for a modest fee. The black community in Covington always responded well to the spring variety shows at Lincoln-Grant School.

The musical tradition at Grant was also enhanced by in school performances by black entertainers such as Maurice Rocco and Rose Murphy, as well as concerts by black college choirs. The Knoxville College Concert Choir and the Fisk Jubilee Singers performed at Lincoln-Grant School on separate occasions. Those vocal groups were touring the United States and other countries in order to raise money for their colleges, and recruit students. Somehow, probably with the influence of Mrs. Jackson and other alumni, they had been persuaded to perform at Lincoln-Grant School.

The Knoxville Choir was good, but the Fisk Jubilee Singers left a lasting impression on the author. The Jubilee Singers looked very stunning and professional as they entered the Lincoln-Grant stage adorned in their formal, dark attire. They represented their institution well both in their appearance and their performance. The special stage lighting had its effect as those rich, trained voices echoed throughout the Lincoln-Grant school auditorium to an audience of hushed, still students. The whole student body and the teachers focused on every nuance of the group's captivating renditions of various Negro Spirituals. The author immediately identified with them as examples of the kind of college student that he wanted to become.

Photograph 113: William Grant High School Choir, 1940s.

Source: Lincoln-Grant Reunion Program Booklet, 1979. Courtesy of Theodore H. H. Harris, Class of 1962.

Photograph 114: William Grant High School Chorus, 1950.
SOURCE: *GRANTONIAN*, 1950. COURTESY OF WILLA HOFFMAN JACKSON.

First row (left to right): *Vera Rhodes, Sarah Weaver, Ann Turner, Bettye Mills, Juanita Griffin, Mary S. Webb, Nettie Humphries, Betty Jones.*

Second row: *Ezell Lee, Rebecca Bell, Sue Cavil, Mattie Royal, Dorothy McQueen, Goldie Walker, Mary Hall, Gladys Behanan.*

Third row: *Margie Payne, Dorothy Humphries, Virginia Rice, Mary M. Webb, Peggy Williams, Wilma Thacker.*

Fourth row: *George Harrison, Edward Cunningham, Raymond Clifford, George Patterson, Richard Jarman, William Riley, Millard Garrett, Van Roy Clemmens.*

Fifth row: *David Redden, Granville Ingguls, William Hargraves, James Watkins, Theodore Hon, Donald George, James Riley, Walter Page, Robert Rhodes.*

Not pictured: *Elizabeth Gooch, Directress.*

Photograph 115: Lincoln-Grant School Choir, 1956.
SOURCE *GRANT WARRIOR* YEARBOOK, 1956.
COURTESY OF THE COVINGTON INDEPENDENT PUBLIC SCHOOLS.

Row one: *G. Slaughter, J. Hall, V. Alderson, G. Tyler, S. Pennington, M. Brown, J. Porterfield, Mrs. R. Phillips (teacher), L. Lattimore, H. Johnson, D. Green, V. Green, S. Rhodes, J. Tyler.*

Row two: *M. Givens, M. Bonner, R. Wilkinson, A. Johnson, B. Humphrey, A. Jefferson, B. Jouett, V. Sheffey, L. Givens, C. Jones, K. McIntie.*

Row three: *N. Brown, M. Ferrell, E. Wright, N. Simpson, J. Jasper, W. Hoffman, R. Hampton, G. Martin.*

Row four: *L. Wilkerson, J. Walton, L. Stewart, A. Green.*

Row five: *F. Wideman, J. McCullough, F. Jackson, P. Brown.*

Row six: *J. Moore, A. Roberts, T. Walton.*

Photograph 116: Lincoln-Grant Band, 1940s.
PHOTO PROVIDED BY RICHARD B. L. FOWLER.

An early Lincoln-Grant band, presumed to be in the 1940s. At that point, the band did not have standard band uniforms—only band caps supplied by the school, and their personal white shirts, dark trousers or skirts, and dark neckties.

Photograph 117: Lincoln-Grant Band, 1950.
SOURCE: *GRANTONIAN*, 1950. COURTESY OF WILLA HOFFMAN JACKSON.

ROSTER
COMBINED CONCERT AND BEGINNERS BAND

Flutes
George, Donald
Butler, Lois
Clarinets
Hargraves, Wm. II
Deal, Frank
Jackson, Collins
Hargraves, Beatrice
Crittenden, Theresa
LaBordeaux, Clementine
Dunson, Juanita
Stewart, Rod
Payne, Virginia
Herron, Charles
Ware, Pauline
Thacker, Shirley
Crittenden, Jacob
Bozeman, Barbara
Merritt, Wm. II
Reed, William
Cheek, Betty
Johnson, Alma
Hutchinson, Conrad III
Moore, James
Warmack, Bonnie
Hopkins, Sylvia
Ward, Shirley
Golsby, Geraldine
Webb, Raymond
Humphrey, Betty

Saxaphones
Riley, Lawrence
Hargraves, Wm. F.
Barrow, B. T.
Pearl, Brennan
Carr, Charles
Baker, Robert
Horns
Gentry, Fielden
Crowder, Jacqueline
Roland, Leroy
Burton, Lenora
Humphries, Joan
Cornets
Kelly, Robert
Crawford, Albert
Kenney, Clifford
Gentry, Joyce
Smith, Napoleon
Weaver, John
McCullough, Jerry
Baritones
Humphries, Fred
Simpson, William
Trombones
Davis, Earl
Johnson, Noah
Davis, Elsworth
Stickney, Wilbur
Wilkerson, Lois

Basses
Slaughter, James
Lattimore, Kenwood
Thompson, Eddie
Bass Viol
Adams, Gloria
Drums
Walton, James
Jackson, Robert
Sheffey, Donald
Crowder, Russell
Reed, Henry
Marks, Arthur
Bells
Webb, Ernestine
Drum Major
Ingguls, Granville
Drum Majorettes
Arvin, Gail
Thacker, Wilma
Crowder, Jacqueline

Conrad Hutchinson, Jr.
Bandmaster
Wm. F. Hargraves II
Student Cond.

Photograph 118: Lincoln-Grant Bands and Spring Festival.
SOURCE: LINCOLN-GRANT REUNION PROGRAM BOOKLET, 1979.
COURTESY OF THEODORE H. H. HARRIS, CLASS OF 1962.

Photograph 119: Lincoln-Grant Band, 1956.

SOURCE: *GRANT WARRIOR YEARBOOK*, 1956. COURTESY OF THE COVINGTON INDEPENDENT PUBLIC SCHOOLS.

Row one: *(Majorettes):* E. Hopkins, C. Stewart, C. Page, B. Slaughter, G. Slaughter, P. Offutt. **Row two:** unidentified student, W. Sharpe, J. Moore, K. Frye, L. Hartso, F. Wideman, P. Alexander; unidentified student, C. Sharpe, M. Walton, C. Rhodes, J. Wideman, unidentified student. **Row three:** C. James, R. Lattimore. **Row four:** J. Walton, N. Saxon(?), J. McCullough, L. Cammack, A. Green, R. Z. Orr, W. Riley.

Photograph 120: Lincoln-Grant Orchestra, 1950.
SOURCE: *GRANTONIAN*, 1950. COURTESY OF WILLA HOFFMAN JACKSON.

Photograph 121: Maurice Rocco and Rose Murphy, Celebrities.
SOURCE: *GRANTONIAN*, 1950. COURTESY OF WILLA HOFFMAN JACKSON.

CHAPTER 9

Athletics

■ THE BEGINNING

The story of athletics at Lincoln-Grant School centers on the game of basketball, although once upon a time there was a football team when the school was located in the Seventh Street Colored School building. The team practiced and trained at an outdoor facility located away from the school building. As Jim Reis reports, "The first sport apparently offered at [Grant] was football in the 1920s. . . . The William Grant High School Football team soon became a powerhouse among African-American schools in the state. At one point the high school team even played and beat the freshman team at Wilberforce College."[215] Coached by Paul Redden (on a volunteer basis), and assisted by Chester Rice, a manual training teacher at the school, the Grant football team also won the black high school state championship in 1929. However, football as a competitive sport was discontinued at some point after the school was relocated to the new building on Greenup Street. The plans for the new building included a gym with bleachers for spectators and a full interior basketball court, but no outdoor space for a football field. At that point, basketball became the only competitive sport at Lincoln-Grant School.

The athletic program at the new Lincoln-Grant School building on Greenup Street also included gym classes for all students in the upper grades, and voluntary intramural activities in such areas as volleyball, gymnastics, and baseball. Touch football on the hard surface of the school playground was both an in school and an after school activity. Swimming would be largely a sum-

---

215. Reis, "Many tried, few defeated."

mertime, nonschool, community-based activity in a segregated swimming pool located near the Jacob Price Homes. Exposure to a broader range of athletic activities, both in school and in the community would give those with athletic abilities outside of basketball an avenue to develop those abilities.

The athletic model for competitive sports in Kentucky's black schools followed the same path as the academic side of segregated education. An early belief in the inferior status of black athletes was just as potent as the view of academic mediocrity advanced by whites in the early days. That belief system was supported and sustained by Kentucky law, which prohibited the interaction of white and black schools. Consequently, no thought was given to interracial athletic competition among the high schools in Kentucky prior to the mid-1950s. Racial segregation in athletics resulted in the formation of a separate black athletic high school league in Kentucky. Membership in that league would play an important role in shaping the athletic program at Lincoln-Grant School.

One citation provides "an historical overview of the Kentucky High School Athletic League [KHSAL] athletics organization for the Negro Schools of Kentucky. There were 69 member schools, and KHSAL remained active until 1958 when Kentucky schools and athletic associations began to desegregate. Basketball and football were recognized by KHSAL."[216] During its existence, KHSAL provided an additional link among Kentucky's black high schools as their athletic teams competed with each other.

Another citation states, "Like other African American school teams in Kentucky, WGHS [William Grant High School] was a member of the Kentucky High School Athletic League (KHSAL). The counter league, the Kentucky High School Athletic Association (KHSAA), was for whites only until school integration began in the mid-1950s."[217]

Membership in the Kentucky High School Athletic League helped to shape the evolution of the basketball program at Lincoln-Grant. The black athletic league had come into existence the same year that Lincoln-Grant School moved to the new building on Greenup Street. As Stout indicates, "The basketball regular season did not start until after Dec. 31. Each member school could not play more than 20 games prior to the regional tournament. Any school violating that rule would be ineligible for tournament play."[218] The league had also imposed an age limit of twenty for eligibility to play high school basketball, and established standards for basketball referees. Although some member schools violated some of the rules, and were suspended from the league, the basketball program at Grant was consistently in compliance with the rules of the League.

---

216. "Grade Schools & High Schools in Kentucky," Notable Kentucky African Americans Database. See Shadows of the Past, by Louis Stout," 27.

217. Ibid., see Brock, James "Jim," 6.

218. Louis Stout, *Shadows of the Past, A History of the Kentucky High School Sthletic League* (Lexington, Ky.: Host Communications, 2006) 11.

■ GYM TEACHERS AND COACHES

Mr. Paul Redden, a graduate of Wilberforce University, whose teaching career in Covington had begun at the Seventh Street Colored School as a grade school teacher and volunteer football coach, would formally become the gym teacher and head coach at Lincoln-Grant after its relocation to Greenup Street. He would begin the great basketball tradition of the school. Mr. Redden was a professional, who knew that all of his students would not become star athletes. He was patient with those who were less athletically skilled, while encouraging them when they did well. Mr. Redden would leave a firm imprint of more than two decades on Grant's athletic programs when he left Lincoln-Grant to take a job at Knoxville College in Tennessee in 1952.

Mr. Walter Gilliard, a William Grant graduate from the class of 1942 ½, succeeded Mr. Redden as the gym teacher and head basketball coach in 1952, after receiving a B.A. degree earlier from Kentucky State College. Gilliard, who continued a strong basketball tradition at Grant for a three-year period, left Grant to join Lincoln Institute, a black boarding school in Shelby County, Kentucky, at the end of the 1954/55 school year. After earning a master's degree from the University of Kentucky and a Ph.D. Degree in education from Kent State University, Dr. Gilliard would ultimately become a professor and administrator in the area of higher education in Ohio.

There were several Junior Varsity basketball coaches at Lincoln-Grant over a period of time. The most long-term Junior Varsity coach was Mr. Birtill Barrow, a teacher of high school science and Spanish at the school. For a number of years, Mr. Barrow carried his firm demeanor from the classroom to the basketball court. Jerry McCullough also coached the Grant Cubs (grade school basketball players) while he was a student athlete at the school.

Mr. James Brock, a graduate of Tuskegee Institute, followed Mr. Gilliard as the gym teacher and head basketball coach in 1955. Brock would function as Grant's head basketball coach for the next ten years, while building a lasting basketball legacy for the school.

Mr. Brock was unable to teach, or function as the head coach, for a period of time during the 1959 school year due to illness. David Johnson, who had just graduated from Jackson State College in Mississippi, was called in for a four-month period to teach physical education and serve as the temporary head basketball coach. When Mr. Brock returned to his duties, Mr. Johnson became a fifth-grade teacher at Lincoln-Grant, as well as an assistant to Brock. He also replaced Mr. Barrow as the Junior Varsity coach. Johnson was transferred to First District School as an elementary teacher in 1965 after the closing of William Grant High School. He later became involved with the Neighborhood Youth Core and other community organizations in the city of Covington.[219]

A perspective on the progress of the William Grant Warriors under Coach

---

219. Conversation with Mr. David Johnson, May 27, 2010.

James Brock was captioned as follows: "The 1956-57 WGHS [Grant Warrior] team was the first African American basketball team to win a district tournament in the KHSAA [white high school] tournament."[220] Jones further states, "As more African American students were allowed to attend the formerly all white schools, there was an impact on the pool of high school athletes that had been restricted to the all black schools. In 1965, the year that William Grant High School closed, the basketball team won only five games. The season was a far cry from the winning seasons that had garnered the school a win-loss record of 185-69 during Brock's years as head coach."[221]

Mr. Brock left the Covington Independent Public Schools for another position in Ohio after the closing of William Grant High School in 1965. Jones concludes that Brock's stellar coaching career resulted in his induction into the Northern Kentucky Black Hall of Fame and the KHSAA Hall of Fame in 2000.[222]

■ FROM SEGREGATED TO INTEGRATED ATHLETIC COMPETITION

During the days of pure segregation, the Grant Warrior basketball team, a member of the Central Region of KHSAL played "away" games at other black high schools located in places such as Louisville and Lexington, Kentucky, as well as Lockland, Ohio. Among the strongest competitors were Louisville Central, Lexington Dunbar, DePorres, a predominantly black Catholic high school in Cincinnati, and Lockland Wayne. However during the 1956/57 school year, after school integration was mandated, and the black schools in Kentucky began to join the white athletic association, the William Grant High School basketball team was allowed to compete for the district championship against white high schools in the area. That year the team won the 34th district championship by defeating Erlanger Lloyd. The Warrior co-captains, Jerry McCullough and Leslie Stewart proudly accepted the winner's trophy from Superintendent James Caywood of Kenton County on that occasion.

The team also played against Dixie Heights, another Northern Kentucky white high school, in December 1957. The author personally attended that game, which resulted in the defeat of the Dixie Heights basketball team. There was no overt racial name-calling or racially hostility, although the Dixie Heights fans were very disappointed in the loss to Grant.

The team continued the great tradition of basketball at Grant as the Thirty-fourth District champs in 1960. The Grant Warriors also won a couple of regional championships, and even qualified to join the "Sweet 16" for the state in 1964. However, eventually some of the better players at Grant would enroll

---

220. "Grade Schools & High Schools in Kentucky," Notable Kentucky African Americans Database. See Brock, James "Jim," 6.

221. Ibid.

222. Ibid.

at Holmes High School and other predominantly white schools as the integration of the public schools in Northern Kentucky took firm hold in the mid-1960s, followed by the eventual closing of William Grant High School.

■ STAR ATHLETES

One former Lincoln-Grant athlete who emerged to professional status in a sport other than basketball was Don Johnson. Stout reports, "Don Johnson certainly rates as one of Grant High's greatest athletic products. Johnson participated in three sports during his days at Grant High, making his mark in basketball, baseball, and track and field. However, Johnson's athletic future was spent on the baseball diamond, where he spent time in the Old Negro League playing for the Chicago American Giants and later for the Philadelphia Stars."[223]

Stout continues, "How Johnson was discovered rates as an interesting story in itself. While watching a game between the Indianapolis Clowns and the Chicago American Giants, he was recognized by one of the Giants [*sic*] players. Seems the player had seen Johnson play in a fast-pitch softball game and had been mightily impressed with Johnson's talent. The player then persuaded the Chicago manager to let Johnson suit up and play. The rest is, as they say, history."[224]

In the year, 2009 a baseball field that is dedicated to Donald Johnson exists behind the vacant Lincoln-Grant building on Greenup in Covington. The plaque in front of the field reads as follows: "Donald Johnson was born in Covington, Ky on July 1, 1926. He graduated from Lincoln Grant High School & continued his education at Dayton University. In 1947 he signed with the Cincinnati Reds & later signed with the Cleveland Indians. After an injury, he joined the Negro League and played in Philadelphia & Chicago, achieving a lifetime batting average of .335. He won multiple titles & in 1999 was honored with induction into the Negro Baseball Hall of Fame." [225]

LeRoy Hambrick, who attended Southgate Elementary School in Newport, and graduated from William Grant High School in 1938, was another successful athlete. "Athletics was the positive element in the lives of Hambrick and his brothers. They played baseball in the streets, basketball using a beer barrel mailed to a post, and other games which their imagination created. In spite of [racial] segregation, Hambrick and others played with the . . . white kids because they were 'just kids.' A lasting friendship with Ralph Mussman, former city manager of Newport, developed from these activities."[226]

223. Stout, *Shadows of the Past,* 34.
224. Ibid.
225. The author's search of the Covington Board of Education records did not find the name of Donald Johnson among William Grant High School graduates, although it is obvious that Johnson did attend Lincoln-Grant School. It is possible that he was a GED graduate.

LeRoy Hambrick received an A.B. Degree from Clark College, Atlanta, Georgia [and the] M. A. Degree from New York University. . . . His athletic prowess began early in his life. He received letters in football, basketball, baseball and track under Coach Paul Redden. He was a Golden Glove Boxing Champion. In Atlanta, he was a Teacher, Coach and Official. LeRoy Hambrick is a member of the Georgia Interscholastic Association, the Georgia High school Association, the Southern Intercollegiate athletic Conference and the National Football League where he is an Alternate official.[227]

Several basketball players from William Grant also achieved distinction, including Leslie Stewart, who played for Villa Madonna (Thomas More) College as one of that school's first black student athletes, and Dickie Beal, who played at Holmes High School after the Covington schools were integrated.

Tom Thacker was a star focus of the William Grant High School basketball team. A newspaper article in the *Enquirer* focused on Thacker's induction into the Northern Kentucky Hall of Fame that year reports, "As a freshman [at Grant] Tom helped lead Grant to a second-place finish and made the all-tourney team of the all-black state tournament. As a sophomore, his team was the first from an all-black school to win a game in the previously all-white Kentucky High School Athletic Association Tournament, [Coach] Brock says. As a junior and senior, Tom's team made it to the Sweet 16 of the KHSAA tournament."[228]

Thacker attended the University of Cincinnati, where he followed in the footsteps of the great basketball legend, Oscar Robertson. The newspaper article cited above continues, "UC fans will recall it was Thacker who, 0-for-6 against UCLA in the 1962 NCCAA Tournament semifinals, hit a 12-footer with 3 seconds left to win the game on UC's way to a second straight national title." Similar to Robertson, Tommy Thacker was drafted by the Cincinnati Royals in the first round of the 1963 National Basketball Association (NBA) draft after graduating from UC. After playing with the Royals, Thacker "went on to win rings with the 1968 Boston Celtics and 1971 Indiana Pacers."[229]

The Los Angeles Lakers drafted George Stone, another basketball player from Grant, into the NBA in the 9th round (9th pick, 115th overall) of the 1968 NBA draft. Assistant Coach David Johnson and Coach James Brock had discovered Stone's basketball talent while he was a student at William Grant. From that point he became a "standout" forward for the William Grant Warriors. Stone graduated from William Grant High School in 1964. He then went to on to Marshall University to make his athletic contributions to the "Thundering Herd."

---

226. Quotes are excerpts from a Lincoln Grant Reunion program held July 12–14, 1885, during which Hambrick was a guest speaker.
227. Ibid.
228. *Enquirer,* "Thacker's road to UC, NBA began at Grant," January 16, 2008.
229. Ibid.

As a [six-foot, seven inch] forward from Marshall University, Stone played four seasons (1968–1972) in the American Basketball Association [ABA] as a member of the Los Angeles Stars, Utah Stars, and Carolina Cougars. He averaged 13.6 points per game over the course of his career and ranked tenth in ABA history in three-point field goal percentage (.323). He also won a league championship with the Utah Stars in 1971.[230]

Athletics at Lincoln-Grant (and other black high schools) served the purpose of keeping many young black men and women in school. There would be no competitive sports for females at Lincoln-Grant, although several young women became cheerleaders, and participated in intramural sports, such as volleyball. The relationship of coaches to their student athletes was important in sustaining an interest in staying in school and playing sports, for which some were very gifted. The strength of character and personal discipline developed by the coaches and physical education teachers at Lincoln-Grant would have a lasting influence on the lives of many young black men and women who passed through the doors of Lincoln-Grant School.

230. "George Stone (basketball)," *Wikipedia, the free encyclopedia*, http://en.wikipedia.org/wiki/George_Stone(basketball) (accessed May 28, 2010).

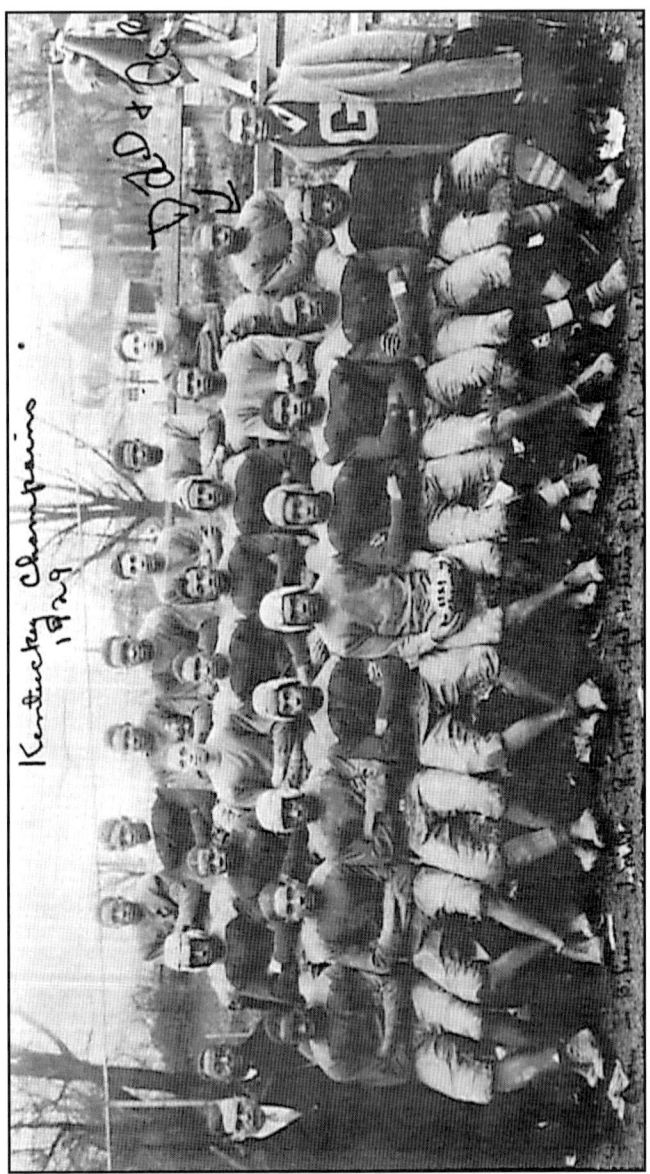

Photograph 122: Lincoln-Grant Football Team, 1929.
PHOTO PROVIDED BY THEODORE H. H. HARRIS, CLASS OF 1962.

The Lincoln-Grant football team (1929) was coached by Paul Redden (standing on right with "G" on sweater). Standing on left are Principal Henry R. Merry and Chester Rice, Manual Training Teacher at Lincoln-Grant. The team had a strong reputation during that period, but football was discontinued in favor of basketball after the school was relocated to a new building on Greenup Street in 1932.

194 7or 1948 "Twenty Counts" at Cov. Ball Field

Photograph 123: "Twenty Counts" Baseball Team, 1947 or 1948.
PHOTOGRAPH COURTESY OF THE KENTON COUNTY PUBLIC LIBRARY, COVINGTON, KENTUCKY.

"Twenty Counts" was a community baseball team for African Americans, which included older players who were former students at Lincoln-Grant School, or graduates of William Grant High School. This 1947 or 1948 photograph was taken at a Covington ball field that accommodated African American players shows:

Front row, left to right: *Marvin McIntie, Jack Reed, Johnny Herndon, unidentified, Otis Madison, Vic Elmer, and Leon Whatley.*

Second row, left to right: *Charles Stewart, Donald Johnson (Negro Baseball Hall of Fame, 1999), Hillard "Doughboy" Baskin, Vernon James, Robert Baughman, Raymond Gray, and "Cowboy" Gary.*

Photograph 124: Grant Warrior Basketball Team, 1947.
SOURCE: *GRANT WARRIOR ARCHIVES.*

Coach Paul Redden, second row, standing, last person on right.

Photograph 125: Senior and Junior Cheerleaders, 1950.
SOURCE: *GRANTONION* YEARBOOK, 1950.

Photograph 126: Lincoln-Grant Varsity Basketball Team, 1950.
SOURCE: *GRANTONION YEARBOOK*, 1950.

First row: *D. Herndon, G. Patterson, J. Riley, unidentified, C. Jackson(?)*
Second row: *Coach Redden, T. Hon, J. Clemmons, R. Rhodes, D. George(?)*
Third row: *unidentified, L. Riley, unidentified, R. Jackson, W. Riley, F. Deal, D. Redden, D. Williams.*

Photograph 127: Grant Warriors, 1954.
PHOTOGRAPH COURTESY OF DR. WALTER GILLIARD, CLASS OF 1942-1/2.

Kneeling: *C. Herron, G. Walton, C. Fields, W. Hall, L. Wilkinson, and R. Stewart.*

Standing: *Coach Walter Gilliard, unidentified, J. A. Walton, N. Smith, C. Green, J. McCullough, and Principal Henry R. Merry.*

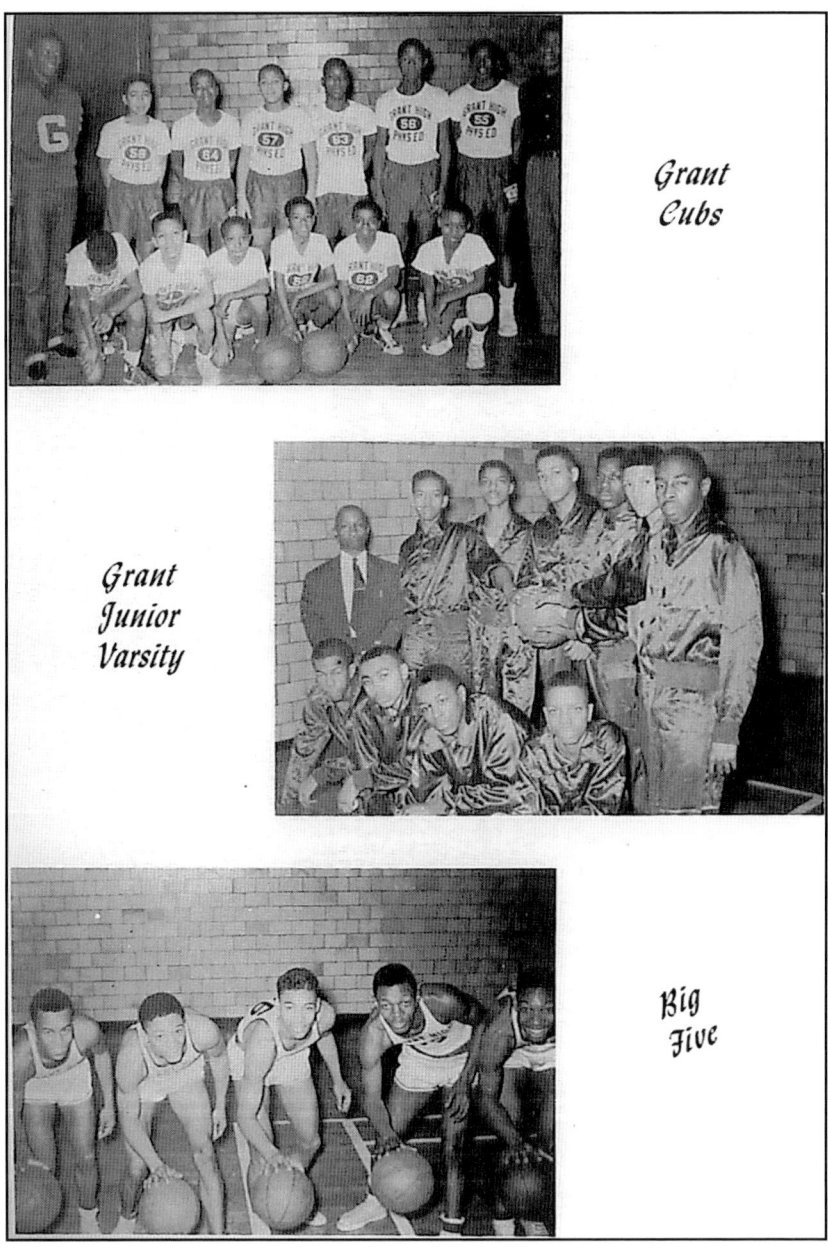

Grant Cubs

Grant Junior Varsity

Big Five

Photograph 128: Grant Cubs, Junior Varsity and "Big Five," 1956.
SOURCE: *GRANT WARRIOR* YEARBOOK, 1956.
COURTESY OF THE COVINGTON INDEPENDENT PUBLIC SCHOOLS.

Varsity

First row: Coach Brock, W. Riley, scorekeeper. Second row: W. Reed, J. McCullough, L. Stewart, T. Butler. Third row: T. Thacker, A. Roberts, L. Wilkinson, R. Phipps, R. Humphries. Fourth row: A. Ballard, L. Cammack, F. Jackson.

SCHEDULE

60	Alumni	41
38	Maysville	23
101	Catholic Louisville	74
70	Elizabethtown	36
72	Ky. State B Team	53
46	Xenia	41
56	Maysville	61
74	Elizabethtown	46
66	Central	81
81	Lincoln Inst.	72
55	Deporres	62
90	Lincoln Inst.	78
79	Catholic	57
48	Cincinnati· Y. M.	17
66	Covington Y. M.	56

CENTRAL DISTRICT TOURNAMENT

84	Elizabethtown	57
84	Lincoln Institute	70

FINALS

50	Central	102

CHEERLEADERS

G. Tyler, J. Warmack, P. Gray, M. Ferrell, L. Smith, R. Patterson.

Photograph 129: Lincoln-Grant Varsity and Cheerleaders, 1956.
SOURCE: *GRANT WARRIOR* YEARBOOK, 1956.
COURTESY OF THE COVINGTON INDEPENDENT PUBLIC SCHOOLS.

Photograph 130: Grant Warriors, 1957A.
SOURCE: *GRANT WARRIOR* YEARBOOK, 1957.
COURTESY OF THE COVINGTON INDEPENDENT PUBLIC SCHOOLS.
PHOTOGRAPHER: CURTIS BENION, CLASS OF 1958.

Grant Warriors

Left to right: A. Ballad, R. Humphery, W. Reed, Co-Captain L. Stewart, G. Butler,
A. Roberts, T. Thacker, L. Cammack, W. Guest, J. Young, A. Davis, Center J.
McCullough, Captain James Brock, Coach.

Photograph 131: Grant Warriors, 1957B.
SOURCE: *GRANT WARRIOR* YEARBOOK, 1957.
COURTESY OF THE COVINGTON INDEPENDENT PUBLIC SCHOOLS.

Photograph 132: Grant Warriors, 34th District Champions, 1957.
SOURCE: *GRANT WARRIOR* YEARBOOK, 1957.
COURTESY OF THE COVINGTON INDEPENDENT PUBLIC SCHOOLS.

*Jerry McCullough and Leslie Stewart, co-captains of the Warrior team of William
Grant High School receive the 34th District basketball trophy from Superintendent
James Caywood of Kenton County.*

Photograph 133: Grant Warriors, 1959/60.
PHOTOGRAPH COURTESY OF CHARLES E. DICKERSON, CLASS OF 1958.

Left to right: *William Jackson, Joe Nelson, Clinton Rhodes, George Offutt, Eugene Claxton, Leonard Phipps, William Sharpe, George Hunter, Wayne Mays, Charles James, Robert Brown, Barry Storms.*

Photograph 134: David Hunter, Coach James Brock, and Robert Storms, 1964.
PHOTOGRAPH COURTESY OF RICHARD B. L. FOWLER, CLASS OF 1963.

Hunter and Storms were both honors graduates of the William Grant Class of 1964, and leaders on the 1964 Warrior Basketball Team.

CHAPTER 10

Bluegrass Echoes: The Bonds and Boundaries of Black Schools

Lincoln-Grant School did not stand alone as a racially segregated, black school. There were similar schools in major cities, including Louisville and Lexington, as well as several smaller towns located in more remote parts of the state. Athletic competition, usually through basketball, kept many of the black high schools connected to each other. A few of those schools, with which the author is acquainted, are cited below.

■ PAUL LAURENCE DUNBAR HIGH SCHOOL
LEXINGTON, KENTUCKY

In 1921 William H. Fouse [who was the principal of Lincoln-Grant School from 1908 to 1912] was instrumental in convincing the city of Lexington and the Education Board to build a new school for Negro children. Two years later the school was completed at 545 North Upper Street [in Lexington] with Fouse as the principal. The school was named after poet Paul Laurence Dunbar, whose mother Matilda and father Joshua were from Kentucky.[231]

Fouse would ultimately elevate the status of the Paul Laurence Dunbar High School as "the first African American high school accredited by the Southern Association of Colleges and Schools."[232] He helped to create "the first school bank and the first insurance program within Dunbar," while also

---

231. "Grade Schools & High Schools in Kentucky." Notable Kentucky African Americans Database. See Paul Laurence Dunbar High School (Lexington, KY), 24.
232. Jones, "The Early Kinship."

developing regional literacy and art competitions, "and a championship debate team." Fouse became the supervisor of African American schools for the city of Lexington, and "developed the Bluegrass Oratorical Association and the Bluegrass Athletic Association."[233] Dunbar High School compared favorably to Lincoln-Grant School both academically and athletically. Dunbar won the state tournament in 1948 and 1950. It is reported that a majority of high school graduates from Dunbar went on to pursue college studies. The school closed in 1967.

■   CENTRAL HIGH SCHOOL—LOUISVILLE, KENTUCKY

Another black high school in Kentucky that was highly regarded by the Lincoln-Grant constituency for its academic and athletic prowess was Louisville Central. "Previously known as Louisville Colored High School, the school opened in 1882 after leaders of the Louisville, KY African American community appealed to the Louisville Board of Education for a high school for African Americans. The school was initially located at the corner of Sixth and Kentucky Streets, with J. M. Maxwell serving as principal and C. W. House the only teacher. Funding initially came from African American taxes only. In 1952 the school was moved to the new Central High School building on Twelfth and Chestnut Streets."[234]

Louisville Central was an athletic competitor of Lincoln-Grant. The author recalls traveling from Covington to Louisville by chartered bus for a basketball game between Grant and Central as a high school student during the early 1950s. Upon our arrival at the school building in Louisville, the Lincoln-Grant students were quite favorably impressed by Central's relatively new, expansive school facility and gymnasium. We were actually amazed by the fact that such an extensive school facility had been created for black high school students in Kentucky. (Our sense of being so overwhelmed by the building may have also contributed to the loss of the basketball game to Central that evening). Louisville Central won the State Tournament in 1932, 1949, 1951, 1952, and 1956. It also won the National High School Athletic League National Basketball Championship in 1952 and 1956.

> Career courses were part of the educational offerings. Central was the largest and most progressive high school in the state for African Americans; there were 1400 students and 57 faculty members. Today, Central High School Magnet Career Academy, a four-year accredited comprehensive high that offers a pre-college curriculum, is located at 1130 W. Chestnut Street in Louisville.[235]

233. Ibid.
234. "Grade Schools & High Schools in Kentucky." Notable Kentucky African Americans Database. See Louisville Central High School/Central High School Magnet Career Academy, 21.
235. Ibid.

■ LINCOLN INSTITUTE—LINCOLN RIDGE, KENTUCKY

Occasionally, while the author was a student at Lincoln-Grant, a student would transfer from Lincoln-Grant School to Lincoln Institute, a boarding school in Shelby County, located approximately 103 miles south of Covington. (Being sent off to a boarding school was a "big deal" for a black student in Covington at that time). In addition to sharing first names, Lincoln Institute seemed to have a special relationship with Lincoln-Grant School with regard to student transfer. The setting in Lincoln Ridge would capture much of the natural beauty of the hills of Kentucky, and bring a sense of serenity and calm to boarding school students who came from all over the state.

Although it was connected to Berea College, Lincoln Institute had an extensive academic history of its own, and a distinct identity that focused on primary and secondary vocational education.

> The Lincoln Institute was formed in response to the 1904 Day Law, which was upheld by the 1908 Supreme Court decision forbidding the education of whites and blacks in the same Kentucky school. The law was aimed at Berea College, which had been integrated since 1863. . . . Lincoln Institute opened in 1912 in Shelby County, KY. It offered vocational instruction, unlike the classical education that had been offered at Berea. The first African American president was Dr. Whitney M. Young, Sr.; he led Lincoln Institute for over 40 years as it became a prominent boarding school for African American children.[236]

The Lincoln-Grant basketball team competed regularly against the team at Lincoln Institute. The Lincoln Institute team won the state tournament in 1937, 1938, and again in 1955. The two schools were so familiar with each other that Lincoln-Grant basketball players and fans shortened the Lincoln Institute name to "Institute." Jones reports, "The campus is presently leased by the federal government for the Whitney M. Young, Jr. Job Core Center."[237]

■ LOCAL BLACK HIGH SCHOOLS IN THE CINCINNATI AREA

In spite of the fact that Ohio did not have laws prescribing racial segregation, there were two schools in the Cincinnati area with histories similar to Lincoln-Grant School, as well as an athletic relationship to Grant. DePorres, a predominantly black Catholic High School in downtown Cincinnati was attractive to a few Lincoln-Grant students of the Catholic faith, who wanted to complete their high school education there. The other historically black school, Lockland Wayne, located in the city of Lockland, north of Cincinnati, was primarily an athletic competitor in basketball.

---

236. Ibid., see Lincoln Institute (Lincoln Ridge, KY), 20.
237. Jones, "The Early Kinship."

There were also three predominantly black high schools in the Cincinnati Public School district that attracted selected students from Lincoln-Grant. Some students changed their residence from Covington to Cincinnati in order to attend Woodward High School, Taft Senior High School, and Hughes High School. While Taft was always a predominantly black school, Woodward and Hughes, which began as predominantly white high schools, would also eventually became predominantly black.

The complexity of the black, segregated high school network was extensive. The forged outreach to other similarly situated black schools formed a sort of kinship and bonding among black students and teachers from different geographical areas that was far-reaching. But the layers of policies, procedures, actions and segregated interschool relationships that had become ingrained over so many years would soon be eradicated.

Figure 26: Black Segregated High Schools in Kentucky.[a]

Ashland Booker T. Washington High School	Lebanon Rosenwald High School
Bardstown Training High School	Lexington Douglas High School
Beaver Dam Bruce High School	Lexington Dunbar High School
Benham Colored High School	Louisville Catholic High School
Bowling Green High Street	Louisville Central High School
Campbellsville Durham Colored High School	Lynch Colored High School
Covington William Grant High School	Madisonville Rosenwald High School
Cynthiana Banneker High School	Mayfield Dunbar High School
Danville Bate High School	Maysville Fee High School
Drakesboro Community High School	Middlesboro Lincoln High School
Elizabethtown Bond-Washington High School	Morganfield Duncan High School
Elkton Todd County Training High School	Mt. Sterling Dubois High School
Frankfort Mayo-Underwood High School	Murray Douglas High School
Franklin Lincoln High School	Nicholasville Rosenwald-Dunbar H.S.
Georgetown Ed Davis High School	Owensboro Western High School
Glasgow Ralph Bunche High School	Paducah Lincoln High School
Harlan Rosenwald High School	Paris Western High School
Harrodsburg West Side High School	Pikeville Perry Cline High School
Hazard Liberty High School	Princeton Dotson High School
Henderson Douglass High School	Richmond High School
Hickman Riverview High School	Russellville Knob City High School
Hopkinsville Attucks High School	Simpsonville Lincoln Institute
Horse Cave High School	Somerset Dunbar High School
J. W. Million High School	Stanford Lincoln High School
Jenkins Dunham High School	Versailles Simmons High School
Lancaster Mason High School	Winchester Oliver High School

a. Stout, *Shadows of the Past.*

Part III

Changing Times
1954–1976

United States Supreme Court Building
Washington, D.C.

CHAPTER 11

The Personal Impact
of Changes in Racial Policy

■ NEW LEADERSHIP: PRINCIPAL CHARLES L. LETT

This author had just entered high school as a freshman at William Grant by legitimately accessing on a daily basis the third floor of a school building that he had attended since kindergarten. The "police action" involved in the Korean Conflict had officially paused on July 27, 1953, and Harry S. Truman, the plain spoken Democrat from Missouri who had the audacity to order the racial integration of the United States armed forces in 1948, had yielded the U.S. presidency to a popular Republican military general named Dwight David Eisenhower. The initial chants of "We like Ike" would diminish significantly as the thirty-fourth president of the United States led the country into the Vietnam War, which had official U.S. involvement in 1959, near the end of his second term in office. During a period of U.S. history that was dominated nationally by McCarthyism and charges of communist activity on the part of some prominent U.S. citizens, a large number of male students and graduates from William Grant High School (and a few females) voluntarily joined their preferred branches of the armed services. Many, who made those choices rather than being drafted through the selective service system, readily embraced their sense of duty to God and country. Although a few chose the U.S. Marine Corps or the U.S. Navy, larger numbers joined the U.S. Air Force, under the "buddy system" during the 1950s.

My worldview was evolving into that of a young black man looking more broadly at what I could accomplish in life as I approached adulthood. The constellation in my family household was also changing. Two of my brothers would graduate from William Grant High School, one in 1954 and the other in

1955. Each would join the United States Air Force immediately upon graduation, and reduce our home to three children and two parents. A third brother to the author would graduate from William Grant High School in 1957, and later receive his undergraduate degree from Villa Madonna (Thomas More) College in Covington. The author's only sister would attend Lincoln-Grant through the eighth grade, and become the first black graduate of LaSallette Academy, a Catholic all-girls' school in Covington, in 1961. She would also earn a bachelor's degree from Thomas More College.

The social adjustments of the students and faculty at Lincoln-Grant School were subtle, and vaguely attached to the shifting winds of a changing society. I recall during my freshman year the preparations for the retirement of Mr. Henry R. Merry, who had been our school principal for as long as I could remember. Mrs. Jackson, our English teacher was very directly involved in organizing the students and faculty for Mr. Merry's retirement, even to the point of having students in every grade learn a special song, "We'll (I'll) be Loving You Always," which the entire student body would sing at a final school assembly for an emotional Mr. Merry in the spring of 1955. There would also be a testimonial dinner for Mr. Merry at the Manse Hotel on Friday, June 3, 1955, with Superintendent Glenn Swing as the main speaker. That community event would include "musical selections by the students of Lincoln Grant School."[238]

Whether planned and encouraged by the city school administration or not, Mr. Merry's retirement at the approximate age of seventy would coincide with the beginning of a new era in public school education in Covington, and in the nation at large, as a new principal, Charles L. Lett took the reigns of Lincoln-Grant School in 1955.

Photograph 135: Principal Charles L. Lett.
Mr. Charles L. Lett, was principal of Lincoln-Grant School from 1955 until 1963.
SOURCE: *GRANT WARRIOR*, 1956. COURTESY OF THE COVINGTON INDEPENDENT PUBLIC SCHOOLS.

Mr. Lett had initiated his educational career as a seventh grade student teacher at Lincoln-Grant in 1950 under the supervision of Mr. Clarence Williams, a veteran seventh grade teacher. Somewhat ironically, Mr. Lett would quickly ascend the promotional ladder at Lincoln-Grant School and become Mr. Williams's "boss." After graduating from Kentucky State College around 1950, Mr. Lett apparently taught at a

---

238. *Kentucky Times Star,* "To Be Honored" (H. R. Merry), May 23, 1955, 6A.

Figure 27: Memory Page for Mr. William Hargraves, Board of Education Minutes, December 23, 1953, p. 391.

William Frederick Hargraves

Through the sudden death of William F. Hargraves, on Saturday, December 12, the Covington Public School System suffered a distinct and irreparable loss in its teaching staff.

Mr. Hargraves, a teacher of history and social science at William Grant High School, had been an employee of the Board of Education since September, 1929. He was a superior instructor, a good scholar, and possessed the highest attributes of character. He was well liked by pupils and fellow workers, and he rendered to the community an invaluable service through his many activities and interests.

Mr. Hargraves graduated from Miami University at Oxford, Ohio, in 1925, with a B.A. degree. Later, he received an M.A. degree from the same institution. When he came to Covington, in 1929, President Raymond M. Hughes, of Miami University said in his recommendation, "I regard him as unusually well fitted for teaching in high school. He is the first boy of his race to be awarded a degree from Miami, and has made distinctly the best record of any Colored student we have had. He uses good English, is industrious, trustworthy and pleasant to work with. I recommend him without reservation."

In recognition of his superior service and the loss to the Board of Education through his death, I respectfully recommend that a page in the Minute Book be dedicated to his memory.

Respectfully submitted,
Glenn O. Swing
Superintendent of Schools

Having a Memory Page dedicated in the Board of Education Minutes as a permanent memorial to one's work in the Covington Public Schools was a rare honor for anyone, black or white. Mr. Hargraves was the only black person in the history of the school system to receive that honor during that period. Mr. Lett initially replaced Mr. Hargraves as a teacher of Social Studies at William Grant High School.

black grade school outside of Covington until a teaching opening occurred at William Grant High School in 1953. The untimely death of Mr. William Hargraves, our high school Social Studies teacher, in December 1953 would create a vacancy that Mr. Lett would be called to fill. (In a rare tribute, Superintendent Swing recommended the dedication of a memory page in the Board of Education Minutes to Mr. Hargraves. See figure 29).

Mr. Lett was married to Anna Sleet Lett, a 1943 William Grant graduate. He functioned as the social studies teacher at William Grant for a year and a half. Lett was then appointed as the eighth permanent principal of Lincoln-Grant School, while he simultaneously pursued graduate work on a part-time basis at the University of Cincinnati. As students, we did not realize that Charles L. Lett had been selected to begin the final chapter in the existence of Lincoln-Grant School.

I remember Mr. Lett's administrative tenure during my remaining three years at William Grant High School as primarily student centered. He had more direct contact with students than his predecessor, as he attempted to influence our educational development both individually and collectively. Unlike Mr. Merry, Mr. Lett was often visible in the hallways, while informally conversing with students in person and in random groups between classes and during the lunch hour. As high school students, we identified more closely with a young principal who seemed only a few years older than many of us. Mr. Lett was probably chosen for his younger age and his presumed resilience in dealing with a projected new era of public school education.

■ BROWN V. BOARD OF EDUCATION

Change was on the way. It would emerge gradually in Northern Kentucky, without undue fanfare or formal proclamation of its arrival. It would come upon the city of Covington furtively, and much to the eventual surprise and anguish of many local people, who had been lulled into a sense of complacency and racial rigidity since the eighteen hundreds. A seismic shift in the ground beneath us was occurring. Indeed, a sea change in our social order was taking place in the nation without our grasping immediately its enormity, its complexity, or the far-reaching impact of its impending effects upon our lives.

Others far removed from the city of Covington would accomplish the real work, the "heavy lifting." The case began in Clarendon County, South Carolina, with the repeated denial of a request for a single school bus for black children in 1950. Although white children in the county were transported to separate schools by as many as thirty school buses, black children in that county walked to school from as far away as five miles. The case, which began as a quest for equal treatment, had expanded to the view that separate schools for black and white children violated the Equal Protection Clause of the Fourteenth Amendment to the U.S. Constitution. After arguments were brought before the South Carolina Supreme Court, a three-judge panel ruled in favor of the school board in a split decision, with one judge dissenting. The case then moved to the U.S. Supreme Court. While Northern Kentucky continued to languish in its usual racial convictions and traditions, *Brown v. Board of Education, 347 U.S. 483* would be first argued before the Supreme Court of the United States of America on December 9, 1952, in behalf of black children in the states of Kansas, South Carolina, Virginia, and Delaware. The Court combined several cases from different geographical areas under *Oliver L. Brown et al. v. the Board of Education of Topeka, Kansas, et al.* because all sought the same legal remedy for segregated schools in America—that "separate but equal" schools in America should be ruled inherently unequal.

The U.S. Supreme Court considered the case for several months, but was unable to arrive at a decision. Following the death of one member of the Court, and the appointment of Chief Justice Earl Warren, the case was reargued on December 8, 1953. With new leadership, the Warren Court decided the case in favor of black children on May 17, 1954. Attorneys Charles H. Houston and Thurgood Marshall[239] would do a masterful job of convincing the justices of the U.S. Supreme Court to conclude unanimously that "segregation of students in public schools violates the Equal Protection Clause of the Fourteenth Amendment"[240] That decision was reaffirmed on May 31, 1955.

Lincoln-Grant School and other black schools in Kentucky were similarly situated, and could have easily been included in the case. But segregated schools geographically far removed from Covington had taken the lead in a legal endeavor that would affect all racially segregated schools in the United States, as it rendered *Plessy v. Ferguson* and the Day Law in Kentucky null and void. The 1896 Supreme Court ruling and its 1904 Kentucky companion had been interpreted very broadly in support of maintaining racially segregated schools like Lincoln-Grant for decades with ease and comfort, and without the least concern for any sort of legal challenge. But, lo and behold, in one fail swoop, through one unanimous ruling by the United States Supreme Court, racial segregation, in theory, would become illegal, and all of the well-crafted, layered policies and practices of educational segregation and discrimination that had existed for decades would suddenly become irrelevant! But the thorny, protracted process of implementing the Court's decision would neither be quick, nor easy.

As students at Lincoln-Grant we knew remotely about the possibility of racial integration of the schools, since it was sometimes discussed on the radio and television, as well as in the local newspapers (which were relatively silent on the matter). But we did not immediately relate what was going on in Wash-

---

239. Thurgood Marshall would later be named to the U.S. Supreme Court as the first black associate justice.

240. *Brown v. Board of Education*, 347 U.S. 483 (1954) (USSC+), Supreme Court of the United States, 2008.

ington, D.C., at the U.S. Supreme Court level to our school and our way of life in Covington, Kentucky. It was as though some theoretical discussion about integration was taking place in a reality far removed from the one that we knew. I simply did not believe that racial integration in Covington, if it ever came to be, would have any impact upon my life in the near future. I could not at that point even envision in my own head what racial integration in Northern Kentucky would look like.

During at least four years of legal maneuvering, our teachers and the school principal had said nothing to us as students regarding potential desegregation of the schools. To the best of my knowledge, the possibility of racial desegregation was not mentioned in our history or social studies classes, or discussed informally in any way in our classrooms, although the more informed adults in our school and community had to be aware of the impending Supreme Court ruling, and the possibility of a favorable outcome. Perhaps they didn't want to alarm us, or say anything until such a decision became final—just in case it went the other way, and there was "business as usual." Perhaps our teachers were dubious and uncertain about the change that such a ruling might bring to their way of life. After all, a majority of them had been secure in their teaching positions at Lincoln-Grant School for several years—even decades for a few. What would racial integration of the schools in Covington mean for them and their educational careers?

Photograph 136 (inset left): Superintendent Glenn O. Swing, 1957.
Photograph 137 (inset right): Assistant Superintendent David Evans, 1957.
SOURCE: GRANT WARRIOR YEARBOOK, 1957.
COURTESY OF THE COVINGTON INDEPENDENT PUBLIC SCHOOLS.

Both men were key administrators during the initial desegregation efforts.

Photograph 138: Holmes High School Building, ca. 1941.
COURTESY OF THE KENTON COUNTY PUBLIC LIBRARY.

Photo 139: A Holmes High School Senior Class (Male Students) Prior to Integration.
PHOTOGRAPH COURTESY OF THE KENTON COUNTY PUBLIC LIBRARY, COVINGTON, KENTUCKY.

Photo 140: A Holmes High School Senior Class (Female Students) Prior to Integration.
PHOTOGRAPH COURTESY OF THE KENTON COUNTY PUBLIC LIBRARY, COVINGTON, KENTUCKY.

Photograph 141:
Col. William F. Hargraves, II,
USAF (retired).
PHOTOGRAPH COURTESY OF THE
KENTON COUNTY PUBLIC LIBRARY,
COVINGTON, KENTUCKY.

Col. Hargraves, a former USAF pilot, is the son of two Lincoln-Grant teachers, and a 1950 honors graduate of William Grant High School.

Photograph 142:
Airman William Joseph Stewart.
PHOTOGRAPH COURTESY OF THE
KENTON COUNTY PUBLIC LIBRARY,
COVINGTON, KENTUCKY.

Airman Stewart, a 1965 graduate, is also one of many young men from Lincoln-Grant School who served in the U.S. armed forces during the 1950s and 1960s.

Photograph 143: William Grant High School Class of 1954.
PHOTO COURTESY OF AARON BALLARD, CLASS OF 1959.

Top row: *Jean Collins, Norma Jean Fox, Willa Nell Paige, Juanita Clemens, Dorothy Louise Crawford.*

Second row from top: *Arthur Elmer Stewart, Carlton Lewis Mabrey Jr., Donald Redmonn Sheffey, Edgar Morris Gray, James Augustus Walton.*

Third row from top: *Dorothy Mae Lightfoot, Lois Estolia Butler, Shirley Mae Davis, Judith Ann Storms, Betty Jean Roberts.*

Bottom row: *(Faculty) William N. Jackson, Roscoe C. Vaught, Mrs. Jewell R. Jackson, H. R. Merry (Principal), William Hargraves, Birtill T. Barrow.*

Photograph 144: William Grant High School Class of 1955.
PHOTO COURTESY OF WILLA HOFFMAN JACKSON, CLASS OF 1957.

Top row: *Napoleon Smith, Hercules Davis Jr., John Richard Crawford, Charles Lee Herron, Lennard Alonzo (Linus) Green.*

Second row from top: *Wessley Karl Hall, Helen Devra Lee, Genevieve Slaughter, John Etta Rice, Bobbie Lou Florence, George Willie Walton.*

Third row from top: *Ruth Ann Payne, Mae Delores Lewis, Beatrice Anne Hargraves (Valedictorian), Dorothy Mae Allen, Josephine Elizabeth George.*

Bottom row: *(Faculty) William N. Jackson, Roscoe C. Vaught, Mrs. Jewell R. Jackson, H. R. Merry (Principal), Charles L. Lett, Birtill T. Barrow.*

Photograph 145: William Grant High School Class of 1956.
PHOTO COURTESY OF BARBARA JOUETT, CLASS OF 1956

Top row: *Clementine LaBordeaux, Jessie Mae Hall, Barbara Jean Jouett, Vera Elaine Sheffey.*

Second row from top: *Frederick Jackson, Albert Eugene Green, Paul William Brown, Louis Wilkinson.*

Third row from top: *Joyce Elaine Porterfield, Alma Louise Johnson (Salutatorian), Jacqueline Marquis Tyler (Valedictorian), Anna Belle Jefferson.*

Bottom row, faculty: *Harvey C. Cobbs, Mrs. Jewell R. Jackson, Charles L. Lett (Principal), Roscoe C. Vaught, Birtill T. Barrow.*

Photograph 146: William Grant High School Class of 1957.
Grant Warrior, 1956.
Courtesy of the Covington Independent Public Schools.

Top row from left: *Rosetta Collins, R. Patterson, Norma Brown.*

Second row from top: *Rosetta Hampton, Toney Walton, Joan Jasper.*

Third row from top: *Barbara Gentry, J. McCullough.*

Bottom row: *Willa Hoffman, Robert Phipps, Auguster Roberts, Raymond Webb, Allen Thomas, Charles Jouett.*

■ INITIATING SCHOOL INTEGRATION IN COVINGTON: STUDENT EXPERIENCES

As a student I was so immersed in going to school and reaching adulthood that I paid little attention to the larger picture on desegregation of the schools and its possible impact upon my life. But I was unexpectedly jolted into another level of consciousness along with other students in the fall of 1955, when many of the black students from Newport and other areas outside of Covington (some of whom had been with me in the same grades for several years) did not re-enroll at Lincoln-Grant School. There seemed to be a sudden void in the Lincoln-Grant building that fall. It was as though some of our vital parts had been surreptitiously taken from us. I was saddened by the loss of some of my close friends, and somewhat discouraged about a shrinking student body at our school. We would lose additional students to integrated schools the following year.

In due course, after our initial student loss, Mr. Lett told us that, because of new laws governing school integration, black students who did not live in the city of Covington, with the exception of those who were seniors, were now *required* to attend the white schools in the districts where they lived. During a brief school assembly that may have included the high school students only, Mr. Lett explained to us in simple language, why we had so abruptly lost a large portion of our student body, while assuring us that our own school, Lincoln-Grant, would remain in service for Covington students.

But almost immediately after the assembly there was an unsettling student rumor floating around the third floor of the building which asserted that Lincoln-Grant School would soon either be racially integrated, or closed down. As high school students who were getting close to our senior year we felt some level of anxiety about these changing, uncertain circumstances, but I did not believe that my education at William Grant High School would be involuntarily affected at that time, given Mr. Lett's assurances on the matter.

However, as time progressed, a few unusual activities beyond the Lincoln-Grant building occurred. Jessie Moore, a freshman female student at William Grant during the 1955/56 school year, had attempted to enroll at the all-white Holmes High School as a sophomore the following year. However, her request was initially denied on the grounds that her enrollment at that time would not fit the plan for gradual integration that the Covington School Board and superintendent had in mind. As a result of a complaint filed in her behalf with support from Mrs. Alice Shimfessel, the president of the local chapter of the NAACP, Jessie was eventually allowed to enroll at Holmes. Although her stay at Holmes lasted only a few weeks, due to overwhelming racial harassment from white students, the action taken by Jessie Moore and her community supporters may have also triggered additional desegregation efforts by the Covington Board of Education.

The 1956/57 William Grant High School choir was assembled for its usual choir period in the second floor music room of the Lincoln-Grant building on Greenup Street one day in the fall of 1956 when Mrs. Ruth Brown Phillips, our vocal music teacher, broached an unusual request. She stated in a casual manner that she needed a few people from our high school choir to go with her to sing at a Christmas assembly at Holmes High School in a few weeks. We were all temporarily perplexed by that unexpected request, and no one responded immediately. I had captured distant glimpses of the Holmes campus on rare occasions when I either drove up Madison Avenue, or cut someone's grass on that side of town. I had never seen the building complex completely, since it was well shielded from the day-to-day Madison Avenue traffic, and definitely "off limits" to black people. Holmes High School was mostly a fleeting image in my head, which until that point, I had not engaged at length, nor yearned for —a large, campus style, multiple building arrangement with rolling lawns, green shrubbery, and baseball and football fields, as well as provisions for other sports, and a presumed plethora of curricular and extracurricular activities—for white people only. Holmes had been very thoroughly insulated from us by more than a hundred years of racial segregation.

After a bit of coaxing from Mrs. Phillips, who explained that the performance would involve singing only a few familiar songs during a brief assembly, several students, including me, reluctantly volunteered to participate. Mrs. Phillips also asked me to accompany her on the piano for a solo that she would sing. She prepared a small vocal ensemble to sing for that occasion, and she and I practiced her solo a few weeks before the event. With knowledge of Jessie Moore's experience, we were guarded about the prospect of going out to Holmes, even for a brief school assembly.

Some of our teachers drove us in two or three cars from Lincoln-Grant to the Holmes campus on the day of the event. As students, we didn't know what to expect. When we arrived at Holmes that cold, wintry school day, we were greeted enthusiastically by two or three white male administrators, who rushed outside to our cars to escort us into the building. Once inside, we were shown to a room near the auditorium by one of the music teachers, a middle-aged white lady who was probably Mrs. Phillips's counterpart at Holmes. The Holmes music teacher seemed to come in and out of the room sporadically, while smiling nervously—wanting to give us our space as a group, but not wanting to seem unfriendly—as we put on our choir robes and warmed up vocally for a brief period in that room. She was trying really hard to make us feel comfortable. The members of our vocal ensemble were also a bit nervous about this new experience of singing at a "white" school.

After a few minutes, we were escorted to the main auditorium, and briefly introduced to the assembly by the Holmes vocal music teacher, who then faded quickly into a seat near the front to observe us with the rest of the audience. I took a seat at the piano to accompany Mrs. Phillips, as she ascended to the stage to initiate our performance in the Holmes auditorium with a vocal solo before a large audience of white students and teachers. This was a totally new experience for all concerned. Mrs. Phillips was in an elevated position on the stage, while I was seated at an upright piano located to the side, and slightly below stage level. We both seemed really in the "spotlight" for a brief moment, she more than I, as the Holmes audience quickly became hushed.

As the auditorium lights dimmed, and we were about to perform, Mr. Barrow and Mr. Gaines, two Lincoln-Grant teachers who had driven us to the school, quietly entered the auditorium from two rear doors. Mr. Barrow exuded a slight smile and cautious optimism, while Mr. Gaines, standing quietly with folded arms, seemed to observe the situation more circumspectly. Perhaps they and the white administrators were prepared to remove us from the auditorium immediately in case of any racial incidents. I took some comfort in noting their presence from the stage area.

I played a short introduction on the piano, and Mrs. Phillips began to sing the Negro Christmas Spiritual, "Sweet Little Jesus Boy." The audience focused quietly on our performance, as her steady, soprano voice flowed evenly throughout the darkened auditorium. I remember Mrs. Phillips's sense of confidence, as she quietly whispered to me immediately after our performance, "See, I told you it would go well." She then brought our vocal ensemble on stage to sing at least two additional Christmas selections. We received polite applause from the all-white audience after each selection.

Our ensemble then exited the stage, and returned to the music room, as the Holmes music teacher took over for what seemed to be a conclusive Christmas carol (probably something like "Joy to the World") with audience participation. I remember hearing the loud, exuberant voices of some of the white students as they sang the group song while we exited the auditorium. I was not sure how to interpret the apparent "enthusiasm" of some of the white students. Their sense of anxiety was probably similar to ours, and singing loudly (if not mockingly from a few students) in our direction as we left the auditorium was perhaps a way of expressing it. Holmes vocal groups did not perform at that assembly while we were present, nor was there any personalized social interaction with individual white students before, during, or after the assembly.

After our group returned to the music room, we removed our robes in preparation for returning to Lincoln-Grant School. We had only been in the music room for a brief period of time when the Holmes music teacher quickly rushed into the room from the auditorium. I remember being surprised that the assembly had ended so abruptly, and that she had gotten back to the music room in such haste. (When we exited the auditorium she was still directing the group song from the front of the auditorium).

The music teacher congratulated Mrs. Phillips on our performance. She and one or two younger looking white female students in special dresses, who seemed to be of junior high school age, showed us to a table set up with a few refreshments in the front of the room. But as a group we were disinclined to partake of the punch and cookies that were offered. We did not want to seem like hungry people who were anxious to eat, and yet we did not want to offend their hospitality. The entire experience had the feel of cautious, uncertain inter-actions on everyone's part, black and white. No one seemed to know quite what to do next. Our group soon left Holmes High School without any racial inci-dents, and returned to Lincoln-Grant, where we were relieved to be back in our "comfort zone.'

While I was unaware of it at the time, that little one-way "cultural exchange" was an initial step in a long-range plan for integrating the Covington Public Schools. We had just taken a "baby step" in that process. Larger steps would be enacted later in a gradual, orderly move toward complete integration.

Retrospectively, the concept of initiating integration of the schools through music seemed a sensible way to start the process, since humanity is usually connected through the common bond of musical expression regardless of race, ethnicity, or country of origin. And it was perhaps better to use music, a unify-ing experience, rather than athletics, which would have reinforced an "us and them," competitive approach. But the missing element in this initial effort was the concept of reciprocity. As we had been bold enough to go to Holmes and sing before an all-white assembly, a small group from Holmes should have come to Grant, perhaps the following Spring, and performed in our auditorium. That, I believe would have taken some of the awkwardness out of the situation, and caused us to feel less like "entertainers" in a white school. But there was no reciprocal visit to Lincoln-Grant by Holmes music students. And to the best of my knowledge, no white teachers or students ever came to Lincoln-Grant School for any reason during that period.

Nothing else happened for a while other than that event, the loss of our black "tuition pupils" from other school districts, and the beginning of our bas-ketball team playing games against white high school teams in the area. How-ever, during the spring of 1957 (near the end of my junior year in high school) I was called into the principal's office for a conference. Mr. Lett, the principal, wanted to know if I would be interested in attending summer school at Holmes High School.

My initial, nonverbal reaction was mixed. Why me? What would be the reaction of white students? Would other black students from Grant also attend? Mr. Lett seemed to anticipate my unspoken questions, as he quickly continued the conversation without giving me a chance verbalize them. He indicated that I had been chosen because of my academic achievements and my exemplary school record. He wanted me to take plane geometry, which was not offered at Lincoln-Grant. This would be a five- or six-week session and I would not have to pay anything. Mr. Lett also assured me that if it didn't work out, I could dis-continue the class, since I did not need it for graduation. He wanted me to dis-cuss his request with my parents, think about it, and give him an answer in a few days.

What Mr. Lett did not say was that this was a preplanned, racial experi-ment, which had been collaboratively set up with the Covington school admin-istration. I would become one of the "ground-breaking" black students for integration in Covington, by attending Holmes High School during the first summer school session of 1957. One other black student from Lincoln–Grant would attend Holmes during the second summer session. These two *in vivo* summer classroom experiences would be yet another step toward integrating the Covington Public Schools. Notwithstanding the groundbreaking effort of Jessie Moore, my brother, Toney would also take a summer school history course at Holmes at one point.

After talking the proposal over with my parents, I agreed, and went to Holmes for the five or six weeks of summer school. At that point I was driving my own car. I arrived on campus in my older, sporty Mercury coupe that first day, and parked in the school lot. As I entered the building, and went to the school office, I encountered a cordial, all-white office staff. Office personnel, that had obviously been prepared in advance to receive me, showed me immediately to my classroom. Mr. Erl, a middle-aged white male geometry teacher smiled and greeted me while rising quickly from his desk. His words of welcome were something like, "Well, hello, Joseph." (He already knew my name). "Come right in and have a seat wherever you'd like." Two or three white students were already present and seated, as others also drifted into the classroom. Although none greeted me individually, the students did not seem hostile. Since they did not seem surprised by my presence, I assume the white students had been prepared in advance for my enrollment in the class. I took a seat near a window, toward the front of the room, and eventually, a few more white students arrived. Soon the roll was called, and class began.

The class of approximately twenty students seemed like a normal classroom situation for me, except for the race of the other participants and my own sense of racial self-consciousness in the situation. Mr. Erl was partially bald, and smiled often as he looked over his black horn-rimmed glasses from time to time to observe how I was "fitting in" with the white students. He was very optimistic, and encouraging to me personally. Mr. Erl called on me in class frequently during those few weeks. He seemed to be very delighted that I usually answered correctly, and was such a good academic example for the other students, some of whom appeared to be struggling in the class.

The total experience was positive for me. I encountered no hostility from the white students in the class. In fact they gave me little attention during the entire summer session other than an occasional glance of curiosity, particularly when I verbalized correct answers to relatively difficult geometry questions in class. I earned a grade of "A" in the class.

As I left the Holmes campus on my last day, I encountered the next black student from Lincoln-Grant, who would attend Holmes during the second summer session. We greeted each other as his eyes projected slight uncertainty about what he would experience at Holmes. He asked me privately, "How is it out here?" We both understood the intent of the question. I said, "It was o.k." I then got into my car and left him to his own experiences at Holmes that summer. Apparently, the outcome for him was also positive. With that experience behind me, I was looking forward to concluding my senior year at William Grant High School.

In time, I would come to understand the historical roles that Jessie Moore, my brother, Toney, the other black summer school student and I had played in integrating the Covington Public Schools. But something else occurred through that experience for me personally—something that would reinforce my confidence in my own abilities and my reach toward a broader life goal. I realized that I could get excellent grades in reasonably complex subject matter in a white school sitting next to white kids as easily as I could in a black school sitting next to black children. I suddenly had living proof that my intellectual abilities transcended my racial identity!

That experience, along with the consistent encouragement that I had received from my parents and the teachers at Lincoln-Grant for many years, would indeed motivate me anew to "keep climbing." I had begun to believe that I could become almost anything that I wanted to become in life—within realistic expectations for that era. I knew, for instance, that I would not become president of the United States of America. But a black high school principal, or the president of a black college? Perhaps. A medical doctor, a science teacher, or a college professor? Maybe.

Figure 28: Holmes High School Report Card, SS 1957.

Course No.	Days Absent	Times Tardy	Phys. Ed.	English	Latin	French	Spanish	History	Government	Mathematics	Biology	Phys. Geog.	Physics	Chemistry	Bookkeeping	Com. Law	Shorthand	Typewriting	Printing	Woodwork	Mech. Draw.	Homemaking	Clothing	Psychology	Sociology	Economics	Music	Art
1st Report	2	0								B																		
2nd Report	0	0								A																		
3rd Report	0	0								A																		
4th Report										A																		
5th Report																												
6th Report																												
Exam										A																		
Average										A																		

HOLMES SENIOR HIGH   **REPORT OF PUPIL PROGRESS**   HOME ROOM_____
COVINGTON PUBLIC SCHOOLS
GLENN O. SWING, SUPERINTENDENT   Pl. Geom.
Record of _____ Watten, Joseph   SS 1957

I (parent, guardian) have carefully inspected this report.
First Report_____   Fourth Report _____
Second Report_____   Fifth Report_____
Third Report_____   Sixth Report _____
(over)

Subsequent to those initial experiments with integration, the Covington school administration set up a plan that would take several years to complete. At the beginning of the 1957/58 school year all seniors at Grant who lived in Covington were offered the opportunity to transfer to Holmes and complete our high school education there. As he discussed the situation with the Grant seniors as a group, Mr. Lett explained that all of our credits from William Grant High School would be accepted at Holmes, and those who chose to enroll there would simply complete their senior year successfully at Holmes, and receive a Holmes High School diploma instead of one from William Grant High School. Mrs. Jackson, our senior class advisor, was present during the discussion, and was available to us for any subsequent questions after Mr. Lett left the room.

All of us chose to remain at Grant except two of my classmates, who opted to transfer to Holmes at the beginning of the 1957/58 school year. I recall their agreement and resolve to go out to Holmes together. But apparently, when the full white student body returned to Holmes that fall, there were some racial incidents with my two classmates. After voluntarily enrolling at Holmes that fall, they quickly returned to Grant after two weeks. As we pressed them for the details of their experience at Holmes, and why they had returned to Grant so abruptly, they simply indicated that they were not willing to endure the contin-ual barrage of racial harassment that they had received from a number of white Holmes High School students that fall.

Black seniors at Grant who had been bused from other school districts to Grant for years were given a similar choice. They could either continue to attend Grant, and graduate from there, or they could complete their senior year at the previously all-white school in their district, and receive their high school diploma in that district. One young lady from Newport, Jessie Mays, who had left Grant to attend Newport High School as a sophomore, returned to Grant for her junior and senior years with us. Her family actually moved from Newport to Covington so that she could re-enroll at Grant as a senior. Another young lady from Newport, Blanch Utz, made a similar choice, and joined our senior class in the fall of 1957. Both young ladies would graduate from William Grant High School with us in 1958.

After our class graduated, there would continue to be optional, voluntary attendance at Holmes or Grant by black high school students in Covington. Lincoln-Grant School would remain intact as an all-black, K-12 school at that point. There would not be sustained, yearlong attendance by black students at Holmes High School until the 1958/59 school year, when two or three female students from William Grant enrolled voluntarily at Holmes in the fall of 1958. While those students also encountered some rough periods during the school year, they persevered to become the first black graduates of Holmes High School in June 1959.

The gradual introduction of black students into white schools over a period of years would minimize friction between black and white students. Keeping Lincoln-Grant School basically intact would also give some of its black teach-ers a chance to retire or go elsewhere, thus diminishing the problem of black teacher placement in the Covington school system. Over time, several of the younger Lincoln-Grant teachers transferred to The Cincinnati Public Schools and other Ohio districts, as some of those schools seemed eager to integrate their teaching staffs more completely following the 1955 Supreme Court ruling.

Photograph 147: Senior Class Picture, 1958.
Joseph M. Walton, Personal Collection.

Top row: *Mrs. Jewell R. Jackson, Senior Class Advisor.*

Second row from top: *Eleanor Slaughter, Jessie Mays, Joseph Walton, William Riley, Curtis Benion, George Butler.*

Third row from top: *James Moore, Janice Warmack, Mamie Ferrell, Andrew Clifford, Charles Simpson, Edmonia Wright.*

Bottom row: *Geraldine Tyler, LaVera Givens, Blanch Utz, Robert E. Jackson, Charles Dickerson, William Walker.*

Not pictured: *Leslie Stewart, Rosetta Wilkinson.*

■ COLLEGE BOUND

But even though I had been a part of some of the initial efforts to integrate the schools in Covington, as a seventeen year old, I did not have intense interest in either the national picture on integrating the public schools, the intricate technicalities of school integration in Northern Kentucky, or becoming one of the first black students to receive a high school diploma from Holmes High School. I was focused on concluding my high school years at Grant, and moving on to the next phase of my life.

My high school years at Grant were great! My teachers regarded me as a model student, a leader and a high achiever, and I was respected by my peers, and nicknamed "the brain" while I was in high school. I enjoyed the role of an enthusiastic spectator at our basketball games, playing in the band, singing in the school choir and going to the school proms, particularly the senior prom, when my date and I were crowned King and Queen of the prom. My classmates elected me vice-president of my junior class and president of the senior class. And during my senior year, I earned the spot of valedictorian of our graduating class based on my high school grades. In my opinion, none of that would have occurred if I had transferred to Holmes High School for my senior year.

The William Grant High School class of 1958 was a proud group of students. We were closely knit, and self-confident, even to the point of slight arrogance. We had "made it" after thirteen years of many of us hanging together in the Lincoln-Grant building. In spite of several of our original classmates dropping out along the way, or being taken away by integration, the eleven males and nine females in our class were on the verge of gaining the grand prize of a high school diploma. I remember standing around during an informal hallway conversation on the third floor near our lockers one spring day in 1958, enjoying the moment as a high school senior with a couple of my buddies. We felt that we were "at the top of our game" in life. The three of us actually had the audacity to articulate our belief that at that point in our lives we had gained all of the knowledge that we needed to be successful in whatever path we chose in life! Of course, we would have rather rude awakenings as our lives progressed. We would find out that there was so much more that we still did not know!

There were no special programs such as affirmative action and minority scholarships for persons of color who wanted to go to college in the late 1950s. Participation in higher education had to begin with personal determination and creative ways of financing one's way. Everything that would be achieved would be accomplished on undeniably good merit, and the bar seemed higher for blacks. The analysis completed by Leconia Franklin Crosby in his 1929 master's thesis revealed that over a ten-year period from 1919 through 1929 about 40 percent of the William Grant High School graduates went on to college. My estimates for the class of 1958 are somewhat lower, perhaps 35 percent of our class. I believe that a paucity of economic resources among black high school graduates in Covington, a general tone of segregation and very high standards of acceptance by colleges and universities affected those percentages. Some Grant graduates pursued other forms of post-secondary training, went directly into the workforce, or joined the armed services. But my teachers and parents had *always* encouraged me to further my education. I was determined to extend my education beyond high school, and nothing that I could imagine would thwart my efforts.

There was never any doubt in my mind that I was "college bound." I even bought a book by that title which described the process of applying for college as well as various approaches to financing a college education. During my senior year, I applied for several private scholarships listed in a separate scholarship book that I had also purchased, although I sensed that the scholarships in the books were set up primarily for white students. I ultimately received *none* of them. But I was so sure that I was going away to college—somewhere—that I went downtown and purchased a very expensive new leather suitcase, which I didn't actually get to use until years later.

I thought about possible colleges to attend in four categories: (1) Ivy league institutions, including Harvard, Yale, and Columbia; (2) Large, land-grant type of institutions such as The Ohio State University and Michigan State; (3) local institutions, including the University of Cincinnati and Xavier University; and (4) *premier* historically black institutions, namely Fisk University, Howard University and Morehouse College. I obtained catalogues and admission materials from most of them. I did not consider white Kentucky institutions due to their reputations of segregation, and prejudice against black students. The only possibility for Kentucky would have been Kentucky State College (the designated "colored" college in Kentucky), which in my mind was primarily a teachers college at that time.

Each year the senior class had a fundraiser in order to get money for the annual senior class trip. Our senior class elected to go to Central State University in Xenia, Ohio, for a visit, and then on to the Mammoth Cave in Kentucky by chartered bus. I benefited educationally from observing the stalactites, stalagmites and other cave phenomena, and I enjoyed touring the Central State Campus. However, I knew that Central State would not be among my college choices. I was determined to attend a predominantly white institution to "prove my intellectual worth," although I would realize later that such proof was unnecessary. My intellectual worth had been sufficiently validated at Lincoln-Grant School, and reaffirmed by my summer school experience at Holmes High School.

Since we had no school counselor, several teachers became involved in helping me in my quest for a college education. Mr. Barrow, the science teacher who made a special effort to help me prepare for the Scholastic Achievement Tests (SAT), secured study materials and brought them to school for me to use. He also personally drove me to Hughes High School in Cincinnati to take the SAT one Saturday. Mr. Barrow had a new car (a Ford automobile, I think), which I offered to help him drive to Hughes High School. But Mr. Barrow very quickly put that request to rest by simply saying with a wry smile, "I drive my own car." He dropped me off at Hughes and returned in the afternoon to take me back home.

Mrs. Jackson wanted me to go to Fisk University, her undergraduate alma mater. She indicated that I would probably qualify for a "full ride" academic scholarship at Fisk, but I wanted to go to Harvard.

Mr. Lett and some of my teachers urged me to become a physician or major in science or engineering, but I wanted to major in music. My oldest brother advised me to major in "anything but music." The collective wisdom was that my overall academic talent was much too valuable to waste on such a major. I disagreed, and chose music as a major, with support from Mrs. Blackwell, our vocal music teacher and Mr. Crowder, the band instructor. They encouraged me to follow my own dreams, and major in music, if that was where my heart was.

Mr. Crowder prepared me for my audition for the College-Conservatory of Music of Cincinnati. It was he who initially made me aware of the fact that one does not just send in a transcript and an SAT score and become admitted to a school of music. One in fact had to choose a major instrument, and audition successfully before faculty members at the institution. Mr. Crowder told me that I first needed to decide on a major instrument to study in college, since I had mastered four musical instruments by then. Naturally, I chose the piano as my major instrument, since I had played it for most of my life. I am not sure why I decided on the organ as a minor, except for the fact that I had been interested in learning to play that instrument for some time, and I felt that there could be a reasonable transfer of knowledge from one keyboard instrument to the other. Next, we had to choose a "classical" piano selection for my audition, since I could not simply go in and play a simple popular melody for the audition. We selected a short piano excerpt by Beethoven. As best as I can remember, it was the *Adagio Cantabile from Sonata Number 8,* "Pathetique," which I was able to perfect in a few weeks.

Ultimately I applied to three institutions of higher education, in order of preference: Harvard University, The Ohio State University, and the University of Cincinnati's combined degree program with the College-Conservatory of Music of Cincinnati. I was accepted by UC/CCM with a level of enthusiasm and genuineness, as well as an offer of a partial academic scholarship. But an admissions officer from The Ohio State University (OSU) wrote me a rather terse, unfriendly letter indicating that they gave preference to residents of the state of Ohio, and that since I was a resident of Kentucky I was not welcome there, unless I could pay my own way, including out-of state tuition. I naively did not understand the out-of-state tuition provision by OSU, since the University of Cincinnati and the College-Conservatory of Music had waived it. While my application was not rejected on an academic basis, OSU offered no scholarships or financial support. That would make my enrolling there not even remotely possible. Clearly, I had no financial resources to meet the OSU conditions. (But later in my life I would vindicate that application process by earning a Ph.D. degree from The Ohio State University by the age of thirty!)

Although my SAT scores were not superb in some areas, my application to Harvard had some strength, since I was granted an interview. I received a call at home from a local alumni representative from Harvard, who set up a meeting with me at a restaurant in downtown Cincinnati early in the spring of my senior year. I was guardedly excited that my application to such a prestigious institution had generated a personal interview.

I remember entering the upscale restaurant on the day of the interview to the questioning eyes of the restaurant personnel, who seemed to communicate through their body language that I was "out of place" by coming into that restaurant with the apparent expectation of either being served or looking for employment. But I was quickly greeted, and "rescued" by the Harvard interviewer, a white man in a business suit, who appeared to be somewhere in his thirties. He had apparently been waiting for my arrival in another part of the restaurant. The Harvard man seemed anxious to assure the restaurant personnel that I was his invited guest, by smiling in my direction, extending his hand, and quickly ushering me to an "out-of-the way" table near a window. The "interview" would not be lengthy. As we waited to be served, he explained briefly that the admission process to Harvard was different, in that it involved an interview by a Harvard alumnus (who seemed to have the sole power to recommend acceptance or rejection of the applicant).

The alumni representative seemed rushed, and not at all sincere in his approach to me. I immediately sensed an air of feigned warmth toward me. He made a few positive comments about my application at the beginning of the meeting. But as the interview progressed, he quickly started discouraging me with admonitions like "Harvard is not a strong school for music. You may want to go elsewhere. And financial aid—you will need complete financial aid, which we could not offer you." (Was he inferring that *partial* financial aid could be offered? I was not sure). I knew that Harvard did not have a premier music program such as Julliard or The New England Conservatory of Music, but it did offer a course of study in music, as indicated in its bulletin. Otherwise, I would not have applied. I was interested in Harvard because of its overall reputation for academic excellence, as well as its program in music.

The interview was rather awkward, as the Harvard representative kept shaking his head in a negative way, and making open-handed expressions that indicated his "helplessness" in my case, while trying to talk me out of attending Harvard. I believe he even mentioned the fact that my graduation class was rather small (only twenty people), and by inference that my very strong grades didn't carry as much weight as those of someone from a much larger senior class. "Do you feel that you would be a good fit for Harvard?" he queried. I responded positively, but he obviously felt otherwise. The interviewer never said that my application to Harvard was rejected, or that I did not qualify academically. He just kept encouraging me to tell him that I did not plan to enroll at Harvard.

After he thoroughly expressed all the negatives to me, he pushed the interview to a conclusion by saying something like, "I assume you have offers to attend other colleges. You did apply elsewhere, didn't you?" he asked with a tinge of anxiety in his voice. I said yes. He seemed relieved that he was not cutting me out of attending college altogether, as he smiled disingenuously, and continued with, "So can we conclude that you do *not* intend to enroll at Harvard?" Reluctantly, I felt that I had little choice but to say, "yes" under the circumstances that he had just presented to me, i.e. no offer of financial support. I don't remember eating lunch, although I might have consumed a small part of a beverage as we talked about my not attending Harvard. He then smiled again somewhat mechanically, wished me good luck in the future, and shook my hand as though he had accomplished his mission.

I left the interview feeling that a man whose sole purpose was to get rid of me had succeeded in talking me into a concession. My gut feeling was that I had just been "pushed aside" by an interviewer who had no intention of encouraging my attempts to gain acceptance to Harvard. Was the fact that I was a "colored boy" from a "colored" high school with no apparent parental support or Harvard "connections" a major factor in this process? It seemed so.

With The Ohio State University and Harvard application processes behind me, I took the only offer on the table, and accepted a renewable $250 scholarship offer to attend the combined music education program offered jointly by the College-Conservatory of Music of Cincinnati and the University of Cincinnati. The scholarship offer actually came from CCM rather than UC. As one administrator at CCM explained, the scholarship offer was based on my status as a "top bee" academically, as well as my musical audition. I also received a one-time scholarship from the black Ladies Union Club of Kentucky in the amount of $150. That gave me $400 toward $950 a year that I needed for tuition. I would continue to live at home and commute from Covington, thus mitigating the need for room and board.

I would earn the additional $550 by working full-time as a janitor at Walgreen's in Newport and part-time as a busboy the summer after I graduated from high school. My parents could make no direct monetary contribution to my education, but they did allow me to continue living at home without asking me to contribute to their household expenses. I was grateful for that, as well as their continued moral support and encouragement.

Prior to my second year of college I would receive another one-time $150 scholarship from the Omega Psi Phi Fraternity upon the recommendation of Mr. Barrow. Also, quite unexpectedly, based on my academic performance during my freshman year, I would qualify for an additional $250 award at the end of that academic year. Thus, I had help from several mentors in securing small scholarships from different organizations. Through a variety of sources including scholarships, student loans, full-time summer employment, and part-time jobs during the school year, I would be able to assemble the financial resources to support my undergraduate education at UC and CCM.

I would occasionally wonder if I had made the right decision by not applying to Fisk University, where according to Mrs. Jackson, I could have gotten a "full ride" scholarship, including full tuition and room and board at a prestigious, historically black institution with a strong program in music. Mrs. Jackson was a Fisk University alum, and her connections there could probably have guaranteed that outcome. But, to paraphrase Robert Frost (perhaps inappropriately), "I had chosen the road less traveled by—the one that was grassy and wanted wear"—and I would have to live with the consequences of that choice.

■ GRADUATION DAY

There were twenty seniors in my high school graduating class, and we had looked forward to graduation day with great anticipation. It finally arrived on Wednesday, June 11, 1958. Our commencement had been previously publicized in a *Kentucky Times Star* newspaper article on June 7, 1958.[241] It would be followed by another article on June 12, 1958, which showed all of the graduates on stage with Principal Charles L. Lett just prior to the beginning of the ceremonies. [242]

I had given the valedictory address the previous Sunday at the baccalaureate exercises. My speech, which I had written in the context of the "Sputnik Era" had been edited by Mrs. Jackson, and was entitled "The Greatest Challenge." Within the text, I stressed the value of people of various nations and races getting along with each other, in view of atomic weapons and scientific advances that had the potential to destroy the entire world. I emphasized the importance of positive human relationships, as I cited Rudyard Kipling's hymn, "Recessional." I remember delivering the address with fervor and excitement.

Roughly a month after graduation day, I recorded my reactions and impressions in a typed two-page document entitled "My High School Commencement," without realizing at that time that I would use it many decades later in the current work. Those relatively contemporaneous comments follow (with some minor post-hoc editing).

I do not recall what I did early on graduation day. I do, however, remember being downtown (in Covington) around 3:30 p.m. on that Wednesday afternoon. I ran into one of my fellow graduates, who saw me going into the shoe shop to have my shoes shined. He was employed as a "shine boy" at the shoe shop, and suggested that if I would bring my shoes to his home after he got off from work, he would shine them for me at no charge. I accepted his offer, and

---

241. *Kentucky Times Star,* "Grant Exercises Set for Wednesday—Twenty to Graduate," June 7, 1958, 1A.

242. *Kentucky Times Star,* "Grant High School Graduates," June 12, 1958, 6A. The *Kentucky Times Star* would also carry a picture of the final all-white graduating class for Holmes High School on June 5, 1958. Subsequent Holmes High School graduating classes would reflect African American graduates.

took my shoes to his house that afternoon, since he lived only a few blocks from me on Bush Street. We discussed our after-graduation plans while he shined my shoes. It seems that, while I was headed for college, my buddy planned to work fulltime. He had secured a well-paying job that would begin immediately after graduation. A couple of years after graduation he would marry and start a family. We philosophized about the meaning of this stage of our lives—graduating and becoming adults. I looked at my watch, and it was 7:15 p.m. We were due at school for the graduation ceremony before 8:00 p.m.!

I rushed home, cleaned up, put on my suit and newly shined shoes, and arrived at Grant at 8:00 p.m. to find that most of my classmates were in place and prepared to take a group picture by a representative of the local newspaper. Mrs. Jackson scolded me for being late. Some of my invited guests handed me two graduation presents while I was changing into my cap and gown in the in the aisle of the auditorium. A stranger volunteered to hold my gifts while I put on my cap and gown. We were then rushed to the stage for a preliminary group picture which would appear in the *Times Star.* I felt self-conscious as we sat on the stage for the group picture before the ceremony started, since the guests who had arrived early were carefully scrutinizing us.

After the group picture we went to "dressing rooms" designated separately for female and male graduates in order to make last minute adjustments in our academic regalia and take a final restroom break before the ceremony began. That time soon arrived as the graduates who were also band members entered the auditorium via the back entrance to play the first band selection, *Atlantis* by V.F. SaFranck. The band selection was well performed. After that number, the three of us hurried back around to the back of the auditorium through the side hallways. It was time for us to march in.

The graduation ceremony would begin precisely at 8:30 p.m. in the Jones Auditorium. My parents, siblings (except for my brother, George, who was away in the air force) and my future sister-in-law attended as well as some of the neighbors on Tenth Street. I was pleased to have the support of my family, and many close friends and neighbors who had watched me grow up in Covington.

As class valedictorian, I was designated to lead the processional to the tune of *Pomp and Circumstance.* I took my place in line and looked behind me to see the young lady who was the class salutatorian, followed by an alphabetical arrangement of the remaining eighteen graduates. I then peered curiously into the audience where the auditorium lights had been lowered, as I tried to see exactly where my family was seated. Having confirmed their location, I then viewed the well-illuminated stage to which we were about to march. The anticipatory excitement of the event was building within me. Mr. Crowder looked around from the orchestra pit to make sure that the graduates were ready for the processional. Having confirmed with Mrs. Jackson that we were indeed ready, the march was about to begin. The band played the introduction to the processional, as I got ready to start marching.

We had practiced the graduation march during the week with Mrs. Jackson as she coached us on stepping off from the back of the auditorium to the beat of the music. Each of us would step off with our left foot after every eighth count. "One, two, three, four, five, six, seven, eight." We were told to hold our shoulders erect and march proudly down the aisle. This was *our* moment. There was structure, accuracy, and order to our processional.

With Mrs. Jackson in the background, I stepped off. I was slightly anxious, but I remembered to march proudly and square my corners carefully, as Mrs. Jackson had stressed. The shiny concrete floor of the auditorium had a slight downward slope, so we had to march carefully, lest we slip and stumble. Finally, I reached my seat on the stage. I scrutinized the large crowd in the audience, and then glanced at my marching classmates. They all looked great. Everyone was in step—even those who were viewed as rhythmically challenged. Soon we were all on stage.

The graduates who were also band members again rose and went to the orchestra pit to play the *Hymn of Freedom* by Brahms. The selection was well performed. That was the last note and musical selection that I would play on the school-owned baritone horn, my musical companion for about three years. A fellow band member had volunteered to take charge of the baritone horn and return it to the band room after my final selection. The three of us returned to the stage as the entire assembly rose for the invocation. We sat again, and then the choir, which was seated on our left hand side in the audience, and the graduates who were in the choir (including me) stood. As the choir filed onto the stage, I moved quickly across the stage to the piano. All was set as I accompanied the choir, which gave an almost excellent rendition of *Gloria* by Mozart.

The Lincoln-Grant building was not air-conditioned, but as graduates we were impervious to the humidity of the June weather that evening. As the graduation ceremonies progressed, a few ladies in the audience solved the problem by fanning themselves with graduation programs, or occasionally using their fans from the C. E. Jones and E. B. Delaney and Son Funeral Homes that had been brought from home in anticipation of the heat. Some of the men in the auditorium mopped their brows intermittently with well-used, crumpled handkerchiefs as the program developed, while the more patrician members of the stage party simply endured the heat. They pretended not to sweat.

The choir recessed, and the graduates returned to their seats on stage. Next Mr. Swing, the school superintendent, introduced the commencement speaker, Dr. Yokley, a black female professor and department head from Kentucky State University, who rose and spoke for about thirty or thirty-five minutes. During that time, my father, who was seated near the front of the auditorium with my mother and the rest of my family members, started to "nod off." The young lady seated next to me poked me with her elbow, and started to tease me nonverbally about the fact that my father was falling asleep during the commencement address. I was, of course, embarrassed—until her father started nodding also.

The young lady and I then started noting that a number of fathers and mothers in the audience were also beginning to fall asleep. Suddenly, it became an amusing situation to observe from the stage. It was as though a little elf was sprinkling "twilight dust" throughout the auditorium causing people here and there to become sleepy. Nudging each other whenever another person "nodded off" helped us pass the time during a relatively lengthy commencement address. The exchanges between the young lady and me while Dr. Yokley spoke apparently caught the attention of Mr. Swing, who was seated right in front of us. He turned his head toward us, while not looking at us directly. That was an unspoken directive from the Superintendent of Schools for the young lady and me to be absolutely quiet. We quickly hushed, and became more attentive to the speaker. Dr. Yokley's address on A Liberal Education (a work that we had studied during our junior year) finally ended.

At the conclusion of Dr. Yokley's commencement address the graduates who were choir members joined the a cappella choir in its renditions of "Dark Water" by James, and Bright's version of the Negro spiritual, "I Hear a Voice A'Prayin'." The piano accompaniment for "Dark Water" was provided by the class salutatorian, who performed well, despite the reservations of some of the choir members about her ability to provide an adequate piano accompaniment. They thought she might "mess up," but she did well.

Next came the presentation of the class of 1958 by our principal, Mr. Lett. His saying "The Class of 1958" the second time represented our signal to stand in unison as a class together on the stage.

Mr. Bernard Kathman, chairman of the Covington Board of Education went to the podium and extended brief words of congratulations to the class of 1958. Then the presentation of diplomas began. The graduates were arranged in two rows of ten divided into four rotating sections with five graduates to a section. As valedictorian, my name was called first. Mr. Lett said "Joseph Moses Walton, the Valedictorian" as I proudly squared my corners and received my diploma from Mr. Kathman. I returned to the opposite end of our section of five, while forgetting to move my tassel to the other side, until one of my fellow graduates whispered rather loudly, "Tassel! Change your tassel!"

After the presentation of diplomas was completed, I again crossed the stage to the piano, where I would be one of two piano accompanists for Waring's arrangement of "The Battle Hymn of the Republic." Due to the complexity of the piano accompaniment, Mrs. Blackwell had asked Mrs. Edwards, a musical colleague of hers to play one part on one piano, while I played the other on a different piano. There was also to be a trumpet part at the beginning of the song, but that failed. After some initial awkwardness Mrs. Edwards started the music, as I joined her on the other piano. The song was well performed by the choir.

Finally, we sang the Lincoln-Grant Alma Mater for the last time, and recessed into the arms of our waiting relatives and friends to the strains of "War March of the Priests." Our guests greeted us with hugs, kisses, and congratulations as we prepared to leave Lincoln-Grant School for good. I said goodbye to my fellow graduates for the last time as we left the school grounds. Several of us had been together for thirteen years, since kindergarten. Now we would take divergent paths as we moved on to the next phase of our lives.

Figure 29: Commencement Program, William Grant High School Class of 1958.

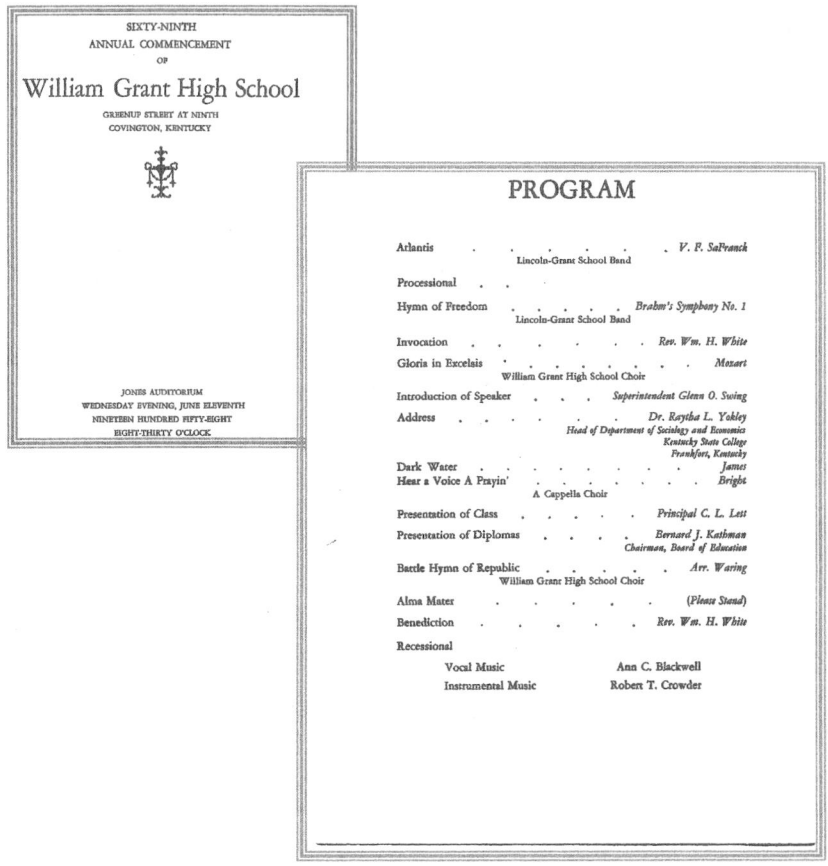

Photograph 148: William Grant High School Class of 1958.
PHOTOGRAPH COURTESY OF JOSEPH M. WALTON, CLASS OF 1958, PERSONAL COLLECTION.

Top row: *Rosetta Wilkinson, George Thomas Butler, Eleanor Slaughter, Andrew Jackson Clifford, Blanche Euchee. Utz.*
Second row from top: *William Riley Jr., Edmona Wright, Robert Eugene Jackson, Janice Marie Warmack, James David Moore.*
Third row from top: *Leslie Lee Stewart, Jessie Mae Mays, Charles Edward Dickerson, Mamie Elizabeth Ferrell (Mabrey), Charles Stanford Simpson.*
Fourth row from top: *Curtis Benion, William Edward Walker, Joseph Moses Walton, Geraldine Tyler, LaVera Ann Givens.*
Bottom row: *(Faculty) Harvey C. Cobbs (Social Studies), Mrs. J. R. Jackson (English), Charles L. Lett (Principal), B. T. Barrow (Science), Roscoe C. Vaught (Mathematics).*
G.E.D. Graduates: *Robert W. Perkins, Donald W. Mabrey (Minutes, Board of Education, January 31, 1958, 184).*

Photograph 149: William Grant High School Class of 1959.
Photograph courtesy of Aaron Ballard, Class of 1959.

Top row: *Aaron Ballard Jr., Milton Louis Jasper, Alma Patterson, Helen Delores Johnson, Marian Willis Givens, Frederick Wideman Jr., Louis Albert Cammack.*
Second row from top: *Lorraine Lattimore, Jackie Young, Nancy Carolyn Simpson, Betty Ann Henderson, Delores Green, Ruth Ann Mann, Nathaniel Weldon Saxon, Janice Barnes.*
Third row from top: *William Jackson Reed Jr., Elizabeth Jackson, Sonia Lee Payne, Alfonza Davis, Margaret Ann Webb, Doris Green, Ronald LaMar Cottie.*
Not pictured: *Tom Thacker (Summer, 1959).*
Bottom row: *(Faculty) Harvey C. Cobbs (Social Studies), Mrs. J. R. Jackson (English), Charles L. Lett (Principal), B. T. Barrow (Science), Roscoe C. Vaught (Mathematics).*

Photograph 150: William Grant High School Class of 1960.
COPY OF CLASS PORTRAIT PROVIDED BY BARBARA JOUETT, CLASS OF 1956.

Top row: *Wayne Mays, Patricia A. Offutt, Vivian Green, George R. Offutt Jr.*

Second row from top: *Willie J. Oden, Clinton M. Rhodes, Helen D. Hinton, James C. Young, Leonard Phipps Jr.*

Third row from top: *Ella Reed, Robert L. Scott, Carole J. Lattimore, Bertha M. Payne.*

Bottom row: *(Faculty) Harvey C. Cobbs (Social Studies), Mrs. J. R. Jackson (English), Charles L. Lett (Principal), B. T. Barrow (Science), Roscoe C. Vaught (Mathematics.*

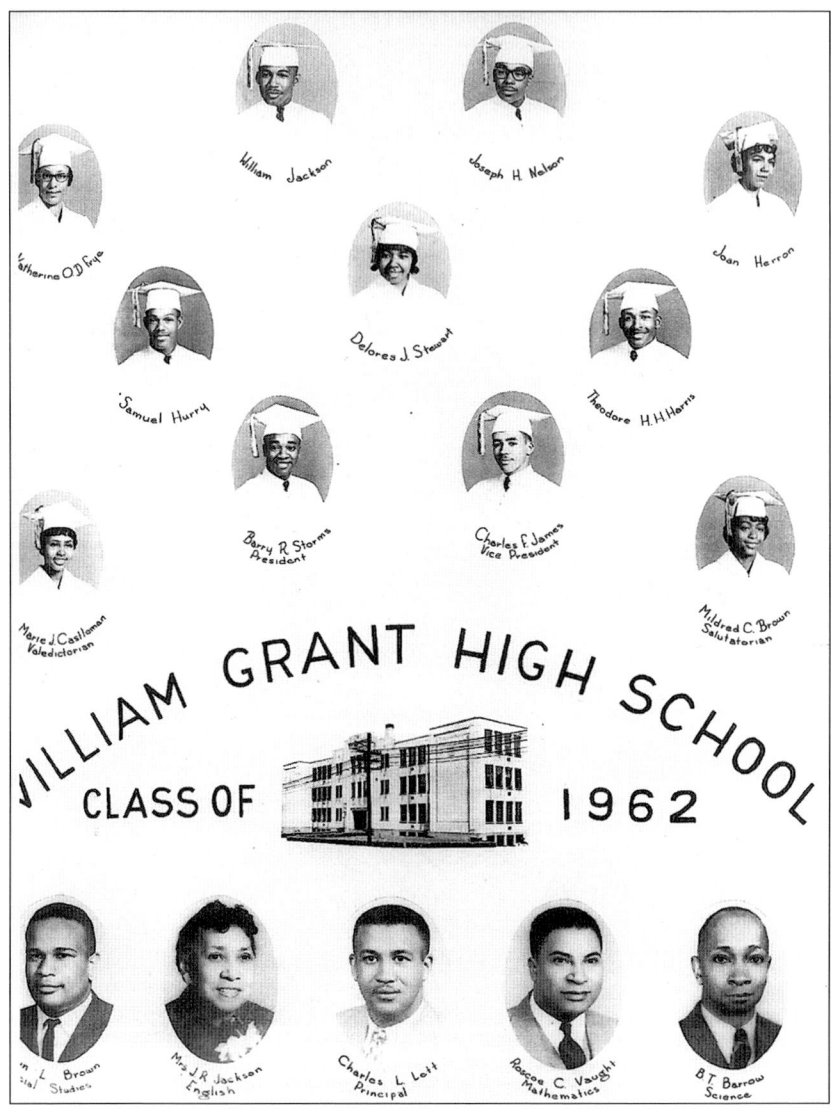

Photograph 151: William Grant High School Class of 1962.
PHOTOGRAPH COURTESY OF CHARLES JAMES, CLASS OF 1962.

Top row: *Katherine Olivia Dawson Frye, William Jackson, Joseph Henry Nelson, Joan Elizabeth Herron.*

Second row from top: *Samuel Hurry, Deloris Jean Stewart, Theodore Herbert Henry Harris.*

Third row from top: *Marie Jeanette Castleman, Barry Richard Storms, Charles Frederick James, Mildred Carole Brown.*

Bottom row: *(Faculty) Irvin L. Brown (Social Studies), Mrs. J. R. Jackson (English), Charles L. Lett (Principal), Roscoe C. Vaught (Mathematics), B. T. Barrow (Science).*

Photograph 152: William Grant High School Class of 1963.
PHOTOGRAPH COURTESY OF RICHARD B. L. FOWLER, CLASS OF 1963.

Top row: *Bennie Leigh Ward, John Franklin Payne, Michael Brian Burton, Charles Victor Patterson, Eugene Claxton.*

Second row from top: *William Herman Payne, Loistene Beal, Clinton Jackson, Sherry Jarrell, William Bell.*

Third row from top: *Margo Lee Brown, Otis Andrews, Richard Barkley Fowler (honor student), Franklin David Stewart, David Allen Webb (honor student).*

Bottom row: *(Faculty) Irvin L. Brown (Social Studies), Mrs. J. R. Jackson, (English), Charles L. Lett (Principal), Roscoe C. Vaught (Mathematics), B. T. Barrow (Science).*

Photograph 153: William Grant High School Class of 1964.
COPY OF CLASS PORTRAIT PROVIDED BY BARBARA JOUETT, CLASS OF 1956.

Top row: *Sandra Lillian Ward, Gerald McKinley Offutt, Kenneth L. Simpson, Donald Grant, Charles E. Stewart, Betty Jo Huddleston.*

Second row from top: *Charles Fann, Sherron Antonio Davis II, Judy Ann Miller, Walter W. Patterson, Rita Elizabeth Meeks, John Tyler, Colonger Baugh.*

Third row from top: *George E. Stone, Anna Marie Gray, Estella Elizabeth Banks, Robert Storms, David Hunter, Marcella Jennings, Loroma Jackson.*

Not pictured: *Edgar Jouett.*

Bottom row: *(Faculty) Arnetta Searcy (Social Studies), Mrs. J. R. Jackson (English), Matthew L. Mastin (Principal), Roscoe C. Vaught (Mathematics), B. T. Barrow (Science).*

Photograph 154: William Grant High School Class of 1965.

Top row: *Rudolph Valentino Meeks, John Allen Stone, William Joseph Stewart, Lawrence Maurice Jouett.*

Second row from top: *Pauline Perrin, Wallace Lee Engleman, Lillie Marie Penny, Dwight Campbell, La Rita Guy Jamar (honor student).*

Third row from top: *Eloise Young (honor student), Deborah Grant, Walter Bedford Jr., Priscilla Perrin, Donna Jean Herndon.*

Bottom row: *(Faculty) Arnetta Searcy (Social Studies), Mrs. J. R. Jackson (English), Matthew L. Mastin (Principal), Roscoe C. Vaught (Mathematics), Birtill T. Barrow (Science).*

JEWELL SMITH JACKSON
Fisk University, A. B.
University of Cincinnati, M. E.
English
Advisor Senior Class

BIRTILL T. BARROW
Bates College, A. B.
Columbia University, M. A. Graduate Study:
Harvard University
Science

HARVEY C. COBBS
Central State College, B. A.
Social Sciences

ROSCOE C. VAUGHT
Knoxville College, A. B., University of
Wisconsin, M. Ph.
Mathematics

CLARENCE H. WILLIAMS
Wilberforce University, B. S. Graduate Study:
University of Cincinnati, Villa Madonna College
Eighth Grade

SARA M. FITCH
Kentucky State College, B. S. Graduate
Study: University of Kentucky, University of Cincinnati
Eighth Grade

MINNIE M. CORBIN
Wilberforce University, University of Cincinnati, B. S. in Ed.
Seventh Grade

W. H. CRAIG
Fisk University, B. A.
University of Cincinnati, M. A., M. Ed.
Ohio State
Seventh Grade

ELIZABETH M. BOONE
Fisk University, B. A.
Graduate Study: University of Cincinnati
Sixth Grade

CARRIE McATEE TAYLOR
University of Louisville, A. B., Graduate
Study: Columbia University

Photograph 155: Lincoln-Grant Faculty, 1955/56.
SOURCE: *GRANT WARRIOR*, 1956.
PHOTOGRAPH COURTESY OF THE COVINGTON INDEPENDENT PUBLIC SCHOOLS.

Top row from left: *Jewell Smith Jackson, Birtill T. Barrow.*

Second row: *Harvey C. Cobbs, Roscoe C. Vaught.*

Third row: *Clarence H. Williams, Sara M. Fitch.*

Fourth row: *Minnie M. Corbin, W. H. Craig.*

Fifth row: *Elizabeth M. Boone, Carrie McAtee Taylor.*

Photograph 156: Lincoln-Grant Faculty, 1955/56.
SOURCE: *GRANT WARRIOR*, 1956.
PHOTOGRAPH COURTESY OF THE COVINGTON INDEPENDENT PUBLIC SCHOOLS.

Top row from left: *Charles D. Houston Jr., Sadye Irene Bunyan.*

Second row: *James E. Brock, Mattie Ruth Brown.*

Third row: *Eleanora Warren Henderson, Sara Sleet Wright.*

Fourth row: *Robert T. Crawder* [sic]*, Samuel C. Gaines.*

Fifth row: *Chester A. Rice, Maudlyn S. Garrett.*

Photograph 157: Lincoln-Grant Faculty, 1955/56.
SOURCE: *GRANT WARRIOR*, 1956.
PHOTOGRAPH COURTESY OF THE COVINGTON INDEPENDENT PUBLIC SCHOOLS.

Top row: *Lauraida Fitch, Mary F. Michaux.*

Second row: *Etta L. Hundley, Eva B. Clark.*

Third row: *Edmonia A. Wilson, Catharine W. Webb.*

Fourth row: *Alberta B. Vaughn, Clara G. Bowers.*

Fifth row: *Florence J. White, Gertrude C. Coles.*

CHAPTER 12

School Desegregation

"Oh, the tangled web that was woven,
when the path of racial segregation was chosen."

The development of two parallel educational delivery systems with a primary goal of racial separation in Northern Kentucky was historically methodical and deliberate. The Commonwealth of Kentucky and other Southern states had uniformly established laws that mandated segregated schools, and the effects of those laws would persist for almost an entire century of public education.

The sense of inequality between Lincoln-Grant and the white schools in Covington had been obliquely manifest through a more limited school curriculum, and such actions as the reassignment of outdated textbooks from the white district schools to Lincoln-Grant when new editions were made available, as well as reports of Lincoln-Grant Domestic Science classes washing and ironing the uniforms of Holmes students. In general Lincoln-Grant seemed not to be the first priority of the Covington Board of Education in most matters. But most patently evident were the racially based actions of the Covington school administration that had, over many decades, built staunch, long-term, insulated walls between black and white students and teachers in Northern Kentucky, with reassurance from the existing laws of the Commonwealth of Kentucky as well as the previous rulings of the U.S. Supreme Court.

Now, all of that had to be undone. And since the racial segregation of schools was a reflection of the larger society, desegregation had to be accomplished concurrently in the areas of housing, public facilities, and employment hiring practices. The task ahead would not be an easy one.

The 1954 Supreme Court decision would place all of the nation's segregated schools, including those in Northern Kentucky, in a political and social dilemma about how to proceed, especially in view of the Court's 1955 ruling, which confirmed the 1954 decision, and further instructed that the desegregation of the nation's schools must move forward "with all deliberate speed." In addition to the legal mandate, there was also pressure from the nation's oldest civil rights organization. An article from the *Kentucky Post* revealed that the Kentucky Conference of the National Association for the Advancement of Colored People (NAACP) was prepared to take legal action against school systems in the Commonwealth of Kentucky that "do not show that they are working 'in good faith' toward integration. James A. Crumlin, Louisville, president of the state NAACP Conference, said petitions will be filed soon with school boards in all counties to learn their plans for desegregation."[243]

The desegregation of the white schools in Campbell and Boone counties would take effect almost immediately in 1955 and 1956. During a special meeting of the Board of Education of the Walton-Verona Independent School District, which was attended by eighty-nine persons, including "fourteen Negroes," the community voted, by a show of hands, 41 to 18 in favor of implementing integration immediately. Although eighteen people voted against immediate integration by a show of hands, no one in the audience vocalized opposition to the plan.[244] The fact that there were small, isolated numbers of black students in pockets of the outlying areas, would make their integration into some of those school systems less complicated, at least on the surface. The reality that in some areas, black and white children had "played together" for years, while attending separate schools, would also make integration easier.

And although there were larger numbers of black students in Newport, there would also be a reasonably seamless absorption of black students into the Newport School System. Reis reports, "African-American students began transferring to other public schools in Newport in 1955. A *Kentucky Post* account on Sept. 7, 1955, said Newport was among the first schools in the state to comply in response to a U.S. Supreme Court ruling."[245] The Catholic schools in Covington would also immediately open their doors to black children.

The ultimate integration of the Covington Public Schools would be much more complex because of a much larger student body as well as the existence of a fully functioning K-12, all-black school that had been in existence for close to a century. The desegregation of the Covington Public School System was set in motion by a July 29, 1955, resolution of the Covington Board of Education as found on the following page:

The initial resolution adopted by the board seemed like a study guide designed to "buy time" rather than a plan for immediate action on integrating the Covington Public Schools. Indeed, items IV.(1), (2), and (5) should have been easily accessible, while item IV. (3) would have been unnecessary if black

---

243. *Kentucky Post*, "Action Demanded On De-Segregation," July 31, 1955.

244. *Kentucky Post and Times Star*, "Walton-Verona Vote for De-Segregation," July 20, 1955.

245. Reis, Southgate Street School stood alone for decades."

Figure 30: Board Resolution on Desegregation, 1955.[a]

Desegregation

I. *The Supreme Court of the United States decreed on May 17, 1954 that segregation of the races in the public schools is unconstitutional. This decision was reaffirmed May 31, 1955. The Covington Independent School System operated under the Statutes of the State of Kentucky which specified a segregated system with separate but equal facilities has since its inception adhered to the principle that a school system should function on a basis that is to the best interest of its children regardless of race, color, creed, or economic status. That principle shall remain uppermost in the minds of the Board of Education as it considers the future destiny of the school system.*

II. *There is at present an understandable indecision at the State level as to the proper directives to individual school boards regarding the interpretation and the implementation of the Supreme Court decision.*

III. *On June 23, 1955, the Kentucky State Board of Education enacted the following regulations:*

    (a) that the State Board of Education authorize its chairman, the Superintendent of Public Instruction, to direct to the attention of local school authorities the court's instruction that local school boards begin immediately a study of appropriate methods to implement the decision of the Supreme Court as applicable to their respective local conditions.

    (b) that the State Board of Education urge local school authorities to proceed as rapidly as conditions warrant.

IV. *In order to be prepared for eventualities in this connection, it is respectfully recommended that the local Board of Education approve a committee consisting of the Superintendent of Schools, the Assistant Superintendent of Schools, the Attorney for the Board, The Principal of Lincoln-Grant School, and the Director of Pupil Personnel of the Covington Independent Public Schools to proceed with a detailed study of the problems inherent to desegregation and that these studies be conducted in the following areas and that subsequently the committee report to the Board of Education its recommendation:*

    (1) Scholastic boundaries of individual schools with relation to racial groups contained therein

    (2) age-grade distribution of pupils

    (3) adaptation of curriculum

    (4) the problems of integration of the Parent-Teacher Association of Lincoln-Grant School with other Parent-Teacher Associations.

    (5) general capacity of all school buildings in the areas affected by an integration program.

a. Minutes, Covington Board of Education, July 29, 1955, 3–4.

and white schools in Covington had been "equal" in their curricular offerings.

Unlike some contemporaneous attempts to block school integration at any cost, such as those infamous actions involving the Arkansas National Guard, which were undertaken by Governor Faubus at Central High School in Little Rock, Arkansas, in 1957, or Senator Harry F. Byrd of Virginia, who sought to close the public schools in that state, rather than integrate them, there were no demonstrations or extreme actions in Covington regarding the initial integration of the public schools. But eventual eradication of a dual system of education that had been in existence since the inception of public education in the city would neither be immediate, nor without significant complications.

Superintendent Glenn O. Swing, who had been Covington's school superintendent since 1927, would be the primary architect of the original plan for desegregating the Covington Public Schools. He had previously served as principal of Holmes High School from 1919, when the high school moved to the Holmesdale Estate, until his election as superintendent. David Evans had been assigned as principal of Holmes Junior High School for two separate years as well as executive principal of Holmes Senior High School for two additional years in the 1950s before becoming Swing's assistant. Obviously, both men had invested many years in the *status quo* of the Covington Public Schools. After administering a racially segregated system of education for their entire administrative careers, could Swing and Evans really bring about radical change by integrating the Covington Public Schools? Swing retired in 1960, approximately six years after the Supreme Court had mandated desegregation. He passed away in 1962, with seemingly little fanfare for an administrator with such longevity in heading the Covington school system.

The desegregation plan advanced by Mr. Swing, and inherited by his successor, David Evans, seemed limited to one-way voluntary student transfer from Lincoln-Grant School, and the integration of interschool athletic competition. The initial desegregation plan seemed adequate on paper as a public relations piece, but in reality, it did not translate into significant change in the racial balance of the Covington Public Schools. Implementation of the plan in Covington would soon become overshadowed by events at the national level, which caused the next few years to become filled with a sense of national uncertainty and civil unrest.

The nation's conscience would be shocked by the untimely assassination of President John Fitzgerald Kennedy on November 22, 1963. The brief era of "Camelot" and the national sense of optimism ushered in by the aura of the Kennedys in 1961 had suddenly ended as Kennedy's successor and former vice president, Lyndon Johnson, took over the helm of the nation. The U.S. citizenry would become emotionally and psychologically drained by a sustained "loss of national innocence" due to the brutal murder of the thirty-fifth president of the United States. A national sense of despair and civil unrest would also be continued as a result of the blatant murders of civil rights activists and innocent young black people in the South during the 1960s, as well as our long-term involvement in a war abroad.

President Johnson would continue to support the efforts toward racial equality that had been initiated by Kennedy and his brother, former Attorney General Robert F. Kennedy. But even as Johnson personally quoted the title of the civil rights protest song, "We Shall Overcome," his administration would become mired in the confluence of a never-ending war and general civil unrest. Eventually, the country would enter a period when group protests over political issues would become the most dominant mode of public expression. Protests over the war in Vietnam, as well as issues of gender equity and racial integration would take place in many areas of the country. The nonviolent protests initiated during the early 1960s by Rev. Martin Luther King would culminate in King's assassination in 1968, followed by the murder of Robert F. Kennedy. The nation sought a different direction and a sense of relief from turmoil through the election of Richard Nixon. However, Nixon's eventual impeachment and resignation from the U.S. presidency would sustain national uncertainty.

Those national events, along with local approaches to integrating the schools, seemed to impede real progress toward racial integration in Covington. As time progressed, the sense of "sluggishness" about the complete desegregation of the Covington Public Schools would cause some community leaders as well as the United States Department of Health, Education and Welfare (HEW) to question the aggressiveness of desegregation efforts in the Covington Public Schools. After ten years, the process was not moving forward. Voluntary student transfer was limited by the fact that not many black students wanted to get out of their "comfort zone" at Lincoln-Grant School, which remained fundamentally segregated. And there was virtually no racial integration of the teaching staff in the Covington Public Schools. Federal funds for various programs would be withheld from the Covington school system because of a lack of compliance with desegregation orders. In addition, there was mounting pressure on Superintendent David Evans by local human rights organizations.

Evans reported to the members of the Covington Board of Education in January 1965 that he had been visited by "two members of the Human Rights Commission of Covington, Rt. Reverend Mons[ignor] John F. Murphy and Reverend C. C. Nunnery . . . to discuss the progress of the Covington Schools as it applied to desegregation. Most of the discussion centered around the fact that there was no integration in the faculties of our schools." Evans said that he "tried to explain that there was no disposition on the part of the Board to circumvent the assignment of teachers of any particular race to any given school and that the responsibility for the assignment of teachers lay with the superintendent, subject to the Board's approval." Evans "further explained that teachers were hired on the basis of their merits and were assigned to the positions where it was felt the[y] could perform most effectively." Evans then expressed an optimistic view: "I have no doubt that sometime soon we will have candidates for teaching positions among our negro [*sic*] applicants of a caliber which will justify their being selected for appointment to any one of our schools. However, I would be reluctant to make such a recommendations [*sic*] only for the purpose of integrating faculties. Finding white teachers who will accept an assignment in a predominantly negro school has proven more difficult. Certainly, I do not favor making arbitrary changes in assignment without the acquiescence of the teachers involved."

Mr. Evans's statement to the board raised questions about his view of "negro applicants" for teaching positions, as well as the suitability of currently employed black teachers at Lincoln-Grant to teach white children, and indeed, his true commitment to the integration of the Covington Public Schools. His tentativeness about the effectiveness of local desegregation efforts was further reflected in the following statement at the same board meeting:

> As I indicated to you in the Bulletin, the 1964 Civil Rights Act, or Title VI, may cause us some difficulty. At the present time, all Federal funds[s] for NDEA Title III and Title V and for the Federal Lunch and Milk program are being withheld. Each Board of Education will be required to sign a statement of assurance that it is complying fully with the desegregation decision of the Supreme Court, if it is to receive financial assistance from federal sources in the future. I feel that we can safely say that there is no discrimination exercised in our system as far as any policy exists in the treatment and assignment of pupils. Most of our pupils attend the school in the district in which they live; however exceptions are made when good reasons are presented and there is room in another school to which they wish to transfer at the beginning of the school year. We permit all negro children to choose between Lincoln-Grant and the district school of their residence.[246]

■ THE CLOSING OF WILLIAM GRANT HIGH SCHOOL—1965

The consistent probing of the U.S. Department of Health, Education and Welfare, and the pressure of local civil rights groups caused Mr. Evans and his staff to develop a plan for desegregation that went beyond the voluntary movement of students. It was decided that William Grant High School would be closed down. Starting in the fall of 1965, all black high school students in Covington would be required to attend Holmes High School, and Lincoln-Grant would continue to function only as an elementary school.

On June 24, 1965, Superintendent Evans presented the assignments to the Board of Education for its approval, as found on the following page. (The designations of "1st, 6th, 8th, and 10th" refer to the names of elementary "District Schools.")

These changes represented a large step in the desegregation process,

---

246. Superintendent's Report to the Covington Board of Education, January 1965.

Figure 31: Closing William Grant High School:
Reassigning Teachers from Lincoln-Grant School, June 1965.

Re-assignment of Teachers from Lincoln-Grant

All teachers who were affected by the closing of the high school division of the Lincoln-Grant School have been made aware of their new assignments for the 1965-66 school year. In Addition to these, one elementary teacher from the school will be reassigned. Listed below are the names of the teachers involved and the teaching assignment of each.

Teacher	School	Teaching Assignment
Birtill T. Barrow	John G. Carlisle	General Science
James Brock	Holmes	General Science 7-8
		Jr. H. Basketball Coach
Robert Crowder	Holmes et al.	Asst. Band Director
		Grade School Bands
William Daniels	Lincoln-Grant	Art—Lincoln-Grant and Self-contained 7th grades at 1st, 6th, 8th and 10th
Joyce Boynton	Holmes	Business Science—Typing
William Martin	Lincoln-Grant	Holmes Choir Chorus
		Lincoln-Grant 7-8
		Self-contained 7th grades at 1st, 6th, 8th and 10th
Roscoe Vaught	John G. Carlisle	General Science 7-8
Jewell Jackson	Holmes	English
Sara Wright	Holmes	Home Economics
Augustine Shannon	John G. Carlisle	Elementary
Arnetta Searcy	Holmes	World History

although it was immediately obvious from the above listing that black teachers from Lincoln-Grant School had received new assignments that were not comparable in status to those that they had held at Lincoln-Grant. On July 29, 1965, Evans reported to the Board of Education "We have received confirmation from the U.S. Department of Health, Education, and Welfare that our plan for desegregation has been approved for 1965–66, subject to periodic review. Certain figures on enrollment need to be sent to Washington at a later date."

The final high school commencement at Lincoln-Grant School had taken place in the Jones Auditorium in the spring of 1965, as the students who comprised the William Grant High School class of 1965, took their graduation walk.[247] The graduation of the class of 1965 had formally ended an era of high school segregation in the Covington Independent Public Schools, which began in 1886. A number of William Grant High School students had already transferred to Holmes High School voluntarily, and were receiving their high school diplomas from that institution at the same time. All ninth, tenth and eleventh-grade students who had remained at Grant through the 1964/65 school year would be transferred automatically to Holmes in the fall of 1965, as dictated in the new plan submitted by Mr. Evans.

The closing of William Grant High School would coincide with the death of Mr. Henry R. Merry, who had retired as the Lincoln-Grant principal in 1955. He passed away on May 18, 1965, in Covington. His brief obituary in the *Kentucky Post and Times Star* dated May 19, 1965, is reflected in figure 32.

Figure 32: Death Notice, Mr. Henry R. Merry, 1965.

Henry R. Merry, 80, of 1111 Russell street [sic]*, Covington, died at 12:30 p.m. Tuesday at St. Elizabeth Hospital.*

Mr. Merry was retired principal of Lincoln Grant High School, Covington. [sic] *He had served as principal from 1923* [sic] *to 1955.*

He was a trustee at St. James AME Church, Covington, and belonged to the Utopian Club, Covington.

His only survivor is a daughter, Mrs. Elizabeth Mary [sic] *Boone, Cincinnati.*

Services will be at 11 a.m. Saturday at St. James AME Church. Burial will be in the Mary E. Smith Memorial Cemetery, Elsmere.

Jones & Simpson Funeral Home, Covington, is in charge.

Mr. Charles Lett, the principal of Lincoln-Grant from 1955 until 1963 left the school system to pursue a career in another state on the west coast before the high school closed. Mrs. Jewell Jackson, the very influential English teacher and senior class advisor, who had witnessed the entire evolution of Lincoln-Grant School from the Seventh Street Colored School building from which she graduated in 1916 through the Greenup Street building where she taught until William Grant High School closed in 1965, was assigned to Holmes High School to complete her lengthy career as a teacher in the Covington Public Schools. She was living testimony to almost the entire history and legacy of Lincoln-Grant School.

Mrs. Jackson would teach at Holmes for only one year before retiring due to her health. She would then pass away on September 18, 1966. An article printed in the *Cincinnati Enquirer* on September 20, 1966, is shown in figure 33.[248]

247. Minutes, Covington Board of Education, June 24, 1965, 343.

248. *Cincinnati Enquirer*, "Mrs. Jackson Was Veteran Teacher," September 20, 1966, 18: 2.

Figure 33: Death Notice, Mrs. Jewell R. Jackson, 1966.

Mrs. Jackson Was A Veteran Teacher

Services for Mrs. Jewell R. Jackson, 67, who taught 46 years in Covington, will be at 11 a.m. Wednesday in the Mt. Zion Methodist Church, Walters and Altonna [sic] *Aves., Walnut Hills.*

Burial will be in the family plot at Flemingsburg, Ky.

Mrs. Jackson died Sunday night in Bethesda Hospital. She had been ill for a year and had been hospitalized for 10 days preceding her death.

She taught at William Grant High School, Covington, from 1920 until June 1965. She then taught one year at Holmes high School before illness forced her to retire in June.

Mrs. Jackson lived at 3420 Pleasantview Ave, Evanston.

On June 19, Mrs. Jackson was honored by the public at Covington's Ninth St. Methodist Church for her service to education. She was cited at that occasion as the only graduating student of William Grant High School's Class of 1916.

Her husband, Robert C. Sr., has been [sic] *science and mathematics teacher at Hoffman School, Durrell Ave and Victory Parkway for 13 of his 25 years as a teacher. A son, Robert C. Jr., is a Taft High School science instructor. Three grandchildren also survive.*

Friends may call at the residence from 6 to 9 p.m. today. The Alpha Kappa Alpha sorority will conduct a memorial service at 7:30 p.m.

Five other Lincoln-Grant teachers, Mrs. Sara Wright (a 1935 graduate of William Grant High School), Mr. William Martin (class of 1949), Mr. Birtill Barrow, Mr. Roscoe C. Vaught, and Mr. Robert Crowder would sustain their teaching careers at Holmes and other school buildings for several years after William Grant High School closed down. Two relatively new high school teachers, Ms. Arnetta Searcy and Ms. Joyce Boynton would also be assigned to Holmes. Mr. Aaron Ballard, who graduated from Grant in 1959, would become a teacher at Holmes Junior High School after teaching briefly at Lincoln-Grant. Mr. Ballard would also have a long career as a teacher, and eventually become the first black principal of a racially mixed school in the Covington Public School System other than Lincoln-Grant (Twelfth District).

Photograph 158: William Grant High School Tenth Grade Class, 1958/1959.
Photograph 159: Holmes High School Class of 1966.
PHOTOGRAPHS COURTESY OF THEODORE H. H. HARRIS, CLASS OF 1962.

Above: *There were thirty-one tenth grade students enrolled at William Grant High School during the 1958/59 school year. However, by 1962, only eleven of those students would form the William Grant High School Class of 1962. A significant number of William Grant Students would voluntarily transfer to Holmes High School during that period.*

Below: *Black students who were automatically transferred to Holmes High School following the closing of William Grant High School at the end of the 1965 school year. The students depicted in the picture were identified as members of the Holmes High School Class of 1966.*

■ INTEGRATING THE COVINGTON PUBLIC SCHOOL SYSTEM: A THORNY ISSUE

The U.S. Department of Health, Education and Welfare (HEW) and local civil rights groups would continuously monitor the desegregation plans for the Covington Public School System. Although the Covington schools seemed generally in compliance with the Civil Rights Act of 1964, HEW and local civil rights groups would continue to question two primary areas of the desegregation efforts: (1) the lack of significant racial diversity in teaching assignments throughout the system, particularly at the elementary level, and (2) the continued lack of integration at Lincoln-Grant (Elementary) School.

On March 24, 1966, David Evans reported the following to the board:

> We have received forms of Assurance of Compliance with the Revised Statement of Policies for School Desegregation Plans under Title VI of the Civil Rights Act of 1964. I have completed these forms and have them ready for signature. I feel that we are in full compliance with the plan which was submitted last year. With the closing of the high school grades at Lincoln-Grant and the integration of faculties at John G. Carlisle and Holmes High School, we accomplished a great deal. I have invited all Kentucky colleges to submit names of both negro and white applicants for teaching positions and I am hopeful that we will receive applications from well qualified negro teachers so that our faculty integration may be expanded. Up to this time, no white teacher has evidenced a willingness to accept an assignment at the Lincoln-Grant School but that, too, will come in time.

But Mr. Evans's sense of optimism about the current desegregation plan did not hold. The closing of William Grant High School and the assignment of the remaining black high school teachers (and one elementary teacher) to Holmes and John G. Carlisle were not sufficient actions for HEW.

At the end of the David M. Evans administration in 1966 "The Covington Board of Education was directed by the United States Department of Health, Education, and Welfare to rezone the first and fourth school districts so as to include a zone for the Lincoln-Grant School. New regulations of the Civil Rights Act, Title VI, made this mandatory."[249] The rezoning would reconfigure the previous boundaries of Lincoln-Grant School to include a number of white elementary students, and also expand racial diversity in contiguous elementary schools. HEW representatives would also concur with a name change, from Lincoln-Grant to the Twelfth District Elementary School. The new name would give the school a sense of parity with the other elementary district schools, as opposed to its distinction as a historically black school.

Matthew Mastin, Mr. Lett's successor became the principal of Lincoln-Grant in 1963. He would guide the school through all of its transitions until his

---

249. Minutes, Covington Board of Education, June 23, 1966, 563.

death from a heart attack on Wednesday, September 13, 1972. James K. Burns, the final principal of the school, would succeed him.

Superintendent Evans would be followed by Bert Bennett, who presided over the school system from 1966 to 1975. In spite of the changes enumerated above, the Covington Public Schools seemed to be drifting toward resegregation because of the lack of a pro-active approach to continued integration of the schools. But the status quo was not sufficient for HEW, which kept its monitoring devices in place. Some school systems in the country had turned to extensive school busing to achieve racial balance while raising a controversial issue in many communities, but that did not seem to be the case in Covington.

At a board meeting in August 1972, Superintendent Bert Bennett reported the following:

> I received a call from HEW in Washington relative to our desegration [sic] efforts and from all indications our plan and implementation of teacher assignments are fully acceptable and we will receive a letter from HEW indicative of this.
>
> They are still questioning our black and white pupil ratio at the Twelfth District School and asked what plans we had for reducing the percentage of black pupils. I indicated very definitely that we had none. It is very strange that this call came directly on the heels of President Nixon's veto of the Education Bill passed by Congress. His veto was a result of the excessive appropriations contained in the bill. However, also incorporated in the act was an anti-busing section, and as a result, we have no anti-busing clause. I believe, however, that a much stronger anti-busing act has passed one house of Congress and at this time is not tied to any money bill. This should forestall any additional pressure from HEW.

Superintendent Bennett was clearly opposed to the concept of busing to achieve racial balance. He apparently did not please either HEW or the majority of board members in his approach to running the school district. On January 23, 1975, the board decided not to renew Mr. Bennett's contract. Mr. Bennett would assume the title of associate superintendent under a new system administrator. He would later be selected to head the Kenton County Public School System.

Several new Board of Education members with a fresh determination to integrate the Covington Public Schools fully were elected. The new board chose a different superintendent, Dr. Gary Blade. The new superintendent, who headed the system from 1975 to 1979, would certainly "ruffle a few feathers" as he made substantive changes in the policies and practices of the Covington Public Schools. The evidence from the board minutes would suggest that, in addition to mandating changes in the personnel area through well-defined job descriptions and attention to other details, Dr. Blade and the new board would tackle the problem of the desegregation of the Covington Public Schools through a reorganization plan that would shake up the entire community.

Dr. Blade would delve into every detail of the system's functioning from the superintendent's office to the last custodian on the system's roster, as he developed job descriptions for virtually every position in the system. There would be specificity, which included duties and educational requirements for every category of job in the system. Blade would also become the secretary to the Board of Education, a position traditionally not held by the superintendent. But when he took on that duty, the minutes of the board would explode with the details of every board action, including full job descriptions, and complete letters from parents and community leaders who didn't necessarily agree with his policies and procedures.

Blade's predecessors had apparently developed a one-dimensional, reactive stance in relation to the HEW mandates, while engaging a myopic view of integration in the Covington schools that focused primarily on voluntary student transfers from Lincoln-Grant School and the closing of William Grant High School. That approach placed HEW in the position of dictating local actions from Washington, D.C., as it forced changes in the Covington Public Schools through strong oversight, and a "stick and carrot" approach, which included the withholding of federal funding for various school programs until certain mandates had been satisfied, or filing lawsuits against districts that were in non-compliance with desegregation orders.

Blade and the new board would implement a different approach. The July 11, 1975, board minutes reflected the following: "Mr. Mang moved that the Board direct the Superintendent to proceed along the lines of the plan he presented to reduce the racial disproportion of the schools of the Covington Independent Schools." The motion passed unanimously and was followed by unanimous approval of the following board resolution: "Be it resolved that the Board recognizes the existence of disproportionate percentages of black children enrolled in the Covington Schools and commits the Board to the development and implementation of a plan which will correct these disproportionate enrollments on a long term basis." With the adoption of that resolution the ball had begun rolling for major changes in the Covington Public Schools.

During a follow-up meeting of the board, Superintendent Blade "read a letter from HEW and responded" with three possibilities as to a response, while suggesting his own:

1   React by trying to fight the case . . .
2   Accept their proposal . . .
3   The third possibility, and the one I'd like to recommend is that I get in touch with HEW and tell them we recognize we have a problem in complying with the district court ruling. They have suggested that we consider permanent solutions. We have looked at their suggestions and found that they will not result in a permanent solution and we can't come up with a permanent solution for implementation by August 25. We would ask HEW to send representatives to Covington for an on site visit and provide access to all data available to

us. We can express our willingness to comply and develop a plan that looks like it is more permanent; that if need be we will prepare some sort of a resolution or policy which says we will develop a plan agreeable to HEW with implementation by August 1976. This plan will be submitted by a date agreeable to HEW early next year. Should we not do so we will implement their plan in August 1976. However, I believe we can come up with a plan better suited for Covington.

The board unanimously adopted Dr. Blade's third suggestion. On August 21, 1975, Dr. Blade made additional changes in the elementary teaching staff at Lincoln-Grant School to engage better racial balance, and even changed the name of the school from "12th District School" back to "Lincoln-Grant School." The racial makeup of the school was the issue, not its name. By September 2, 1975, the Lincoln-Grant School student population had gone from 57.23 percent black on October 2, 1974, to 29.9 percent. The teaching staff at Lincoln-Grant, already only 25 percent black, would be further reduced to 20 percent black as minority teachers were moved to other schools to enhance racial balance among the teaching staffs in other schools. Dr. Blade's predecessor, in response to HEW mandates, had obviously accomplished some of that work.

After only a few months on the job, Dr. Blade and the members of the Covington Board of Education had taken the following actions toward the desegregation of the Covington Pubic Schools:

1 The appointment of "a citizens advisory committee and a faculty advisory committee to work jointly or separately, at their mutual options, to advise the Board on long term solutions to our problem of racial disproportion in enrollment."

2 An alternative, voluntary desegregation plan which would allow "those living in (the) area bounded by the center line of Robbins on the North, Licking River on the East, the center of 13th Street on the south and the C. & O. Railroad on the West" to "transfer their elementary school child to any public school in the Covington Independent School District if there is space and if the transfer would improve the racial balance within the school system.

3 The reassignment of the Covington teaching staff in large numbers to enhance racial balance in the schools.

4 The beginning of an in-depth study of each school which would result in a cost/benefit analysis broken down into a per pupil cost for each school building.

As a result of the tenacity of the board and the superintendent, the following changes in the racial composition of students and professional staff at the Covington schools were reflected in the Board of Education minutes on September 18, 1975:

Figure 34: Comparative Covington School Enrollment Statistics by Race, 1974 and 1975.

Students	1-Oct-74				2-Sep-75			
	Black	White	Total	Black %	Black	White	Total	Black %
John G. Carlisle	66	627	693	9.52	159	583	742	27.3
Third District	16	403	419	3.81	12	369	381	3.1
Fourth District	158	298	456	34.4	69	320	389	17.7
Sixth District	3	478	481	0.62	74	434	508	14.6
Glenn O. Swing	13	574	587	2.21	22	549	571	3.9
Latonia Elementary	0	538	538	0	5	522	527	0.9
Ninth District	1	441	442	0.22	3	435	430	0.7
Eleventh District	0	205	205	0	0	197	197	0
Lincoln-Grant (formerly 12th Dist.)	174	130	304	57.23	61	143	204	29.9
Total Elementary	431	3694	4125	10.4	405	3552	3949	10.2
Covington Jr. H.	181	596	777	23.3	163	543	706	23.1
Holmes Jr. H.	19	1059	1078	1.8	37	1078	1115	3.3
	200	1655	1855	10.8	200	1621	1821	11
Holmes High Sch.	105	1170	1275	8.2	104	1114	1218	8.5
Professional Staff								
John G. Carlisle	3	36	39	7.7	3	38	41	7.3
Third District	3	20	23	13.4	5	20	25	20
Fourth District	3	21	24	12.5	4	20	24	16.6
Sixth District	1	21	22	4.5	1	22	23	4.3
Glenn O. Swing	2	25	27	7.4	2	27	29	6.9
Latonia Elementary	2	24	26	7.7	2	24	26	7.7
Ninth District	4	25	29	13.8	4	19	23	17.4
Eleventh District	1	9	10	10	1	10	11	9.1
Lincoln-Grant	5	15	20	25	3	12	15	20
Alternative School	0	0	0	0	1	3	4	25
Total Elementary	24	196	220	10.9	26	195	221	11.8
Covington Jr. H.	2	42	44	4.5	2	42	44	4.5
Holmes Jr. H.	3	50	53	5.7	2	51	53	3.8
	5	92	97	5.2	4	93	97	4.1
Holmes High Sch.	4	61	65	6.2	3	66	69	4.3

■ THE CLOSING OF LINCOLN-GRANT SCHOOL—1976

By October 22, 1975, the HEW people responded with an acknowledgement of the revised desegregation plan. The conclusion of the HEW letter to Dr. Blade stated, "The above information shows that the district's alternative plan has resulted in further desegregation than was contemplated in the original interim plan. You are to be congratulated for this additional effort which has resulted in the elimination of racially disproportionate student enrollments at the Fourth and formerly Twelfth District schools in compliance with the *Adams vs. Weinberger* order."

But while HEW was extremely pleased, rumblings were just beginning in the Covington community. Dr. Blade was about to release another, more comprehensive plan. His in-depth cost analysis of every school in the Covington system had revealed wide disparities in per pupil cost for operation. On February 17, 1976, he concluded the following:

Figure 35: Board Recommendation Closing Lincoln-Grant School Building, February 17, 1976

> *It is clear . . . that the highest costs per pupil are in the low enrollment schools of Eleventh District and Lincoln-Grant and in Covington Jr. High School. Since all of these high cost schools are also located in the area of most rapid enrollment decline, they were considered very carefully in our effort to plan for the reorganization of the school district. . . . At this point, I believe the best of the plans considered would close 11th District and Lincoln-Grant Schools, reconvert Covington jr. High to 1st District grades K-7, and would enroll grades K-7 students in each of the remaining schools except G.O.S. and 6th Dist[rict] . . .[a]*

a. Minutes, Covington Board of Education, February 17, 1976.

Dr. Blade then presented the cost data for his proposal. The plan, ostensibly driven by cost savings, would at the same time accomplish optimal racial balance in the schools. It would also generate major protests from a Citizens Committee, individual parents and parent groups in the Eleventh District. Interestingly, there would be no overt objections from the black community regarding the closing of Lincoln-Grant School, which had already been downsized to very low enrollment through rezoning and staff reassignments, and had in fact become a predominantly white school. The local president of the NAACP, Mr. Eddie Thompson, had offered the assistance of the NAACP to the new superintendent earlier in the school year, and that organization expressed no written objection to Dr. Blade's proposal. Led by William Martin, the black community urged the closing of Lincoln-Grant and its conversion to a community center. Martin, who had been a music teacher in the Covington Public Schools, would take over the building after its closing, and reopen it as the Northern Kentucky Community Center. His primary goal was to preserve the heritage and history of Lincoln-Grant School in the community while also providing a community center to serve the local community. Those purposes for the building would be sustained for a number of years, until Martin's death.

In the meantime, the Eleventh District people would literally be up in arms about the potential closing of that school. The Eleventh District School was the only one in the Covington Public Schools that had no black students at all. Blade's proposal would cause the Eleventh District to become the only district in the system without an elementary school. The protests were abundant!

To appreciate the depth of indignation from that area of Covington, one must understand how the city districts were independently built in the 1800s and eventually merged into a single school system with an elementary school in each district. "West Covington (where the Eleventh District School was located) was established as an independent city in 1858. That same year, the town officials financed the construction of a public school on Main Street (Parkway Avenue). West Covington was annexed by the City of Covington in 1916, and at that time the West Covington School was renamed Eleventh District School. A new Eleventh District School building was built on Parkway Avenue and dedicated in 1923."[250] And Dr. Blade was about to disturb that history significantly by closing the school! People whose parents and grandparents had attended Eleventh District, and whose children now attended that school would confront Superintendent Blade with vehemence and angry protests.

Blade temporarily postponed the changes. He listened and took advice from the community, but ultimately he would submit the plan, unchanged, to HEW for its approval. HEW endorsed the proposal enthusiastically. HEW endorsement would give Dr. Blade the external support that he needed to implement the plan. And so it was done. Dr. Blade had already ordered buses to transport children as necessary. He formally closed Eleventh District School in 1979. The school building would eventually be converted into apartments. And at that point, the Covington Public Schools would be fully racially integrated at all levels. As indicated above, Dr. Blade left the Covington Public School System in 1979 after an active, radical period in the history of the school system. The *Kentucky Enquirer* reported, "last June, after serving four years, Dr. Gary Blade resigned as superintendent of Covington Independent Schools. He became superintendent of the Fairfield Ohio School District last Aug. 1 [1979]."[251]

250. Kenton County Public Library, "Images of America—Covington," 2003.
251. *Kentucky Enquirer*, "Update [Dr. Gary Blade]," February 22, 1980, 1.

Photograph 160: Superintendent and Mrs. David Evans, 1960s.
COURTESY OF THE KENTON COUNTY PUBLIC LI.BRARY, COVINGTON, KENTUCKY.

Photograph 161: Superintendent Gary Blade (extreme right) and Colleagues.
PHOTOGRAPH COURTESY OF THE KENTON COUNTY PUBLIC LIBRARY, COVINGTON, KENTUCKY.

Photograph 162 (left): Superintendent Bert Bennett.
Photograph 163 (right): Superintendent Gary Blade.
COURTESY OF THE KENTON COUNTY PUBLIC LI.BRARY, COVINGTON, KENTUCKY.

Dr. Gary Blade was superintendent of the Covington Independent Public Schools, 1975–79.

Photograph 164: A Racially Integrated Class at the Twelfth District School, 1969.
PHOTOGRAPH COURTESY OF THE KENTON COUNTY PUBLIC LIBRARY, COVINGTON, KENTUCKY.

A racially integrated class at the Twelfth District Elementary School (formerly Lincoln-Grant), 1969.

Photograph 165: Principal Matthew L. Mastin.
PHOTOGRAPH COURTESY OF THE KENTON COUNTY PUBLIC LIBRARY, COVINGTON, KENTUCKY.

Matthew Mastin served as principal of Lincoln-Grant (Twelfth District) School from 1963 until his unanticipated death on September 13, 1972.

Photograph 166: Eleventh District School Protest.
Photograph courtesy of the Kenton County Public Library, Covington, Kentucky.

Photograph 167: Eleventh District School.
Photograph courtesy of the Kenton County Public Library, Covington, Kentucky.

Photograph 168: Black Student Protest, Holmes High School.
PHOTOGRAPH COURTESY OF THE KENTON COUNTY PUBLIC LIBRARY, COVINGTON, KENTUCKY.

Holmes High School students protest the lack of African American history and culture courses at the school in 1970.

Photograph 169: Black Student Protest, Holmes High School.
Photograph courtesy of the Kenton County Public Library, Covington, Kentucky.

Holmes High School students protest the lack of African American history and culture courses at the school in 1970.

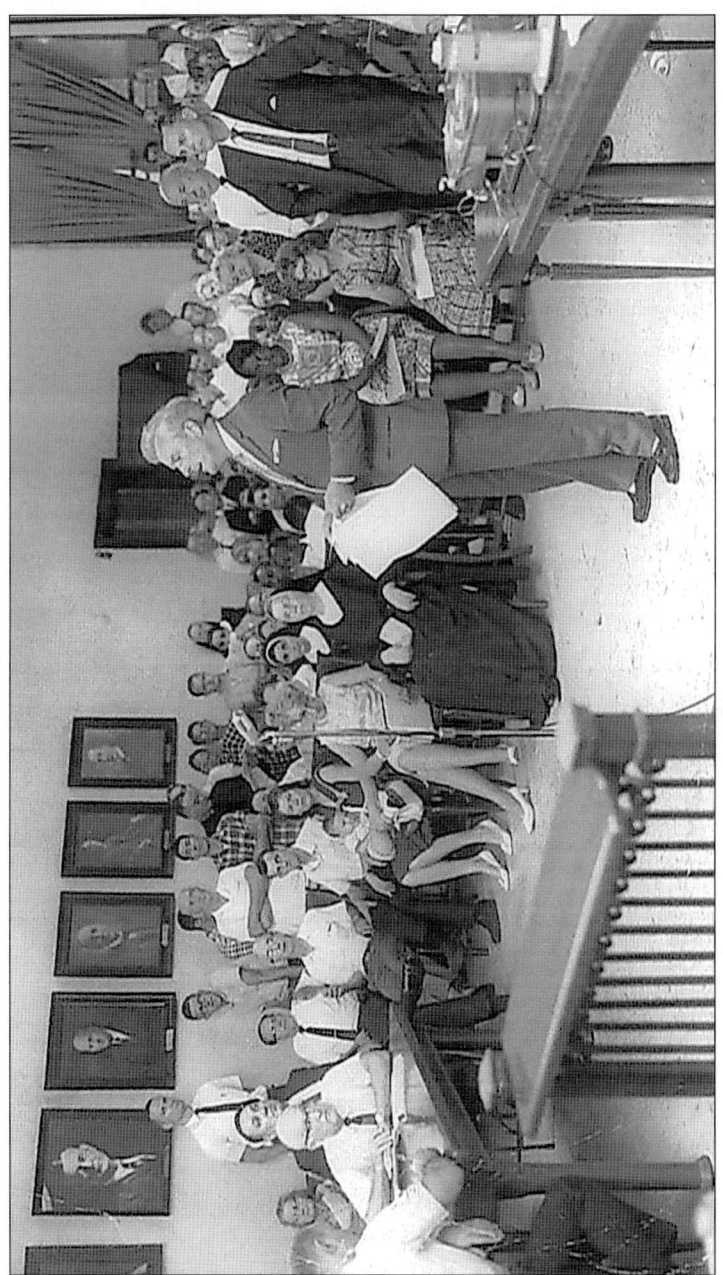

Photograph 170: Open Housing Discussion at City Hall, 1976.
PHOTOGRAPH COURTESY OF THE KENTON COUNTY PUBLIC LIBRARY, COVINGTON, KENTUCKY.

A 1976 public meeting regarding an Open Housing Ordinance regarding race in Covington.

Photograph 171: Protest Against Segregation, 1960s.
PHOTOGRAPH COURTESY OF THE KENTON COUNTY PUBLIC LIBRARY, COVINGTON, KENTUCKY.

CHAPTER 13

Racial Changes in Covington

The entire process of completely desegregating the Covington Public Schools had taken twenty-one years, the work of several different board of education memberships, four superintendents, three principals of Lincoln-Grant School, and the steady work of a comprehensive professional staff over more than two decades. Almost a century of racial segregation in the Covington Public Schools had finally ended!

Over time the character of the local black community would change with an influx of displaced black residents from Cincinnati into the Jacob Price Homes and other areas on the east side of Covington, as well as the arrival of different minority groups, including some Hispanic residents. Jacob Price Homes would become racially integrated as low-income white families moved in. As black students were dispersed more deeply into outlying, previously all-white schools there would be conflict over the relevance of those schools to the black community.

Covington, and the nation at large would become involved in protests and demontrations over racial and gender issues as well as the Vietnam War during the 1960s and '70s. Those matters would extend to Holmes Junior and Senior High School, where the relevance of the curriculum to African Americans and other issues would become dominant themes of dissent. Nordheim reported "a very brief period of fighting at the Junior and Senior High Schools," followed by the expulsion of students who "struck" teachers.[252] Some would refer to those activities as "race riots" in the Covington Public Schools. But Covington, for all of its faults about race, never seemed capable of the extreme racial violence found in some communties across the nation.

---

252. Nordheim, *Echoes*.

Eventually, racial tension in the Covington Public Schools would decrease, and resolve into a "matter of fact" coexistence of black and white students in a community that has historically had a mixed, "approach-avoidance" view of racial relationships. However, irrespective of school integration in Covington, and a degree of racial conciliation, many people, both black and white, had begun a steady exodus from the city.

According to one city historian "the city's [economic and population] decline did not become pronounced until the 1960's. . . . The city's population [had] remained somewhat stagnant for three decades. But post–World War II urban flight, coupled with a substantial reduction in the city's manufacturing sector, caused a significant decline in the city's workforce as well as its resident population."[253]

The author of Covington's history further indicates that the 1970s and early 1980s would become "the nadir for the city, at least with respect to its downtown." However, "beginning in the mid- to late-1980s, Covington began its revival. New buildings were constructed, jobs were created, and the population loss began to stabilize."[254] New building projects would continue into the twenty-first century, as the city struggled to increase its workforce, and maintain a viable, reputable system of public school education.

■   THE LEGACY

When William Grant deeded the property on Seventh Street in Covington for the education of black students in the 1880s, he could not have forseen the sequence of events described herein. He probably did not envision a new building for black students on Greenup Street in 1932 and the eventual development of a teaching staff that would produce students who could compete intellectually and academically on a variety of fronts with other students, without regard to race or social standing. And though there was a place in William Grant's heart for black people, even he may not have been able to predict the demise of racially segregated public schools in the United States of America some one hundred years later, when children of all races would learn together in the same classrooms. But, with thanks to William Grant, Jacob Price, C. E. Jones, Isaac Black, many other historical community leaders, and a dedicated, highly competent black teaching staff, the legacy of William Grant High School is well reflected in the various achievements of its graduates, and others who attended the school for a substantial number of years and graduated from other high schools.

The story of Lincoln-Grant School could be told from the perspective of any of its former students and graduates. The medical doctor and hospital administrator who attended Lincoln-Grant through the eighth grade and trans-

253. "Covington, Kentucky," *Wikipedia.*
254. Ibid.

ferred to a public school in Cincinnati could tell his story, as could the retired educator who lost both of his parents and only sister at an early age. A foster mom raised the latter young man with a village of community support that that encouraged him to complete his education, including a master's degree. Ulti- mately, he opened the door to integrated public school administration in Cov- ington for black people. The stories of at least three professional athletes from Lincoln-Grant would be worthwhile as documented accounts of student suc- cess. And even the casualties of some who may have taken errant pathways could be acknowledged for their instructive value. Collectively, Lincoln-Grant School yielded students whose lives were made better because of their affilia- tion with the school, regardless of whether their goals and achievements in life were lofty or more commonplace.

Initially, this author was hesitant to attempt a listing of the accomplish- ments of Lincoln-Grant students and graduates in anything more than general terms, because of the possibility of omitting some graduates who had achieved much in their lives, and understating the accomplishments of others. Also, there was the risk of naming only those who were engaged in professional careers, while neglecting others whose day-to day contributions would go unnoticed. Since the pinnacle of this work comes down to how students at Lincoln-Grant were prepared for life, and what they have contributed to society, ultimately a decision was made to proceed down this path with the following precautions: (A) The listing below includes *graduates* of William Grant High School only. (Some students with notable achievements were transferred to Holmes High School and other high schools in Boone and Campbell counties because of inte- gration, and still others completed their grade school education at Grant and voluntarily went to other high schools in the greater Cincinnati area). (B) The listing below is also limited by this author's knowledge and restricted ability to research the contributions and achievements of graduates completely due to the passage of time or the unavailability of subjects.

Below is an alphabetical listing of a *limited* group of William Grant High School graduates along with brief descriptions of their known achievements at a particular point in history. Additional accomplishments, which may be far greater than those listed herein, may have been omitted:

Figure 36: Selected Achievements of William Grant High School Graduates.

Allen, Mary E., Class of 1889, Teacher, Lincoln-Grant School
Ballard, Aaron, Jr., Class of 1959, Teacher and Principal, Covington Public Schools
Bedford, Walter, Jr., Class of 1965, Attorney at Law, Louisville, Kentucky
Brean, David Zellars, Class of 1942-1/2, Professional Artist, Harlem Renaissance
Brean, Emily Elizabeth, Class of 1945, Private Duty Nurse, Cincinnati
Bunyan (Clark), Eva, Class of 1937, Teacher, Covington and Cincinnati Public Schools
Bunyan, George Walter, Jr., Class of 1940-1/2, Attorney and Judge, Cincinnati
Bunyan, Sadye Irene, Class of 1945, Teacher and Supervisor, Covington and Cincin-

nati Schools

Carneal (Porterfield), Wilma, Class of 1922, Teacher, Lincoln-Grant School

Corbin, Minnie M., Class of 1922, Teacher, Lincoln-Grant School

Conway, Woodson Coleman, Class of 1935, Teacher, Cincinnati Public Schools

Crosby, Leconia Franklin, Class of 1917, Teacher, Lincoln-Grant School

Delaney, John William Thomas, Jr., Class of 1929, Attorney and Mortician, Covington

Fleming, Nathan, Class of 1894, Teacher, Lincoln-Grant School

Fowler, Richard Barkley, Class of 1963, Pastor, Ninth Street Baptist Church, Covington

Gilliard, Walter, Class of 1942-1/2, Teacher, Lincoln-Grant School and University Adm

Gooch, Elizabeth, Class of 1902, Teacher, Lincoln-Grant School

Hambrick, LeRoy, Class of 1939, Professional Athlete and Sports official.

Hargraves, Beatrice Anne, Class of 1955, Teacher, Toledo Public Schools

Hargraves, William F., II, Class of 1951, Colonel and Pilot, U.S. Air Force

Harris, Theodore Herbert Henry, Class of 1962, African American historian

Houston, Charles D., Jr., Class of 1945, Teacher and Administrator, Covington and Cincinnati Public Schools

Hundley, Etta Louise, Class of 1911, Teacher, Lincoln-Grant School

Jackson, Robert Connelly, Jr., Class of 1951, Teacher, Cincinnati Public Schools

Johnson, Robert Page, Class of 1897, Teacher, Latonia Colored and Lincoln-Grant Schools

Lovelace (Langham), Vanda, 1953, Manager of Accounts, U.S. Treasury Department

Martin, William Henry, Jr., Class of 1949, Teacher and Community Administrator, Covington

Mays (Lattimore), Jessie May, Class of 1958, Administrator, Fifth-Third Bank

Merry (Boone), Elizabeth Page, Class of 1928, Teacher, Covington and Cincinnati Public Schools

Merry, Charles Raymond, Class of 1931, Medical Doctor (MeHarry Medical College)

McCullough, Jerry, Class of 1957, Television Minister

Payne, Frank William, Class of 1939, Professional Pianist and Jazz Musician

Rhodes, Robert Norman, Class of 1950, President Nixon's Economic Council

Russel, Mr. Francis Marion, Class of 1895, Principal, Southgate School, Newport, Kentucky

Sheffey, Sigsbee Wilson, Class of 1917, Custodian, Lincoln-Grant School

Sleet (Wright), Sarah Mamie, Class of 1935, Teacher, Covington Public Schools

Smith (Conley), Bessie, Class of 1910, Teacher, Beaverlick School, Boone County, Kentucky

Smith, Lulu, Class of 1896, Teacher, Seventh Street Colored School

Smith (Jackson), Jewell Rebecca, Class of 1916, Teacher, Covington Public Schools

Smith, Napolean, Class of 1955, VP, Urban Economic Development Company, and Restaurant Owner

Stone, George E., Class of 1964, Professional Basketball Player, American Basketball Association

Sudduth, Horace S., Class of 1908, Owner, Manse Hotel, Cincinnati, Ohio
Summers (Northington), Mary, Class of 1945, Northern Kentucky African/American Heritage Task Force
Thacker, Tom, Class of 1959, Professional Basketball Player, NBA
Thomas, Allen, Class of 1957, Career, U.S. Army
Thompson, Eddie James, Class of 1953, Professional Boxer; President, Covington NAACP
Walker, Melvin W., Class of 1929, Decorated Hero, WWII; Educator, Cleveland Schools
Walton, James Augustus, Class of 1954, Teaching Assistant, Cincinnati Public Schools and Minister, Mt. Zion Baptist Church of Woodlawn
Walton, George Willie, Class of 1955, Bus Driver, City Transit Companies; and Evangelist
Walton, Joseph Moses, Class of 1958, Professor and Administrator, University of Akron, Ohio
Walton, Toney, Jr., Class of 1957, Teacher, Cincinnati Public Schools
Warren (Henderson), Eleanora Odesa, Class of 1915, Teacher, Lincoln-Grant School
Williams (Webb), Catharine, Class of 1917, Teacher, Lincoln-Grant School
Williams, Clarence, Class of 1927, Teacher, Covington Public Schools
Young, Tillie, Class of 1892, Teacher, Lincoln-Grant School
Zellers (Brean), Bessie Mae, Class of 1906, Private Music Teacher, Covington

■ THE REUNION

After the closing of the Lincoln-Grant School building in 1976, and its reopening as a the Northern Kentucky Community Center, the alumni, under the leadership of William Martin, director of the center, sponsored periodic school reunions, which brought together many former Lincoln-Grant students, alumni, former teachers and friends. After Mr. Martin's death, individual classes sponsored class reunions usually centered on their fiftieth anniversary. The following poem, written by this author, was inspired by the fiftieth anniversary celebration of the William Grant High School Class of 1958 on June 18, 2008.

THE REUNION

AUTHORED BY JOSEPH M. WALTON, PH.D., JULY 2008

And so we all gathered, from far and near,
Old friends and relations, some distant, some dear.
From North, South, East and West we came—
Older figures, familiar faces—and childhood names.

We greeted each other as some would recall
Growing up together, the start of it all.
A pleasant ambience from memories of old
That some would recount, and others withhold.

There was music without dancing, a lively spirit
As the program developed with a cherised lyric
That most would remember as the School Song,
While a few hoped the singing wouldn't last very long.

A moment of silence to honor our dead.
Then there was more music, as we waited to be fed
With sustenance for both body and soul
From diligent hands, and orators bold.

Photograph 172: Reunion Celebration.
PHOTO BY GREG JONES.

There were speeches, acknowledgments and presentations
As we moved through the evening, with manifestations
Of the reason for the gathering, the purpose of the affair
That would eventually end with a circle of prayer.

We shared a common history from a segregated past,
United as one through a racial caste.
Some thought it was fair, given the color of our skin,
To educate us in one building, from beginning to end.

"Separate but equal?" A dubious question.
Pride and dignity in the face of oppression
Were the personal qualities that would sustain us
While racial seclusion sought to contain us.

Why separate people according to race,
And limit them to a specific place?
"But its according to the law" some would say with chagrin
Of an era that was vanquished with the stroke of a pen!

"We hold these truths . . . " " . . . And justice for all."
"United we stand; Divided we fall."
Those quotes had begun to approach reality
In a nation still uncertain about racial equality.

Racial patterns changed slowly as the themes of yesterday
Receded into history, while time faded away.
Memories dim gradually as the years move on,
And those of our vintage will one day all be gone.

Our stories will then exist in the written word,
And nothing will be spoken by those who once heard
The daunting echoes of a racial endeavor
That some people felt should have lasted forever.

For future generations, the lessons from the past
Should be printed indelibly and should always last.
So that those yet unborn will not be defeated
By a racial divide—that should never be repeated.

We must have faith and always believe
That anything is possible, if we want to achieve
The maximum value from the lives we are given,
Before that Great Reunion with our Creator in Heaven.

Epilogue

Authoring *The Life and Legacy of Lincoln-Grant School* has been much like fitting together the disparate, scattered (and sometimes hidden) pieces of a giant, historical puzzle. This work began with several questions: When was Lincoln-Grant School created? What was its early history, and how were the racially based educational practices that sustained it carried out with such a sense of ease, and routine, objective social comfort for more than a century? What was involved in its desegregation and final closing? The threads of the questions were rooted in the author's personal experiences as a product of the school several decades ago. The answers would be revealed many years later, through the current examination and analysis of many aspects of racially segregated public school education in Northern Kentucky from 1866 to 1976. Gradually, as this book developed over a period of several years, the pieces of the puzzle seemed to fit together. It is hoped that the answers to the questions raised above are largely settled through the present work.

Some of the revelations contained herein constitute new information for this author. One noteworthy finding was confirmation of the fact that not all black people in Covington were slaves when the city was founded in 1815. The relative ease with which some free people of color traveled back and forth between Covington and Cincinnati well before the Civil War was novel information—especially since the most dominant image portrayed for that period is that of slave hunters chasing black people across the Ohio River with hound dogs, as they ran for freedom. Of course, slavery, largely domestic in nature, did exist in Northern Kentucky, and some black slaves were indeed pursued in that manner. But not all black people had that status prior to the American Civil War.

The level of education, familiarity with the law, and sophistication with language skills of several of those involved in founding the black school in Covington constituted surprisingly refreshing information, as did the statewide and regional organizations among newly freed black citizens that influenced the state legislature immediately after the Civil War ended. The fact that the school was founded by a black Covington minister and businessman, who was assisted by one of the first black attorneys in the Commonwealth of Kentucky, was significant information. This author was also impressed by the fact that the early principals for the school during the late eighteen hundreds and early nineteen hundreds included a black man with a college degree from Oberlin College, and another with a degree from Otterbein College. I knew that the teachers at Lincoln-Grant School who taught and mentored me from kindergarten through the twelfth grade during the 1940s and 1950s were well-educated—some with master's degrees from prestigious places. However I was surprised to learn that the depth of well-educated teachers and school principals extended so deeply into Lincoln-Grant's early history.

But perhaps the most aggregious and discouraging finding of the present work is the discovery of how the unwavering will to maintain racially segregated schools in Kentucky invaded and influenced every avenue of public life in the Commonwealth. The lengths and depths that were pursued for the sole purpose of keeping black and white children from being educated in the same buildings in Kentucky and other southern states were somewhat atonishing. The duplication of effort at every turn, the cumbersome, peculiar arrangements of travel and teaching assignments, and the blatant inequality of educational opportunity involved in running a dual educational system in the Commonwealth of Kentucky seemed excessively aberrant. Collectively, those racially segregated arrangements would seem to be unsustainable over time—yet they persisted in Covington and other parts of Northern Kentucky for better than a hundred years!

"The song has ended, but the melody lingers on," according to one jazz composer. The yellow, brick, exterior shell of the Lincoln-Grant edifice still stands vertical and stoically reticent, though benignly neglected from apparent lack of use. The building's aging crevices and rusting metal window frames are partially concealed in front by overgrown trees and shrubbery. The halls of the building remain empty, depleted, and silent in the year, 2009; the status of the Greenup Street facility as a vibrant learning center for black youth in Northern Kentucky is a phenomenon of the past.

Behind the building, a bright, multi-colored, public playground built mostly of a sturdy, polymer material, provides activities for younger neighborhood children of any race. Further to the east, close to an earthen, grass-covered floodwall that assists in the containment of the Licking River, is a baseball field with a dedication plaque that reads: Donald Johnson—Baseball Hall of Famer.

As the seasons come and go, the building reflects the bright afternoon sun, the the sullen cloudiness of the day, a wintry scene, or a the multiple foilage of a fall morning, while emitting only the quiet echos of an era that ended more than forty years ago. When night descends upon Greenup Street, the stars occasionally shine brightly overhead. It is as though they are illuminating and celebrating the personal, educational, and career achievements of the former students and graduates who emerged from Lincoln-Grant School to make their unique contributions to society. The foundation for all of our accomplishments was developed initially in makeshift buildings in downtown Covington, and later at the corner of Ninth and Greenup streets in a school building with an odd, hyphenated name, that was dedicated exclusively to people of color. But even as that yellow, brick building sinks deeper into Covington's history, the memories of Lincoln-Grant School continue to live in the hearts and minds of many of its graduates, former teachers, and others who passed through its doors.

The world seems different now. The current leader of the free world, the forty-fourth president of the United States of America, is Barrack Obama, a man of African-American descent. That historic event, which occured on January 20, 2009, could not have been imagined by most people in the late eighteen hundreds or even by many during the beginning of the twenty-first century. The connection of the most recent presidential election to the life and legacy of Lincoln-Grant School is a nonsequitur for many whose early educational and social histories were rooted in racial segregation. But, reflective of the linear progression of our human existence on the planet earth, it would seem inevitable that, at some point in American history, African Americans would move closer and closer to the realization of full equality in the United States of America.

Photograph 173: Lincoln-Grant School Building, 2007.
PHOTOGRAPH BY JOSEPH WALTON, 2007..

Photograph 174: The Walton Family, 1969.
FROM THE AUTHOR'S PERSONAL COLLECTION.

In Memory of Our Parents

Seated, left to right: *Martha Walton Mason (LaSallette Academy, 1961), and our parents, Georgie and Toney Walton, Sr.*

Standing, left to right: *Toney, James, George, and Joseph Walton (William Grant High School Classes of 1957, 1954, 1955, and 1958, respectively).*

The Rise and Fall of Segregated Public Schools in Covington

1866. Public Education for black people in Covington initiated by Jacob Price and others.

1874. Commonwealth of Kentucky establishes laws for separate common schools for black people.

1876. Covington charter amendment establishes public education for black people.

1886. William Grant High School established.

1888. Seventh Street Colored School opened.

1889. First graduating class from William Grant High School.

1896. U.S. Supreme Court upholds "Separate but Equal" via *Plessy v. Ferguson*.

1932. New building for Lincoln-Grant opened on Greenup Street.

1954. U.S. Supreme Court orders desegregation of all U.S. public schools through *Brown v. Board of Education*.

1965. William Grant High School closed; high school students sent to Holmes High School. Elementary section remains open, eventually becomes integrated.

1976. Lincoln-Grant Elementary School closed and turned into a community center.

A Chronology of Events:
Segregated Schools in Covington, Kentucky
1815–1976

1815. City of Covington incorporated by the Kentucky General Assembly.

1815–1866. No provision for the education of black people in Covington. Informal education in private venues for freedmen, or education across the river in Cincinnati, Ohio.

1820. Private schools established for white children; William Letcher Grant born.

1825. Free public school education available in Covington for white children.

1838. A state system of education established for white children.

1839. Jacob Price, a free man of color, born in Woodford County, Kentucky.

1841. A Covington city ordinance establishes a Board of Visitors for white public schools.

1850. Covington City Charter makes provision for a Board of Trustees to replace the Board of Visitors for white public schools. High school for white youth a part of charter.

1852. Samuel Singer born in Covington, apparently a free black person. Educated in Cincinnati until 1868.

1853. Covington Central High School, later known as Covington Holmes High School, established for white children.

1859. Jacob Price, a free man of color, relocates to Covington from Woodford County; William Grant defeated for a congressional seat.

1860. Abraham Lincoln, who stated, "Government cannot endure permanently half slave, half free" elected president of the United States.

1861. Confederate States of America is formed; Abraham Lincoln sworn in as sixteenth president; American Civil War begins. Eleven-state confederacy does *not* include Kentucky.

1863. Emancipation Proclamation freeing all slaves issued by President Lincoln.

1864. Lincoln re-elected as president of the United States; Jacob Price becomes a minister at the First (Colored) Baptist Church on Bremen Street.

1865. President Lincoln assassinated; Civil War ends; U.S. Congress approves Thirteenth Amendment to the U.S. Constitution, abolishing slavery. Freedmen's Bureau established at the federal level on March 3, 1865.

1866. A group of concerned citizens, including Jacob Price meet in the Covington City Hall to establish a public school for African American children. First classes held in the home of Jacob Price at 61 Bremen Street (now Pershing Street).

1868. Samuel Singer leaves Covington. Apparently takes up residence in Ohio; eventually attends Oberlin College.

1869. First graduating class from Holmes (Central) High School, one white student, Miss Amelia Orr, who becomes a second grade teacher in the Covington School System.

1870. The Fifteenth Amendment granting black males the right to vote in federal and state elections was incorporated into the U.S. Constitution.

1873. School for black children moved from various black churches to a vacated white district school building in Covington.

1874. Kentucky Legislature establishes "Common Schools" for "colored" children.

1876. City of Covington ordinance amendment establishes public school for "colored" children. Examination for the school principalship held, John McLeod elected.

1879. Darius Moffett becomes principal of the school in Covington for African Americans.

1880. William Grant deeds property on Seventh Street in Covington for African American school. Samuel R. Singer graduates from Oberlin College.

1881. Singer succeeds Mr. Moffet as the third principal of the Colored School in Covington. Jacob Price establishes successful lumber business in region.

1882. William Grant dies, and is buried in Linden Grove Cemetery in Covington. Charles E. Jones, who later became the owner of C. E. Jones Funeral Home is born in Covington.

1886. A high school for black students is established in Covington, and named for William Grant.

1888. Seventh Street (Colored) School built on property deeded by William Grant.

1889. First graduating class from William Grant High School, two female students, Annie Price (daughter of Rev. Jacob Price), and Mary E. Allen, who later became a teacher at the school.

1890. Public library established in Covington under school board control.

1896. *Plessy v. Ferguson* ruling upholds racial segregation in a train car in Louisiana, thereby providing the path for legally based racial segregation in all public venues, including public schools.

1897. Covington Public Library becomes freestanding, not under school board control.

1899. William Grant High School academic program changed from three years to four.

1900. Covington teachers required to have at least a year of training in a normal school. Samuel Singer is suspended as principal of William Grant High School.

1901. Covington Public Library is racially integrated. Frank L. Williams becomes the fourth principal of the black school in Covington.

1902. First graduates of William Grant High School four-year program.

1911. Holmesdale property deeded to Covington Public Schools for new high school building for white children.

1914. Evening classes for black and white students established in Covington Public Schools. Fire at home of Jacob Price in Covington. At age of seventy-four, Price jumps from second floor window to safety.

1916. Construction of new Holmes High School building initiated on Holmesdale property.

1919. New Holmes High School building occupied by white students; Glenn O. Swing becomes principal of Holmes.

1920. The Nineteenth Amendment to the U.S. Constitution, which granted women in the United States the right to vote was finally ratified by all states in the Union.

1923. Jacob Price dies; funeral held at First (Colored) Baptist Church on Ninth Street in Covington; buried in Evergreen Cemetery, Southgate, Kentucky.

1924. Mary Singer Price, wife of Jacob Price dies.

1926. Henry R. Merry, who served as acting principal from 1923 to 1924, becomes permanent principal of Lincoln-Grant School.

1927. Glenn O. Swing elected superintendent of Covington Schools.

1929. Covington Board of Education chooses site at Ninth and Greenup streets for a new Lincoln-Grant School building. Anonymous persons start fires in an attempt to destroy the Seventh Street School building and the black First Baptist Church, located near the new school site.

1931. Construction of the new Lincoln-Grant building at Ninth and Greenup.

1932. New Lincoln-Grant building at Ninth and Greenup occupied by black students in March; first graduating class in new building.

1939. Government-sponsored homes for black people, named for Rev. Jacob Price opened on Covington's east side close to Lincoln-Grant School.

1947. Charles E. Jones, owner of C. E. Jones Funeral Home in Covington dies at the age of sixty-five. Jones was a prominent community leader in the fight for a new Lincoln-Grant building in the 1930s.

1954. U.S. Supreme Court *Brown v. Board of Education* decision striking down "separate but equal," and ruling segregated schools unconstitutional.

1955. William Grant High School students from Boone and Campbell counties integrated into those school districts. Desegregation efforts initiated in Covington after Supreme Court decision reaffirmed. Henry R. Merry retires from Lincoln-Grant, Charles L. Lett becomes new principal of Lincoln-Grant.

1957. Summer school trial of integration begins at Holmes; Optional enrollment of black seniors at Holmes High School initiated.

1960. Glenn Swing retires as superintendent of Covington Schools; David Evans becomes new superintendent.

1962. Glenn O. Swing dies.

1963. Charles Lett, principal of Lincoln-Grant leaves Covington Public Schools, and is succeeded by Matthew L. Mastin.

1965. William Grant High School closed, and black students transferred to Holmes High School; elementary grades remain open at Lincoln-Grant. Retired principal Henry R. Merry dies at the age of eighty.

1966. Lincoln-Grant School name changed to Twelfth District School; building significantly integrated. Mrs. Jewell R. Jackson, former English teacher at William Grant High School passes away.

1972. Matthew Mastin, principal of Lincoln-Grant, dies of heart attack; succeeded by James K. Burns.

1974. Name of school building changed back to Lincoln-Grant School.

1976. Lincoln-Grant School building closed and reopened as the Northern

Kentucky Community Center. Former Covington schoolteacher William Martin was the founding director of the center.

Historical Locations of Lincoln-Grant School From 1866 to 1976

Year	Name of Building	Street Location	Grade Levels	Principal
1866	Bremen Street Baptist Church	61 Bremen St.	Uncertain	None
1875	Madison St. School Robbins St. School	Madison St. Robbins St.	Elementary Elementary	John S. McLeod John S. McLeod
1879	Colored School		Elementary	Darius L. V. Moffett
1888	Seventh St. Colored School William Grant High School	25 E. 7th St. 25 E. 7th St.	Elementary & High School	Samuel R. Singer Samuel R. Singer
1932	Lincoln-Grant School William Grant High School	9th & Greenup Sts. 9th & Greenup Sts.	Elementary & High School	Henry R. Merry Henry R. Merry
1966	Twelfth District School	9th & Greenup Sts.	Elementary	Matthew L. Mastin
1974	Lincoln-Grant School	9th & Greenup Sts.	Elementary	James K. Burns
1976	N. Kentucky Community Center	9th & Greenup Sts.	N/A	N/A

Principals of Lincoln-Grant School, 1871–1976

1871–1879. John S. McLeod**

1879–1881. Darius L.V. Moffet**

1881–1900. Samuel R. Singer**

1901–1908. Frank L. Williams**

1908–1912. William H. Fouse**

1912–1913. Miss Frankie B. Watkins (temporary)

1913–1923. Robert L. Yancey

1923–1924. Henry R. Merry (acting)

1924–1926. Robert L. Yancey

1926–1955. Henry R. Merry

1955–1963. Charles L. Lett

1963–1972. Matthew L. Mastin**

1972–1976. James K. Burns**

---

* Primary Sources: B. L. Nordheim, *Echoes of the Past. A History of the Covington Public School System*, 131–132; Official Minutes, Covington Board of Education; and Theodore H. H. Harris, African American Historian.

**The original name of Lincoln-Grant School was the Seventh Street Colored School, which also contained William Grant High School as of 1886. The Seventh Street Colored School, which was preceded by a series of buildings in different locations referred to as the "Colored School" in the early board minutes, was renamed Lincoln School in the early 1900s. The name, Lincoln-Grant School evolved around 1912 as a description of both the elementary portion (Lincoln School) and the high school division (William Grant High School). The Lincoln-Grant name was carried forward until 1966, when the school was renamed Twelfth District School from 1966 until 1974 (following the closing of the high school division, William Grant High School in 1965). The name reverted back to Lincoln-Grant School from 1974 until the school building was closed in 1976 due to low enrollment. The high school section of the school was always designated as William Grant High School.

Number of Grant High School Graduates by Year of Graduation, 1889–1965

1965	14	1942-1/2	14	1930-1/2	1	1907	3
1964	21	1942	13	1930	10	1906	5
1963	15	1941-1/2	7	1929	13	1905	4
1962	11	1941	11	1928	8	1904	5
1961	13	1940-1/2	6	1927	5	1903	5
1960	13	1940	9	1926	4	1902	2
1959	22	1939-1/2	2	1925	2	1901	0
1958	22	1939	11	1924	3	1900	2
1957	13	1938-1/2	4	1923	5	1899	7
1956	12	1938	16	1922	10	1898	3
1955	18	1937-1/2	5	1921	2	1897	3
1954	15	1937	10	1920	4	1896	2
1953	15	1936-1/2	3	1919	5	1895	2
1952	15	1936	21	1918	4	1894	2
1951	22	1935-1/2	3	1917	9	1893	2
1950	25	1935	13	1916	1	1892	2
1949	25	1934-1/2	1	1915	4	1891	3
1948	18	1934	18	1914	5	1890	0
1947	26	1933-1/2	2	1913	8	1889	2
1946	25	1933	9	1912	3		
1945	23	1932-1/2	1	1911	9	Total	792
1944	11	Jun '32	14	1910	1		
1943-1/2	4	Feb '32	2	1909	*		
1943	18	1931	6	1908	5	* None listed	

[Note: Figures may vary from actual "cap and gown" graduates for some years due to the inclusion of GED and GI graduates.]

Alphabetical Listing of
William Grant High School Alumni
1889–1965

Note: The names for the graduating classes from 1889 to 1900 were provided in an authenticated letter from William Grant High School principal Samuel R. Singer (see figure 6). The letter was included in a published, 1929 University of Cincinnati master's thesis by Leconia Franklin Crosby. The primary source for the names of alumni from all other classes is the *Official Covington Board of Education Minutes.* Supplemental information was obtained from the *Kentucky Post* for the early 1900s, and two William Grant High School Commencement Programs (1939 and 1958). Specific names of all graduates in the classes of 1903 and 1904 are not included because neither the Board of Education Minutes nor any supplementary sources listed all of the individual names for those two classes. However, according to the Board of Education Minutes for 1903 and 1904, there were "five graduates, 1 boy and 4 girls," in the class of 1903. The following year "there were five graduates, all girls [in the class of 1904]. Miss Mary Margeret Page was the salutatorian and Miss Maymie Milla Williams was the valedictorian." The names of 785 graduates are listed on the following pages. However the official number of William Grant alumni should be 792, based on the records cited above.

Adams, Gloria Ann (1951)
Adams, Mary (1937 ½)
Alexander, Edna Earl (1946)
Allen, Alfred Green (1934)
Allen, Dorothy Mar (1955)
Allen, Hazel Bernice (1947)
Allen, Imogene (1946)
Allen, Mary E. (1889)
Andrews, Otis (1963)
Arvin, Elmer Downey (1933)
Arvin, Gail Elaine (1952)
Arvin, Mary Ann (1952)
Arvin, Velma Marie (1929)
Ayres, Ralph (1927)
Ayres, Robert Lee (1929)

Bailey, Richard (1929)
Baker, Bessie Maie (1933)
Baker, Clarence William (1941 ½)
Baker, Elizabeth (1936)
Baker, Juanita Elsie (1935)
Baker, Lura Carnelia (1932)
Baker, Robert Lee (1950)
Baker, Rosetta (1936)
Baker, Vivian Jane (1934)
Ballard, Aaron, Jr. (1959)
Banks, Estella Elizabeth (1964)
Banks, Russell Grant (1941)
Bannister, William Frank (1938 ½)
Barnes, Janice (1959)
Baskin, Annie (1937 ½)
Baskin, Ella Mae (1943 ½)
Baskin, Hilliard (1942)
Baskin, Lorene (1946)
Baskin, Mattie Mae (1934)
Baskin, Nettie Ida (1936)
Baugh, Colonger (1964)
Baughman, Anderson Louis (1941 ½)
Baughman, Katie Lee (1943)
Bedford, Walter, Jr. ((1965)
Beal, Loistene (1963)
Beal, William, G.I. (1949)
Beam, Earl (1927)
Bedford, Walter, Jr. (1965)
Behanan, Addie Mae (1953)
Behanan, Gladys Winifred (1950)
Bell, William (1963)
Benion, Curtis (1958)
Black, Alice Adeline (1942)

Black, June Thomasina (1947)
Blackwell, John Stanley (1912)
Bland, Helen (1938)
Booher, Armilda (1939)
Bothwell, Amos (1942)
Bothwell, Joyce Gentry (1952)
Boyer, Carrie Bernice (1934)
Bozeman, Mildred (1938)
Bradford, Sarah Helen (1948)
Bradford, Thomas Richard (1926)
Brean, David Zellars (1942 ½)
Brean, Emily Elizabeth (1945)
Brean, John W. (1938 ½)
Brown, Mary Louise (1940 ½)
Brown, Ella B. (1897)
Brown, Henry Bufford (1941 ½)
Brown, Margo Lee (1963)
Brown, Mildred Carole (1962)
Brown, Norma Regina (1957)
Brown, Paul William (1956)
Brown, Robert Edward (1961)
Brown, Vernon Tone (1941 ½)
Bryant, Robert (1947)
Buckner, Julia A. (1922)
Bufford, Thelma Mae (1942)
Bunyan, Eva (1937)
Bunyan, George Walter, Jr. (1940 ½)
Bunyan, Marguerite Louise (1936)
Bunyan, Sadye Irene (1945)
Burnside, John Neil (1911)
Burton, Charles (1938)
Burton, Mary DuVal (1933)
Burton, Michael Brian (1963)
Butler, Anna Louise (1932)
Butler, George Thomas (1958)
Butler, James Guthrie (1934)
Butler, Lois Estolia (1954)
Butler, Romeo S. (1905)
Byrd, Mayme Walker (1911)

Caldwell, Beatrice (1923)
Caldwell, Martha (1923)
Cammack, Louis Albert (1959)
Campbell, George Dwight (1965)
Carneal, Cora E. (1922)
Carneal, Wilma Lucille (1926)
Castleman, Anna Pearl (1952)
Castleman, Marie Jeanette (1962)
Castleman, Pearl (1937)

Cavil, Sue Belle (1953)

Chapman, Margaret Holloway (1931)

Childs, Gertrude (1938 ½)

Chinn, Alice (1900)

Clark, George Rogers (1949)

Clarke, Eugene (1943)

Claxton, Betty Jean (1947)

Claxton, Eugene (1963)

Clemens, Juanita (1954)

Clemons, Van Roy, Jr. (1951)

Clifford, Andrew Jackson (1958)

Clifford, Raymond Louis (1953)

Clinkenbeard, Dorothy Rochelle (1943)

Clinkenbeard, Marian Lewis (1946)

Collins, Jean (1954)

Collins, Richard Henry (1943)

Collins, Rosetta (1957)

Collins, Ruby Hill (1931)

Conley, Countee Cullen (1947)

Conley, Edwyn Paul (1944)

Conley, Leonard (1914)

Conley, Lee (1949)

Conley, Russell (1937)

Conrad, Charles Richard (1946)

Conrad, Robert (1936)

Conway, Clara Margaret (1939)

Conway, Geraldine (1941 ½)

Conway, Julius, Jr. (1946)

Conway, Woodson Coleman (1935)

Corbin, Minnie M. (1922)

Cork, Robert William (1930)

Correll, Emma Mae (1917)

Cottie, Ronald LaMar (1959)

Cottrell, Mary Lee (1949)

Cottrell, Rosa Lee (1947)

Cowan, Chester Arthur, Jr. (1946)

Crawford, Alfred (1951)

Crawford, Dorothy Louise (1954)

Crawford, Frank (1892)

Crawford, Fredderic Douglas (1947)

Crawford, John Richard (1955)

Crosby, Elizabeth F. (1922)

Crosby, James Henry (1917)

Crosby, Leconia Franklin (1917)

Cunningham, Edward Jerome (1951)

Cunningham, Mary Louise (1947)

Cunningham, Norma Jean (1947)

Dale, Doris Mae (1946)

Dancer, Hallie Boyd (1895)

Dandridge, William Chester (1950)

Davis, Sherron Antonio, II (1964)

Davis, Alfonza (1959)

Davis, Ellena (1928)

Davis, Francis (1914)

Davis, Grace Frances (1908)

Davis, Earl Wayne, Jr. (1952)

Davis, Junior, Hercules (1955)

Davis, Mary Gredderdine (1942)

Davis, Rosa Katherine (1941)

Davis, Shirley Mae (1954)

Davis, William Assa (1936)

Davis, William Henry (1911)

Deal, Frank Louis (1950)

Decoursey Mary Louise (1935)

Delaney, Ada Florena (1913)

Delaney, John William Thomas, Jr. (1929)

Delaney, Julia (1896)

Delaney, Pinkie Esther (1898)

Dews, Robert Edward (1929)

Dickerson, Charles Edward (1958)

Doddy, John Wilbur (1946)

Douglas, Elmer G. (1899)

Dowell, Norma Jean (1948)

Doyle, Rowena Mentlo (1942 ½)

Duff, Susie M. (1899)

Duke, Jessie B. (1899)

Dunson, Juanita (1953)

Dunson, Neil (1936)

Engleman, Wallace Lee (1965)

English, Theodore (1948)

Estill, Edith Elizabeth (1919)

Estill, Leland Fletcher (1915)

Fann, Charles (1964)

Ferrell, Mamie Elizabeth (1958)

Finnell, Everett (1942)

Fishback, Etta Mae (1942)

Fisher, John Earl (1940)

Flagler, Marjorie Marie (1945)

Fleming, Anna Palm (1917)

Fleming, Katherine (1919)

Fleming, Nathan (1894)

Fleming, Thomas Wilson (1922)

Florence, Bobbie Lou (1955)

Florence, Elbert Lee, G.I.* (1947)

Fortune, Hattie Woodford (1936)
Fortune, Priscilla (1937)
Foster, Lorenzo, Jr. (1945)
Fowler, Richard Barkley (1963)
Fox, Geraldine Elizabeth (1929)
Fox, Homer Weaver (1952)
Fox, Norma Jean (1954)
Fox, Tilly (1907)
Frakes, Harold (1945)
Francis, Nellie Lou (1932)
Frateman, Mae Margaret (1932)
Frazier, Lee (1938)
Frazier, Robert Albert (1934)
French, Betty Sue (1948)
Frierson, Madeleine Dilcia (1932)
Frierson, Russell Lamont (1929)
Frye, Carrie (1894)
Frye, Katherine Olivia Dawson (1962)
Frye, William Dawson (1941)

Gaines, Effinger (1939 ½)
Garrett, Irvin (1943 ½)
Garrett, Josephine Russell (1929)
Garrett, Kathryn Louise (1932)
Garrett, Matthew F. (1922)
Garrett, Matthew Turner (1945)
Garrett, William Millard (1950)
Gee, Eileen Vivian (1924)
George, Donald (1951)
George, Josephine Elizabeth (1955)
George, Margaret Louise (1944)
Gilliard, Viola Louise (1945)
Gilliard, Walter (1942 ½)
Givens, Della (1914)
Givens, George Henry (1912)
Givens, LaVera Ann (1958)
Givens, Marian Willis (1959)
Givens, Virginia Bells (1935)
Glenn, William (1945)
Goggins, Lawrence Reid (1936)
Gooch, Elizabeth Wotten (1902)
Gooch, Elsie Amelia (1898)
Gooch, Henry H. (1899)
Gordon, Wallace Edward (1917)
Grant, Arthur (1893)
Grant, Deborah (1965)
Grant, Donald (1964)
Grant, James William, G.I. (1950)
Grant, Lois Dean (1961)

Grant, Thurston Thomas (1943)
Grant, Virginia Olivette (1928)
Gray, Allen Barnes (1952)
Gray, Anna Marie (1964)
Gray, Arnold Spencer (1948)
Gray, Edgar Morris (1954)
Gray, Marshall (1938)
Green, Albert Eugene (1956)
Green, Alexander (1948)
Green, Delores (1959)
Green, Doris (1959)
Green, Lennard Alonzo (Linus) (1955)
Green, Naomi Elizabeth (1946)
Green, Vivian (1960)
Greene, Anna Frances (1934)
Greene, Rosetta (1946)
Griffin, Juanita Pearl (1950)

Haggard, Charles (1891)
Haggard, Maurice Charles (1913)
Hall, Edward Lee (1928)
Hall, Ernestine (1950)
Hall, Frank (1942 ½)
Hall, James Robert (1949)
Hall, Jessie Mae (1956)
Hall, Mary Elizabeth (1951)
Hall, Wessley Karl (1955)
Hambrick, Leroy (1938)
Hamilton, Jessie Farnsworth (1930)
Hamilton, Lillyan (1933)
Hamlin, Hazel Agnes (1932)
Hampton, Clifford Edward (1915)
Hampton, Rosetta (1957)
Hancock, Jerome (1930)
Hardin, Annie Lue (1942)
Hardin, Melvin Frances (1923)
Hargraves, Beatrice Anne (1955)
Hargraves, William Frederick, II (1950)
Harper, Charles Edward (1948)
Harper, Myrtle Olivia (1946)
Harper, Sarah (1937)
Harper, William Rayford (1930)
Harris, Anna Catherine (1961)
Harris, Arcenia Bell (1948)
Harris, Esther Lydia (1933)
Harris, Josephine Lavelle (1932)
Harris, Marion Elizabeth (1945)
Harris, Nathaniel (1938)
Harris, Ruth (1937)

Harris, Theodore Herbert Henry (1962)
Harris, Ada Mae Trequela (1942 ½)
Harrison, George Walter (1953)
Harrison, Leona Marie (1930)
Haskins, Wilson (1907)
Hatcher, Julia Mae (1913)
Hawkins, Alberta Henrietta (1932 ½)
Hawkins, Lucille (1926)
Haynes, Virginia Lee (1930)
Hedges, Desota Lee (1949)
Hedges, Norma Rose (1949)
Helm, Ann Maie (1933)
Henderson, Betty Ann (1959)
Hendricks, Margaret Wilma (1935 ½)
Henry, Melba Padilla (1947)
Herndon, Alice Elizabeth (1945)
Herndon, Donna Jean (1965)
Herron, Charles Lee (1955)
Herron, Joan Elizabeth (1962)
Higbee, Gladys (1937 ½)
Higgins, Henry Morris (1939)
Hillard, James Thomas (female) (1913)
Hillman, Charles W. (1891)
Hillman, John Garrard (1912)
Hinton, Helen D. (1960)
Hinton, Joshua (1939)
Hinton, Lucy Lee (1936)
Hinton, Woodrow (1935 ½)
Hisle, Dorothy Chase (1942 ½)
Hisle, John W., Jr. (1940)
Hisle, Ruth Willis (1936)
Hoffman, Willa Mae (1957)
Holley, Leon (1938)
Holloway, Bradshaw (1929)
Holloway, John, G.I. (1949)
Hood, Carrie Lee (1920)
Hopkins, Andrew Leroy (1936)
Hopkins, Viola Olivette (1935)
Horner, Mattie Mae (1908)
Houston, Charles D., Jr. (1945)
Howlett, Joseph Robert (1934)
Huddleston, Betty Jo (1964)
Hughes, Alena (1939)
Hughes, Lucille (1942)
Humphrey, Cpl. Frederick L., G.I. (1955)
Humphrey, Dorothy Benetta (1951)
Humphries, Nettie Frances (1950)
Humphries, Vernon James (1947)
Hundley, Etta Louise (1911)

Hunter, David (1964)
Hurry, Samuel (1962)
Hutchins, Leara (1938 ½)
Hutchins, Margaret Lucinda (1948)
Hutchins, Walter Hadley (1946)
Hutsel, John Thomas (1941 ½)
Hutsell, Lucenia Ruth (1941)

Ingguls, Granville Robert (1950)
Ingram, Mary (1949)

Jackson, Clinton (1963)
Jackson, Doris Mae (1949)
Jackson, Elizabeth (1959)
Jackson, Evelyn Louise (1947)
Jackson, Frank Lewis (1961)
Jackson, Frederick (1956)
Jackson, Collins, Jr. (1950)
Jackson, Loroma (1964)
Jackson, Robert Connelly (1951)
Jackson, Robert Eugene (1958)
Jackson, William (1962)
Jamar, La Rita Guy (1965)
Jamar, Rosa Lena (1943)
James, Charles Andrew (1942 ½)
James, Charles Frederick (1962)
James, Estella Mae (1935)
Jarman, Christine Marie (1944)
Jarman, Katie Lee (1935)
Jarman, Lillian Mildred (1945)
Jarman, Madeline Bernice (1946)
Jarman, Richard Douglas (1950)
Jarrell, Sherry (1963)
Jasper (Douglas), Raymond (1952)
Jasper, Joan Carol (1957)
Jasper, Lueaver (1953)
Jasper, Milton Louis (1959)
Jefferson, Anna Belle (1956)
Jefferson, Charles Donald (1952)
Jennings, Marcella (1964)
Johnson, Abraham Winston (1948)
Johnson, Alma Louise (1956)
Johnson, Ann Mae (1923)
Johnson, Dorothy Beatrice (1946)
Johnson, Florence Emma (1943)
Johnson, Frances Aurelia (1942)
Johnson, Gloria Jacqueline (1941)
Johnson, Grace Belle (1899)
Johnson, Helen Delores (1959)

Johnson, Helen Louise (1950)
Johnson, Hiram (1947)
Johnson, Homer Melvin, G.I. (1949)
Johnson, James Henry (1917)
Johnson, James Henry (1929)
Johnson, Jessie Rebecca (1920)
Johnson, James Henry, Jr. (1946)
Johnson, Lorraine (1947)
Johnson, Orval Lee (1940)
Johnson, Ruth Belle (1902)
Johnson, Robert Page (1897)
Johnson, Sylvia Marie (1951)
Johnson, Thelma Frances (1961)
Johnson, William Earl (1949)
Johnsonne, Sarah Katheryn (1933 ½)
Jones, B. H. (1906)
Jones, Betty Jean (1950)
Jones, Carl (1931)
Jones, Edith Helena (1920)
Jones, Mary Frances (1946)
Jones, Melvena (1907)
Jones, Raslee (1949)
Jones, Robert O., G.I. (1949)
Jones, Zenobia Elizabeth (1918)
Jordan, Marie A. B. (1936)
Jouett, Barbara Jean (1956)
Jouett, Charles (1957)
Jouett, Edgar (1964)
Jouett, Lawrence Maurice (1965)
Jouett, Melvin Douglas (1961)

Kelley, Coleman (1930)
Kelly, Robert Franklin (1951)
Kenny, Clifford (1950)
Kenny, Lucille Elizabeth (1948)
Kilby, Albert Brown (1936)
Kilby, Luvenia M. (1905)
Knight, Henry, G.I. (1950)

LaBordeaux, Clementine (1956)
Lair, Isaac (1891)
Lambkins, Katherine Vivian (1918)
Lambkins, William Delbert (1935)
Langford, Katie (1930)
Lattimore, Carole J. (1960)
Lattimore, Lorraine (1959)
Lattimore, Winnefred Rebecca (1942 ½)
Leachman, Lucille(1948)
Lee, Bernice (1951)

Lee, Ezelle Lavonne (1951)
Lee, Helen Devra (1955)
Lewis, William, Jr. (1933)
Lewis, Mae Delores (1955)
Lewis, William (1937)
Lightfoot, Dorothy Mae (1954)
Lindley, Christine (1942 ½)
Lindley, Harry Lee (1946)
Litmon, William Robert (1945)
Littleton, Harriet Elizabeth (1934)
Littleton, Lillian Louise (1946)
Littleton, Robert Painter (1941)
Locust, Nannie Beatrice (1935)
Lovelace, Vanda (1953)
Lyons, Kenneth (1937 ½)

Mabrey, Donald W., GED (1958)
Mabrey, Helena Theressa (1949)
Mabrey, Carlton Lewis, Jr. (1954)
Madison, Curtis Cortez (1934)
Madison, Marie Peggy (1932)
Madison, William James (1934)
Mallory, Freddie M. (1922)
Malone, Alice Lynch (1941)
Mann, Ruth Ann (1959)
Marshall, Ella Frances (1906)
Marshall, Mary Louise (1911)
Martin, Walter, Jr. (1944)
Martin, William Henry, Jr. (1949)
Martin, Lena Louise (1943 ½)
Martin, Mary Alyce (1945)
Martin, Willana (1947)
Martin, William Henry (1913)
Maxwell, Frozene (1947)
Mays, Jessie Mae (1958)
Mays, Wayne (1960)
McCary, Bertram (1924)
McClellan, William, Jr. (1945)
McConico, Anna Margaret (1952)
McCoy, Melvena (1936)
McCoy, Oliver, G.I. (1955)
McCullough, Jerry (1957)
McCullough, William Prentice (1948)
McEntie, Clarice Lee (1941)
McEntie, Marvin Sanders (1940 ½)
McGaines, Charles (1897)
McQueen, Stewart (1931)
Meeks, Rita Elizabeth (1964)
Meeks, Rudolph Valentine (1965)

Merritt, William Bradley (1939)

Merry, Charles Raymond (1931)

Merry, Elizabeth Page (1928)

Miles, Ernest Lee (1936)

Miller, Judy Ann (1964)

Miller, William Oscar (1899)

Mills, Bettye Jean (1950)

Mitchell, Ella Pollard (1934)

Mitchell, Jennie Belle (1933)

Montgomery, Elizabeth Ann (1947)

Moore, James David (1958)

Morgan, Mary Elizabeth (1915)

Morris, Ethel Lee (1940)

Morris, Clarence, Jr. (1950)

Morton, Ella Marie (1932)

Morton, Ida Mae (1908)

Morton, Ottee (1937)

Moss, Goldia Mae Elizabeth (1932)

Murphy, Ida Kathryn (1940)

Murphy, Sarah E. (1922)

Nelson, Joseph Henry (1962)

O'Neal, Elizabeth (1961)

Oden, Willie J. (1960)

Offutt, Gerald McKinley (1964)

Offutt, George R., Jr. (1960)

Offutt, Patricia A. (1960)

Orr, William Henry (1943 ½)

Page, Carole Ann (1961)

Page, Edora Wallace (1940)

Page, Mary Margeret (1904)

Paige, Willa Nell (1954)

Parrish, Jasa France (1943)

Patterson, Alma Jane (1959)

Patterson, Charles Victor (1963)

Patterson, George Andrew (1951)

Patterson, Mary Beatrice (1935 ½)

Patterson, Robbie Merle (1957)

Patterson, Sylvia Lee (1952)

Patterson, Walter W. (1964)

Paxton, Helen Estelle (1928)

Paxton, Melvenna Velma (1932)

Payne, Bertha M. (1960)

Payne, Dorothy (1944)

Payne, Frank William (1939)

Payne, John Franklin (1963)

Payne, John Marshall (1942)

Payne, Margie Lou (1951)

Payne, Ruth Ann (1955)

Payne, Sonia Lee (1959)

Payne, William Herman (1963)

Penn, Leconia (1934)

Penny, Lillie Marie (1965)

Perkins, Robert W., GED (1958)

Perrin, Pauline (1965)

Perrin, Priscilla (1965)

Perry, Josephine Helen (1946)

Perry, William Winfred (1947)

Phelps, Benjamin (1936 ½)

Phipps, Leonard, Jr. (1960)

Phipps, Robert Lee (1957)

Pinkins, Ramona (1934)

Porterfield, Joyce Elaine (1956)

Price, Annie (1889)

Price, John Maurice (1930)

Puckett, Vernell Leroy (1941 ½)

Ragan, Maude Belle (1911)

Redden, David Lee (1951)

Redden, Paul Lawrence, Jr. (1947)

Reed, Charlotte Elizabeth (1942 ½)

Reed, Ella (1960)

Reed, Henry Edgar (1935)

Reed, William Jackson, Jr. (1959)

Reed, Maria Antoinette (1929)

Reed, William Jackson (1939)

Regan, Ruby (1919)

Reid, Commodore Russell (1933)

Reid, Norman Patterson (1950)

Rhodes, Clinton M. (1960)

Rhodes, Jaqueline (1947)

Rhodes, Marian Arletta (1945)

Rhodes, Robert Norman (1950)

Rice, John Etta (1955)

Rice, Mildred Odessa (1944)

Rice, Virginia Mae (1953)

Riley, Alice Viola (1944)

Riley, Edward Alfred (1946)

Riley, Harry Franklin (1946)

Riley, James Arthur (1951)

Riley, William, Jr. (1958)

Riley, Lawrence Russell (1952)

Riley, Mary Lou (1947)

Riley, Sarah Elizabeth (1943)

Riley, William Herbert (1953)

Roberts, Auguster Clark (1957)

Roberts, Betty Jean (1954)
Robinson, Emma B. (1922)
Robinson, Kathryn Hood (1950)
Robinson, Lucille (1936)
Robinson, Martha Louise (1943)
Robinson, Valerie Audrey (1924)
Roland, Frances Elizabeth (1947)
Ross, Anna Pearl (1934 ½)* (as listed in
    Board Minutes)
Ross, Anna Pearl (1934)** (as listed in
    Board Minutes)
Roundtree, Inez Louise (1943)
Roundtree, Lillie Mae (1940 ½)
Royal, Mattie Lee (1953)
Russell, Mr. Francis Marion (1895)
Russell, Charles Waldroth (1911)
Russell, Thelma (1948)

Saunders, George Andrew (1936)
Saxon, Mary Elizabeth (1961)
Saxon, Nathaniel Weldon (1959)
Scott, Robert L. (1960)
Sechrest, Geneva (1942)
Sechrest, Phoebe (1938)
Sharp, William Henry (1930)
Sharpe, Carita Jean (1951)
Sharpe, William Henry, Jr. (1961)
Shauntee, Adam Keller, Jr. (1944)
Shauntee, Julia Ann (1945)
Shauntee, Mary Etta (1948)
Shaw, Carrie Lue (1920)
Sheffey, Donald Redmonn (1954)
Sheffey, John Robert (1949)
Sheffey, Sigsbee L. Wilson, Jr. (1943)
Sheffey, Sigsbee Wilson (1917)
Sheffey, Vera Elaine (1956)
Sheffey, Virginia Lee (1945)
Sheffield, Arthur Arvin (1942)
Sheffield, Minnie (1932)
Simon, Edward (1937 ½)
Simpson, Charles Stanford (1958)
Simpson, Joyce Ann (1961)
Simpson, Kenneth L. (1964)
Simpson, Marjorie Katherine (1942 ½)
Simpson, Nancy Carolyn (1959)
Slaughter, Aretha (1938)
Slaughter, Eleanor (1958)
Slaughter, Genevieve (1955)
Slaughter, John Dockett (1941)

Slaughter, James, Jr. (1951)
Slaughter, Marie Annette (1953)
Sleet, Alice Estella (1939)
Sleet, Anna Mae (1943)
Sleet, Earl Zinn (1936)
Sleet, Emma Addlene (1943)
Sleet, Emma Elizabeth (1932)
Sleet, Glenna (1937)
Sleet, Lula Mae (1935)
Sleet, Mary Magdalena (1940)
Sleet, Mattie (1937)
Sleet, Richard (1938)
Sleet, Robert Matthew (1941)
Sleet, Sarah Mamie (1935)
Slegins, Louise Vivian (1949)
Smith, Bessie (1910)
Smith, Charles Vanderbilt (1930 ½)
Smith, Mary Louise (1935)
Smith, Alfred Alden (1934)
Smith, Ethel Ruth (1952)
Smith, James Harvey (1926)
Smith, Jerome (1927)
Smith, Jewell Rebecca (1916)
Smith, John Alden (1913)
Smith, Johnnie Mae (1938)
Smith, Josephine Ellen (1905)
Smith, Lulu (1896)
Smith, Maggie Mae (1952)
Smith, Napoleon (1955)
Smith, Pauline (1940 ½)
Smith, Preston (1938)
Smith, Preston W. (1914)
Smith, Robert Lee (1944)
Smith, William James (1951)
Snowden, Alberta Watkins (1940 ½)
Snowden, Norman Douglas (1947)
Spears, Julia Mae (1913)
Spears, Martha (1939 ½)
Spears, Mary Adelaide (1946)
Spiller, Mattie Love (1917)
Spriggs, Charles B., G.I. (1948)
Stewart, Arthur Elmer (1954)
Stewart, Charles E. (1964)
Stewart, Charles William (1945)
Stewart, Deloris Jean (1962)
Stewart, Ella Pearl (1943)
Stewart, Franklin David (1963)
Stewart, Leslie Lee (1958)
Stewart, Marguerite (1914)

Stewart, Sarah Beatrice (1918)

Stewart, William Joseph (1965)

Stockdale, James (1949)

Stone, George E. (1964)

Stone, John Allen (1965)

Storms, Barry Richard (1962)

Storms, Judith Ann (1954)

Storms, Robert (1964)

Sudduth, Horace S. (1908)

Summers, Mary Adeline (1945)

Sweatt, Georgene (1940)

Sweatt, Mary M. (1936 ½)

Talley, James Edward (1942 ½)

Talley, La Verne (1949)

Talley, Marion Louise (1946)

Talley, William Lincoln (1944)

Taylor, Andrew Embry (1913)

Taylor, Anna Bell (1925)

Taylor, Granville Norman (1928)

Taylor, Harry William (1928)

Temple, Jessie May Louise (1929)

Terrell, Amanda Belle (1928)

Thacker, Juanita (1949)

Thacker, Tom (1959)

Thomas, Allen, Jr. (1957)

Thompson, Dorothy (1936)

Thompson, Eddie James (1953)

Thompson, Perry Clifton (1911)

Thornton, Alva Samuel (1919)

Thornton, Jacoliah Ethel (1906)

Thornton, Mildred Gertrude (1911)

Turner, Ann Louise (1953)

Tyler, Geraldine (1958)

Tyler, Jacqueline Marquis (1956)

Tyler, John (1964)

Tyler, John Obie (1936)

Utz, Blanche Euchee (1958)

Van Cleave, Edythe Pearl (1934)

Vaughn, Braden S. T. (1905)

Walker, Melvin Waddell (1929)

Walker, William Edward (1958)

Wallace, James Allen, G.I. (1949)

Wallace, Ozetta (1893)

Walton, George Willie (1955)

Walton, James Augustus (1954)

Walton, Joseph Moses (1958)

Walton, Toney, Jr. (1957)

Ward, Bennie Leigh (1963)

Ward, Sandra Lillian (1964)

Ware, Sarah Elizabeth (1940)

Warmack, Janice Marie (1958)

Warren, Eleanora Odessa (1915)

Washington, Clarence (1938)* (as listed in Board Minutes)

Washington, Clarence (1939)** (as listed in Board Minutes)

Washington, Ida May (1951)

Waters, Lida Belle (1942 ½)

Watkins, Charlena (1938)

Watkins, Gladys Geneva (1945)

Watkins, Hester Lee (1947)

Watkins, James Douglas (1953)

Watkins, Minerva (1938)

Watkins, Ruth Waveline (1943)

Waugh, Albert J. (1922)

Waugh, Anna Mae (1923)

Waugh, William Wallace Edward (1932)

Weathers, Olivia (1952)

Weaver, John (1953)

Weaver, Sarah Alice (1951)

Webb, David Allen (1963)

Webb, Jencie (1919)

Webb, James, Jr. (1948)

Webb, Lucy Mae (1921)

Webb, Margaret Ann (1959)

Webb, Mary Elaine (1950)

Webb, Mary Margaret (1950)

Webb, Raymond Edward (1957)

Webb, Samuel Reginald (1932)

Wells, Forest (1943)

Wells, Marian Marie (1925)

Wells, Richard Leonard (1944)

Whaley, Robert A., G.I. (1949)

Whatley, Ivery Lee (1946)

Whatley, Samuel James (1941)

Wheeler, Elizabeth D. (1900)

White, Mae Louise (1943)

Whittaker, Mary (1939)

Wideman, Joan Elizabeth (1961)

Wideman, Frederick, Jr. (1959)

Wiedmon, Frederick Barbarossa (1933 ½)

Wilkinson, Louis (1956)

Wilkinson, Rosetta (1958)

Williams, Catharine (1917)

Williams, Clarence (1927)
Williams, Devolzia (1951)
Williams, Josephine (1947)
Williams, Mary Elizabeth (1945)
Williams, Mary Jane (1948)
Williams, Maymie Milla (1904)
Williams, Peggy Lee (1950)
Williams, Ruth Laverne (1942 ½)
Williams, Susie Pearl (1908)
Williams, William (1936 ½)
Wilson, Robert Kirk (1918)
Wilson, Ruth Ann (1945)
Wimzie, John, G.I. (1949)
Wood, Rosamond Frank (1931)
Woodson, Josephine B. (1899)
Wright, Edmonia (1958)

Yates, Lawrence (1927)
Yates, Leroy Hortense (1906)
Yates, Mildred (1934)
Yelder, Ella Weese (1949)
Young, Eloise (1965)
Young, Jackie (1959)
Young, James C. (1960)
Young, Raymond Eugene (1961)
Young, Susie Emma (1898)
Young, Tillie (1892)
Young, Velma Thomas (1921)

Zellers, Bessie Mae (1906)

Bibliography

Books and Other Major Sources

"Brown v. Board of Education, 347 U.S. 483 (1954)." Supreme Court of the United States. *The National Center for Public Policy Research.* http:www.nationalcenter.org/ brown.html (accessed January 17, 2008).

"Brown v. Board of Education." *Wikipedia, The Free Encyclopedia.* http://wikipedia.org/ wiki/Brown_v._Board_of_Education (accessed January 17, 2008).

"Bureau of Refugees, Freedmen and Abandoned Lands." *Wikipedia, The Free Encyclopedia.*http://en.wikipedia.org/ wikiBureau_of_Refugees_Fredmen_and_Abandoned_Lands (accessed March 19, 2008).

"Civil Rights Act of 1866" *Answers.com.* http://www.answers.com/topic/civil-rights-act-of-1866 (accessed October 18, 2009).

"Covington, Kentucky." *Trailsrus: Civil War in Kentucky.* http://www.trailsrus.com/civil-war/region4/covington.html (accessed September 12, 2007).

"Covington, Kentucky." *Wikipedia, The Free Encyclopedia.* http://en.wikipedia.org/wiki/ Covington,_Kentucky (accessed June 17, 2009).

Cozzens, Lisa. "After the Civil War: *Plessy v. Ferguson.*" http://www.watson.org-lisa/ blackhistory/post-covo;war/plessy.html (accessed November 23, 2002).

———. "Early Civil Rights Struggles: Brown V. Board of Education.*.."* *African American History.* http://www.watson.org/lisa/blackhistory/early-civilrights/brown.html (accessed January 17, 2008).

Crosby, Leconia. F. "A Study of Pupil Marks, William Grant High School, Covington, Ky. 1918–1929." Master's thesis, University of Cincinnati, 1929.

"Fourteenth Amendment to the United States Constitution." *Wikipedia, the free encyclopedia.* http://en.wikipedia.org/wiki/Fourteenth_Amendment_to_the-United_States_Constitution (accessed October 18, 2009).

Franklin, John Hope. *The Color Line: Legacy for the Twenty-First Century.* Columbia:

University of Missouri Press, 1993.

Franklin, John Hope and Alfred A. Moss, Jr., *From Slavery to Freedom: A History of African Americans.* 7th ed. New York: McGraw-Hill, Inc., 1994.

Gavin, Phillip. "U.S. Civil War 1861–1865." *The History Place: The Past into the Future.* http://www.historyplace.com/civilwar/ (accessed September 17, 2007).

"George Stone (basketball)." *Wikipedia, the free encyclopedia.* http://en.wikipedia.org/wiki/George_Stone(basketball) (accessed May 28, 2010).

"Grade Schools & High Schools in Kentucky." Notable Kentucky African Americans Database. *University of Kentucky Libraries.* http://www.uky.edu/Libraries/NKAA/subject.php?sub_id=124 (accessed May 29, 2009).

Jackson, Eric R. *Northern Kentucky.* Black America Series. Charleston, S.C.: Arcadia Publishing, 2005.

Jones, Reinette F. "The Early Kinship: Kentucky Negro Public Education, Libraries, and Librarians." University of Kentucky. College of Communications Librarian. htpp://www.uky.edu/Subject/earlykin.html (accessed May 29, 2009).

Kenton County Public Library. *Covington/Kenton County Library.* Public Images of America. Charleston, S.C.: Arcadia Pub., 2003.

"Kentucky." *Wikipedia, The Free Encyclopedia.* http://en.wikipedia.org/wiki/Kentuky (accessed June 17, 2009).

New Georgia Encyclopedia. "Rosenwald Schools." http://www.georgiaencyclopedia.org/nge/Article.jsp?id=h-1113 (accessed May 23, 2007).

"Newport's First Black School, Southgate Street School Elementary and High School." African American Records. *Campbell County Kentucky GenWeb.* http://www.rootsweb.com/-kycampbe/southgateschool.htm (accessed March 25, 2007).

Nordheim, Betty Lee. *Echoes of the Past. A History of the Covington Public School System.* [Covington, Ky.:The Covington Independent Public Schools, 2002.]

Official Minutes of the Covington Board of Education. Covington Independent Public Schools. Covington Kentucky, 1894–1976.

"Ohio River Information." *U.S. Army Corps of Engineers, Pittsburgh District.* http://www.lrp.usace.army.mil/nav/ohioback.htm (accessed September 12, 2007).

"Ohio River." *Wikipedia, The Free Encyclopedia.* http:en.wikipedia.org/wiki/Ohio_River (accessed September 12, 2007).

"Our History." *City of Covington, Kentucky.* http://www.covingtonky.com/index.asp?page=history (accessed August 3, 2007).

"Our Savior Church." *Mother of God Church.* http"//www.mother-of-god.org/our_sister_church.htm (accessed December 13, 2009).

"Price, Jacob (Rev.)*"* Covington Biographies. Genealogy and Kentucky History. *Kenton County Public Library.* http://www.kenton.lib.ky.us/gen/kenton/covington/covbio/pages/price.htm (accessed April 13, 2007).

Reinhart, Joseph R. "Kentucky's German-Americans in the Civil War." http://www.geocities.com/kygermans/kgew.html?200712 (accessed September 12, 2007).

Ryan, Rev. Paul E. "Church of Our Savior, Covington, Kentucky," excerpted from *History of the Diocese of Covington, Kentucky, on the Occasion of the Centenary of the Diocese, 1853–1953.* http://www.nkyviews.com/kenton/text/kenton_text_ryan_cov_colored_church.htm (accessed December 13, 2009).

Stout, Louis. *Shadows of the Past. A History of the Kentucky High School Athletic League.* Lexington, Ky.: Host Communications, 2006.

Tilford-Weathers, Thelma. C. *A History of Louisville Central High School 1882–1982.* Louisville, Ky.: Printed by General Printing Co., 1982.

Articles by Theodore H. H. Harris, African American Historian

Harris, Theodore H. H. "A History of the Stained Glass Windows and the Tribes of Israel of First Baptist Church, 120 East Ninth Street Covington, Kentucky." *Kenton County Historical Society Bulletin,* (August 1991): 1–2. http//www.kentonlib.ky.us~histsoc/ (accessed September 1, 2009).
———. "Covington amended charter for African-American schools." *Cincinnati Enquirer,* February 9, 2009.
———. "Creating Windows of Opportunity: Isaac E. Black and the African American Experience in Kentucky, 1848–1914." *The Register of the Kentucky Historical Society* 98, no. 2 (Spring 2000) 155–178.
———. "History of African American Education in Campbell County." (http://www.rootssweb.ancestry.com/~kycambe/historyeducation.htm (accessed March 19, 2008).
———. "Lincoln-Grant school pushed for excellence in academics." *Cincinnati Enquirer,* February 16, 2009.
———. "Organizing for the Education of Black Children, 1866–1872." *Kenton County Historical Society Bulletin* (July 2002): 3. http//www.kentonlib.ky.us~histsoc/ (accessed September 1, 2009).

Articles by Jim Reis, *Kentucky Post* Writer

Reis, Jim. "Education for blacks began in secret schools." Pieces of the Past, *Kentucky Post,* n.d. Accessed from the Kenton County Public Library, Covington, Kentucky, History and Genealogy Department Archival Files, 2007.
———. "Long road to new school." *Kentucky Post,* February 7, 2000.
———. "Many tried, few defeated William Grant in '50s, '60." Pieces of the Past, *Cincinnati Post,* February 23, 1998. http://www.kypost.com/opinion/pieces022398html (accessed March 25, 2007).
———. "School namesake an astute politician." *Kentucky Post,* January 19, 2004. http://www.kypost.com/2004/01/19/reissd011904.html (accessed March 25, 2007).
———. "Several schools taught black students."*Kentucky Post,* February 17, 2003.
———. "Southgate Street School stood alone for decades." *Kentucky Post,* February 17, 2003.

Historical Newspaper Articles

Cincinnati Enquirer, "Covington—Board of Education [Course of Study at William Grant High School changed from 3 to 4 years]," July 7, 1899.
———, "Mrs. Jackson Was Veteran Teacher," September 20, 1966.
———, "Stampede of Slaves—A Tale of Horror," January 29, 1856.
Commercial Tribunal, "Covington [There will be no commencement of the William Grant High School this year]," June 16, 1901.
Covington Journal, "Civil Rights at Church [Isaac Black Refused Seat]," March 27, 1875.
———, "Colored People of Covington Appointed J. W. Grant and Isaac Black to represent them," July 10, 1869.
———, "Colored People's Education Convention," February 22, 1873.
———, "[Colored] School Board Met—Elected Officers and Employed Teacher from Cincinnati [Mary L. Forte]," October 19. 1872.

————, "Covington's Members [of the state legislature—William Letcher Grant]," February 20, 1876.

————, "Stampede of Slaves—Arrest of the Fugitives (Runaway Slaves from Boone County are Caught)," June 17, 1854.

————, "The Colored Educational Convention," February 15, 1873.

————, "The Negro as a Politician," October 19, 1872.

Daily Commonwealth, "Col. Wm. L. Grant [serious illness and impending death]," May 3, 1882.

————, "Death of Moses B. Grant," December 10, 1883.

————, "Death of Mrs. Laura S. Grant," January 26, 1883.

————, "S. R. Singer, a talented son of John Singer, Esq.," June 30, 1880.

Enquirer, "Thacker's road to UC, NBA began at Grant," January 16, 2008.

Kentucky Enquirer, "Update [Dr. Gary Blade]," February 22, 1980.

Kentucky Post, "Accuses the Principal—Charges Made Against Samuel Singer," July 30, 1900.

————, "Action Demanded On De-Segregation," July 31, 1955.

————, "Architects To Bid On Plans For School," January 5, 1931.

————, "Ask Aid of Foundation For School," January 5, 1931.

————, "Believes Fires of Incendiary Origin," June 3, 1929.

————, "Board Retains Principal Fouse at Grant School," August 4, 1911.

————, "Celebration at Church," December 23, 1933.

————, "Colored Commencement," June 16, 1904.

————, "Colored High Pupils Graduate," June 15, 1911.

————, "Colored High School Exercises [Ruth Belle Johnson and Elizabeth Wooten Gooch.]," June 20, 1902.

————, "Colored School Will Hold Commencement Exercises in Newport," June 17, 1904.

————, "Commencement Of Colored High [27th Annual Commencement Program.]," June 14, 1916.

————, "Covington is Outgrowing old Bounds," June 17, 1914.

————, "Friday's Program – Second Annual Commencement of the High School Department of the Southgate Street School (colored)," June 18, 1896.

————, "Graduates from William Grant Colored High School Will Receive Diplomas—Eighth Annual Commencement," June 17, 1897.

————, "Ground Broken At School Site—City Officials at Lincoln-Grant Ceremonies," May 4, 1931.

————, "Homer Sluss Chosen to Succeed Hall," June 3, 1904.

————, "Latonia," June 17, 1914.

————, "Negro Educator Placed on Trial in Police Court. [W. H. Fouse]," January 6, 1912.

————, "Negro Pastor Dies—Rev. Jacob Price Organized First Negro Church," March 2, 1923.

————, "Prof. Morris Leaves Head of Schools," August 2, 1907.

————, "Prof. Singer Will Resign—Result of the Board of Education's Stand—Trustees told Him He Must Get Out," August 22, 1900.

————, "School Head is 'On Carpet'—Negro Principal Scored for Bond Attitude," September 30, 1925.

————, "School Unsafe—Fire Hazard Seen in Negro Building—10 and 12 E. 6th," May 1, 1923.

———, "Seeks support for bonds; Covington Lags in School Facilities, Speaker [H. R. Merry] says," November 3, 1928.

———, "Singer Must Resign at Once," August 18, 1900.

———, "Singer out of Schools—Supt. Morris took definite action—The colored principal will have to retire," August 23, 1900.

———, "Six Graduate Tonight From Colored Hi," June 17, 1914.

———, "Two Young Girls—To Graduate From Covington Colored High School," June 18, 1896.

———, "Will Honor Negro Prof. [Frank L. Williams]," August 29, 1908.

———, "Yancey In Charge," March 13, 1913.

Kentucky Post and Times Star, "Henry R. Merry," deaths, May 19, 1965.

———, "Walton-Verona Vote for De-Segregation," July 20, 1955.

Kentucky Times Star, "Commencement in Mid-Season—First," December 21, 1917.

———, "Grant High School Graduates," June 12, 1958.

———, "Grant Exercises Set for Wednesday—Twenty to Graduate," June 7, 1958.

———, "To Be Honored" (H. R. Merry), May 23, 1955.

The Post, "To Dedicate New School," March 31, 1932.

Singer, Samuel R. and Mrs. Frances R, Parrot, Marriage Licenses," *Daily Commonwealth,* June 30, 1880.

The Ticket, "Meeting of School Board," August 12, 1876; August 19, 1876.

Other Sources

Boh, John. "The Old Colored Church on Madison Avenue." *Kenton County Historical Society Bulletin,* (May 1992): 3–6. http//www.kentonlib.ky.us~histsoc/ (accessed September 1, 2009).

Fann, Patricia Humphries. "History of William Grant." Accessed from The Kenton County Public Library, Covington, Kentucky, History and Genealogy Department Archival Files, 2007.

Grantonian, 1950 (Lincoln-Grant School Yearbook).

Grant Warrior, 1956 (Lincoln-Grant School Yearbook).

———, *1957* (Lincoln-Grant School Yearbook).

Harden, Crystal. "Holmes High to Celebrate History." Posted: September 29, 2003. http://www.covingtonky.com/index.asp?fn=news&id=1130 (accessed March 25, 2007).

"Latonia Race Track." *Wikipedia, The Free Encyclopedia.* http://en.wikipedia.org/wiki/Latonia_Race_Track (accessed June 17, 2009).

Lincoln-Grant and William Grant Reunion Program Booklets, 1979, 1982 and 1985.

"Where the River Bends: A History of Northern Kentucky. Historical Timeline, 1866–1939." http://www.ket.org/historynky/timeline/timeline02.htm (accessed March 19, 2008).

Index

Photograph 175: Drs. Joseph and Nancy Walton.
PHOTOGRAPH BY GREG JONES.

About the Author

Joseph M. Walton and his family moved to Covington, Kentucky, from South Carolina in the early 1940s. He attended Lincoln-Grant School from kindergarten through the twelfth grade, and graduated from William Grant High School as class valedictorian. Walton was among the first black students to enroll at Covington Holmes High School, a previously all-white school during the summer of 1957 for an early stage of initiating the racial integration of that school through a brief, summer school geometry course.

Joseph M. Walton earned a Bachelor of Science in Education degree from the University of Cincinnati. He was initially employed as a teacher in the Cincinnati Public Schools while completing a Master of Education degree in school administration at Xavier University in Cincinnati, and beginning work on a doctoral degree at The Ohio State University.

The author and his wife, Nancy Riley Walton eventually moved to Columbus, Ohio where he completed a Doctor of Philosophy (Ph.D.) degree in education at The Ohio State University. He then launched a lengthy career at The University of Akron located in northeastern Ohio, where his wife also earned a Ph.D. degree in education. In addition to serving as a faculty member and attaining the rank of full professor, Walton held several administrative posts, including Acting Dean of Graduate Studies and Research, Associate Provost for Academic and Faculty affairs, and Executive Assistant to the President of the university. He recently retired as Professor Emeritus of Education.

The author of several academic publications, Walton and his wife now reside in the greater Cincinnati area. They have four adult children and several grandchildren, as well as a great-grandchild.